W9-CIC-030

Developing the Curriculum

FIFTH EDITION

Peter F. Oliva

Longman

New York   San Francisco   Boston
London   Toronto   Sydney   Tokyo   Singapore   Madrid
Mexico City   Munich   Paris   Cape Town   Hong Kong   Montreal

To our children, Eve and Marc, and our grandchildren,
Gregory, Cory, Anthony, and Amanda, whose curricular
needs have always been a paramount concern

Publisher: Priscilla McGeehon
Supplement Editor: Jennifer Ackerman
Production Manager: Denise Phillip
Project Coordination, Text Design, and Electronic Page Makeup: Thompson Steele, Inc.
Cover Design Manager: Nancy Danahy
Cover Designer: Joe DePinho
Cover Illustrations/Photos: © PhotoDisc, Inc. and © Tony Stone
Manufacturing Buyer: Roy Pickering
Printer and Binder: The Maple-Vail Book Manufacturing Group
Cover Printer: The Lehigh Press, Inc.

Library of Congress Cataloging-in-Publication Data

Oliva, Peter F.
    Developing the curriculum / Peter F. Oliva.—5th ed.
        p.   cm.
    Includes bibliographical references and indexes.
        ISBN 0-321-03789-8
            1. Curriculum planning—United States. 2. School supervision—United States. I. Title.

LB2806.15.O45 2001
375'.001'0973—dc21   00-35589

Please visit our Web site at http://www.awl.com

ISBN 0-321-03789-8

1 2 3 4 5 6 7 8 9 10—MA—03 02 01 00

CONTENTS

PART IV CURRICULUM DEVELOPMENT: PROBLEMS AND PRODUCTS   487

14. PROBLEMS IN CURRICULUM DEVELOPMENT   487

15. CURRICULUM PRODUCTS   578

PREFACE

In its fifth edition, this textbook remains a comprehensive analysis of the *process* of curriculum development. Process is the main feature that distinguishes this text from many other curriculum texts. The book illuminates how curriculum workers go about the process of developing the curriculum. The book's major purpose is to give the student a comprehensive view of the field.

Basically, the substance of the text has not changed. However, a number of changes have been made to make the book more current and more usable in the classroom. Key revisions to be found in this fifth edition are:

- Thorough updating to reflect changes that have taken place since the fourth edition was published.
- Reorganization of Chapter 14 on Problems in Curriculum Development.
- Incorporation of views of many curriculum developers and theorists not included in the previous edition.
- The addition of useful Internet web sites at the end of some chapters, especially Chapter 14.
- Coding of bibliographical references at the end of Chapter 14 to help students who wish to research particular topics.

The passing of time has not altered the process described in the first four editions. Like its preceding editions this book is intended for students in courses such as Curriculum Development, Curriculum Planning, and Curriculum Improvement. It is meant to be especially helpful to preservice and inservice curriculum coordinators, principals, assistant principals for curriculum, department chairpersons, instructional team leaders, and grade coordinators, who will find the book to be a practical guide to curriculum development.

This text has proved useful at the master's degree level through the doctoral level. It fits especially well those courses in curriculum development that are required of persons preparing to be instructional leaders, administrators, and supervisors. In addition, the book contains a great deal of information and suggestions suitable to inservice professionals. Wherever possible, I have included examples of practices from actual schools.

The text has a particular sequence to it. It begins with an examination of the theoretical dimensions of curriculum development. After curriculum has been defined and its relationship to instruction clarified, the text looks at roles of various personnel who have primary responsibility for developing the curriculum. A number of models of curriculum development are then described.

Following the model I have presented in Chapter 5, subsequent chapters outline a step-by-step process for engaging in curriculum development. Integrating curriculum and instruction, the model is a distillation of ideas of many thinkers and researchers on curriculum, instruction, and supervision. The process of curriculum development is examined from stating philosophical beliefs and broad aims of education to specifying curriculum and instructional goals and objectives, implementing the curriculum and instruction, and evaluating instruction and the curriculum.

Because the primary focus of the book is on curriculum development, less emphasis is given to instruction, a whole area of study in itself.

Each chapter begins with a number of cognitive objectives (competencies) to be achieved by the student on completion of study of the chapter. Several questions for discussion are found at the end of each chapter. The supplementary exercises that follow the questions for discussion are designed to serve two purposes: (1) to reinforce the goals and content of each chapter and (2) to extend the treatment of topics beyond the material presented in the chapter. These exercises range in difficulty from simple to complex. Some provide for individual student work, others for group work. Some require only thought and opinion; others call for extensive research. In one respect the discussion questions and supplementary exercises substitute for an instructor's manual. Instructors are encouraged to select those exercises most appropriate for their own students. Instructors who wish to do so can easily turn many of the supplementary exercises into questions for class discussion. To further enhance the usefulness of the text, each chapter concludes with an often extensive bibliography of pertinent books, journal articles, and other media. I have resisted well-intended suggestions to limit end-of-chapter exercises to a few thought-provoking activities and to provide a brief preselected bibliography. I have preferred instead to offer many activities from which the instructor may choose and to provide references presenting many views to help students doing research on a topic.

Both old and new references have been deliberately woven into the text to clarify and support points under discussion. The old references are included in order to (1) acquaint the student with persons who have contributed to the field, (2) trace the development of curricular thought, and (3) show that earlier thinking was often ahead of its time. The new references are included, of course, to present current views on curriculum development. In as many cases as possible I have chosen to let sources speak to the reader in their own words. At the end of some of the chapters you will find references to pertinent audio-visual materials.

At the end of the book are six appendices. Appendix A is a list of exit competencies, a summary of behaviors students should be able to demonstrate at the end of the course. Appendix B lists Educational Resources Information Center (ERIC) clearinghouses; Appendix C, regional educational laboratories; Appendix D, national research and development centers; Appendix E, National Institutes within the Office of Educational Research and Improvement, U.S. Department of Education; and Appendix F, Curriculum Journals.

The book is not meant to be a one-person prescription on curriculum development. I approach this text from the standpoint of an instructor who wishes students to obtain an overview of curriculum development. I have conscientiously tried to acquaint the reader with people, places, and ideas from both the past and present. Where I have treated controversial issues, that is issues on which there is considerable disagreement, I have made a great effort to portray all sides to the issue, citing both proponents and opponents.

One clarifying note about the structure of the book. You will note the rubrics of Curriculum Past, Curriculum Present, and Curriculum Future in Chapter 9. The book returns to Curriculum Present and, to a lesser extent, Curriculum Future in Chapter 14. I chose to include in Curriculum Present, Chapter 9, those curriculum developments which were more established and less controversial. I have presented in Chapter 14 a number of recent developments that are for many people problem areas engendering considerable disagreement.

One of the difficulties any writer in the field of curriculum development faces is that the field is so broad. A primary task of the writer, as with any teacher, is to select the content to be included. Hence if I have missed your favorite person or theme, I beg your indulgence.

I would like to emphasize that this textbook, with its questions for discussion, exercises, and bibliographies, is meant to be used, not just read. Therefore, it is designed as a teaching aid for the instructor and a sourcebook for the student.

Many people have contributed to the writing and publishing of this and earlier editions. Through their insights into curriculum and instruction, teachers, administrators, and students with whom I have worked have helped to shape my thinking. I am deeply indebted not only to the reviewers, who so generously gave of their time to review the manuscripts of all editions of this book. I especially wish to thank my editors, Priscilla McGeehon and Virginia Blanford at Addison-Wesley-Longman for their continuing support. I continue to appreciate all the help given me by the staff of the library at the University of Central Florida, especially, the reference, interlibrary loan, circulation, and serials/AV departments.

As always, I welcome comments from users of the book.

Peter F. Oliva
124 Carriage Hill Drive
Casselberry, FL 32707

PART I

THE CURRICULUM: THEORETICAL DIMENSIONS

CHAPTER 1

CURRICULUM AND INSTRUCTION DEFINED

After studying this chapter you should be able to:

1. **Define curriculum.**
2. **Define instruction.**
3. **Explain in what ways curriculum can be considered a discipline**
4. **Create or select a model of the relationship between curriculum and instruction and describe your creation or selection.**

CONCEPTIONS OF CURRICULUM

Gaius Julius Caesar and his cohorts of the first century B.C. had no idea that the oval track upon which the Roman chariots raced would bequeath a word used almost daily by educators twenty-one centuries later. The track—the *curriculum*—has become one of the key concerns of today's schools, and its meaning has expanded from a tangible racecourse to an abstract concept.

In the world of professional education, the word *curriculum* has taken on an elusive, almost esoteric connotation. This poetic, neuter word does possess an aura of mystery. By contrast, other dimensions of the world of professional education like adminis*tration*, instruc*tion*, and supervi*sion* are strong, action-oriented words. Administration is the *act* of administering; instruction is the *act* of instructing; and supervision is the *act* of supervising. But in what way is *curriculum* an act? While administrators administer, instructors instruct, and supervisors supervise, no school person *curricules,* and though we can find the use of the term *curricularist,*[1] it is only a rare *curricularist* who *curricularizes.*

---

[1]See, for example, Allan C. Ornstein and Francis P. Hunkins. *Curriculum: Foundations, Principles, and Issues,* 2nd ed. (Boston: Allyn and Bacon, 1993), pp. 9,10.

The quest for a definition of curriculum has taxed many an educator. Dwayne Huebner ascribed ambiguity and a lack of precision to the term *curriculum*..[2] Elizabeth Vallance observed, "The curriculum field is by no means clear; as a discipline of study and as a field of practice, *curriculum* lacks clean boundaries . . . ."[3] Indeed, curriculum seems at times analogous to the blind men's elephant. It is the pachyderm's trunk to some; its thick legs to others; its pterodactyllike flopping ears to some people; its massive, rough sides to other persons; and its ropelike tail to still others.

Though it may be vehemently denied, no one has ever seen a curriculum, not a real, total, tangible, visible entity called a curriculum. The interested observer may have seen a written plan that may have been called a curriculum. Somehow the observer knows, probably by word of mouth, that in every school in which teachers are instructing students a curriculum exists. A written plan provides the observer with an additional clue to the existence of a certain something called a curriculum. But if by some bit of magic the observer could lift the roof of a school in session and examine the cross section thereof, the curriculum would not be apparent. What the observer would immediately perceive would be many instances of teacher–pupil interaction we call *instruction*.

The search for evidence of the mysterious creation called curriculum is not unlike efforts to track down Bigfoot, the Yeti, the Almasty, Sasquatch, South Bay Bessie, Scotland's Loch Ness Monster, or Sweden's Great Lake Monster. Bigfoot, the Yeti, the Almasty, and Sasquatch have left their tracks in the mud and the snow; Bessie and Nessie have rippled the waters of their lakes; but no one has yet succeeded in producing incontrovertible photographs of these reputed creatures. (Was the Nessie that we've seen in some photos really a toy submarine with a phony sea serpent's head?)

Nor has anyone ever photographed a curriculum. Shutterbugs have instead photographed pupils, teachers, and other school personnel. Perhaps if someone videotaped every instance of behavior in every classroom, corridor, office, and auxiliary room of a school every day and then investigated this record as thoroughly as military leaders analyze air reconnaissance photos, a curriculum could be discerned.

CERTIFICATION AND CURRICULUM

State certification laws compound the problem of defining curriculum because few, if any, professionals can become certified in *curriculum*. Whereas all professionals in training must take courses of one type or another called *curriculum*, there is not a certifiable field labeled *curriculum*. Professionals are certified in administration, guidance, supervision, school psychology, elementary education, and many fields of teaching. But in *curriculum* per se? Not as a rule, although courses in the field of curriculum are mandated for certification in certain fields of specialization, such as administration and supervision.

Nevertheless, numbers of curriculum workers, consultants, coordinators, and even professors of curriculum can be identified. These specialists, many of whom may hold

---

[2]Dwayne Huebner, "The Moribund Curriculum Field: Its Wake and Our Work," *Curriculum Inquiry* 6, no. 2 (1976): 156.
[3]Elizabeth Vallance, "Curriculum as a Field of Practice," in Fenwick W. English, ed., *Fundamental Curriculum Decisions,* 1983 Yearbook (Alexandria, Va.: Association for Supervision and Curriculum Development, 1983), p. 159.

state certification in one or more fields, cannot customarily hang on the wall a certificate that shows that endorsement has been granted in a field called *curriculum*.

While a certifiable field of specialization called curriculum may be lacking, the word itself is treated as if it had tangible substance, for it can undergo a substantial variety of processes. Curriculum—or its plural, curricula or curriculums (depending on the user's penchant or abhorrence for the Latin)—is built, planned, designed, and constructed. It is improved, revised, and evaluated. Like photographic film and muscles, the curriculum is developed. It is also organized, structured, and restructured, and, like a wayward child, reformed. With considerable ingenuity the curriculum planner—another specialist—can mold, shape, and tailor the curriculum.

INTERPRETATIONS OF CURRICULUM

The amorphous nature of the word curriculum has given rise over the years to many interpretations. Madeleine R. Grumet labeled curriculum as a "field of utter confusion."[4] Depending on their philosophical beliefs, persons have conveyed these interpretations, among others:

- Curriculum is that which is taught in school.
- Curriculum is a set of subjects.
- Curriculum is content.
- Curriculum is a program of studies.
- Curriculum is a set of materials.
- Curriculum is a sequence of courses.
- Curriculum is a set of performance objectives.
- Curriculum is a course of study.
- Curriculum is everything that goes on within the school, including extra-class activities, guidance, and interpersonal relationships.
- Curriculum is that which is taught both inside and outside of school directed by the school.
- Curriculum is everything that is planned by school personnel.
- Curriculum is a series of experiences undergone by learners in school.
- Curriculum is that which an individual learner experiences as a result of schooling.

In the foregoing definitions you can see that curriculum can be conceived in a narrow way (as subjects taught) or in a broad way (as all the experiences of learners, both in school and out, directed by the school). The implications for the school to be drawn from the differing conceptions of curriculum can vary considerably. The school that accepts the definition of curriculum as a set of subjects faces a much simpler task than the school that takes upon itself responsibilities for experiences of the learner both inside and outside of school.

A variety of nuances is perceived when the professional educators define curriculum. The first definition, for example, given in Carter V. Good's *Dictionary of Education* describes curriculum as "a systematic group of courses or sequences of subjects required for graduation or certification in a field of study, for example, social studies

---

[4]Madeleine R. Grumet, *Bitter Milk: Women and Teaching* (Amherst, Mass.: The University of Massachusetts Press, 1988), p. 4

curriculum, physical education curriculum . . . ."[5] Let's see how a few writers on the subject define curriculum. One of the earliest writers on curriculum, Franklin Bobbitt, perceived curriculum as

> . . . that *series of things which children and youth must do and experience* by way of developing abilities to do the things well that make up the affairs of adult life; and to be in all respects what adults should be.[6]

Hollis L. Caswell and Doak S. Campbell viewed curriculum not as a group of courses but as "all the experiences children have under the guidance of teachers."[7] J. Gaylen Saylor, William M. Alexander, and Arthur J. Lewis offered this definition: "We define curriculum as a plan for providing sets of learning opportunities for persons to be educated."[8]

The Saylor, Alexander, and Lewis definition parallels the one given by Hilda Taba in a discussion of criteria for providing sets of learning opportunities for curriculum development: "A curriculum is a plan for learning."[9] She defined curriculum by listing its elements:

> All curricula, no matter what their particular design, are composed of certain elements. A curriculum usually contains a statement of aims and of specific objectives; it indicates some selection and organization of content; it either implies or manifests certain patterns of learning and teaching, whether because the objectives demand them or because the content organization requires them. Finally, it includes a program of evaluation of the outcomes.[10]

Ronald C. Doll defined the curriculum of a school as:

> . . . the formal and informal content and process by which learners gain knowledge and understanding, develop skills, and alter attitudes, appreciations, and values under the auspices of that school.[11]

Daniel Tanner and Laurel N. Tanner proposed the following definition:

> The authors regard curriculum as *that reconstruction of knowledge and experience that enables the learner to grow in exercising intelligent control of subsequent knowledge and experience.*[12]

Albert I. Oliver equated curriculum with the educational program and divided it into four basic elements: "(1) the program of studies, (2) the program of experiences, (3) the program of services, and (4) the hidden curriculum."[13]

---

[5]From Carter V. Good, ed., *Dictionary of Education,* 3rd ed. (New York: McGraw-Hill, 1973), p. 157. Reproduced with permission of The McGraw-Hill Companies.

[6]Franklin Bobbitt, *The Curriculum* (Boston: Houghton Mifflin, 1918), p. 42.

[7]Hollis L. Caswell and Doak S. Campbell, *Curriculum Development* (New York: American Book Company, 1935), p. 66.

[8]J. Galen Saylor, William M. Alexander, and Arthur J. Lewis, *Curriculum Planning for Better Teaching and Learning,* 4th ed. (New York: Holt, Rinehart and Winston, 1981), p. 8.

[9]Hilda Taba, *Curriculum Development: Theory and Practice* (New York: Harcourt Brace Jovanovich, 1962), p. 11.

[10]Ibid., p. 10.

[11]Ronald C. Doll, *Curriculum Improvement: Decision Making and Process,* 9th ed. (Boston: Allyn and Bacon, 1996), p. 15.

[12]Daniel Tanner and Laurel Tanner, *Curriculum Development: Theory into Practice,* 3rd ed. (New York: Merrill, 1995), p. 189.

[13]Albert I. Oliver, *Curriculum Improvement: A Guide to Problems, Principles, and Process,* 2nd ed. (New York: Harper & Row, 1977), p. 8.

The programs of studies, experiences, and services are readily apparent. To these elements Oliver has added the concept of a hidden curriculum, which encompasses values promoted by the school, differing emphases given by different teachers within the same subject areas, the degree of enthusiasm of teachers, and the physical and social climate of the school.

A different approach to defining curriculum was taken by Robert M. Gagné, who wove together subject matter (content), the statement of ends (terminal objectives), sequencing of content, and preassessment of entry skills required of students when they begin the study of the content.[14] Mauritz Johnson, Jr. agreed basically with Gagné when he defined curriculum as a "structured series of intended learning outcomes."[15] Johnson perceived curriculum as "the output of a 'curriculum development system' and as an input into an 'instructional system'."[16]

Geneva Gay, writing on desegregating the curriculum, offered a broad interpretation of curriculum:

> If we are to achieve equally, we must broaden our conception to include the entire culture of the school—not just subject matter content.[17]

Evelyn J. Sowell offered the definition: "what is taught to students, both intended and unintended information, skills, and attitudes."[18]

Herbert K. Kliebard observed that "what we call *the* American curriculum is actually an assemblage of competing doctrines and practices."[19]

Jon Wiles and Joseph Bondi not only accepted the definition of curriculum as a plan for learning[20] but also saw "the curriculum as a goal or set of values, which can be activated through a development process culminating in experiences for students."[21]

Expressing the view that the word "'curriculum' has come to mean only a course of study," D. Jean Clandinin and F. Michael Connelly held curriculum to be no less than "a course of life" led by teachers as curriculum makers.[22]

Departing from a definition of curriculum as "school materials" William F. Pinar, William M. Reynolds, Patrick Slattery, and Peter M. Taubman described curriculum as "symbolic representation."[23] Said these authors:

---

[14]See Robert M. Gagné, "Curriculum Research and the Promotion of Learning," *AERA Monograph Series on Evaluation: Perspectives of Curriculum Evaluation,* no. 1 (Chicago: Rand McNally, 1967), p. 21.

[15]Mauritz, Johnson, Jr., "Definitions and Models in Curriculum Theory," *Educational Theory* 17, no. 2 (April 1967), p. 130.

[16]Ibid., p. 133.

[17]Geneva Gay, "Achieving Educational Equality Through Curriculum Desegregation," *Phi Delta Kappan* 72, no. 1 (September 1990): 61–62.

[18]Evelyn J. Sowell, *Curriculum: An Integrative Introduction* (Englewood Cliffs, N.J.: Merrill, 1996), p. 367.

[19]Herbert M. Kliebard, "The Effort to Reconstruct the Modern American Curriculum," in *The Curriculum: Problems, Politics, and Possibilities,* 2nd ed., in Landon E. Beyer and Michael W. Apple, eds. (Albany, N.Y.: State University of New York Press, 1998), p. 21.

[20]Jon Wiles and Joseph Bondi, *Curriculum Development: A Guide to Practice,* 5th ed. (Upper Saddle River, N.J.: Merrill, 1998), p. 31.

[21]Ibid., p. 12.

[22]D. Jean Clandinin and F. Michael Connelly, *Teacher as Curriculum Maker.* In Phillip W. Jackson, ed., *Handbook of Research on Curriculum: A Project of the American Educational Research Association* (New York: Macmillan, 1992), p. 393.

[23]William F. Pinar, William M. Reynolds, Patrick Slattery, and Peter M. Taubman, *Understanding Curriculum: An Introduction to the Study of Historical and Contemporary Curriculum Discourses* (New York: Peter Lang, 1996), p. 16.

Curriculum understood as symbolic representation refers to those institutional and discursive practices, structures, images, and experiences that can be identified and analyzed in various ways, i.e., politically, racially, autobiographically, phenomenologically, theologically, internationally, and in terms of gender and deconstruction.[24]

DEFINITIONS BY PURPOSES, CONTEXTS, AND STRATEGIES

Differences in substance of definitions of curriculum, while they exist, are not as great or as common as differences in what the curriculum theorists include in their conceptions of the term. Some theorists elaborate more than others. Some combine elements of both curriculum and instruction, a conceptual problem that will be examined later in this chapter. Others find a definition of curriculum in (1) purposes or goals of the curriculum, (2) contexts within which the curriculum is found, or (3) strategies used throughout the curriculum.

Purposes.   The search for a definition of curriculum is clouded when the theoretician responds to the term not in the context of what curriculum is but what it *does* or *should do*—that is, its purpose. On the purposes of the curriculum we can find many varying statements.

When curriculum is conceptualized as "the development of reflective thinking on the part of the learner" or "the transmission of the cultural heritage," purpose is confused with entity. This concept could be stated more correctly: "The purpose of the curriculum is transmission of the cultural heritage," or "The purpose of the curriculum is the development of reflective thinking on the part of the learner." A statement of what the curriculum is meant to achieve does little to help us sharpen a definition of what curriculum is.

Contexts.   Definitions of curriculum sometimes state the settings within which it takes shape. When theoreticians speak of an essentialist curriculum, a child-centered curriculum, or a reconstructionist curriculum, they are invoking two characteristics of the curriculum at the same time—purpose and context. For example, an essentialistic curriculum is designed to transmit the cultural heritage, to school young people in the organized disciplines, and to prepare boys and girls for the future. This curriculum arises from a special philosophical context, that of the essentialistic school of philosophy.

A child-centered curriculum clearly reveals its orientation—the learner, who is the primary focus of the progressive school of philosophy. The development of the individual learner in all aspects of growth may be inferred but the plans for that development vary considerably from school to school. The curriculum of a school following reconstructionist philosophical beliefs aims to educate youth in such a way that they will be capable of solving some of society's pressing problems, and therefore change society for the better. Setting forth a "feminist argument," Madeleine R. Grumet argued that *"what is the most fundamental to our lives as men and women sharing a moment on this planet is the process and experience of reproducing ourselves."*[25]

---
[24]Ibid.
[25]Madeleine R. Grumet, *Bitter Milk: Women and Teaching* (Amherst, MA.: The University of Massachusetts Press, 1988), pp. 3–4.

Holding the view that "schools are ritual centers cut off from the real living places where we love and labor,"[26] she defined curriculum as a "project of transcendence, our attempt while immersed in biology and ideology to transcend biology and ideology."[27] Again we see a particular orientation or context within which the curriculum is lodged.

Strategies.   While purpose and context are sometimes offered as definitions of curriculum, an additional complexity arises when the theoretician equates curriculum with instructional strategy. Some theoreticians isolate certain instructional variables such as processes, strategies, and techniques and then proceed to equate them with curriculum. The curriculum as a problem-solving process illustrates an attempt to define curriculum in terms of an instructional process—problem-solving techniques, the scientific method, or reflective thinking. The curriculum as group living, for example, is an effort at definition built around certain instructional techniques that must be used to provide opportunities for group living. The curriculum as individualized learning and the curriculum as programmed instruction are, in reality, specifications of systems by which learners encounter curricular content through the process of instruction. Neither purpose, context, nor strategy provides a clear basis for defining curriculum.

In a class by itself is the definition of curriculum as ends or terminal objectives. W. James Popham and Eva L. Baker classified curriculum as ends and instruction as means when they said, "Curriculum is all the planned learning outcomes for which the school is responsible."[28] In designing the curriculum, planners would cast these outcomes or objectives in operational or behavioral terms.

The operational or behavioral objectives are, in effect, instructional objectives. According to the proponents of behavioral objectives, a compilation of all the behavioral objectives of all the programs and activities of the school would constitute the curriculum. The curriculum would then be the sum total of all instructional objectives. You will encounter in this text an approach that distinguishes curriculum goals and objectives from instructional goals and objectives. You will see later that curriculum objectives are derived from curriculum goals and aims of education, and instructional objectives are derived from instructional goals and from curriculum goals and objectives. Both curriculum objectives and instructional objectives can be stated in behavioral terms.

Some advocates of behavioral objectives seem comfortable with the notion that once the terminal objectives (the ends) are clearly specified, the curriculum has been defined. From that point on instruction takes over. This view of curriculum as specification of objectives is quite different, for example, from the concept of the curriculum as a plan, a program, or a sequence of courses.[29]

In this text curriculum is perceived as a plan or program for all the experiences that the learner encounters under the direction of the school. In practice, the curriculum consists of a number of plans, in written form and of varying scope, that delineate

---

[26]Ibid., p. 21.
[27]Ibid., p. 20.
[28]W. James Popham and Eva L. Baker, *Systematic Instruction* (Englewood Cliffs, N.J.: Prentice-Hall, 1970), p. 48.
[29]See, for example, Gagné, "Curriculum Research."

the desired learning experiences. The curriculum, therefore, may be a unit, a course, a sequence of courses, the school's entire program of studies—and may take place outside of class or school when directed by the personnel of the school.

RELATIONSHIPS BETWEEN CURRICULUM AND INSTRUCTION

The search to clarify the meaning of curriculum reveals uncertainty about the distinctions between curriculum and instruction and their relationships to each other. We may simplistically view curriculum as that which is taught and instruction as the means used to teach that which is taught. Even more simply, curriculum can be conceived as the "what" and instruction as the "how." We may think of the curriculum as a program, a plan, content, and learning experiences, whereas we may characterize instruction as methods, the teaching act, implementation, and presentation.

Distinguishing instruction from curriculum, Johnson defined instruction as "the interaction between a teaching agent and one or more individuals intending to learn."[30] James B. Macdonald viewed curricular activity as the production of plans for further action and instruction as the putting of plans into operation. Thus, according to Macdonald, curriculum planning precedes instruction, a premise with which I am in agreement.[31]

In the course of planning for either the curriculum or instruction, decisions are made. Decisions about the curriculum relate to plans or programs and thus are *programmatic,* while those about instruction (and thereby implementation) are *methodological.* Both curriculum and instruction are subsystems of a larger system called schooling or education.

MODELS OF THE CURRICULUM–INSTRUCTION RELATIONSHIP

Definitions of the two terms are valuable but can obscure the interdependence of these two systems. They may be recognized as two entities, but like cojoined twins, one may not function without the other. That the relationship between the "what" and the "how" of education is not easily determined can be seen in several different models of this relationship. For lack of better terminology, the following labels are coined for these models: (1) dualistic model, (2) interlocking model, (3) concentric models, and (4) cyclical model.

Dualistic Model.   Figure 1.1 depicts the dualistic model. Curriculum sits on one side and instruction on the other and never the twain shall meet. Between the two entities lies a great gulf. What takes place in the classroom under the direction of the teacher seems to have little relationship to what the master plan says should go on in the classroom. The planners ignore the instructors and in turn are ignored by them. Discussions of curriculum are divorced from their practical application to the classroom. Un-

---

[30]Johnson, "Definitions," p. 138. See also Saylor, Alexander, and Lewis, *Curriculum Planning,* pp. 9–10, for a definition of instruction.

[31]James B. Macdonald and Robert R. Leeper, eds., *Theories of Instruction* (Alexandria, Va.: Association for Supervision and Curriculum Development, 1965), pp. 5–6.

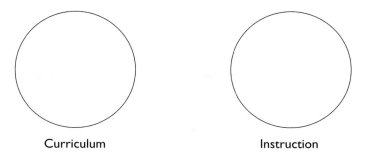

Figure 1.1 The dualistic model

der this model the curriculum and the instructional process may change without significantly affecting one another.

Interlocking Model.   When curriculum and instruction are shown as systems entwined, an interlocking relationship exists. No particular significance is given to the position of instruction or curriculum in either of the versions of this model presented in Figure 1.2. The same relationship is implied no matter which element appears on the left or the right. These models clearly demonstrate an integrated relationship between these two entities. The separation of one from the other would do serious harm to both.

Curriculum planners would find it difficult to regard instruction as paramount to curriculum and to determine teaching methods before program objectives. Nevertheless, some faculties proceed as if instruction were primary by dispensing with advance planning of the curriculum and by letting it more or less develop as it unfolds in the classroom.

Concentric Models.   The preceding models of the relationship between curriculum and instruction reveal varying degrees of independence from complete detachment to interlocking relationships. Mutual dependence is the key feature of concentric models. Two conceptions of the curriculum–instruction relationship that show one as the sub-

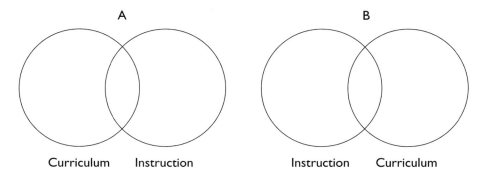

Figure 1.2 The interlocking model

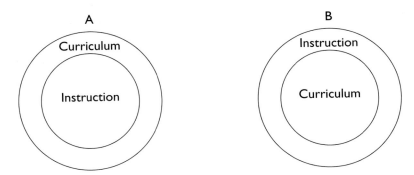

Figure 1.3   The concentric model

system of the other can be sketched (see Figure 1.3). Variations A and B both convey the idea that one of the entities occupies a superordinate position while the other is subordinate.

Concentric model A makes instruction a subsystem of curriculum, which is itself a subsystem of the whole system of education. Concentric model B subsumes curriculum within the subsystem instruction. A clear hierarchical relationship comes through in both these models. Curriculum ranks above instruction in model A and instruction is predominant in model B. In model A instruction is a very dependent portion of the entity curriculum. Model B makes curriculum subservient to and derivative from the more global instruction.

Cyclical Model.   The cyclical conception of the curriculum-instruction relationship is a simplified systems model that stresses the essential element of feedback. Curriculum and instruction are separate entities with a continuing circular relationship. Curriculum makes a continuous impact on instruction and, vice versa, instruction has impact on curriculum. This relationship can be schematically represented as in Figure 1.4. The cyclical model implies that instructional decisions are made after curricular decisions, which in turn are modified after instructional decisions are implemented and evaluated. This process is continuous, repetitious, and never-ending. The evaluation of instructional procedures affects the next round of curricular decision making, which

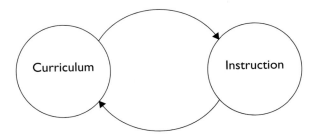

Figure 1.4   The cyclical model

again affects instructional implementation. While curriculum and instruction are diagrammed as separate entities, with this model they are not to be conceived as separate entities but as part of a sphere—a circle that revolves, causing continuous adaptations and improvements of both entities.

Each curriculum–instruction model has its champions who espouse it in part or in whole, in theory or in practice. Yet how can we account for these numerous conceptions, and how do we know which is the "right" one to hold?

Common Beliefs.   As newer developments occur in education, as research adds new insights on teaching and learning, as new ideas are developed, and as times change, beliefs about curriculum and instruction also undergo transformation. The "rightness" or "wrongness" of concepts like curriculum and instruction cannot be established by an individual educator or even by a group of educators. One index of "correctness" might be the prevailing opinion of most educators at a particular stage in history—a rather pragmatic but nevertheless viable and defensible position. Though no one to my knowledge has made a count of prevailing postulates regarding curriculum and instruction, most theoreticians today appear to agree with the following comments:

- Curriculum and instruction are related but different.
- Curriculum and instruction are interlocking and interdependent.
- Curriculum and instruction may be studied and analyzed as separate entities but cannot function in mutual isolation.

In my judgment, serious problems are posed by the dualistic conceptual model of the relationship between curriculum and instruction with its separation of the two entities and by concentric models that make one a subsystem of the other.

Some curriculum workers feel comfortable with an interlocking model because it shows a close relationship between the two entities. Of all the curriculum-instruction models that have crossed my path, however, I feel that the cyclical has much to recommend it for its simplicity and for its stress on the need for the continuous influence of each entity on the other.

CURRICULUM AS A DISCIPLINE

In spite of its elusive character, curriculum is viewed by many, including me, as a discipline—a subject of study—and even, on the graduate level of higher education, as a major field of study. Curriculum is then both a field within which people work and a subject to be taught. Graduate and, to some extent, undergraduate students take courses in curriculum development, curriculum theory, curriculum evaluation, secondary school curriculum, elementary school curriculum, middle school curriculum, community college curriculum, and, on fewer occasions, university curriculum.

Can there be a discipline called curriculum? Are the many college courses in curriculum mere frosting, as some of the critics of teacher education maintain, or is there cake beneath the surface? Is there a curriculum field or occupation to which persons can devote their lives?

THE CHARACTERISTICS OF A DISCIPLINE

To arrive at a decision as to whether an area of study is a discipline, the question might be raised, "What are the characteristics of a discipline?" If the characteristics of a discipline can be spelled out, we can determine whether curriculum, for example, is a discipline or not.

Principles. *Any discipline worthy of study has an organized set of theoretical constructs or principles that govern it.* Certainly, the field of curriculum has developed a significant set of principles, tried and untried, proved and unproved, many of which are appropriately the subjects of discussion in this text. Balance in the curriculum, discussed in Chapter 14, is a construct or concept. Curriculum itself is a construct or concept, a verbalization of an extremely complex idea or set of ideas. Using the constructs of balance and curriculum, we can derive a principle or rule which, stated in simple terms, says "A curriculum that provides maximum opportunities for learners incorporates the concept of balance." Sequencing of courses, career education, open-space education, behavioral objectives, and a whole-language approach to the teaching of language arts are examples of constructs incorporated into one or more curriculum principles.

A major characteristic of any theoretical principle is its capacity for being generalized and applied in more than one situation. Were curriculum theories but one-shot solutions to specific problems, it would be difficult to defend the concept of curriculum as a discipline. But the principles of curriculum theory are often successful efforts to establish rules that can be repeated in similar situations and under similar conditions. Many people will agree, for example, that the concept of balance should be incorporated into every curriculum. We encounter more controversy, however, over a principle that might be stated as, "The first step in curriculum planning is the specification of behavioral objectives." Though some maintain this principle has become universal practice and therefore might be labeled "truth," it has been tried and accepted by many educators, rejected by some, and tried and abandoned by others.

Knowledge and Skills. *Any discipline encompasses a body of knowledge and skills pertinent to that discipline.* The field of curriculum has adapted and borrowed subject matter from a number of pure and derived disciplines. Figure 1.5 schematically shows areas from which the field of curriculum has borrowed constructs, principles, knowledge, and skills. Selection of content for study by students, for example, cannot be done without referring to the disciplines of sociology, psychology, and subject areas. Organization of the curriculum depends upon knowledge from organizational theory and management, which are aspects of administration. The fields of supervision, systems theory, technology, and communications theory are called on in the process of curriculum development. Knowledge from many fields is selected and adapted by the curriculum field.

The "child-centered curriculum" as a concept draws heavily on what is known about learning, growth, and development (psychology and biology), on philosophy (particularly from one school of philosophy, progressivism), and on sociology. The "essentialist curriculum" borrows from the subject areas of philosophy, psychology, and sociology and, of course, the academic disciplines.

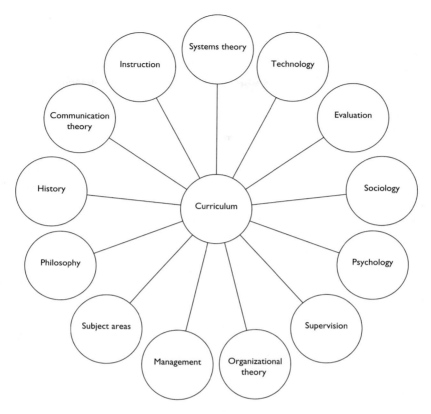

Figure 1.5   Sources of the curriculum field

You might ask whether the field of curriculum contributes any knowledge of its own to that borrowed from other disciplines. Certainly, a good deal of thinking and research is going on in the name of curriculum. New curricular ideas are being generated continuously. These ideas, whether they be cooperative learning, computer literacy, or character education (to mention but three fairly recent concepts), borrow heavily from other disciplines.

The skills used by curriculum specialists are also borrowed from other fields. Let's take an example from the field of social psychology. Generally accepted is the notion that a curriculum changes only when the people affected have changed. This principle, drawn from the field of social psychology, and applied in the field of curriculum development, was perhaps most dramatically demonstrated by the Western Electric researches conducted by industry in the 1930s.[32] Here researchers discovered that factory workers assembling telephone relays were more productive when they were

---

[32]See F. J. Roethlisberger and William J. Dickson, *Management and the Worker* (Cambridge, Mass.: Harvard University Press, 1939) for discussion of the Western Electric researches.

consulted and made to feel of value to the organization. Making the workers feel important resulted in greater productivity than manipulating the physical environment, for example, lighting in the factory. The feeling of being part of the research studies also created its own aura, the so-called Hawthorne Effect, named for the Western Electric's Hawthorne plant in Chicago. Since the feeling of involvement can in itself contribute to high productivity, this effect is one that researchers learn to discount, for it can obscure the hypothesized or real causes for change. However, the educational practitioner who is aware of the Hawthorne Effect may take advantage of it to promote learning.

Criticisms have been made of the Western Electric researches.[33] In spite of the criticisms, however, the findings still appear generally sound. An instructional leader—let's call him or her a supervisor—is the person who acts as a catalyst or agent for bringing about change in people. How does the supervisor do this? He or she makes use of knowledge and skills from a number of fields: communication theory, psychology of groups, and other areas. How does the supervisor help teachers to carry out the change once they have subscribed to it? He or she applies principles and skills from management, from knowledge of the structure of disciplines, and from other areas.

Consequently, we can conclude that the field of curriculum requires the use of an amalgamation of knowledge and skills from many disciplines. That curriculum theory and practice are derived from other disciplines does not in any way diminish the importance of the field. The observation of its derived nature simply characterizes its essence. Curriculum's synthesis of elements from many fields in some ways makes it both a demanding and an exciting arena in which to work.

In a cyclical fashion the derived discipline of *curriculum* in turn makes its own potent impact upon the disciplines from which it is derived. Through curricular research, experimentation and application, subject areas are modified; learning theories are corroborated, revised, or rejected; administrative and supervisory techniques are implemented or changed; and philosophical positions are subjected to examination.

Theoreticians and Practitioners.   *A discipline has its theoreticians and its practitioners.* Certainly, the field of curriculum has an array of workers laboring in its name. Mention has already been made of some of the titles they go by: planners, consultants, coordinators, directors, and professors of curriculum, to name but a few. We can include them under the generic title of curriculum worker or curriculum specialist.

Curriculum specialists make a number of distinctive contributions to their field. Specialists know what types of curricula have worked in the past, under what conditions, and with what success. Since the name of the game is improvement, specialists must be well-grounded in the historical development of the curriculum and must possess the capacity to use that knowledge to help the schools avoid historical pitfalls.

Curriculum specialists generate or help to generate new curriculum concepts. In this capacity specialists draw on the past and conceive new arrangements, adaptations of existing approaches, or completely new approaches. Alternative forms of schools, for example, are newer arrangements and approaches for the same general goal—education of the young.

---

[33]See, for example, Berkeley Rice, "The Hawthorne Defect: Persistence of a Flawed Theory," *Psychology Today* 16, no. 2 (February 1982): 70–74.

While curriculum specialists are indulging in the "big think," hoping to bring to light new theories—a worthy goal not to be dismissed lightly—other, and perhaps more, curriculum specialists are experts in application of theory and research. They know techniques of curriculum planning that are most likely to result in higher achievement on the part of learners. They are familiar with variations in the organizational patterns. They must be not only knowledgeable but also creative and able to spark innovations that give promise of bringing about higher achievement in learners.

The concept of "core" curriculum dating from the 1930s and the 1940s, for example, that integrated two or more subjects, was a promising, creative innovation. In one of its shapes the core curriculum, which we will discuss in Chapter 9, fused English and social studies into a block of time—ordinarily two to three periods—at the junior high school level, using content based on adolescent needs and interests. But was this innovative concept truly original, unique to the field of curriculum, or was it adapted and drawn from a variety of disciplines? Examination of the subconcepts of the core curriculum shows that it owed a great deal to other disciplines. The adolescent-needs base followed in some core programs came from student-centered, progressive learning theories, as did the problem-solving approach used in instruction. One reason for the inauguration of this type of core curriculum in schools in the 1930s and 1940s could be attributed to dissatisfaction with the subject matter, as evidenced by, among other factors, the low holding power of schools of the times.

CURRICULUM PRACTITIONERS

CURRICULUM SPECIALISTS

Curriculum specialists often make a unique contribution by creatively transforming theory and knowledge into practice. Through their efforts a new, at first experimental, approach gradually becomes a widespread practice. As students of the discipline of curriculum, they also examine and reexamine theory and knowledge from their field and related fields. Their awareness of past successes and failures elsewhere helps them to chart directions for their own curricula.

Curriculum specialists are in the best position to stimulate research on curricular problems. Specialists carry out and encourage study of curricular problems, comparisons of plans and programs, results of new patterns of curriculum organization, and history of curriculum experiments, to indicate but a few areas of research. Specialists encourage the use of results of research to continue efforts to improve the curriculum.

While classroom teachers daily concern themselves with problems of curriculum and instruction, the curriculum specialist is charged with the task of providing leadership to the teachers. Since there are so many different types of specialists in so many different locations, you will find it difficult to generalize on their roles. Some curriculum workers are generalists whose roles may be limited to leadership in curricular or programmatic planning or whose roles may also encompass instructional planning and decision making.

Some curriculum workers confine their spheres of action to certain levels or subjects, such as elementary, middle, or secondary school curriculum; community college curriculum, special education, science education, early childhood education; and others. What can be observed is that the roles the curriculum leader plays are shaped by the job, by the supervising administrator, and by the specialist himself or herself. At varying times the curriculum specialist must be

- a philosopher
- a psychologist
- a sociologist
- a human relations expert
- a theoretician
- a historian
- a scholar in one or more disciplines
- an evaluator
- a researcher
- an instructor
- a systems analyst

TEACHERS

Up to this point the discussion has centered on the curriculum specialists and their place in the scheme of the field called curriculum. We must not deemphasize an even larger group of professionals—the teachers. Just as the curriculum leader works primarily in one realm (curriculum) of the continuum that we call curriculum–instruction and secondarily in the other realm (instruction), so too the teacher works primarily in one realm (in this case, instruction) and secondarily in the other (in this case, curriculum).

The teacher, too, is a curriculum worker who engages in curriculum planning in varying degrees, on different occasions, generally under the leadership of a supervisor, be that person a coordinator, consultant, lead teacher, team leader, grade coordinator, department head, assistant principal, or principal. How the teacher-instructor and the curriculum specialist work together in the two fields of curriculum and instruction is a recurrent theme of this book.

SUPERVISORS

An additional clarification should be made at this point—that is, the relationship between the roles of persons designated as curriculum specialists and those persons who are called supervisors. Some consider the titles synonymous.

In this text a *supervisor* is perceived as a specialist who works in three domains: instructional development; curriculum development; and staff, primarily teacher, development.[34] When the supervisor works in the first two domains, he or she is an instructional/curriculum specialist or, in common but somewhat inaccurate parlance, a

---

[34]See Peter F. Oliva and George E. Pawlas, *Supervision for Today's Schools,* 6th ed. (New York: Wiley, 2001).

curriculum specialist. Thus, the curriculum worker or specialist is a particular type of supervisor, one with more limited responsibilities than a "complete" or general supervisor. Both the curriculum specialist and the supervisor fulfill similar roles when they work with teachers in curriculum development and instructional development, but the curriculum specialist is not primarily concerned with such activities as organizing inservice programs and evaluating teachers, which are more properly responsibilities of the general supervisors.

ROLE VARIATIONS

As with so many jobs in the field of education, difficulty arises in attempting to draw firm lines that apply under all conditions and in all situations. To understand more fully the roles and functions of educational personnel, we must examine local practice. Teachers, curriculum specialists, and supervisors all engage in activities to improve both curriculum and instruction. At times their roles are different and at other times their roles are similar. These personnel, all specialists in their own right, frequently trade places to accomplish the task of improvement. Sometimes they are one and the same person—the teacher who is his or her own curriculum specialist and supervisor. Whatever the structure of leadership for the improvement of curriculum and instruction, all teachers and all specialists must ultimately participate in this challenging task. Since curriculum and instruction are the mind and heart of schooling, all personnel, all students, and the community as well participate in the improvement of what is offered in the school and how it is implemented.

Chapters 3 and 4 will describe roles of personnel involved in curriculum development, including teachers, students, department heads, lead teachers, team leaders, grade coordinators, administrators, curriculum specialists, supervisors, and laypersons.

SUMMARY

Curriculum and instruction are viewed as separate but dependent concepts. Curriculum is defined in a variety of ways by theoreticians. This text follows the concept of curriculum as a plan or program for the learning experiences that the learner encounters under the direction of the school.

Instruction is perceived in these pages as the means for making the curriculum operational, that is, the techniques that teachers use to make the curriculum available to the learners. In short, curriculum is program and instruction is method.

A number of models showing the relationship between curriculum and instruction have been discussed. While all models have their strengths and weaknesses, the cyclical model seems to have particular merit for its emphasis on the reciprocity between curriculum and instruction.

Planning should begin with the programmatic—that is, with curriculum decisions, rather than with instructional decisions. Appropriate planning begins with the broad aims of education and proceeds through a continuum that leads to the most detailed objectives of instruction.

Curriculum is perceived as a discipline, albeit a derived one that borrows concepts and principles from many disciplines.

Many practitioners work in the field of curriculum, including specialists who make a career of curriculum planning, development, and research. Teachers, curriculum specialists, and instructional supervisors share leadership responsibilities in efforts to develop the curriculum.

As a discipline, curriculum possesses (l) an organized set of principles, (2) a body of knowledge and skills for which training is needed, and (3) its theoreticians and practitioners.

QUESTIONS FOR DISCUSSION

1. Does it make any difference which definition of curriculum you adopt? Why? Give examples of the effects of following different definitions of curriculum.
2. Should curriculum be an area certified (credentialed) by the state? Why?
3. What is the purpose of distinguishing curriculum from instruction?
4. What would you include in a preparation program for curriculum specialists?
5. Does planning start with the curriculum or with instruction? Why?

SUPPLEMENTARY EXERCISES

1. Locate and report three definitions of curriculum that differ from those quoted in this chapter.
2. Describe the characteristics of a discipline.
3. Describe whether curriculum is a discipline, a pseudodiscipline, or not a discipline, and state your reasons for your decision.
4. Make a brief presentation on the distinctions between a curriculum specialist and a supervisor, using selected quotations from the professional literature or from persons in positions with those titles.
5. Show the differences between the terms: curriculum worker, curriculum specialist, curriculum planner, curriculum coordinator, curriculum consultant, and instructional supervisor.
6. Locate in the literature and describe one or more models of the relationship between curriculum and instruction that are different from those that appear in this chapter.
7. Create and describe your own model of the relationship between curriculum and instruction.
8. Evaluate the model of the relationship between curriculum and instruction below suggested by Deborah Westcot, graduate student in the Georgia Southern College–University of Georgia Cooperative Doctoral Program winter 1986.

In the field of mathematics known as topology, the Möbius strip (see the illustration on page 19) presents only one continuous surface. When applied to the relationship be-

Figure 1.6   The Möbius strip

tween curriculum and instruction, curriculum flows into instruction and instruction flows into curriculum.

9. Take each of the disciplines from which the field of curriculum borrows and describe at least one contribution (principle, construct, concept, or skill) borrowed from that discipline.
10. Decide whether there are any sources of the curriculum field not shown in Figure 1.5.
11. State what you believe is meant by the following terms: curriculum planning, curriculum development, curriculum improvement, curriculum revision, curriculum reform, and curriculum evaluation.
12. Report on the Western Electric researches mentioned in this chapter and explain their significance for curriculum development. Include in your answer your description of the Hawthorne Effect. Evaluate some of the criticisms of the Western Electric researches.
13. Consult one or more of the following references (see bibliography) on the meaning of "hidden curriculum": James A. Beane et al.; Henry Giroux and David Purpel; John D. McNeil; Albert I. Oliver; Allan C. Ornstein and Francis P. Hunkins.
14. Explain what George S. Morrison means by formal curriculum, informal curriculum, hidden curriculum, and integrated curriculum (see bibliography).
15. Define types of curricula described by Allan A. Glatthorn and by John I. Goodlad (see bibliography).

BIBLIOGRAPHY

Armstrong, David G. *Developing and Documenting the Curriculum.* Boston: Allyn and Bacon, 1989.

Beane, James A., Toepfer, Conrad F., Jr., and Alessi, Samuel J., Jr. *Curriculum Planning and Development.* Boston: Allyn and Bacon, 1986.

Beauchamp, George A. *Curricular Theory,* 4th ed. Itasca, Ill.: F. E. Peacock, 1981.

Beyer, Landon E. and Apple, Michael W., eds. *The Curriculum: Problems, Politics, and Possibilities,* 2nd ed. Albany, N.Y.: State University of New York Press, 1998.

Bobbitt, Franklin. *The Curriculum.* Boston: Houghton Mifflin, 1918.

Caswell, Hollis L. and Campbell, Doak S. *Curriculum Development.* New York: American Book Company, 1935.

Clandinin, D. Jean and Connelly, F. Michael. "Teacher as Curriculum Maker," in Philip W. Jackson, ed., *Handbook of Research on Curriculum: A Project of the American Educational Research Association.* New York: Macmillan, 1992, pp. 363–401.

Doll, Ronald C. *Curriculum Improvement: Decision Making and Process,* 9th ed. Boston: Allyn and Bacon, 1996.

Eisner, Elliot W., ed. *Confronting Curriculum Reform.* Boston: Little, Brown, 1971.

———. *The Educational Imagination: On the Design and Evaluation of School Programs,* 2nd ed. New York: Macmillan, 1985.

——— and Vallance, Elizabeth, eds. *Conflicting Conceptions of Curriculum.* Berkeley, Calif.: McCutchan, 1974.

Elmore, Richard F. and Furman, Susan H., eds. *The Governance of Curriculum,* 1994 Yearbook. Alexandria, Va.: Association for Supervision and Curriculum Development, 1994.

Frymier, Jack R. and Hawn, Horace C. *Curriculum Improvement for Better Schools.* Worthington, Ohio: Charles A. Jones, 1970.

Gagné, Robert M. "Curriculum Research and the Promotion Learning." *AERA Monograph Series on Evaluation: Perspectives of Curriculum Evaluation,* no. 1. Chicago: Rand McNally, 1967.

Gay, Geneva. "Achieving Educational Equality Through Curriculum Desegregation." *Phi Delta Kappan* 72, no. 1 (September 1990): 61–62.

Giroux, Henry A., Penna, Anthony N., and Pinar, William F., eds. *Curriculum and Instruction: Alternatives in Education.* Berkeley, Calif.: McCutchan, 1981.

——— and Purpel, David, eds. *The Hidden Curriculum and Moral Education.* Berkeley, Calif.: McCutchan, 1983.

Glatthorn, Allan A. *Curriculum Leadership.* Glenview, Ill.: Scott, Foresman, 1987.

———. *Curriculum Renewal.* Alexandria, Va.: Association for Supervision and Curriculum Development, 1987.

Goodlad, John I. and associates. *Curriculum Inquiry: The Study of Curriculum Practice.* New York: McGraw-Hill, 1979.

Gress, James R. and Purpel, David E. *Curriculum: An Introduction to the Field,* 2nd ed. Berkeley, Calif.: McCutchan, 1988.

Grumet, Madeleine R. *Bitter Milk: Women and Teaching.* Amherst, Mass.: The University of Massachusetts Press, 1988.

Henson, Kenneth T. *Curriculum Development for Education Reform.* New York: HarperCollins, 1995.

Huebner, Dwayne. "The Moribund Curriculum Field: Its Wake and Our Work." *Curriculum Inquiry* 6, no. 2 (1976): 156.

Jackson, Philip W., ed. *Handbook of Research on Curriculum: A Project of the American Educational Research Association.* New York: Macmillan, 1992.

Johnson, Mauritz, Jr. "Definitions and Models in Curriculum Theory." Educational Theory 17, no. 2 (April 1967): 127–140.

Kliebard, Herbert M. "The Effort to Reconstruct the Modern American Curriculum." In Landon E. Beyer and Michael W. Apple, eds., *The Curriculum: Problems, Politics, and Possibilities,* 2nd ed. Albany, N.Y." State University of New York Press, 1998.

Macdonald, James B. and Leeper, Robert R., eds. *Theories of Instruction.* Alexandria, Va.: Association for Supervision and Curriculum Development, 1965.

McNeil, John D. *Curriculum: A Comprehensive Introduction,* 5th ed. New York: HarperCollins, 1996.

Molnar, Alex, ed. *Current Thought on Curriculum,* 1985 Yearbook. Alexandria, Va.: Association for Supervision and Curriculum Development, 1985.

Morrison, George S. *Contemporary Curriculum K–8.* Boston: Allyn and Bacon, 1993.

Oliva, Peter F. and Pawlas, George E. *Supervision for Today's Schools,* 6th ed. New York: Wiley, 2001.

Oliver, Albert I. *Curriculum Improvement: A Guide to Problems, Principles, and Process,* 2nd ed. New York: Harper & Row, 1977.

Ornstein, Allan C. and Behar, Linda S., eds. *Contemporary Issues in Curriculum.* Boston: Allyn and Bacon, 1995.

——— and Hunkins, Francis P. *Curriculum Foundations, Principles, and Issues,* 2nd ed. Boston: Allyn and Bacon, 1993.

Pinar, William F., Reynolds, William M., Slattery, Patrick, and Taubman, Peter M. *Understanding Curriculum: An Introduction to the Study of Historical and Contemporary Discourses.* New York: Peter Lang, 1996.

Popham, W. James and Baker, Eva L. *Systematic Instruction.* Englewood Cliffs, N.J.: Prentice-Hall, 1970.

Posner, George J. *Analyzing the Curriculum.* New York: McGraw-Hill, 1992.

Pratt, David. *Curriculum: Design and Development.* New York: Harcourt Brace Jovanovich, 1980.

Rice, Berkeley. "The Hawthorne Defect: Persistence of a Flawed Theory." *Psychology Today,* 16, no. 2 (February 1982): 70–74.

Roethlisberger, F. J. and Dickson, William J. *Management and the Worker.* Cambridge, Mass.: Harvard University Press, 1939.

Saylor, J. Galen, Alexander, William M., and Lewis, Arthur J. *Curriculum Planning for Better Teaching and Learning,* 4th ed. New York: Holt, Rinehart and Winston, 1981.

Schubert, William H. *Curriculum: Perspective, Paradigm, and Possibility.* New York: Macmillan, 1986.

Schwab, Joseph J. *The Practical: A Language for Curriculum.* Washington, D.C.: National Education Association, Center for the Study of Instruction, 1970.

Slattery, Patrick. *Curriculum Development in the Postmodern Era.* New York: Garland Publishing, 1995.

Smith, B. Othanel, Stanley, William O., and Shores, J. Harlan. *Fundamentals of Curriculum Development,* rev. ed. New York: Harcourt Brace Jovanovich, 1957.

Sowell, Evelyn J. *Curriculum: An Integrative Introduction.* Englewood Cliffs, N.J.: Merrill, 1996.

Taba, Hilda. Curriculum Development: *Theory and Practice.* New York: Harcourt Brace Jovanovich, 1962.

Tanner, Daniel and Tanner, Laurel. *Curriculum Development: Theory into Practice,* 3rd ed. New York: Merrill, 1995.

———. *History of the School Curriculum.* New York: Macmillan, 1990.

Tyler, Ralph W. *Basic Principles of Curriculum and Instruction.* Chicago: University of Chicago Press, 1949.

Unruh, Glenys G. and Unruh, Adolph. *Curriculum Development: Problems, Processes, and Progress.* Berkeley, Calif.: McCutchan, 1984.

Vallance, Elizabeth. "Curriculum As a Field of Practice." In Fenwick W. English, ed. *Fundamental Curriculum Decisions,* 1983 Yearbook, 154–164. Alexandria, Va.: Association for Supervision and Curriculum Development, 1983.

Walker, Decker. *Fundamentals of Curriculum.* San Diego: Harcourt Brace Jovanovich, 1990.

Wiles, Jon and Bondi, Joseph. *Curriculum Development: A Guide to Practice,* 5th ed.. Upper Saddle River, N.J.: Merrill, 1998.

Zais, Robert S. *Curriculum: Principles and Foundations.* New York: Harper & Row, 1976.

CHAPTER 2
PRINCIPLES OF CURRICULUM DEVELOPMENT

After studying this chapter you should be able to:

1. Describe the ten axioms for curriculum development discussed in this chapter.
2. Illustrate in what way the curriculum is influenced by changes in society.
3. Describe limitations affecting curriculum changes in a school system and within which curriculum workers must function.

CLARIFICATION OF TERMS

Education is one of the institutions the human race has created to serve certain needs, and, like all human institutions, it responds or should respond to changes in the environment. The institution of education is activated by a curriculum that itself changes in response to forces affecting it. The curriculum of the cave dweller, albeit informal and unstructured, was quite different from increasingly formal types of schooling that the human race invented over subsequent periods of history. Techniques for coping with the woolly mammoth may well have been of paramount concern to prehistoric man.[1] But the woolly mammoth has disappeared, and men and women today must learn to cope with other sources of anxiety like poverty, crime, drug addiction, job insecurities, homelessness, environmental problems, health problems, malnutrition, decreasing natural resources, intercultural conflicts, and the military and industrial hazards of nuclear power. At the same time humankind must learn to apply the technological tools that are proliferating in both number and complexity at a dizzying rate—a cause of anxiety in itself—to solve these and other problems.

---

[1]For delightful reading, the little classic by Harold Benjamin (J. Abner Peddiwell) entitled *The Saber-Tooth Curriculum* (New York: McGraw-Hill, 1939) is recommended.

Although no educator—teacher, curriculum coordinator, administrator, or professor—would dream of arguing that techniques for coping with the woolly mammoth should be part of the curriculum of schools at the dawn of the twenty-first century A.D., in the third century of the American republic, the woolly mammoth syndrome still persists. Schools "woolly mammoth" children when they offer a curriculum that does the following:

- Allows learners to leave school without an adequate mastery of the basic skills.
- Ill equips learners to find and hold employment when they finish school.
- Fails to train students in the use of the latest technological tools.
- Fails to promote attitudes of concern for others, cooperation with others, responsibility for one's actions, tolerance for others, and preservation of the environment.
- Holds learners to low expectations.
- Portrays the average American child as being of Caucasian extraction; living with a father, mother, and two children, a boy and a girl, residing in a $200,000 single-family home equipped with all the modern conveniences and luxuries and two cars in the garage.
- Uses materials that show all children as members of healthy, happy, prosperous, white, Anglo-Saxon, Protestant families joyously living in the suburbs.
- Omits exposure to the fine arts, including the development of aesthetic appreciation.
- Leaves out the practical knowledge and skills necessary for survival and success in a complex, technological society, such as computer science, knowledge about insurance and taxes, writing a resume and letter of application for a job, interviewing for a position, intelligent consumerism, listening and discussion skills.
- Distorts truths of the past ("Honest Abe had no faults"), the present ("Every person who is willing to work can find an adequate job"), and the future ("There is no need for residents of fast-growing sections of the country to worry about running out of potable water").
- Appeals to short-term interests of students and ignores long-range needs; or, vice versa, appeals to long-range needs and ignores short-term interests.

If the curriculum is perceived as a plan for the learning experiences that young people encounter under the direction of the school, its purpose is to provide a vehicle for ordering and directing those experiences. This process of providing the vehicle and keeping it running smoothly is known as *curriculum development*.

It may be helpful at this point to review the slight distinctions among the following terms: *curriculum development, curriculum planning, curriculum improvement,* and *curriculum evaluation. Curriculum development* is the more comprehensive term; it includes planning, implementation, and evaluation. Since curriculum development implies change and betterment, *curriculum improvement* is often used synonymously with curriculum development, though in some cases improvement is viewed as the result of development.

Curriculum planning is the preliminary phase of curriculum development when the curriculum workers make decisions and take actions to establish the plan that teachers and students will carry out. Planning is the thinking or design phase.

Curriculum implementation is translation of plans into action. During the stage of curriculum planning certain patterns of curriculum organization or reorganization are chosen. These patterns are put into operation at the implementation stage. Ways of delivering the learning experiences, for example, using teaching teams, are taken out of the planning context and made operational. Since curriculum implementation translates plans into action in the classroom, thereby transforming the realm of curriculum into the realm of instruction, the role of the teacher changes from curriculum worker to instructor.

Those intermediate and final phases of development in which results are assessed and successes of both the learners and the programs are determined are *curriculum evaluation*. On occasion, curriculum revision is used to refer to the process for making changes in an existing curriculum or to the changes themselves and is substituted for *curriculum development or improvement*. We shall return to the distinctions among curriculum planning, implementation, and evaluation when models of curriculum development are diagrammed and discussed in Chapter 5.

Through the process of curriculum development we can discover new ways for providing more effective pupil learning experiences. The curriculum developer continuously strives to find newer, better, and more efficient means to accomplish the task of educating the young.

TYPES OF CURRICULUM DEVELOPERS

Some curriculum developers excel in the conceptualizing phase (planning), others in carrying out the curricular plan (implementation), and still others in assessing curriculum results (evaluation). Over the centuries the human race has had no shortage of curriculum developers. In a positive vein Moses, Jesus, Buddha, Confucius, and Mohammed could all be called curriculum consultants. They had their respective conceptions of the goals of the human race and recommended behavior that must be learned and practiced to achieve those goals. On the negative side, at a later period in history, Hitler, Stalin, Mussolini, and Mao Zedong had definite notions and programs to train the young in what to believe and how to behave in a totalitarian society.

The ranks of the politicians in a democracy have produced curriculum consultants, some more astute than others. To the weary professional curriculum worker, it sometimes seems that every federal, state, and local legislator is a self-appointed, self-trained curriculum consultant who has his or her own pet program to promulgate. The statutes of the state legislatures, as we shall see in Chapter 3, provide numerous examples of legislative curriculum making.

Singling out all the politicians who have turned themselves into curriculum consultants through the years would be impossible. But the kite-flier who experimented with electricity, invented a stove, created a new educational institution called the Academy, and in between found time to participate in a revolution—Benjamin Franklin—made some farsighted curriculum proposals for his academy. Franklin's statement of recommendations almost seems to have been drawn out of a report on a high school's program of studies by a present-day visiting committee of a regional accrediting association. Franklin proposed for his academy (later to become the University of

Pennsylvania) a curriculum much more suited to its time than its predecessor, the Latin Grammar School.[2]

Curriculum advisers have been found not only among politicians but also among academicians, journalists, the clergy, and the public at large. Professional educators have received a great deal of both solicited and unsolicited help in shaping school curricula. An unending procession of advisers from both within and outside the profession of education over many decades has not been at a loss to advocate curriculum proposals. No matter how significant or minor, no matter how mundane or bizarre, all proposals have shared one common element: advocacy of change.

What has led so many people to be dissatisfied with so much of what education is all about? Why is the status quo rarely a satisfactory place to be? And why does it turn out, as will be illustrated, that yesterday's status quo is sometimes tomorrow's innovation? For answers to these questions some general principles of curriculum development should be considered by teachers and specialists who participate in efforts to improve the curriculum.

SOURCES OF CURRICULUM PRINCIPLES

Principles serve as guidelines to direct the activity of persons working in a particular area. Curriculum principles are derived from many sources: (1) empirical data, (2) experimental data, (3) the folklore of curriculum, composed of unsubstantiated beliefs and attitudes, and (4) common sense. In an age of science and technology, the attitude often prevails that all principles must be scientifically derived from the results of research. Yet even folklore and common sense can have their use. The scientist has discovered, for example, that some truths underlie ancient folk remedies for human maladies and that old wives' tales are not always the ravings of demented witches. While a garland of garlic hung around the neck may or may not fend off werewolves and asafetida on the end of a fishline may or may not lure fish onto the hook, the aloe plant does, after all, yield a soothing ointment for burns, and the peppermint herb has relieved many a stomachache.

Common sense, which is often distrusted, combines folklore, generalizations based on observation, and learning discovered through experimentation with intuition and reasoned guesses. It can function not only as a source of curriculum principles but as a methodology as well. For example, Joseph J. Schwab proposed a common-sense process he called "deliberation" to deal with curriculum problems. Minimizing the search for theoretical constructs and principles, his method depends more on practical solutions to specific problems.[3] Schwab pointed out the pitfalls of relying on theory alone. He rejected "the pursuit of global principles and comprehensive patterns, the search for stable sequences and invariant elements, the construction of taxonomies of

---

[2]For discussion of the Academy, see Nelson L. Bossing, *Principles of Secondary Education* (Englewood Cliffs, N.J.: Prentice-Hall, 1955), pp. 97–107.

[3]Joseph J. Schwab, *The Practical: A Language for Curriculum* (Washington, D.C.: National Education Association, Center for the Study of Instruction, 1970).

supposedly fixed or recurrent kinds" and recommended "three other modes of operation . . . the practical, the quasi-practical, and the eclectic."[4]

Of particular interest is Schwab's contrast of the theoretical and practical modes. Schwab explained:

> The end or outcome of the theoretical is knowledge, general or universal statements which are supposed to be true, warranted, confidence-inspiring. Their truth, warrant, or untrustworthiness is held, moreover, to be durable and extensive. . . . The end or outcome of the practical, on the other hand, is a *decision,* a selection and guide to possible action. Decisions are never true or trustworthy. Instead a decision (before it is put into effect) can be judged only comparatively, as probably better or worse than alternatives. . . . A decision, moreover, has no great durability or extensive application. It applies unequivocally only to the case for which it is sought.[5]

When curriculum planning is based on deliberation, judgment and common sense are applied to decision making. Some professional educators have faulted the application of common sense or judgment as a methodology, so imbued are they with a scientific approach to problem solving. In 1918 Franklin Bobbitt took note of scientific methodology in curriculum making, citing the application of measurement and evaluation techniques, diagnosis of problems, and prescription of remedies.[6] At a later date Arthur W. Combs was moved to warn against too great a reliance on science for the solution of all educational problems.[7] Whereas science may help us find solutions to some problems, not all answers to educational problems of the day can be found in this way. Certainly, hard data are preferred over beliefs and judgments. But there are times in the absence of hard data when curriculum workers must rely on their intuition and make judgments on the basis of the best available evidence.

Unless a principle is established that is irrefutable by reason of objective data, some degree of judgment must be brought into play. Whenever judgment comes into the picture, the potential for controversy arises. Consequently, some of the principles for curriculum development provoke controversy, while others are generally accepted as reasonable guidelines. Controversy occurs as often as a result of differing values and philosophical orientations of curriculum workers as it does from lack of hard data for making decisions.

TYPES OF PRINCIPLES

Curriculum principles may be viewed as whole truths, partial truths, or hypotheses. While all function as operating principles, they are distinguished by their known effectiveness or by degree of risk. It is important to understand these differences before examining the major guiding principles for curriculum development.

---

[4]Ibid., p. 2.
[5]Ibid., pp. 2–3.
[6]See Franklin Bobbitt, *The Curriculum* (Boston: Houghton Mifflin, 1918), pp. 41–42.
[7]See Arthur W. Combs, *The Professional Education of Teachers* (Boston: Allyn and Bacon, 1965), p. 74.

WHOLE TRUTHS

Whole truths are either obvious facts or concepts proved through experimentation, and they are usually accepted without challenge. For example, few will dispute that students will be able, as a rule, to master an advanced body of content only after they have developed the prerequisite skills. From this principle come the practices of pre-assessment of entry skills and sequencing of content.

PARTIAL TRUTHS

Partial truths are based on limited data and can apply to some, many, or most situations, but they are not always universal. Some educators assert, for example, that student achievement is higher when students are grouped homogeneously for instruction. Some learners may achieve better results when placed in groups of like ability, but others may not. The practice of homogeneous or ability grouping may be successful with some groups but not with others. It may permit schools to achieve certain goals of education, such as mastery of content, but prevent them from achieving other goals, such as enabling students to learn to live and work with persons of differing levels of ability. Partial truths are not "half-truths," containing falsehoods, but they do not always tell the whole story.

HYPOTHESES

Finally, some principles are neither whole nor partial truths but are *hypotheses* or tentative working assumptions. Curriculum workers base these ideas on their best judgments, folklore, and common sense. As one example, teachers and administrators have talked for many years about optimum size for classes and for schools. Educators have advocated class sizes of as few as twenty-five students in high school classes and fewer in elementary classes. They have been less certain as to how many pupils should be housed in a single school. Figures used as recommendations for class and school size are but estimates based on best judgments. School planners have reasoned that for purposes of economy and efficiency, class and school sizes can be too small. They also know from intuition or experience that class and school sizes can grow so large as to create situations that reduce educational productivity. However, the research delivers no magic number that will guarantee success in every course, classroom, and school.

While practice based on whole truth is a desideratum, the use of partial truths and the application of hypotheses contribute to the development of the field. Growth would be stymied if the field waited until all truths were discovered before any changes were made. Judgments, folklore, and common sense make the curriculum arena a far more stimulating place to work than if everything were already predetermined. If all theories, beliefs, and hypotheses could be either proved or disproved—a most improbable event—we would have reached that condition of perfection that would make life among the curriculum developers exceedingly dull.

TEN AXIOMS

Instead of talking in terms of whole truths and partial truths, since so many of the principles to which practitioners subscribe have not been fully tested, we might be more accurate if we speak of *axioms*. *Merriam-Webster's Collegiate® Dictionary,* 10th Edition, defines an axiom as "**1:** a maxim widely accepted on its intrinsic merit **2:** a statement accepted as true as the basis for argument or inference: POSTULATE **3:** an established rule or principle or a self-evident truth."[8] Or perhaps "axiom" should be replaced with "theorem." The first two definitions of "theorem" in this dictionary are "**1:** a formula, proposition or statement in mathematics or logic deduced or to be deduced from other formulas or propositions **2:** an idea accepted or proposed as a demonstrable truth often as a part of a general theory: PROPOSITION."[9] As students of mathematics know well, even though an axiom may be a postulate and a theorem may be a proposition, both axioms and theorems serve the field well. They offer guidelines that establish a frame of reference for workers seeking ways of operating and resolving problems. Several generally accepted axioms that apply to the curriculum field may serve to guide efforts that curriculum workers make for the purpose of improving the curriculum.

INEVITABILITY OF CHANGE

Axiom 1. *Change is both inevitable and necessary, for it is through change that life forms grow and develop.* Human institutions, like human beings themselves, grow and develop in proportion to their ability to respond to change and to adapt to changing conditions. Society and its institutions continuously encounter problems to which they must respond or perish. Glen Hass called attention in 1987 to the following major contemporary problems facing society, all of which remain continuing issues:

- environment
- changing values and morality
- the family
- the Microelectronics Revolution
- the changing world of work
- equal rights
- urban and suburban crises
- crime and violence
- alienation and anxiety
- international tensions[10]

The public school, one of our society's fundamental institutions, faces a plethora of contemporary problems, some of which threaten its very existence. We need cite only the intense competition from both secular and sectarian private schools; proposals for tax credits and vouchers which may be used at any school, public, private, or

---

[8]By permission. From *Merriam-Webster's Collegiate® Dictionary,* 10th Edition © 1999 by Merriam Webster, Incorporated.
[9]By permission. From *Merriam-Webster's Collegiate® Dictionary,* 10th Edition © 1999 by Merriam Webster, Incorporated.
[10]Glen Hass, *Curriculum Planning: A New Approach,* 5th ed. (Boston: Allyn and Bacon, 1987), pp. 45–48.

parochial; the advent of charter schools and the increase in the number of home schools to illustrate the scope of problems currently confronting the public school. Change in the form of responses to contemporary problems must be foremost in the minds of curriculum developers.

CURRICULUM AS A PRODUCT OF ITS TIME

Axiom 2.   The second axiom is a corollary of the first. Quite simply, a *school curriculum not only reflects but is a product of its time*. Though it may seem to some that the curriculum is a tortoise moving infernally s-l-o-w-l-y, it has really undergone more transformations than the number of disguises assumed by a skilled master change artist.

David Turney, for example, commented on the slowness of change when he said:

> Real social change is painfully slow. It proceeds like a glacier whose movement is measured in feet per year. Educational and especially curriculum change is a part and parcel of social change and proceeds at about the same rate.[11]

Turney felt that at least a decade must be allowed as a minimum period of time for a basic change in education to be made. The reader has no doubt heard the comment (itself an axiom) that it takes fifty years to effect an innovation in the school's curriculum. Many also believe that it takes an additional fifty years before the innovation is universally adopted by the schools. The fifty-year axiom illustrates well that axioms, which are created by human beings, are themselves subject to change as conditions in society change. Prior to the advent of television, computer networks, and other sophisticated media, this axiom may have had an element of truth; but today's news and ideas flash across the country, indeed across the world, instantaneously. Fifty years were certainly not required for thousands of schools across the country to put into practice (and in some cases later abandon) team teaching, instructional television, open-space education, values clarification, behavioral objectives, computer literacy, cooperative learning, and whole language, to mention only a few curricular innovations. But as a word of caution, although an innovation may not require fifty to one hundred years, it may require three, five, or ten years or more—to some a long period of time—before it becomes a relatively common practice.

Clearly, the curriculum responds to and is changed by social forces, philosophical positions, psychological principles, accumulating knowledge, and educational leadership at its moment in history. Changes in society clearly influence curriculum development as, for example, the increased pluralism of our nation, the growth of technology, and the need for health education. You will note the pervasive effects of social forces when we discuss programs and issues in Chapters 9 and 14.

The impact of the rapid accumulation of knowledge may be one of the more dramatic illustrations of forces affecting the curriculum. Certainly some adaptations in the school's program ought to be made as a result of discoveries of lifesaving vaccines and medications; inventions such as the computer, the laser, and interactive video; and scientific accom-

[11]David Turney, "Sisyphus Revisited," *Perspectives on Curriculum Development 1776–1976.* 1976 Yearbook (Alexandria, Va.: Association for Supervision and Curriculum Development, 1976), p. 232.

plishments like the moon landings, the Mars flights, the Galileo probes, and other land, sea, and space explorations.

The presence of persuasive educational groups and individuals has been responsible for the adoption of curricular innovations at given moments in history and in numerous cases has caused permanent and continuing curriculum change. The effects of the *Cardinal Principles of Secondary Education* by the Commission on the Reorganization of Secondary Education,[12] *Education for All American Youth* by the Educational Policies Commission,[13] and *A Nation at Risk* by the National Commission on Excellence in Education[14] are illustrations of the impact persuasive groups have on the curriculum.

We may even point to individuals over the course of history, speaking either for themselves or for groups that they represented, who can be credited (or blamed, depending on one's perspective) for changes that have come about in the curriculum. Who can calculate the impact on education, for example, of Benjamin Franklin in the eighteenth century or Horace Mann in the nineteenth? What would the progressive education movement of the early twentieth century have been without John Dewey, William H. Kilpatrick, and Boyd Bode? How many secondary schools in the late 1950s and early 1960s "Conantized" their programs on the recommendations of James B. Conant, the former president of Harvard University? What impact has Maria Montessori had on elementary school programs? What responses of the curriculum in the latter half of the twentieth century can be traced to the teachings of Jean Piaget and of B. F. Skinner? What changes will come about as a result of recommendations made by Mortimer J. Adler,[15] Ernest L. Boyer,[16] John I. Goodlad,[17] and Theodore R. Sizer[18] (In Chapter 9 we will examine many of these recommendations).

We could fashion for ourselves a little chart—see Table 2.1—to illustrate the effects of several forces during periods of history on both the curriculum and instruction. In barest skeletal form we might break American educational history into three periods: 1650–1750, 1750–1850, and 1850 to the present. We might then chart some of the curricular and instructional responses to philosophical, psychological, and sociological forces of their time as the table shows. These forces and responses often overlap from one period to the next.

We could embellish the chart by refining the periods of history and adding other elements, but this skeletal description serves to illustrate that a curriculum is the product of its time. James B. Macdonald made the same point in this way:

> It should be clear to most knowledgeable and thoughtful observers of the American scene during the past twenty-five years, that any reforms in institutional setting, whether in education, occupations, churches, families, recreation, or whatever, are in-

---

[12]Commission on the Reorganization of Secondary Education. *Cardinal Principles of Secondary Education* (Washington, D.C.: U.S. Office of Education, Bulletin 35, 1918). See Chapter 3 of this text.

[13]Educational Policies Commission, *Education for All American Youth* (Washington, D.C.: National Education Association, 1944). See Chapter 3 of this text.

[14]The National Commission on Excellence in Education, David P. Gardner, chairman. *A Nation at Risk: The Imperative for Educational Reform* (Washington, D.C.: U.S. Government Printing Office, 1983). See Chapter 3 of this text.

[15]Mortimer J. Adler, *The Paideia Proposal: An Educational Manifesto* (New York: Macmillan, 1982).

[16]Ernest L. Boyer, *High School: A Report on Secondary Education in America* (New York: Harper & Row, 1983).

[17]John I. Goodlad, *A Place Called School: Prospects for the Future* (New York: McGraw-Hill, 1984).

[18]Theodore R. Sizer, *Horace's Compromise: The Dilemma of the American High School* (Boston: Houghton Mifflin, 1984).

TABLE 2.1

FORCES AFFECTING CURRICULUM AND INSTRUCTION

PERIOD	FORCES	CURRICULAR RESPONSES	INSTRUCTIONAL RESPONSES

1650–1750	*Philosophy*
	Essentialism
	
	Psychology
	Faculty psychology—
	  mind as a muscle
	Sociology
	Theocracy—Calvinist
	Male chauvinism
	Agrarian society
	Rich–poor dichotomy
		Latin Grammar School:
		  School for boys
		The Bible
		The three R's
		Classical curriculum
			Strict discipline
			Rote learning
			Use of sectarian
			  materials
			Mental discipline

1750–1850	*Philosophy*
	Essentialism
	Utilitarianism
	
	Psychology
	Faculty psychology
	
	Sociology
	Industrial Revolution
	Westward movement
	Rise of middle class
	Increased urbanization
		Academy:
		Education for girls
		Instruction in:
		  English
		  Natural history
		  Modern languages
		    plus three R's
		    and classical
		    curriculum
		Tax-supported schools
		Kindergartens
			Mental discipline
			Recitation
			Strict discipline
			Some practical
			  applications

1850 to present:	*Philosophy*
	Essentialism
	Progressivism
	
	Psychology
	Behavioristic
	Experimental
	Gestalt
	Perceptual
	
	Sociology
	Settling the West
	Mechanized society
		1850–1925:
		High schools
		
		1925–1950:
		Child-centered
		  curriculum
		Experimentalism
		Centralization and
		  consolidation of
		  schools
		Life adjustment
		
		1950 to present:
		Career education
		Open-space education
			Practical applications
			Electives
			Problem-solving
			  methods
			Attention to whole
			  child
			
			Individualization
			  and groupings for
			  instruction

(*Continued*)

Table 2.1 Continued

PERIOD	FORCES	CURRICULAR RESPONSES	INSTRUCTIONAL RESPONSES

1850 to present: (*Continued*)	Internationalism
	Urbanization
	Immigration
	Internationalism
	Urbanization
	Immigration
	Armed conflicts
	Civil rights
	Big business
	Big labor
	Equal rights
	Changes in family
	Environmental problems
	Diminishing resources
	Rapid growth
	  of technology
	Space exploration
	Public demand
	  for schools'
	  accountability
	Unemployment
	Drug and alcohol
	  abuse
	Crime
	Homeless persons
	Racial tensions/
	  ethnic conflicts
	Movements for human
	  rights
	Persons with disabilities
	Aging population
	Sexual behavior
	Religious differences
	Growth of democratic
	  movements
	  worldwide
	Economic crises
	Global warming
	End of cold war
	Continuing health needs
		Alternative schools
		Magnet schools
		Basic skills
		Alternative schools
		Magnet schools
		Charter schools
		Home schools
		Basic skills
		Middle schools
		Computer education
		Values/character education
		Environmental education
		Multicultural education
		Global education
		Health education/clinics
		Sexuality education
		Adult education
		Literacy education
		Bilingual education
		Consumer education
		Cultural literacy
		  (core knowledge)
		Technological
		  education
			Mediated instruction
			Education for self-discipline
			Achievement testing
			Effective teaching models
			Cooperative learning
			Whole language
			Use of community resources

tricately related to multiple social pressures and set in the context of a general cultural ethos.[19]

Consequently, the curriculum planner of today must identify and be concerned with forces that impinge on the schools and must carefully decide how the curriculum should change in response to these often conflicting forces.

CONCURRENT CHANGES

Axiom 3.   *Curriculum changes made at an earlier period of time can exist concurrently with newer curriculum changes at a later period of time.* The classical curriculum of the Latin Grammar School was continued, in spite of the reluctance of Benjamin Franklin, in the Academy. Indeed, even the first high school, established in Boston in 1821, was known as the English Classical School. It was not until three years later that the English Classical School became the English High School.

Curriculum revision rarely starts and ends abruptly. Changes coexist and overlap for long periods of time. Ordinarily, curricular developments are phased in gradually and phased out the same way. Because competing forces and responses occur at different periods of time and continue to exist, curriculum development becomes a frustrating, yet challenging task.

Philosophical positions have differed on the nature of humankind, the destiny of the human race, good and evil, and the purposes of education have existed at every period of history. The powerful schools of essentialism and progressive thought continually strive to capture the allegiance of the profession and the public. The college preparatory curriculum, for example, vies with the vocational curriculum for primacy. Instructional strategies that are targeted at the development of the intellect compete with strategies for treating the child in body, mind, and spirit. Even the discredited tenets of faculty psychology ("mind as a muscle," mental discipline) linger in school practices.

The competing responses to changing conditions have almost mandated an eclecticism, especially in the public schools. Curriculum developers select the best responses from previous times or modify them for future times. Except at the most trivial level, either/or choices are almost impossible to make in complex social areas like education. Yet some people continue to look for and argue for either/or solutions. To some, education will perish if all teachers do not write behavioral objectives. To others, the growth of preadolescents will surely be stunted unless they are educated in a middle school. Some elementary school administrators seek to provide a quality education with teaching teams. Others hold firmly to the traditional self-contained classroom.

Some themes are repeated through history. Critics have, for example, lambasted the schools periodically for what they conceive as failure to stress fundamental subject matter.[20] The history of curriculum development is filled with illustrations not only of

---

[19]James B. Macdonald, "Curriculum Development in Relation to Social and Intellectual Systems," in Robert M. McClure, ed., *The Curriculum: Retrospect and Prospect,* 70th Yearbook, Part I, National Society for the Study of Education (Chicago: University of Chicago Press, 1971), pp. 98–99.

[20]See, for example, Arthur Bestor, *Educational Wastelands: The Retreat from Learning in Our Public Schools* (Urbana, Ill.: University of Illinois Press, 1953); Hyman Rickover, *Swiss Schools and Ours: Why Theirs Are Better* (Boston: Little, Brown, 1962); and Richard Mitchell, *The Graves of Academe* (Boston: Little, Brown, 1981).

recurrent philosophical themes, like the subject matter cacophony, but also with recurrent and cyclical curricular responses. Many of our schools have changed from an essentialistic to a progressive curriculum and back again.

Schools have moved from self-contained to open-space to self-contained; elementary schools have shifted from self-contained to nongraded to self-contained; schools have taught the "old math," then the "new math," and afterwards reverted to the former; they have followed the phonics method of teaching reading, changed to "look/say" methods, then gone back to phonics; they have stressed modern languages, then abandoned them, then reincorporated them in the curriculum. On the other hand, some schools, particularly the essentialistic, have remained unchanged while social transformations have swirled around them.

The schools of the early days in America stressed basic skills taught in a strict disciplinary climate. The early twentieth century schools went beyond basic skills—some would say away from basic skills—to concern for pupils' diverse needs and interests in a more permissive environment. Schools of the present emphasize the basic skills, subject matter, academic achievement, pupil assessment, and codes of conduct as well as personal development in a culturally diverse society.

As curricular themes are often recapitulated, some teachers and curriculum developers are disposed to maintain the status quo, concluding that their current mode of operation, while it may be out of favor at the present moment, will be in style again sometime in the future. "Why change and then have to change back?" they ask.

When the status quo no longer serves the needs of the learners or of society, the maintenance of the status quo is inexcusable, for it prohibits responses appropriate to the times. Even if prior responses return at a later date, they should result from a reexamination of the forces of that particular time. Thus, the reemergence of prior responses will be new responses, not *old* in the sense of being unchanging and unchangeable.

CHANGE IN PEOPLE

Axiom 4. *Curriculum change results from changes in people.* Thus curriculum developers should begin with an attempt to change the people who must ultimately effect curriculum change. This effort implies involving people in the process of curriculum development to gain their commitment to change. Sad experience over a long period of time has demonstrated that changes handed down from on high to subordinates do not work well as a rule. Not until the subordinates have internalized the changes and accepted them as their own can the changes be effective and long lasting. Many school personnel lack commitment because they are denied this involvement in change and their contributions to change have been deprecated.

The importance of effecting change in people has been stressed by curriculum experts for many years. Alice Miel, for example, wrote:

> To change the curriculum of the school is to change the factors interacting to shape the curriculum. In each instance this means bringing about changes in people—in their desires, beliefs, and attitudes, in their knowledge and skill. Even changes in the physical environment, to the extent that they can be made at all, are dependent upon changes in the persons who have some control over that environment. In short, the nature of cur-

riculum change should be seen for what it really is—a type of social change, change in people, not mere change on paper.[21]

Vernon Anderson advised curriculum developers that no curriculum change could be lasting without a change in the way people think. He gave this principle paramount importance.[22]

Jack Frymier and Horace Hawn spoke to the same theme:

> Tinkering with minutiae in curriculum may cause some minor changes to occur in the educational process but for anyone seriously interested in effecting significant change, the people who are involved must be themselves changed.[23]

A lack of enthusiastic support from those affected by change spills over to the students, who often adopt negative attitudes as a result.

Some curriculum planners interpret this axiom to mean that one hundred percent commitment of all affected parties must be achieved before a curriculum change can be implemented. Would that it were possible to obtain one hundred percent consensus on any issue in education! Somewhere between a simple majority and universal agreement would appear to be a reasonable expectation. Involvement of persons affected in the process itself will succeed in garnering some support even from those who may disagree with the final curricular product.

The curriculum planner should ensure that all persons have an opportunity to contribute to a proposed change before it is too far along and irreversible. No persons should be involved in the charade practiced in some school systems whereby teachers and others are brought into the planning process for window dressing when it is a foregone conclusion that the curriculum change will be implemented whether the participants accept it or not. The "curriculum planner knows best" attitude has no place in curriculum design and implementation.

In recent years we have been witnessing a pronounced movement toward empowerment of teachers and laypersons, that is, enabling them to exercise a degree of control over what happens in their schools. For further discussion of empowerment, see Chapter 4, which expands on the process for instituting and effecting curriculum change.

COOPERATIVE ENDEAVOR

Axiom 5. *Curriculum change is effected as a result of cooperative endeavor on the part of groups.* Albert I. Oliver underscored the group nature of curriculum development when he said:

> It cannot be stressed too strongly that curriculum improvement is a cooperative endeavor. In the past, action on the curriculum was often limited to small-group work or to administrative decree; today, on the other hand, many groups and individuals are being encouraged to participate in a spirit of genuine cooperation.[24]

---

[21]Alice Miel, *Changing the Curriculum: A Social Process* (New York: D. Appleton Century, 1946), p. 10.

[22]Vernon E. Anderson, *Curriculum Guidelines in an Era of Change* (New York: Ronald Press, 1969), p. 19.

[23]Jack R. Frymier and Horace C. Hawn, *Curriculum Improvement for Better Schools* (Worthington, Ohio: Charles A. Jones, 1970), p. 24.

[24]Albert I. Oliver, *Curriculum Improvement,* 2nd ed. (New York: Harper & Row, 1977), p. 37.

Oliver saw the cooperative nature of curriculum development as "more a matter of growth of individuals" than as "the installation or construction of certain materials."[25] Therefore, according to Oliver, "the more individuals can identify themselves with a curriculum activity, the more readily will they accept new phases. Genuine participation tends to generate 'psychological ownership' of the resulting program."[26]

Although an individual teacher working in isolation might conceivably, and sometimes does, effect changes in the curriculum by himself or herself, large and fundamental changes are brought about as a result of group decision.

Several groups or constituencies are involved in curriculum development in differing roles and with differing intensities. Students and laypersons often, though perhaps not as frequently as might be desired, join forces with educational personnel in the complex job of planning a curriculum.

Teachers and curriculum specialists constitute the professional core of planners. These professionally trained persons carry the weight of curriculum development. They work together under the direction of the school administrator whose task it is to oversee their activities and to facilitate their efforts at all stages of development. The administrator may take the bows for the school's successful activities but by the same token will also receive barbs for efforts gone awry.

Students enter the process of curriculum development as direct recipients of both benefits and harm that result from curriculum change, and parents are brought in as the persons most vitally concerned with the welfare of their young. More often than in days gone by, administrators, either willingly on their own or by directives from higher authority, invite students and parents to participate in the process of curriculum planning. Some school systems go beyond parents of children in their schools and seek representation from the total community, parents and nonparents alike. People from the community are asked more frequently now what they feel the schools should offer and what they believe the schools are omitting from their programs.

Generally, any significant change in the curriculum should involve all the aforementioned constituencies, as well as the school's noncertificated personnel. The more people affected by the change, the greater its complexity and costs, the greater the number of persons and groups that should be involved. The roles of various individuals and groups in curriculum development are examined in Chapter 4.

Although some limited gains certainly take place through independent curriculum development within the walls of a classroom, significant curriculum improvement comes about through group activity. Results of group deliberation are not only more extensive than individual efforts, but the process by which the group works together allows group members to share their ideas and to reach group consensus. In this respect group members help each other to change and to achieve commitment to change. Carl D. Glickman averred: "Any comprehensive changes made without the understanding and support of at last a core majority of educators and parents will fail, not necessarily because of the changes themselves but because of the way they came about."[27] Drawing on a report from Public Agenda by Jean Johnson and John

---

[25]Ibid.
[26]Ibid.
[27]Carl D. Glickman, *Revolutionizing America's Schools* (San Francisco: Jossey-Bass, 1998), p. 38.

Immerwahr,[28] Glickman affirmed that the public wants to maintain the status quo and stressed the importance of involving parents and citizens in curriculum planning when he said:

> The hard facts are that most parents and citizens do not believe in or want much alternation in their schools' educational structures. They want grade levels, letter grades, ability grouping, single classrooms, and textbooks. They want today's school to look like the schools they attended. They want teachers to emphasize the basic skills and direct instruction. They are skeptical about new ways of assessing student learning, group or cooperative learning, critical thinking, and student problem solving. . . . Regardless of how insupportable is the case for keeping schools as they are, without a way for educators, parents, and citizens to understand, discuss, and participate in new possibilities, change efforts for the long term will be for naught."[29]

In analyzing the failures of curriculum reform efforts Larry Cuban made clear that "defining the official school curriculum (as opposed to the 'taught,' 'learned,' and 'tested,' curricula) is one of the few endeavors left that allows groups in a democratic society, continually pulled this way and that by highly prized but competing values to debate what they want for the next generation."[30]

DECISION-MAKING PROCESS

Axiom 6. *Curriculum development is basically a decision-making process.* The curriculum planner in cooperation with those involved must make a variety of choices, including the following:

1. *Choices among disciplines.* The absence of philosophy, anthropology, Eastern languages, and sometimes even art and music from the curriculum of schools indicates that choices have been made about the subjects to which students will be exposed.
2. *Choices among competing viewpoints.* Planners must decide, for example, whether they agree that bilingual education best serves the needs of segments of society. If they decide in the positive, they must further decide what type of bilingual education is appropriate for their schools. Planners must make decisions about programs such as interscholastic athletics for girls; whether pupils with learning disabilities should be assigned to special classes; whether to group pupils by ability, achievement, age, or heterogeneously; and whether programs of sexuality education should be offered.
3. *Choices of emphases.* Shall a school system, for example, give extra help to poor readers? Shall school systems provide programs for the gifted? Shall extra efforts be made for disadvantaged students? Should school funds be diverted from one group of students to aid another group?

---

[28]Jean Johnson and John Immerwahr, *First Things First: What Americans Expect form the Public Schools: A Report from Public Agenda* (New York: Public Agenda, 1994).

[29]Glickman, *Revolutionizing*, p. 39.

[30]Larry Cuban, "The Lure of Curricular Reform and Its Pitiful History," *Phi Delta Kappan* 75, no. 2 (October 1993): 183.

4. *Choices of methods.* What is the best way, for example, to teach reading? phonics? look/say? "systems" reading? whole language? What is the best way to teach writing? Shall methods emphasize skills or creativity and self-esteem? What are the more effective materials to use? How do we eliminate cultural bias from the curriculum?

5. *Choices in organization.* Is a nongraded school, for example, the better approach to an organizational arrangement that will provide maximum opportunities for learners? Should alternative forms of schooling within and outside the system be provided? Shall elementary programs be delivered in an open-space or pod setting, with totally self-contained classrooms, or with the use of resource persons to assist a teacher in a self-contained classroom? Should schools operate year-round and if so, shall they be single track or multitrack?

Two necessary characteristics of a curriculum planner are the ability to effect decisions after sufficient study of a problem and the willingness to make decisions.[31] The indecisive person had best not gravitate to a career as a curriculum planner. Those persons for whom every *i* must be dotted and every *t* crossed before a move can be made are far too cautious for curriculum planning. Every decision involves calculated risk, for no one—in spite of what some experts may claim—has all the answers to all the problems or a single panacea for every problem. Some decisions will end in dismal failure. But unless the test is made, it can never be known what will succeed and what will not. The most that can be expected of a fallible human being is that decisions will be made on the basis of available evidence that suggests success for the learners and that promises no harm for them as a result of a decision taken. In the history of curriculum development we can find evidence of many roads that were not taken. Those roads might have turned out to be expressways to learning, though of course, the pessimistic champion of the status quo would assure us that the roads not taken would have been overgrown ruts that ended at the brink of a precipice or circular paths that would lead us right back to where we were.

The curriculum planner needs to be aware as John D. McNeil pointed out, that "curriculum decision making is a political process."[32] Although the task of making curricular choices may be difficult in complex, advanced societies, the opportunity to make choices from among many alternatives is a luxury not found in every country.

CONTINUOUS PROCESS

Axiom 7. *Curriculum development is a never-ending process.* Curriculum planners constantly strive for the ideal, yet the ideal eludes them. John R. Verduin, Jr. made this point succinctly: "Continuous examination, evaluation, and improvement of the curriculum is, therefore, of vital importance."[33] Perfection in the curriculum will never be

---

[31]For description of a decision-making process, see Chapter 13 of this text regarding material from Phi Delta Kappa Committee on Evaluation, Daniel L. Stufflebeam, committee chairman, *Educational Evaluation and Decision Making* (Itasca, Ill.: F. E. Peacock, 1971).

[32]John D. McNeil, *Curriculum: A Comprehensive Introduction,* 5th ed. (New York: HarperCollins, 1996), p. 290.

[33]John R. Verduin, Jr., *Cooperative Curriculum Improvement* (Englewood Cliffs, N.J.: Prentice-Hall, 1967), p. 33.

achieved. The curriculum can always be improved, and many times better solutions can be found to accomplish specific objectives. As the needs of learners change, as society changes, and as new knowledge appears, the curriculum must change. Curriculum evaluation should affect subsequent planning and implementation. Curriculum goals and objectives and plans for curricular organization should be modified as feedback reveals the need for modification.

Curriculum development is not finished when a single curricular problem has been temporarily solved nor when a newer, revised program has been instituted. Continual monitoring is necessary to assure that the program is on track and the problem does not recur. Further, adequate records should be kept by curriculum committees so that curriculum workers in future years will know what has been attempted and with what results.

COMPREHENSIVE PROCESS

Axiom 8. *Curriculum development is a comprehensive process.* Historically, curriculum revision has been a hit-or-miss procedure: patching, cutting, adding, plugging in, shortening, lengthening, and trouble-shooting. In agreeing with the necessity for comprehensive planning, Hilda Taba explained:

> Some commentators have pointed out that the whole history of curriculum revision has been piecemeal—a mere shifting of pieces from one place to another, taking out one piece and replacing it with another without a reappraisal of the whole pattern. The curriculum has become "the amorphous product of generations of tinkering"—a patchwork. This piecemeal approach is continuing today, when additions and revisions in certain areas are made without reconsidering the entire pattern, and when attention in one part of the school system is recommended without corresponding changes in the next.[34]

Curriculum planning has often been too fragmentary rather than comprehensive or holistic. Too many curriculum planners have focused on the trees and not seen the forest. The popular expression that the whole is greater than the sum of its parts applies well to curriculum development. Although parts of the curriculum may be studied separately, planners must frequently and periodically view the macrocurriculum, that is, the curriculum as a whole, as distinguished from the sum of its parts.

Curriculum development spills not only into the forest but beyond. A comprehensive view encompasses an awareness of the impact of curriculum development not only on the students, teachers, and parents directly concerned with a programmatic change but also on the innocent bystanders, those not directly involved in the curriculum planning but affected in some way by the results of planning.[35] Sexuality education, for example, may affect not only teachers, students, and parents of students for whom the program is intended but also teachers, students, and parents of those who are not

[34]Hilda Taba. *Curriculum Development: Theory and Practice* (New York: Harcourt Brace Jovanovich, 1962), p. 8.

[35]See Michael Scriven. "The Methodology of Evaluation." *Perspectives of Curriculum Evaluation.* AERA Monograph Series on Evaluation no. 1 (Chicago: Rand McNally, 1967), p. 77.

scheduled for the instruction. Some from the groups involved may not wish to be included. Some from the groups not in the program may wish to receive the instruction. Some from both groups may reject the subject as inappropriate for the school.

The comprehensive approach to curriculum planning requires a generous investment of physical and human resources. Curriculum workers must engage in, without meaning to be redundant, planning for curriculum planning or what some people might refer to as "preplanning." Some predetermination must be made prior to initiating curriculum development as to whether the tangible resources, the personnel, and sufficient time will be available to allow a reasonable expectation of success. Not only must personnel be identified, but their sense of motivation, energy level, and other commitments must also be taken into consideration by the curriculum leaders. Perhaps one of the reasons that curriculum development has historically been fragmentary and piecemeal is the demand the comprehensive approach places on the school's resources.

SYSTEMATIC DEVELOPMENT

Axiom 9. *Systematic curriculum development is more effective than trial and error.* Curriculum development should ideally be made comprehensive by looking at the whole canvas and should be made systematic by following an established set of procedures. That set of procedures should be agreed upon and known by all those who participate in the development of the curriculum. Curriculum planners are more likely to be productive and successful if they follow an agreed-upon model for curriculum development that outlines or charts the sequence of steps to be followed. In Chapter 5 we will examine several models for curriculum development.

If the curriculum worker subscribes to the foregoing axioms and consents to modeling his or her behavior on the basis of these axioms, will success be inevitable? The answer is an obvious no, for there are many limitations on curriculum workers, some of which are beyond their control. Among the restrictions on the curriculum planner are the style and personal philosophy of the administrator, the resources of the school system, the degree of complacency in the school system and community, the presence or absence of competent supervisory leadership, the fund of knowledge and skills possessed by the participants in curriculum development, and the availability of professional materials and resource persons.

One of the great limitations—sometimes overlooked because it is so obvious and encompassing—is the existing curriculum. Many treatises have been written by curriculum experts on the characteristics of different types of curriculum. The earmarks of an activity curriculum, a subject matter curriculum, a broad-fields curriculum, and variations of core curriculum are described in the literature in detail.[36] From a purely cognitive base such discussions are useful. But the inference is sometimes drawn that the choice of a type of curriculum is an open one—that if the planners know and believe in the characteristics of an activity curriculum, for example, they will have the option of organizing and implementing that type of curriculum. It is as if a curriculum planner could start from scratch and design a totally new curriculum, which is rarely the case, and which leads us to the tenth axiom.

---

[36]See B. O. Smith, William O. Stanley, and J. Harlan Shores, *Fundamentals of Curriculum Development,* rev. ed. (New York: Harcourt Brace Jovanovich, 1957). See also Chapter 9 of this text.

STARTING FROM THE EXISTING CURRICULUM

Axiom 10.   *The curriculum planner starts from where the curriculum is, just as the teacher starts from where the students are.* Curriculum change does not take place overnight. Few quantum leaps can be found in the field of curriculum, and this condition may be a positive value rather than a negative one, for slow but steady progress toward change allows time for testing and reflection.

Since most curriculum planners begin with already existing curricula, we would be more accurate if, instead of talking about curriculum organization, we talked about curriculum reorganization. The investment of thought, time, money, and work by previous planners cannot be thrown out even if such a drastic remedy appeared valid to a new set of planners. The curriculum worker might well follow the advice in the *Book of Common Prayer,* where the believer is told to "hold fast to that which is good."

SUMMARY

The system that we call education responds to changes as conditions in its suprasystem (society) change. Curriculum change is a normal, expected consequence of changes in the environment.

The curriculum worker's responsibility is to seek ways of making continuous improvement in the curriculum. The task of the curriculum worker is facilitated if the worker follows some generally accepted principles for curriculum development. Ten general principles or axioms are presented in this chapter. The principles stem not only from disciplines outside of professional education but also from the folklore of curriculum, observation, experimental data, and common sense.

Axioms suggested as guidelines to curriculum developers are:

- Curriculum change is inevitable and desirable.
- The curriculum is a product of its time.
- Curriculum changes of earlier periods often coexist and overlap curriculum changes of later periods.
- Curriculum change results only as people are changed.
- Curriculum development is a cooperative group activity.
- Curriculum development is basically a process of making choices from among alternatives.
- Curriculum development never ends.
- Curriculum development is more effective if it is a comprehensive, not piecemeal, process.
- Curriculum development is more effective when it follows a systematic process.
- Curriculum development starts from where the curriculum is.

Both teachers and curriculum specialists fill roles as curriculum workers in cooperation with other school personnel. Teachers, curriculum specialists, supervisors, administrators, students, parents, and other community representatives can all play significant roles in effecting curriculum change.

Curriculum developers start from the given and work within specific parameters. Ordinarily, change is relatively slow, limited, and gradual.

QUESTIONS FOR DISCUSSION

1. In what ways is today's public school curriculum suitable for the times?
2. In what ways is today's public school curriculum not suitable for the times?
3. What are some curriculum principles derived from common sense?
4. Are there any curriculum developments that have been based on whole truths? If so, give examples.
5. Are there any curriculum developments that have been based on false premises? If so, give examples.

SUPPLEMENTARY EXERCISES

1. Develop your own chart of the effects of forces on curriculum and instruction by periods of history of the United States. Your chart should expand on the periods of history and present additional details.
2. Formulate and support one or two additional axioms pertaining to curriculum development. These may be original ones that you will be able to defend, or they may be axioms drawn from the professional literature.
3. Look up and write a paper on the contributions of one of the following persons to the development of curriculum thought or practice: Franklin Bobbitt, Boyd Bode, John Dewey, Robert Hutchins, William H. Kilpatrick, Jean Piaget, B. F. Skinner, and Ralph Tyler.
4. Look up and write a paper on one of the following groups and describe its impact on curriculum development in the United States: the Committee of Ten, the Commission on the Reorganization of Secondary Education, the Educational Policies Commission, the National Science Foundation, and the National Commission on Excellence in Education.
5. Choose three social developments, events, pressures, or forces in the United States within the last fifteen years that have caused changes in the school's curriculum, and briefly explain those changes.
6. Look up one or more books or articles by an author who has been critical of public education (such as Arthur Bestor, Rudolph Flesch, Paul Goodman, John Holt, John Keats, James D. Koerner, Jonathan Kozol, Max Rafferty, Hyman Rickover, and Mortimer Smith in the 1950s; George B. Leonard in the 1960s; Paul Cooperman, Ivan Illich, and Charles E. Silberman in the 1970s; Richard Mitchell, E. D. Hirsch, Jr., Diane Ravitch, and Chester E. Finn, Jr., in the 1980s; and William J. Bennett, Lynne V. Cheney, Lewis J. Perelman, Harold W. Stevenson and James W. Stigler, Thomas Toch, and Ernest R. House in the 1990s) and summarize their criticisms in a written or oral report. Tell where you believe the critics were right and where you believe they were wrong. (You will be given an opportunity in the exercises at the end of Chapter 9 to report on some of the more recent studies on the reform of education.)
7. Read *The Practical: A Language for Curriculum* by Joseph J. Schwab and explain to the class what Schwab means by three modes of operation for curriculum development: the practical, the quasi-practical, and the eclectic. Tell what Schwab

means when he says, "The field of curriculum is moribund." State whether you agree with Schwab. (See bibliography.)

8. Consult some references on the history of American education and prepare comparative descriptions of the curriculum of (1) the Latin Grammar School, (2) the Academy, and (3) the English High School.

9. Explain what Larry Cuban meant by the four curricula: official, taught, learned, and tested. (See bibliography).

BIBLIOGRAPHY

Adler, Mortimer J. *The Paideia Proposal: An Educational Manifesto.* New York: Macmillan, 1982.

Anderson, Vernon E. *Curriculum Guidelines in an Era of Change.* New York: Ronald Press, 1969.

———. *Principles and Procedures of Curriculum Improvement,* 2nd ed. New York: Ronald Press, 1965.

Beane, James A., Toepfer, Conrad F., Jr., and Alessi, Samuel J., Jr. *Curriculum Planning and Development.* Boston: Allyn and Bacon, 1986.

Benjamin, Harold R. W. (Peddiwell, J. Abner). *The Saber-Tooth Curriculum.* New York: McGraw-Hill, 1939.

Bennett, William J. *The De-Valuing of America: The Fight for Our Children and Our Culture.* New York: Summit Books, 1992.

Berman, Louise M. and Roderick, Jessie A. *Curriculum: Teaching the What, How, and Why of Living.* Columbus, Ohio: Merrill, 1977.

Bestor, Arthur. *Educational Wastelands: The Retreat from Learning in Our Public Schools.* Urbana, Ill.: University of Illinois Press, 1953.

Bobbitt, Franklin. *The Curriculum.* Boston: Houghton Mifflin, 1918. Also, New York: Arno Press and The New York Times, 1975.

Bossing, Nelson L. *Principles of Secondary Education.* Englewood Cliffs, N.J.: Prentice-Hall, 1955.

Boyer, Ernest L. *High School: A Report on Secondary Education in America.* New York: Harper & Row, 1983.

Charters, W. W. *Curriculum Construction.* New York: Macmillan, 1923. Also, New York: Arno Press and The *New York Times,* 1971.

Combs, Arthur W. *The Professional Education of Teachers: A Perceptual View of Teacher Preparation.* Boston: Allyn and Bacon, 1965.

Commission on the Reorganization of Secondary Education. *Cardinal Principles of Secondary Education.* Washington, D.C.: U.S. Office of Education, Bulletin 35, 1918.

Cuban, Larry. "The Lure of Curriculum Reform and Its Pitiful History." *Phi Delta Kappan* 75, no. 2 (October 1993): 182–185.

Davis, O. L., Jr. *Perspectives on Curriculum Development 1776–1976.* 1976 Yearbook. Alexandria, Va.: Association for Supervision and Curriculum Development, 1976.

Doll, Ronald C. *Curriculum Improvement: Decision Making and Process,* 9th ed. Boston: Allyn and Bacon, 1996.

Draper, Edgar Marion. *Principles and Techniques of Curriculum Making.* New York: D. Appleton-Century, 1936.

Educational Policies Commission. *Education for All American Youth.* Washington, D.C.: National Education Association, 1944.

Firth, Gerald R. and Kimpston, Richard D. *The Curricular Continuum in Perspective.* Itasca, Ill.: F. E. Peacock, 1973.

Frymier, Jack R. and Hawn, Horace C. *Curriculum Improvement for Better Schools.* Worthington, Ohio: Charles A. Jones, 1970.

Gagné, Robert M. *The Conditions of Learning,* 2nd ed. New York: Holt, Rinehart and Winston, 1970. 3rd ed., 1977.

Glickman, Carl D. *Revolutionizing America's Schools.* San Francisco: Jossey-Bass, 1998.

Goodlad, John I. *A Place Called School: Prospects for the Future.* New York: McGraw-Hill, 1984.

Gwynn, J. Minor and Chase, John B., Jr. *Curriculum Principles and Social Trends,* 4th ed. New York: Macmillan, 1969.

Hass, Glen. *Curriculum Planning: A New Approach,* 5th ed. Boston: Allyn and Bacon, 1987.

Henson, Kenneth T. *Curriculum Development for Education Reform.* New York: HarperCollins, 1995.

Herrick, Virgil E. and Tyler, Ralph W. *Toward Improved Curriculum Theory.* Supplementary Educational Monograph, no. 71, March, 1950. Chicago: University of Chicago Press, 1950.

Johnson, Jean and Immerwahr, John. *First Things First: What Americans Expect from the Public Schools: A Report from Public Agenda.* New York: Public Agenda, 1994.

Knezevich, Stephen J. *Administration of Public Education,* 4th ed. New York: Harper & Row, 1984.

Leonard, Gorge B. *Education and Ecstasy with the Great School Reform Hoax.* Berkeley, Calif.: North Atlantic Books, 1987.

McClure, Robert M., ed. *The Curriculum: Retrospect and Prospect.* 70th Yearbook. Chicago: National Society for the Study of Education, University of Chicago Press, 1971.

Macdonald, James B., Anderson, Dan W., and May, Frank B. *Strategies of Curriculum Development: Selected Writings of the Late Virgil E. Herrick.* Columbus, Ohio: Merrill, 1965.

McNeil, John D. *Curriculum: A Comprehensive Introduction,* 5th ed. New York: HarperCollins, 1996.

Miel, Alice. *Changing the Curriculum: A Social Process.* New York: D. Appleton-Century, 1946.

Mitchell, Richard. *The Graves of Academe.* Boston: Little, Brown, 1981.

The National Commission on Excellence in Education, David P. Gardner, chairman. *A Nation at Risk: The Imperative for Educational Reform.* Washington, D.C.: U.S. Government Printing Office, 1983.

Oliver, Albert I. *Curriculum Improvement: A Guide to Problems, Principles, and Process,* 2nd ed. New York: Harper & Row, 1977.

Orlofsky, Donald E. and Smith, B. Othanel. *Curriculum Development: Issues and Insights.* Chicago: Rand McNally, 1978.

Perelman, Lewis J. *School's Out: Hyperlearning, the New Technology, and the End of Education.* New York: William Morrow, 1992.

Phi Delta Kappa Commission on Evaluation, Daniel L. Stufflebeam, committee chairman. *Educational Evaluation and Decision Making.* Itasca, Ill.: F. E. Peacock, 1971.

Rubin, Louis, ed. *Curriculum Handbook: The Disciplines, Current Movements, and Instructional Methodology.* Boston: Allyn and Bacon, 1977.

———. *Curriculum Handbook: Administration and Theory.* Boston: Allyn and Bacon, 1977.

———. *Curriculum Handbook: The Disciplines, Current Movements, Instructional Methodology, Administration and Theory,* abridged ed. Boston: Allyn and Bacon, 1977.

Rickover, Hyman. *Swiss Schools and Ours: Why Theirs Are Better.* Boston: Little, Brown, 1962.

Saylor, J. Galen, Alexander, William M., and Lewis, Arthur J. *Curriculum Planning for Better Teaching and Learning,* 4th ed. New York: Holt, Rinehart and Winston, 1981.

Schwab, Joseph J. *The Practical: A Language for Curriculum.* Washington, D.C.: National Education Association, Center for the Study of Instruction, 1970.

Scriven, Michael. "The Methodology of Evaluation." *Perspectives of Curriculum Evaluation.* AERA Monograph Series on Evaluation, no. 1. Chicago: Rand McNally, 1967.

Sizer, Theodore R. *Horace's Compromise: The Dilemma of the American High School.* Boston: Houghton Mifflin, 1984.

Smith, B. O., Stanley, William O., and Shores, J. Harlan. *Fundamentals of Curriculum Development,* rev. ed. New York: Harcourt Brace Jovanovich, 1957.

Stevenson, Harold J. and Stigler, James W. *The Learning Gap: Why Our Schools Are Failing & What We Can Learn from Japanese & Chinese Education.* New York: Summit Books, 1992.

Taba, Hilda. *Curriculum Development: Theory and Practice.* New York: Harcourt Brace Jovanovich, 1962.

Tanner, Daniel and Tanner, Laurel N. *Curriculum Improvement: Theory Into Practice,* 3rd ed. New York: Merrill, 1995.

Turney, David. "Sisyphus Revisited." *Perspectives on Curriculum Development 1776–1976.* 1976 Yearbook. Alexandria, Va.: Association for Supervision and Curriculum Development. 1976.

Unruh, Glenys H. *Responsive Curriculum Development: Theory and Action.* Berkeley, Calif.: McCutchan, 1975.

Verduin, John R., Jr. *Cooperative Curriculum Improvement.* Englewood Cliffs, N.J.: Prentice-Hall, 1967.

Walker, Decker. *Fundamentals of Curriculum.* Orlando, Fla.: Harcourt Brace Jovanovich, 1990.

Wiles, Jon and Bondi, Joseph C. *Curriculum Development: A Guide to Practice,* 5th ed. Upper Saddle River, N.J.: Merrill, 1998.

Zais, Robert S. *Curriculum: Principles and Foundations.* New York: Harper & Row, 1976.

PART II

CURRICULUM DEVELOPMENT: ROLES OF SCHOOL PERSONNEL

CHAPTER 3

CURRICULUM PLANNING: A MULTILEVEL, MULTISECTOR PROCESS

After studying this chapter you should be able to:

1. Describe types of curriculum planning that are conducted at five levels and in three sectors.
2. Design an organizational pattern for curriculum development at the individual school level.
3. Design an organizational pattern for curriculum development at the school district level.

ILLUSTRATIONS OF CURRICULUM DECISIONS

Daily, curriculum decisions like the following are being made in some school district somewhere in the United States:

- An elementary school uses computer-assisted instruction in teaching the basic skills.
- Computer laboratories have been established in both the middle and senior high schools of the same school district.
- A middle school has decided to incorporate more material on the achievements of various ethnic groups into its social studies program.
- An entire school district has decided to put a program of sexuality education into the curriculum at all levels.
- A senior high school faculty is concentrating on the development of students' thinking skills.
- A school system has revised a plan for bilingual education.
- An elementary school has decided to replace its reading series with that of another publisher.

- A school district has put into operation a program of character education.
  A school system has approved a plan for meeting the needs of the academically talented and gifted.
- The secondary schools of a district have put into operation a plan for increasing opportunities for girls to participate in team sports and for placing these sports on a par with boys' athletic activities.
- An urban school district is establishing a magnet secondary school that will emphasize science, mathematics, and technology.

VARIATIONS AMONG SCHOOLS

Countless curricular decisions like those in the preceding examples are made constantly. Some decisions are relatively simple—adding a course here, deleting a course there, or making some minor changes of content. Other decisions are sweeping and far-reaching—for example, the institution or abandonment of open-education plans or the conversion of a 6–3–3 plan for school organization (six years of elementary school, three of junior high, and three of senior high) to a 4–4–4 plan (four years each of elementary, middle, and high school). These changes are both administrative and curricular decisions.

Some of the more dynamic school systems maintain a lively pace of curriculum decision making and are continuously effecting changes in the curriculum as a result of these decisions. Often more than one type of change occurs simultaneously in some districts and schools.

Some systems follow a reasoned, measured process for arriving at planning decisions and carrying out those decisions; others enter into an almost frenzied, superheated process in which dozens of curricular ideas are dancing around without decisions or resolution; other school districts demonstrate lethargy and apathy toward curricular decision making and are, for all intents and purposes, stagnant.

The foregoing illustrations of curriculum decisions are typical examples occurring within individual school districts. These illustrations might have been stated to show that the same kind of decisions were being made at the same time in more than one school district. These illustrations of curriculum decisions could apply to multiple school districts scattered throughout the United States and might be reported as follows:

- A number of elementary schools have decided to replace their reading series with that of another publisher. We might extend this illustration by pointing out that they have all chosen the same publisher!
- Several school districts have decided to put a program of character education into the curriculum at all levels.
- Several middle schools have decided to incorporate more material on the achievements of various ethnic groups in their social studies programs.

How can we account for the simultaneous development of curriculum plans in different parts of the country? Shall we attribute it to legal pressures from federal or state sources? Among the foregoing illustrations only two—bilingual education programs and increased opportunities for girls to participate in team sports—may be said to have evolved as a result of legal processes. In 1974 the United States Supreme Court opened the doors to bilingual education programs with its decision in the *Lau v. Nichols* case.[1] As a consequence of this decision the San Francisco school system was required to provide special instruction to children of Chinese ancestry who were having difficulty with the English language. Furthermore, federal funds have been appropriated to assist school systems to develop and implement bilingual education programs. The participation of girls in team sports has been advanced through enactment by the U.S. Congress of Title IX of the Educational Amendments of 1972, which bars discrimination on the basis of gender. Certainly, federal and state legislation and court decisions have brought about curricular change, as we will explore more fully later. But we must also look elsewhere for other causes or partial causes of simultaneous development of curricular plans.

SIMULTANEOUS DEVELOPMENTS

Though it is unlikely, similar curriculum developments in different school systems may unfold at the same time by pure chance. This situation resembles that of two astronomers, unknown to each other and separated by oceans, who suddenly discover a new planet, or two scientific researchers who find within days of each other a cure for a disease plaguing humankind.

It is more likely that our country's efficient systems of transportation and communication can be pointed to as principal reasons for concurrent curriculum development. These pervasive technological systems make possible the rapid transmission of the beneficial pollen (or not so beneficial virus, depending on one's point of view) of curricular ideas.

These gigantic systems have an impact on all the constituencies of a school district—the administrators, teachers, students, parents, and other members of the community. Transportation makes it possible for people from all parts of the country to get together in formal and informal settings and discuss contemporary problems of the schools. It would be interesting, for example, to measure the effects of national professional conferences on the spread of curricular innovation. Although the pessimist would assert that a great deal of drivel flows at many professional conferences, enough kernels of wisdom are shared and taken back home where they are planted, nurtured, and brought to fruition. Could not several of the preceding illustrations have come about through the exchange of ideas on a person-to-person basis at a state, regional, or national meeting?

With possibly an even greater impact, communication systems permit the dissemination of reports of educational and social problems in various parts of the country and descriptions of how communities have sought to cope with these problems. The commercial press and television consistently make the public aware of social problems that call for some curricular responses, such as AIDS, drug abuse, crime, unemployment, ethnic conflicts, environmental hazards, and the lack of basic skills on the part

---

[1]*Lau v. Nichols,* 414 U.S. 563 (1974).

of young people. The media have been instrumental in revealing widespread dissatisfaction with the public schools to the point where lay constituencies are demanding that curriculum changes be made.

While the commercial media are pointing out social problems and, on occasion, educational responses to these problems, the professional media are engaged in healthy dialogue. The United States is blanketed with professional journals filled with educators' philosophical positions; proposals for change; and reports of projects, research, and experimentation. National and state professional organizations, the United States Department of Education, and state departments of education frequently release monographs, guides, and research reports of promising curricular projects. Both popular and professional books on education make their contributions to the quest for curricular solutions to many social and educational problems. Who is to assess, for example, the impact made on the schools by writers and educators such as Earl Kelley, who stressed the importance of an individual's self-concept;[2] Ralph Tyler, who suggested a systematic way of arriving at instructional objectives;[3] Benjamin Bloom and his associates, who offered a way of classifying educational objectives and advocated mastery learning;[4] James B. Conant, who made recommendations that were widely adopted by secondary schools;[5] Jerome S. Bruner, who wrote on the structure of disciplines;[6] Charles E. Silberman, who painted a grim picture of schools;[7] and John I. Goodlad, who directed an extensive study of schools and made recommendations for improvement?[8]

Through modern means of communication and transportation, curriculum innovations—good, bad, and indifferent—are transmitted rapidly to a world thirsty for new and better ways of meeting its educational obligations to children and youth. It is extremely difficult in an enterprise as large as education to pinpoint the source of a particular curriculum change, and it is not usually necessary to do so. What is important to the student and practitioner in curriculum planning is to understand that processes for effecting change are in operation. These processes extend beyond the classroom, the school, even the school district.

LEVELS OF PLANNING

Curriculum planning occurs on many levels, and curriculum workers—teachers, supervisors, administrators, or others—may be engaged in curriculum efforts on several levels at the same time. The levels of planning on which teachers function can be conceptualized as shown in Figure 3.1.[9] All teachers are involved in curriculum planning at

---

[2]Earl C. Kelley, *Education for What Is Real* (New York: Harper & Row, 1947).

[3]Ralph W. Tyler, *Basic Principles of Curriculum and Instruction* (Chicago: University of Chicago Press, 1949).

[4]Benjamin S. Bloom, ed., *Taxonomy of Educational Objectives: The Classification of Educational Goals: Handbook I: Cognitive Domain* (White Plains, N.Y.: Longman, 1956). Benjamin S. Bloom, J. Thomas Hastings, and George F. Madaus, *Handbook on Formative and Summative Evaluation of Student Learning* (New York: McGraw-Hill, 1971).

[5]James B. Conant, *The American High School Today* (New York: McGraw-Hill, 1959).

[6]Jerome S. Bruner, *The Process of Education* (Cambridge, Mass.: Harvard University Press, 1960).

[7]Charles E. Silberman, *Crisis in the Classroom: The Remaking of American Education* (New York: Random House, 1970).

[8]John I. Goodlad, *A Place Called School: Prospects for the Future* (New York: McGraw-Hill, 1984).

[9]Adapted from Peter F. Oliva, *The Secondary School Today*, 2nd ed. (New York: Harper & Row, 1972), p. 280.

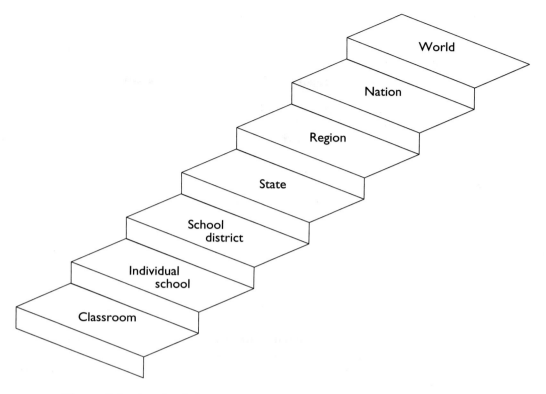

Figure 3.1   Levels of planning

the classroom level, most teachers participate in curriculum planning at the school level, some take part at the district level, and fewer and fewer engage in planning at the state, regional, national, and international levels. A few teachers, however, do participate in curriculum planning at all levels.

IMPORTANCE OF CLASSROOM LEVEL

The model in Figure 3.1, with its ascending stairs and even with its use of the term "levels," may lead to some erroneous conclusions. You might decide, since the steps clearly sketch a hierarchy, that planning at the classroom level is least important and planning at each successive level is increasingly more important. Nothing could be further from the truth. If we are concerned about levels of importance, and indeed we are, we should concede that classroom planning is far more important than any of the successive steps. At the classroom level, the results of curriculum planning make their impact on the learners.

In some ways it would appear pertinent if we turned the model around and placed classroom planning at the top and international planning at the bottom. Unfortunately, reversing the step model would introduce another possible misinterpretation. Since the classroom is the focal point for curriculum planning and the main locale for curriculum development efforts, this stage is shown as the first step. Designating the international level as the initial step would be extremely inaccurate since very few teachers or curriculum specialists work at that level and then usually only after they have demonstrated competence in the other levels.

The step model may convey to some readers that curriculum workers move through each stage or level in a fixed sequence. Although most teachers are involved in curriculum planning at both the classroom and school levels, some will proceed no further than those two levels. Some teachers and curriculum specialists work in sequence from one level to the next or simultaneously at all levels, whereas others may skip whole levels. Although curriculum planning usually begins in the classroom, it may start at whatever level curriculum workers feel a need to initiate change.

Since the steps in the preceding model are of equal width and rise, the model can give the impression that curriculum planners have an equal opportunity to participate at all levels and spend equal amounts of time in planning at each level. Opportunities for curriculum planning become fewer at each successive step up the staircase. Consequently, if the step model is retained to show the levels of planning, it would be better to visualize the rise between steps as progressively higher and the width of each step as progressively narrower.

The persons with whom we are most concerned in this textbook—the curriculum workers at the school and district levels—will be able to devote only limited time to curriculum planning at levels beyond the district.

As long as we conceptualize levels of planning as loci of work rather than of importance and understand that curriculum specialists do not necessarily work at all levels or in a fixed sequence of levels, the concept of levels of planning is valid and useful.

SECTORS OF PLANNING

Some curriculum theorists might feel somewhat more comfortable if, instead of speaking of levels of planning, we talked of sectors of planning. The concept of sectors eliminates the hierarchical and sequence problems of the step model and says simply that curriculum planning goes on in eight sectors—the classroom, the team/grade/department, the individual school, the school district, the state, the region, the nation, and the world. The sector model, illustrated in Figure.3.2, shows teachers and curriculum workers spending the largest part of their time in the individual school and school district and decreasing amounts of their time in sectors beyond the district boundaries. The broken lines signify that an individual teacher or curriculum planner may work at separate times or simultaneously in more than one sector. On the other hand, the teacher or curriculum planner may confine himself or herself to the classroom sector.

Models of levels or of sectors of planning address the questions of where decisions are made and what organizational processes are used for developing plans. These models do not, of course, answer the questions of why decisions are made, a topic explored in later chapters.

In discussing levels or sectors of planning, we should distinguish between levels or sectors in which individual planners work and those where decisions are actually made. These are not necessarily the same. Let's take, for example, the case of a fifth-

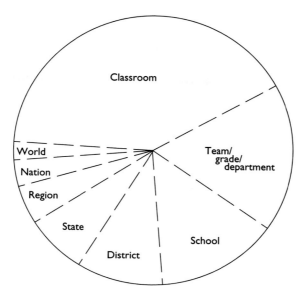

Figure 3.2   Sectors of planning

grade teacher. This teacher may possess sufficient leadership skills, motivation, and knowledge to become involved in curriculum planning either at successive times or simultaneously in the classroom, team/grade/department, school, and district levels. This individual may be involved at each level in making curriculum decisions that affect him or her as well as others in the school system.

On the other hand, this fifth-grade teacher may be engaged in curriculum planning at only the classroom level and may not be actively involved in the process above that level. Nevertheless, decisions about classroom curriculum that the individual teacher wishes to make must often be referred to a higher level of decision making, especially if these decisions will affect other teachers. For example, the individual teacher cannot unilaterally replace an adopted textbook that is part of an articulated series used at several grade levels. Decision making, then, will and must take place at higher levels whether or not the individual teacher actively participates in them.

A HIERARCHICAL STRUCTURE

Since many curriculum decisions must be, in effect, ratified at successive levels, we do have a hierarchical structure in operation throughout the United States. Each successive level of the hierarchy up to and including the state level, possesses the power to approve or reject curriculum proposals of the level below it.

In practice, responsibility for curriculum planning is spread across the levels of classroom, school, district, and state. Whereas teachers and curriculum specialists may participate in curriculum projects at the state level, their curriculum efforts at that level are purely advisory. Only the state board of education, the state department of education, or the state legislature can mandate incorporating the projects' results in the schools' programs. School systems must follow specific state regulations and statutes

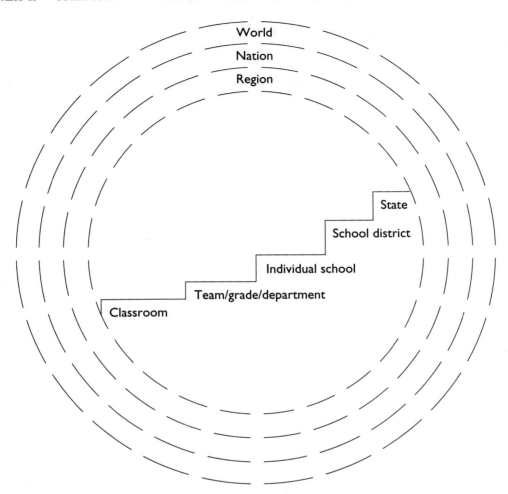

Figure 3.3 Levels and sectors of planning. For purposes of simplicity this figure does not show two levels—the area level that is a subdivision of the district and the intermediate unit that is a level between the district and the state. The area level is found in large urban school systems and the intermediate level, primarily a service unit, in some states.

after which, allowing for state curriculum mandates, may they demonstrate initiative in curriculum planning.

LIMITATIONS OF HIERARCHICAL STRUCTURE

Beyond the state level, hierarchical power structure does not hold true. In our decentralized system of education, authority for education is reserved to the states. The regional, national (with appropriate qualifications), and international sectors may seek to bring about curriculum change only through persuasion by working through state and local levels.

The national level represents a unique blend of control through both authority and persuasion. Some maintain that in spite of our decentralized system, the federal government exercises too much control over the schools, including the curriculum of those schools.

The history of federal legislation in support of vocational education and education of the handicapped, for example, reveals that the national level exerts a potent influence on the curriculum of the schools throughout the country. The dollar, distributed by the federal government is, of course, in itself a powerfully persuasive instrument. However, officials at the national level can intervene in state and local school matters only subsequent to federal legislation that they are empowered and required to enforce.

It is a moot question, however, whether the enactment of federal legislation and the enforcement of federal decisions can be called curriculum planning in its true sense. For example, whereas school districts must comply with federal legislation that bans all forms of discrimination in the schools' programs, they are under no obligation to submit grant proposals for optional types of aid.

Consequently, we might design a model that shows the levels of curriculum planning through the state level and the sectors beyond the state level. Such a model is shown in Figure 3.3.

CURRICULUM EFFORTS AT THE VARIOUS LEVELS

When the graduates of teacher education programs, with degrees and state certificates fresh in hand, sign contracts for their first teaching positions, they generally have only the vaguest of notions of the extent to which they will be involved in curriculum planning and development. Teacher education institutions do not ordinarily require courses in curriculum development at the undergraduate level. A typical preservice training program, ignoring the problem of differing delivery systems, consists of general education (liberal studies); foundations of education (social, psychological, philosophical, and historical) or introduction to education; methods of teaching (both general and specific); and student teaching in addition to a field of specialization (elmentary or middle school education or secondary school academic discipline). Some teacher candidates are exposed to an undergraduate course in curriculum, which provides them with an overview of the sources of the curriculum; presents a survey of programs in elementary, middle, and secondary education; and raises some curriculum issues. Despite their limited undergraduate training in curriculum development, teachers engage in instructional and curricular decision making from day one. Novice teachers are, as a rule, reasonably well trained to make the instructional or methodological decisions but are less well equipped to make the curricular or programmatic decisions, even though they may be well grounded in subject matter.

Teachers and curriculum specialists work within and across many levels and sectors. Each level performs distinct curricular efforts and has its own organizational processes for making curriculum decisions. Let's examine these levels more fully and point to the internal structures professionals have created to improve the curriculum. By contrast, in Chapters 4 and 7 you will see how external structures—those outside the teaching profession itself—impinge on internal structures.

For curriculum decision making to take place, appropriate organizational structures are essential. In the following pages of this chapter we will examine such structures in some detail. In Chapter 4 you will find a fuller treatment of the roles of various individuals and groups in the curriculum development process.

THE CLASSROOM LEVEL

At first blush it seems that all programmatic decisions have been made for the teacher at the time he or she is employed. A full-blown program is already in operation at the school where the teacher is to be assigned. The school board contracts with the applicant to fill an advertised position, be it early childhood education, sixth grade, middle-school English, or senior-high school chemistry. The principal makes the teaching assignment and informs the teacher about school policies and regulations. If the school is large enough to require the services of supervisory personnel other than the principal, the teacher may be referred to one of the supervisors for further orientation. The supervisor designated by the principal (for example, the assistant principal, a grade coordinator, or a department head) acquaints the teacher with the adopted textbooks and whatever other curriculum materials are used, such as statements of objectives, syllabi, and curriculum guides.

The new teacher begins to feel with some justification as if all the important decisions about the curriculum have already been made by others—the school, the district, the state, the nation, the public. Have we not in our educational history encountered materials that were supposed to be "teacher-proof"? No need for a teacher at all with teacher-proof materials!

Perhaps the life of the teacher would be easier and less complicated if the curriculum were prescribed. On the other hand, it is safe to say that the teacher's life would be immensely duller were there no curriculum decisions to be made. If teachers subscribe to the axioms that change is inevitable and never-ending, they will come to view their role first and foremost as decision maker. The teacher then not only makes decisions or participates in shared decision making but also gathers data on which to base decisions, implements decisions, and evaluates programs. In what specific curriculum endeavors, we may ask, is the individual classroom teacher likely to participate? Let's respond to that question in two ways.

Two Cases.   First, let us take the hypothetical cases of two high-powered, experienced, highly motivated teachers—a fourth-grade teacher and a tenth-grade teacher of social studies. We will further posit that (1) the fourth-grade teacher is a male and the tenth-grade teacher, a female, (2) both are employed in the same school district, and (3) both participate in curriculum planning at all levels and sectors. Our fourth-grade teacher, whom we will refer to as Teacher F, is the grade coordinator in a school that houses three sections of the fourth grade. Our tenth-grade teacher, Teacher N, is a member of a social studies department numbering eight faculty members. We will examine their curriculum development activities at one point in time—the cold and windy month of March.

During this period Teacher F was selecting supplementary materials for his pupils' science lessons (classroom level). He was reviewing with the other teachers the next day's mathematics lesson for slower students in the classes and examining a new fourth-grade reading program (grade level). He was also participating in making recommendations for implementing a new human growth and development program in the school (school level), serving on a committee studying ways to implement federal legislation regarding the handicapped (district level), serving on a statewide committee to define minimal competencies in language arts (state level), taking part in a panel discussion at a regional conference on effective teaching (regional level), finishing a proposal for federal funding of a project for children-at-risk (national sector and local level), and planning activities for a program on contributions of immigrants to American culture (international sector and local level).

While Teacher F has been making his contributions toward keeping the curriculum of his school system lively, Teacher N has been no less occupied. She has just finished resequencing the content of a course in geography that she regularly teaches (classroom level); is working with all the tenth-grade social studies teachers on a new course in consumer economics (department level); will attend later in the week as her department representative a meeting of the school's curriculum council to discuss ways for the school to use community resources more effectively (school level); has been serving on the same district committee as Teacher F, which is charged with the task of making recommendations for an improved curriculum for the handicapped (district level); has been invited to participate on a committee to consider changes in the state's minimal requirements for high school graduation (state level); served a week ago on a visiting committee for a distant high school that is seeking accreditation (regional sector); has been notified by the National Endowment for the Humanities that a proposal she submitted will be funded (national sector and local level); and has been invited by the World Council for Gifted and Talented Children to present a paper at a conference in Europe (international sector). While relatively few teachers have the opportunity, ability, or perhaps the inclination to participate in curriculum efforts at all levels and in all sectors suggested by these two hypothetical cases, none of these curricular activities is beyond the realm of possibility. Teachers have engaged in all these activities at some time or other.

A second way to respond to the question "In what specific endeavors is the individual classroom teacher likely to participate?" is to survey typical curriculum efforts that take place at each level and in each sector. An examination of some of the curriculum responsibilities at the classroom level reveals that the individual teacher has a rather large task cut out for him or her. A number of tasks in curriculum development at the classroom level may be identified.

Tasks of Teachers.   Teachers carry out activities in curriculum design when they write curricular goals and objectives, select subject matter (content), choose materials, identify resources in the school and community, sequence or resequence the subject matter, decide on the scope of the topics or course, revise the content, decide on types of instructional plans to use, construct the plans, try out new programs, create developmental and remedial programs in reading or other subject matter, seek ways to provide for all kinds of individual differences in the classroom, incorporate content mandated by levels above the classroom, and develop their own curricular materials.

Curriculum implementation is equated by some curriculum experts with instruction. Some hold the view that curriculum implementation does not start until the teacher interacts with the students. I would include in this concept the final stages of curriculum planning or design when the nitty-gritty decisions are made about how programs will be put into operation and how instruction will be designed and presented. Within this context teachers are occupied at the classroom level when they select appropriate emphases within the subjects, decide which students will pursue what subject matter, allot times for the various topics and units to be taught, determine if the facilities are appropriate and how they will be modified (if necessary), decide how materials and resources may best be made available to the learners, assign duties to volunteer aides, write instructional goals and objectives, and select and carry out strategies for classroom presentation and interaction.

Teachers have the responsibility of evaluating both the curriculum and instruction. In some ways it is difficult to separate the two dimensions of evaluation and to tell where instructional evaluation ceases and curriculum evaluation begins. In a very real sense evaluating instruction is evaluating curriculum implementation. We may clarify the distinctions between the two dimensions of evaluation in the following way: *Curriculum evaluation* is the assessment of programs, processes, and curricular products (material, not human). *Instructional evaluation* is (1) the assessment of student achievement before, during, and at the end of instruction and (2) the assessment of the effectiveness of the instructor. Thus, teachers work at the task of curriculum evaluation when they seek to find out if the programs are meeting the curriculum objectives; try to learn if the programs are valid, relevant, feasible, of interest to the learners, and in keeping with the learners' needs; review the choices of delivery systems, materials, and resources; and examine the finished curriculum products, such as guides, unit plans, and lesson plans, that they have created. Teachers conduct instructional evaluation when they assess the learners' entry skills before the start of instruction; give progress tests; write, administer, score, and interpret final achievement tests; and permit students to evaluate their performance as instructors.

These examples of activities transpiring at the classroom level demonstrate that curriculum planning and development are complex and demanding responsibilities of the teacher. As we discuss curriculum planning at the various levels in the following pages of this chapter, it may seem that individual teachers have little autonomy. Surely, many hold that view, and to some extent there is truth in that belief. The impingement of federal, state, and local school system mandates affecting the teachers' prerogatives in the areas of curriculum and instruction is a serious concern. In spite of the infringement on the teachers' professional responsibilities, many curricular and instructional decisions remain to be made, especially in selecting delivery systems, adapting techniques to students' learning styles, diagnosing student problems, and prescribing remediation.

Teachers may take comfort from the fact that they have at least as a group, if not individually, considerable opportunity to shape curricular decisions at the classroom, local school, and district levels and some opportunity at the state level.

THE TEAM, GRADE, AND DEPARTMENT LEVEL

One of the axioms in Chapter 2 stated that curriculum development is essentially a group undertaking. Once the teacher leaves the sanctuary of the self-contained elementary, middle, or secondary school classroom and joins other teachers, curriculum development takes a new turn. It calls for a cooperative effort on the part of each teacher, places a limit on solitary curriculum planning, and calls for a more formal organizational structure. It is at the team, grade, or department level that curriculum leadership begins to emerge, with leaders coming to be distinguished from followers.

For decades the graded school system with its orderly hierarchical structure and self-contained classrooms has been and continues to be the prevailing model of school organization. In the late 1970s, however, the self-contained classroom with its one teacher and one group of students was jostled by the appearance of open-space or open-area schools. Scores of elementary, middle, and junior high schools were built as or converted into open-space facilities. In these schools, in place of walled, self-contained classrooms came large open spaces in which the learning activities of a large group of youngsters were directed by a team of teachers assisted in some cases by paraprofessionals. A semblance of territoriality was created by assigning each of the members of the teaching team to a particular group of youngsters whose home base was a sector of the large open area. In theory and in practice, groups and subgroups were formed and reformed continuously depending on their learning needs, goals, and interests and on the teachers' individual competencies. Although open-space schools can still be found, the movement has reversed itself, and in many cases open classrooms have been converted or reconverted into self-contained classrooms. Sentiment among teachers, parents, and students has continued to favor the self-contained classroom.

Specific curriculum innovations are discussed in this text primarily to delineate the process of curriculum development and to help the curriculum worker to effect and evaluate curriculum change. Organizational patterns appear in this chapter to illustrate teachers' participation in curriculum planning at various levels beyond the classroom. Teachers in schools organized into self-contained units participate at the grade or department level. Teachers in open-space elementary schools share curriculum planning responsibilities at both the team and grade level. Teachers in middle schools customarily take part in curriculum development at the team (usually interdisciplinary), grade, and department levels. Secondary school teachers join with their colleagues in curriculum planning primarily at the department level, also on the grade level, and, in the case of team teaching efforts, at the team level.[10]

With the children for whom they are specifically responsible in mind, the teachers in a team, given grade, or particular department are called on to make curricular decisions like the following:

- determining content to be presented
- sequencing subject matter
- adapting instruction for exceptionalities
- establishing or revising team, grade, or departmental objectives
- selecting materials and resources suitable to the children under their supervision
- creating groupings and subgroupings of learners
- establishing a means of coordinating progress of students in the various sections and classrooms
- writing tests to be taken by all students of the team, grade, or department

---

[10]See Chapter 9 of this text for a discussion of the graded school, open-space schools, team teaching, and other organizational arrangements.

- writing curriculum materials for use by all teachers
- agreeing on team-wide, grade-wide, and department-wide programs that all students and teachers will attend
- agreeing on ways students can learn to demonstrate socially responsible behavior and self-discipline
- agreeing on or reviewing minimal standards that pupils must demonstrate in the basic skills
- cooperating in the establishment and use of laboratories and learning centers
- agreeing on implementation of the school's marking practices
- agreeing on the institution of new programs and abandonment of old programs within their jurisdiction
- evaluating their programs, students, and instructors

These are but a sampling of the many kinds of cooperative decisions that members who constitute the team, grade, or department must make. Team leaders or lead teachers, grade coordinators, or chairpersons are generally free to make many, though not all, decisions that affect only their own classes. When a decision is likely to have an impact on teachers other than the individual classroom teacher, it becomes a matter for joint deliberation by the parties to be affected or, at higher levels, by their representatives.

To enable the decision-making process to become more efficient, curriculum leaders either emerge or need to be designated. Team leaders or lead teachers, grade coordinators, or chairpersons are appointed by the principal or elected by the teachers themselves. Those administrators who are inclined to a bureaucratic approach to administration prefer the former system, and those who are disposed to a collegial approach permit the latter system. In either case, if the most experienced and skilled teachers are chosen for leadership positions, they may establish themselves as curriculum specialists, key members of a cooperating group of curriculum workers.

Although many schools have their own unique organizational arrangements, we might show common organizational patterns for curriculum planning through the team, grade, and departmental levels, as in the diagrams of Patterns 1 through 4 shown in Figures 3.4 through 3.7. Later in this chapter we will look at parallel patterns of organization for curriculum development on a schoolwide and districtwide basis.

Patterns 1 through 4 are examples of four out of the numerous ways in which teams, grades, and departments are organized for carrying out their assigned tasks, a major one of which is curriculum development. Each pattern should be viewed in the mind's eye as expanded to include all teachers, teams, grades, and departments in the school. The channels shown in the diagrams can be followed for both administrative and curricular decision making, limited, of course, in these illustrations to decisions affecting only a specific teacher, team or teams, grade, or department. In a moment we will look at the means of organizing on a schoolwide basis and for making decisions that affect more than a particular teacher, team or teams, grade, or department.

Arrowheads at both ends of a line in the pattern charts convey a philosophy and practice of collegiality. This element of collegiality extends even to the various leaders' relationships with the administrator. Many charts, especially those showing administrative decision making in a bureaucratic model, include lines with arrows in only one direction—from the top down.

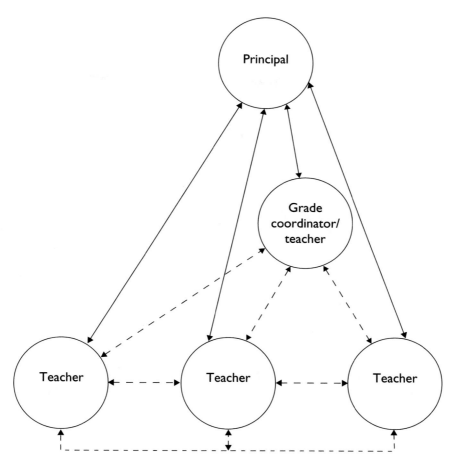

Figure 3.4 Pattern I: Sections of a grade in an elementary school with self-contained classes.

In the less common small school with only one class of each grade with one teacher in a self-contained unit, the individual teacher is both the leader and follower and has sole responsibility for making curriculum decisions (with the administrator's cooperation and approval) for the classroom and grade levels, in this case identical. The teacher and principal, who is viewed by many as the school's instructional leader, relate to each other directly. Whereas the presence of single sections of a particular grade prevents cooperative curriculum planning within grade levels, cooperation is possible, if the principal encourages it, at the school level and across grade levels.

In some schools housing multiple sections of each grade the principal follows the model of the less common small school, trying to relate to each teacher on an individual basis and not encouraging cooperative planning by the faculty within and across grade levels. Interchange among those affected by curriculum change is essential to intelligent and effective curriculum planning.

Patterns 1 through 4 introduce a dimension of cooperative planning. Pattern 1 shows an organizational plan for sections of a grade in a school which adheres to a self-

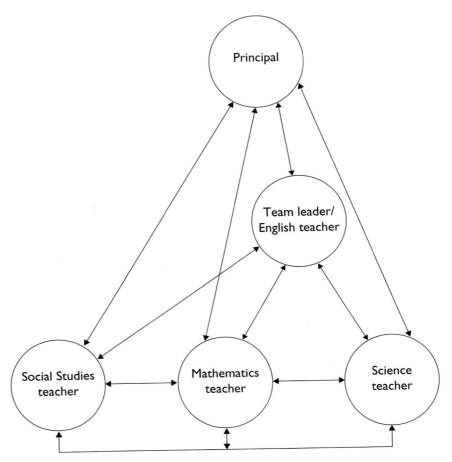

Figure 3.5   Pattern 2: Organization of a middle-school interdisciplinary team.

contained model. We could show a more bureaucratic structure if we charted the arrows pointing in only one direction, emanating from the principal, and eliminating lines between teachers. The interaction between teachers in Figure 3.4, Pattern 1 is shown as broken lines to conceptualize degrees of cooperation. If the principal fosters a collegial style, the lines between teachers would appear as solid rather than broken.

By changing a few titles: "grade coordinator/teacher" to "team leader/teacher," and "teacher" to "team member" we could convert the diagram into an organizational pattern for an interdisciplinary team as shown in Figure 3.5, Pattern 2 (with each teacher's field added). Since team teaching is an essential principle of middle-school operation, the lines from teacher to teacher are drawn solid. Interaction among team members is an expected part of middle-school teaching.

Figure 3.6, Pattern 3 charts an organizational plan showing two teams at the same grade level of a middle school. In this hypothetical case one teacher—the leader of Team I—serves as both a team leader and as grade coordinator. There will be times when the principal will wish to meet with the faculty of a grade level—seventh-grade teachers, for example—to discuss matters pertinent to the entire grade level or that cut

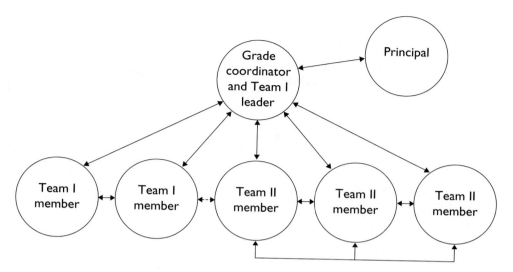

Figure 3.6   Pattern 3: Two teams at the same grade level of a middle school.

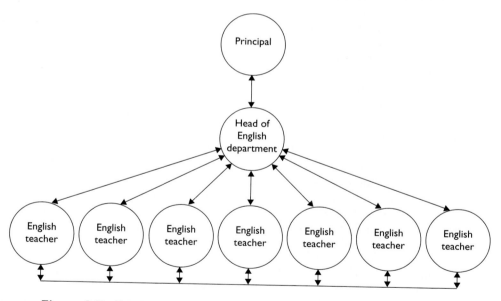

Figure 3.7   Pattern 4: Organizational pattern of all members of a secondary school department. One faculty member happens to also serve as a grade coordinator.

across team lines, for example, a new seventh-grade reading program. The broken line between Teams I and II signifies that interchange between teams is likely to be limited primarily to grade-level matters.

Figure 3.7, Pattern 4 is the typical, traditional, departmental vehicle by which much of the work of the secondary school is conducted. Teachers in a particular discipline at all grade levels of the school concern themselves with matters significant to their field of instruction. We need to point out that the school may and should have a corresponding plan for grade-level organization composed of all teachers of a particular grade level with one person, perhaps one of the department heads, designated as grade coordinator. Principals will meet with grade faculties to consider matters pertinent to the grade level and cutting across department lines, for example, providing for smoother transition of pupils from the last year of middle school to the first year of secondary school.

Patterns 1 through 4 show structures for curriculum development at the team, grade, and department levels. Curriculum matters that can be settled and contained within a team, grade, or department are handled at that level. However, curriculum planning sends out waves that affect, sometimes even engulf, persons beyond the planners and the client group for whom the plans were made. Hence, we must look to the next level—the school level—for curriculum decision making that transcends the team, grade, or department.

THE SCHOOL LEVEL

Although many curriculum decisions may be made at the classroom or team/grade/department level, other decisions can be reached only at a schoolwide level. The institution must provide some mechanism whereby the curriculum is articulated and integrated. The administrator must ensure a process whereby the implications of curriculum decisions made anywhere within the institution will be understood and, hopefully, agreed to by the faculty as a whole.

Of all the levels and sectors of curriculum planning, the individual school has emerged as the most critical. Current administrative philosophy promotes an approach to school administration known generally as "school-based (or site-based) management" in which authority is decentralized and the school principal is granted considerable autonomy over not only curriculum planning but also the budget, hiring and firing of school personnel, inservice education of staff, and supervision and evaluation of staff.[11] Several writers have identified the individual school as the primary locus for curriculum change. Alice Miel long ago observed, "If really widespread participation is desirable, there appears to be no better way than to make the individual school the unit of participation, the primary action agency in curriculum development."[12] Almost forty years later Goodlad endorsed the concept of the school as the unit for improvement.[13]

The decade of the 1980s, with its quest for reform of the schools, saw many states shift more and more decision making to the state level as they grappled for ways to improve their schools. Local schools felt the pressure of state curricular mandates that in some cases went beyond the specification of subjects and units to the specification of instructional objectives to be accomplished at every level in every course.

Emphasis has now shifted away from heavy centralized state and district administration toward more responsibility for operation of the schools on the local school

---

[11]See Jane L. David, "Synthesis of Research on School-Based Management," *Educational Leadership* 46, no. 8 (May 1989): 45–53.

[12]Alice Miel, *Changing the Curriculum: A Social Process* (New York: D. Appleton Century, 1946), p. 69.

[13]Goodlad, *A Place Called School*, pp. 31 and 318–319.

level. Tight state budgets as well as educational reasons have accelerated the move toward decentralization from state to local level. An even more dramatic loosening of state controls over education is seen in several states in the late 1990s in the movement toward permitting private organizations and individuals to organize and operate "charter schools," funded by tax moneys and free of many state regulations.

The preceding chapter demonstrated that curriculum specialists conceive of curriculum development as a cooperative group undertaking. Given the many dimensions of the school administrator's job, intensified by the concept of school-based management, a participatory approach to administration is sound not only philosophically but also practically. Shared decision making, whether in respect to curriculum planning or to other aspects of the administrator's job, makes for a more efficient and effective school.

Foreign observers are often amazed, if not shocked, by the uniqueness of each American school. Two elementary schools in the same community, for example, may be completely different in ambience, student body, staffing, scheduling, resources, and to some extent, curricula. Achievement levels, motivation of the students, enthusiasm of the faculty, leadership skills of the principal, neighborhood, support from the parents, and curricular emphases make for differences from school to school. Consequently, Americans are not surprised when they find that organizational arrangements differ school by school within the nation, within the state, indeed, within the same locality. Educational diversity is both a blessing and a dilemma for curriculum planners. It is a strength of our system of education in that it permits schools to respond to needs evidenced in the individual school and locality. It presents a problem for curriculum workers who seek to create state and even national curricula that specify commonalities and minimal competencies, an issue that we will address later.

Constituencies of the School.   To varying degrees, the democratic process is accepted more and more in school systems across the country. Nowhere is its presence more clearly felt than in the participatory procedures that seek to involve the major constituencies of the school in curriculum development. Usually identified as the principal constituencies are the administrators and their staffs, teachers, students, and citizens of the community. On occasion, nonprofessional employees of the school system are acknowledged in this way and become involved in the planning process—but rarely as major participants.

Jack R. Frymier and Horace C. Hawn stated a principle that summarizes their belief in the necessity for involving persons in curriculum planning on a broad scale:

> *People Who Are Affected Must Be Involved.* Involvement is a principle fundamental to democracy and to learning theory. The very essence of democracy is predicated upon the assumption that those who are affected by any change should have some say in determining just what that change shall be. This is guaranteed in our political-social system through citizen participation and through our efforts to persuade representatives once they have been chosen. Devising ways of involving people in decision making is a difficult and time-consuming chore, but *unless decisions are made democratically they will be less than the best.* . . . Significant and lasting change can only come about by such involvement. All who are affected by curriculum development and change must have a genuine opportunity to participate in the process.[14]

---

[14]Jack R. Frymier and Horace C. Hawn, *Curriculum Improvement for Better Schools* (Worthington, Ohio: Charles A. Jones, 1970), pp. 28–29.

Robert S. Zais raised a question, however, about the validity of the participatory model of curriculum decision making. Speaking of the democratic "grass-roots model,"[15] Zais said:

The grass-roots model of curriculum engineering[16] . . . is initiated by teachers in individual schools, employs democratic group methods of decision making, proceeds on a "broken front," and is geared to the specific curriculum problems of particular schools or even classrooms.

The intensely democratic orientation of the grass-roots model is responsible for generating what have probably become the curriculum establishment's two least-questioned axioms: First, that a curriculum can be successfully implemented only if the teachers have been intimately involved in the construction and development processes, and second, that not only professional personnel, but students, parents, and other lay members of the community must be included in the curriculum planning process. To deny the validity of either of these claims (neither of which has been satisfactorily demonstrated) is not necessarily to deny *any* role to teachers or lay participants; rather it is to suggest the need to define more precisely the *appropriate* role that administrators, teachers, curriculum specialists, and nonprofessionals should play in curriculum engineering.[17]

Decisions and Organizational Patterns. Curriculum committees or councils exist in many schools. The school's curriculum committee meets and makes recommendations on such matters as the following:

- adding new programs for the school, including interdisciplinary programs
- deleting existing programs
- revising existing programs
- conducting schoolwide surveys of teacher, student, and parental opinion
- evaluating the school's curriculum
- planning ways to overcome curricular deficiencies
- planning for school accreditation
- choosing articulated series of textbooks
- using library and learning centers
- planning for exceptional children
- verifying the school's compliance with state mandates and federal legislation
- sanctioning schoolwide events like career days and science fairs
- supervising assessment of student achievement
- reviewing recommendations of accrediting committees and planning for removal of deficiencies

---

[15]Zais attributes the classification "grass-roots model" to B. Othanel Smith, William O. Stanley, and J. Harlan Shores, *Fundamentals of Curriculum Development* (New York: Harcourt Brace Jovanovich, 1957). See Robert S. Zais, *Curriculum: Principles and Foundations* (New York: Harper & Row, 1976), p. 448.

[16]Zais refers to the definition of "curriculum engineering" by George A. Beauchamp, *Curriculum Theory*, 2nd ed. (Wilmette, Ill.: Kagg Press, 1968), and uses the term to encompass "curriculum construction," "curriculum development," and "curriculum implementation." Zais, *Curriculum*, p. 18. See also the third edition of Beauchamp's *Curriculum Theory* (1975), Chapter 7.

[17]Zais, *Curriculum*, pp. 448–449.

Figure 3.8   Pattern A1: Principal works with a faculty curriculum council. Subcommittees of the faculty curriculum council are appointed as needed.

- reducing absenteeism
- increasing the holding power of the school

Although curriculum specialists may not agree to what degree they should encourage or permit the involvement of various constituencies, how each group will be constituted, and which group has the primary role, the literature on curriculum development almost unanimously endorses the concept of the democratic, participatory approach. Although it is possible that the collective judgment of specialists in the field could be in error, their judgments—based on experience, training, observation, and research—provide a foundation for accepting the validity of the democratic approach to curriculum development.

Several organizational arrangements exist on the school level for considering curriculum matters. The diagrams that follow depict some of these patterns of organization. In Patterns A1 and A2 (Figures 3.8 and 3.9) the administrator(s) share decision making with the group that most curriculum experts agree is of primary importance in curriculum development—the teachers. Patterns A3 and A4 (Figures 3.10 and 3.11) expand cooperation into collaborative models that include groups in addition to teachers.

We should not forget that in any organizational model in which decision making is shared, groups other than the duly appointed administrators serve only in advisory

Figure 3.9   Pattern A2: Principal works with a faculty curriculum council and involves total faculty.

capacities. Both professionally and legally the administrator does not and cannot surrender "line" authority for making ultimate decisions and supervising the staff.

The following patterns of organizing for curriculum development at the local school level maintain the customary line-and-staff relationship that we have already seen at the team/grade/department level and will see again at the school district level. They also serve as illustrations of ways schools may be organized for carrying out curriculum development and convey a sense of the variations possible for accomplishing this task.

The principals in Patterns A1 and A2 use a faculty curriculum council or faculty curriculum committee. In practice, faculty committees that serve to advise school administrators on curriculum matters are constituted either by election of teachers by their colleagues or by appointment of teachers by school administrators. In some cases, team leaders, grade coordinators, or department heads—elected in some schools, appointed in others—may make up the faculty curriculum committee. I would advocate the democratic election of representatives to curriculum committees and councils at all levels of the school system.

The principal of Pattern A2 has provided a systematic way by which the total faculty acting as a body approves or disapproves decisions of the faculty curriculum council. Although only one subcommittee is pictured in each of these figures, it is understood that the faculty council would appoint as many subcommittees of the faculty as needed.

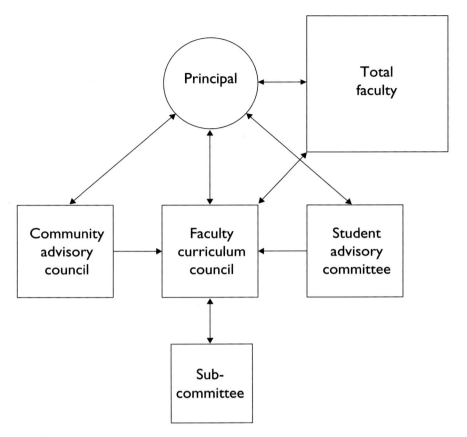

Figure 3.10   Pattern A3: Principal involves lay citizens and students as well as faculty.

Citizens of the community and students join forces with the faculty and administrators to produce collaborative Patterns A3 and A4. The principal of Pattern A3 keeps the three constituencies separate. The model shows, however, the possibility of interaction among the several working groups.

Pattern A4 integrates all three constituencies into one expanded curriculum committee. Patterns A2, A3, and A4 all incorporate the total faculty within the model.

Pattern A4, an integrated, collaborative model, appears the most democratic, but it would be wrong to conclude that it is therefore the most efficient. As anyone who has grappled with the concept of "parity" as dictated by some federal programs—public school teachers, university specialists, and lay people working together as equal partners from proposal stage to final evaluation—has discovered, "parity" is not necessarily the most efficient way to do business. In reference to the expanded curriculum committee the professionals—the teachers and administrators—must often talk a language filled with concepts that must be explained to lay citizens and students and must make distinctions between desired outcomes and processes. Technical decisions that must be made are often beyond the competence of lay citizens and students. Only if an

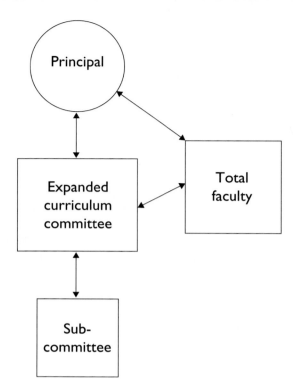

Figure 3.11   Pattern A4: Principal involves lay citizens, students, and faculty in a combined curriculum committee.

expanded curriculum committee is composed of persons who are well informed about the processes of education and are highly motivated can this pattern meet with any degree of success.

Students and lay people often participate with teachers and administrators on school-level committees. In the next chapter, we will examine the roles of these constituent groups in curriculum development. We might ask at this point: What are typical curriculum tasks of the schoolwide curriculum committee? The school curriculum committee or council must articulate its work with curriculum development efforts at the classroom and team/grade/department levels and, in effect, coordinate the work of lower levels. It receives proposals for curricular change from the lower levels, especially proposals that affect more than one team, grade, or department or that are interdisciplinary in nature.

The school curriculum council considers proposals that require human and material resources, budgetary expenditures, and changes in staffing. The council conducts or supervises assessment of the educational needs of pupils. It coordinates the development of a statement of school philosophy. It specifies and regularly reviews curriculum goals and objectives for the school.

The curriculum council plans the evaluation of the curriculum. It studies results of student assessment and proposes changes based on the data gathered. The council studies the educational needs of the community and implements programs to meet legitimate needs. The council seeks solutions to short-range curricular problems while also establishing and refining long-range plans.

The council is both proactive and reactive in its manner of operating. Whereas it may react to proposals presented by both the principal and the faculty, it also generates its own proposals and possible solutions to curricular problems.

At the time of a pending school evaluation by a regional accreditation team, the curriculum council may act as a steering committee and assign specific tasks to various committees. The council coordinates an intensive self-study prior to the visit of the accrediting team.

The council must ensure articulation between and among the various teams, grades, and departments of the school, making certain that teachers are following agreed-upon sequences and meeting minimal prescribed objectives. Requests from higher levels and various sectors for the school's cooperation on curriculum projects are routed to the curriculum council.

The local school curriculum council occupies a strategic position and fulfills a key role in the process of curriculum development. Of all groups at all levels and sectors of planning, the schoolwide curriculum council is in the position to make significant contributions to curriculum improvement.

Limitation to Decentralization.   A decentralized site-based approach to management, per se, is no greater guarantee of successful curriculum making than is a centralized approach orchestrated by the district or state level. Michael G. Fullan called attention to the need for coordinating top-down and bottom-up strategies.[18] Site-based management and shared decision making should not be perceived as the delegation of all authority and responsibility to the individual school. A bottom-up approach without cooperation of higher levels may be no more successful in effecting lasting curriculum improvement than a top-down approach without cooperation of lower levels. Fullan averred, " . . . the claim of superiority of grassroots initiatives is primarily theoretical."[19] Commented Fullan, "In sum, decentralized initiatives, as far as the evidence is concerned, are not faring much better than centralized reforms."[20] Current efforts toward empowerment at the local level have sought to balance the heavier control formerly exerted by district and state levels. However, the local school cannot work in isolation. Collaboration among levels and sectors remains essential. The 1994 Yearbook of the Association for Supervision and Curriculum Development on the governance of curriculum highlighted the need for educators to develop "boundary-spanning skills" and apply those skills in "working across institutional boundaries in the education system."[21]

---

[18]Michael G. Fullan, "Coordinating Top-Down and Bottom-Up Strategies for Educational Reform," in *The Governance of Curriculum,* Richard F. Elmore and Susan H. Fuhrman, eds., 1994 Yearbook (Alexandria, Va.: Association for Supervision and Curriculum Development, 1994), pp. 186–202.

[19]Ibid., p. 187.

[20]Ibid., p. 189.

[21]Richard F. Elmore and Susan H. Fuhrman, "Governing Curriculum: Changing Patterns in Policy, Politics, and Practice," *The Governance of Curriculum,* in Richard F. Elmore and Susan H. Furhman, eds., 1994 Yearbook (Alexandria, Va.: Association for Supervision and Curriculum Development, 1994), pp. 7, 8.

THE SCHOOL DISTRICT LEVEL

None of the previously discussed levels—classroom, team/grade/department, or individual school—can work as isolated units. They function within the context of the school district under the direction of the duly constituted school board and its administrative officer, the superintendent. Their efforts must be coordinated among themselves and with the central district office. Goals and objectives of the subordinate units must mesh with those of the district level. Consequently, the superintendent must provide a mechanism whereby district-level curriculum planning may be conducted.

Curriculum planning on a districtwide level is often conducted through the district curriculum council composed of teachers, administrators, supervisors, lay persons, and, in some cases, students. The size of the district curriculum council and the extent of its representation depend upon the size of the school district. Representatives may be either elected by members of their respective groups or appointed by district-level administrators, frequently on the recommendation of school principals.

Decisions and Organizational Patterns. Districtwide committees meet to consider problems such as these:

- adding new programs for the district
- abandoning districtwide programs
- reviewing student achievement in the various schools and recommending ways to improve programs of any deficient schools
- writing or reviewing proposals for state and federal grants
- gathering data on student achievement for presentation to parent groups and lay advisory councils
- supervising district compliance with state mandates and federal legislation
- evaluating programs on a districtwide basis
- articulating programs between levels

The patterns that follow show typical organizational arrangements for curriculum development at the district level. The patterns increase in complexity as the size of the school district increases. The district represented in Pattern B1 (Figure 3.12) uses a curriculum council composed of professionals only—administrators and supervisors named by the superintendent and teachers selected by their principals or elected by their faculties to represent them on the council. Subcommittees of professionals from anywhere in the school system are appointed by the curriculum council to conduct specific phases of curriculum development. The community advisory council serves in an advisory capacity to the superintendent and may or may not consider curriculum matters. Subordinate school units are responsible to the superintendent through the principals.

Pattern B2 (Figure 3.13) is essentially like Pattern B1 except that this school district extends membership on the curriculum council to students and lay persons.

Pattern B3 (Figure 3.14) charts the organizational structure for curriculum development in a large county school system broken down into four administrative units or subdistricts, each of which is placed under the control of an area superintendent. The area superintendents report on matters of curriculum and instruction to the assistant superintendent for curriculum and instruction who, in turn, is responsible to the super-

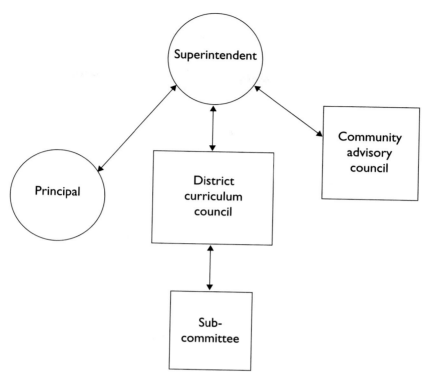

Figure 3.12 Pattern B1: Small school district.

intendent. Each area superintendent charges a director of instruction (actually curriculum *and* instruction) or a director of elementary and secondary schools with the job of leadership in curriculum development. In each of the four areas, a curriculum council made up of administrators, supervisors, and teachers representative of the area works with the director of instruction in the vital task of improving the curriculum in their subdivision of the district. Subcommittees are appointed by the curriculum councils as they are needed in their areas. Principals are supervised by the directors of instruction. In some cases the directors of instruction supervise only in curriculum and instruction; in other cases, they supervise in all areas, including administrative matters. The area superintendents enlist the aid of community advisory councils, which advise them on curricular and other matters. To maintain coordination among the four areas of the district, the assistant superintendent has established a districtwide curriculum coordinating council.

Decisions made at the area level, which is a subdistrict of the larger school district, affect all the schools within that area, whereas decisions made at the district level are binding on all schools of the entire system. The district curriculum council serves in a coordinating capacity. It acts on proposals from subordinate levels; develops or causes to be developed statements of district philosophy, goals, and objectives; and establishes minimal competencies to be achieved by all students in the entire district. It

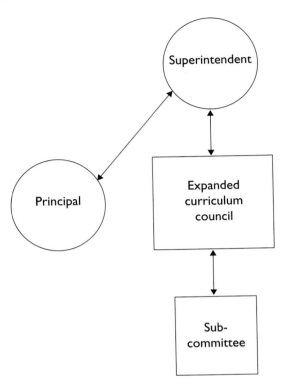

Figure 3.13 Pattern B2: Small school district with expanded curriculum council composed of administrators, teachers, students, and lay people.

makes recommendations concerning districtwide programs and projects; develops plans to secure federal moneys; and reviews district efforts to cooperate with state, regional, and national governmental and nongovernmental agencies on curriculum matters. The district curriculum committees, such as the curriculum coordinating council of Pattern B3, can be extremely influential groups; they, in the last analysis, make recommendations about the curriculum that the chief administrator may, if he or she approves, take to the public's representatives—the school board—for action.

Sequence for Decision Making. We might visualize the sequence for decision making by the curriculum groups at the various levels within a school system in the form of waves starting in the individual teacher's classroom and terminating with the district curriculum coordinating council, as pictured in Figure 3.15.

Teachers new to a school system should be informed, perhaps through a faculty handbook, of the district's structures for curriculum development. Teachers should be aware not only of the process of curriculum development in the district but also of the opportunities for curricular leadership.

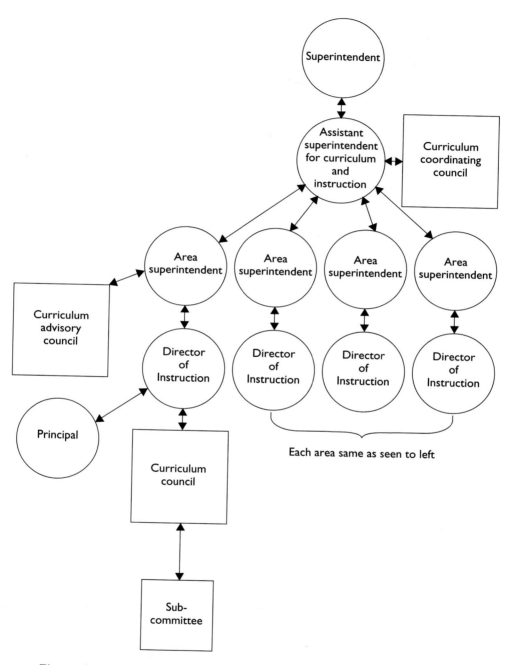

Figure 3.14   Pattern B3: Large county school district with four district subordinate areas (subdistricts).

Figure 3.15 Sequence of decision making.

Each level receives information, ideas, and proposals from the lower levels and, in turn, sends information, ideas, and proposals to them. Each level acts within the limitations of its own "territory." Councils at any level may initiate action as well as react to suggestions made to them. Councils must be responsive to both subordinate and higher levels. If a council wishes to initiate a plan that affects lower levels, it must involve persons from those levels beginning at the earliest planning stages. If a council wishes to initiate or endorse a plan that goes beyond its "territory" or that might be likely to create repercussions anywhere in the system, it must seek approval at higher levels.

Before we discuss curriculum development at the next level—the state—we should consider the following observations about the previously discussed organizational patterns for curriculum development:

- Although an administrator—the principal or superintendent—has been shown at the top of each model, the patterns should not be considered simply administrative models in which orders are given by the administrator to his or her subordinates. The arrows at both ends of the lines from administrator to curriculum committees signify that exchange is a two-way rather than a one-way process. The administrator holds the power for final decision making and must take the consequences if decisions prove to be unwise. The administrator's presence at the top of each pattern does not in itself make the pattern undemocratic.

  The key difference between a democratic and an undemocratic process is the involvement of people. No administrator worth his or her keep can turn over the decision-making process completely to others, yet every administrator can seek to obtain the widest possible participation of people in that process.

- The patterns presented are rather typical arrangements that permit the work of curriculum development to be carried out by the professionals in the school system and by others whose aid they solicit. Other patterns also exist. Zais, for example, analyzed a number of existing and proposed models for curriculum development.[22]

- Realistically, we must admit that a significant amount of curriculum change is brought about *outside* of the established structure. Individual teachers and small committees often effect changes that are well received and disseminated through the school system and sometimes beyond. B. Frank Brown observed many years ago that a few teachers, by their example, may be instrumental in bringing about curriculum revision, a process he referred to as "spinning out."[23] The public and teachers' organizations are often ahead of the designated curriculum leaders.

- The patterns described in this chapter are models of structure—the organizational arrangements whereby the professionals and those who assist them may apply their knowledge and skills to curriculum improvement. We should distinguish these organizational patterns from models for the process of curriculum development, which we will consider in Chapter 5.

THE STATE LEVEL

To many curriculum workers on the local and district levels, participation in curriculum development beyond their boundaries seems like a remote undertaking. Administrators, teachers, and others are aware, sometimes painfully, that curriculum revision does go on outside the school district and that it does have an impact on the schools of the district. Although state involvement in curricular and instructional development has varied over the years, relatively few school personnel in proportion to the number of employees are actively involved in curriculum making outside the district and then rarely on a sustaining basis.

As we move further and further away from the district level, the percentage of school personnel actively and continuously participating in curriculum development shrinks in size. Were the state not in a superordinate position over the local school districts and were the state not directly responsible for the educational system within its borders, we should classify the state as a sector rather than a level. Clearly, however, under the Tenth Amendment to the U.S. Constitution and under the state constitutions, the state holds primary power over education.

Channels Within Education.   The state operates in the arena of curriculum development through a number of channels within the education profession. The state department of education and school people from the various districts of the state who are called on to assist the state department of education constitute the professional channel for curriculum development under the aegis of the state.

State Departments of Education.   The state department of education, often a large bureaucracy that is sometimes criticized for its size and power, exercises direct responsibility over the curriculum of the schools of the state. Led by a chief state school officer (superintendent or commissioner of education), the state department of education—an agency of the executive branch of the state government—consists of a number of assis-

---

[22]Zais, *Curriculum,* Chapter 19.

[23]B. Frank Brown, *The Nongraded High School* (Englewood Cliffs, N.J.: Prentice-Hall, 1963), pp. 209–210.

tant superintendents, heads of branches, curriculum specialists, and other staff members. The state department of education provides general leadership to the schools; it interprets, enforces, and monitors legislated regulations as well as its own regulations that attain the force of law.

The state department of education wields great power over the districts of the state. In curriculum matters it accredits and monitors school programs, disburses state and federal-through-state moneys for specific programs, enforces standards for high school graduation, and sets specifications for amounts of time to be devoted to specific content areas. The state department of education develops statewide standards of philosophy, goals, and objectives. Additionally, the state department of education makes available consultant help to the individual schools and districts and conducts evaluation of school programs.

At times, decisions are made on the state level without advance consultation with the local school personnel of the state. At other times, however, the state department of education seeks advice and assistance from individuals and from ad hoc committees that they create for the purpose of studying specific problems and recommending solutions. Administrators and teachers are often asked to participate in organizing, conducting, or attending conferences and workshops held throughout the state on specific topics—for example, drug abuse, programs for the handicapped, eliminating gender discrimination, writing curriculum guides, conducting research studies, identifying teacher competencies, specifying minimal competencies that students are expected to achieve at each grade level, and selecting textbooks for state adoption.

The state department of education takes a leadership role in disseminating information regarding curriculum innovations and practices among the schools of the state. It issues both regular and periodic bulletins, monographs, and newsletters, frequently containing articles written by persons from local school districts, to keep school personnel throughout the state up-to-date on recent developments in curriculum, instruction, and other matters.

The state's presence in all school matters has been a commanding one. Yet local school personnel do find limited opportunity to participate in curriculum decision making through established state channels. As site-based management increases, local school personnel will find greater opportunities for participation. Further, the educational climate of the late 1990s has resulted in downsizing of state departments of education with subsequent reduction of their staffs, responsibilities, and authority.

State Professional Organizations. In a less formal way curriculum workers find opportunities for curriculum planning and consideration of curriculum problems through activities of the state professional organizations. Conference programs of such organizations as the state chapters of the National Council of Teachers of English, the National Council for the Social Studies, and the Association for Supervision and Curriculum Development customarily focus on curriculum concerns. Although conference participants may engage in curriculum planning in only the most rudimentary and often passive way, the sharing of curriculum ideas often lays the groundwork for subsequent curriculum reform. This type of curriculum activity cannot, of course, be equated with more structured efforts under the state department of education. Nor can we truly label the examination of curriculum problems by state professional organizations as a level of planning since no element of authority exists in this type of voluntary activity. More appropriately, the state professional organizations constitute a sector that seeks to effect curriculum change through research, example, and persuasion. Nevertheless, we would be remiss if we did not credit state professional organizations for the influence they often exert in bringing about changes in the curriculum of the local school systems of the state.

Channels Outside of Education.

Other departments of the executive branch, the state legislature, and the state judicial branch form channels outside the profession of education that have an impact on the curriculum of all the schools of the state. Within the executive branch the governor and the state board of education wield tremendous power over the state educational system. The governor presents a budget to the legislature in which he or she recommends supporting or curtailing programs. The state board sets policies that bind all the schools of the state.

Legislative Decisions.

State legislatures throughout the country consistently demonstrate a penchant for curriculum making. Mandates from the state legislatures in some cases with leadership from the executive branch have been the prime movers for educational reform in the 1980s and early 1990s. Susan H. Fuhrman cited Florida, Georgia, Indiana, Mississippi, South Carolina, and Texas as examples of states that overhauled their educational systems. Among the many modifications, forty-five states revised requirements for high school graduation and over forty states instituted programs to assess student achievement.[24]

The legislature of the state of Florida provides an example of legislative curriculum making. Among the many curriculum prescriptions are the following extractions from Florida statutes.

Florida Statute 233.061, addressing a wide variety of designated needs, required instruction on the following:

Declaration of Independence
Arguments in support of a republican form of government
U.S. Constitution and its relation to government structure
Flag education, including proper display and salute
The elements of civil government
History of the Holocaust
History of African Americans
The elementary principles of agriculture
The true effects of all alcoholic and intoxicating liquors, beverages, and narcotics
Kindness to animals
The history of the state
The conservation of natural resources
Comprehensive health education
The study of Hispanic contributions to the United States
The study of women's contributions to the United States

---

[24]Fuhrman, "Legislatures and Education Policy," *Governance*, p. 31.

Florida Statute 233.0612, authorized school districts to provide the following instruction:

Character development and law education
The objective study of the Bible and religion
Traffic education
Free enterprise and consumer education
Programs to encourage patriotism and greater respect for country
Drug abuse resistance education
Comprehensive health education
Care of nursing home patients
Acquired immune deficiency syndrome
Voting instruction, including the use of county voting machines
Before-school and after-school programs

In mandating character-development education in the spring of 1999 the Florida legislature became very specific, stipulating for the elementary schools a secular character-development program similar to those of Character Counts![25]

Florida Statute 229.57, made sweeping provision, later modified, for state assessment of student progress when it directed the state commissioner of education to:

"Develop and administer in the public schools a uniform, statewide program of assessment to determine, periodically, educational status and progress and the degree of achievement of approved minimum performance standards. The uniform statewide program shall consist of testing in grades 3, 5, 8, and 11. . . ."

Although some legislation is a result of grassroots movement within the state and some statutes evolve from recommendations made by the state superintendent of public instruction and the state department of education, many acts of the state legislature stem from the personal beliefs and desires of the legislators themselves. Even the state judicial branch finds itself entangled in curriculum decision making from time to time. Two famous cases may serve to illustrate involvement of the state courts in curriculum making.

The Supreme Court of Michigan ruled in 1874 in a case brought against the school district of Kalamazoo by a taxpayer of that community that the school board of Kalamazoo could, indeed, spend public funds to provide a secondary school education for youth of their district.[26]

In 1927 the Supreme Court of Tennessee replied to the appeal of defense attorneys of John Thomas Scopes of the world-famous "monkey trial" by upholding the constitutionality of the Tennessee law that forbade teaching in the public schools any theory that denied human creation by a Divine Being.[27] Periodically, state legislatures have attempted to mandate the teaching of "scientific creationism" in the public schools as a

---

[25]See Chapter 6 for reference to Character Counts! Coalition.
[26]Stuart v. *School District No. 1, Village of Kalamazoo,* 30 Mich. 69 (1874).
[27]See Lyon Sprague de Camp, *The Great Monkey Trial* (Garden City, N.Y.: Doubleday, 1968).

counterbalance to the theory of evolution. The scientific creationism/evolution issue, to which we will return in Chapter 14, continues to surface in some state executive and legislative bodies.

SECTORS BEYOND THE STATE

When curriculum planners leave the state level and move onto the broader scene, they work in quite a different context. Participation in planning in the regional, national, and international sectors is ordinarily a voluntary activity. Except in the case of federal legislation, information sharing and persuasion rather than statutory power are the tools of the regional, national, and international sectors. No assurance of any kind exists that curriculum decisions reached in these sectors will or can be put into operation in the schools.

Although fewer opportunities exist for curriculum workers to engage in planning in the regional, national, and international sectors, the opportunities that do arise can be exciting for the participants.

THE REGIONAL SECTOR

Participation in planning in the regional, national, and international sectors is not comparable to that in the previously described levels. On occasion, curriculum specialists of a particular region of the United States, from around the nation, or even from a number of foreign countries may assemble and develop curriculum materials that they will then disseminate or try out in their own schools. The most notable illustrations of this type of cooperative endeavor were the efforts of the scholars from various parts of the country who in the late 1950s developed the so-called new math and new science programs.

As a general rule, curriculum activities in the regional, national, and international sectors are more likely to consist of sharing problems, exchanging practices, reporting research, and gathering information. Conferences of the professional organizations—for example, the South Atlantic Modern Language Association—are the most common vehicle whereby school personnel participate in regional curriculum study. With considerable frequency teachers, administrators, and curriculum specialists are invited to take part in the activities of the regional associations (New England, Middle States, North Central, Northwest, Southern, and Western) that accredit schools and colleges. This participation consists of three types. First, participants are elected or invited to serve on various committees and commissions of the associations—for example, the Commission on Elementary Schools, the Commission on Secondary Schools, and the regional associations' state committees. Second, committees of professionals review, revise, and write for each subject area the criteria that schools follow in evaluating their programs. The third and most extensive of the three types of participation is service on accreditation visiting committees that go into schools in the region to ascertain strengths and weaknesses of the schools' programs and to make recommendations for improvements and accreditation of the schools.

Much of the participation in which school personnel take part in the regional sector falls into the category of curriculum evaluation in contrast to planning or implementation of the curriculum.

THE NATIONAL SECTOR

U.S. Department of Education.   The national scene is peppered with a variety of public, private, and professional curriculum activities, and school personnel from the state level and below play key roles in some of these activities. In the public governmental sector, the Department of Education exercises a strong influence. Called the United States Office of Education until Education was separated from the U.S. Department of Health, Education, and Welfare in 1980 during President Jimmy Carter's administration, the Department of Education with its large bureaucracy gathers data, disseminates information, provides consultative assistance, sponsors and conducts research, funds projects, and disburses money appropriated by Congress. Local school people find the opportunity to participate in national curriculum efforts by writing and submitting proposals for grants to conduct curricular research or to put particular programs into operation in their school systems.

Federal Funding.   To choose recipients of funds for proposals awarded competitively, the Department of Education calls in readers who are specialists in the particular fields in which grants are being given. These readers evaluate and make recommendations on proposals to be awarded by the specific office within the Department of Education. Persons from all over the United States journey to Washington (or sometimes to other sites) to read proposals. In so doing, they grow professionally and bring back new ideas for curriculum development in their own institutions.

Federal funding permits numerous committees to carry out curriculum projects that the U.S. Congress deems significant. Title I of the Elementary and Secondary School Act of 1965 (which later became Chapter 1 of the Education Consolidation and Improvement Act of 1981), for example, provided for programs to aid the culturally disadvantaged.

Grants from the federal government over the years have enabled national study groups to prepare curriculum materials, some of which (as in foreign languages, mathematics, and science) have been used extensively.

Federal aid has stimulated and resulted in the involvement of curriculum workers both directly as participants and indirectly as consumers of products and services of the Educational Resources Information Center (ERIC), the National Diffusion Network, the Regional Educational Laboratories, the National Research and Development Centers, and the National Institutes of the U.S. Department of Education's Office of Educational Research and Improvement.[28]

In the late 1960s, the publicly funded National Science Foundation joined with the U.S. Office of Education to assist social studies and humanities specialists led by Jerome S. Bruner[29] to develop *Man: A Course of Study,* a multimedia curriculum for

---

[28]For recent lists of centers, laboratories, and institutes, see Appendices B, C, D, and E.

[29]Author of *The Process of Education* (Cambridge, Mass.: Harvard University Press, 1960).

elementary school pupils.[30] Heralded by many, *Man: A Course of Study* presents an interesting case of problems of curriculum development on a national scale. Imbued with the ambitious goal of analyzing the human condition, *Man: A Course of Study* became controversial subject matter by contrasting life in the United States with life among members of an Eskimo tribe.

John D. McNeil pointed out that criticisms of *Man: A Course of Study* (MACOS) came from different curricular concerns—from the humanists who "criticized Bruner for failing to recognize the potential of MACOS for fostering emotional growth," from "social reconstructionists opposed [to] MACOS on the ground that it was created by a scholarly elite," and from the U.S. Congress, where a congressman, "criticized the course on the House floor as depicting 'abhorrent and revolting behavior by a nearly extinct Eskimo tribe'" and "said the material was full of references to adultery, cannibalism, killing of female babies and old people, trial marriage, wife-swapping, and violent murders."[31]

Local schools in various regions of the country have participated in curriculum evaluation on a national scale through the National Assessment of Educational Progress, which is funded by the Office of Educational Research and Improvement. Under the direction of the National Assessment of Educational Progress (NAEP), objectives have been specified, criterion-referenced measurement instruments have been created, and assessments have been conducted in a number of subject areas.[32] From these data curriculum developers in the local school systems can draw inferences about appropriate objectives of the areas tested, achievements of pupils in their region as compared to other regions, and their own state and local assessment programs.

Historically, the U.S. Department of Education has exercised a degree of leadership in curriculum development for the schools of the nation. Downsizing of government for budgetary and political reasons has set in with such force at the federal level that in the spring of 1995 the survival of the U.S. Department of Education was in doubt. Proposals of the Republican-controlled Congress called for abolition of the Department of Education along with the Departments of Commerce and Energy.

In this discussion of curriculum efforts on a national scale, I have mentioned the executive branch of the U.S. government (the Department of Education) and the legislative branch (the Congress). We should not neglect to note that on occasion the judicial branch of the federal government assumes the role of curriculum maker. For example, the U.S. Supreme Court has ruled that public schools may not conduct sectarian practices,[33] that released time for religious instruction under certain conditions is permissible,[34] that the theory of evolution may be taught,[35] that special instruction in English must be given to non-English-speaking pupils,[36] and that prayer in the public schools is a violation of the First Amendment of the U.S. Constitution.[37] The

---

[30]*Man: A Course of Study* (Washington, D.C.: Curriculum Development Associates, 1970).

[31]John D. McNeil, *Curriculum: A Comprehensive Introduction,* 5th ed. (New York: HarperCollins, 1996), p. 86.

[32]See Chapter 12 of this text for additional details about the National Assessment of Educational Progress.

[33]*Illinois ex rel McCollum v. Board of Education,* 333 US 203, 68 S Ct. 461 (1948).

[34]*Zorach v. Clauson,* 343 US 306, 72 S. Ct. 679 (1952).

[35]*Epperson v. Arkansas,* 393 US 97, 89 S. Ct. 266 (1968).

[36]*Lau v. Nichols,* 414 US 663 (1974).

[37]*School District of Abington Township, Pa. v. Schempp & Murray v. Curlett,* 374 US 203, 83 S. Ct. 1560 (1963).

U.S. Supreme Court justices do not seek the role of curriculum specialists but by virtue of the cases that come before them sometimes find themselves in that role.

Professional Education Associations. The professional education associations afford opportunities for educators to engage in curriculum deliberations. The National Education Association (NEA) has repeatedly called together influential groups to evaluate purposes and programs of the schools. The NEA's Committee of Ten, for example, issued a report in 1893 that recommended the same courses (foreign languages, history, mathematics, and science) and the same allotment of time for each course for both college-bound and non-college-bound students.[38] Gerald R. Firth and Richard D. Klimpston commented on the influence of the Committee of Ten's report:

> The recommendations of courses to be taught, coupled with a statement that the courses should be offered in the same manner to both the college-bound and the non-college-bound, became a powerful force influencing the secondary school curriculum well into the 20th century.[39]

One of the more significant attempts at curriculum decision making at the national level was the National Education Association's appointment of the Commission on the Reorganization of Secondary Education which produced in 1918 one of the most influential and foresighted documents in the history of American education. The document, *Cardinal Principles of Secondary Education,* made nineteen generalizations or principles, some of which applied at all levels of education. In speaking of the role of secondary education in achieving the main objectives of education the Commission listed (in Principle IV) seven objectives that have become widely known and discussed as the *Seven Cardinal Principles.*[40]

These seven objectives were:

1. health
2. command of fundamental processes [currently known as the basic skills]
3. worthy home membership
4. vocation
5. citizenship
6. worthy use of leisure
7. ethical character

The Commission's report, possessing no authority other than its persuasiveness, was broadly received and accepted as a valid statement of goals for secondary education of its time. Many high schools have attempted to implement the Commission's Cardinal Principles. Although some criticism of the Seven Cardinal Principles exists, many educators feel that this statement of the purposes of secondary education is as relevant today as it was when first issued so many years ago.[41]

---

[38]National Education Association, *Report of the Committee of Ten on Secondary School Studies* (New York: American Book, 1894).

[39]Gerald R. Firth and Richard D. Klimpston, *The Curricular Continuum in Perspective* (Itasca, Ill.: F. E. Peacock, 1973), p. 70.

[40]Commission on the Reorganization of Secondary Education, *Cardinal Principles of Secondary Education* (Washington, D.C.: United States Office of Education, Bulletin no. 35, 1918), pp. 5–10.

[41]For criticism of the Seven Cardinal Principles, see Chapter 9 of this text.

Between 1938 and 1961 the prestigious Educational Policies Commission of the National Education Association formulated statements of the purposes of education. Three of these statements have had an enduring effect on American education.

In 1938 the Educational Policies Commission defined the purposes of education as fourfold: self-realization, human relationship, economic efficiency, and civic responsibility.[42] Six years later, in the midst of World War II, the Educational Policies Commission released its report on *Education for All American Youth,* which set forth ten imperative needs of American youth.[43]

Refining the earlier Seven Cardinal Principles, the Educational Policies Commission in 1944 stated the purposes of secondary education as follows:

1. All youth need to develop salable skills.
2. All youth need to develop and maintain good health, physical fitness, and mental health.
3. All youth need to understand the rights and duties of the citizen of a democratic society.
4. All youth need to understand the significance of the family.
5. All youth need to know how to purchase and use goods and services intelligently.
6. All youth need to understand the methods of science.
7. All youth need opportunities to develop their capacities to appreciate beauty in literature, art, and music.
8. All youth need to be able to use their leisure time well.
9. All youth need to develop respect for other people, to grow in their insight into ethical values and principles, to be able to live and work cooperatively with others, and to grow in the moral and spiritual values of life.
10. All youth need to grow in their ability to think rationally, to express their thoughts clearly, and to read and listen with understanding.[44]

Once again, this time in 1961, the Educational Policies Commission turned its attention to the purposes of education and decided that the central purpose of American education was to develop the ability to think.[45]

On the current scene, the Association for Supervision and Curriculum Development (ASCD), a professional association with a special interest in curriculum improvement, engages its members and others in numerous curriculum studies. It disseminates the results of studies through its journals, yearbooks, and monographs. Of special help to persons interested in the curriculum field are the ASCD's National Curriculum Study Institutes in which participants under the leadership of recognized experts focus on particular curriculum problems.

Development of curricula in certain specialized fields has been made possible by the National Science Foundation in cooperation with professional associations. The

[42]Educational Policies Commission, *The Purposes of Education in American Democracy* (Washington, D.C.: National Education Association, 1938).

[43]Educational Policies Commission, *Education for All American Youth* (Washington, D.C.: National Education Association, 1944).

[44]Educational Policies Commission, *American Youth*, pp. 225–226.

[45]Educational Policies Commission, *The Central Purpose of American Education* (Washington, D.C.: National Education Association, 1961).

National Science Foundation, the American Mathematical Society, the National Council of Teachers of Mathematics, and the Mathematical Association of America joined forces in the 1950s to produce the School Mathematics Study Group (SMSG) program for grades four through twelve. Involved in the production of this program were mathematicians, mathematics educators, and high school teachers. At about the same time and through a similar collaborative effort, the American Institute of Biological Sciences, with financial backing by the National Science Foundation, brought forth the Biological Sciences Curriculum Study (BSCS) programs (in three versions) for high school biology.

Professional education organizations have made and continue to make significant contributions to the curriculum field, most recently in the generation of national standards as we will see in Chapter 14.

Private Foundations and Business Corporations.   Over the years a goodly number of private foundations and organizations sponsored by business and industrial corporations have demonstrated a keen interest in supporting projects designed to improve education in the United States. The Ford Foundation has given generous backing to experimentations with novel staff patterns in the schools and the use of educational television. The Kellogg Foundation has zeroed in on studies of educational administration. As examples of foundations' interest in the curriculum of the schools we might mention the Carnegie Corporation's support in the field of mathematics and the Alfred P. Sloan Foundation's aid in the field of science. In the early l950s the Carnegie Corporation financially aided professors in arts and sciences, education, and engineering at the University of Illinois to develop a school mathematics program for grades nine through twelve, which became known as the University of Illinois Committee on School Mathematics (UICSM) math. Shortly thereafter, in the late 1950s, the Carnegie Corporation funded another mathematics project: the development of a program for grades seven and eight by teachers of mathematics, mathematicians, and mathematics educators at the University of Maryland.

The Alfred P. Sloan Foundation entered into curriculum development in the late 1950s by supporting, along with the National Science Foundation and the Ford Foundation's Fund for the Advancement of Education, the production of a new program for high school physics known as Physical Science Study Committee (PSSC) physics.

Several observations can be made about these illustrations of national curriculum development in mathematics and science. First, these programs were created through the collaboration of scholars and practitioners, professors and teachers, combinations that have been tried with rather low frequency, unfortunately. Second, all these undertakings took considerable effort and cost a significant amount of money. Without the largesse of the federal government, public and private foundations, and professional organizations, these materials would most probably never have seen the light of day. Third, as you may have already noted, all these developments occurred in the decade of the 1950s and continued into the early 1960s. The 1950s were a time when there was a great deal of ferment in education, and money flowed into educational pursuits as if from the proverbial horn of plenty. As a response to the technology of the then–Soviet Union and in the name of national defense, the availability of funds for educational projects and research made the 1950s a heady time for educators. No such concerned collaborative activity on such a broad scale has occurred since, and we may well ponder whether it is ever likely to happen again. Finally and most significantly, in spite of the curriculum fervor of the 1950s (Could it be *because* of the fervor of the 1950s?), some of the new math and new science programs have gone into eclipse, causing us to muse with François Villon, "Where are the snows of yesteryear?"

In the 1980s the Carnegie Corporation with the Atlantic Richfield Foundation funded the study of American high schools directed by Ernest L. Boyer, president of the Carnegie Foundation for the Advancement of Teaching.[46] Six philanthropic foundations—the Charles E. Culpepper Foundation, the Carnegie Corporation, the Commonwealth Fund, the Esther A. and Joseph Klingenstein Fund, the Gates Foundation, and the Edward John Noble Foundation—supported Theodore R. Sizer's study of the American high school. Cosponsors of Sizer's study were the National Association of Secondary School Principals and the National Association of Independent Schools.[47]

Funds for John Goodlad's study of schooling in America were provided by eleven foundations, including the Danforth Foundation, the Ford Foundation, the International Paper Company Foundation, the JDR[3rd] Fund, the Martha Holden Jennings Foundation, the Charles F. Kettering Foundation, the Lilly Endowment, the Charles Stewart Mott Foundation, the Needmore Fund, the Rockefeller Foundation, and the Spencer Foundation; funding was also provided by Pedamorphosis, Inc., the National Institute of Education, and the U.S. Office of Education.[48]

The Danforth Foundation, which long concerned itself with professional growth and development of secondary school administrators, has over the years also taken an interest in promoting international education in the schools. The John D. and Catherine T. MacArthur Foundation aided the Paideia Group, which issued the *Paideia Proposal,* calling for the same course of study for all students in the twelve years of basic schooling, the only exception being the choice of a second language.[49]

In recent years Microsoft Corporation has made available without charge to K–12 schools software to enable them to become familiar with the Internet. Microsoft joined forces with MCI to offer schools the opportunity to establish an informative web page or register web pages with Global SchoolNet Foundation's *Global Schoolhouse.*[50] In September 1999 Bill Gates, CEO of Microsoft, and his wife announced creation of 1,000 college scholarships a year for 20 years to minority students.

AT&T's Learning Network has supported efforts to develop technological skills of students and teachers in the federally designated Empowerment Zones of Harlem and the Bronx. Empowerment Zones in the United States are characterized by their need for economic development and cooperation between the public and private organizations.[51] The Oklahoma Foundation for Excellence has directed efforts to prevent students from dropping out of school and made awards recognizing excellence among students and teachers in the public schools of Oklahoma while the Steppingstone Foundation has sought to help students in inner-city schools of Boston gain access to

---

[46]Ernest L. Boyer, *High School: A Report on Secondary Education in America* (New York: Harper & Row, 1983).

[47]Theodore R. Sizer, *Horace's Compromise: The Dilemma of the American High School* (Boston: Houghton Mifflin, 1984).

[48]Goodlad, *A Place Called School.*

[49]Mortimer J. Adler, *The Paideia Proposal: An Educational Manifesto* (New York: Macmillan, 1982).

[50]For information about *Global Schoolhouse* and its sponsors consult Web site at URL http://www.gsh.org.

[51]For information on Empowerment Zones see Web site at http://www.ezec.gov.

independent and public-examination schools of Boston. The DeWitt-Wallace Reader's Digest Fund has extended aid to public-school libraries in urban school districts across the country.

You can readily see that private foundations and business corporations play a significant role in promoting change in the school's curriculum.

Other Influential Voices.   In 1990 President George Bush and the National Governors Association set forth six national educational goals. Expanding on the Bush reform efforts, the U.S. Congress in 1994 enacted President Bill Clinton's educational reform package known as *Goals 2000 Educate America Act,* which added two goals beyond the earlier six and authorized funding to promote achievement of those goals. We will examine these goals and their significance in Chapter 6.

Tests and Texts.   Before we leave the national sector, we should mention an aspect of curriculum development that has evoked considerable discussion. Standardized tests of achievement and textbooks used in the schools have played a great part in molding the contemporary curriculum. Combined with the movement toward specification of minimal competencies for high school graduation, achievement tests profoundly affect what is being taught and how it is being taught. Under these conditions, curriculum decisions have been, in effect, put into the hands of the test makers and textbook writers. Some curriculum experts see the reliance on tests and textbooks marketed throughout the country as constituting a "national curriculum." Elliot W. Eisner expressed concern about the influence of the testing movement:

> One may wax eloquent about the life of the mind and the grand purposes of education, but must face up to the fact that school programs are shaped by other factors as well. Communities led to believe that the quality of education is represented by the reading and math scores students receive come to demand that those areas of the curriculum be given the highest priority. When this happens, teachers begin to define their own priorities in terms of test performance. Indeed, I do not believe it is an exaggeration to say that test scores function as one of the most powerful controls on the character of educational practice.[52]

Other educators identify federal aid for specific categories as creating types of national curricula. Considerable activity in planning, implementing, and evaluating curriculum transpires in the national sector. Although curriculum activities on the national scene are many and diverse, opportunities for personal involvement are rather limited for the rank-and-file teacher and curriculum specialist. Their roles are more often as recipients of curriculum plans developed by others, implementors of plans, and sometimes evaluators.

The Public.   We would be remiss if we did not include the public in our survey of groups that influence curriculum development. We have but to examine some of the controversial issues discussed in Chapter 14 as evidence of public participation in efforts to change the curriculum.

---

[52]Elliot W. Eisner, *The Educational Imagination: On the Design and Evaluation of School Programs,* 2nd ed. (New York: Macmillan, 1985), p. 4.

Most often the public's efforts are diffuse with subgroups advocating change of one type whereas other subgroups take opposite positions.

The public's views, however, succeed in effecting change when issues are put before them, albeit from legislator-curriculum planners, in the form of proposals to be voted on by the voting public. The electorate of California, for example, in the spring of 1998 voted to remove bilingual education from the public schools.

THE INTERNATIONAL SECTOR

International Professional Associations.   Involvement of American curriculum workers on the international scene is made possible through membership in international professional associations, primarily those based in the United States. The International Reading Association, for example, attracts reading specialists from around the world but primarily from the United States and Canada. The World Council for Gifted and Talented Children holds conferences in various parts of the world. One of the more pertinent international organizations for those interested in curricular activities on an international scale is the World Council for Curriculum and Instruction (WCCI), which is open to all educators who have an interest in "global fellowship."[53] This organization, comprising members from more than seventy countries, provides advice and assistance on curricular matters, carries out transnational projects, and sponsors triennial conferences in various locations throughout the world.

If teachers and administrators are willing to spend a period of time abroad, they can become intimately involved in curriculum development overseas by accepting employment in the U.S. Department of Defense Schools (which, given current retrenchments in the defense establishment, are shrinking in numbers) or in the private American Community/International Schools whose curricula are mainly those offered stateside. Or they may become active in developing curricula of foreign national schools through employment with the Peace Corps or the Agency for International Development.

The United Nations Educational, Scientific, and Cultural Organization (UNESCO), with headquarters in Paris, affords opportunities for curriculum study, research, teaching, and technical assistance from members of the United Nations. The Institute of International Education in New York City directs an international exchange of students and teachers supported in part by Fulbright funds. The Council for International Exchange of Scholars in Washington, D.C., administers Fulbright grants that enable faculty from institutions of higher education to conduct research and teach in foreign countries.

Opportunities for firsthand participation in actual curriculum construction on a cross-national basis are rare, and this dearth of opportunity is, perhaps, to be expected. The curricular needs and goals of education in various countries are so divergent as to make impractical the building of a particular curriculum that will fit the requirements of the educational system of every country.

Comparative Studies of Student Achievement.   Significant efforts primarily in the realm of assessment of student achievement should be noted. Studies comparing

---

[53]World Council for Curriculum and Instruction, Box 171, Teachers College, Columbia University, New York, N.Y. 10027.

achievement of students in a number of countries and in a variety of disciplines have been conducted by the International Association for Evaluation of Educational Achievement (IEA) and the International Assessment of Educational Progress (IAEP). You will find discussion of international comparative studies in Chapter 12 of this text.

United States–USSR Textbook-Study Project.   One of the more interesting international curriculum studies of modern times was the United States and, the then USSR, Textbook-Study Project sponsored by the National Council for the Social Studies, the Council of Chief State School Officers, the Association of American Publishers, the Association for the Advancement of Slavic Studies, and the former Soviet Union's Ministry of Education.[54] Begun in 1977 as a phase of cultural exchange agreements between the two countries, the project ceased functioning after the Soviet march into Afghanistan in 1979. The project resumed operation in 1985, drafted a report in 1987, and presented a subsequent report on the conclusion of a seminar in Moscow in 1989.

Educators from both countries examined history and geography textbooks used in the secondary schools of each country to ascertain what one nation's students were taught about the other nation. These educators searched for errors of fact and distortions in the textbooks. Project efforts pointed to the need for textbooks published in each country to present a more accurate picture of the other country. This exciting approach to international curriculum study could well furnish a model that the United States could and, I believe, should replicate with other countries.

Global Awareness.   To this point we have concentrated on opportunities for collaborative cross-cultural curriculum research and development. A somewhat different curriculum activity was the funding by the U.S. Department of Education of programs in American schools for the development of global awareness among our children and youth. In spite of international tensions, American commitment to the development of students' and teachers' understanding of foreign peoples remains high. Recommendations of such groups as the President's Commission on Foreign Languages and International Studies in the late 1970s have helped stimulate study of foreign languages and cultures.[55] Among the many recommendations of the President's Commission were these:

- regional centers for upgrading competencies for foreign language study
- summer institutes abroad for foreign language teachers and others
- reinstatement of foreign language requirements in schools and colleges
- the integration of international studies throughout the school curricula
- the expansion of international exchange of students, teachers, administrators, and policymakers
- requirement of two to three courses in international studies for all bachelor's degree candidates
- establishment of regional international studies centers at colleges and universities

---

[54]Robert Rothman, "Americans, Soviets, Critique Texts." *Education Week* 7, no. 12 (November 25, 1987): 5; and Oliva's correspondence from the National Council for the Social Studies, dated December 4, 1990.

[55]See Malcolm G. Scully, "Require Foreign-Language Studies, Presidential Panel Urges Colleges," *The Chronicle of Higher Education* 19, no. 11 (November 13, 1979): 1 ff.

A decade later, citing America's global role, The National Commission on Excellence in Education in its famed *Nation at Risk* report included foreign language study among its recommendations. According to the Commission's report:

> Achieving proficiency in *foreign language* ordinarily requires from 4 to 6 years of study and should, therefore, be started in the elementary grades. We believe it is desirable that students achieve such proficiency because study of a foreign language introduces students to non-English speaking cultures, heightens awareness and comprehension of one's native tongue, and serves the Nation's needs in commerce, diplomacy, defense, and education.[56]

A rationale for global education was the focus of the 1991 Yearbook of the Association for Supervision and Curriculum Development. The yearbook includes descriptions of ways to introduce global studies into the curriculum.[57] In the late 1990s global education, enhanced by cheaper transportation, communication, and technology, has seen a resurgence in the schools as evidenced, for example, by the Global Education Network of the Association for Supervision and Curriculum Development[58] and the creation of the American Forum on Global Education.[59]

Although opportunities for actual curriculum development on the international scene are limited, many opportunities exist for school personnel to study and compare curricula of the world's nations. Professional organizations like Phi Delta Kappa, the National Education Association, the Association for Supervision and Curriculum Development, and the Comparative and International Education Society conduct frequent study tours for those interested in examining firsthand the curricula of other countries and meeting their educational leaders. Many teachers have taken advantage of opportunities to serve as leaders of educational study tours abroad. Furthermore, development of both awareness and understanding of other cultures (both within and outside of our borders) remains a high priority of our elementary and secondary curricula.

SUMMARY

Curriculum planning is viewed as occurring on five levels: classroom, team/grade/department, individual school, school district, and state. Each level in ascending order exercises authority over levels below it.

In addition, planning takes place in regional, national, and world sectors. Sectors are distinguished from levels because powers of the sectors over the five levels are

---

[56]National Commission on Excellence in Education, *A Nation at Risk: The Imperative for Educational Reform* (Washington, D.C.: U.S. Government Printing Office, 1983), p. 26.

[57]Kenneth A. Tye, ed., *Global Education: From Thought to Action.* 1991 Yearbook (Alexandria, Va.: Association for Supervision and Curriculum Development, 1990).

[58]See Association for Supervision and Curriculum Development, "Making Connections Through Global Education," *Curriculum Update,* summer 1998, p. 8

[59]The American Forum on Global Education, 120 Wall Street, Suite 2600, New York, N.Y. 10005. Web site: http://www.globaled.org.

nonexistent or limited.

Teachers and curriculum specialists will find their most frequent opportunities to participate actively in curriculum development at the first four levels. Some curriculum workers are called on by the state to serve on curriculum projects. A limited number of school-based persons take part in a variety of curriculum efforts sponsored by regional, national, and international organizations and agencies.

This chapter diagrams a variety of organizational patterns for carrying out curriculum activities in the individual school and school district. A teacher or curriculum specialist may be requested to serve on a number of curriculum committees and councils within a school system.

Forces outside the schools also influence curriculum decision making. Curriculum development is perceived as a multilevel, multisector process and as a collaborative effort.

QUESTIONS FOR DISCUSSION

1. To what degree should teachers be involved in curriculum planning at the individual school level? at the district level?
2. What are the strengths and limitations of the concept of levels of planning?
3. What are the strengths and limitations of the concept of sectors of planning?
4. What do you believe is the best way for organizing a curriculum council on the individual school level?
5. What do you believe is the best way for organizing a curriculum council on the school district level?

SUPPLEMENTARY EXERCISES

1. Chart the organizational pattern for curriculum development in your school and district.
2. Write a short paper describing the extent to which the organizational patterns operating in your school system can be called participatory.
3. Tell how curriculum committees and councils, if any, are selected and constituted in your school district.
4. Describe any curricular changes within the last three years brought about by an individual teacher in his/her classroom.
5. Describe activities of a team, grade, or department of a school faculty in the last three years in the area of curriculum development.
6. Describe the roles and powers of (a) the state superintendent of public instruction, (b) the state board of education, and (c) the state department of education in curricular and instructional matters within your state.
7. Study an organizational chart of your state department of education and identify those offices that are charged with providing curricular and instructional leadership in the state. Describe some of the services of these offices.

8. Report on several programs that have come about or been affected as a result of state legislation.
9. Describe any curriculum developments that have come about as a result of regional activities.
10. Report on the purposes and activities of the accrediting associations of your region.
11. Report on several programs that have come about or been affected as a result of federal legislation.
12. Describe any support that may have come to schools of your community and/or state from private foundations or business/industrial corporations.
13. Report on any national curriculum studies that you would call significant.
14. Report on at least two state and two federal court decisions that have had an impact on the curriculum of your school system.
15. Describe any curriculum development in your school that might be attributed to international influences.
16. Report on the purposes and recent activities of at least two state, two national, and two international professional organizations concerned with curriculum development.
17. Write a description of the processes by which textbooks are selected in your state or district.
18. If you work in a private school and if your school is accredited by an association or associations other than the regional association, describe the purpose and activities of that association or associations.
19. In Chapter 11 of his book, John D. McNeil (see bibliography) discusses the politics of curriculum making. Report several ways in which curriculum making is a political process.
20. Describe what Michael W. Apple meant by "Curriculum . . . is the social product of contending forces." (See bibliography). See also Chapter 4, "Understanding Curriculum as Political Text," in William F. Pinar et al. (see bibliography).

BIBLIOGRAPHY

Apple, Michael W. "Social Crisis and Curriculum Accords." *Educational Theory* 38, no. 2 (Spring 1988): 191–201.

Ayers, William. "*Perestroika* in Chicago's Schools" *Educational Leadership* 48, no. 8 (May 1991): 69–71.

Beauchamp, George A. *Curriculum Theory,* 4th ed. Itasca, Ill.: F. E. Peacock, 1981.

Bruner, Jerome S. *The Process of Education.* Cambridge, Mass.: Harvard University Press, 1960.

Carroll, Joseph M. "The Copernican Plan: Restructuring the American High School." *Phi Delta Kappan* 71, no. 5 (January 1990): 358–365.

Commission on the Reorganization of Secondary Education. *Cardinal Principles of Secondary Education.* Washington, D.C.: United States Office of Education, Bulletin no. 35, 1918.

Doll, Ronald C. *Curriculum Improvement: Decision Making and Process,* 9th ed. Boston: Allyn and Bacon, 1996.

Educational Policies Commission. *The Central Purpose of American Education.* Washington, D.C.: National Education Association, 1961.

———. *Education for All American Youth.* Washington, D.C.: National Education Association, 1944.

———. *The Purposes of Education in American Democracy.* Washington, D.C.: National Education Association, 1938.

Eisner, Elliot W. *Confronting Curriculum Reform.* Boston: Little, Brown, 1971.

———. *The Educational Imagination: On the Design and Evaluation of School Programs,* 2nd ed. New York: Macmillan, 1985.

Firth, Gerald R. and Kimpston, Richard D. *The Curricular Continuum in Perspective.* Itasca, Ill.: F. E. Peacock, 1973.

Frymier, Jack R. and Hawn, Horace C. *Curriculum Improvement for Better Schools.* Worthington, Ohio: Charles A. Jones, 1970.

Gomez, Joseph J. "The Path to School-Based Management Isn't Smooth, but We're Scaling the Obstacles One by One." *American School Board Journal* 176, no. 10 (October 1989): 20–22.

Hass, Glen, ed. *Curriculum Planning: A New Approach,* 5th ed. Boston: Allyn and Bacon, 1987.

Kimbrough, Ralph B. and Nunnery, Michael Y. *Educational Administration: An Introduction,* 3rd ed. New York: Macmillan, 1988.

McNeil, John D. *Curriculum: A Comprehensive Introduction,* 5th ed. New York: HarperCollins, 1996.

Mendez, Roy. "The Curriculum Council: One Way to Develop the Instructional Leadership Role." *NASSP Bulletin* 67, no. 464 (September 1983): 18–21.

Oliva, Peter F. *The Secondary School Today,* 2nd ed. New York: Harper & Row, 1972.

Oliver, Albert I. *Curriculum Improvement: A Guide to Problems, Principles, and Process,* 2nd ed. New York: Harper & Row, 1977.

Pinar, William F., Reynolds, William M., Slattery Patrick, and Taubman, Peter M. *Understanding Curriculum: An Introduction to the Study of Historical and Contemporary Curriculum Discourses.* New York: Peter Lang, 1996.

Prasch, John. *How to Organize for School-Based Management.* Alexandria, Va.: Association for Supervision and Curriculum Development, 1990.

"Restructuring Schools to Match a Changing Society." *Educational Leadership* 45, no. 5 (February 1988): 3–79.

"Restructuring Schools: What's Really Happening." *Educational Leadership* 48, no. 8 (May 1991): 3–76.

Rubin, Louis, ed. *Curriculum Handbook: The Disciplines, Current Movements, and Instructional Methodology.* Boston: Allyn and Bacon, 1977.

Saylor, J. Galen, Alexander, William M., and Lewis, Arthur J. *Curriculum Planning for Better Teaching and Learning,* 4th ed. New York: Holt, Rinehart and Winston, 1981.

Shanker, Albert. "The End of the Traditional Model of Schooling—and a Proposal for Using Incentives to Restructure Our Public Schools." *Phi Delta Kappan* 71, no. 5 (January 1990): 344–357.

Tye, Kenneth A., ed. *Global Education from Thought to Action.* 1991 Yearbook. Alexandria, Va: Association for Supervision and Curriculum Development, 1990.

Walberg, Herbert J., Bakalis, Michael J., Bast, Joseph L., and Baer, Steven, "Restructuring the Nation's Worst Schools." *Phi Delta Kappan* 70, no. 10 (June 1989): 802–805.

Walker, Decker. *Fundamentals of Curriculum.* Orlando, Fla.: Harcourt Brace Jovanovich, 1990.

Wiles, Jon and Bondi, Joseph C. *Curriculum Development: A Guide to Practice,* 5th ed. Upper Saddle River, N.J.: Merrill, 1998.

Zais, Robert S. *Curriculum: Principles and Foundations.* New York: Harper & Row, 1976.

CHAPTER 4

CURRICULUM PLANNING: THE HUMAN DIMENSION

After studying this chapter you should be able to:

1. Describe the roles of (a) the principal, (b) the curriculum leader, (c) the teachers, (d) the students, and (e) the parents and other citizens in curriculum development.
2. Describe the knowledge and skills needed by the curriculum leader.

THE SCHOOL AS A UNIQUE BLEND

Let us for a few moments step into the shoes of the superintendent of a hypothetical school district. It is mid-May. The school year is almost over and summer school plans are ready to be implemented. The superintendent has just concluded a meeting with his principals on the budget and staffing needs for next year. In thirty minutes he will meet with an assistant superintendent and one of the principals of the district, who intend to bring charges of insubordination against one of the teachers in the principal's school. For a half hour the superintendent muses on what improvements in curriculum and instruction have been accomplished in the school district this year. Since his energies have been channeled into public relations, budgeting, personnel problems, transportation, new buildings, and other administrative matters, he has delegated responsibility for curriculum and instruction. He holds in his hands the assistant superintendent's report updating developments in the district this year.

The superintendent is struck by the large amount of time and effort that the school district is expending toward improving curriculum and instruction. He is impressed by the sizable number of people involved in this activity. He notes that most teams of teachers meet practically daily; most grade faculties or departments meet as groups regularly, some of them on a weekly basis; every school has its own curriculum council, which meets at least once a month; a number of curriculum committees meet at various times on districtwide problems of curriculum and instruction. The superintendent certainly cannot fault the quantity of effort expended by the professionals in curriculum development.

As to quality, he is less certain. He reviews some of the accomplishments to date and is struck by the unevenness of developments from school to school. The accomplishments at some schools far outshine those of others. Several innovative programs are in experimental stages in some schools. Other schools have defined their philosophies, goals, and objectives. Some have conducted thorough reexaminations of their curricula, whereas others have been content with the status quo. Several groups of teachers have revised their particular curricula. Other groups have developed some new curriculum guides. Some schools have responded to previously unmet curricular needs of their students, and others have failed to come up with solutions to some of their more pressing curricular problems. The superintendent is surprised (though he realizes that he should not be) that a few schools obviously surpass the others in both quantity and quality of curriculum efforts. A few schools have tackled curriculum development with a vigor that has effected significant change. He finds repeated references in the report to positive changes made by a few schools. He concludes that some schools are imbued with the spirit of change and are willing to move forward and out, while others find the established ways of operating more comfortable. The superintendent wonders why such great variations in curriculum development exist from school to school. Whom should he credit in those schools that seem to be engaged in productive curriculum efforts? The principals? The teachers? The curriculum leaders, whoever they are? The students? The parents? The signs of the zodiac? Just plain luck? Or a combination of all these factors?

The superintendent is aware that schools differ considerably from one another. Their physical facilities, resources, and locales all differ. Yet these more or less tangible factors do not explain the great differences in strides made by schools in curriculum and instruction. Yes, we may say that schools differ in many ways, but schools are only brick, concrete, mortar, steel, wood, glass, and a host of other building materials. It is not the schools that differ but the people who either support them or operate within them. The superintendent must credit not the schools in the abstract but the people who make them function. In his short period of reflection, the superintendent reinforces a long-held, verified belief—that curriculum development is a "people" process, a human endeavor. Curriculum development is a process in which the human players accept and carry out mutually reinforcing roles. Given a predisposition to change and a subtle blending of skills and knowledge, a faculty can achieve significant successes in curriculum improvement even in a substandard physical environment. The "people" factor far outweighs the physical setting.

DIFFERENCES AMONG FACULTY

Let's leave the meditating superintendent and focus our attention on another place, another time. It is early in the school year. The principal of a medium-size secondary school is presiding over the initial organizational meeting of the school's curriculum council. Representatives of the nine departments of the school are about to elect their chairperson. With freshness, high spirits, and a modicum of levity, the curriculum council is getting under way. The principal wonders what progress the school will make this year in curriculum improvement. She realizes as she looks around the room that success in improving the curriculum depends largely on human differences among individual curriculum workers and between curriculum groups.

Each school is characterized by its own unique blend of persons, each with different skills, knowledge, experience, and personality. The principal mentally lists some of the ways individuals within the curriculum council, which represents the faculty, differ. Certainly, the philosophical beliefs of the various council members diverge greatly. It will take considerable effort to reach some kind of consensus on the goals of this school, let alone the general goals of education. The council members differ in their knowledge about and ability to apply learning theory. Some are outstanding instructors, others only passable. Variations exist in the members' knowledge of curriculum history and theory and in experience in curriculum development.

Some younger members, new to teaching and the particular school, are less knowledgeable about children in general and in this setting than older teachers who have taught several years, many of them in this school. As soon as the council settles down to work it becomes apparent that there are great differences in individuals' skills in interacting with others; in the leadership skills of the various council members; in the followership skills; in organizational, writing, and oral skills.

Some of the council members will show themselves as being more perceptive of parental roles and the needs of the community. Personal traits like friendliness, reliability, motivation, sense of humor, enthusiasm, and frustration level are significant differences among individuals that contribute to the success or failure of group efforts like curriculum development. Outside commitments, family obligations, and allocations of time differ from person to person and can affect the process of curriculum planning.

The human variables in the process are many and complex. Success or failure will depend to a great extent on how the council members relate to one another, on how each member relates to other teachers on the faculty, and how they, in turn, relate to one another. The way the council and faculty interact with parents, others in the community, and the students can make or break curriculum efforts.

DEPENDENT VARIABLES

The differences among individuals and groups participating in curriculum development are dependent rather than independent variables. The presence or absence of a particular skill or trait and the degree to which an individual possesses it have an impact on all other individuals who take part in the process. Not only are the leaders' leadership skills and the followers' followership skills significant in themselves, but the manner in which they come together is even more important. Competence in leadership must ideally be met with competence in followership. Whether in military service, industry, or education, a superb leader is going nowhere without committed followers. In the same manner superb followers are going nowhere without competent leadership.

In accounting for success or failure in a cooperative enterprise, we should also look to differences among groups as well as among individuals. It is trite but pertinent to say that the whole is greater than the sum of its parts. A group is not simply the addition of each individual member to make a sum but something more than the sum, something special created by an inexplicable meshing of the human elements. Working together, members of a group must become unified as they move toward common goals in a spirit of mutual respect. Thus a curriculum council *as a group* can demonstrate competence in leadership. Success in curriculum development is more likely to be achieved when the leadership skills of the council interface with those of the faculty, resulting in a total team approach to the solution of curriculum problems. When we compare schools' achievements in curriculum improvement, we quickly discover great variations in the leadership skills of (1) the person or persons directing the curriculum study, (2) the curriculum committees or councils, (3) the total faculty, and (4) the preceding three entities working together. The contributions to curriculum improvement that may be made by students, parents, and others from the community enhance the work of the professionals.

THE CAST OF PLAYERS

We would not be far off the mark if we perceived the process of curriculum development as a continuing theatrical production in which actors play specific roles. Some of these roles are determined by society and the force of law; others are set by players themselves. Some roles are mandated, whereas others spring out of the players' personalities.

When discussing roles of various groups, J. Galen Saylor and William M. Alexander applied the analogy of drama to the process of curriculum planning:

> In addition to leading roles of students and teachers in the curriculum planning drama, important supporting actors include the members of lay advisory groups, curriculum councils and committees, teacher teams, and curriculum development units. . . . all of these roles are affected by their interaction with various groups and agencies outside the curriculum theatre.[1]

Although the metaphor of curriculum planning as drama can be overworked, we must admit that a good deal of role-playing does occur, much of it unconsciously, in the group process itself. For the moment, let's talk about the conscious roles the curriculum participants are called on to play. For purposes of analysis we will focus our attention on roles of constituent groups (administrators, students, lay people, curriculum workers: teachers, curriculum consultants, and supervisors). To achieve clarity we will focus on the individual school level. When we discuss below roles of administrators, teachers, and students in curriculum development, we should keep in mind the interactions among these constituencies not only in curriculum development but also in the total life of the school. We should be developing as Roland S. Barth termed it, a "community of learners," striving for high standards in an atmosphere of low anxiety.[2]

---

[1] J. Galen Saylor and William M. Alexander, *Planning Curriculum for Schools* (New York: Holt, Rinehart and Winston, 1974), p. 59.

[2] Roland S. Barth, *Improving Schools from Within: Teachers, Parents, and Principals Can Make a Difference* (San Francisco: Jossey-Bass, 1990).

Addressing the concept of schools as learning communities, Thomas J. Sergiovanni and Robert J. Starratt believed that "schools should be understood as learning communities"[3] [where] ". . . community norms are intermingled with the norms that define teaching as a profession.[4]

ROLE OF THE ADMINISTRATOR

Whether the chief administrator of the school, the principal serves actively as curriculum leader or passively by delegating leadership responsibilities to subordinates, curriculum development is doomed to failure without his or her support. Although some school administrators claim, in keeping with some current conceptions of the administrator's role, that they are instructional leaders, others admit that they are primarily managers.

As long ago as the mid-1950s the Southern States Cooperative Program in Education, sponsored by the W. K. Kellogg Foundation, listed "instructional and curriculum development" as the number one critical task for administrators.[5] With research on effective teaching and effective schools that pointed up the crucial importance of effective leadership, the decade of the 1980s brought a plethora of articles and speeches stressing the role of the principal as instructional leader. In addressing the importance of the principal in this role, David C. Dwyer, Bruce G. Barnett, and Ginny V. Lee, for example, wrote, "The principal is the vital actor in the school setting who can bridge context and school, policy and program, means and ends."[6]

Although the role of the principal as instructional leader is recognized by many, perhaps most, administrators as an important task, instructional and curriculum development do not head the list of priorities of many school principals. Thelbert L. Drake and William H. Roe observed that the principal is torn between his or her desired role as instructional leader and his or her actual role as administrator and manager:

> By reading the literature, attending state and national meetings, and discussing the position with incumbents, one gained a mental picture of a professional person being torn apart, on the one hand by an intense interest and desire to lead in instruction and learning, and on the other hand by the responsibility "to keep school," the latter being the proper administration and management of "things." In this little drama an eternal struggle seemed to take place, and in the end, the strong instructional leadership role had to be set aside because of the immediacy and press of everyday duties.[7]

The reasons for the low priority assigned by many principals to what used to be their main raison d'être are found both within the personality of the principal and in the pressure from outside forces. Some of the factors that lead principals away from spending time on instructional leadership are the priority that the higher officers place

[3]Thomas J. Sergiovanni and Robert J. Starratt, *Supervision: A Redefinition,* 6th ed. (New York: McGraw-Hill, 1998), p. 62.
[4]Ibid.
[5]Southern States Cooperative Program in Educational Administration, *Better Teaching in School Administration* (Nashville, Tenn.: McQuiddy, 1955).
[6]David C. Dwyer, Bruce G. Barnett, and Ginny V. Lee, "The School Principal: Scapegoat or the Last Great Hope?" *Leadership: Examining the Elusive.* 1987 Yearbook (Alexandria, Va.: Association for Supervision and Curriculum Development, 1987), p. 45.
[7]Thelbert L. Drake and William H. Roe, *The Principalship,* 4th ed. (New York: Macmillan, 1994), p. 23.

on efficiency of operation, limitations placed on principals' fields of operation by teachers' organizations, and preservice programs for administrators that emphasize business and personnel management, minimizing curriculum and instructional development.

Glenys G. Unruh observed that training programs for administrators may be at least partially at fault for the lower priority placed on curriculum and instruction by some principals.[8] With continuing emphasis on the individual school as the locus of change, on public demand for improvement in students' achievement, and on the assessment of teacher performance, there are signs that the principals' priorities have shifted somewhat. Professional associations for administrators recognize the importance of instructional leadership. Preservice and inservice education programs for school administrators are incorporating training in the technical, supervisory, and human relations skills needed by the instructional leader. Thus, more and more principals will be able to play a direct, central role in curriculum development. Hopefully, instructional leadership will eventually top the list of tasks actually performed by all principals.

Whether the principal plays a direct or indirect role, his or her presence is always keenly felt by all the players. The participants are aware that the principal by both tradition and law is charged with responsibility for conducting all the affairs of the school and for decision making in that school. In that sense, all curriculum groups and subgroups of the school are advisory to the principal.

"Theory X" and "Theory Y."   Through management style the principal exerts a force on all operations within the school. The success of the curriculum developers may depend to some extent on whether the principal is a "Theory X" or "Theory Y" person. Douglas McGregor has classified two sets of assumptions that he believes managers have about people into the categories Theory X and Theory Y.[9] These theories are widely quoted in the literature on management. According to McGregor, managers following Theory X believe the following:

- The average person dislikes work and tries to avoid it.
- Most people must be forced to work and threatened with punishment to get them to work.
- The average person lacks ambition and avoids responsibility.
- The average person must be directed.
- The need for security is the chief motivation of the average person.

Authority, control, task maintenance, and product orientation dominate the thinking of the Theory X administrator. On the other hand, the administrator who subscribes to Theory Y holds these beliefs:

- The average person welcomes work.
- The average person seeks responsibility.

---

[8]Glenys G. Unruh, "Curriculum Politics," in Fenwick W. English, ed. *Fundamental Curriculum Decisions.* 1983 Yearbook (Alexandria, Va.: Association for Supervision and Curriculum Development, 1983), p. 109.

[9]Douglas M. McGregor, *The Human Side of Enterprise* (New York: McGraw-Hill, 1960).

- Most people will demonstrate self-reliance when they share a commitment to the realization of common objectives.
- The average person will be committed to an organization's objectives if he or she is rewarded for that commitment.
- Creativity in problem solving is a trait found rather widely among people.

Whereas the typical administrator will be more inclined toward one theory, he or she will manifest behavior that will at times lean toward the other. There are occasions, for example, when the Theory Y administrator must exercise authority and follow Theory X principles. Nevertheless, the position among many specialists in curriculum development, supervision, and administration counsels a Theory Y approach. Twenty years ago Thomas J. Sergiovanni and Fred D. Carver counseled: "In our view, the unique role of the school as a humanizing and self-actualizing institution requires that school executives adopt the assumptions and behavior manifestations of Theory Y."[10]

The human-relations-oriented principal nurtures the curriculum development process by establishing a climate in which the planners feel valued and in which they satisfy, to use Abraham Maslow's term, "the need for self-actualization."[11] The principal must encourage and facilitate the process. Since the principal holds the power for final decision making within the school, he or she must give serious consideration to recommendations made by the school's curriculum study groups. Further, the principal must always demonstrate sincere interest in the curriculum development process. Personal traits such as a negative attitude or indifference by the school's chief administrator will effectively block progress in improving the school's curriculum. The principal's personality may, indeed, be a more powerful determinant of progress than his or her training, knowledge, or conscious intentions.

Theory Y principals might well find compatible with their views of administration some of the principles of Theory Z organizations.[12] Based on practices traditionally followed by Japanese business and industry, Theory Z organizations emphasize collective decision making and responsibility over individual decision making and responsibility. Theory Z organizations welcome the establishment of "quality control circles," or simply, "quality circles," small groups of employees whose task it is to study and propose ways of solving problems and improving the effectiveness of the organization.[13]

Regardless of their style or approach—and here we may generalize to all levels of the school system—administrators and their assistants must assume responsibility for providing leadership in many areas. They must establish the organizational framework so that curriculum development may proceed, secure facilities and needed resources,

---

[10]Thomas J. Sergiovanni and Fred D. Carver, *The New School Executive: A Theory of Administration,* 2nd ed. (New York: Harper & Row, 1980), p. 49.

[11]Abraham H. Maslow, *Motivation and Personality,* 2nd ed. (New York: Harper & Row, 1970), p. 46.

[12]See William G. Ouchi, *Theory Z: How American Businesses Can Meet the Japanese Challenge* (Reading, Mass.: Addison-Wesley, 1981).

[13]Ibid., pp. 261–268; see also the videotape *Quality Circles: Problem Solving Tool for Educators,* Association for Supervision and Curriculum Development, 1984. For a view of the negative side of Japanese management, see Joel Kotkin and Yoriko Kishimoto, "Theory F," *Inc.* 8, no. 4 (April 1986): 53–60.

coordinate efforts of the various groups, offer consultative help, keep the groups on task, resolve conflicts, communicate school needs to all groups, maintain a harmonious working climate, assure collection of needed data, provide for communication among groups, advise groups on latest developments in education, and make final decisions for their particular level.

ROLE OF STUDENTS

Before turning our attention to the main participants in the curriculum development process (the curriculum leaders and their fellow workers), let's briefly consider the roles of two supporting groups—the students and the adult citizens from the community. With increasing frequency, students, depending upon their maturity, are participating both directly and indirectly in the task of improving the curriculum. In some cases, notably at the high-school level (and above), students are accorded membership on curriculum councils. More commonly, student input is sought in a more indirect fashion. There are still many administrators and teachers who take a dim view of sharing decision making with the student clientele. On the other hand, it is becoming increasingly more common for administrators and teachers to solicit student reactions to the curriculum. Surveys are conducted to obtain student perceptions of their programs; individual students and groups are interviewed. Suggestions for improvement in the curriculum and for ways of meeting students' perceived needs are actively sought.

The recipient of the program—the student—is often in the best position to provide feedback about the product—the curriculum. Advice from the student constituency of the school may well provide clues for intelligent curriculum decision making.

Some schools seek information and advice from the chosen student leaders—the student government—whereas others look toward a wider sampling of opinion about programs. Even in those schools in which student input is not actively sought and in which channels have not been established for gathering data from students, the learners speak loudly by their achievements in class. When standardized and state assessment test scores are consistently below grade level, the faculty can conclude that some adjustments are necessary in respect to either the curriculum or instruction. When diagnostic tests reveal deficiencies on the part of learners, something is being conveyed about the school's program.

John McNeil pointed out how students can silently make an impact on the curriculum:

> Informally, however, students have much influence over what is taught. Often they can vote with their feet by refusing to enroll in courses that feature the curriculum of academic specialists. The failure of students to respond to the Physical Science Study Committee's "physics" was an argument for curriculum change. Alternative schools and underground newspapers are other instances of student power.[14]

In Chapter 7 we will consider the student as a source of the curriculum. Here we are primarily concerned with the student's role as a participant in curriculum development.

---

[14]John D. McNeil, *Curriculum: A Comprehensive Introduction*, 5th ed. (New York: HarperCollins, 1996), pp. 300–301.

Student Involvement.   Student involvement in curriculum improvement has grown in recent years along with the concomitant movement toward students' rights. Ronald Doll spoke of the connection between student participation in curriculum development and the students' rights movement as follows:

> Changes have occurred in the role of pupils, especially at the secondary school level, in planning the curriculum. The revolutionary movement in colleges in the 1960s had almost immediate effect on many high schools and indeed on some elementary schools. Student rights came to include the right to participate with adults in planning the uses to which pupils' time in schools was to be put. Though this right had existed in some better-known schools for many years and had been advocated to a limited extent by authors in the curriculum field, it now meant permission to speak freely and at length in curriculum meetings, often on a footing equal to that of experienced adults. To some teachers and principals, pupils' newly acquired status represented a refreshing view of human potential and a deserved position in the educational hierarchy; to others it seemed an especially time-consuming and plaguing form of contemporary insanity.[15]

Students can help out greatly by indicating to the professional curriculum planners how they perceive a new proposal or program. They can provide input from the standpoint of the recipients of the program, the persons for whom the program was designed. The more alert students can point out pitfalls that the professional planners might be able to avoid. The students can communicate reactions of their peers and they can further relate the nature and purpose of curriculum changes to their parents and other citizens of the community. Students can excel in describing how they perceive a development and how they feel about it.

The degree to which students may participate and the quality of that participation depend on a number of variables such as intelligence, motivation, and knowledge. The most significant variable is the students' maturity. For that reason students in senior high schools and in higher education find more opportunities to take part in curriculum development than students in elementary, middle, and junior high schools.

A particularly valuable contribution to curriculum improvement that students can make is to evaluate the teachers' instruction. Although some teachers resist student evaluations of their performance—as one senior-high school principal was heard to comment, "Students have no business evaluating teachers"—evaluations done anonymously by the learners can provide valuable clues for modifying a curriculum and improving methods of instruction.

George H. Wood saw students in a proactive role when he said, "A curriculum for democratic empowerment engages students in choices about and control over the most central element of their school experience—the curriculum itself."[16] Wood saw empowered students as "having control over knowledge and information" and possessing the opportunity to "produce rather than memorize knowledge."[17]

Although students do enter actively into the process of curriculum development in some school systems, their involvement by and large still tends to be sporadic and ancillary.

[15]Ronald C. Doll, *Curriculum Improvement: Decision Making and Process,* 9th ed. (Boston: Allyn & Bacon, 1996), p. 423.

[16]George H. Wood, "Teachers as Curriculum Workers," in James T. Sears and J. Dan Marshall, eds., *Teaching and Thinking About Curriculum: Critical Inquiries* (New York: Teachers College Press, 1990), p. 102.

[17]Ibid., p. 103.

ROLE OF ADULT CITIZENS OF THE COMMUNITY

The roles of parents and other members of the community in the affairs of the school have changed considerably over the years. Historically, the community *was* the school. Parents tutored their young at home for lack of or in preference to a formal school; the well-to-do imported tutors from Europe to live in their homes and to instruct their children. The church provided instruction in its religious precepts, and young men learned trades as apprentices on the job. Women in colonial America would bring youngsters into their homes and for a small payment from each of their families, teach them the three R's.[18]

As formal schools evolved, the community turned the task of educating the young (for many years only the young white males) over to the school. A gap opened between the community and the school. Both the community and the institution it established developed the attitude that the community should get on with its business and leave teaching to those who know how to do it best—the school personnel. An invisible wall was erected between community and school, resembling the one between church and state.

Some parents with their state's consent have turned in recent years to instructing their children at home. Although relatively small, the home-school movement, discussed in Chapter 14, is significant enough to be of concern to the public schools.

Erosion of the Wall Between School and Community.   Although some school administrators prefer to cling to an outmoded concept of community/school relationships, the wall separating school from community has crumbled. The process of erosion began slowly and has accelerated in recent years. The involvement of parents and other community members can be readily observed in school affairs today. The literature on professional education is filled with discussions of the necessity for involving the community in the educational process.

For the greater part of the twentieth century, community involvement was interpreted as passive support to the schools. The school would send bulletins and notices home to inform parents about issues and activities. The Parent-Teacher Association (PTA) would meet and discuss educational issues, hear about the school's achievements, and plan a rummage sale to raise funds for some school improvement. With much fanfare the school would conduct a "Back-to-School Night," which brought in parents in record numbers. Booster clubs would raise money for athletics and the band. During this period the community rarely participated in decision making even of an advisory nature. The old sentiment prevailed that school matters were best left to the school people. The community's role was to support and strengthen decisions made by the school.

Erosion of the wall between school and community was hastened when administrators and teachers began to realize that parents might supply them with certain types of information that could aid in decision making. Consequently, still resorting to a

---

[18]This practice is commonly referred to in the literature on the history of education as the "dame school" or "kitchen school."

somewhat passive role for parents, the school sent home questionnaires for parents to fill out and return. While the school and community were taking careful, modest steps toward bridging the gulf between them, American society in the twentieth century was bubbling. First, the sociologists and then the educators began to subject the American community to intense scrutiny, identifying networks of influential persons who are referred to in the literature as "the power structure."[19] Educators started to give attention to the politics of education as they realized that the school was as much a part of the total political structure as other social institutions. The astute school administrator became intensely conscious of public relations and sought to involve community members in support of the school. Some might say that the educators' attention to community concerns was more effect than cause as discontent, anxiety, and pressure on educators from outside the schools had been growing and increasing in intensity for several decades.

Social Problems.   Four major and a couple of minor wars, several revolutions, a number of sociological movements, and an ailing economy changed the tapestry of twentieth-century America. The technological revolution, increasing cultural diversity, the sexual revolution, the heightened divorce rate, the change in family structure, the equal rights movement, the student rights movement, the declaration of unconstitutionality of segregation, a period of severe inflation, and America's transformation from a creditor to a debtor nation, all created problems for the schools, problems that could no longer be solved by the schools themselves. With America's social and economic problems came a disenchantment with the programs of the schools and the low achievement of the pupils. From this dissatisfaction arose the concept of accountability of school personnel for the success or failure of their products—the students.

Today, community involvement in school activities—beyond the duly-constituted boards of education—is widespread, encouraged, and generally valued. Members of the community aid in curriculum development in a variety of ways. Parents and other citizens serve on numerous advisory committees. Schools frequently call on parents and others to serve as resource persons and volunteer aides. Across the country, especially in urban areas, local businesses have entered into partnerships with the schools, supplementing and enriching the schools' curricula by providing expertise, materials, and funds.

The school principal always faces a dilemma in deciding how lay people should be involved and who these people should be. Some principals seek the participation of parents of children in their own schools. Some try to involve a broader spectrum of the community, including parents and nonparents and representatives from all socioeconomic levels of the area served by the schools. Some limit participation by plan or by default to parents who happen to be available to attend meetings during the day. The

---

[19]See the following: Robert S. Lynd, *Middletown: A Study in American Culture* (New York: Harcourt Brace Jovanovich, 1929) and Robert S. Lynd and Helen M. Lynd, *Middletown in Transition: A Study in Cultural Conflicts* (New York: Harcourt Brace Jovanovich, 1937); Ralph B. Kimbrough, *Community Power Structure and Analysis* (Englewood Cliffs, N.J.: Prentice-Hall, 1964); Ralph B. Kimbrough and Michael Y. Nunnery, *Educational Administration: An Introduction,* 3rd ed. (New York: Macmillan, 1988), Chapter 13.

chief participants under this condition tend to be middle-class housewives. Some principals seek out the community decision makers from among the citizens who make up the power structure.

State and National Initiatives.   State and national efforts have supplemented local initiatives to involve the community in school affairs. Roald F. Campbell, Luvern L. Cunningham, Raphael O. Nystrand, and Michael D. Usdan described a number of organizations that advocate the participation of citizens in the affairs of the schools.[20] In 1976 the Florida legislature not only established school advisory councils but also charged the principal of every public school in the state with the responsibility of publishing by November 1 of each year an annual report of school progress that must be distributed to the parent or guardian of each student in the school.[21]

Amending the 1976 legislation on school advisory councils, the Florida legislature in 1993 required school boards to establish school (or district in the case of student populations of less than 10,000) advisory councils whose task it is to assist in preparation and evaluation of mandated school improvement plans and to help the principal on request in preparing the school's annual budget. The statute set forth the composition of the councils:

> Each advisory council shall be composed of the principal and an appropriately balanced number of teachers, education support employees, students, parents, and other business and community citizens who are representative of the ethnic, racial, and economic community served by the school.[22]

Campbell and his coauthors noted the impact of federal legislation on citizen involvement in the affairs of the local schools:

> Most federal legislation enacted since the early 1970s required citizen consulting and advisory mechanisms. The number of federally mandated advisory councils was staggering: there were approximately 14,000 district-wide Title I Parent Advisory Committees and 44,000 building-level committees with a total of nearly 900,000 members; another 150,000 persons served on Head Start, Follow Through, and other district and building-level groups.[23]

Thus local, state, and federal initiatives have promoted the involvement of members of the community in affairs of the school. The universal use of program advisory groups in connection with federally funded vocational education programs, for example, has exerted a significant influence on the curriculum of local school systems.

Looking to the future, Campbell and his coauthors identified community groups with which administrators must be concerned and made the following prediction:

> Interest groups representing blacks, American Indians, and other ethnic groups will continue to focus on the schools as a major mechanism for equalizing educational, social, and economic opportunities for their constituencies.

---

[20]Roald F. Campbell, Luvern L. Cunningham, Raphael O. Nystrand, and Michael D. Usdan, *The Organization and Control of American Education,* 6th ed. (Columbus, Ohio: Merrill, 1990), pp. 329–342.

[21]Florida Statute 229.575 (3).

[22]Florida Statute 229.58 (1).

[23]Campbell et al., *Organization and Control,* p. 166.

Taxpayer groups, concerned about periodic inflation, recession, and energy shortages in an uncertain economy, will continue to scrutinize school expenditures.[24]

They also observed, "Hispanics are the nation's most rapidly growing population group and their political influence certainly will continue to expand in the days ahead as they are projected to become the largest racial ethnic group by the end of the century."[25]

The makeup of the school advisory councils must reflect the socioeconomic demographics of the community. To ensure this end, the Florida legislature, for example, in setting the structure of the councils, authorized the school boards to add members to the councils when they determined that the councils were not representative of their various ethnic, racial, and economic groups.

The wise administrator realizes that strong community support can make his or her job much simpler and for that reason devotes considerable time to building that support. Some schools have been turned into community schools in which the resources of the school are shared with the community and vice versa.

Models for citizen participation in school affairs differ widely from community to community. In some communities citizens play a purely advisory role; in others they share directly in the decision-making process. In some localities members of the community serve on standing committees that meet regularly; in other locations they serve on ad hoc groups that undertake a specific task and are then disbanded. In some school districts parents and others are invited to address themselves to any and all problems of the schools, whereas in other communities their areas of responsibility are clearly defined.

Members of the community can serve the schools in a variety of ways. They may be consulted in the curriculum designing stage. They may participate as resource persons, volunteer tutors, and school aides. The resources of individuals, businesses, institutions, and other agencies are tapped to enhance the learning experiences of the students.

With guidance from the school, parents can assist their children in their studies at home. They are able to describe the effect of new programs on their children and can be very specific in telling teachers about problems their children are experiencing.

Parents and others share in curriculum development by responding to surveys sent out by the school. They may invite children to their places of work and thereby contribute to the children's knowledge of the world around them. They may supervise student work experiences in the community.

Parents and others can inform the professional planners about potential conflicts that are likely to arise in the community over teaching of controversial issues. They can help the school authorities review instructional materials and books for bias and distortion. Parents and other residents are often able to suggest programs that would help meet certain educational needs in the community. By actively seeking citizen participation, the principal is able to develop a reservoir of good will toward the school that will stand him or her in good stead when problems inevitably develop. The principal is more readily able to gain support for new programs and to defuse potential controversies if parents and others perceive the school as their institution and as a place

---

[24]Ibid., p. 380.
[25]Ibid., p. 359.

where their voices may be heard and their opinions valued. Community participation in curriculum development is a natural consequence of the public's legal power over education in a democratic society.[26]

ROLE OF THE CURRICULUM WORKERS

Primary responsibility for curriculum development is assigned to teachers and their elected or appointed leaders, both of whom we will refer to as "curriculum workers." This group of persons working together carries the heaviest burden in seeking to improve the curriculum. In Chapter 3 we saw that curriculum groups function at several levels and in several sectors. To make the following discussion clearer, however, let's conceptualize the curriculum council of a particular school. Let's choose an elementary school with grades kindergarten through six that is fortunate enough to have a full-time curriculum coordinator on its staff. By agreement of the total faculty, the grade coordinators (seven of them) join with the curriculum coordinator (appointed by the principal) to form the school's curriculum council. In our hypothetical school, by tacit understanding between the principal and the faculty, the coordinator serves as chairperson or leader of the council.

Let's imagine that we are neutral observers watching this council at its first session of the year. We watch the group get organized; we listen to its discussion; we study the faces of the council members; we observe the interplay between the coordinator and the council members and among the council members themselves. We cannot help speculating about whether this curriculum group will have a productive year. The question crosses our mind, "What conditions make for a productive year in curriculum development?" We wonder, "Could we predict whether a curriculum council is likely to be productive?"

After a great deal of thought, we might conclude that success in terms of productivity is more likely to come about if the group:

- sets its goals at the beginning of its work
- is made up of compatible personalities
- has members who bring to the task expertise, knowledge, and technical competence
- is composed of persons who are motivated and willing to expend time and energy
- accepts its appropriate leadership and followership roles
- has persons who can communicate with each other
- has developed skills in decision making
- has members who keep their own personal agendas in appropriate relationship to the group's goals

What are the roles, we may ask, of those persons whom we call curriculum workers? How do teachers function in curriculum development? What role does the curriculum leader play?

---

[26]For discussion of limitations on the state's power to compel school attendance, you may wish to read *Teach Your Own: A Hopeful Path for Education* (New York: Delacorte Press/Seymour Lawrence, 1981) by John Holt, an advocate of home schooling. See also Chapter 14 of this text.

Role of the Teachers.   Throughout this text teachers are repeatedly seen as the primary group in curriculum development. Numerous examples are given of teacher involvement in curriculum development. Teachers constitute either the majority or the totality of the membership of curriculum committees and councils. Teachers participate at all stages in curriculum development. They initiate proposals and carry them out in their classrooms. They review proposals, gather data, conduct research, make contact with parents and other lay people, write and create curriculum materials, evaluate resources, try out new ideas, obtain feedback from learners, and evaluate programs. Teachers serve on committees mainly at the classroom, team/grade/department, school, and district levels or sectors and on occasion may serve at other levels or sectors.

New teachers typically view themselves primarily as instructors and are often scarcely aware of the responsibilities that are likely to be expected of them in the curriculum area. Beginning teachers' lack of awareness of their professional obligations in curriculum development is not surprising given that preservice teacher education programs, as a rule and understandably, emphasize the mastery of instructional skills over curriculum development competencies.

At the very least, preservice teachers should be oriented to the obligations and opportunities they will encounter in curriculum development. Becoming aware that they will serve on various councils and committees, that curriculum development takes place at many levels and in many sectors, and that instruction and curriculum are different domains, both worthy of involvement, should be part of their training. Thus the teachers, in cooperation with the administrators and other professionals, can bring appropriate knowledge and skills to bear in efforts to improve the curriculum. *Only* the teachers, by their presence at the classroom level, can assure that curricular plans are carried out.

Assumption of a primary role by teachers not only in curriculum development but also in the general affairs of the school is the goal of efforts at "empowerment," which permits teachers as professionals to take part in the decision-making process.[27] The empowerment movement of the 1980s and 1990s seeks to raise the status of teachers and thereby improve the school's program and effectiveness.

Conducted by the Carnegie Foundation for the Advancement of Teaching, a 1990 survey of more than 21,000 public elementary and secondary school teachers revealed that teachers were not very happy with their lot.[28] The Carnegie study found that more than half (sixty-one percent) of the teachers rated the morale of their school as fair or poor. Forty-five percent of the teachers were dissatisfied with the control they have over their professional life as a teacher. Eighty-two percent gave a grade of "C" or below to school reform efforts of recent years.

Significant to the issue of empowerment is the finding that many teachers feel left out of the decision-making process. You might conjecture that if teachers are involved in decision making at all, they would most likely participate in the areas of curriculum,

---

[27]See Gene Maeroff, *The Empowerment of Teachers: Overcoming the Crisis of Confidence* (New York: Teachers College Press, 1988). See also G. Alfred Hess, Jr., ed., *Empowering Teachers and Parents: School Restructuring Through the Eyes of Anthropologists* (Westport, Conn.: Bergin & Garvey, 1992).

[28]Carnegie Foundation for the Advancement of Teaching, *The Condition of Teaching: A State-by-State Analysis, 1990* (Princeton, N.J.: Carnegie Foundation for the Advancement of Teaching, 1990). See also John Godar, *Teacher Talk* (Macomb, Ill.: Glenbridge Publishing Ltd., 1990).

instruction, and staff development. Although a large majority (seventy-nine percent) said they participated to a moderate or great extent in selecting textbooks and materials, twenty-one percent said they participated slightly or not at all. A surprising thirty-five percent indicated that they were involved only slightly or not at all in shaping the curriculum, and a majority (fifty-seven percent) reported that they participated slightly or not at all in the design of staff development or in-service education programs. Teacher participation in curriculum development showed but a small (two percent) drop among those involved only slightly or not at all compared to that reported in an earlier Carnegie survey, and the percentage of teachers involved slightly or not at all in planning staff development activities remained at the same level.[29]

You would expect that in-service education programs that are designed for teachers would be chosen and planned with their cooperation. Apparently, the fine 1970s example of teacher empowerment in the area of staff development—the teacher education center—has waned instead of waxed.[30]

Although critics of empowerment argue that teacher involvement in decision making is an unnecessary demand on teachers' time, an inappropriate role, or an infringement on administrative authority, industrial research of the 1930s and the success of Japanese quality circles in recent years have revealed that meaningful involvement in decision making enhances worker morale and consequently increases production.[31] John Naisbitt stated the principle succinctly when he said, "People whose lives are affected by a decision must be part of the process of arriving at that decision."[31] Translated into school terms, this principle indicates that when teachers find themselves to be valued professionals whose opinions carry some weight, they will be more satisfied with their profession. This improvement in teacher morale, in turn, will increase school productivity—that is, student achievement. Wood further connected the empowerment of teachers to the empowerment of students when he said, "Only by linking democracy to empowerment, that is, working for the democratic empowerment of *students* will teachers find a genuine sense of empowerment themselves."[33]

Role of the Curriculum Leader.   As we consider the complexities in carrying out curriculum development we become keenly aware of the curriculum leader's responsibility for the success or failure of the work of a curriculum committee or council. The curriculum leader most often is a member of the faculty but can be an outsider. It is perhaps inaccurate here to refer to a curriculum leader as *the* curriculum leader. A person may serve as a leader for a period of time and then give way to another leader for any number of sound reasons. Some teachers may serve as leaders at one level, such as the grade, whereas others may serve as leaders at another level, such as the school. In a democratic organization individuals serve as either leaders or followers as the situation demands.

---

[29]Carnegie Foundation for the Advancement of Teaching, *The Condition of Teaching: A State-by-State Analysis, 1988* (Princeton, N.J.: Carnegie Foundation for the Advancement of Teaching, 1988).

[30]See Peter F. Oliva and George E. Pawlas, *Supervision for Today's Schools,* 5th ed. (New York.: Longman, 1997), pp. 390–393, for discussion of teacher education centers.

[31]See F. J. Roethlisberger and William J. Dickson, *Management and the Worker* (Cambridge, Mass.: Harvard University Press, 1939); see also William G. Ouchi, footnote 12 of this chapter.

[31]John Naisbitt, *Megatrends* (New York: Warner, 1982), p. 159.

[33]Wood, "Teachers as Curriculum Workers," p. 107.

The curriculum leader (coordinator) may also come from outside the teacher group, as in the case of central office supervisors, curriculum consultants, directors of instruction, and assistant principals for curriculum. Perhaps even in these cases it would be useful to think of the teachers and leaders from outside the faculty as constituting the "extended family," for they are all colleagues, albeit with different functions and duties. The leadership position is filled either by appointment by an administrator or supervisor, election by the group's members, or self-selection from the group.

The principles discussed in the following pages apply to all curriculum leaders regardless of whether they come from inside or outside the teacher group. We may begin to look at the role of the curriculum leader by asking ourselves what special knowledge and skills the leader must bring to the task. The curriculum coordinator must:

- possess a good general education
- have a good knowledge of both general and specific curricula
- be knowledgeable about resources for curriculum development
- be skilled in research and knowledgeable about locating pertinent research studies
- be knowledgeable about the needs of learners, the community, and the society
- be a bit of philosopher, sociologist, and psychologist
- know and appreciate the individual characteristics of participating colleagues

Most significantly, the curriculum coordinator must be a specialist in the group process, possessing a unique set of skills. Many treatises on the functioning of groups reveal that managing groups effectively is not a trivial task. It is an enormously complicated effort that brings into play all the subtleties of environment and personality. Curriculum development is an exercise in group process, a human endeavor that can lead to both joy and frustration.

Success in curriculum improvement depends, of course, on the concerted effort of both group members and leaders. We will focus our attention, however, on the curriculum leader; no matter how well-intentioned, motivated, and skilled the followers of the group are, group effort cannot succeed without competent leadership.

THE CURRICULUM LEADER AND GROUP PROCESS

Neither technical expertise nor knowledge about curriculum theory can substitute for a curriculum leader's knowledge of and aptitude for group process. What, then, we might ask, are some of the basic principles from the research on group process that would help those who take a leadership role in curriculum development? What skills and knowledge about group process are essential to the job? Four sets or clusters of skills about group process appear to be of particular significance:

1. *The change process.* The leader must be knowledgeable about the process of effecting change and be able to translate that knowledge into practice with the group. He or she must demonstrate effective decision-making skills and be able to lead group members in demonstrating them.

2. *Interpersonal relations.* The leader must be knowledgeable about group dynamics. He or she must exhibit a high degree of human relations skills, be able to develop

interpersonal skills among members of the group, and be able to establish a harmonious working climate.

3. *Leadership skills.* The leader must demonstrate leadership skills, including organizational skills and the ability to manage the process. He or she must help members of the group to develop leadership skills so that they may assume leadership roles when necessary.

4. *Communication skills.* The leader must communicate effectively and be able to lead members of the group in communicating effectively. He or she must be a proficient discussion leader.

THE CHANGE PROCESS

Axiom 1 in Chapter 2 presented the proposition that change is both inevitable and desirable. Human institutions, like human beings, must change if they are to continue growing and developing. Institutions, however, tend to preserve the status quo.

Gail McCutcheon cited the ease and comparative safety of the status quo, the requirements of time and effort, the lack of rewards, established school policies, and routines as impediments to change.[34] Nevertheless, neither the status quo nor regression to outmoded practices is a defensible position for living institutions like the schools. They must constantly seek to better themselves.

Curriculum development is the planned effort of a duly organized group (or groups) that seeks to make intelligent decisions in order to effect change in the curriculum. Planned change, far different from trial and error or natural evolution, implies a systematic process to be followed by all participants. Let's begin our examination of the change process by looking at the variables that exist within organizations and that have an impact upon that process.

Four Variables.   Harold J. Leavitt and Homa Bahrami identified four organizational variables: "structure," "information and control methods (i.e., the technology of managing)," "people," and "task."[35]

Every organization establishes its own *structure.* In Chapter 3 we considered some of the organizational patterns that schools have adopted to carry out curriculum development. As already noted, structures differ considerably among school systems and among individual schools. A school's organizational structure is shaped not only by the tasks to be accomplished but also by the idiosyncrasies of administrators, supervisors, and teachers. No single organizational structure will satisfy the personal and professional needs of participants in every school system. Determination of the appropriate organizational structure is one of the prior decisions that curriculum developers must make.

The element of *technology of managing* encompasses both the technological equipment at the school's disposal and the procedures followed to accomplish the school's task.

---

[34]Gail McCutcheon, "Curriculum Theory/Curriculum Practice: A Gap or the Grand Canyon?" in Alex Molnar, ed., *Current Thought on the Curriculum.* 1985 Yearbook (Alexandria, Va.: Association for Supervision and Curriculum Development, 1985), p. 46.

[35]Harold J. Leavitt and Homa Bahrami, *Managerial Psychology: Managing Behavior in Organizations,* 5th ed. (Chicago: University of Chicago Press, 1988), pp. 246–256.

The human variable—*the people*—sets the operation in motion and carries on the task. The differences in people make each school's efforts at curriculum development a unique undertaking. The persons essential to the curriculum development process have been discussed earlier in this text. Experts in the social science of human behavior refer to the main characters in the change process as the *change agent* and the *client system.* In their language a change agent is a person trained in the behavioral sciences who helps an organization change. The client system consists of those persons in the organization with whom the change agent works and who may, themselves, undergo change. This point reinforces Axiom 4 in Chapter 2, which postulates that curriculum change results from changes in people.

Although behavioral scientists argue about whether the change agent must come from within or outside the system, in practical terms schools will ordinarily use their own personnel for developing the curriculum.

Robert J. Alfonso, Gerald R. Firth, and Richard F. Neville identified change theory as one of four theoretical fields assumed to have implications for the behavior of instructional supervisors.[36] John T. Lovell devoted a chapter in a text on supervision to demonstrating that coordinating and facilitating change are important responsibilities of the instructional supervisor.[37]

Alfonso, Firth, and Neville clearly showed that the supervisor from within the system must serve as a change agent:

> If change is to occur, a school system must value it enough to give some person or group responsibility for it, and not leave it to chance occurrence. Supervisors, if they desire change, must make this a priority, or else it will not occur. They should not expect to be agents of change unless they devote a significant amount of time, effort, and creative thought to the change process.[38]

Even when the services of an outside change agent are sought, Alfonso, Firth, and Neville gave this advice:

> If a supervisor wishes to use the services of an outside change agent or consultant, the external agent must be perceived as enhancing the work of the supervisor. If such linkage can take place, or if, in fact, the external agent can be at least temporarily joined to the system, the total change effort will be more successful. Simply "importing" a change agent will not assist the supervisor markedly unless teachers perceive such a person as connected to the system or to the supervisor in some acceptable way.[39]

What are the typical functions of a change agent? Warren G. Bennis listed the following normative goals of change agents:

- improving interpersonal competence of managers;

---

[36]See Robert J. Alfonso, Gerald R. Firth, and Richard F. Neville, *Instructional Supervision: A Behavior System,* 2nd ed. (Boston: Allyn and Bacon, 1981), Chapter 8.

[37]See John T. Lovell and Kimball Wiles, *Supervision for Better Schools,* 5th ed. (Englewood Cliffs, N.J.: Prentice-Hall, 1983), Chapter 6.

[38]Alfonso, Firth, and Neville, *Instructional Supervision,* p. 283.

[39]Ibid., p. 284.

- effecting a change in values so that human factors and feelings come to be considered legitimate;
- developing increased understanding among and within working groups to reduce tensions;
- developing "team management";
- developing better methods of "conflict resolution" than suppression, denial, and the use of unprincipled power;
- viewing the organization as an organic system of relationships marked by mutual trust, interdependence, multi-group membership, shared responsibility, and conflict resolution through training and problem solving.[40]

The *task* of the school is set out in numerous pronouncements of aims, goals, and objectives, for example, the cardinal principles, the ability to think, the transmittal of the cultural heritage, and so on. More accurately, we should speak of the *tasks* of the school rather than *task*. The school performs many tasks in a number of curriculum development areas and provides a vital service—the education of the young. Although the school is not engaged in the tasks of manufacturing and selling products for profit, it does turn out products—a quite different kind of product—the learners themselves, human beings whose behavior is modified as a result of exposure to the school curriculum. Leadership calls for the judicious integration of these four variables.

Kurt Lewin viewed organizations as being in a state of balance or equilibrium when forces of change (driving forces) and forces of resistance (restraining forces) are equal in strength.[41] Changes occur when the organization is forced into a state of disequilibrium. This state of imbalance may be accomplished by augmenting the driving forces or by reducing the restraining forces—either action breaks the force field that maintains the organization in equilibrium.

Following his concept of the force field, Lewin proposed a simple strategy consisting of three steps. Or was it so simple? Lewin suggested that existing targets of change be unfrozen, then changes or innovations made, and finally the new structures refrozen until the start of a new cycle.

How shall we go about unfreezing old programs and practices—in effect, changing old habits? How would we move, for example, from the junior high school to the middle school; from independent to cooperative learning; from discrete linguistic concepts to whole language; from exclusive stress on cognitive learning to provision for cognitive, affective, and psychomotor learning; from emphasis on convergent thinking to more on divergent thinking; or from rote learning to critical thinking? How do we thaw out old patterns?

When we identify the barriers or impediments to change and eliminate those barriers, we can set the organization into disequilibrium. Table 4.1 lists several commonly encountered barriers and suggest tactics for overcoming them. Uppermost in the minds of curriculum planners must be the purpose of change: improvement in the

---

[40]Reprinted with permission from NTL Institute, "Theory and Method in Applying Behavioral Science to Planned Organizational Change," by Warren G. Bennis, pp. 347–348, *Journal of Applied Behavioral Science*, Vol. 1, No. 4, copyright 1965.

[41]See Kurt Lewin, *Field Theory in Social Science* (New York: Harper Torchbooks, 1951). Also in Kurt Lewin, "Frontiers in Group Dynamics," *Human Relations* 1 (1947): 5–41.

TABLE 4.1

COMMON BARRIERS TO CHANGE

BARRIERS	TACTICS
Fear of change on the part of those likely to be affected	The group should proceed slowly. Leader gives repeated reassurance to those affected by change. Involvement of those affected in decision making. The changed status must be made more attractive than the old pattern.
Lack of clear goals	The group must set clear goals before proceeding further.
Lack of competent leadership	Superiors must appoint or peers must elect persons as leaders who are most qualified. Leaders who prove to be incompetent should be removed.
Lack of ability of group members to function as a group	Training in group process should be conducted.
Lack of research on problems before the group	The leader should have the ability to conduct research, to locate pertinent research data, and to interpret research studies to the group.
A history of unsuccessful curriculum efforts	The group must be made to feel that progress is being made continuously.
Lack of evaluation of previous curriculum efforts	Efforts should be made to evaluate previous efforts, and an evaluation plan for current efforts must be designed.
Negative attitudes from the community	School personnel must call parents and citizens in for discussion, involve them in the process, and try to change their attitudes.
Lack of resources	Adequate resources both to carry out curriculum planning and to implement plans decided upon must be available. Personnel needed must be available.
External pressures such as state and federal legislation, regional accreditation, and regulations of the state department of education	Efforts must be made to work within the framework of laws and regulations or to try to get the laws and regulations changed. Responses to laws and regulations, which are broad and general, may vary from school to school.
Lack of experience or knowledge about a particular curricular problem	The group may call in consultants for assistance, or the school may provide training for its personnel.

organization, not change for change's sake nor for creating an image of newness per se but for bettering the products of the school.

Decision Making.   Axiom 6 of Chapter 2 takes the position that curriculum development is basically a decision-making process. A lack of skills in decision making on the part of a curriculum leader and group can be a formidable barrier to change. Are there any principles of decision making that could be helpful to curriculum study groups?

Let's turn to Daniel L. Stufflebeam and the Phi Delta Kappa National Study Committee on Evaluation, which Stufflebeam chaired, for guidance on the process of decision making.[42]

Stufflebeam and his committee ventured that the process of decision making consists of four stages—awareness, design, choice, and action—during which four kinds of decisions must be made—planning, structuring, implementing, and recycling.

Planning decisions are made "to determine objectives." They "specify *major changes that are needed in a program.*" Structuring decisions are made "to design procedures." They "specify the *means to achieve the ends* established as a result of planning decisions." Implementing decisions are made "to utilize, control, and refine procedures." Decisions on implementation are "those involved in *carrying through the action plan.*" Recycling decisions are made "to judge and react to attainments." "These are decisions used in determining the relationship of attainments to objectives and whether to continue, terminate, evolve, or drastically modify the activity."[43]

From the time a perceptive staff member in a school first starts to feel uneasy about a program and senses that something is not right and change is needed, decisions must be made constantly. Since decision making never ends, skills in the process need to be developed.

Creative Individuals. Although the literature on change stresses the necessity of group involvement, change can be and often is brought about by creative individuals and small groups working independently. Many of our great inventors, for example, have been individualists.

What sometimes happens is that an individual experiments with a new idea; a few others who like the idea adopt it; success with the idea builds on success and the idea is widely translated into practice. Creative individual enterprise should be encouraged by administrators and faculty as long as the implications of the activity do not invade areas outside the individual's own sphere. When creative endeavor begins to force demands on others without their sanction or involvement, independence must give way to cooperation.

In summary, curriculum leaders guide cooperating workers in bringing about change. In so doing they must exhibit skill in directing the change process. Both leaders and followers must have skill in decision making if positive curricular changes are to be effected.

INTERPERSONAL RELATIONS

The principal's reminder, "faculty meeting today at 3:30 P.M.," is normally greeted with less than enthusiasm. The typical teacher responses are likely to be "Oh, no, not again!" "I hope it's short," and "Faculty meetings are such a waste of time." At best these group meetings are received with a quiet resignation. Why does a group effort like a faculty meeting, which should be such a potent instrument for group deliberation, provoke such widespread dissatisfaction?

---

[42]Daniel L. Stufflebeam et al., *Educational Evaluation and Decision Making* (Itasca, Ill.: F. E. Peacock, 1971), especially Chapter 3.

[43]Ibid., pp. 80–84.

Let's try to answer that question by picturing a typical faculty meeting of a secondary school. Some fifty faculty members shuffle into a classroom and take their seats while the principal stands at the desk at the front of the room.

We observe the faculty meeting in session and take some notes:

- The classroom is crowded and the pupils' desks are uncomfortable for some of the faculty, particularly the heavier teachers.
- The straight rows are not conducive to group discussion.
- No refreshments were provided to help set a pleasant tone for the meeting.
- It is difficult to understand the purpose of the meeting. Is it information-giving on the part of the principal? A sermon from the principal on responsibilities? An effort to gain faculty approval of policies? An attempt to get faculty opinion on an issue?
- One teacher in the back was reading the daily newspaper.
- One teacher by the window was grading papers.
- Two teachers were talking about an incident that took place in one of the teachers' classrooms that day.
- One teacher, tired, sat with her eyes closed during the meeting.
- The football coaches were absent.
- A couple of teachers spoke repeatedly, whereas the majority remained silent.
- Several teachers watched the clock on the wall.
- The principal became visibly annoyed with the comment of one teacher.
- A restlessness among the teachers was apparent after the first thirty minutes.
- The group rushed out of the room as soon as the meeting ended.

None of the behaviors at this hypothetical meeting was unusual. The behaviors were quite predictable and to a great extent preventable. The general faculty meeting is but one of many group configurations in which teachers and administrators will participate. If the administrator fosters a collegial approach to administration, teachers will find themselves working on a number of committees for a variety of purposes, including curriculum development.

Most new teachers do not fully realize the extent to which teaching is a group-oriented career. Training in group process, for example, is conspicuous by its absence in preservice programs. The mind-set that novice teachers have developed about teaching pictures the teacher as an *individual* planner, presenter, and evaluator. When they begin teaching, they are unaware of the degree to which teaching involves *group* activities in which responsibilities must be shared.

Whereas beginning teachers realize from student teaching that they work with groups of children, they are often not ready to work cooperatively with their professional colleagues. A preparation program for teachers should seek to develop an appreciation of the necessity of working in groups, an attitude of willingness to work cooperatively, an understanding of the working or dynamics of a group, and skills of group participation. If these cognitive and affective objectives are not achieved in preservice teacher education, their attainment should be sought in inservice education programs.

Let's try to improve our understanding of the composition and functioning of groups by examining some of the salient characteristics of group dynamics. We shall not belabor the question of defining *group* but will call two or more persons working together for a mutual purpose a group. The faculty as a body, curriculum councils, departments, advisory committees, and teams are illustrations of formal groups.

Informal groups are self-constituted, ad hoc, impromptu collections of individuals who gather together for some immediate purpose and later disband. Protest groups and cliques of teachers are illustrations of informal groups. Although we are primarily concerned with the functioning of formally constituted groups, we should not overlook the possible impact of informal groups. It is quite possible, for example, for the formal and informal groups within a school to be working at cross purposes. The wise curriculum leader seeks to identify informal groups that may have an impact on curriculum development efforts and to channel their energies into the deliberations of the formal structure.

Recall that in the illustration of the hypothetical secondary school faculty meeting, the sense of purpose was unclear. Both the general purpose and the specific goals of the group must be known. Groups are organized most frequently for the following purposes:

- To receive instructions or information. Faculty meetings are often used for this purpose.
- To help individuals develop personally or professionally. Sensitivity groups, study groups, and workshops in pedagogy are examples of groups with this purpose.
- To recommend solutions to problems. Making such recommendations is a major purpose of curriculum improvement groups.
- To produce something. Curriculum committees, for example, may be charged with the task of creating new programs or writing curriculum guides.
- To resolve conflicts. Curriculum development efforts sometimes result in disagreements among factions, necessitating new groups to resolve these differences.

To some extent all these purposes operate in curriculum development. However, the latter three are the primary purposes, which make curriculum committees action- or task-oriented rather than ego- or process-oriented groups. In all human groups we find individuals who are there to serve the social needs of the organizations—that is, the fulfillment of the group's task—and others who are there to satisfy their own ego needs.

One of the great difficulties for the curriculum leader is keeping a group "on task." Challenging this goal are the many individuals who are impelled to satisfy their own personal needs in a group setting, behavior referred to as "processing." Some processing is essential in any group, particularly early in the group's activity when individuals are getting to know each other and trying to analyze the task. The curriculum leader must ensure some, though not equal, balance between "task orientation" and "process orientation." He or she must see to it that a group moves on with its task while permitting individuals to achieve personal satisfaction as members of the group. Excessive stress on either approach can lead to frustration and withdrawal.

The curriculum leader who is, of course, a key—or *the* key—member of a curriculum planning group, must be aware of the presence of three types of behavior within a group. First, each group is composed of individuals who bring their own individual behaviors to the group. Some will maintain these behaviors, sometimes consciously and at other times subconsciously, regardless of the group setting. Thus, the teacher who is habitually punctual, conscientious, confident, or complaining is likely to bring those traits into the group setting. Some traits have a positive impact on the group, others, a negative one.

Individuals bring their motivations, often covert, into group efforts—their personal desires, feelings, or goals, commonly referred to as the "hidden agenda." Individuals may react negatively to a curriculum proposal, for example, not because they object to the proposal per se but because they dislike the person who made the proposal. Individuals may attack a proposal because they feel their ideas have not been adequately considered. Individuals may strive to ask a group member embarrassing questions because they perceive that person as a potential rival for a leadership position. The curriculum leader must constantly attempt to channel negative behaviors into constructive paths or to eliminate them where possible. He or she must often act as mediator to ensure that the individuals' hidden agendas do not sabotage the official agenda.

Second, individuals in groups often behave in ways that are quite different from their individual behaviors. We have only to turn to studies of mob psychology to demonstrate that individuals change their behavior in group situations. Have we never observed, for example, a group of otherwise sweet, innocent elementary school youngsters taunting a classmate? Have we never seen an otherwise cautious adolescent driver become reckless when driving a car filled with friends? The presence of companion human beings who read and evaluate an individual's behavior causes that individual to behave in a way in which he or she perceives the group members wish him or her to act.

We see great contrasts in behavior between the individual who relies on his or her own inner resources (the inner-directed personality) and the individual who takes cues from those around him or her (the outer-directed personality). Although few individuals are completely immune to outer-direction in our society, some individuals are more adept than others at weighing external influences before acting on them. Some individuals are aware when they are being manipulated by others, whereas others are highly subject to suggestion. Not only do personal behaviors sometimes change in a group setting, but individuals assume, as we shall soon see, special roles that they do not and cannot perform in isolation.

Third, the group itself assumes a personality of its own. We already noted that the functioning of the group is more than the sum of the functioning of each of the individuals who make up the group. The individuals interact with and reinforce each other, creating a unique blend. In this respect some departments of a school are perceived as being more productive (pick your own word: creative, enthusiastic, reactionary, innovative, obstreperous) than others, just as schools are perceived as being different from one another.

The curriculum leader must try to develop pride in the group as a team organization by promoting group morale and by helping the group feel a sense of accomplishment. The group concept is fostered when

- interaction among group members is frequent, on a high professional level, friendly, and harmonious
- personal conflicts among group members are infrequent or nonexistent
- leadership is allowed to develop from within the group so that the group capitalizes on the strengths of its members

- constructive dissent is encouraged
- the group realizes that it is making progress toward meeting its goals, which points out again the necessity for clearly specifying the goals the group expects to attain
- the group feels some sense of reward for accomplishment

Perhaps the most satisfying reward for a group is to see its recommendations translated into practice. A word of appreciation from the administrator also goes a long way in securing the continuous motivation of teachers to participate in curriculum development.

Roles Played by Group Members.   Many years ago Kenneth D. Benne and Paul Sheats developed a classification system for identifying functional roles of group members.[41] They organized their classification system into three categories: group task roles, group building and maintenance roles, and individual roles. Group members take on task roles when they seek to move the group toward attaining its goals and solving its problems. Group members play group building and maintenance roles when they are concerned with the functioning of the group. Group members indulge in individual roles to satisfy personal needs.

Since the Benne-Sheats classification system stands as one of the most creative and comprehensive expositions of roles played by group members, its categories and roles are reproduced:

GROUP TASK ROLES

a. Initiator-contributor. Suggests ideas, ways of solving problems, or procedures.
b. Information seeker. Seeks facts.
c. Opinion seeker. Asks opinions about the values of the suggestions made by members of the group.
d. Information giver. Supplies facts as he/she sees them.
e. Opinion giver. Presents his/her own opinions about the subject matter under discussion.
f. Elaborator. States implications of suggestions and describes how suggestions might work out if adopted.
g. Coordinator. Tries to synthesize suggestions.
h. Orienter. Lets group know when it is off task.
i. Evaluator-critic. Evaluates suggestions made by group members as to criteria which he/she feels important.
j. Energizer. Spurs the group to activity.
k. Procedural technician. Performs the routine tasks which have to be done such as distributing materials.
l. Recorder. Keeps the group's record.

GROUP BUILDING AND MAINTENANCE ROLES

a. Encourager. Praises people for their suggestions.
b. Harmonizer. Settles disagreements among members.

---

[41]Kenneth D. Benne and Paul Sheats, "Functional Roles of Group Members," *Journal of Social Issues* 4, no. 2 (Spring 1948): 43–46.

   c. Compromiser. Modifies his/her position in the interests of group progress.
   d. Gate-keeper. Tries to ensure that everybody has a chance to contribute to the discussion.
   e. Standard setter or ego ideal. Urges the group to live up to high standards.
   f. Group observer and commentator. Records and reports on the functioning of the group.
   g. Follower. Accepts suggestions of others.

INDIVIDUAL ROLES

   a. Aggressor. Attacks others or their ideas.
   b. Blocker. Opposes suggestions and group decisions.
   c. Recognition-seeker. Seeks personal attention.
   d. Self-confessor. Expresses personal feelings not applicable to the group's efforts.
   e. Playboy. Refrains from getting involved in the group's work with sometimes disturbing behavior. [Since the term "Playboy" may give a different connotation in today's climate, we might want to use a term like frivolous or noncommitted individual.]
   f. Dominator. Interrupts others and tries to assert own superiority.
   g. Help-seeker. Tries to elicit sympathy for himself/herself.
   h. Special interest pleader. Reinforces his/her position by claiming to speak for others not represented in the group.[45]

A group will be more effective if the individual and negative roles are minimized or eliminated. Groups can be helped by the leader or by an outside consultant through exposing them to group dynamics theory and a classification system such as the Benne-Sheats model. Help of a more personal nature can be achieved through group interaction that permits feedback to its members. This feedback could be in the form of simple analysis of interaction skills possessed by the various members. Certainly, a group will be more productive if its members already possess a high degree of interaction skill. If, however, a group appears to lack skills in interaction or human relations, it may be advisable to depart from the group's task long enough to seek to develop some fundamental interpersonal skills.

A trained observer who records the performance of individuals participating in a group can provide valuable feedback. To record the performance of individuals in a group the observer can create a simple checksheet by listing the task, building/maintenance, and individual roles in a column on the left and the names of members across the top. The observer then records with a tally the frequency with which a participant plays a particular role.

After the observation period members would be furnished feedback about their performance. The observer must exercise great tact in how he or she presents the information. Some of the individual roles are particularly unflattering, and it will be difficult for some individuals to accept the fact that they behave in this way. Therefore, negative feedback should be supplied to individuals only on request and in confidence.

---

[45]Ibid.

Task-oriented Groups.   Curriculum development groups are or should be essentially task-oriented groups. They are given a specific job to do, carry it out, and then either accept another job or cease to function. Their productivity should be measured first in the quality of improvement that takes place in the curriculum and second in the personal and professional growth of the participants.

Curriculum development consists of a continuing series of interpersonal experiences. Both leaders and followers are obligated to make the process successful. With a modicum of training, professional persons should be able to bury their hidden agendas and to eliminate or suppress negative behaviors that disrupt the group's effort. Fortunately, some human beings have learned during their formative years to demonstrate human relations skills like warmth, empathy, valuing others' opinions and beliefs, intellectual honesty, patience, mutual assistance, and respect for others as persons. They have learned to accept responsibility and to refrain from blaming others for their own deficiencies. They have learned to put aside their own ego needs in deference to the needs of the group. They have learned to enjoy and take pride in group accomplishments. Others who demonstrate a low level of performance in these skills should be encouraged to participate in a human relations training program to improve their interpersonal skills.

Remember that curriculum development is ordinarily a voluntary undertaking. Curriculum workers might ask themselves what motivated them to agree to serve in a group devoted to curriculum improvement. They might uncover motives like the following:

- a desire to please the administrator
- a desire to work with certain colleagues
- a desire to be where the action is
- a desire to grow professionally
- a desire to make a professional contribution to the school system
- a desire to make use of one's skills and talents
- a desire for a new experience
- a desire to socialize
- a desire to use the group as a sounding board for personal beliefs and values

The reasons why individuals agree to participate in group activity are many and varied, sometimes verbalized but often not; sometimes valid in terms of the group's goals, sometimes not. Individuals who are motivated and possess the necessary personal and professional skills should be encouraged to take part in curriculum development.

Characteristics of Productive Groups.   From examining the wealth of literature on group dynamics and group process, how might we summarize the characteristics that make for group effectiveness or productivity? We have already noted in Chapter 1 that research conducted in the Hawthorne plant of the Western Electric Company in Chicago produced evidence that involvement of workers in planning and carrying out a project led to greater productivity. Research by Kurt Lewin, Ronald Lippitt, and Ralph K. White on groups of eleven-year-old children showed their productivity to be greater in a democratic group climate than in an authoritarian or laissez-faire one.[46]

---

[46]Kurt Lewin, Ronald Lippitt, and Ralph K. White, "Patterns of Aggressive Behavior in Experimentally Created Social Climates," *Journal of Social Psychology* 10 (May 1939): 271–299.

Rensis Likert saw a supportive environment, mutual confidence and trust among group members, and a sharing of common goals as contributing to group effectiveness.[47] Ned A. Flanders's studies of classroom verbal interaction led users of his instrument for observing this process to conclude that group leaders need to decrease their own verbal behavior and stimulate members of the group to interact more.[48] John Dewey,[49] and Daniel L. Stufflebeam and associates,[50] wrote of the importance of the skill of problem solving or decision making. Warren G. Bennis, Kenneth D. Benne, and Robert Chin advocated skill in planning for change.[51] Fred E. Fiedler concentrated on the effectiveness of the leader,[52] and Kimball Wiles[53] gave attention to skill in communication as essential to group effectiveness. These latter two sets of skills will be discussed in the next section, but first, based on the foregoing principles, we might conclude that a group is effective when

- leaders and members support each other
- trust is apparent among members
- goals are understood and mutually accepted
- adequate opportunity exists for members to express their own feelings and perceptions
- roles played by group members are essentially positive
- hidden agendas of members do not disrupt the group
- leadership is competent and appropriate to the group
- members possess the necessary expertise
- members have the necessary resources
- members share in all decision making
- communication is at a high level
- leadership is encouraged from within the group
- progress in accomplishing the task is noticeable and significant
- the group activity satisfies members' personal needs
- leaders seek to release potential of the members
- the group manages its time wisely

LEADERSHIP SKILLS

Let's attend the meeting of a school's curriculum committee as a guest of the curriculum coordinator who is serving as chairperson. It is early in the year. We take a seat in

---

[47]Rensis Likert, *New Patterns of Management* (New York: McGraw-Hill, 1961).

[48]Ned A. Flanders, *Analyzing Teacher Behavior* (Reading, Mass.: Addison-Wesley, 1970).

[49]John Dewey, *How We Think*, rev. ed. (Lexington, Mass.: D.C. Heath, 1933).

[50]Stufflebeam et al., *Educational Evaluation*.

[51]Warren G. Bennis, Kenneth D. Benne, and Robert Chin, eds., *The Planning of Change*, 4th ed. (New York: Holt, Rinehart and Winston, 1985).

[52]Fred E. Fiedler, *A Theory of Leadership Effectiveness* (New York: McGraw-Hill, 1967).

[53]Kimball Wiles, *Supervision for Better Schools*, 3rd ed. (Englewood Cliffs, N.J.: Prentice-Hall, 1967). Also Lovell and Wiles, *Supervision for Better Schools*, 5th ed, 1983.

the back of the room and in the course of less than an hour we observe the following behaviors:

- Two teachers are discussing an action of the principal.
- Each person speaks as long as he or she wishes, sometimes going on at length.
- The coordinator engages in dialogue with one individual, ignoring the group.
- Several members ask whether this discussion is in keeping with the group's purposes.
- The coordinator pushes his ideas and is visibly annoyed when someone disagrees with him.
- Two teachers become involved in arguing with each other.
- The coordinator steers the group toward a proposal that he has offered.
- The meeting breaks up without closure and without identifying next steps.

We might conclude that this session of the curriculum committee was less than productive. Would we attribute this lack of productivity to deficiencies on the part of the group members? To lack of leadership on the part of the coordinator? To both? Certainly, group productivity arises from a harmonious blend of skills by group members and the group leader, yet a heavy burden for the productivity of the group rests with the leader. This person has been chosen to set the pace, to provide expertise, and to channel the skills of others. The skilled leader would have been able to avoid and resolve some of the unproductive situations that developed in this curriculum committee.

Traits of Leaders. When asking ourselves and others what traits a leader should possess, we would probably garner the following responses:

- intelligent
- experienced
- assertive
- articulate
- innovative
- dynamic
- charismatic

Some would say, "You must be in the right place at the right time." Others, perhaps more cynical would say a leader must be

- a politician
- a climber
- a friend of a person in power

Like Laurence J. Peter, Jr., some people would observe that persons rise to their level of incompetence.[54]

What the research has found, however, is that it is almost impossible to ascribe any single set of traits to all persons in positions of leadership. Ralph B. Kimbrough

---

[54]See Laurence J. Peter, Jr., and Raymond Hull, *The Peter Principle: Why Things Always Go Wrong* (New York: William Morrow, 1969).

and Michael Y. Nunnery offered four generalizations about leaders and leadership that they believed to be reasonably valid:

1. Leaders tend to be slightly higher in intelligence than the average of the group led and have the administrative skills and technical competence appropriate to the situation.
2. Leaders tend to be emotionally mature, to exhibit self-confidence, to be goal oriented, to initiate action, to be dependable in exercising responsibilities, to have insight into problems faced by the group, and to have a strong continuing drive to succeed.
3. Leaders realize that people are essential for goal achievement. Therefore they attempt to communicate with others, tend to be sociable, show consideration for people, and seek cooperation of others.
4. The presence of such traits and characteristics does not guarantee effective performance as a leader, nor does their absence preclude effective performance; rather, the presence of these traits and characteristics enhances the probability of effective performance as a leader.[55]

Two Approaches.   Leaders tend to lean toward one of two basic approaches to administration: the bureaucratic or the collegial. The first approach has been labeled autocratic; the second, democratic. Edgar L. Morphet, Roe L. Johns, and Theodore L. Reller discussed the assumptions that underlie these two approaches. According to these authors, leaders who follow what they term the traditional, monocratic, bureaucratic approach hold the following beliefs:

- Leadership is confined to those holding positions in the power echelon.
- Good human relations are necessary in order that followers accept decisions of superordinates.
- Authority and power can be delegated but responsibility cannot be shared.
- Final responsibility for all matters is placed in the administrator at the top of the power echelon.
- The individual finds security in a climate in which the superordinates protect the interests of subordinates in the organization.
- Unity of purpose is obtained through loyalty to the administrator.
- The image of the executive is that of a superman.
- Maximum production is attained in a climate of competition.
- The line-and-staff plan of organization should be utilized to formulate goals, policies, and programs as well as to execute policies and programs.
- Authority is the right and privilege of a person holding a hierarchical position.
- The individual in the organization is expendable.
- Evaluation is the prerogative of superordinates.[56]

On the other hand, according to Morphet, Johns, and Reller, leaders who follow what they called the emerging, pluralistic, collegial approach believe the following:

---

[55]Kimbrough and Nunnery, *Educational Administration,* p. 357.
[56]Edgar L. Morphet, Roe L. Johns, and Theodore L. Reller, *Educational Organization and Administration: Concepts, Practices, and Issues,* 4th ed. (Englewood Cliffs, N.J.: Prentice-Hall, 1982), pp. 77–79.

- Leadership is not confined to those holding status position in the power echelon.
- Good human relations are essential to group production and to meeting the needs of the individual members of the group.
- Responsibility, as well as power and authority, can be shared.
- Those affected by a program or policy should share in decision making with respect to that program or policy.
- The individual finds security in a dynamic climate in which responsibility for decision making is shared.
- Unity of purpose is secured through consensus and group loyalty.
- Maximum production is attained in a threat-free climate.
- The line-and-staff organizations should be used exclusively for the purpose of dividing labor and implementing policies and programs developed by the total group affected.
- Laws and regulations legitimatizing authority recognize that need for authority arises from the situation.
- The individual in the organization is not expendable.
- Evaluation is a group responsibility.[57]

In contrasting these two approaches to administration Morphet, Johns, and Reller noted that the traditional approach operates in a closed climate, whereas the democratic approach functions in an open climate. The traditional approach relies on centralized authority with a fixed line-and-staff structure. Authority is spread out and shared under the pluralistic approach; the structure, while sometimes more complex than the traditional structure, is more flexible to allow for maximum participation of members of the organization. The flow of communication is much different under these two approaches. The autocratic or authoritarian approach is imbued with the philosophy of going through channels. Messages may originate from the top of the echelon, which is most common, or from the bottom. Messages from the top down pass through intermediate echelons but may not be stopped by these echelons. On the other hand, messages originating from the bottom proceed through intermediate echelons and may be stopped by any echelon. Subordinates are required to conduct business through channels and may not with impunity "go over the head" of their immediate supervisor. Under a pluralistic approach communications may flow in any direction—up, down, circularly, or horizontally. They may skip echelons and may be referred to persons outside the immediate chain of command. The pluralistic administrator is not "hung up" on channels and personal status. It is the traditional approach that begets the "organization man."

Morphet, Johns, and Reller cautioned, in comparing these two approaches, "It should not be inferred, however, that democratic administration is *ipso facto* good and that authoritarian administration is *ipso facto* bad. History provides numerous examples of successful and unsuccessful democratic administration and successful and unsuccessful authoritarian administration."[58] They noted, though, that some studies reveal monocratic organizations to be less innovative than pluralistic ones.

---

[57]Ibid., pp. 80–82.
[58]Ibid., p. 85.

Some people would identify the traditional leader as an adherent to Theory X; they would classify the pluralistic leader as a follower of Theory Y. Leaders in organizations of the Theory Z type are largely Theory Y practitioners who structure their organizations to secure maximum involvement and commitment from the workers. The pluralistic assumption that the individual is not expendable, for example, has been interpreted in Japanese Theory Z organizations as a guarantee of lifetime employment in the organization in return for full commitment to that organization in the realization of its goals.[59] This guarantee has become less certain in the economic stress of the late 1990s and early 2000s.

Leadership style is a potent factor in the productivity of groups. A classic study of the impact of leadership is the previously mentioned research conducted by Lewin, Lippitt, and White, who studied the effects of three different styles of adult leadership on four groups of eleven year old children. They examined the effects of "authoritarian," "democratic," and "laissez-faire" leadership.

> Under the authoritarian leadership, the children were more dependent upon the leader, more discontent, made more demands for attention, were less friendly, produced less work-minded conversation than under the democratic leadership. There was no group initiative in the authoritarian group climate.
>
> The laissez-faire atmosphere produced more dependence on the leader, more discontent, less friendliness, fewer group-minded suggestions, less work-minded conversation than under the democratic climate. In the absence of the laissez-faire leader, work was unproductive. The laissez-faire group was extremely dependent upon the leader for information. The converse of these situations was true for the democratic group climate. In addition, relations among the individuals in the democratic leadership atmosphere were friendlier. Those under the democratic leadership sought more attention and approval from fellow club members. They depended upon each other for recognition as opposed to recognition by the leader under the authoritarian and laissez-faire systems. Further, in the absence of the leader the democratic group proceeded at their work in productive fashion.[60]

Thus, if a curriculum leader seeks commitment from a group, the authoritarian and laissez-faire approaches are not likely to be effective. The curriculum leader's power (what little there is) is conferred by the group, especially if the leadership is encouraged from *within* the group. The democratic approach is, indeed, the only viable approach open to the curriculum leader who is a staff and not a line person propped up by external authority.

Task- and Relationship-oriented Leaders.   Fred E. Fielder studied the age-old question of whether successful leadership results from personal style or from the circumstances of the situation in which the leader finds himself or herself.[61] Fiedler spoke of the need for an appropriate match between the leader's style and the group situation in which he or

---

[59]See Ouchi, *Theory Z.*

[60]Lewin, Lippitt, and White, "Patterns of Aggressive Behavior." Quoted from Peter F. Oliva, "High School Discipline in American Society," *NASSP Bulletin* 40, no. 26 (January 1956): 7–8.

[61]See Fiedler, *Theory of Leadership.* Also, "Style or Circumstance: The Leadership Enigma," *Psychology Today* 2, no. 10 (March 1969): 38–43.

she must exercise leadership. Developing what is called a "contingency model," Fielder classified leaders as task-oriented or relationship-oriented. We might substitute human relations-oriented for the latter term. In some respects this classification resembles the dichotomy between the autocratic and democratic leader. The task-oriented leader keeps the goals of the organization always in front of him or her and the group. The needs of the organization take precedence over the needs of individuals. The superordinate-subordinate relationship is always clear. The relationship-oriented leader is less task-oriented and more concerned with building harmonious relationships among the members of the organization. He or she possesses a high degree of human-relations skill and is less conscious of status.

Persons exhibiting either of these two styles may find themselves in organizations that are either structured or unstructured, or in mixed situations possessing elements of both structure and lack of structure. Successful leadership depends upon the fortuitous combination of both style and circumstance. Fiedler found that task-oriented leaders perform better than relationship-oriented leaders at both ends of the continuum from structure to lack of structure. They perform well in structured situations where they possess authority and influence and in unstructured situations where they lack authority and influence. Relationship-oriented persons function best in mixed situations in which they possess moderate authority and influence.

Leadership, then, arises from the exigencies of a situation. Stephen J. Knezevich, for example, espoused a situational view of leadership when he said:

> A person is selected to perform the leadership role because of possessing a set of sensitivities, insights, or personal qualities the group may require for realization of group objectives and decisions. . . . The leader is selected and followed because of being capable to achieve what the followers need or want. A leader successful in one community with a unique set of educational needs may not experience similar success when moved to another with a markedly different set of educational problems, personnel, and value orientations. Changing the situation, or group's nature and purposes, results in a significant variation in leader characteristics desired that upsets all but the broadest interpretations of personal attributes.[62]

When a group member who has been in the role of follower assumes the role of leader that person is then expected to demonstrate democratic behaviors associated with his or her new status of leadership. If the original leader remains a part of the group, he or she then assumes the role of follower. Some status leaders find it difficult to surrender power and are compelled to be constantly on center stage. Such behavior will effectively prevent leadership from developing within the group and is likely to impede its progress. When the original leader resists being replaced, the leader's superior with executive, line power may have to correct the situation by urging changes in the original leader's behavior or by removing him or her from the scene.

The research on leadership thus suggests that the leader in curriculum development should

---

[62]Stephen J. Knezevich, *Administration of Public Education*, 4th ed. (New York: Harper & Row, 1984), p. 66.

- seek to develop a democratic approach
- seek to develop a relationship-oriented style
- move between a task-oriented and relationship-oriented style as the situation demands (Jacob W. Getzels, James M. Lipham, and Roald F. Campbell called this flexible style "transactional".[63])
- keep the group on task and avoid excessive processing
- avoid a laissez-faire approach
- encourage the development of leadership from within the group
- maintain openness and avoid a defensive posture
- fulfill his or her role as a change agent by serving as

advisor	interpreter
expert	reinforcer
mediator	spokesperson
organizer	intermediary
explainer	summarizer
discussion leader	team builder

Even with the best leadership some groups experience great difficulties in moving toward accomplishment of their goals. Without effective leadership little can be expected of groups in terms of productivity.

W. Edwards Deming, whose ideas on management are credited with helping Japan's rise as an industrial power blended industrial management principles into a concept known as Total Quality Management (TQM). Although Deming's ideas applied to industry, TQM when applied to education would incorporate principles of shared-management, the notion that quality should be determined in process rather than tested at the end of the process, learners should share responsibility in evaluating their own work, abandonment of performance ratings of individuals and participation of group members in finding solutions to problems. You have encountered some of these principles earlier in this chapter when we discussed quality circles.[64] William Glasser, in a vein similar to Deming's, pointed out obstacles to quality schools in the presence of too much "boss-management," too much coercion, not enough cooperative learning, too much traditional testing, too little emphasis on enhancing the ability to use knowledge, and too little opportunity for learners to evaluate the quality of their work.[65] Neither American industry nor education has fully implemented all principles of quality management. However, we see some evidence in performance assessment, cooperative learning, and constructivist psychology, which encourages the learners to take responsibility for formulating their own knowledge under the guidance of the teacher.

---

[63]Jacob W. Getzels, James M. Lipham, and Roald F. Campbell, *Educational Administration as a Social Process* (New York: Harper & Row, 1968).

[64]See W. Edwards Deming, *Out of the Crisis: Productivity and Competitive Position* (Cambridge, Mass.: Massachusetts Institute of Technology Press, 1986). See also Kenneth T. Delavigne and J. Daniel Robertson, *Deming's Profound Changes: When Will the Sleeping Giant Awaken?* (Englewood Cliffs, N.J.: Prentice-Hall, 1994).

[65]William Glasser, *The Quality School: Managing Students Without Coercion*, 2nd, expanded ed. (New York: HarperPerennial, 1992). See also William Glasser, "The Quality School," *Phi Delta Kappan* 71, no. 6 (February 1990): 424–435.

COMMUNICATION SKILLS

Curriculum development is primarily an exercise in verbal behavior—to some degree written but to a greater degree oral. Through the miraculous gift of language one human being is able to communicate his or her thoughts and feelings to another. Much of the world's business—particularly in a democratic society—is transacted through group discussions. Sometimes it seems as if most administrators, including school personnel, spend the majority of their hours participating in groups, for the standard response to callers is "Sorry, he's [she's] in a meeting."

Thoughts are communicated verbally in the form of oral activity and handwritten and printed documents, visually in the form of pictures, diagrams, charts, and the like, and nonverbally in the form of gestures and actions. Styles of oral communication and writing differ from individual to individual and from group to group. Styles vary among ethnic, regional, and national groups.

The choice of words, the loudness or softness of speech, and the rapidity of the spoken language differ from person to person and from group to group. We find differences in "accent" and in tone or intonation. The flexibility of language, both a strength and a problem, can be seen in a simple example. By using the same words but by varying the intonation or stress pattern, a speaker can convey different meanings as follows:

- *They* said that.
- They *said* that.
- They said *that.*
- They said *that?*

Individuals from some cultures are said to "talk with their hands," indicating frequent use of nonverbal behavior, whereas individuals from other cultures are taught not to be so expressive. Proficiency in communication skills by both the leader and the group members is essential to successful curriculum development. They must demonstrate proficiency in both oral and written communication. At the same time, they must be aware of their own nonverbal behavior and be skilled at reading other people's.

The leader must demonstrate proficiency in two ways: He or she must possess a high degree of communication skill and must also be able to help group members to increase their proficiency in communicating.

For purposes of our discussion, we will assume that the school or district curriculum committees, in which we are most interested, operate through the medium of the English language and that, although they represent a variety of ethnic groups and national origins, they possess at least average proficiency in English language usage. What we have to say about communication goes beyond the mere mechanics of grammar, syntax, spelling, vocabulary, and sentence structure. Deficiencies in the linguistic aspects of communication can be remedied perhaps more easily than some of the more complex psychological, social, and cultural aspects.

It is safe to conjecture that even in a group in which all members possess an excellent command of the language, communication leaves something to be desired. Have you ever sat, for example, in group meetings where

- •two people talk at the same time?
- •one member consistently finishes sentences for people?
- •one member jumps into the discussion without recognition from the chair, elevates his or her voice, and continues to do so until he or she has forced others to be silent?
- •one member, angered with the way the discussion is going, gets up and stomps out of the room?
- •members snicker and make snide remarks whenever a particular member of the group speaks?
- •one member drones on *ad infinitum?*
- •one member cannot resist displaying his or her advanced knowledge of the subject under discussion?
- •one member becomes sullen when another disagrees with his or her ideas?
- •the leader has to explain a point three times before all group members seem to understand?

Do you recognize any of these people? Some of them are, of course, playing the roles discussed earlier. It is possible that many, even most, of the members thought they were communicating something to the group while they were speaking. It is highly probable that what they were communicating was much different from what they thought they were.

Two people vying for the floor may communicate that they both are individuals who demand attention. Or shall we say that they possess a trait, lauded by some, called "assertiveness"? The member who finishes others' sentences may communicate that it is necessary for him or her to think for others. The member who stomps out of the room might attempt to convey that he or she is a person who sticks to his or her principles. More likely, in rejecting the group, the person will be perceived as a "sore loser." We communicate not only through words but through our actions as well.

Common Misunderstandings.   We should clear up some common misunderstandings about communication. First, skill in speaking is sometimes mistaken for communication. The ability to respond quickly and fully—to think on one's feet—is an attribute desired, some say required, of a leader. However, facility in speaking does not ensure that a message is getting across. One need only listen to some political leaders to make the distinction between the ability to articulate and the ability to communicate. People place great stress on oral skills, often to such an extent that they do not realize they are accepting form in the place of substance. A glib tongue may obfuscate a topic under discussion. A speaker should strive to be both articulate and communicative.

Second, group interaction is sometimes taken for communication. Comments like "We had a lively discussion" are meaningless unless we know whether the discussion led to understanding and decision making. Processing, the sharing of personal feelings and opinions, is sometimes equated with communication. Interaction for interaction's sake cannot be accepted as a legitimate activity for work in curriculum development.

Third, the assumption that communication is full, clear, and completely understood is often made without sufficient evidence. Alfonso, Firth, and Neville advised supervisors against making such an assumption: "Communication will always be inaccurate because sender and receiver can never share common perceptions. Supervisors often operate on the assumption that communication is perfect. Instead, they should function on the basis that communication is imperfect and must always be so."[66]

How many times have we heard the words of a speaker, understood them all, yet not comprehended what the speaker was saying? How many times have we heard a member of a group tell another, "I hear you," but mean, "Even though I hear you, I do not know what you are saying"?

What are some common problems people experience in trying to communicate and what can be done to solve them? Let's create three categories: (1) problems with oral communications or those that oral and written communication share, (2) problems with written communication, and (3) problems brought about by nonverbal behavior or the absence thereof.

Oral Communication.   Difficulties in oral communication can arise in the following situations:

1. *Members of the group either unintentionally or deliberately fail to come to the point.* They talk around instead of to an issue. Sometimes they engage in avoidance behavior—that is, they resist coming to grips with the issue. The curriculum leader must help group members to address the issues and to come to the point. When some group members prattle on, others in the group become bored and frustrated. The burden of keeping the group's attention on the issues falls on the group leader.

2. *Members of the group use fuzzy, imprecise language.* They use words with many interpretations, like "relevance," without defining them. They use "psychobabble," like "Tell me where you're coming from" and "I'm into behavioral objectives." They employ words of low frequency, like "nomothetic," "synergy," and "androgogy," that some members of the group may not understand. They lapse into pedagese, like "Each child must develop his or her personal curriculum," without venturing to explain how this may be done. They borrow Madison Avenue jargon, like "Let's run it up the flagpole," or they turn to sports analogies, like "What's the game plan?" The group leader must be alert to difficulties members may have in following a discussion. He or she must ask speakers to repeat and clarify statements and questions as necessary. The leader must keep in mind that some members hesitate to ask for clarifications themselves, feeling that in so doing they may expose their own ignorance.

3. *Members of the group select out of a discussion those things that they wish to hear.* It is a well-known fact that we hear and see selectively. We hear and see those people and things that we wish to hear and we see and reject those people and things that we do not want to see or hear. The leader must help group members to see all facets of a problem, calling attention to points they may have missed.

4. *Members fail to express themselves, particularly if they disagree with what has been said.* Some persons hold back their views from a sense of insecurity. They feel that their opinions are not worthwhile, or they fear embarrassment or ridicule. They may not wish to seem in disagreement with status persons who are in a position to reward or punish them. The group leader must assure members that dissent is possible and encouraged. The leader must foster a climate in which each person can express himself or herself without fear.

[66]Alfonso, Firth, and Neville, *Instructional Supervision*, p. 175.

5. *Members fail to follow an orderly process of discussion.* Communication is impossible when group members are unwilling to discipline themselves and do not take turns in discussing, listening to each other, and respecting each other's views. The group leader must enforce order during the discussion process to ensure that everyone who wishes to be heard has an opportunity.

6. *Discussion is shut off and the group presses for a premature vote.* The group should be striving to reach consensus on issues. The goal is commitment of as many persons as possible. The group leader should keep the goal of consensus in front of the group. Close votes on issues should be reexamined, if possible. A vote may (or may not) secure compliance on the part of the people affected; it does not guarantee, however, commitment that is so necessary to curriculum improvement.

7. *Sessions break up without some sort of closure.* If next steps are not clear, members leave the group sessions confused. The leader has the responsibility for seeking closure on issues when possible, for summarizing the group's work, and for calling the group's attention to next steps.

8. *The communication flow is primarily from leader to members.* The leader should resist the temptation to dominate a discussion and to foist his or her views on the group. He or she should ensure that communication is initiated by members of the group to the leader and to each other as well as from the leader to group members.

9. *Acrimony, hostility, and disharmony exist within a group.* When these conditions occur, the leader must spend time developing a pleasant, harmonious group climate before positive communication can take place among members. Members must learn to work together in an atmosphere of trust and mutual respect. The leader should seek to promote a relaxed, threat-free atmosphere.

Written Communication.   In the course of a group's activity there will be occasions on which the leader and members of the group will wish and need to communicate in written form between group sessions. They will also need to communicate in writing with persons outside the work group. Difficulties arise with this form of communication when the following situations occur:

1. *The writer cannot sense the impact of his or her words in a written communication.* Extra care needs to be taken when structuring a written message. Writers of memos must weigh their choice of words and manner of phrasing their thoughts. Some messages are unintentionally blunt or curt and cause negative responses in the receivers. A message when put in writing may give a far different impression from what the writer intended. The writer should review any written communication in the light of the impact it would have on him or her if he or she were the recipient.

2. *Written communications are excessive in number.* Some persons indulge in memorandum writing with almost the same frequency as some individuals write letters to the editor of a newspaper. Some vent their own frustrations in memo after memo. Some people believe that every thought, word, and deed must be committed to writing in order to (a) preserve them for posterity, (b) maintain an ongoing record for current use, or (c) cover one's posterior, as is crudely suggested. Some recipients—or intended recipients—will not take any action unless they have information in written form. Some organizations have almost immobilized themselves with the ubiquitous memo to the point where there are many communiqués but little communication. The leader should encourage the use of memoranda and other written communications as needed

and discourage their excessive use. Courtesy, clarity, and brevity should be earmarks of written communications.

3. *The use of English is poor.* Many memoranda, particularly from professional people, lose their impact because of poor English. Inaccurate spelling, improper grammar, and poor sentence structure can detract from the message contained in the memoranda and can subject the writers to unnecessary criticism.

Special precautions must be taken when the medium of e-mail is used to deliver messages. E-mail conventions (e.g., the avoidance of sending messages all in capital letters) must be observed to prevent misunderstandings. Further, writers of e-mail must keep in mind that there is no clarifying, correcting, or softening of a message once they've hit the Send button.

The writing of intelligible memoranda that do not create negative responses on the part of recipients is an art that, at least in a cooperative activity like curriculum development, should serve only to supplement, not replace, oral communication.

Face-to-face communication is ordinarily—barring the need for complex or technical data—a far more effective means than writing for conveying ideas among members of small groups of peers such as a typical curriculum development group. Even in the case of complex or technical data presented in written form, follow-up discussion is usually necessary.

Nonverbal Behavior. Human beings communicate with each other without the use of words. A smile, a frown, a wave, a shrug, and a wink all say something. Nonverbal behavior is shaped both biologically and culturally. Most human beings start out life with basically the same physiological equipment—two eyes, arms, legs, and so on. But what they do with that equipment is shaped by the culture in which they grow and develop. Thus it is possible for every human being to smile, but some individuals within a single culture are more prone to smiling than others, and members of a particular culture are more prone to smile than members of another culture. South American Indians, for example, are much more stoic and reserved than the more expressive Latinos of Spanish origin.

Nonverbal behavior is less studied and less understood than verbal behavior. We have great need in our teacher education programs for training in understanding the differences in nonverbal behavior between members of the U.S. culture and foreign cultures in the United States. In our pluralistic society many social and work groups are composed of persons from varying subcultures: white, black, Hispanic, Native American, and Asian, among others. Every individual brings to a group his or her culturally determined ways of behaving. While some cultures prize assertiveness, others stress deference. Signs of respect are accorded to age, status, and experience more often in some cultures than in others. Attitudes of both males and females toward children and of one gender toward the other vary among cultures. Some cultures value physical closeness among individuals and gregariousness. Other cultures strive to maintain distance among individuals both physically and socially. These attitudes are shown in both verbal and nonverbal behavior. Accepted styles of dress vary from culture to culture and even from subculture to subculture.

We need to learn to perceive what our colleagues are trying to communicate to us by the expression on their faces, by the look in their eyes, by the way they hold their mouths or heads, by the movement of their hands, and by the fidgeting of their legs. A group leader should be able to detect fatigue, boredom, hostility, and sensitivity on the part of members of the organization. He or she should be able to sense when one individual is stepping on another's toes and turn the discussion to constructive paths. He or she should strive to effect signs of pleasure, not pain among members of the group. The leader must be especially cautious of nonverbal signals he or she gives and must make every effort to ensure that those signals are positive. Finally, for successful curriculum development both the leader and group members must exhibit a high degree of skill in all modes of communication.[67]

SUMMARY

This chapter focused on the roles played by various persons and groups participating in curriculum development at the individual school level. Some principals perceive themselves as instructional leaders and take an active part in curriculum development, whereas others delegate that responsibility. A Theory X administrator emphasizes authority and control, whereas a Theory Y administrator follows a human-relations approach. Theory Y leaders may adopt Theory Z principles.

Students in some schools, depending on their maturity, participate in curriculum improvement by serving on committees and by providing data about their own learning experiences.

Parents and other citizens participate in curriculum work by serving on advisory committees, responding to surveys, providing data about their children, and serving as resource persons in school and out.

The professional personnel—teachers and specialists—share the greatest responsibility for curriculum development.[68] Both leaders and followers need to develop skills in group process. Among the competencies necessary for the curriculum leader are skills in producing change, in decision making, in interpersonal relationships, in leading groups, and in communicating.

QUESTIONS FOR DISCUSSION

1. What evidence is there that today's principals either are or are not instructional leaders?
2. What are some community groups with which school administrators and supervisors should be concerned?
3. What are the characteristics of a school as a community of learners?

---

[67]For interesting analyses of some aspects of nonverbal behavior see Edward T. Hall, *The Silent Language* (Garden City, N.Y.: Doubleday, 1959); Julius Fast, *Body Language* (New York: M. Evans, 1970); and Desmond Morris, Peter Collett, Peter Marsh, and Marie O'Shaughnessy, *Gestures: Their Origin and Distribution* (New York: Stein and Day, 1979).

[68]This textbook focuses on the roles of the various constituencies of the school in relationship to *curriculum development*. Concerning one of those constituencies—the teachers—you may wish to read three informative books by John I. Goodlad et al. on the role, responsibilities, and preparation of teachers. All three books are from Jossey-Bass, San Francisco, 1990: *The Moral Dimensions of Teaching, Places Where Teachers are Taught,* and *Teachers for Our Nation's Schools.* See also John Goodlad's article in *Phi Delta Kappan,* vol. 70, no. 3, November 1990, pp. 185–194, entitled, "Better Teachers for Our Nation's Schools," a summary of the findings of the Study of the Education of Educators.

4. Do you agree that teachers should be the primary group in curriculum development?

5. How would you as a curriculum leader proceed to bring about change in the curriculum?

SUPPLEMENTARY EXERCISES

1. Write a paper stating the pros and cons and showing your position on the role of the principal as instructional leader.
2. List qualities and qualifications needed by a curriculum leader.
3. Explain what is meant by Theory X, Theory Y, and Theory Z, and draw implications of these theories for curriculum development.
4. Write a paper on developing a Theory Z school.
5. Report on ways pupils are involved in curriculum development in a school district with which you are familiar.
6. Report on ways parents and others from the community are involved in curriculum development in a school district with which you are familiar.
7. Explain the meaning of the term "power structure," and draw implications of the power structure for curriculum development.
8. Analyze the power structure of a community that you know well.
9. Write an essay on the curriculum leader as a change agent.
10. Write a brief report on ways to unfreeze curricular patterns.
11. Identify roles played by group members and how the curriculum leader copes with each. (You should make an effort to describe roles in addition to those mentioned in this chapter.)
12. Describe common barriers to educational change and suggest ways the curriculum leader may work to eliminate them.
13. List steps in the decision-making process.
14. Create an observation chart based on the Benne-Sheats classification system discussed in this chapter and use it in observing a discussion group in action. (You might want to try using this system at a school board meeting.)
15. Observe a discussion group in action and record evidence of task orientation and process orientation. Conjecture on hidden agendas present in the group.
16. Observe a discussion group in action and evaluate the effectiveness of the leader, using criteria discussed in this chapter.
17. Report on the meaning of gestures used within a particular culture.
18. Analyze the gestures you use, if any. If you do not use any gestures, account for this lack of use.
19. Explain the ten kinds of human activity which Edward T. Hall labeled Primary Message Systems (see bibliography).
20. Explain and demonstrate examples of body language as described by Julius Fast (see bibliography).
21. Prepare a written or oral report on the Concerns-Based Adoption Model (CBAM) developed by the University of Texas Research and Development Center for determining stages of teacher concerns about an innovation and levels of teacher use of

innovations. See references to Gene E. Hall and Susan Loucks and to Hall, Loucks, Rutherford, and Newlove in the bibliography. See also description of this model in John P. Miller and Wayne Seller (see bibliography).

BIBLIOGRAPHY

Alfonso, Robert J., Firth, Gerald R., and Neville, Richard F. *Instructional Supervision: A Behavior System,* 2nd ed. Boston: Allyn and Bacon, 1981.

Barth, Roland. *Improving Schools from Within: Teachers, Parents, and Principals Can Make the Difference.* San Francisco: Jossey-Bass, 1990.

Benne, Kenneth D. and Sheats, Paul, "Functional Roles of Group Members," *Journal of Social Issues* 4, no. 2 (Spring 1948): 43–46.

Bennis, Warren G., Benne, Kenneth D., and Chin, Robert, eds. *The Planning of Change,* 4th ed. New York: Holt, Rinehart and Winston, 1985.

Campbell, Roald F., Cunningham, Luvern L., Nystrand, Raphael O., and Usdan, Michael D. *The Organization and Control of American Schools,* 6th ed. Columbus, Ohio: Merrill, 1990.

Carnegie Foundation for the Advancement of Teaching. *The Condition of Teaching: A State-by-State Analysis, 1990.* Princeton, N.J.: Carnegie Foundation for the Advancement of Teaching, 1990.

Delavigne, Kenneth T. and Robertson, J. Daniel. *Deming's Profound Changes: When Will the Sleeping Giant Awaken?* Englewood Cliffs, N.J.: Prentice-Hall, 1994.

Deming, W. Edwards. *Out of the Crisis: Productivity and Competitive Position.* Cambridge, Mass.: Massachusetts Institute of Technology, 1986.

Dewey, John. *How We Think,* rev. ed. Lexington: Mass.: D. C. Heath, 1933.

Doll, Ronald C. *Curriculum Improvement: Decision Making and Process,* 9th ed. Boston: Allyn and Bacon, 1996.

Drake, Thelbert L. and Roe, William H. *The Principalship,* 4th ed. New York: Macmillan, 1994.

Dwyer, David C., Barnett, Bruce G., and Lee, Ginny V. "The School Principal: Scapegoat or the Last Great Hope?" in Linda T. Sheive and Marian B. Schoenheit, eds., *Leadership: Examining the Elusive.* Alexandria, Va.: Association for Supervision and Curriculum Development, 1987, pp. 30–46.

Fast, Julius. *Body Language.* New York: M. Evans, 1970.

———. *The Body Language of Sex, Power, and Aggression.* New York: M. Evans, 1977.

Fiedler, Fred E. *A Theory of Leadership Effectiveness.* New York: McGraw-Hill, 1967.

Flanders, Ned A. *Analyzing Teacher Behavior.* Reading, Mass.: Addison-Wesley, 1970.

Galloway, Charles. *Silent Language in the Classroom.* Bloomington, Ind.: Phi Delta Kappa Educational Foundation, 1976.

George, Paul S. *The Theory Z School: Beyond Effectiveness.* Columbus, Ohio: National Middle School Association, 1983.

Getzels, Jacob, Lipham, James M., and Campbell, Roald F. *Educational Administration as a Social Process.* New York: Harper & Row, 1968.

Glasser, William. *The Quality School: Managing Students Without Coercion.* New York: HarperPerennial, 1992.

Glatthorn, Allan A. *Curriculum Leadership.* Glenview, Ill.: Scott, Foresman, 1987.

———. *Developing a Quality Curriculum.* Alexandria, Va.: Association for Supervision and Curriculum Development, 1994.

Good, Thomas L. and Brophy, Jere E. "School Effects." In Merlin C. Wittrock, ed. *Handbook of Research on Teaching,* 3rd ed., 570–602. New York: Macmillan, 1986.

Goodlad, John I. *The Dynamics of Educational Change: Toward Responsive Schools.* New York: McGraw-Hill, 1975.

Hall, Edward T. *The Silent Language.* Garden City, N.Y.: Doubleday, 1959.

Hall, Gene E. and Loucks, Susan. "Teacher Concerns as a Basis for Facilitating and Personalizing Staff Development." *Teachers College Record* 80, no. 1 (September 1978): 36–53.

———, Loucks, Susan, Rutherford, William L., and Newlove, Beaulah W. "Levels of Use in the Innovation: A Framework for Analyzing Innovation Adoption." *Journal of Teacher Education* 26, no. 1 (Spring 1975): 52–56.

Hess, G. Alfred, Jr., *Empowering Teachers and Parents: School Restructuring Through the Eyes of Anthropologists.* Westport, Conn.: Bergin & Garvey, 1992.

Holt, John. *Teach Your Own: A Hopeful Path for Education.* New York: Delacorte Press/Seymour Lawrence, 1981.

Hord, Shirley M., Rutherford, William L., Huling-Austin, Leslie, and Hall, Gene E. *Taking Charge of Change.* Alexandria, Va.: Association for Supervision and Curriculum Development, 1987.

Kimbrough, Ralph B. and Nunnery, Michael Y. *Educational Administration,* 3rd ed. New York: Macmillan, 1988.

Knezevich, Stephen J. *Administration of Public Education,* 4th ed. New York: Harper & Row, 1984.

Leavitt, Harold J. and Bahrami, Homa. *Managerial Psychology: Managing Behavior in Organizations,* 5th ed. Chicago: University of Chicago Press, 1988.

Lewin, Kurt. *Field Theory in Social Science: Selected Theoretical Papers,* edited by Dorwin Cartwright. New York: Harper Torchbooks, 1951.

———, Lippitt, Ronald, and White, Ralph K. "Patterns of Aggression in Experimentally Created Social Climates." *Journal of Social Psychology* 10 (May 1939): 271–299.

Likert, Rensis. *New Patterns of Management.* New York: McGraw-Hill, 1961.

Lovell, John T. and Wiles, Kimball. *Supervision for Better Schools,* 5th ed. Englewood Cliffs, N.J.: Prentice-Hall, 1983.

Lucio, William H. and McNeil, John D. *Supervision: A Synthesis of Thought and Action,* 2nd ed. New York: McGraw-Hill, 1969.

Lynd, Robert S. *Middletown: A Study in American Culture.* New York: Harcourt Brace Jovanovich, 1929.

——— and Lynd, Helen M. *Middletown in Transition: A Study in Cultural Conflicts.* New York: Harcourt Brace Jovanovich, 1937.

McCutcheon, Gail. "Curriculum Theory/Curriculum Practice: A Gap or the Grand Canyon?" In Alex Molnar, ed. *Current Thought on Curriculum,* 1985 Yearbook, 45–52. Alexandria, Va.: Association for Supervision and Curriculum Development, 1985.

McGregor, Douglas M. *The Human Side of Enterprise.* New York: McGraw-Hill, 1960.

McNeil, John D. *Curriculum: A Comprehensive Introduction,* 5th ed. New York: HarperCollins, 1996.

Madeja, Stanley S. "Where Have All the Disciplines Gone?" *Educational Leadership* 38, no. 8 (May 1981): 602–604.

Maeroff, Gene I. *The Empowerment of Teachers: Overcoming the Crisis of Confidence.* New York: Teachers College Press, 1988.

Martin, David S. *Curriculum Leadership: Case Studies for Program Practitioners.* Alexandria, Va.: Association for Supervision and Curriculum Development, 1989.

Maslow, Abraham H. *Motivation and Personality,* 2nd ed. New York: Harper & Row, 1970.

Miel, Alice. *Changing the Curriculum: A Social Process.* New York: Appleton-Century-Crofts, 1946.

Miller, John P. and Seller, Wayne. *Curriculum: Perspectives and Practice.* White Plains, N.Y.: Longman, 1985.

Morphet, Edgar L., Johns, Roe L., and Reller, Theodore L. *Educational Organization and Administration: Concepts, Practices, and Issues,* 4th ed. Englewood Cliffs, N.J.: Prentice-Hall, 1982.

Morris, Desmond, Collett, Peter, Marsh, Peter, and O'Shaughnessy, Marie. *Gestures: Their Origin and Distribution.* New York: Stein and Day, 1979.

Oliver, Albert I. *Curriculum Improvement: A Guide to Problems, Principles, and Process,* 2nd ed. New York: Harper & Row, 1977.

Ouchi, William G. *Theory Z: How American Businesses Can Meet the Japanese Challenge.* Reading, Mass.: Addison-Wesley, 1981.

Owens, Robert G. *Organizational Behavior in Education,* 5th ed. Boston: Allyn and Bacon, 1995.

Peter, Laurence J. *The Peter Prescription.* New York: William Morrow, 1972.

———. *Why Things Go Wrong: Or, the Peter Principle Revisited.* New York: William Morrow, 1985.

——— and Hull, Raymond. *The Peter Principle: Why Things Always Go Wrong.* New York: William Morrow, 1969.

Roethlisberger, F. J. and Dickson, William J. *Management and the Worker.* Cambridge, Mass.: Harvard University Press, 1939.

Ross, Joel E. *Total Quality Management: Text, Cases, and Readings,* 2nd ed. Delray Beach, Fla.: St. Luice Press, 1995.

Saylor, J. Galen, Alexander, William M., and Lewis, Arthur J. *Curriculum Planning for Better Teaching and Learning,* 4th ed. New York: Holt, Rinehart and Winston, 1981.

Sears, James T. and Marshall, J. Dan, eds. *Teaching and Thinking About Curriculum: Critical Inquiries.* New York: Teachers College Press, 1990.

Sergiovanni, Thomas J. and Carver, Fred D. *The New School Executive: A Theory of Administration,* 2nd ed. New York: Harper & Row, 1980.

Sergiovanni, Thomas J. and Starratt, Robert J. *Supervision: A Redefinition,* 6th ed. New York: McGraw-Hill, 1998.

Stufflebeam, Daniel L. et al. *Educational Evaluation and Decision Making.* Itasca, Ill.: F. E. Peacock, 1971.

Toffler, Alvin. *Future Shock.* New York: Random House, 1970.

———. *The Third Wave.* New York: William Morrow, 1980.

Unruh, Glenys G. "Curriculum Politics." In Fenwick W. English, ed., *Fundamental Curriculum Decisions,* 1983 Yearbook, 99–111. Alexandria, Va.: Association for Supervision and Curriculum Development, 1983.

Wiles, Jon and Bondi, Joseph C. *Curriculum Development: A Guide to Practice,* 5th ed. Upper Saddle River, N.J.: Merrill, 1998.

———. *Supervision: A Guide to Practice,* 4th ed. Englewood Cliffs, N.J.: Merrill, 1996.

Wiles, Kimball. *Supervision for Better Schools,* 3rd ed. Englewood Cliffs, N.J.: Prentice-Hall, 1967.

Willis, Scott. "Creating 'Total Quality' Schools." *ASCD Update* 35, no. 2 (February 1993): 1, 4–5.

Wood, George H. "Teacher as Curriculum Workers," in James T. Sears and J. Dan Marshall, ed., *Teaching and Thinking About Curriculum: Critical Inquiries.* New York: Teachers College Press, 1990, pp. 97–109.

Zenger, Weldon F. and Zenger, Sharon K. *Curriculum Planning: A Ten-Step Process.* Palo Alto, Calif.: R & E Research Associates, 1982.

PART III

CURRICULUM DEVELOPMENT: COMPONENTS OF THE PROCESS

CHAPTER 5

MODELS FOR CURRICULUM DEVELOPMENT

After studying this chapter you should be able to:

1. Analyze each model for curriculum development in this chapter and decide which models, if any, meet the necessary criteria for such a model.
2. Choose one model and carry out one or more of its components in your school.
3. Distinguish between deductive and inductive models for curriculum development.
4. Distinguish between linear and nonlinear models for curriculum development.
5. Distinguish between prescriptive and descriptive models for curriculum development.

SELECTING MODELS

The current literature of education is replete with discussions of modeling. Models, which are essentially patterns serving as guidelines to action, can be found for almost every form of educational activity. The profession has models of instruction, of administration, of evaluation, of supervision, and others. We can even find models of *curriculum* as opposed to models of *curriculum development*.[1]

Unfortunately, the term *model* as used in the education profession often lacks precision. It may be a tried or untried scheme. It may be a proposed solution to a piece of a problem; an attempt at a solution to a specific problem; or a microcosmic pattern for replication on a grander scale.

Some faculties have been *modeling* for years. They have been devising their own patterns for solving educational problems or establishing procedures, though they may not have labeled their activity as *modeling*.

---

[1]For a model of *curriculum*, see Mauritz Johnson, Jr., "Definitions and Models in Curriculum Theory," *Educational Theory* 17, no. 2 (April 1967): 127–140.

VARIATION IN MODELS

Some of the models found in the literature are simple; others are very complex. The more complex ones border on computer science, with charts that consist of squares, boxes, circles, rectangles, arrows, and so on. Within a given area of specialization (such as administration, instruction, supervision, or curriculum development), models may differ but bear great similarities. The similarities may outweigh the differences. Individual models are often refinements or revisions, frequently major, often minor, of already existing models.

Practitioners to whom a model is directed, therefore, have the heavy responsibility of selecting a model in their particular field from the often bewildering variety in the literature. If the practitioners are not disposed to apply models they discover, they may either design their own, by no means a rare event, or reject all models that prescribe order and sequence. They may thus proceed intuitively without the apparent limitations imposed by a model. After proceeding intuitively, the practitioners may then "put it all together" and come out with a working model at the end of the process instead of starting with a model at the beginning.

Four models of curriculum development are presented in this chapter, one of which is my own. I believe that using a model in such an activity as curriculum development can result in greater efficiency and productivity.

By examining models for curriculum development, we can analyze the phases their originators conceived as essential to the process. The purpose in presenting four models is to acquaint the reader with some of the thinking that has gone on or is going on in the field. Three of the chosen models were conceived by persons well known in the curriculum field: Ralph W. Tyler,[2] Hilda Taba,[3] and J. Galen Saylor, William M. Alexander, and Arthur J. Lewis.[4] My own model is presented as an effort to tie together essential components in the process of curriculum development. The supplementary exercises at the end of this chapter will direct you to additional models.

Three of the models (Tyler's; Saylor, Alexander, and Lewis's; and mine) are deductive. They proceed from the general (examining the needs of society, for example) to the specific (specifying instructional objectives, for example). On the other hand, Taba's model is inductive, starting with the actual development of curriculum materials and leading to generalization.

The four models described in this chapter are linear, that is, they propose a certain order or sequence of progression through the various steps. A nonlinear approach would permit planners to enter at various points of the model, skip components, reverse the order, and work on two or more components simultaneously. You might say that the ultimate in a nonlinear approach is the absence of a model when curriculum planners operate intuitively. Actually, linear models should not be perceived as immutable sequences of steps. Curriculum workers would exercise judgment as to entry points and interrelationships of components of the models.

The four models presented in this chapter are prescriptive rather than descriptive. They suggest what ought to be done (and what is done by many curriculum develop-

---

[2]Ralph W. Tyler, *Basic Principles of Curriculum and Instruction* (Chicago: University of Chicago Press, 1949).

[3]Hilda Taba, *Curriculum Development: Theory and Practice* (New York: Harcourt Brace Jovanovich, 1962).

[4]J. Galen Saylor, William M. Alexander, and Arthur J. Lewis, *Curriculum Planning for Better Teaching and Learning*, 4th ed. (New York: Holt, Rinehart and Winston, 1981).

ers). A descriptive model takes a different approach. Proposing a descriptive model, which he termed *naturalistic,* Decker F. Walker included three major elements: platform, deliberation, and design.[5] By *platform* he meant the beliefs or principles that guided the curriculum developers. Platform principles lead to *deliberation,* the process of making decisions from among alternatives available. From the deliberation comes the curriculum *design.* Walker contrasted the naturalistic or descriptive model with the classical or prescriptive model as follows:

> This model is primarily descriptive, whereas the classical model is prescriptive. This model is basically a temporal one; it postulates a beginning (the platform), an end (the design), and a process (deliberation) by means of which the beginning progresses to the end. In contrast, the classical model is a means-end model; it postulates a desired end (the objective), a means for attaining this end (the learning experience), and a process (evaluation) for determining whether the means does indeed bring about the end. The two models differ radically in the roles they assign to objectives and to evaluation in the process of curriculum development.
>
> In the classical model objectives are essential. . . . In the naturalistic model, on the other hand, objectives are only one means among others for guiding our search for better educational programs. . . .
>
> Evaluation in the classical model is a self-corrective process for determining whether learning experiences lead to the attainment of given objectives. . . . In the naturalistic model this kind of evaluation is not *logically* necessary. Design decisions *can* be justified by reference to the platform only. . . . In the naturalistic model evaluation is a useful tool for justifying design decisions, even though it is quite possible and not nonsensical (although probably unwise) for a curriculum developer to neglect systematic formal evaluation.[6]

All of these models specify or depict major phases and a sequence for carrying out these phases. The models, including mine, show *phases* or *components,* not *people.* The various individuals and groups involved in each phase are not included in the models per se. To do so would require a most cumbersome diagram, for we would have to show the persons involved in every component. For example, if we showed the people involved in the component "specification of curriculum goals," we would need to chart a progression of steps from departmental committee to school faculty curriculum committee or extended school committee to principal to district curriculum committee to superintendent to school board. The roles of individuals and groups in the process are discussed elsewhere in this text.

MODELS OF CURRICULUM DEVELOPMENT

Curriculum development is seen here as the process for making programmatic decisions and for revising the products of those decisions on the basis of continuous and subsequent evaluation.

---

[5]Decker F. Walker, "A Naturalistic Model for Curriculum Development," *School Review* 80, no. 1 (November 1971): 51–67.

[6]Ibid., pp. 58–59.

A model can give order to the process. As Taba stated, "If one conceives of curriculum development as a task requiring orderly thinking, one needs to examine both the order in which decisions are made and the way in which they are made to make sure that all relevant considerations are brought to bear on these decisions."[7]

THE TYLER MODEL

Perhaps the best or one of the best known models for curriculum development with special attention to the planning phases can be found in Ralph W. Tyler's classic little book, *Basic Principles of Curriculum and Instruction.* "The Tyler rationale," a process for selecting educational objectives, is widely known and practiced in curriculum circles. Although Tyler proposed a rather comprehensive model for curriculum development, the first part of his model (selection of objectives) received the greatest attention from other educators.

Tyler recommended that curriculum planners identify general objectives by gathering data from three sources: the learners, contemporary life outside the school, and the subject matter. After identifying numerous general objectives, the planners refine them by filtering them through two screens: the educational and social philosophy of the school and the psychology of learning. The general objectives that successfully pass through the two screens become what are now popularly known as instructional objectives. In describing educational objectives Tyler referred to them as "goals," "educational ends," "educational purposes," and "behavioral objectives."[8]

Student as Source. The curriculum worker begins his or her search for educational objectives by gathering and analyzing data relevant to student needs and interests. The total range of needs—educational, social, occupational, physical, psychological, and recreational—is studied. Tyler recommended observations by teachers, interviews with students, interviews with parents, questionnaires, and tests as techniques for collecting data about students.[9] By examining the needs and interests of students, the curriculum developer identifies a set of potential objectives.

Society as Source. Analysis of contemporary life in both the local community and in society at large is the next step in the process of formulating general objectives. Tyler suggested that curriculum planners develop a classification scheme that divides life into various aspects such as health, family, recreation, vocation, religion, consumption, and civic roles.[10] From the needs of society flow many potential educational objectives. The curriculum worker must be something of a sociologist to make an intelligent analysis of needs of social institutions. After considering this second source, the curriculum worker has lengthened his or her set of objectives.

Subject Matter as Source. For a third source the curriculum planner turns to the subject matter, the disciplines themselves. Many of the curricular innovations of the 1950s—the "new math," audio-lingual foreign language programs, and the plethora

[7]Taba, *Curriculum Development,* pp. 11–12.
[8]Tyler, *Basic Principles,* pp. 3, 37, 57.
[9]Ibid., pp. 12–13.
[10]Ibid., pp. 19–20.

of science programs—came from the subject matter specialists. From the three afore-mentioned sources curriculum planners derive general or broad objectives that lack precision and that I would prefer to call instructional goals. These goals may be pertinent to specific disciplines or may cut across disciplines.

Johnson held a different perspective about these sources. He commented that the "only possible source [of the curriculum] is the total available culture" and that only organized subject matter—that is, the disciplines, not the needs and interests of learners or the values and problems of society—can be considered a source of curriculum items.[11]

Once this array of possibly applicable objectives is determined, a screening process is necessary, according to Tyler's model, to eliminate unimportant and contradictory objectives. He advised the use of the school's educational and social philosophy as the first screen for these goals.

Philosophical Screen.   Tyler advised teachers of a particular school to formulate an educational and social philosophy. He urged them to outline their values and illustrated this task by emphasizing our democratic goals:

- the recognition of the importance of every individual human being regardless of race, national, social, or economic status;
- opportunity for wide participation in all phases of activities in the social groups in the society;
- encouragement of variability rather than demanding a single type of personality;
- faith in intelligence as a method of dealing with important problems rather than depending upon the authority of an autocratic or aristocratic group.[12]

In his discussion about the formulation of an educational social philosophy, Tyler personified the school. He talked about "the educational and social philosophy to which the school is committed," "when a school accepts these values," "many schools are likely to state," and "if the school believes."[13] Thus Tyler made of the school a dynamic, living entity. The curriculum worker will review the list of general objectives and omit those that are not in keeping with the faculty's agreed-upon philosophy.

Psychological Screen.   The application of the psychological screen is the next step in the Tyler model. To apply the screen, teachers must clarify the principles of learning that they believe to be sound. "A psychology of learning," said Tyler, "not only includes specific and definite findings but it also involves a unified formulation of a theory of learning which helps to outline the nature of the learning process, how it takes place, under what conditions, what sort of mechanisms operate and the like."[14] Effective application of this screen presupposes adequate training in educational psychology and in human growth and development by those charged with the task of curriculum development. Tyler explained the significance of the psychological screen:

---

[11]Johnson, "Definitions and Models," p. 132.
[12]Tyler, *Basic Principles,* p. 34.
[13]Ibid., pp. 33–36.
[14]Ibid., p. 41.

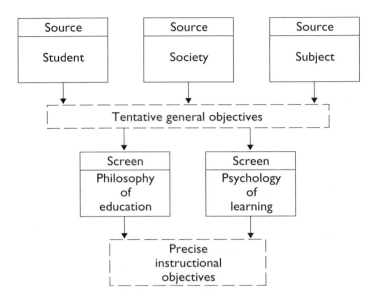

Figure 5.1 Tyler's curriculum rationale. Figure from W. James Popham and Eva L. Baker, *Establishing Instructional Goals* (Englewood Cliffs, N.J.: Prentice-Hall, 1970) p. 87. Based on the work of Ralph W. Tyler, *Basic Principles of Curriculum and Instruction* (Chicago: The University of Chicago Press, 1949), pp. 3–85. Reprinted by permission of the University of Chicago, publisher.

- A knowledge of the psychology of learning enables us to distinguish changes in human beings that can be expected to result from a learning process from those that cannot.
- A knowledge of the psychology of learning enables us to distinguish goals that are feasible from those that are likely to take a very long time or are almost impossible of attainment at the age level contemplated.
- Psychology of learning gives us some idea of the length of time required to attain an objective and the age levels at which the effort is most efficiently employed.[15]

After the curriculum planner has applied this second screen, his or her list of general objectives will be reduced, leaving those that are the most significant and feasible. Care is then taken to state the objectives in behavioral terms, which turns them into instructional, classroom objectives. We will return to the writing of behavioral objectives in Chapters 7, 8, and 10.

Tyler did not make use of a diagram in describing the process he recommended. However, W. James Popham and Eva L. Baker cast the model into the illustration shown in Figure 5.1.[16] In applying the Tyler rationale, Popham and Baker, advocates for the use of behavioral objectives, referred to the stage after the philosophical and psychological screenings as specification of "precise instructional objectives." Tyler

---

[15]Ibid., pp. 38–39.
[16]W. James Popham and Eva L. Baker, *Establishing Instructional Goals* (Englewood Cliffs, N.J.: Prentice-Hall, 1970), p. 87.

saw that stage as the identification of a small number of important objectives, though general in nature, yet still specific enough to incorporate content and behavioral aspects. Tyler left room, however, for curriculum workers to determine educational objectives in keeping with what they believe about learning.[17] In this respect Tyler's objectives, though behavioral in nature, may be somewhat less precise than those proposed by other behavioral objectives advocates.

For some reason, discussions of the Tyler model often stop after examining the first part of the model—the rationale for selecting educational objectives. Actually, Tyler's model goes beyond this process to describe three more steps in curriculum planning: selection, organization, and evaluation of learning experiences. He defined learning experiences as "the interaction between the learner and the external conditions in the environment to which he can react."[18] He suggested teachers give attention to learning experiences

- that will "develop skill in thinking"
- that will be "helpful in acquiring information"
- that will be "helpful in developing social attitudes"
- that will be "helpful in developing interests."[19]

He explained how to organize the experiences into units and described various evaluation procedures.[20] Although Tyler did not devote a chapter to a phase called direction of learning experiences (or implementation of instruction), we can infer that instruction must take place between the selection and organization of learning experiences and the evaluation of student achievement of these experiences.

Expanded Model.   We could, therefore, modify the diagram of Tyler's model by expanding it to include steps in the planning process after specifying instructional objectives. Figure 5.2 shows how such an expanded model might appear.

In discussing the Tyler rationale, Daniel and Laurel Tanner noted its debt to the progressive thought of John Dewey, H. H. Giles, S. P. McCutchen, and A. N. Zechiel.[21]

Although acknowledging that "the influence of Ralph Tyler on the history of curriculum development cannot be underemphasized," Patrick Slattery took the position that "postmodern curriculum development is challenging the traditional curriculum development model of Ralph Tyler."[22] He observed that "postmodern curriculum development is concerned with biographical and autobiographical narrative . . ."[23]

The Tanners faulted the rationale for its failure to show the interdependence of "the four functions in curriculum development (identifying objectives, selecting the means for the attainment of these objectives, organizing these means, and evaluating the outcomes)."[24] If curriculum planners consider the components to be separate and

---

[17]Tyler, *Basic Principles*, pp. 43, 50, 57

[18]Ibid., p. 63

[19]Ibid., Chapter 2.

[20]Ibid., Chapters 3 and 4.

[21]Daniel Tanner and Laurel Tanner, *Curriculum Development: Theory into Practice*, 3rd ed. (Upper Saddle River, N.J.: Prentice-Hall, 1995), p. 234.

[22]Patrick Slattery, *Curriculum Development in the Post Modern Era* (New York: Garland Publishing, 1995), p. 47.

[23]Ibid.

[24]Tanner and Tanner, *Curriculum Development*, p. 236.

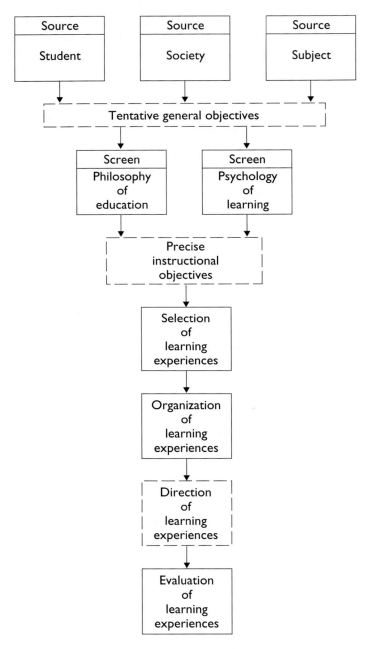

Figure 5.2 Tyler's curriculum rationale (expanded).

fail to understand the interaction among the sources, curriculum development can become too mechanical a process. Tyler himself did not perceive the rationale as a strictly prescribed sequence of steps to be followed without fail by curriculum planners. Evidence of this can be seen in a lesser-known, but more complex, model of the rationale presented with coauthor Mario Leyton Soto. This rendition of the rationale reveals the integration and interdependence of the various components.[25] The Tanners credited the Tyler model, however, as "a basis for consensus and . . . a paradigm for the field."[26]

THE TABA MODEL

Taba took what is known as a grassroots approach to curriculum development. She believed that the curriculum should be designed by the teachers rather than handed down by higher authority. Further, she felt that teachers should begin the process by creating specific teaching-learning units for their students in their schools rather than by engaging initially in creating a general curriculum design. Taba, therefore, advocated an inductive approach to curriculum development, starting with the specifics and building up to a general design as opposed to the more traditional deductive approach of starting with the general design and working down to the specifics.

Five-Step Sequence. Eschewing graphic exposition of her model, Taba listed a five-step sequence for accomplishing curriculum change, as follows:[27]

1. *Producing pilot units* representative of the grade level or subject area. Taba saw this step as linking theory and practice. She proposed the following eight-step sequence for curriculum developers who are producing pilot units.[28]
   a. *Diagnosis of needs.* The curriculum developer begins by determining the needs of the students for whom the curriculum is being planned. Taba directed the curriculum worker to diagnose the "gaps, deficiencies, and variations in [students'] backgrounds."[29]
   b. *Formulation of objectives.* After student needs have been diagnosed, the curriculum planner specifies objectives to be accomplished. Taba used the terms "goals" and "objectives" interchangeably, a point to which we will return later.
   c. *Selection of content.* The subject matter or topics to be studied stem directly from the objectives. Taba pointed out that not only must the objectives be considered in selecting content but also the "validity and significance" of the content chosen.[30]
   d. *Organization of content.* With the selection of content goes the task of deciding at what levels and in what sequences the subject matter will be placed. Matu-

[25]Mario Leyton Soto and Ralph W. Tyler, *Planeamiento Educational* (Santiago, Chile: Editorial Universitaria, 1969). See also Peter F. Oliva, *Developing the Curriculum,* 1st ed. (Boston: Little, Brown, 1982), pp. 159, 161, 162.

[26]Tanner and Tanner, *Curriculum Development,* p. 241.

[27]Taba, *Curriculum Development,* pp. 456–459.

[28]Ibid., pp. 345–379. On page 12 of her book Taba listed the first seven steps. See Chapter 11 of this text for discussion of the creation of units.

[29]Ibid., p. 12.

[30]Ibid.

rity of learners, their readiness to confront the subject matter, and their levels of academic achievement are factors to be considered in the appropriate placement of content.

e. *Selection of learning experiences.* The methodologies or strategies by which the learners become involved with the content must be chosen by the curriculum planners. Pupils internalize the content through the learning activities selected by the planner-teacher.

f. *Organization of learning activities.* The teacher decides how to package the learning activities and in what combinations and sequences they will be utilized. At this stage the teacher adapts the strategies to the particular students for whom he or she has responsibility.

g. *Determination of what to evaluate and of the ways and means of doing it.* The planner must decide whether objectives have been accomplished. The instructor selects from a variety of techniques appropriate means for assessing achievement of students and for determining whether the objectives of the curriculum have been met.

h. *Checking for balance and sequence.* Taba counseled curriculum workers to look for consistency among the various parts of the teaching-learning units, for proper flow of the learning experiences, and for balance in the types of learning and forms of expression.

2. *Testing experimental units.* Since the goal of this process is to create a curriculum encompassing one or more grade levels or subject areas and since teachers have written their pilot units with their own classrooms in mind, the units must now be tested "to establish their validity and teachability and to set their upper and lower limits of required abilities."[31]

3. *Revising and consolidating.* The units are modified to conform to variations in student needs and abilities, available resources, and different styles of teaching so that the curriculum may suit all types of classrooms. Taba would charge supervisors, the coordinators of curricula, and the curriculum specialists with the task of "stating the principles and theoretical considerations on which the structure of the units and the selection of content and learning activities are based and suggesting the limits within which modifications in the classroom can take place.[32] Taba recommended that such "considerations and suggestions might be assembled in a handbook explaining the use of the units."[33]

4. *Developing a framework.* After a number of units have been constructed, the curriculum planners must examine them as to adequacy of scope and appropriateness of sequence. The curriculum specialist would assume the responsibility of drafting a rationale for the curriculum that has been developed through this process.

5. *Installing and disseminating new units.* Taba called on administrators to arrange appropriate in-service training so that teachers may effectively put the teaching-learning units into operation in their classrooms.

---

[31]Ibid., p. 458.
[32]Ibid.
[33]Ibid., pp. 458–459.

Figure 5.3 Saylor, Alexander, and Lewis's conception of the curriculum planning process. From J. Galen Saylor, William M. Alexander, and Arthur J. Lewis, *Curriculum Planning for Better Teaching and Learning,* 4th ed., p. 30. (New York: Holt, Rinehart and Winston, 1981). Reproduced by permission of the publisher.

Taba's inductive model may not appeal to curriculum developers who prefer to consider the more global aspects of the curriculum before proceeding to specifics. Some planners might wish to see a model that includes steps in both diagnosing the needs of society and culture and in deriving needs from subject matter, philosophy, and learning theory. Taba, however, elaborated on these points in her text.[34]

Other planners may prefer to follow a deductive approach, starting with the general—specification of philosophy, aims, and goals—and moving to the specifics—objectives, instructional techniques, and evaluation. The remaining two models described in this chapter are deductive as is Tyler's.

THE SAYLOR, ALEXANDER, AND LEWIS MODEL

Saylor, Alexander, and Lewis conceptualized the *curriculum planning process* in the model shown in Figure 5.3.[35] To understand this model we must first analyze their concepts of *curriculum* and *curriculum plan.* Earlier in this text you encountered their

[34]Ibid., Part 1.
[35]Saylor, Alexander, and Lewis, *Curriculum Planning,* p. 30.

definition of curriculum: "a plan for providing sets of learning opportunities for persons to be educated."[36] However, the curriculum plan is not to be conceived as a single document but rather as "many smaller plans for particular portions of the curriculum."[37]

Goals, Objectives, and Domains.   The model indicates that the curriculum planners begin by specifying the major educational goals and specific objectives they wish to be accomplished. Saylor, Alexander, and Lewis classified sets of broad goals into four domains under which many learning experiences take place: personal development, social competence, continued learning skills, and specialization.[38] Once the goals, objectives, and domains have been established, the planners move into the process of designing the curriculum. The curriculum workers decide on the appropriate learning opportunities for each domain and how and when these opportunities will be provided. For example, will the curriculum be designed along the lines of academic disciplines, according to a pattern of social institutions, or in relation to student needs and interests?

Instructional Modes.   After the designs have been created—and there may be more than one—all teachers affected by a given part of the curriculum plan must create the instructional plans. They select the methods through which the curriculum will be related to the learners.[39] At this point in the model it would be helpful to introduce the term *instructional objectives*. Teachers would then specify the instructional objectives before selecting the strategies or modes of presentation.

Evaluation.   Finally, the curriculum planners and teachers engage in evaluation. They must choose from a wide variety of evaluation techniques. Saylor, Alexander, and Lewis proposed a design that would permit (1) evaluation of the total educational program, as well as (2) evaluation of the evaluation program itself.[40] The evaluation processes allow curriculum planners to determine whether or not the goals of the school and the objectives of instruction have been met.

Saylor, Alexander, and Lewis supplemented their model of the curriculum planning process with companion models depicting the elements of the curriculum system, the process of defining the goals and objectives of educational institutions, and curriculum evaluation.[41] Curriculum planners might find some synthesis of the model of the curriculum planning process with its companion models desirable. We will look at the Saylor, Alexander, and Lewis model of curriculum evaluation in Chapter 13.

SIMILARITIES AND DIFFERENCES AMONG MODELS

The models discussed reveal both similarities and differences. Tyler and Taba outlined certain steps to be taken in curriculum development. Saylor, Alexander, and Lewis charted the components of the curriculum development process (design, implementa-

---

[36]Ibid., p. 8.
[37]Ibid., p. 28.
[38]Ibid.
[39]Ibid., Chapter 6.
[40]Ibid., Chapter 7.
[41]Ibid., pp. 29, 165, 334.

tion, and evaluation) as opposed to actions taken by the curriculum workers (diagnosis of needs, formulation of objectives, and the like). Tyler's concept of sources and screens stands out in his model.

Models are inevitably incomplete; they do not and cannot show every detail and every nuance of a process as complicated as curriculum development. In one sense the originator of a model is saying, often in graphic form, "These are the features you should not forget." To depict every detail of the curriculum development process would require an exceedingly complex drawing or several models. One task in building a model for curriculum development is to determine what the most salient components in the process are—no easy task—and to limit the model to those components. Model builders feel themselves between the Scylla of oversimplification and the Charybdis of complexity to the point of confusion.

In looking at various models we cannot say that any one model is inherently superior to all other models. For example, some curriculum planners have followed the Tyler model for years with considerable success. Decker Walker spoke to the importance of Tyler's work when he said, "Ralph Tyler has had as much influence on the thought and practice of twentieth-century American education as any other individual, with the possible exception of John Dewey."[42] On the other hand, this success does not mean that the Tyler model, for example, represents the ultimate in models for curriculum development or that any model including Tyler's is universally accepted as a basis for curriculum development.[43]

Before choosing a model or designing a new model—certainly a viable alternative—curriculum planners might attempt to outline the criteria or characteristics they would look for in a model for curriculum improvement. They might agree that the model should show the following:

1. major components of the process, including stages of planning, implementation, and evaluation
2. customary, but not inflexible "beginning" and "ending" points
3. the relationship between curriculum and instruction
4. distinctions between curriculum and instructional goals and objectives
5. reciprocal relationships among components
6. a cyclical pattern
7. feedback lines
8. the possibility of entry at any point in the cycle
9. an internal consistency and logic

[42]Decker Walker, *Fundamentals of Curriculum* (San Diego: Harcourt Brace Jovanovich, 1990), p. 111.

[43]For additional evaluation and critiques of the Tyler rationale, see "Is the Tyler Rationale a suitable basis for current curriculum development?" *ASCD Update* 22, no. 6 (December 1980): 4–5. Replies to the question from Fenwick English, Dwayne Huebner, Rodgers Lewis, James Macdonald, Laurel Tanner, and Marilyn Winters. See also:

Herbert M. Kliebard, "The Tyler Rationale," *School Review* 78, no. 2 (February 1970): 259–272.

Herbert M. Kliebard, "Reappraisal: The Tyler Rationale," in William Pinar, ed., *Curriculum Theorizing: The Reconceptualists* (Berkeley, Calif.: McCutchan, 1975), pp. 70–83.

Herbert M. Kliebard, "The Tyler Rationale," in Arno Bellack and Herbert M. Kliebard, eds., *Curriculum and Evaluation* (Berkeley, Calif.: McCutchan, 1977), pp. 56–67.

John D. McNeil, *Curriculum: A Comprehensive Introduction*, 5th ed. (New York: HarperCollins, 1996), pp. 131–134.

William F. Pinar, ed., *Contemporary Curriculum Discourses* (Scottsdale, Ariz.: Gorsuch and Scarisbrick, 1988), pp. 7–8.

10. enough simplicity to be intelligible and feasible
11. components in the form of a diagram or chart

I would agree that these are reasonable criteria to follow, and, to this end, I will now propose a model incorporating these guidelines. The model will accomplish two purposes: (1) to suggest a system that curriculum planners might wish to follow and (2) to serve as the framework for explanations of phases or components of the process for curriculum improvement.

The model is not presented as the be-all and end-all of models for curriculum development but rather as an attempt to implement the aforementioned guidelines. The proposed model may be acceptable in its present form to curriculum planners, especially those who agree with a deductive, linear, and prescriptive approach. It may, at the same time, stimulate planners to improve the model or to create another that would better reflect their goals, needs, and beliefs.

THE OLIVA MODEL

In the following pages we will look briefly at a model consisting of twelve components. The subsequent chapters of Part III elaborate on each component. This model appears in Figure 5.4.

The Twelve Components.   The model charted in Figure 5.4 illustrates a comprehensive, step-by-step process that takes the curriculum planner from the sources of the curriculum to evaluation. In Chapters 6 through 13, we will examine each part of the model. Each component (designated by Roman numerals I through XII) will be described and illustrations will be given to guide curriculum planners and their coworkers. Let us now undertake a cursory overview of the model.

You will note that both squares and circles are used in the model. The squares are used to represent planning phases; the circles, operational phases. The process starts with component I, at which time the curriculum developers state the aims of education and their philosophical and psychological principles. These aims are beliefs that are derived from the needs of our society and the needs of individuals living in our society. This component incorporates concepts similar to Tyler's "screens."

Component II requires an analysis of the needs of the community in which the school is located, the needs of students served in that community, and the exigencies of the subject matter that will be taught in the given school. Sources of the curriculum are seen as cutting across components I and II. Whereas component I treats the needs of students and society in a more general sense, component II introduces the concept of needs of particular students in particular localities, because the needs of students in particular communities are not always the same as the general needs of students throughout our society.

Components III and IV call for specifying curricular goals and objectives based on the aims, beliefs, and needs specified in components I and II. A distinction that will be clarified later with examples is drawn between goals and objectives. The tasks of component V are to organize and implement the curriculum and to formulate and establish the structure by which the curriculum will be organized.

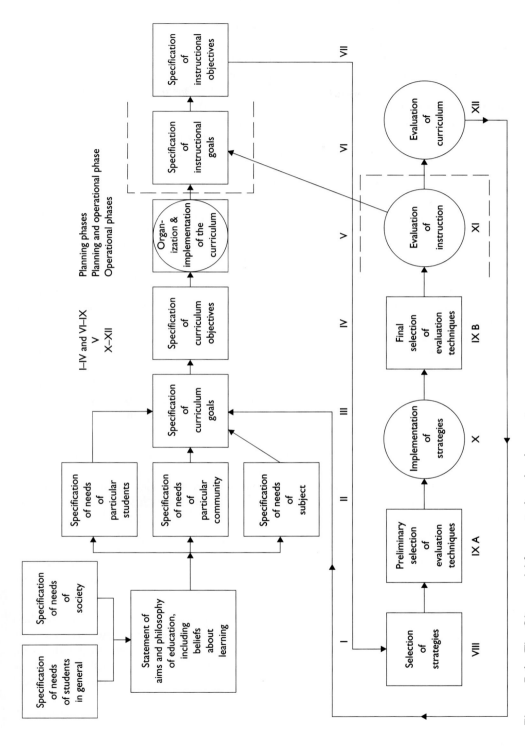

Figure 5.4 The Oliva model for curriculum development.

151

In components VI and VII an increasing level of specification is sought. Instructional goals and objectives are stated for each level and subject. Once again we will distinguish between goals and objectives and will show by illustration how the two differ.

After specifying instructional objectives, the curriculum worker moves to component VIII, at which point he or she chooses instructional strategies for use with students in the classroom. Simultaneously, the curriculum worker initiates preliminary selection of evaluation techniques, phase A of component IX. At this stage the curriculum planner thinks ahead and begins to consider ways he or she will assess student achievement. The implementation of instructional strategies—component X—follows.

After the students have been provided appropriate opportunity to learn (component X), the planner returns to the problem of selecting techniques for evaluating student achievement and the effectiveness of the instructor. Component IX, then, is separated into two phases: the first *precedes* the actual implementation of instruction (IXA) and the second *follows* the implementation (IXB). The instructional phase component (component X) provides the planner with the opportunity to refine, add to, and complete the selection of means to evaluate pupil performance.

Component XI is the stage at which evaluating instruction is carried out. Component XII completes the cycle with evaluation not of the student or the teacher but rather of the curricular program. In this model components I–IV and VI–IX are planning phases, whereas components X–XII are operational phases. Component V is both a planning and operational phase.

Like some other models, this model combines a scheme for curriculum development (components I–V and XII) and a design for instruction (components V–XI).

Important features of the model are the feedback lines that cycle back from the evaluation of the curriculum to the curriculum goals and from the evaluation of instruction to the instructional goals. These lines indicate the necessity for continuous revision of the components of their respective subcycles.

Use of the Model.   The model can be used in a variety of ways. First, the model offers a process for the complete development of a school's curriculum. The faculty of each special area—for example, language arts—can, by following the model, fashion a plan for the curriculum of that area and design ways in which it will be carried out through instruction, or the faculty may develop schoolwide, interdisciplinary programs that cut across areas of specialization such as career education, guidance, and extraclass activities.

Second, a faculty may focus on the curricular components of the model (components I–V and XII) to make programmatic decisions. Third, a faculty may concentrate on the instructional components (VI–XI).

Two Submodels.   This twelve-phase model integrates a general model for curriculum development with a general model for instruction. Components I–V and XII constitute a curriculum development submodel which I will refer to as the curriculum submodel. Components VI–XI constitute an instructional submodel. To distinguish between the curricular and instructional components, I have enclosed the instructional submodel within broken lines.

When the curricular submodel is followed, the curriculum planners must keep in mind that the task has not been completed until the curriculum goals and objectives are subsequently translated by them or others into instruction. Furthermore, when the instructional submodel is followed, the instructional planners must be aware of the curriculum goals and objectives of the school as a whole or of a given subject area or areas.

In order to keep the model as uncluttered as possible at this point, I have not attempted to show all the nuances of the model. At several places in subsequent chapters, certain refinements and embellishments of the model will be described.

For those who prefer a model in the form of steps instead of a diagram, below is a listing of the steps shown in Figure 5.4. The model sets forth the following steps:

1. Specify the needs of students in general.
2. Specify the needs of society.
3. Write a statement of philosophy and aims of education.
4. Specify the needs of students in your school(s).
5. Specify the needs of the particular community.
6. Specify the needs of the subject matter.
7. Specify the curriculum goals of your school(s).
8. Specify the curriculum objectives of your school(s).
9. Organize and implement the curriculum.
10. Specify instructional goals.
11. Specify instructional objectives.
12. Select instructional strategies.
13. Begin selection of evaluation techniques.
14. Implement instructional strategies.
15. Make final selection of evaluation techniques.
16. Evaluate instruction and modify instructional components.
17. Evaluate the curriculum and modify curricular components.

Steps 1–9 and 17 constitute a curriculum submodel; steps 10-16, an instructional submodel.

SUMMARY

Four models of curriculum development are presented in this chapter. Models can help us to conceptualize a process by showing certain principles and procedures. Whereas some models are in the form of diagrams, others are lists of steps that are recommended to curriculum workers. Some models are linear, step-by-step approaches; others allow for departure from a fixed sequence of steps. Some models offer an inductive approach; others follow a deductive approach. Some are prescriptive; others, descriptive.

Those who take leadership in curriculum development are encouraged to become familiar with various models, to try them out, and to select or develop the model that is most understandable and feasible to them and to the persons with whom they are working.

I have presented for consideration a model consisting of twelve components. This model is comprehensive in nature, encompassing both curricular and instructional development.

QUESTIONS FOR DISCUSSION

1. On what bases would you choose a model for curriculum development?
2. Who should decide which model for curriculum development to follow?
3. In your opinion which is better: an inductive or a deductive model for curriculum development?
4. What are the strengths and limitations of a linear model for curriculum development?
5. In your opinion which is better: a prescriptive or a descriptive model for curriculum development?

SUPPLEMENTARY EXERCISES

1. Define "sources" and "screens" as used by Ralph W. Tyler.
2. Explain why Tyler's model has been referred to as "linear" in nature and identify the presence or absence of linearity in each of the other models in this chapter.
3. Write a brief position paper, giving reasons for your position, on the question: "Is the Tyler rationale a suitable basis for current curriculum development?"
4. Cast Taba's steps for curriculum development into a diagrammed model.
5. Identify one or more domains in addition to the four suggested by Saylor, Alexander, and Lewis, or, alternatively, design your own pattern of domains.
6. Explain the meaning of the broken lines in the diagram of the Oliva model.
7. Explain why components X, XI, and XII of the Oliva model are shown as circles whereas the other components, except for component V, are shown as squares. Explain why component V is depicted with both a square and a circle.
8. Describe the four models of curriculum planning found in Geneva Gay's chapter in the 1980 Yearbook of the Association for Supervision and Curriculum Development (see bibliography). These models are the academic model, the experiential model, the technical model, and the pragmatic model.
9. Summarize George A. Beauchamp's concept of curriculum engineering (see bibliography).
10. Find or design a nonlinear model for curriculum development. For one example, see Mario Leyton Soto and Ralph W. Tyler, *Planeamiento Educacional* (see bibliography). This model is discussed in Peter F. Oliva, *Developing the Curriculum*, 1st ed. Little, Brown and Company, 1982, pp. 159, 161, 162.
11. Define curriculum engineering as used by Robert S. Zais (see bibliography) and report on one of the following models for curriculum engineering discussed by Zais:
    a. The Administrative (Line-Staff) Model
    b. The Grass-roots Model
    c. The Demonstration Model
    d. George Beauchamp's System
    e. Carl Rogers's Interpersonal Relations Model
12. Robert M. Gagné maintained that there is no such step in curriculum development as "selection of content" (see bibliography). State whether you agree and give reasons, citing quotations from the literature that support your position.

13. Describe the model of curricular and instructional planning and evaluation proposed by Mauritz Johnson, Jr., in *Intentionality in Education* (see bibliography).
14. Describe the Generic Curriculum Planning Model presented by Arthur W. Steller (see bibliography).
15. Describe the curriculum development models presented by Jerry J. Bellon and Janet R. Handler; H. H. Giles, S. P. McCutchen, and A. N. Zechiel; Francis P. Hunkins; George J. Posner and Alan N. Rudnitsky; David Pratt; and Decker F. Walker (see bibliography).
16. Report on any model for curriculum development described by John P. Miller and Wayne Seller that is different from the models described in this chapter (see bibliography).
17. Report on the curriculum planning model described by Weldon F. Zenger and Sharon K. Zenger (see bibliography) and tell how it differs from the models described in this chapter.
18. Define the term "postmodern curriculum development" as used by some writers on curriculum (see Pinar et al., 1996 and Slattery in bibliography.]

BIBLIOGRAPHY

Beauchamp, George A. *Curriculum Theory,* 4th ed. Itasca, Ill.: F. E. Peacocck, 1981.

Bellon, Jerry J. and Handler, Janet R. *Curriculum Development and Evaluation: A Design for Improvement.* Dubuque, Iowa: Kendall/Hunt, 1982.

Bloom, Benjamin S., ed. *Taxonomy of Educational Objectives: The Classification of Educational Goals: Handbook I: Cognitive Domain.* New York: Longman, 1956.

Foshay, Arthur W., ed. *Considered Action for Curriculum Improvement.* 1980 Yearbook. Alexandria, Va.: Association for Supervision and Curriculum Development, 1980.

Gagné, Robert M. "Curriculum Research and the Promotion of Learning." *Perspectives of Curriculum Evaluation,* AERA Monograph Series on Evaluation, no. 1, 19–23. Chicago: Rand McNally, 1967.

Gay, Geneva, "Conceptual Models of the Curriculum-Planning Process." In Arthur W. Foshay, ed. In *Considered Action for Curriculum Improvement.* 1980 Yearbook, 120–143. Alexandria, Va.: Association for Supervision and Curriculum Development, 1980.

Giles, H. H., McCutchen, S. P., and Zechiel, A. N. *Exploring the Curriculum.* New York: Harper, 1942.

Jackson, Philip W., ed. *Handbook of Research on Curriculum.* New York: Macmillan, 1992.

Johnson, Mauritz, Jr. "Definitions and Models in Curriculum Theory." Educational Theory 17, no. 2 (April 1967): 127–140.

———. *Intentionality in Education.* Albany, N.Y. Center for Curriculum Research and Services, 1977.

Kliebard, William M. "Reappraisal: The Tyler Rationale." In William Pinar, ed. *Curriculum Theorizing: The Reconceptualists.* Berkeley, Calif.: McCutchan, 1975, pp. 70–83.

———. "The Tyler Rationale." In Arno Bellack and Herbert M. Kliebard, eds. Curriculum and Evaluation. Berkeley, Calif.: McCutchan, 1977, pp. 56–67.

———. "The Tyler Rationale." *School Review* 78, no. 2 (February 1970): 259–272.

Krathwohl, David R., Bloom, Benjamin S., and Masia, Bertram B. Taxonomy of Educational Objectives: *The Classification of Educational Goals: Handbook II: Affective Domain.* New York: Longman, 1964.

Leyton Soto, Mario and Tyler, Ralph W. *Planeamiento Educacional.* Santiago, Chile: Editorial Universitaria, 1969.

McNeil, John D. *Curriculum: A Comprehensive Introduction,* 5th ed. New York: HarperCollins, 1996.

Miller, John P. and Seller, Wayne. *Curriculum : Perspectives and Practice.* White Plains, N.Y.: Longman, 1985, Chapter 9.

Oliva, Peter F. and George E. Pawlas. *Supervision for Today's Schools,* 6th ed. Part III. New York: Wiley, 2001.

Ornstein, Allan C. and Behar, Linda S., eds. *Contemporary Issues in Curriculum.* Boston: Allyn and Bacon, 1995.

Pinar, William, F., ed. *Contemporary Curriculum Discourses.* Scottsdale, Ariz.: Gorsuch and Scarisbrick, 1988.

———. *Curriculum Theorizing: The Reconceptualists.* Berkeley, Calif.: McCutchan, 1975.

————, Reynolds, William D., Slattery, Patrick, and Taubman, Peter M. *Understanding Curriculum: An Introduction to the Study of Historical and Contemporary Discourses.* New York: Peter Lang, 1996.

Popham, W. James. *Evaluating Instruction.* Englewood Cliffs, N.J.: Prentice-Hall, 1973.

Pratt, David. *Curriculum Design and Development.* New York: Harcourt Brace Jovanovich, 1980.

Saylor, J. Galen, Alexander, William M., and Lewis, Arthur J. *Curriculum Planning for Better Teaching and Learning,* 4th ed. New York: Holt, Rinehart and Winston, 1981.

Slattery, Patrick. *Curriculum Development in the Postmodern Era.* New York: Garland, 1995.

Steller, Arthur W., "Curriculum Planning," in Fenwick W. English, ed., *Fundamental Curriculum Decisions.* 1983 Yearbook. Alexandria, Va.: Association for Supervision and Curriculum Development, 1983.

Taba, Hilda. *Curriculum Development: Theory and Practice.* New York: Harcourt Brace Jovanovich, 1962.

Tanner, Daniel and Tanner, Laurel. *Curriculum Development: Theory into Practice,* 3rd ed. New York: Merrill, 1995.

Tyler, Ralph W. *Basic Principles of Curriculum and Instruction.* Chicago: University of Chicago Press, 1949.

Walker, Decker F. "A Naturalistic Model for Curriculum Development." *School Review* 80, no. 1 (November 1971): 51–67.

Wiles, Jon and Bondi, Joseph. *Curriculum Development: A Guide to Practice,* 4th ed. New York: Merrill, l993.

Zais, Robert S. *Curriculum: Principles and Foundations.* New York: Harper & Row, 1976. Chapter 19.

Zenger, Weldon F. and Zenger, Sharon K. "Planning for Curriculum Development: A Model for Administrators." *NASSP Bulletin* 68, no. 471 (April 1984): 17–28.

CHAPTER 6

PHILOSOPHY AND AIMS OF EDUCATION

After studying this chapter you should be able to:

1. Explain how aims of education are derived.
2. Cite commonly voiced statements of the aims of education.
3. Write statements of the aims of education.
4. Outline major beliefs of four well-known schools of philosophy.
5. Draft a school philosophy that could be submitted to a school faculty for discussion.

USING THE PROPOSED MODEL

A comprehensive model for the process of curriculum development, consisting of twelve phases or components, was presented in Chapter 5. For a moment, let's take another look at it (see Figure 5.4), and then I'll underscore some of its characteristics.

Examining the model reveals the following special characteristics:

1. *The model flows from the most general (aims of education) to the most specific (evaluation techniques).* Beginning here and in the remaining chapters of Part III, I will describe each component and define its terms in such a way as to show this flow.

2. *The model can be followed by curriculum planning groups (or even to some extent by individuals) in whole or in part.* The model allows for a comprehensive, holistic study of the curriculum. Given the many demands on the time of teachers, administrators, and others, it is likely that a complete look at the curriculum from the aims of education (component I) to evaluation of the curriculum (component XII) will be carried out only periodically. Although somewhat arbitrary, reassessment and revision of the various phases might be considered on the schedule shown in Box 6.1.

BOX 6.1

SUGGESTED SCHEDULE FOR REASSESSING CURRICULUM DEVELOPMENT COMPONENTS

Aims of education	In depth:	every 10 years
	Limited:	every 5 years
Assessment of needs	In depth:	every 3 years
	Limited:	every year
Curriculum goals	In depth:	every 2 years
	Limited:	every year
Curriculum objectives	In depth:	every 2 years
	Limited:	every year
Instructional goals	In depth:	every year
	Limited:	continuously
Instructional objectives	In depth:	every year
	Limited:	continuously
Organization and implementation of the curriculum	In depth:	every 10 years
	Limited:	every year
Other components	Continuously	

Faculties may wish to set their own schedules for considering the various components. Those components that are closest to the faculty, involve fewer persons, are more easily manageable, and are less costly in time and money might be reassessed with greater frequency than those components that are more remote, involve many persons, are more difficult to manage, and are more costly.

3. *A single curriculum group, like the curriculum committee of an individual school, department, or grade, will not carry out all phases of the model by itself.* Various groups, subgroups, and individuals will assume responsibility for different parts of the model. One group (for example, the school's curriculum council) may work on the first component, the aims of education. A subgroup may conduct a needs assessment and study the sources of curricular needs. The school's curriculum council may attempt to define schoolwide curriculum goals and objectives while committees within the various disciplines identify curriculum goals and objectives within particular fields. Individual faculty members and groups in various grades and departments will be engaged in specifying instructional goals and objectives. Decisions at any phase that have relevance to the entire school may be presented to the total faculty for its information and support or rejection. Throughout the process, decisions made by any of the subgroups must be presented so that rela-

tionships among the various components are clearly understood. In this respect the curriculum council of the school will serve as a coordinating body.

4. *With modifications, the model can be followed at any level or sector of curriculum planning.* Parts of the model may also be applied at the various levels and sectors that were discussed in Chapter 3.

AIMS OF EDUCATION

PROLIFERATION OF TERMS

The educational literature uses a proliferation of terms, rather loosely and often interchangeably, to signify terminal expectations of education. Educators speak of "outcomes," "aims," "ends," "purposes," "functions," "goals," and "objectives." Although these terms may be used synonymously in common language, it is helpful if distinctions are made in pedagogical language.

In this book the term "outcome" applies to terminal expectations generally. "Aims" are equated with "ends," "purposes," "functions," and "universal goals." The aims of education are the very broad, general statements of the purposes of education; they are meant to give general direction to education throughout the country. Decker F. Walker and Jonas F. Soltis likened aims of education to wishes for "something desirable for people in general *that is only possible for them to have because of something they learn.*"[1]

In this text "curriculum goals," "curriculum objectives," "instructional goals," and "instructional objectives" are separate entities of special relevance to the local school or school system. Curriculum goals are defined as general, programmatic expectations without criteria of achievement or mastery, whereas curriculum objectives are specific, programmatic targets with criteria of achievement and, therefore, are measurable. The curriculum objectives stem from the curriculum goals.[2] Both curriculum goals and curriculum objectives trace their sources to the school's philosophy and the statement of aims of education.

Instructional goals are statements of instructional targets in general, nonobservable terms without criteria of achievement, whereas instructional objectives are expected learner behaviors formulated, with possible exceptions for those in the affective domain, in measurable and observable terms.[3] Instructional objectives are derived from instructional goals, and both instructional goals and instructional objectives originate from the curriculum goals and objectives.

The aims of education have special relevance to the nation as a whole. We will talk about aims of our educational system, society, and country. Presumably, in former days we could have set forth regional aims for the North, South, Midwest, and West. As we move into the twenty-first century, however, it would seem an anachronism to promote regional aims as if the broad purposes of education in California, for

[1]Decker F. Walker and Jonas F. Soltis, *Curriculum and Aims*, 3rd ed. (New York: Teachers College Press, 1997) p. 12.
[2]See Chapter 8 for discussion of curriculum goals and objectives.
[3]See Chapter 10 for discussion of instructional goals and objectives.

example, were different from those in New York or the purposes of education in Indiana different from those of Mississippi.

GLOBAL AIMS

It is possible, even desirable, to define aims of education on a global scale, and sometimes such definitions are attempted. The United Nations Educational, Scientific, and Cultural Organization (UNESCO) is the foremost exponent of attempts on a worldwide scale to state aims of education for humanity. Among the aims of education that UNESCO seeks to promote are these:

- fostering international understanding among all peoples of the world
- improving the standard of living of people in the various countries
- solving continuing problems that plague humanity, such as war, disease, hunger, and unemployment

Similar organizations, such as the Organization of American States, are also concerned with the aims of education on an international scale. The few Americans who participate in such organizations find some opportunity for expressing aims of education that can apply across national boundaries. More common are statements of aims of education by the respective nations of the world to guide the development of their own educational systems.

In any discipline, the field of curriculum notwithstanding, the specialist seeks to find or develop generalizations or rules that apply in most situations. On the other hand, the specialist must always be aware that exceptions may be found to most rules. Although we may hold to the view that curriculum development is a group process and is more effective as a result of that process, we must admit that individuals can carry out any of the components of the suggested model of curriculum development. It would seem at first sight, for example, that defining aims of education to which the entire country might subscribe would certainly be a group project. However, as we shall see, several significant statements of aims of education have been made over the years by prominent individuals. When statements are generated by individuals instead of groups, members of the social structure for which the aims are intended become, in effect, consumers and interpreters of the ideas of individuals—certainly a tenable procedure.

That statements of aims, goals, and objectives may originate from individuals rather than groups should not invalidate them. It might be said that "while individuals propose, the group will dispose." Groups should react to coherent statements in a deliberative manner. The model of curriculum development should not be construed to eliminate spontaneous, individual efforts at curriculum development. Some of the most successful innovations in schools have been effected as the result of the work of independently motivated mavericks on the school's staff.

STATEMENTS OF PURPOSES

We are confronted with aims of education when we read statements of purposes promulgated by various societies around the world, for example:

- to inculcate family values
- to prepare youth to fit into a planned society
- to promote free enterprise
- to further the glorious revolution
- to create citizens who will serve the fatherland
- to prepare an enlightened citizenry
- to nurture the Islamic culture
- to correct social ills
- to promote the Judeo-Christian heritage

We encounter aims of education in a descriptive form when someone makes declarations like the following:

- Education is life, not preparation for life.
- Education is the molding of the young to the values of the old.
- Education is the transmission of the cultural heritage.
- Education is vocational training.
- Education is the liberal arts.
- Education is training in socialization.
- Education is intellectual development.
- Education is personal development.
- Education is socialization of groups and individuals.
- Education is the development of technological skills.

We can even find implied aims of education in slogans like these:

- If you think education is expensive, try ignorance.
- If you can read this sign, thank a teacher.
- A sound mind in a sound body.

Presumably ever since primitive peoples discovered that the flint axe was more effective for killing game than a wooden club, that animal skin protected their bodies against the elements, and that roast boar was superior to raw, they continually discussed what training they must provide their Neanderthal young so that they could cope with their environment. In their own primitive way they must have dealt with the heady topic of the purposes of education in Neanderthal Land.

Today, many thousands of years later, people still affirm coping with the environment as a central purpose of education. The common term to express this purpose is "survival skills." Instead of learning coping skills like stalking a gazelle, frightening a tiger, and spearing a fish, today's children must master the basic academic skills, learn to conserve resources, learn to live on a more densely populated planet, develop computer literacy, and know how to earn a legitimate living. Sometimes, as has been the case throughout the history of humankind, the martial arts become survival skills. Not only do the martial arts become a priority when a nation is confronted by an enemy from beyond its borders, but it is an unfortunate commentary on today's civilization that many children and adults are flocking to self-defense and weapons classes so that they can protect themselves from predators on the streets of many urban areas.

DERIVATION OF AIMS

The aims of education are derived from examining the needs of children and youth in our American society, from analyzing our culture, and from studying the various needs of our society. Given the historic development of nations with their own institutions, mores, and values, and often their own language, no two countries exhibit exactly the same needs. One does not have to be an anthropologist to recognize that the needs of Japanese, Chinese, Russian, English, Mexican, or Tahitian youngsters are not identical to those of American youth. The automobile, for example, has become a "need" of American high school youth if we judge by the school parking lot crammed with vehicles of students. Nor is it a rare occurrence any more to see not only American adults in stores or cars with a cellular phone glued to their ears but also students trotting around school campuses with this "needed" application of satellite technology.

Few countries have such a heterogeneous population as the United States. A comment often heard about people in the Sunbelt cities of America, "Everybody here is from some place else," might be extended to America in toto. We are a nation of immigrants who have brought, as some say, both the best and the worst traits of the societies that we left. We cannot even claim the Native Americans, who were here first, as indigenous to America, for theory holds that they themselves migrated out of Asia across the Bering Strait.

Such heterogeneity makes it extremely difficult to reach consensus on aims of education and particularly on values central to aims. Many years ago the National Education Association attempted to identify moral and spiritual values that it believed should be taught in the public schools.[4] They listed the following ten values:

1. human personality
2. moral responsibility
3. institutions as the servants of men
4. common consent
5. devotion to truth
6. respect for excellence
7. moral equality
8. brotherhood
9. the pursuit of happiness
10. spiritual enrichment

The assumption was made that these are common values held by a majority of the people of the society at that particular time. On how many of these values could we still reach consensus? James Patterson and Peter Kim surveyed in 1991 the current status of Americans' adherence to moral values and found a pronounced absence of consensus on values. Some of the beliefs and behaviors revealed by this study run counter to the more traditional conception of moral and spiritual values.[5] The specter of indoctrination has loomed so large that educators are often hesitant to identify broad-based,

---

[4]Educational Policies Commission, *Moral and Spiritual Values in the Public Schools* (Washington, D.C.: National Education Association, 1951), pp. 17–34.

[5]James Patterson and Peter Kim, *The Day America Told the Truth: What People Really Think About Everything That Really Matters* (New York: Prentice-Hall, 1991).

common, secular values to which Americans as a whole can subscribe. Less concerned about indoctrination than about the absence of moral education, the National Conference of Catholic Bishops and the Synagogue Council of America issued a joint report in the spring of 1990 in which they advocated a new effort on the part of the public schools to teach shared moral values.[6]

We are witnessing renewed interest in character education in the schools. William J. Bennett and Michael S. Josephson, for example, have directed recent attention to the need for ethical values in our society. *The Book of Virtues: A Treasury of Great Moral Stories,* edited by Bennett, spoke to values such as to self-discipline and faith.[7]

Josephson, founder of the Institute of Ethics, has enlisted the aid of a number of national organizations to foster character education. Input gathered from young people and adults identified six broad ethical values worthy of promoting: trustworthiness, respect, responsibility, fairness and justice, caring, and citizenship. Each of these broad values subsumes a number of related values.[8] A consortium of twenty-seven organizations known as the Character Counts! Coalition encourage the teaching of these values to young people in school and out. The U.S. Congress gave added emphasis to the teaching of values when it proclaimed a National Character Counts Week. Affirming an interest in character education the U.S. Department of Education in the Spring of 1999 awarded grants under its Partnership in Education Pilot Projects for school districts and communities in nine states[9] to develop programs to teach common values and ethics.

The 26th Annual Phi Delta Kappa/Gallup Poll found that fifty-seven percent of public school parents in 1994 supported character education in the public schools. The poll discovered overwhelming support for specific values similar to those addressed by Bennett and Josephson, namely values like respect for others, hard work, and fairness.[10] We will return to the question of teaching values when we examine the issue of religion in the schools in Chapter 14.

Salad Bowl Versus Melting Pot. As our heterogeneous population reveals plural rather than common values, the "salad bowl" concept now challenges the old "melting pot" idea. Some people argue that since few, if any, common values exist in our society, we should no longer strive to assimilate values but should collect and assemble the diverse values in a saladlike concoction that preserves the essence of each (like a tasty fruit salad, for example).[11] If we make this dilemma an either/or question, we create a false dichotomy. We need the salad bowl concept to preserve the values on which Americans are divided, such as materialistic versus nonmaterialistic goals, pro-

[6]See press report, *The New York Times,* June 20, 1990: A12.

[7]William J. Bennett, ed., *The Book of Virtues: A Treasury of Great Moral* Stories (New York: Simon and Schuster, 1993). See also William J. Bennett, *Our Children and Our Country: Improving America's Schools and Affirming the Common Culture* (New York: Simon and Schuster, 1988), Chapter 9 on moral literacy and character formation.

[8]Michael Josephson, *Excerpts from Easier Said Than Done: A Common Sense Approach to Ethical Decision Making,* Unpublished draft. Marina del Rey, Calif.: Josephson Institute of Ethics, 1995, p. 53. Reprinted by permission.

[9]Georgia, Illinois, Kansas, New Hampshire, New Mexico, North Carolina, North Dakota, Oklahoma, and Pennsylvania.

[10]Stanley M. Elam, Lowell C. Rose, and Alec M. Gallup, "The 26th Annual Phi Delta Kappa/Gallup Poll of the Public's Attitudes Toward the Public Schools," *Phi Delta Kappan* 76, no. 1 (September 1994): 49–50.

[11]See Theodore R. Sizer, "Education and Assimilation: A Fresh Plea for Pluralism," *Phi Delta Kappan* 58, no. 1 (September 1976): 31–35.

choice versus "right to life," and sectarian versus secular goals. On the other hand, we need the melting pot concept to preserve fundamental, overarching values that guide us as a nation.[12]

In recent years the salad bowl/melting pot controversy has intensified. Whether to promote multicultural values or common values of American society is a highly charged issue both in public schools and on college campuses. We will return to this issue in Chapter 14. As we examine statements of aims of education, we soon discover that these statements are, in effect, philosophical positions based on some set of values and are derived from an analysis of society and its children and youth.

STATEMENTS BY PROMINENT INDIVIDUALS AND GROUPS

To gain a perception of statements of educational aims, let's sample a few of the better known ones proffered by various individuals and groups over the years. In 1916 John Dewey described the functions of education in a number of ways, including its socialization of the child and its facilitation of personal growth.[13] Putting these concepts into the form of aims of education, we could say that, according to Dewey, the aims of education are (1) to socialize the young, thereby transforming both the young and society, and (2) to develop the individual in all his or her physical, mental, moral, and emotional capacities.

Dewey made it clear that the school is an agency for socializing the child:

> I believe that all education proceeds by the participation of the individual in the social consciousness of the race. . . . the only true education comes through the stimulation of the child's powers by the demands of the social situations in which he finds himself. . . . this educational process has two sides—one psychological and one sociological—and that neither can be subordinated to the other, or neglected, without evil results following. Of these two sides, the psychological is the basis. . . . knowledge of social conditions, of the present state of civilization, is necessary in order properly to interpret the child's powers. . . . In sum, I believe that the individual who is to be educated is a social individual, and that society is an organic union of individuals. . . . I believe that the school is primarily a social institution.[14]

Dewey elaborated on his conception of education as growth in the following terms:

> One net conclusion is that life is development, and that developing, growing, is life. Translated into its educational equivalents, that means (i) that the educational process has no end beyond itself; it is its own end; and that (ii) the educational process is one of continual reorganizing, reconstructing, transforming. . . . Normal child and normal adult alike, in other words, are engaged in growing. . . . Since in reality there is nothing to which growth is relative save more growth, there is nothing to which education is subordinate save more education.[15]

---

[12]See Richard Mitchell, *The Leaning Tower of Babel and Other Affronts by the Underground Grammarian* (Boston: Little, Brown, 1984), pp. 113–116.

[13]John Dewey, *Democracy and Education: An Introduction to the Philosophy of Education* (New York: Macmillan, 1916; New York: Free Press, 1966), Chapters 2 and 4.

[14]John Dewey, *My Pedagogic Creed* (Washington, D.C.: Progressive Education Association, 1929), pp. 3–6.

[15]Dewey, *Democracy and Education*, pp. 59–60.

The National Education Association's Commission on the Reorganization of Secondary Education in 1918 spoke to the role of education in our democratic society in this way: "Education in a democracy, both within and without the school, should develop in each individual the knowledge, interests, ideals, habits, and powers whereby he will find his place and use that place to shape both himself and society toward even nobler ends."[16]

The Educational Policies Commission of the National Education Association in 1937 related the aim of education to democracy as follows:

> In any realistic definition of education for the United States, therefore, must appear the whole philosophy and practice of democracy. Education cherishes and inculcates its moral values, disseminates knowledge necessary to its functioning, spreads information relevant to its institutions and economy, keeps alive the creative and sustaining spirit without which the latter is dead.[17]

In 1943—in the midst of the Second World War—James B. Conant, president of Harvard University, appointed a committee of professors from the fields of education and the liberal arts and sciences to examine the place of general (i.e., required, liberal) education in American society. The Harvard Committee on General Education took the position that the aim of education was "to prepare an individual to become an expert both in some particular vocation or art and in the general art of the free man and the citizen."[18] To accomplish this aim the Harvard committee recommended a prescribed set of subjects, including English, science, mathematics, and the social studies, for all secondary school pupils.[19]

Statements of aims of education repeatedly address great themes like democracy and the progress of humanity. In 1961 the National Education Association's Educational Policies Commission elaborated on the role of education in solving the problems of humanity:

> Many profound changes are occurring in the world today, but there is a fundamental force contributing to all of them. That force is the expanding role accorded in modern life to the rational powers of man. By using these powers to increase his knowledge, man is attempting to solve the riddles of life, space, and time which have long intrigued him.[20]

Before the Committee on Appropriations of the United States House of Representatives of the Eighty-Seventh Congress in 1962, Vice-Admiral Hyman G. Rickover, generally acknowledged as the father of the nuclear submarine, testified on distinctions between American and British educational systems and formulated for the committee the aims of education as he saw them:

---

[16]Commission on the Reorganization of Secondary Education, *Cardinal Principles of Secondary Education* (Washington, D.C.: United States Office of Education, Bulletin 35, 1918), p. 9.

[17]Educational Policies Commission, *The Unique Function of Education in American Democracy* (Washington, D.C.: National Education Association, 1937), p. 89.

[18]Harvard Committee on General Education, *General Education in a Free Society* (Cambridge, Mass.: Harvard University Press, 1945), p. 54.

[19]Ibid., pp. 99–100.

[20]Educational Policies Commission, *The Central Purpose of American Education* (Washington, D.C.: National Education Association, 1961), p. 89.

> The school's major objective should be to send its graduates into the world equipped with the knowledge they will need to live successfully, hence happily. . . . A school system performs its proper task when it does a first-rate job of equipping children with the requisite knowledge and intellectual skill for successful living in a complex modern society. . . . There is general agreement abroad that a school must accomplish three difficult tasks: First, it must transmit to the pupil a substantial body of knowledge; second, it must develop in him the necessary intellectual skill to apply this knowledge to the problems he will encounter in later life; and third, it must inculcate in him the habit of judging issues on the basis of verified fact and logical reasoning.[21]

Mortimer J. Adler expressed the aim of education and schooling as follows: "The ultimate goal of the educational process is to help human beings become educated persons. Schooling is the preparatory stage; it forms the habit of learning and provides the means for continuing to learn after all schooling is completed."[22]

John I. Goodlad addressed the themes of social purposes served by the schools, educational goals and aims, and school goals. He divided the school goals into four categories: academic, vocational, social and civic, and personal. He and his colleagues analyzed approximately a hundred goals from various sources and refined them into a list of ten categories that they saw as encompassing generally accepted goals for schooling in the United States (Box 6.2).

Theodore R. Sizer, who was instrumental in the formation of the Coalition of Essential Schools in 1984, wove into his narrative of the fictitious Franklin High School the purposes of schooling and at the same time pointed up an American dilemma: " . . . some Americans do not see the schools as engines both of information and of intellectual liberation. Indeed, they find the latter—especially when so described—to be intolerable."[23]

Conflict over what education should be like dates back to ancient times as Herbert M. Kliebard pointed out in quoting from Aristotle's *Politics:*

> At present opinion is divided about the subjects of education. All do not take the same view of what should be learned by the young, either with a view to plain goodness or with a view to the best life possible; nor is opinion clear whether education should be directed mainly to understanding, or mainly to moral character. If we look at actual practice, the result is sadly confusing; it throws no light on the problem whether the proper studies to be followed are those which are useful in life, or those which make for goodness, or those which advance the bounds of knowledge. Each sort of study receives some votes in favor.[24]

This amazingly pertinent observation from ancient Greece more than 2000 years before the Christian era might well have come from the word processor of an author at the beginning of the twenty-first century. In Chapter 9 you will encounter additional

---

[21]H. G. Rickover, *Education for All Children: What We Can Learn From England: Hearings Before the Committee on Appropriations, House of Representatives, Eighty-Seventh Congress, Second Session* (Washington, D.C.: U.S. Government Printing Office, 1962), pp. 14, 17, 18.

[22]Mortimer J. Adler, *The Paideia Proposal: An Educational Manifesto* (New York: Macmillan, 1982), p. 10.

[23]Theodore R. Sizer, *Horace's School: Redesigning the American High School* (Boston: Houghton Mifflin, 1992), p. 127.

[24]Herbert M. Kliebard, "The Effort to Reconstruct the Modern American Curriculum," in *The Curriculum: Problems, Politics, and Possibilities,* 2nd ed. (Albany, N.Y.: State University of New York Press, 1998), p. 21 as quoted from Aristotle, *Politics* (New York: Oxford University Press, 1945), p. 244.

BOX 6.2

GOALS FOR SCHOOLING IN THE U.S.

A. Academic Goals
   1. Mastery of basic skills and fundamental processes
      1.1 Learn to read, write, and handle basic arithmetical operations.
      1.2 Learn to acquire ideas through reading and listening.
      1.3 Learn to communicate ideas through writing and speaking.
      1.4 Learn to utilize mathematical concepts.
      1.5 Develop the ability to utilize available sources of information.
   2. Intellectual development
      2.1 Develop the ability to think rationally, including problem-solving skills, application of principles of logic, and skill in using different modes of inquiry.
      2.2 Develop the ability to use and evaluate knowledge, i.e., critical and independent thinking that enables one to make judgments and decisions in a wide variety of life roles—citizen, consumer, worker, etc.—as well as in intellectual activities.
      2.3 Accumulate a general fund of knowledge, including information and concepts in mathematics, literature, natural science, and social science.
      2.4 Develop positive attitudes toward intellectual activity, including curiosity and a desire for further learning.
      2.5 Develop an understanding of changes in society.
B. Vocational Goals
   3. Career education-vocational education
      3.1 Learn how to select an occupation that will be personally satisfying and suitable to one's skills and interests.
      3.2 Learn to make decisions based on an awareness and knowledge of career options.
      3.3 Learn salable skills and specialized knowledge that will prepare one to become economically independent.
      3.4 Learn habits and attitudes, such as pride in good workmanship, that will make one a productive participant in economic life.
      3.5 Learn positive attitudes toward work, including acceptance of the necessity of making a living and an appreciation of the social value and dignity of work.
C. Social, Civic, and Cultural Goals
   4. Interpersonal understandings
      4.1 Develop a knowledge of opposing value systems and their influence on the individual and society.
      4.2 Develop an understanding of how members of a family function under different family patterns as well as within one's own family.
      4.3 Develop skill in communicating effectively in groups.
      4.4 Develop the ability to identify with and advance the goals and concerns of others.
      4.5 Learn to form productive and satisfying relations with others based on respect, trust, cooperation, consideration, and caring.

(Continued)

Box 6.2 Continued

    4.6 Develop a concern for humanity and an understanding of international relations.

    4.7 Develop an understanding and appreciation of cultures different from one's own.

5. Citizenship participation

    5.1 Develop historical perspective.

    5.2 Develop knowledge of the basic workings of the government.

    5.3 Develop a willingness to participate in the political life of the nation and the community.

    5.4 Develop a commitment to the values of liberty, government by consent of the governed, representational government, and one's responsibility for the welfare of all.

    5.5 Develop an understanding of the interrelationships among complex organizations and agencies in a modern society, and learn to act in accordance with it.

    5.6 Exercise the democratic right to dissent in accordance with personal conscience.

    5.7 Develop economic and consumer skills necessary for making informed choices that enhance one's quality of life.

    5.8 Develop an understanding of the basic interdependence of the biological and physical resources of the environment.

    5.9 Develop the ability to act in light of this understanding of interdependence.

6. Enculturation

    6.1 Develop insight into the values and characteristics, including language, of the civilization of which one is a member.

    6.2 Develop an awareness and understanding of one's cultural heritage and become familiar with the achievements of the past that have inspired and influenced humanity.

    6.3 Develop understanding of the manner in which traditions from the past are operative today and influence the direction and values of society.

    6.4 Understand and adopt the norms, values, and traditions of the groups of which one is a member.

    6.5 Learn how to apply the basic principles and concepts of the fine arts and humanities to the appreciation of the aesthetic contributions of other cultures.

7. Moral and ethical character

    7.1 Develop the judgment to evaluate events and phenomena as good or evil.

    7.2 Develop a commitment to truth and values.

    7.3 Learn to utilize values in making choices.

    7.4 Develop moral integrity.

    7.5 Develop an understanding of the necessity for moral conduct.

D. Personal Goals

8. Emotional and physical well-being

    8.1 Develop the willingness to receive emotional impressions and to expand one's affective sensitivity.

    8.2 Develop the competence and skills for continuous adjustment and emotional stability, including coping with social change.

(Continued)

Box 6.2 Continued

8.3 Develop a knowledge of one's own body and adopt health practices that support and sustain it, including avoiding the consumption of harmful or addictive substances.

8.4 Learn to use leisure time effectively.

8.5 Develop physical fitness and recreational skills.

8.6 Develop the ability to engage in constructive self-criticism.

9. Creativity and aesthetic expression

9.1 Develop the ability to deal with problems in original ways.

9.2 Develop the ability to be tolerant of new ideas.

9.3 Develop the ability to be flexible and to consider different points of view.

9.4 Develop the ability to experience and enjoy different forms of creative expression.

9.5 Develop the ability to evaluate various forms of aesthetic expression.

9.6 Develop the willingness and ability to communicate through creative work in an active way.

9.7 Seek to contribute to cultural and social life through one's artistic, vocational, and avocational interests.

10. Self-realization

10.1 Learn to search for meaning in one's activities, and develop a philosophy of life.

10.2 Develop the self-confidence necessary for knowing and confronting one's self.

10.3 Learn to assess realistically and live with one's limitations and strengths.

10.4 Recognize that one's self-concept is developed in interaction with other people.

10.5 Develop skill in making decisions with purpose.

10.6 Learn to plan and organize the environment in order to realize one's goals.

10.7 Develop willingness to accept responsibility for one's own decisions and their consequences.

10.8 Develop skill in selecting some personal, life-long learning goals and the means to attain them.

SOURCE: From John I. Goodlad, *A Place Called School: Prospects for the Future.* (New York: McGraw-Hill, 1984), pp. 51–56. Reproduced with permission of The McGraw-Hill Companies.

beliefs of individuals and groups about the aims of education when we examine some of the recommendations made during the 1980s for reform of the schools. You will also encounter in Chapter 14 philosophical and often conflicting positions and recommendations of other individuals and groups demanding reform and restructuring of the schools in the 1990s.

STATEMENTS FROM THE FEDERAL GOVERNMENT

Perhaps the most influential recent statement of aims in recent years was issued by President George Bush and the National Governors' Association. In September 1989 at the University of Virginia, the president and the governors' association developed a statement of six performance goals. The president presented this statement to the nation in his State of the Union address in January 1990.

In the spring of 1991 President Bush announced proposals for implementing the six national goals. Known as *America 2000,* the proposals—promoted by the U.S. Department of Education under the leadership of Lamar Alexander, U.S. Secretary of Education—included the creation of 535 experimental schools (one in each congressional district) for the purpose of demonstrating effective curricula and instructional techniques; voluntary national examinations in English, mathematics, science, history, and geography at the fourth-, eighth-, and twelfth-grade levels; and parental choice of school.

These proposals were in keeping with recommendations of the Commission on the Skills of the American Workforce, which advocated national standards and national examinations.[25] The proposed goals met with varying reactions from educators around the country. Many educators would welcome realization of these noble goals but doubted very much that they could be reached in the short time to the year 2000. Educators have expressed concern about the lack of federal funding to implement the proposals, the effects of parental choice on the public schools, the expenditure of over 500 million dollars for experimental schools, and the burden of new national examinations.

Educators wonder about the need for new national examinations since the National Assessment of Educational Progress already assesses student achievement in thirty-seven states.[26] The new examinations, however, would purportedly concentrate more on thinking skills in the various disciplines than do current multiple-choice examinations.

National assessment tests, however, may lead to a national standardized curriculum, a possibility that some educators find unacceptable. These educators fear that national examinations will dictate the curriculum rather than vice versa. They also believe that a national curriculum would prevent schools from tailoring the curriculum to local needs. Some aver that national standards and assessments would penalize those students in educational and social settings where they have encountered barriers to learning

The Congress moved to implement *America 2000* by creating the National Council on Education Standards and Testing whose duty it was to oversee development of (1) national standards, beginning in the five disciplines: English, mathematics, science, history, and geography with the possibility of adding other disciplines at a later date and of (2) a voluntary system of national assessment based on the standards.

Piloting of new examinations began in seventeen states in the spring of 1992 under the direction of the New Standards Project formed by the University of Pittsburgh's Research and Development Center and the National Center on Education and the Economy. Field testing of examinations in the various disciplines was projected over the next five years. The Pew Charitable Trusts and the John D. and Catherine T. MacArthur Foundation have provided substantial financial support to the New Standards Project.

Following the initiative begun in the Bush administration, in the spring of 1994 the Congress passed and President Bill Clinton signed the *Goals 2000 Educate America Act* authorizing federal support to the states for plans to improve the schools, reit-

---

[25]Commission on the Skills of the American Workforce, *America's Choice: High Skills or Low Wages* (Washington, D.C.: Commission on Skills of the American Workforce, 1991).

[26]See Chapter 12 for further discussion of the National Assessment of Educational Progress and Chapter 14 on the issue of national standards.

erating in slightly edited form the six national goals earlier proposed, and adding two goals calling for staff development for teachers and increased parental involvement. The eight national goals stipulated that by the year 2000

- All children in America will start school ready to learn.
- The high school graduation rate will increase to at least 90 percent.
- All students will leave grades four, eight, and twelve having demonstrated competency in challenging subject matter including English, mathematics, science, foreign languages, civics and government, economics, arts, history, and geography; and every school in America will ensure that all students learn to use their minds well, so they may be prepared for responsible citizenship, further learning, and productive employment in our nation's modern economy.
- U.S. students will be first in the world in mathematics and science achievement.
- Every adult American will be literate and will possess the knowledge and skills necessary to compete in a global economy and exercise the rights and responsibilities of citizenship.
- Every school in the United States will be free of drugs, violence, and the unauthorized presence of firearms and alcohol and will offer a disciplined environment conducive to learning.
- The nation's teaching force will have access to programs for the continued improvement of their professional skills and the opportunity to acquire the knowledge and skills needed to instruct and prepare all American students for the next century.
- Every school will promote partnerships that will increase parental involvement and participation in promoting the social, emotional, and academic growth of children.[27]

That not all curriculum theorists subscribed to *America 2000* can be seen in the remarks of Henry A. Giroux:

> "Under the guise of attempting to revitalize the language of leadership and reform, these reports signify a dangerous attack on some of the most fundamental aspects of democratic public life and the social, moral, and political obligations of responsible, critical citizens."[28]

Addressing *Goals 2000: The Educate America Act,* Maxine Greene saw problems with this "new national agenda for education" that called for achievement of subject-matter standards and for national assessment: the presumption that "it is realizable, poverty and inequality notwithstanding," "the implication that standards and tests can simply be imposed," and the "untapped diversity among American youth today."[29]

---

[27]U.S. Department of Education, *National Goals for Education* (Washington, D.C.: U.S. Department of Education, July 1990). See also Penelope M. Earley, *Goals 2000: Educate America Act: Implications for Teacher Educators* (ERIC document ED367661, 1994).

[28]Henry A. Giroux, *Living Dangerously: Multiculturalism and the Politics of Difference* (New York: Peter Lang, 1993), p. 14.

[29]Maxine Greene, *Releasing the Imagination: Essays on Education, the Arts, and Social Change* (San Francisco: Jossey-Bass, 1995), p. 17.

Said Greene, "The familiar paradigms seem still to be in use; the need for alternative possibilities in the face of economic and demographic changes is repressed or ignored."[30]

Citing the family as the crucial element in raising educational standards, critics of the legislation decried the expenditure of millions of dollars, which they maintained would not guarantee improvement in the schools. They objected to involvement of the federal government in education which they believed takes autonomy away from the local schools and deprives them of their uniqueness.

That federal support to education does not necessarily lead to federal control can be seen in a number of provisions of these national proposals: national assessments are to be voluntary; national standards and assessments are being developed with input from educators and experts from around the country; in applying for support, states will propose their own plans for improvement. The state of Florida, for example, expressly designed its improvement program, labeled *Blueprint 2000,* to involve a wide spectrum of decision makers at the local level and to grant greater autonomy to the local schools. Although the state presents seven goals with twenty-two standards to be adopted statewide, *Blueprint 2000* clearly states:

> Although Florida has approached school reform before, this initiative is different. The state will no longer dictate process or program to local schools and districts, but will require that schools make progress toward meeting the rigorous standards and outcomes presented in this document [*Blueprint 2000*]. *Blueprint 2000* reinforces local control by supporting the authority of those closest to the students to determine the how of public education. A decentralized system gives schools and districts greater freedom to design programs that better meet the needs of individual children. Along with this freedom comes responsibility, and the Commission encourages all local decision makers (parents, students, teachers, administrators, school board members, postsecondary educators, and community members) to become full partners in accepting and carrying out this responsibility.[31]

It did not take a soothsayer to predict that the ambitious *America 2000* goals would not be realized by the year 2000. In fact, none of the goals have been fully achieved. Many people both within and outside of the teaching profession, however, would maintain that the goals remain worthy targets.

You will note that the statements of aims of education cited in this chapter vary from advocacy of cognitive competencies alone to concern for the development of cognitive, affective, and psychomotor competencies. We will revisit the issues of national standards and national assessment in Chapter 14.

PHILOSOPHIES OF EDUCATION

Greene defined philosophy as "a way of framing distinctive sorts of questions having to do with what is presupposed, perceived, intuited, believed, and known."[32] "Educational philosophy," wrote Greene, "is a matter of doing philosophy with respect to the

---

[30]Ibid.

[31]The Florida Department of Education, *Blueprint 2000* (Tallahassee, Fla.: The Florida Department of Education, 1993), p. i. See Chapter 8 for further discussion of Florida's Goals and Standards.

[32]Maxine Greene, *Teacher as Stranger: Educational Philosophy for the Modern Age* (Belmont, Calif.: Wadsworth, 1973), p. 7.

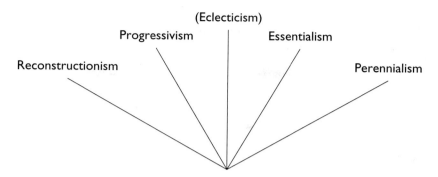

Figure 6.1 Four philosophies of education. In the middle is Eclecticism, the borrowing of beliefs from more than one school of philosophy.

educational enterprise as it engages the educator. . . . To do educational philosophy is to become critically conscious of what is involved in the complex business of teaching and learning."[33]

Statements of aims of education are positions taken that are based on a set of beliefs—a philosophy of education. Clearly, the authors of the illustrations of aims cited in the preceding section held certain assumptions about education, society, and how young people learn. An aim of education, then, is a statement of beliefs central to the author's philosophical creed that is directed to the mission of the school.

We will now examine four major philosophies of education that have demanded the attention of educators. Only two of these philosophies appear to have large followings in today's schools. Although these philosophies are known by various names and there are schools of philosophy within schools, we shall refer to these four as *reconstructionism, progressivism, essentialism, and perennialism.*

These four schools of thought can be charted from the most liberal to the most conservative as shown in Figure 6.1. At the far left is the most liberal of these four philosophies, reconstructionism, and at the far right, the most conservative, perennialism. Although essentialism and progressivism have been widely accepted and practiced by educators, neither reconstructionism nor perennialism has found widespread endorsement in the schools. The American public appears to be far too conservative to espouse reconstructionism, and at the same time far too liberal to accept perennialism, as a prevailing philosophy. Since reconstructionism and perennialism have had less impact on the schools than the two other philosophies, we will discuss them first and then come back to the two more pervasive philosophies: essentialism and progressivism.

A word of explanation about the following discussion: Although this text chooses to elaborate on *philosophies of education,* we must recognize that *philosophies of education* stem from more general *philosophies of life.* As J. Donald Butler commented, ". . . aims of education cannot just be pulled out of a hat, but must be derived from more fundamental and general thinking about value, reality, and knowledge,"[34] Discussion

---

[33]Ibid.

[34]J. Donald Butler, *Four Philosophies and Their Practice in Education and Religion,* 3rd ed. (New York: Harper & Row, 1968), p. 487.

of general philosophies is beyond the scope of this text. Numerous books describe various schools of philosophy. I would recommend two excellent, readable references:

> Butler (see footnote 34). Butler described naturalism, idealism, realism, and pragmatism. He included also treatments of existentialism and language analysis.
>
> Will Durant, *The Story of Philosophy: The Lives and Opinions of the World's Greatest Philosophers From Plato to John Dewey* (New York: Simon and Schuster, 1926). Durant described the thinking of fifteen great philosophers.

RECONSTRUCTIONISM

Hilda Taba pointed out that John Dewey "consistently saw the function of the school in both psychological and social terms."[35] She explained:

> A flowering of the idea that education is a social process, the primary and the most effective instrument of social reconstructionism, came with the work and writings of Dewey and his followers. The main thesis of this group was that the school is not merely a residual institution to maintain things as they are; education has a creative function to play in shaping of individuals and through them in the shaping of the culture. . . . In subsequent development one fork of this dual orientation of Dewey on the function of education matured into an elaboration of the social responsibilities of the school, while the other centered more emphatically on individual development.[36]

Branching out from Dewey's philosophy, the reconstructionists followed a path that led them to propose using the school to achieve what they considered to be improvements in society. George S. Counts, in his much-discussed book, *Dare the School Build a New Social Order?*, challenged educators to reconsider the role of schools in our society.[37] In essence, reconstructionism holds that the school should not simply transmit the cultural heritage or simply study social problems but should become an agency for solving political and social problems. The subject matter to which all youngsters should be exposed consists of unsolved, often controversial, problems of the day such as unemployment, health needs, housing needs, and ethnic problems. Group consensus is the methodology by which solutions to the problems are sought.

Theodore Brameld made clear the values of the reconstructionists. Most people want the following:

a. sufficient nourishment
b. adequate dress
c. shelter and privacy
d. erotic expression and celebration
e. physiological and mental health
f. steady work, steady income
g. companionship, mutual devotion, belongingness
h. recognition, appreciation, status

---

[35]Hilda Taba, *Curriculum Development: Theory and Practice* (New York: Harcourt Brace Jovanovich, 1962), p. 23.
[36]Ibid.
[37]George S. Counts, *Dare the School Build a New Social Order?* (New York: John Day, 1932).

   i. novelty, curiosity, variation, recreation, adventure, growth, creativity

   j. literacy, skill, information

   k. participation, sharing

   l. fairly immediate meaning, significance, order, direction[38]

Some educators agree that young people should consider pressing social, economic, and political problems and even attempt to reach consensus on possible solutions. They do take exception, however, when teachers propose their own specific solutions which raises the specter of indoctrination, a practice unacceptable to most schools of philosophy.

With its heavy emphasis on controversial social issues and its major premise to make the school a primary agency for social change, reconstructionism has not made great inroads into the largely middle-class, centrist schools of the United States.

PERENNIALISM

In the tradition of Plato, Aristotle, and the scholasticism of the Catholic thinker St. Thomas Aquinas, the contemporary perennialists see the aims of education as the disciplining of the mind, the development of the ability to reason, and the pursuit of truth. Unlike progressivists, who, as we shall see later, hold that truth is relative and changing, the perennialists believe that truth is eternal, everlasting, and unchanging. In their pursuit of truth, the secular perennialists joined hands with the sectarian perennialists. The secular perennialists advocated a highly academic curriculum with emphasis on grammar, rhetoric, logic, classical and modern languages, mathematics, and—at the heart of the perennialist curriculum—the great books of the Western world. In the great books of the past, one searched for truth, which in perennialist thinking is the same today as it was then and always shall be. To these academic disciplines the sectarian perennialists would add study of the Bible and theological writings.

Robert M. Hutchins, former president of the University of Chicago, was perhaps the best known exponent of the philosophy of perennialism in America. Hutchins and other perennialists eschewed immediate needs of the learners, specialized education, and vocational training. Hutchins made these points clear when he stated: "The ideal education is not an ad hoc education, not an education directed to immediate needs; it is not a specialized education, or a preprofessional education; it is not a utilitarian education. It is an education calculated to develop the mind."[39]

The perennialist agrees with the essentialist that education is preparation for life but opposes the progressivist who holds that education *is* life. If taken seriously, perennialism would afford an education suitable to that small percentage of students who possess high verbal and academic aptitude.

The perennialist looks backward for the answers to social problems. We must wonder, for example, how useful Lucretius' *De Rerum Natura* is for this and future generations in solving environmental problems. One criticism that appears to be overlooked in most critiques of perennialism is its ethnocentricity. The perennialist showcase features the great books of the Western world, considered by some as the greatest

---

[38]Theodore Brameld, *Patterns of Educational Philosophy: Divergence and Convergence in Culturological Perspective* (New York: Holt, Rinehart and Winston, 1971), p. 418.

[39]Robert M. Hutchins, *On Education* (Santa Barbara, Calif.: Center for the Study of Democratic Institutions, 1963), p. 18.

works of all humanity. Excluded are the great writings of the Eastern world, of which many of us are abysmally ignorant. An outstanding curriculum project would bring together, perhaps under the auspices of UNESCO, a group of world scholars who would draw up a set of great books of the entire world. East and West have much to say to each other.

In conclusion, perennialism has not yet proved an attractive philosophy for our educational system.

ESSENTIALISM

Historically, essentialism and progressivism have succeeded in commanding the allegiance of the American public. Both have been and remain potent contenders for public and professional support. Walker and Soltis highlighted the conflict between the two schools of thought when they said:

> The first half of the twentieth century witnessed a running battle between progressive educators, who saw in the ideas of Dewey and other progressives new ways to think about the curriculum, and the traditionalists, who were sure that the basic curriculum did not need change because it had proven itself essential to the education of individuals who would maintain an intellectually sound and civilized society. Many battles were fought over these opposing views, leaving a profound mark on elementary school practices especially and curriculum theory generally that is still visible today.[40]

With only slight inaccuracies, we can mark the periods of supremacy of one school over another. From 1635 with the establishment of the Boston Latin School to 1896 with the creation of John Dewey's Laboratory School at the University of Chicago—a period of 261 years—the doctrines of essentialism (with a patina of sectarian perennialism from 1635 to the advent of the English High School in 1824) held sway. Starting in 1896, moving slowly, and gathering steam in the 1930s and 1940s until 1957 (the year of Sputnik), progressivism emerged for a short time as the most popular educational philosophy. Its path was somewhat rocky, however, strewn as it was with the loss of the Progressive Education Association and essentialist criticisms from sources like the Council on Basic Education, Arthur Bestor, Max Rafferty, John Keats, Albert Lynd, and Mortimer Smith. Since 1957 essentialism has reclaimed its predominant position. Since the late 1990s, however, the fostering of pupil self-esteem has been strongly emphasized; contemporary essentialist critics of education would say "overemphasized."

The aim of education according to essentialist tenets is the transmission of the cultural heritage. Unlike the reconstructionists, who would actively change society, the essentialists seek to preserve it. Again, unlike the reconstructionists, who would seek to adjust society to its populace, the essentialists seek to adjust men and women to society.

Cognitive Goals.   The goals of the essentialist are primarily cognitive and intellectual. Organized courses are the vehicles for transmitting the culture, and emphasis is placed on mental discipline. The three R's and the "hard" (i.e., academic) subjects form the

---

[40]Walker and Soltis, *Curriculum and Aims*, p. 18.

core of the essentialist curriculum. In one sense the essentialist tailors the child to the curriculum, whereas the progressivist tailors the curriculum to the child.

The subject matter curriculum, which we will examine in Chapter 9, is an essentialist plan for curriculum organization, and the techniques of Assign-Study-Recite-Test are the principal methods. Erudition, the ability to reproduce that which has been learned, is highly valued, and education is perceived as preparation for some future purpose—for college, vocation, life.

In spite of the mitigating influence of Jean Jacques Rousseau, Johann Pestalozzi, and Friedrich Froebel, essentialism has for generations dominated European education and all the areas of the globe to which it has been exported. Essentialist thinking fits in well with centralized administrative structures as represented in the European and most colonial ministries of education. The ministries, following essentialist concepts, can select, promote, and control the content to which young people are exposed. They can promote and reward the young in respect to their mastery of subject matter. They can screen youth for the universities on the basis of stringent examinations that call for recapitulation of subject matter.

William C. Bagley, one of the foremost advocates of essentialistic philosophy, strongly criticized the child-centered approach and urged teachers to follow essentialistic principles.[41] James B. Conant, in a series of reports on the junior and senior high school conducted in the late 1950s and mid-1960s, revealed an essentialistic outlook in his major recommendations.[42] Conant championed emphasis on the academic disciplines.[43]

Behavioristic Principles. The essentialists found the principles of the behavioristic school of psychology to be particularly harmonious with their philosophical beliefs. V. T. Thayer called attention to the urbanization of America and immigration taking place in the late 1800s and the early 1900s in explaining the reason for the essentialists' espousal of behavioristic principles:

> The changes in American society to which we have drawn attention affected education on all levels. But the contrast between programs of education keyed, on the one hand, to the inner nature of the young person and, on the other hand, to the demands of society were most obvious on the junior high school level. Here genetic psychology was emphasizing the dynamic and distinctive potentialities of the young person, with the clear implication that nature was to be followed; whereas life outside the school, in the home and community, in business and industry, stressed the importance of education for adjustment, one that would give specific and detailed attention to the formation of desirable habits and skills and techniques. Confronted with this necessity of choice, educators turned to a psychology that would further education for adjustment.[44]

---

[41]See William C. Bagley, "An Essentialist's Platform for the Advancement of American Education," *Educational Administration and Supervision* 24, no. 4 (April 1938): 251–252.

[42]See James B. Conant, *The American High School Today* (New York: McGraw-Hill, 1959); Conant, *Recommendations for Education in the Junior High School Years* (Princeton, N.J.: Educational Testing Service, 1960); Conant, *The Comprehensive High School* (New York: McGraw-Hill, 1967).

[43]See Chapter 9 for further discussion of the Conant reports.

[44]V.T.Thayer, *The Role of the School in American Society* (New York: Dodd, Mead, 1960), pp. 251-252.

Behaviorism casts the learner in a passive role as the recipient of the many stimuli to which he or she must respond. Known in its variants as connectionism, association, S-R (stimulus-response) bond, and conditioning, behaviorism brought into the classroom drill, programmed instruction, teaching machines, standardized testing, and, of course, behavioral objectives. The movement toward specification and demonstration of competencies in both general and teacher education owes a debt to the behaviorists. Selection of content by the adult for the immature learner and reinforcement, preferably immediate and positive, are central to behavioristic thought. Noted among the behaviorists are Ivan Pavlov, the Russian scientist who performed the classic experiment in which a dog was taught to salivate at the ringing of a bell; John B. Watson, who maintained that with the right stimuli he could shape a child into whatever he wished; Edward L. Thorndike, who is considered by many to be the father of the controversial standardized test; and B. F. Skinner, who popularized teaching machines.

Teachers of the behavioristic-essentialist school fragment content into logical, sequential pieces and prescribe the pieces the learner will study. Typically, they begin instruction by giving the learners a rule, concept, or model (for example, the formula for finding the area of a rectangle) and then provide many opportunities to practice (drill) using this guide. With adequate practice the learner can presumably use the rule, concept, or model whenever he or she needs it. The learning has become a habitual part of the individual's behavior. Though human beings are prone to forget content not used regularly, the behaviorists and essentialists maintain that if the content has been thoroughly mastered, it can easily be retrieved.

Current and continuing emphasis on the basic skills clearly derives from the essentialists. Thus present educational programs and practices maintain a strong essentialistic orientation.

PROGRESSIVISM

In the late nineteenth and early twentieth centuries progressivism swept through the educational structure of America, challenging the time-honored doctrines of essentialism. Led by John Dewey, William H. Kilpatrick, John Childs, and Boyd Bode, the progressivists maintained that it was time to subordinate subject matter to the learner. Borrowing from some European philosophers like Rousseau, who advocated rearing a child in a relaxed environment without forcing learning, the progressivists created the child-centered school. Its prototype was the University of Chicago Laboratory School. Moving east from Chicago to New York, John Dewey formulated progressive beliefs in a series of publications that included *Democracy and Education*,[45] *Experience and Education*,[46] *How We Think*,[47] and *My Pedagogic Creed*.[48] By insisting that the needs and interests of learners must be considered and by recognizing that learners bring their bodies, emotions, and spirits to school along with their minds, progressivism captured the attention and allegiance of educators.

---

[45]Macmillan, 1916.
[46]Macmillan, 1938.
[47]D. C. Heath, 1933.
[48]Progressive Education Association, 1929.

Dewey clearly stated the differences between the essential and the progressive curriculum:

> The fundamental factors in the educative process are the immature, underdeveloped being; and certain social aims, meanings, values incarnate in the matured experience of the adult. The educative process is the due interaction of these forces. . . . From these elements of conflict grow up different educational sects. One school fixes its attention upon the importance of subject matter of the curriculum as compared with the contents of the child's own experience. . . . Hence the moral: ignore and minimize the child's individual peculiarities, whims, and experiences. . . . As educators our work is precisely to substitute for these superficial and casual affairs stable and well-ordered realities; and these are found in studies and lessons.
>
> Subdivide each topic into studies; each study into lessons; each lesson into specific facts and formulae. Let each child proceed step by step to master each one of these separate parts, and at last he will have covered the entire ground. . . . Problems of instruction are problems of procuring texts giving logical parts and sequences, and of presenting these portions in class in a similar definite and graded way. Subject matter furnishes the end, and it determines method. The child is simply the immature being who is to be matured; he is the superficial being who is to be deepened; his is narrow experience which is to be widened. It is his to receive, to accept. . . .
>
> Not so, says the other sect. The child is the starting point, the center, and the end. His development, his growth, is the ideal. It alone furnishes the standard. To the growth of the child all studies are subservient; they are instruments valued as they serve the needs of growth. Personality, character, is more than subject matter. Not knowledge or information, but self-realization, is the goal. . . . Moreover, subject matter never can be got into the child from without. Learning is active. It involves reaching out of the mind. It involves organic assimilation starting from within. . . . It is he and not the subject matter which determines both quality and quantity of learning.
>
> The only significant method is the method of the mind as it reaches out and assimilates. Subject matter is but spiritual food, possible nutritive material. It cannot digest itself; it cannot of its own accord turn into bone and muscle and blood. The source of whatever is dead, mechanical, and formal in schools is found precisely in the subordination of the life and experience of the child to the curriculum. It is because of this that "study" has become a synonym for what is irksome, and a "lesson" identical with a task.[49]

To the progressives then, education is not a product to be learned—for example, facts and motor skills—but a process that continues as long as one lives. To their way of thinking a child learns best when actively experiencing his or her world as opposed to passively absorbing preselected content. If experiences in school are designed to meet the needs and interests of individual learners, it follows that no single pattern of subject matter can be appropriate for all learners. Brameld explained this point of view held by progessivists like Dewey and Rugg:[50]

> The proper subject matter of a curriculum is any experience that is educative. This means that the good school is concerned with every kind of learning that helps students, young and old, to grow. No single body of content, no system of courses, no

---

[49]John Dewey, *The Child and the Curriculum* (Chicago: University of Chicago Press, 1902), pp. 7–14.
[50]Harold Rugg, et al., *Foundations for American Education* (Yonkers, N.Y.: World Book Company, 1947).

universal method of teaching is inappropriate. For, like experience itself, the needs and interests of individuals and groups vary from place to place, from time to time, from culture to culture.[51]

The progressivist position that the child should undergo educative experiences in the here and now has led to the clichélike indicators of progressive philosophy: "education is life" and "learning by doing." The progressivists urged schools to provide for learners' individual differences in the broadest sense of the term, encompassing mental, physical, emotional, spiritual, social, and cultural differences. In both thought and practice, progressivism shows concern for the student, society, and subject matter, placing the student at the center of the learning process.

At the heart of progressive thinking is an abiding faith in democracy. Hence the progressivists see little place for authoritarian practices in the classroom and the school. They do not hold with the essentialists that the learners are immature subjects of adult preceptors and administrators but rather consider them partners in the educational process. Teachers influenced by progressive thinking see themselves as counselors to pupils and facilitators of learning rather than expounders of subject matter. Cooperation is fostered in the classroom rather than competition. Individual growth in relationship to one's ability is considered more important than growth in comparison to others.

A concern for the many unresolved problems of democracy led to a split in the progressive camp, with reconstructionists advocating that the schools become the instrument for building a new social order. It has been mentioned that the perennialist considers truth to be absolute, enduring, and found in the wisdom of the past; the essentialist presents the cultural heritage as truth, whereas the progressivist takes a pragmatic view and holds truth to be relative, changing, and in many cases as yet to be discovered. For the pragmatist, education is a continuing search for the truth utilizing whatever sources are needed to discover that truth.

Scientific Method.   The scientific method, known also as reflective thinking, problem solving, and practical intelligence, became both a goal and a technique in the progressive school. The scientific method was both a skill to be achieved and a means of finding solutions to problems. In its simplest elements the scientific method consists of five steps:

- identifying a problem
- forming an hypothesis or hypotheses
- gathering data
- analyzing data
- drawing conclusions

The progressivists proposed the scientific method as a general method to be applied in any area of human endeavor. It is generally accepted for both unsophisticated problem solving and for sophisticated research. Taba offered a very legitimate caution about accepting this method of problem solving as complete training in the ability to think:

---

[51]Brameld, *Patterns of Educational Philosophy*, p. 133.

But to maintain that all aspects of thinking are involved in problem solving or in the process of inquiry is one thing. To assume that following these steps also provides sufficient training in all elements of thinking is something else. For training purposes it is important both to master the various aspects of elements of thinking—such as generalizing, concept formation, analysis of assumptions, application of principle—and to use these processes in an organized sequence of problem solving. . . . If these elements are not consciously recognized and mastered, problem solving can turn into a ritualistic process of defining any kind of question, collecting any kind of data, hypothesizing any variety of solutions, and so on.

Subsuming all reflective thinking under the category of problem solving has also caused certain elements of thinking to be neglected, especially those which, although involved in problem solving, are not fully attended to *while* solving problems. Among these are such mental processes as concept formation, abstracting, and various methods of induction.[52]

Experimentalist Psychology.   In behaviorism the essentialists found learning theories harmonious with their philosophy. The progressivists did not have to look far for theories of learning compatible with their views on education. They found a wealth of ideas in the experimentalist psychology of Charles S. Peirce and William James: in the field (gestalt) psychology of Max Wertheimer, Wolfgang Köhler, Kurt Koffka, and Kurt Lewin; and in the perceptual psychology of Earl Kelley, Donald Snygg, Arthur Combs, Abraham Maslow, and Carl Rogers.

The experimentalists encourage the active involvement of the learner in all his or her capacities in the educational process. Brameld credited James's efforts to promote experimentalist-progressive thought:

The influence of James has, of course, been very great throughout the twentieth century. His famous *Principles of Psychology* is still, in various respects, the foremost single achievement in the field by any American scholar-scientist. . . . the dominant point of view is one of living organisms that function through experience, action, flowing feelings, habit patterns. Concern is nearly always with the total self viewed in a range of overlapping perspectives—spiritual, emotional, bodily.[53]

Gestalt Psychology.   In contrast to the behaviorists' presentation of subject matter in parts, the gestaltists concentrated on wholes, the "big picture," so to speak. They advised teachers to organize subject matter in such a way that learners could see the relationships among the various parts. This advice fit in perfectly with the progressivists' concern for "the whole child." The unit method of teaching in which content from all pertinent areas is organized into a holistic plan in order to study a particular topic or problem became a popular and enduring instructional technique. Writing unit plans is common practice among teachers today. For example, the topic of the Victorian Era provides a unifying theme for the study of the history, philosophy, government, literature, science, and fine arts of the period.

The gestaltists pointed out that the learners achieve insight when they discern relationships among elements of a given situation. The gestaltists encourage inquiry or discovery learning in order to sharpen the skill of insight. Both the experimentalists and

---

[52]Taba, *Curriculum Development,* p. 184.
[53]Brameld, *Patterns of Educational Philosophy,* pp. 96–97.

gestaltists agree that the closer content to be mastered is to real-life situations and the closer problems are to the previous experiences of the learner, the more likelihood there is for successful mastery of the material.

Perceptual Psychology.   Of more recent vintage, perceptual psychology focused on the development of the learner's self-concept. The goal of the perceptualists is the development of the "self-actualizing" or "fully functioning" personality. Abraham H. Maslow defined self-actualization as follows:

> Self-actualization is defined in various ways, but a solid core of agreement is perceptible. All definitions accept or imply: (a) acceptance and expression of the inner core of self, i.e., actualization of these latent capacities and potentialities, "full functioning," availability of the human and personal essence; and (b) minimal presence of ill health, neurosis, psychosis, or loss or diminution of the basic human and personal capacities.[54]

The perceptualists concentrate their efforts on developing persons who feel adequate. Arthur W. Combs listed the following "four characteristics of the perceptual field which always seem to underlie the behavior of truly adequate persons"[55] (a) a positive view of the self, (b) identification with others, (c) openness to experience and acceptance, and (d) possession of a rich field of perceptions gained from both formal schooling and informal sources.[56]

According to the perceptual psychologists, teachers must help young people to develop an adequate concept of themselves and must be willing to deal with both their perceptions of the world and the world as it is. The perceptualist maintains that it is more important to know how the learner perceives the facts than what the facts of a given situation are. We all have a tendency to selectively perceive our environment. We recognize familiar faces before we pay attention to unfamiliar persons. We pick out words we know and ignore those that we do not know. We are sure that our version of the truth of any situation is the right one, for that is the way we perceive it. The perceptualists emphasize dealing with people's perceptions of the world around them.

An individual's feeling of adequacy or inadequacy can often be attributed to other people's perceptions. If a child is told by a parent that he or she is a weakling, the child may agree that it is so. If a child is told by teachers that he or she has an artistic talent, the child may seek to develop that ability. If a child is told that he or she is a poor reader, lacks aptitude for mathematics, or is short on musical talent, the child may accept these perceptions and internalize them. The child is exemplifying then what is referred to in the literature as the self-fulfilling prophecy. We are not only what we eat, as health food devotees tell us—we are what others have made us, as the perceptual psychologists maintain. Combs described how the self-concept is learned in the following passage:

[54]Abraham H. Maslow, "Some Basic Propositions of a Growth and Self-Actualization Psychology," in *Perceiving, Behaving, Becoming,* 1962 Yearbook (Alexandria, Va.: Association for Supervision and Curriculum Development, 1962), p. 36.

[55]Arthur W. Combs, "A Perceptual View of the Adequate Personality," in *Perceiving, Behaving, Becoming,* 1962 Yearbook (Alexandria, Va.: Association for Supervision and Curriculum Development, 1962), p. 51.

[56]Ibid., pp. 51–62.

People *learn* who they are and what they are from the ways in which they have been treated by those who surround them in the process of their growing up. . . . People discover their self-concepts from the kinds of experiences they have had with life; not from telling, but from experience. People develop feelings that they are liked, wanted, acceptable, and able from *having been* liked, wanted, accepted, and from having been successful. One learns that he is these things, not from being told so, but only through the experience of *being treated as though he were so.* Here is the key to what must be done to produce more adequate people. To produce a positive self, it is necessary to provide experiences that teach individuals they are positive people.[57]

The perceptualists attacked the notion that children must experience failure. Said Combs, "Actually, the best guarantee we have that a person will be able to deal with the future effectively is that he has been successful in the past. People learn that they are able, not from failure, but from success."[58]

The progressive philosophers identified readily with the experimentalist, gestalt, and perceptual schools of psychology. Their combined efforts to humanize education captured the imagination of educators, particularly those in teacher education, flourished for a relatively brief period, peaked, but left an indelible mark on our educational system. Because of progressivism, essentialism will never be the same.

Critical Inquiry.   You will encounter in your readings discussions of *critical inquiry.* According to Kenneth A. Sirotnik

> critical inquiry is a rigorous, time-consuming, collaborative, informed, school-based dialectic around generic questions such as: What is going on in the name of X? (X is a place-holder for things like educational goals and schooling functions; instructional practices like the use of time, tracking students, and achievement testing; organizational practices like leadership, decision making, and communication, etc.). How did it come to be that way? Whose interests are being served (and not being served) by the way things are? What information and knowledge do we have—and need to get— that bear upon the issues? . . . Is this the way we want it? . . . What are we going to *do* about all this? . . .[59]

Noting that goal statements for the public schools often differ from classroom realities, Sirotnik would view as more accurate statements of what goes on as: "to develop in students abilities to think linearly, depend on authority, speak when spoken to, work alone, become socially apathetic, learn passively and nonexperientially, recall information, follow instructions, compartmentalize knowledge, and so on."[60]

"At the heart of critical inquiry, therefore," said Sirotnik, "is the willingness and ability of people to engage in competent discourse and communication.[61]

Constructivist Psychology.   Like experimentalist, gestalt, and perceptual psychology, constructivism complements progressive philosophy. Constructivists hold that the

---

[57]Ibid., p. 53.

[58]Ibid.

[59]Kenneth A. Sirotnik, "What Goes on in Classrooms? Is This the Way We Want It." in Landon E. Beyer and Michael W. Apple, eds., *The Curriculum: Problems, Politics, and Possibilities,* 2nd ed. (Albany, N.Y.: State University of New York Press, 1998), pp. 66–67.

[60]Ibid., p. 64.

[61]Ibid., p. 67.

teacher is a facilitator of learning, students must be taught to take responsibility for their own learning, learning is an active process (recall the progressives' "learning by doing"), learning must be present in ways meaningful to students, basic skills will be learned in authentic situations not by separate concentration on the skills themselves. Numerous programs and practices in schools today follow constructivist doctrine.

Nell Noddings explained:

> Constructivism—variously described as a philosophy, an epistemology, a cognitive position, or a pedagogical orientation—currently dominates mathematics and science education. One of its basic premises is that all knowledge is constructed knowledge; knowledge is not the result of passive reception. This premise is common to all forms of constructivism and is also a basic tenet of cognitive psychology. . . . Constructivists in education trace their roots . . . to [Jean] Piaget.[62]

Like other schools of psychology, constructivism does not dictate any particular program or method of instruction to accomplish its aim—the development of thinking individuals able to use knowledge effectively in society.

Constructivism is accepted by many educators, rejected by others. As examples of constructivist practices we can cite whole language, authentic assessment, guided discovery, holistic grading, and integrated curriculum. Karen H. Harris and Steve Graham pointed out that the "back-to-basics" movement was a backlash against constructivist practices.[63] The public (and many teachers) do not appear ready to fully espouse constructivist practices. As often happens, however, teachers commonly blend elements of constructivism with more traditional approaches.

The Eight-Year Study.   The cause of the progressives was boosted by the Eight-Year Study, conducted by the Progressive Education Association between 1933 and 1941. Many educators recognize this study as one of the most significant pieces of educational research ever conducted in the United States. There have been few longitudinal studies that followed subjects over a period of years. Few studies have been as sweeping or have involved as many people. Students, high school teachers and administrators, curriculum consultants, researchers, and college professors all played significant roles in the study.

The Progressive Education Association was disenchanted with the typical high school college preparatory curriculum with its customary prescribed constants required for college admission. The Association wanted to see more flexibility in the secondary school curriculum but realized that such a change would not be possible as long as the colleges demanded a prescribed set of courses. It therefore enlisted the cooperation of more than 300 colleges and universities that agreed to accept graduates from a limited number of high schools without regard to the usual college entrance requirements. Obtaining the cooperation of so many colleges and universities for an experiment of this nature, which might shatter traditional notions of what is needed to succeed in college, was a feat in itself. Wilford M. Aikin, H. H. Giles, S. P. McCutchen, Ralph W. Tyler, and A. N. Zechiel were instrumental in conducting the study.[64]

---

[62]Nell Noddings, *Philosophy of Education* (Boulder, Col.: Westview Press, 1995), p. 115

[63]Karen H. Harris and Steve Graham, "Constructivism: Principles, Paradigms, and Integration," *The Journal of Special Education* 28, no. 3 (March 1994): 240.

[64]See Wilford M. Aikin, *The Story of the Eight-Year Study* (New York: Harper & Row, 1942).

The colleges and universities consented to admit graduates from thirty public and private schools regardless of their programs for a five-year period, from 1936 to 1941. Beginning in 1933 these thirty experimental schools were able to modify their programs in any way they saw fit.

Once admitted to cooperating colleges and universities, graduates of the experimental schools were matched with counterparts in the same institution who came from conventional high schools, and their performance in college was analyzed. More than 1400 matched pairs of students were involved in this study. The findings of the Eight-Year Study are summarized as follows:

> The graduates of the experimental schools, as it turned out, did as well as or better than their counterparts in college in all subjects except foreign languages. The graduates of the experimental schools excelled their counterparts in scholastic honors, leadership positions, study habits, intellectual curiosity, and extraclass activities. The Eight-Year Study showed rather conclusively that a single pattern of required courses is not essential for success in college.[65]

The Eight-Year Study gave impetus to novel curriculum experiments like the core curriculum, which along with the progessivist experience curriculum will be discussed in Chapter 9.

Decline of Progressivism.   In spite of its contributions—placing the child at the center of the educational process, treating the whole child, appealing to children's needs and interests, providing for individual differences, and emphasizing reflective thinking—progressivism has declined in acceptance by both the public and educators. It is probably not too far from the truth to maintain that the public was never completely enamored of progressive doctrines.

It was not Sputnik per se followed by the panicky rush to the "substantive" courses—science, mathematics, and foreign languages—that caused the turn away from progressivism. Trouble had been brewing for a number of years prior to the Soviet achievement in space.

The essentialist curriculum has always been the easiest to understand and the simplest to organize and administer. It appears clear-cut and can be readily preplanned by teachers and administrators drawing on their knowledge of the adult world. We must not overlook the force that tradition plays in our society. The essentialist curriculum has been the one to which most Americans have been exposed and which, therefore, they know best and wish to retain.

There can be no doubt that some of the so-called progressive schools went to extremes in catering to the needs and interests of children. The high school graduate who must write in block printing because he or she was not required to master cursive writing raised eyebrows among the American public. Appealing to the child's immediate needs and interests, some progressive schools seemed to sacrifice long-range needs and interests of which the immature learner was scarcely aware.

A feeling developed that the graduates of progressive schools were not learning the basic skills or the elements of the nation's cultural heritage. The public was uncomfortable with assertions from educators such as "The child should be taught to read

---

[65]Peter F. Oliva, *The Secondary School Today*, 2nd ed. (New York: Harper & Row, 1972), p. 120.

only after he or she expresses a felt need for reading" or "There's no need to memorize the multiplication tables, you can always look them up or use a calculator."

Compared to the apparent tidiness of the essentialist curriculum and the relative ease of measuring achievement of subject matter, the progressivist curriculum appeared at times disorganized and impossible to evaluate. In attempting to deal with the whole child, the progressive school seemed to many parents to be usurping the functions of the home, and many harried teachers agreed with them.

Some of the more zealous progressivists led even Dewey to warn:

> Apart from the question of the future, continually to appeal even in childhood to the principle of interest is eternally to excite, that is, distract, the child. Continuity of activity is destroyed. Everything is made play, amusement. This means overstimulation; it means dissipation of energy. Will is never called into action. The reliance is upon external attractions and amusements. Everything is sugar-coated for the child, and he soon learns to turn everything that is not artificially surrounded with diverting circumstances.[66]

Mass education alone has contributed to the decline of progressive practices. What might work in a class of twenty-five will not necessarily work in classes of thirty-five or above. No one has yet demonstrated satisfactorily how a high school teacher of English can provide for cognitive differences among 150 students per day, let alone be effective. As long ago as 1959 James B. Conant advocated a maximum of 100 pupils per high school English teacher—a standard yet to be realized in many schools.[67]

Criticisms of progressive education by the essentialists, the behaviorists, and the scholastics converged to restore essentialism to its currently strong position. The numerous reports on educational reform in the 1970s and 1980s, some of which will be discussed in Chapter 9, revealed dissatisfaction, however, with the essentialistic curriculum. Some contemporary curriculum theorists characterize the historic role of schools as an outmoded, inappropriate factory or industrial model, imposed by society on young people who are its products destined for the workforce, rewarding conformity and deemphasizing the preparation of, in the words of George H. Wood, "independent thinkers who are committed to the public good and willing to act on their own initiative,"[68] Linda Darling-Hammond described present school structure whose origins lie in principles of top-down organizational management, as a "conveyor belt" wherein impersonal treatment of students and rote learning predominate. Efforts at improvement like "required courses, textbooks, testing instruments, and management systems," based on a "manufacturing industries" model, according to Darling-Hammond, have been assumed to lead to student learning and have sought to produce a standard product.[69] She held that factory-model schools erect barriers to democratic education, commenting:

[66]John Dewey, *Interest and Effort in Education* (Boston: Houghton Mifflin, 1913), pp. 4–5.

[67]Conant, *The American High School Today*, p. 51.

[68]George H. Wood, "Teachers as Curriculum Workers," in James T. Sears and J. Dan Marshall, eds., *Teaching and Thinking About Curriculum: Critical Inquiries* (New York: Teachers College Press, 1990), p. 100

[69]Linda Darling-Hammond, *The Right to Learn: A Blueprint for Creating Schools That Work* (San Francisco: Jossey-Bass, 1997), pp. 16–17.

Relatively few schools offer all their students a rich, active curriculum that teaches for understanding. Even fewer manage to educate a diverse set of students for constructive social interaction and shared decision making . . . the right to learn in ways that develop both competence and community has been a myth rather than a reality for many Americans.[70]

Critical of education tied to economic goals Michael W. Apple commented, "the most powerful economic and political groups in the United States and similar nations have made it abundantly clear that for them a good education is only one that is tied to economic needs (but, of course, only as these needs are defined by the powerful)."[71] Noting that democratic ideals have long been featured in school reform Jean Anyon questioned their adequacy in the restructuring of urban schools, Anyon argued that "until the economic and political systems in which the cities are enmeshed are themselves transformed so they may be more democratic and productive for urban residents, educational reformers have little chance of effecting long-lasting educational changes in city schools."[72]

Dissatisfaction emanates also from a small group of curriculum theorists known as the reconceptualists. This group of theorists, for the most part college professors of curriculum, has expressed concern about the hidden curriculum, the values that are not directly taught but that children nevertheless experience in school. These values include the rules students live by, their relationships with peers and adults in the school, and the values embedded in the content of their studies.

The reconceptualists argue for fundamental changes in curriculum and instruction. Some view curriculum *development* as outdated and offer in its place curriculum *understanding*.[73] They draw support for their position from the humanities, especially history, philosophy, and literary criticism. William Pinar explained the interests of reconceptual theorists:

The reconceptualists tend to concern themselves with the internal and existential experience of the public world. They tend to study not "change in behavior" or "decision making in the classroom," but matters of temporality, transcendence, consciousness, and politics. In brief, the reconceptualist attempts to understand the nature of educational experience.[74]

Pinar noted in 1975 that reconceptualists constituted three to five percent of all curriculum theorists. Another sixty to eighty percent were what Pinar called "traditionalists" whose primary mission is guiding practitioners in the schools. The others were "conceptual empiricists" whose interests lie in the behavioral sciences, of which the curriculum is one."[75] Although percentages for each of these three groups may vary somewhat today, observation of the current curriculum scene leads to the conclusion

---

[70]Ibid., p. 7.

[71]Michael W. Apple, *Cultural Politics and Education* (New York: Teachers College Press, 1996), p. 5.

[72]Jean Anyon, *Ghetto Schooling: A Political Economy of Urban Educational Reform* (New York: Teachers College Press, 1997), pp. 12–13.

[73]See William F. Pinar, William M. Reynolds, Patrick Slattery, and Peter M. Taubman, *Understanding Curriculum: An introduction to the Study of Historical and Contemporary Curriculum Discourses* (New York: Peter Lang, 1996), p. 6.

[74]William Pinar, ed., *Curriculum Theorizing: The Reconceptualists* (Berkeley, Calif.: McCutchan, 1975), pp. xii–xiii.

[75]Ibid., p. xii.

that the "traditionalists" still constitute the largest group, followed by the "conceptual empiricists," with the "reconceptualists" composing the smallest. Pinar et al. saw reconceptualization as still underemphasized in traditional curriculum textbooks.[76]

Critical Theory.   In discussing the reconceptualization of the curriculum field, Peter S. Hlebowitsh observed that "many contemporary challenges in curriculum studies have been inspired by a critical theory of education."[77] Influenced by the Institute of Social Research in Frankfort, Germany[78] critical theorists are concerned with injustices in society and the part the school plays in sustaining those injustices, for example, in "tracking, vocational education, special education, and teacher education."[79] Nell Noddings explained, "From the perspective of critical theorists, philosophy must be engaged with the great struggles and social movements of its times."[80]

The critical theorists offer no prescribed programs or pedagogical processes, stressing instead the need for empowerment of the individual with the goal of improving both the school and society. Noddings observed that "Philosophers of education have been greatly influenced by critical theory . . . ."[81]

In spite of the many conflicting philosophical views and at the risk of overgeneralizing we might conclude the public and a majority of educators at the start of the twenty-first century endorse educational programs and practices in American schools that represent a judicious mixture of essentialist and progressive philosophy.

FORMULATING A PHILOSOPHY

In a holistic approach to curriculum development, the curriculum committee designated to lead the process examines statements of aims of education, chooses those that appear most significant, and tries its skill at fashioning its own statements.

The curriculum committee should be cognizant of the major principles of the leading schools of philosophy, particularly essentialism and progressivism. They should know where they stand as individuals and as a group in the philosophical spectrum. They may discover that they have adopted, as have perhaps a majority of educators, an eclectic approach to philosophy, choosing the best from several philosophies. They may find that there is no such thing as a pure essentialist or a pure progressivist but rather, more commonly, one is an essentialist who leans toward progressive thinking (a progressive essentialist) or, conversely, a progressivist who leans toward essentialist ideas (an essentialistic progressivist).

Curriculum workers should take the time to think through their own philosophies and to formulate them into some kind of coherent statement. The formulation of philosophy is not an activity that most Americans—pragmatists as they are—engage in

---

[76]Pinar et al., *Understanding Curriculum,* p. 17.

[77]Peter S. Hlebowitsh, *Radical Curriculum Theory: A Historical Approach* (New York: Teachers College Press, 1993), p. 4.

[78]For discussion of the Institute for Social Research see Henry A. Giroux, *Pedagogy and the Politics of Hope: Theory, Culture, and Schooling: A Critical Reader* (Boulder, Col.: Westview Press, 1997), pp. 35–70.

[79]Hlebowitsh, *Radical Curriculum Theory,* p. 4

[80]Noddings, *Philosophy,* p. 67.

[81]Ibid., p. 68.

with either zeal or frequency. Unlike French schools that include philosophy in their secondary school curriculum, in our high schools philosophy is conspicuous by its absence. Even on the college level philosophy professors rarely have to beat off hordes of students clamoring at their doors.

Educators should reexamine their beliefs periodically to see if they reflect changes in society and the continuous expansion of knowledge. Schools would do well to draw up a statement of philosophy, review and revise it every five years, and thoroughly reexamine and revise it every ten years. This recommendation has been followed by schools that wished to achieve and maintain accreditation by the regional associations of colleges and schools.[82] Whether or not a school seeks regional accreditation, it should formulate a school philosophy to establish a framework for the practices of that school.

A school's philosophy should always be the result of cooperative efforts by teachers and administrators and preferably with the additional help of parents and students. Statements of philosophy are sometimes written and promulgated by a school administrator as the philosophy of that school. Such an activity might be engaged in to meet the terms for a report to the regional accreditation association, yet it misses the spirit of the exercise. The writing of a school philosophy should be an effort to gain consensus among divergent thinkers and to find out what aims and values the group holds in common. For this reason even a statement of philosophy drawn up by a faculty committee should be presented to the total faculty for acceptance, rejection, or modification. In a very real sense, the faculty's statement of philosophy becomes a manifesto signifying "This is what we believe" or "This is where we stand" as of now.

VALUE IN WRITING A PHILOSOPHY

Some hold that writing statements of philosophy is a waste of time, that such an effort takes too much valuable time that could be better spent in other ways, and that most efforts wind up with empty platitudes. Philosophical statements *can* become meaningless slogans, but they do not *have* to be. Should we call the following phrases of political philosophy from the Declaration of Independence—"all men are created equal"—and "they are endowed by their Creator with certain unalienable rights," including "Life, Liberty, and the Pursuit of Happiness"—empty platitudes? Why, we might ask, did our forebears not just sever relations between the motherland and the colonies instead of prattling about unalienable rights? Perhaps they recognized that they must set the stage and provide a rationale around which other like-minded persons might rally.

A school's philosophy is not of the same order or in the same class as the Declaration of Independence, yet it does set the stage and does offer a rationale that calls for the allegiance of those who proclaim it. If a statement of philosophy is to serve this purpose, it must be a truthful one and not simply platitudinous window dressing. If a school faculty believes that the major purposes of its school are to develop cognitive skills, to preserve the social status quo, or to direct the growth and development of the gifted and academically talented, it should say so. A frank statement of philosophical beliefs is much more defensible than a sanctimonious statement of platitudes that

---

[82]See Chapters 7 and 13 of this text for discussion of regional accreditation.

many faculty may not support and that many teachers do not translate into classroom practice.

As curriculum workers we must disabuse ourselves of the notions that it is somehow indecent to expose our beliefs and that we must feel either silly or guilty when setting forth ideals. The formulation of a school philosophy can be a valuable in-service educational experience, giving teachers and administrators a chance to exchange views and to find a common meeting ground.

A school's philosophy should include statements of belief about the purposes of education, society, the learner, and the role of the teacher. Examples of statements of philosophy written by school personnel follow below. These statements are typical of philosophies written by faculties throughout the United States. They speak about democracy, the individual, and the learning process. Statements of some schools are brief; others lengthy. Some schools include goals and objectives in their statements of philosophy. Here we are concerned primarily with a school's philosophy. In Chapter 8 we will discuss the writing of curriculum goals and objectives and will provide examples of those.

These statements of philosophy reveal the schools of thought to which the faculties subscribe. In spite of the essentialistic turn in American education, progressive beliefs are still strong. Despite the current emphasis on developing the intellect, these examples show concern for the whole child. In spite of increased stress on the development of cognitive abilities, the examples provided give attention to the affect.

PROBLEMS IN DEVELOPING AND IMPLEMENTING A PHILOSOPHY

Before examining the examples of school philosophies, we should mention that curriculum workers often encounter two sets of problems in developing and implementing a school's philosophy. First, those who are charged with drafting a statement usually enter into the process with differing assumptions, sometimes unexpressed, about the learning process, the needs of society, and the roles of individuals in that society. The various participating individuals may well espouse differing and conflicting philosophies of life that color their beliefs about education. Somehow the differing views need to be aired and reconciled. If consensus cannot be reached, perhaps no statement of philosophy can be drafted or that which is drafted will be so inconsequential as to be useless.

A second set of problems arises from the statement of philosophical beliefs in rather general, often vague, terms that permit varying interpretations. When a statement of philosophy has been completed and, presumably consensus has been reached on the *wording,* curriculum leaders will experience the continuing problem of striving to achieve consensus (sometimes even among those who drafted the statement) on *interpretations* of the wording.

EXAMPLES OF SCHOOL PHILOSOPHIES

Let's look at examples of school philosophies, in this case those of two large urban school districts: Omaha, Nebraska (Box 6.3) and Orange County (Florida) Public Schools (Box 6.4). Increasingly common in addition to statements of philosophy are

---

BOX 6.3

STATEMENT OF PHILOSOPHY OF THE SCHOOL DISTRICT OF OMAHA

The Board of Education of the Omaha Public Schools is responsible for meeting the challenge of providing a comprehensive educational program in an atmosphere that is open, concerned, and responsive to the needs of students and the community. To this end, the Board of Education establishes policies that are translated into practices and procedures by the Superintendent and staff to maintain and improve the quality of teaching and learning in the Omaha Public Schools. The following statements express the philosophy that guided the school district in formation of its goals and objectives:

IT IS BELIEVED:

- All students have an inherent right to an education that will enable them to reach their highest possible intellectual, social, physical, and ethical development.
- Education must concentrate on the complete development of students as individuals and as citizens.
- Quality education programs and a committed staff provide learners with the knowledge and skills necessary for full participation in our changing society.
- The responsibility of education in a democracy is to make it possible for all citizens to understand themselves and the world about them, so that they can live effectively in the world of expanding experiences and constant change.
- Education requires systematic and sustained effort by students, staff, parents, and community.
- Education is a life-long process.

SOURCE: *Practices & Procedures* School District of Omaha, Nebraska, February 1995. Reprinted with permission

---

statements of mission and specification of aims or goals and subgoals. Box 6.3 reproduces Omaha's statement of philosophy. Not reproduced but equally significant are a mission statement, several educational aims, and a number of goals and subgoals. Box 6.4 contains Orange County's mission statement and its exposition of district values and beliefs. Not shown but equally important are statements of expectations of students and staff and its district goals. You will encounter additional examples of school statements of belief in Chapter 8.

In the following examples, you will notice references to democratic concepts, to respect for the individual, and to the necessity of providing programs to develop the pupil in all his or her capacities. Although some may fault the style or prose of a given school philosophy, what we have to keep in mind is the purpose of the statement—to communicate to professionals and the public the beliefs held by the personnel of a school or a school system. A philosophy serves its purpose when significant beliefs are successfully communicated.

From our beliefs about education, schooling, learning, and society, we can proceed to subsequent steps of the curriculum development process. Component I of the suggested model for curriculum development calls for a statement of educational aims and philosophy. In respect to aims of education, curriculum workers should

BOX 6.4

MISSION STATEMENT OF ORANGE COUNTY (FLORIDA) PUBLIC SCHOOLS

Our district is committed to enhancing educational programs, facilities, and support services to ensure learner success both now and in the future. The following district mission expresses our commitment to learning:

Our mission is to ensure that all learners acquire the skills, knowledge, and attitudes necessary to succeed.

Success refers to performance in the classroom, home, workplace, and community. Learners include both students and staff. Our mission will be accomplished through the collaborative actions of staff, students, and community. Continuous quality improvement and customer satisfaction underlie all of our efforts.

DISTRICT VALUES AND BELIEFS

Efforts to accomplish the district mission and to achieve district and state goals are anchored by the following values and beliefs:

Students
- All students are treated with dignity and respect.
- All students can learn.
- Students are partners in educational decision-making.
- Students share responsibility for the quality of their education.
- Students actively engage in a meaningful learning process where success is the focus and time is structured to suit student needs.
- Students are empowered.

Learning
- Learning is unique to each individual.
- Learning is lifelong.
- Learning is facilitated by realistically high expectations, the application of skills and knowledge, collaboration and cooperation, personalized experiences, interactive approaches, an articulated curriculum, authentic assessment, successful experiences, and supportive technology.
- Instruction is based on research on how students learn.

Staff
- Quality education for students is the highest priority of all staff.
- All staff are engaged in the continuous quality improvement of programs, products, and services.
- Staff development is cooperatively planned and tailored to meet individual needs.
- Staff interactions and activities are characterized by integrity, mutual respect, and fairness.
- Staff are empowered partners in important district and school decision-making processes.

(Continued)

Box 6.4 Continued

Parents and Community
- Parents are partners in the education of students and in important district and school decision-making processes.
- Community members are partners in important district and school decision-making processes.

School and Worksites
- All schools and worksites are safe and secure for all.
- Decision-making responsibilities are placed as close as possible to where work is done and where teaching and learning take place.
- Innovation and prudent risk-taking at both the school and district level are encouraged and rewarded.
- Leadership is shared.

SOURCE: Orange County (Florida) Public Schools. Reprinted by permission.

- be aware that educational aims are derived from and are part of one's educational philosophy
- be cognizant of national statements of aims of education made by prominent individuals and groups
- evaluate national statements and select from those statements, revising as they deem necessary, the aims of education that they find acceptable
- draw up a statement of educational aims (in keeping with pronounced statewide aims) to which they subscribe or, alternately, incorporate the aims of education they have selected into a statement of philosophy

In respect to the philosophical dimension of component I, curriculum workers should be able to

- identify principal beliefs of leading schools of educational philosophy
- analyze statements of philosophy and identify the schools to which they belong
- analyze and clarify their own educational philosophies

SUMMARY

A holistic approach to curriculum development begins with an examination of the aims of education in society. Aims are perceived as the broad purposes of education that are national and, on occasion, international in scope.

Over the years a number of prominent individuals and groups expressed their positions on the appropriate aims of education for America. The curriculum worker should be able not only to formulate his or her own statement of aims but should also be knowledgeable about historic and significant statements of aims.

In this chapter we examined four philosophies of education—reconstructionism, progressivism, essentialism, and perennialism—two of which, essentialism and progressivism, are deemed to have special significance for our schools.

Essentialism, with its emphasis on subject matter, has been the prevailing philosophy of education throughout most of our country's history. Progressivism, however, with its emphasis on the child's needs and interests, has had a profound impact on educational programs and practices. Curriculum workers are urged to clarify their own philosophies and to draw up a statement of their school's philosophy that can be communicated to other professionals and to the public. Samples of school philosophies are included in this chapter not as models of content—that is, statements to be borrowed—but rather as examples of process. Curriculum developers should put together their own statement of beliefs in their own words. It is very likely that their statements will be eclectic in nature, borrowing from both essentialism and progressivism.

The development of a statement of aims of education and a school philosophy is seen as the first phase or component of a comprehensive model for curriculum development.

QUESTIONS FOR DISCUSSION

1. Why has the essentialistic philosophy of education been so enduring?
2. How can you keep a statement of philosophy from becoming mere verbalism?
3. If a state has adopted a statement of aims, is there any place for district or individual school statements?
4. Is truth relative or absolute? Explain with examples.
5. From what sources are aims of education derived?

SUPPLEMENTARY EXERCISES

1. Compare, citing appropriate references, aims of education in a democratic society with those of a totalitarian society.
2. State at least three premises of each of the following schools of philosophy:
   a. reconstructionism
   b. perennialism
   c. essentialism
   d. progressivism
3. Write a report, using appropriate references, contrasting essentialism and progressivism.
4. Search the literature and prepare a report on the research or beliefs of one (or more) of the following people, citing quotations from one or more of that person's works:

Jean Anyon	Jerome Bruner
Michael Apple	John Childs
William C. Bagley	Arthur Combs
Louise M. Berman	James B. Conant
Theodore Brameld	George Counts
Deborah P. Britzman	John Dewey

Friedrich Froebel
Henry A. Giroux
Maxine Greene
Madeleine Grumet
Georg W. F. Hegel
Johann F. Herbart
Dwayne Huebner
Robert M. Hutchins
William James
Immanuel Kant
Earl Kelley
William H. Kilpatrick
Herbert M. Kliebard
Kurt Koffka
Wolfgang Köhler
Kurt Lewin
Sarah Lawrence Lightfoot
Gail McCutchen
James B. Macdonald
Abraham Maslow
Alice Miel

Maria Montessori
Jeanie Oakes
Ivan Pavlov
Charles S. Peirce
Johann Pestalozzi
Philip Phenix
Jean Piaget
William F. Pinar
Hyman G. Rickover
Carl Rogers
Jean Jacques Rousseau
Harold Rugg
Kenneth A. Sirotnik
B. F. Skinner
Patrick Slattery
Donald Snygg
Herbert Spencer
Florence B. Stratemeyer
Edward L. Thorndike
John Watson
Max Wertheimer

5. Identify several practices in the schools that follow behavioristic principles.
6. Identify several practices in the schools that follow (a) experimentalist principles, (b) gestalt principles, (c) principles of perceptual psychology, and (d) constructivist principles.
7. Demonstrate with appropriate references how particular learning theories are related to certain schools of philosophy.
8. Write a short paper with appropriate references on the place and use of memorization in the classroom.
9. Write a paper on reflective thinking and show how it can be applied in the field of specialization you know best.
10. Write a report summarizing the findings of the Eight-Year Study.
11. Locate in the literature any curriculum proposals within the past five years that you would label either perennialist or reconstructionist.
12. Summarize the major beliefs of the following schools of philosophy and draw implications, if any, for the curriculum:
    a. naturalism
    b. idealism
    c. realism
    d. pragmatism
    e. existentialism
    f. scholasticism
13. Write an analysis of beliefs of the reconceptualists.
14. Write a report explaining and evaluating the beliefs of critical theorists.
15. Explain what is meant by critical inquiry.

BIBLIOGRAPHY

Adler, Mortimer J. *The Paideia Proposal: An Educational Manifesto.* New York: Macmillan, 1982.

Aikin, Wilford M. *The Story of the Eight-Year Study.* New York: Harper & Row, 1942.

Anyon, Jean. *Ghetto Schooling: A Political Economy of Urban Educational Reform.* New York: Teachers College Press, 1997.

Apple, Michael W. *Cultural Politics and Education.* New York: Teachers College Press, 1996.

———. *Ideology and Curriculum,* 2nd ed. New York. Routledge, 1990.

———. "The Politics of Curriculum and Teaching." *NASSP Bulletin* 75, no. 532 (February 1991): 39-50.

Aronowitz, Stanley and Giroux, Henry A. *Education Under Siege: The Conservative, Liberal, and Radical Debate over Schooling.* South Hadley, Mass.: Bergin & Garvey, 1985.

Ayers, William C. and Miller, Janet L., eds. *A Light in Dark Times: Maxine Greene and the Unfinished Conversation.* New York: Teachers College Press, 1998.

Bagley, William C. "An Essentialist's Platform for the Advancement of American Education." *Educational Administration and Supervision* 24, no. 4 (April 1938): 241–256.

Bennett, William J., ed. *The Book of Virtues: A Treasury of Great Moral Stories.* New York: Simon and Schuster, 1993.

———. *Our Children and Our Country: Improving America's Schools and Affirming the Common Culture.* New York: Simon and Schuster, 1988.

Beyer, Landon E. and Apple, Michael W., eds. *The Curriculum: Problems, Politics, and Possibilities,* 2nd ed. Albany, New York: State University of New York Press, 1998.

Bode, Boyd H. *How We Learn.* Boston: D. C. Heath, 1940.

———. "Pragmatism in Education." *New Republic* 121, no. 16 (October 17, 1949): 15–18.

Brameld, Theodore. *Patterns of Educational Philosophy: A Democratic Interpretation.* Yonkers, N.Y.: World Book Company, 1950.

———. *Patterns of Educational Philosophy: Divergence and Convergence in Culturological Perspective.* New York: Holt, Rinehart and Winston, 1971.

Broudy, Harry S. *Building a Philosophy of Education,* 2nd ed. Englewood Cliffs, N.J.: Prentice Hall, 1961.

Brooks, Jacqueline Grennon and Brooks, Martin G. *In Search of Understanding: The Case for Constructivist Classrooms.* Alexandria, Va.: Association for Supervision and Curriculum Development, 1993.

Burrett, Kenneth and Rusnak, Timothy. *Integrated Character Education.* Bloomington, Ind.: Phi Delta Kappa, 1993.

Butler, J. Donald. *Four Philosophies and Their Practice in Education and Religion,* 3rd ed. New York: Harper & Row, 1968.

Caine, Renate Nummela and Caine, Geoffrey. *Making Connections: Teaching and the Human Brain.* Alexandria, Va.: Association for Supervision and Curriculum Development, 1991.

Castenell, Louis A., Jr. and Pinar, William, eds. *Understanding Curriculum as Racial Text: Representations of Identity and Difference in Education.* Albany, N.Y.: State University of New York Press, 1993.

"Character Education." *Educational Leadership* 51, no. 3 (November 1993): 6–97.

Combs, Arthur W. "A Perceptual View of the Adequate Personality." In *Perceiving, Behaving, Becoming,* 1962 Yearbook. Alexandria, Va.: Association for Supervision and Curriculum Development, 1962, pp. 50–64.

——— and Snygg, Donald. *Individual Behavior: A Perceptual Approach to Behavior,* rev. ed. New York: Harper & Row, 1959.

Commission on the Reorganization of Secondary Education. *Cardinal Principles of Secondary Education.* Washington, D.C.: United States Office of Education, Bulletin 35, 1918.

Conant, James B. *The American High School Today.* New York: McGraw-Hill, 1959.

———. *The Comprehensive High School.* New York: McGraw-Hill, 1967.

"The Constructivist Classroom." *Educational Leadership* 57, no. 3 (November 1999): 6–78.

———. *Recommendations for Education in the Junior High School Years.* Princeton, N.J.: Educational Testing Service, 1960.

Counts, George S. *Dare the School Build a New Social Order?* New York: John Day, 1932.

Cremin, Lawrence A. *The Transformation of the School: Progressivism in American Education, 1876–1975.* New York: Alfred A. Knopf, 1961.

Darling-Hammond, Linda. *The Right to Learn: A Blueprint for Creating Schools That Work.* San Francisco: Jossey-Bass, 1997.

Dewey, John. *The Child and the Curriculum.* Chicago: University of Chicago Press, 1902.

———. *Democracy and Education: An Introduction to the Philosophy of Education.* New York: Macmillan, 1916; New York: Free Press, 1966.

———. *Interest and Effort in Education.* Boston: Houghton Mifflin, 1913.

———. *My Pedagogic Creed.* Washington, D.C.: Progressive Education Association, 1929.

Durant, Will, *The Story of Philosophy: The Lives and Opinions of the World's Greatest Philosophers from Plato to John Dewey.* New York: Simon & Schuster, 1926.

Ebel, Robert L. "What Are Schools For?" *Phi Delta Kappan* 54, no. 1 (September 1972): 3-7.

Educational Policies Commission. *The Central Purpose of American Education.* Washington, D.C.: National Education Association, 1961.

———. *Moral and Spiritual Values in the Public Schools.* Washington, D.C.: National Education Association, 1951.

———. *The Unique Function of Education in American Democracy.* Washington, D.C.: National Education Association, 1937.

Eisner, Elliot W. "Curriculum Ideologies." In Philip W. Jackson, ed. *Handbook of Research on Curriculum.* New York: Macmillan, 1992, pp. 302–326.

——— and Vallance, Elizabeth, eds. *Conflicting Conceptions of Curriculum.* Berkeley, Calif.: McCutchan, 1974.

Elam, Stanley M., Rose, Lowell C., and Gallup, Alec M. "The 26th Annual Phi Delta Kappa/Gallup Poll of the Public's Attitudes Toward the Public Schools." *Phi Delta Kappan* 58, no. 1 (September 1976): 31–35.

Freire, Paulo. *Pedagogy of Hope: Reliving Pedagogy of the Oppressed.* New York: Continuum, 1992.

———. *Pedagogy of the Oppressed,* rev. 20th anniversary edition. New York: Continuum, 1993.

Giroux, Henry A. "Curriculum Planning, Public Schooling, and Democratic Struggle. *NASSP Bulletin* 75, no. 532 (February 1991): 12–25.

———. *Living Dangerously: Multiculturalism and the Politics of Difference.* New York: Peter Lang, 1993.

———. *Pedagogy and the Politics of Hope: Theory, Culture, and Schooling: A Critical Reader.* Boulder: Col.: Westview Press, 1997.

———. *Theory and Resistance in Education: A Pedagogy for the Opposition.* South Hadley, Mass.: Bergin & Garvey, 1983.

——— and Purpel, David, eds. *The Hidden Curriculum and Moral Education: Deception or Discovery?* Berkeley, Calif.: McCutchan, 1983.

Goodlad, John I. *A Place Called School: Prospects for the Future.* New York: McGraw-Hill, 1984.

Greene, Maxine. *Landscapes of Learning.* New York: Teachers College Press, 1970.

———. *The Public School and the Private Vision: A Search for America in Education and Literature.* New York: Random House, 1965.

———. *Releasing the Imagination: Essays on Education, the Arts, and Social Change.* San Francisco: Jossey-Bass, 1995.

Harris, Karen R. and Steve Graham. "Constructivism: Principles, Paradigms, and Integration." *The Journal of Special Education* 28, no. 3 (March 1994): 233–247.

Harvard Committee on General Education. *General Education in a Free Society.* Cambridge, Mass.: Harvard University Press, 1945.

Hlebowitsh, Peter S. *Radical Curriculum Theory Reconsidered: A Historical Perspective.* New York: Teachers College Press, 1993.

Hutchins, Robert M. *The Higher Learning in America.* New Haven, Conn.: Yale University Press, 1936.

———. *On Education.* Santa Barbara: Center for the Study of Democratic Institutions, 1963.

Jelinek, James John, ed. *Improving the Human Condition: A Curricular Response to Critical Realities,* 1978 Yearbook. Alexandria, Va.: Association for Supervision and Curriculum Development, 1978.

Johnson, Harold T. *Foundations of Curriculum.* Columbus, Ohio: Charles E. Merrill, 1968.

Kilpatrick, William H., ed. *The Educational Frontier.* New York: Appleton-Century-Crofts, 1933.

Kirschenbaum, Howard. "A Comprehensive Model for Values Education and Moral Education." *Phi Delta Kappan* 73, no. 10 (June 1992): 771–776.

Kleibard, Herbert M. "The Effort to Reconstruct the Modern American Curriculum" in Landon E. Beyer and Michael W. Apple, eds., *The Curriculum: Problems, Politics, and Possibilities,* 2nd ed. Albany, N.Y.: State University of New York Press, 1998, pp. 21–33.

———. *The Struggle for the American Curriculum 1898–1958.* Boston: Routledge & Kegan Paul, 1986.

Lickona, Thomas. "The Return of Character Education." *Educational Leadership* 51, no. 3 (November 1993): 6–11.

Maslow, Abraham H. "Some Basic Propositions of a Growth and Self-Actualization Psychology." In Arthur W. Combs, ed. *Perceiving, Behaving, Becoming.* 1962 Yearbook. Alexandria, Va.: Association for Supervision and Curriculum Development, 1962.

———. *Toward a Psychology of Being,* 2nd ed. New York: Van Nostrand Reinhold, 1968.

Miller, John P. and Seller, Wayne. *Curriculum: Perspectives and Practice.* White Plains, N.Y.: Longman, 1985.

Mitchell, Richard. *The Leaning Tower of Bable and Other Affronts by the Underground Grammarian.* Boston: Little, Brown, 1984.

Molnar, Alex, ed. *Current Thought on Curriculum,* 1985 Yearbook. Alexandria, Va.: Association for Supervision and Curriculum Development, 1985.

National Education Goals Panel. *National Education Goals Report: Building a Nation of Learners.* Washington, D.C.: U.S. Government Printing Office, 1994.

———. *The National Education Goals Report. Vol. I. The National Report. Vol. II. State Reports.* Washington, D.C.: U.S. Government Printing Office, 1994.

"National Goals: Let Me Count the Ways." *The Education Digest* 56, no. 2 (October 1990): 8-26.

"The National Goals—Putting Education Back on the Road." *PhiDeltaKappan* 72, no.4 (December 1990): 259-314.

National Governors' Association. *Educating America: State Strategies for Achieving the National Education*

Goals. Washington, D.C.: National Governors' Association, 1990.

————. *Time for Results: The Governors' 1991 Report on Education.* Washington, D.C.: National Governors' Association, 1991.

Noddings, Nell. *Philosophy of Education.* Boulder, Col.: Westview Press, 1995.

Oliva, Peter F. *The Secondary School Today,* 2nd ed. New York: Harper & Row, 1972.

Ornstein, Allan C. and Behar, Linda S., eds. *Contemporary Issues in Curriculum.* Boston: Allyn and Bacon, 1995.

Ornstein, Allan C. and Hunkins, Francis P. *Curriculum: Foundations, Principles, and Issues.* Englewood Cliffs, N.J.: Prentice-Hall, 1988.

———— and Levine, Daniel U. *An Introduction to the Foundations of Education,* 3rd ed. Boston: Houghton Mifflin, 1985.

Patterson, James and Kim, Peter. *The Day America Told the Truth: What People Really Believe About Everything that Really Matters.* New York: Prentice-Hall, 1991.

Piaget, Jean. *The Child's Conception of the World.* New York: Littlefield, 1975.

————. *Insights and Illusions of Philosophy.* New York: World, 1971.

Pinar, William, ed. *Curriculum Theorizing: The Reconceptualists.* Berkeley, Calif.: McCutchan, 1975.

————, Reynolds, William M., Slattery, Patrick, and Taubman, Peter M. *Understanding Curriculum: An Introduction to the Study of Historical and Contemporary Curriculum Discourses.* New York: Peter Lang, 1996.

Rickover, Hyman G. *Education for All Children: What We Can Learn from England: Hearing Before the Committee on Appropriations, House of Representatives, Eighty-Seventh Congress, Second Session.* Washington, D.C.: U.S. Government Printing Office, 1962.

Rugg, Harold et al. *The Foundations and Technique of Curriculum-Construction,* 26th Yearbook of the National Society for the Study of Education, Part 2, *The Foundations of Curriculum-Making,* ed. Guy Montrose Whipple, Bloomington, Ind.: Public School Publishing Company, 1927; New York: Arno Press and *The New York Times,* 1969.

————. *Foundations for American Education.* Yonkers, N.Y.: World Book Company, 1947.

Schiro, Michael. *Curriculum for Better Schools: The Great Ideological Debate.* Englewood Cliffs, N.J.: Educational Technological Publications, 1978.

Sears, James T. and Marshall, J. Dan. *Teaching and Thinking About Curriculum: Critical Inquiries.* New York: Teachers College Press, 1990.

Sirotnik, Kenneth A. "What Goes On In Classrooms? Is This the Way We Want It?" in Landon E. Beyer and Michael W. Apple, eds. *The Curriculum: Problems, Politics, and Possibilities,* 2nd ed. Albany, N.Y.: State University of New York Press, 1998, pp. 58–76.

Sizer, Theodore R. "Education and Assimilation: A Fresh Plea for Pluralism." *Phi Delta Kappan* 58, no. 1 (September 1976): 31–35.

————. *Horace's School: Redesigning the American High School.* Boston: Houghton Mifflin, 1992.

———— and Sizer, Nancy Faust. "Grappling," *Phi Delta Kappan* 81, no. 3 (November 1999): 184–190.

Taba, Hilda. *Curriculum Development: Theory and Practice.* New York: Harcourt Brace Jovanovich, 1962.

Tanner, Daniel and Tanner, Laurel N. *Curriculum Development: Theory into Practice,* 3rd ed. New York: Merrill, 1995.

————. *History of the School Curriculum.* New York: Macmillan, 1990.

Thayer, V. T. *The Role of the School in American Society.* New York: Dodd, Mead, 1960.

U.S. Department of Education. *America 2000: An Education Strategy.* Washington, D.C.: U.S. Government Printing Office, 1991.

————. *America 2000: Sourcebook.* Washington, D.C.: U.S. Government Printing Office, 1991.

U.S. Department of Education. *National Goals for Education.* Washington, D.C.: U.S. Department of Education, 1990.

Walker, Decker. *Fundamentals of Curriculum.* Orlando, Fla.: Harcourt Brace Jovanovich, 1990.

Walker, Decker F. and Soltis, Jonas F. *Curriculum and Aims,* 3rd ed. New York: Teachers College Press, 1997.

"What Schools Should Teach." *Educational Leadership* 46, no. 1 (September 1988): 2–60.

Wiles, Jon and Bondi, Joseph C. *Curriculum Development: A Guide to Practice,* 5th ed. Upper Saddle River, N.J.: Merrill, 1998.

Wood, George H. "Teachers as Curriculum Workers," in James T. Sears and J. Dan Marshall, eds. *Teaching and Thinking About Curriculum: Critical Inquiries.* New York: Teachers College Press, 1990, pp. 97–109.

VIDEOTAPES

Constructivism. Video clips, case studies, learning activities, readings. 1997. Jacqueline Grennon Brooks and Martin C. Brooks, developers. Association for Supervision and Curriculum Development, 1703 N. Beauregard St., Alexandria, Va. 22311-1714.

WEB SITES

Character Counts!: http://www.charactercounts.org

Character Education Partnership: http://www.character.org

Character First! Education: http://www.cfeducation.com

Josephson Institute of Ethics: http://www.josephsoninstitute.org

CHAPTER 7

NEEDS ASSESSMENT

After studying this chapter you should be able to:

1. Identify and describe major sources of curriculum content.
2. Outline levels and types of needs of students.
3. Outline levels and types of needs of society.
4. Show how needs are derived from the structure of a discipline.
5. Describe the steps in conducting a needs assessment.
6. Construct an instrument for conducting a curriculum needs assessment.

CATEGORIES OF NEEDS

At the beginning of the twenty-first century the following items of content among thousands of items were being taught at specified grades somewhere in the United States:

- Kindergarten: Identification of the primary and secondary colors.
- First grade: Identification of U.S. coins.
- Second grade: Demonstration of ability to use period, comma, question mark, and quotation marks correctly.
- Third grade: Distinguishing between a solid, liquid, and gas.
- Fourth grade: Identification of common musical instruments.
- Fifth grade: Demonstration of skill of administering first aid to victims of accidents.
- Sixth grade: Performance of selected calisthenic skills.
- Seventh grade: Demonstration of use of library reference works.
- Eighth grade: Tracing historical development of own state.
- Ninth grade: Using a circular saw properly.
- Tenth grade: Describing preparation needed for selected careers.
- Eleventh grade: Demonstrating skill in using a computer for data and word processing.

• Twelfth grade: Writing a research paper.

We could have listed hundreds of items that young people are called on to master in the course of their education from elementary through secondary school. For the moment these twelve items will suffice for our purpose.

In reviewing these and other items, we could raise a number of questions. How did these particular items of content get there? What needs do the items fulfill? Have the right items been selected? What has been omitted that should have been included, and what might be eliminated from the curriculum? How do we find out whether an item is filling a need? Which needs are being met satisfactorily and which are not being met? What kinds of needs are there to which curriculum planners must pay attention?

The first section of this chapter discusses needs of students and society, classified by levels and types, and needs derived from the subject matter. The second section describes a process for conducting a curriculum needs assessment. When carrying out this process, curriculum planners study the needs of learners, society, and subject matter. With the help of the community, students, teachers, and administrators identify and place in order of priority programmatic needs that the school must address.

In the preceding chapter we saw that statements of educational aims and philosophy are based upon needs of students in general and needs of society. Needs of both students and society are evident in the following phrases drawn from statements of aims and philosophy:

• to promote the Judeo-Christian heritage
• to promote free enterprise
• to develop a well-rounded individual
• to develop a skilled worker
• to promote the pursuit of happiness
• to enrich the spirit
• to develop the ability to use the basic skills
• to develop the ability to think
• to develop a linguistically, technologically, and culturally literate person
• to develop communication skills
• to develop respect for others
• to develop moral, spiritual, and ethical values

Statements of aims and philosophy point to common needs of students and society and set a general framework within which a school or school system will function. In formulating curriculum goals and objectives for a particular school or school system, curriculum developers must give their attention to five sources as shown by components I and II of the model for curriculum development: (1) the needs of students in general, (2) the needs of society, (3) the needs of the particular students, (4) the needs of the particular community, and (5) the needs derived from the subject matter. You will recall that Ralph Tyler, in a similar vein, listed three sources from which tentative general objectives are derived: student, society, and subject.[1]

---

[1] See Chapter 5.

We can expand upon the needs of both students and society in a greater level of detail than is shown in the model for curriculum development by classifying the needs of students and society into two broad categories—levels and types—thereby emphasizing points that curriculum planners should keep in mind.

A CLASSIFICATION SCHEME

To focus our thinking, let's take a look at the following four-part classification scheme:

- needs of students by level
- needs of students by type
- needs of society by level
- needs of society by type

Before analyzing each category, I must stress that the needs of the student cannot be completely divorced from those of society or vice versa. The needs of one are intimately linked to those of the other. True, the two sets of needs sometimes conflict. For example, an individual's need may be contrary to society's when he or she shouts "Fire" to gain attention in a crowded theater when there is no fire. An individual's desire to keep an appointment may result in his or her speeding on the highway and thereby endangering the lives of other members of society. In these two examples, the apparent needs of the person and those of society are antithetical.

The needs of the person and the needs of society are, fortunately, often in harmony. An individual's desire to amass wealth, if carried out legally and fairly, is compatible with a democratic, productive society. The wealth may benefit society in the form of investment or taxes. An individual's need for physical fitness is congruent with society's demand for physically fit people. The literate citizen is as much a need of society as literacy is a need of the individual. Consequently, it is sometimes difficult to categorize a particular need as specifically a need of the person or of society. That degree of refinement is not necessary. As long as the curriculum planner recognizes the need, its classification is secondary.

Lest there be a misunderstanding, the needs of the particular student do not completely differ from those of students in general but do vary from those of other students who share the same general needs. Students manifest not only their own particular needs but also the needs of young people generally in our society. The needs of a particular community do not completely vary from those of society in general but do differ in some respects from those of other communities that share the same general societal needs. The thousands of communities in the United States are, in spite of local distinctions of needs, resources, and cultural idiosyncrasies, parts of the total culture linked by mass media and transportation.

INTERESTS AND WANTS

Before proceeding with a discussion of needs of students, we should distinguish between student *interests* and *wants* in curriculum development. *Interest* refers to attitudes of predisposition toward something (for example, auto mechanics, history, dramatics, or basketball). *Want* includes wishes, desires, or longings for something, such as the want for an automobile, spending money, or stylish clothes.

None of the models for curriculum development in Chapter 5 builds into it either the interests or wants of students. The reasons why interests and wants of students are not shown in the proposed model for curriculum development are the following:

1. The model would become unduly complex and burdensome were these facets of student behavior to be incorporated as well as needs.
2. Interests and wants can be immediate or long-range, serious or ephemeral. Immediate and ephemeral interests and wants have less relevance than long-range and serious interests and wants.
3. Both interests and wants may actually be the bases of needs. For example, an interest in the opposite sex, which may be derived from a basic human drive, may indicate a need for curriculum responses in the areas of human and social relationships. A want may actually be a need. The want to be accepted, for example, is, in fact, the psychological need to be accepted. Alternatively, the want for a pair of expensive, designer jeans, though some may possibly argue, is not a need. If, then, interests and wants can be the bases for needs and are sometimes needs themselves, it would be redundant for them to be shown separately in a model for curriculum improvement.
4. Needs are given a higher priority in the grand scheme of curriculum development than interests and wants. Curriculum workers are on more solid ground when they seek to give closer attention to needs than to interests or wants.

Curriculum workers and instructional personnel know full well, of course, that they cannot ignore interests and wants of students, for these can be powerful motivators. Certainly, as far as interests go, the literature is filled with admonitions for educators to be concerned with student needs and interests to the point where the two concepts, needs and interests, are one blended concept, needs-and-interests.

Interests and wants of students must be continuously considered and sifted in the processes of both curriculum development and instruction. Although curriculum developers cannot cater to whimsical interests and wants of students, they cannot ignore legitimate and substantial interests and wants.

NEEDS OF STUDENTS: LEVELS

The levels of student needs of concern to the curriculum planner may be identified as (1) human, (2) national, (3) state or regional, (4) community, (5) school, and (6) individual.

HUMAN

The curriculum should reflect the needs of students as members of the human race, needs that are common to all human beings on the globe, for example, food, clothing, shelter, and good health. Franklin D. Roosevelt, in his State of the Union address to the U.S. Congress in 1941, iterated four universal needs of humanity, widely known as the Four Freedoms. These are: freedom from want, freedom from fear, freedom to worship God in one's own way, and freedom of speech and expression.

The American student shares in common with his brothers and sisters all over the world certain fundamental human needs that the curriculum should address. The study of anthropology could help a curriculum planner to recognize fundamental human needs.

NATIONAL

At the national level, the general needs of students in American society are assessed. Chapter 6 already presented efforts to identify nationwide needs of students through statements of aims of education. We might identify as needs of students throughout the nation, development of the ability to think, mastery of basic skills, preparation for a vocation or college, the ability to drive a car, consumer knowledge and skills, and a broad, general knowledge. Some of the national needs we might identify are ones held in common by inhabitants of all nations. For example, few would argue that literacy education is not essential to the development and growth of any nation. In that sense literacy education is a worldwide but not a human need because men and women do not need to read or write to exist. Human beings, however, cannot exist without food and water or with overexposure to the elements.

To become aware of nationwide needs of students, the curriculum planners should be well-read, and it is helpful for them to be well-traveled. The curriculum planner should recognize changing needs of our country's youth. For example, contemporary young people must learn to live with the computer, to conserve dwindling natural resources, to protect the environment, and to change some basic attitudes to survive in twenty-first century America.

STATE OR REGIONAL

Curriculum planners should determine whether students have needs particular to a state or region. Whereas preparing for a vocation is a common need of all students in American society, preparing for specific vocations may be more appropriate in a particular community, state, or region. General knowledge and specialized training in certain fields, such as health care, teaching, secretarial science, auto mechanics, woodworking, computer programming, and data processing, may be applied throughout the country. However, states or regions may require students to be equipped with specific knowledge and skills for their industrial and agricultural specializations. Construction workers may be needed, for example, in growing areas of the Sunbelt and not in states or regions that are losing population. Some states and regions exceed others in their need for workers in the hospitality industry.

COMMUNITY

The curriculum developer studies the community served by the school or school system and asks what students' needs are in this particular community. Students growing up in a mining town in West Virginia have some demands that differ from those of students living among the cherry orchards of Michigan. In some urban communities with their melange of races, creeds, colors, and national origins, one of the greatest needs may be to learn to get along with one another. Students who finish school and choose to remain in their communities will need knowledge and skills sufficient for them to earn a livelihood in those communities.

SCHOOL

The curriculum planner typically probes and excels at analyzing the needs of students in a particular school. These needs command the attention of curriculum workers to such an extent that sometimes the demands of the individual students are obscured. The need for remedial reading and mathematics is obvious in schools where test scores reveal deficiencies. The need for the English language may be pressing in a school with a large percentage of children with another native language. Recently integrated or multiethnic school populations show, as a rule, the need for opening communication among groups. Some schools (especially magnet schools specializing, for example, in science, the performing arts, health occupations, or the building trades) reflect the built-in needs of their student body.[2]

INDIVIDUAL

Finally, the needs of individual students in a particular school must be examined. Can it be that the needs of individual students go unattended while focus is on the needs of the many? Has the school addressed the needs of the average, the gifted, the academically talented, the physically or mentally challenged, the diabetic, the hyperactive, the withdrawn, the aggressive, the antisocial, and the creative pupil (to mention but a few categories of individual behavior)? We must ask to what extent the philosophical pledges to serve the needs of individuals are being carried out.

Each level of student needs builds upon the preceding level and makes, in effect, a cumulative set. Thus the individual student presents needs that emanate from his or her (1) individuality, (2) membership in the school, (3) residence in the community, (4) living in the state or region, (5) residing in the United States, and (6) belonging to the human race.

NEEDS OF STUDENTS: TYPES

Another dimension is added when the curriculum planner analyzes the needs of students by types. Four broad types of needs can be established: physical, sociopsychological, educational, and developmental tasks.

PHYSICAL

Biologically determined, the physical needs of young people are common within the culture and generally constant across cultures. Students need movement, exercise, rest, proper nutrition, and adequate medical attention. On leaving the childhood years, students need help with the transition from puberty to adolescence. In the adolescent years they must learn to cope with their developing sexuality. Providing for the dis-

---

[2]For discussion of magnet schools see Chapter 9.

abled is a growing concern in our society. A sound curriculum aids students to understand and meet their physical needs not only during the years of schooling but also into adulthood as well.

SOCIOPSYCHOLOGICAL

Some curriculum developers might divide this category into social and psychological needs, yet it is often difficult to distinguish between the two. For example, an individual's need for affection is certainly a psychological need. Affection, however, is sought from other individuals and in that context becomes a social need. At first glance, self-esteem seems a purely psychological need. If we believe perceptual psychologists like Earl C. Kelley, however, the self is formed through relationships with others: "The self consists, in part at least, of the accumulated experiential background, or backlog, of the individual. . . . This self is built almost entirely, if not entirely, in relationship to others. . . . Since the self is achieved through social contact, it has to be understood in terms of others."[3]

Among the common sociopsychological needs are affection, acceptance and approval, belonging, success, and security. Furthermore, each individual, both in school and out, needs to be engaged in meaningful work. The lack of significant work may well account, at least in part, for the notorious inefficiency of some nations' bloated governmental bureaucracies.

The needs of the mentally and emotionally exceptional child fit more clearly into the psychological category. Attention must be paid to the wide range of exceptionalities: the gifted, the creative, the emotionally disturbed, the mildly retarded, and the severely retarded. Curriculum workers must be able to identify sociopsychological needs of students and to incorporate ways to meet these needs into the curriculum.

EDUCATIONAL

Curriculum planners ordinarily view their task of providing for the educational needs of students as their primary concern. The educational needs of students shift as society changes and as more is learned about the physical and sociopsychological aspects of child growth and development. Historically, schools have gone from emphasizing a classical and theocratic education to a vocational and secular education. They have sought to meet the educational needs of young people through general education, sometimes as the study of contemporary problems of students and/or society. "Life adjustment" courses and career education have been features in our educational history. The basic skills and academic disciplines are currently preferred as the curricular pièce de résistance. The curriculum worker should keep in mind that educational needs do not exist outside the context of students' other needs and society's needs.

DEVELOPMENTAL TASKS

Robert J. Havighurst made popular the concept of a "developmental task," which he viewed as a task that had to be completed by an individual at a particular time in his

---

[3]Earl C. Kelley, "The Fully Functioning Self," in *Perceiving, Behaving, Becoming,* 1962 Yearbook (Alexandria, Va.: Association for Supervision and Curriculum Development, 1962), pp. 9, 13.

or her development if that individual is to experience success with later tasks.[4] He traced the developmental tasks of individuals in our society from infancy through later maturity and described the biological, psychological, and cultural bases as well as the educational implications of each task.

Found between individual needs and societal demands, developmental tasks do not fall neatly into the schemes developed in this chapter for classifying the needs of students and the needs of society. These tasks are, in effect, personal-social needs that arise at a particular stage of life and that must be met at that stage. In middle childhood, for example, youngsters must learn to live, work, and play harmoniously with each other. In adolescence, individuals must learn to become independent, responsible citizens.

Havighurst addressed the question of the usefulness of the concept of developmental tasks in the following way:

> There are two reasons why the concept of developmental tasks is useful to educators. First, it helps in discovering and stating the purposes of education in the schools. Education may be conceived as the effort of society, through the school, to help the individual achieve   certain of his developmental tasks.
>
>   The second use of the concept is in the timing of educational efforts. When the body is ripe, and society requires, and the self is ready to achieve a certain task, the teachable moment has come. Efforts at teaching which would have been largely wasted if they had come earlier, give gratifying results when they come at the *teachable moment,* when the task should be learned.[5]

Curriculum planners in earlier years frequently fashioned an often elaborate planning document known as a scope-and-sequence chart. This chart assigned content to be encountered at each grade level following what was known about child growth and development. Today we recognize the necessity for developmental appropriateness, i.e., providing learning experiences appropriate to the age and background of the individual learner.[6] Addressing the fit between the curriculum and needs of learners, George S. Morrison saw four types of appropriateness: developmental, in terms of growth and development; individual, in terms of special needs of learners; multicultural, in terms of cultural diversity; and gender, in terms of avoiding discriminatory content or practice.[7]

NEEDS OF SOCIETY: LEVELS

The curriculum worker not only looks at the needs of students in relation to society but also at the needs of society in relation to students. These two levels of needs sometimes converge, diverge, or mirror each other. When we make the needs of students the focal point, we gain a perspective that may differ from that accorded us in studying the

---

[4]See Robert J. Havighurst, *Developmental Tasks and Education,* 3rd ed. (New York: Longman, 1972).

[5]Robert J. Havighurst, *Developmental Tasks and Education,* 1st ed. (Chicago: University of Chicago Press, 1948), p. 8.

[6]See Scott Willis, "Teaching Young Children: Educators Seek 'Developmental Appropriateness,'" *ASCD Curriculum Update* (November 1993): 1–8.

[7]George S. Morrison, *Contemporary Curriculum K–8* (Boston: Allyn and Bacon, 1993), pp. 88–90.

needs of society. In analyzing the needs of society, the curriculum worker must bring a particular set of skills to the task. Grounding in the behavioral sciences is especially important to the analysis of the needs of the individual, whereas training in the social sciences is pivotal to the analysis of the needs of society.

As we did in the case of assessing students' needs, let's construct two simple taxonomies of the needs of society: first, as to level, and second, as to type. We can classify the levels of needs of society from the broadest to the narrowest: human, international, national, state, community, and neighborhood.

HUMAN

What needs, we might ask, do human beings throughout the world have as a result of their membership in the human race? Humans as a species possess the same needs as individual human beings—food, clothing, and shelter. Collectively, humankind has a need for freedom from want, from disease, and from fear. As a civilized society, presumably thousands of years removed from the Stone Age. human beings have the need, albeit often unrealized, to live in a state of peace. Human society, by virtue of its position at the pinnacle of evolutionary development, has a continuing need to maintain control over subordinate species of the animal kingdom. When we see the devastation wrought by earthquakes, volcanoes, hurricanes, floods, tornadoes, and drought, we are repeatedly reminded of the need to understand and control the forces of nature. Some of the needs—or demands, if you will—of society are common to the human race.

INTERNATIONAL

Curriculum developers should consider needs that cut across national boundaries and exist not so much because they are basic needs of humanity but because they arise from our loose confederation of nations. The study of foreign languages, for example, is a response to the need for peoples to communicate with each other. The nations of the world need to improve the flow of trade across their borders. They need to work out more effective means of sharing expertise and discoveries for the benefit of all nations. The more fortunate nations can assist the less fortunate to meet their developmental needs by sharing the fruits of their good fortune. The people of each nation continually need to try to understand more about the culture of other nations.

Many years ago I attempted to define a number of understandings that appeared to be essential for American youth to know about the world.[8] Few of these understandings have changed significantly with the passing of time. With the possible exception of the last item in the following list, the same understandings are relevant to the people of every nation, not only Americans.

All American youth need to understand that

1. the world's population is rapidly outstripping its resources.
2. there is more poverty in the world than riches.
3. more than one-third of the world's population is illiterate.
4. there are more "colored" people in the world than white.

---

[8]Peter F. Oliva, "Essential Understandings for the World Citizen," *Social Education* 23, no. 6 (October 1959): 266–268.

5. there are more non-Christians in the world than Christians.
6. our actions at home are sources of propaganda abroad.
7. nationalism is on the march as never before.
8. most of the nations of the world are struggling for technical advances.
9. you can reach by air any point on the globe within thirty-six hours. [Today I would reduce the number of hours of air journey to reflect supersonic flight and would add "you can reach distant spots on the planet almost instantaneously via electronic mail at a miniscule cost."]
10. in spite of our problems at home, thousands of foreigners abroad want to migrate to the land of the free and the home of the brave.

Surely the fact that the world's population of six billion which is projected to reach twenty billion within two decades unless stabilized, ethnic wars such as experienced in recent years in the former Yugoslavia and Rwanda, starvation in countries like Somalia, U.S. and U.N. engagements like the Persian Gulf War, the demise of the Soviet Union, the rise of China to prominence, and the volatility of international financial markets, provide examples of international problems which can have an impact on contemporary curriculum development.

NATIONAL

The curriculum planner must be able to define the needs of the nation with some degree of lucidity. Consequently, our form of government rests upon the presence of an educated and informed citizenry. Education in citizenship is to a great extent the function of the school. One means of identifying national needs is to examine the social and economic problems faced by the country. The United States has an urgent need, for example, to train or retrain persons in occupations that appear to be growing rather than declining. The curriculum planner must be cognizant of careers that are subject to growth and decline.

Between 1988 and 2000, opportunities for employment will vary from occupation to occupation. Some will experience an increase; others, a decrease.

Geoffrey C. Gradler and Kurt E. Schrammel, reporting job projections for the period 1992 to 2005, listed occupations that are expected to grow faster than average; those that are projected to grow at an average rate; and those that will grow slower than average, experience no growth, or decline. Among those predicted for faster than average growth are health service managers, computer programmers, lawyers, physicians, medical assistants. paralegals, counselors, guards, teachers (K-12) and teachers' aides. Average growth is anticipated for chemists, school administrators, economists, geologists, carpenters, retail sales workers, firefighters, and civil engineers. In the slower than average growth, no growth, or declining growth are secretaries, police, mathematicians, petroleum engineers, librarians, telephone operators, and bank tellers.[9]

Gradler and Schrammel summarized projections:

As a whole, this group [professional specialty occupations] is expected to grow faster than average and to increase its share of total employment by 2005. . . . Occupations such as physical therapist, human services worker, operations research analyst, and computer scientist and systems analysis are expected to grow much faster than average. Others, such as physicist and astronomer, mining and nuclear engineer, and dentist

---

[9]Geoffrey C. Gradler and Kurt E. Schrammel, "The 1992–2005 Job Outlook in Brief," *Occupational Outlook Quarterly* 38, no. 1 (Spring 1994): 2–45.

should grow more slowly than average. Most new jobs will be in the education, business, and health services industries.[10]

Not too surprising to persons in education is the observation by the Bureau of Labor Statistics: "On average, employment will grow faster in the major educational groups that require the most education and training. Jobs in these occupations also offer higher than average earnings."[11]

Schools have responded to career needs of young people through vocational education either in comprehensive high schools, vocational schools, or magnet schools. Since World War I emphasis on vocational education has waxed and waned. The Smith-Hughes Act of 1917, the George-Reed Act of 1963, the George-Dean Act of 1936, the Vocational Education Act of 1963, Charles Prosser's resolution calling for "life adjustment education" and the creation of the Commission on Life Adjustment Education in the post World War II years, the Carl D. Perkins Act of 1990, and the School-to-Work Opportunities Act of 1994 all addressed vocational and life needs of youth.

Renewed programs in vocational education from the 1970s to the present take note of deficiencies among the workforce and seek to help students gain skills necessary for successful employment. Among current means of strengthening vocational education are analysis of business and industrial needs of the community; specification of outcomes needed by graduates; integration of academic and vocational education; school-to-work transition programs; establishing partnerships with business and industry; on-the-job experiences concurrent with schooling; and guidance of students in examining a chosen set of vocations (e.g., business, health, communications), a practice known as career clustering.[12]

Of course, a nation's employment needs change from time to time as the economy changes and as new technologies appear. A curriculum worker must stay tuned to changing needs. An excellent illustration of changing national need is the current demand for teachers. When the first edition of this book appeared (1982), openings for teachers in the elementary and secondary schools were limited except in certain fields such as vocational education, mathematics, science, and special education. However, increased pupil enrollments had been predicted, and a general shortage of teachers came to pass. The decrease in enrollments in teacher education programs for a variety of reasons over the past decade further exacerbated the problem. As noted earlier, teaching is projected for faster than average growth. Opportunities for employment vary, of course, from state to state depending on such factors as shifts in population,

---

[10]Ibid., p. 3.

[11]Bureau of Labor Statistics, "The American Work Force: 1992–2205," *Occupational Outlook Quarterly* 37, no. 3 (Fall 1993): 3.

[12]See Comprehensive Career Development Project for Secondary Schools in Tennessee, *Comprehensive Career Development Program: The Second Year: Reflections of Participants.* Practitioners Monograph II (Knoxville, Tenn.: Comprehensive Career Development Project for Secondary Schools in Tennessee, 1990). 15 articles. See also

James M. Brown, "Integrating Academic Skills into Postsecondary Vocational Education Programs through Accommodation Teams," *TASSP Bulletin*, 3, no. 1 (June 1991): 1–3. ERIC document ED333167, 1991.

Tom Holdsworth and Ann Schreiber, *School-to-Work Transition: Local Programs: A Series of Case Studies.* ERIC document ED379432, 1995.

Susan Imel, *School-to-Work Transition: Trends and Issues Alerts.* ERIC document ED378350, 1995.

Bettina A. Lankard, *Integrating Academic and Vocational Education: Strategies for Implementation.* ERIC Digest No. 120. ERIC document ED346317, 1992.

Chester P. Wichowski et al., *School to Work, Learning Outcomes, and Integrating Academic and Vocational Education.* ERIC document ED377360, 1994.

birth rates, and school reform measures. In spite of continuing financial and pupil behavioral problems improvements in teacher salaries, working conditions, and teacher education programs have contributed to making teaching more attractive as a career, completing a cycle of change.

As the nation strives to achieve full employment, it needs employees who feel secure in their work and who do not fear that the competitive free enterprise system will force them into the ranks of the unemployed. In Japan the workers historically have long felt a close identity with their companies and have traditionally been protected against arbitrary dismissals. Although notable stresses in the Japanese economy in recent years have weakened the customary protections which management accorded its workers, to a still greater extent than in America, Japanese employees are retained in their jobs, the economy permitting, on a lifelong basis. Could the collective feeling of security among Japanese workers who give their all to their companies plus the practice of involving workers in decision making have accounted at least in part for the phenomenal success of Japanese industry throughout the world? Does this feeling of security contribute to a feeling of pride in the organization that, in turn, translates into efficiency and quality performance?

The United States Congress responded to a national need—and caused the schools to respond as well—by enacting Public Law 94-192, the Education for All Handicapped Children Act of 1975. Through this and similar legislation, the Congress said that the country could not afford to waste the talents of a sizable segment of the population. The presence of programs in basic skills; citizenship; consumer, global, career, computer, and sexuality education in schools across the country is indicative of curriculum planners' responding to national needs.

The United States has many needs, from improving its educational system to solving ethnic problems to reducing crime to providing for full employment to meeting the health needs of its population to maintaining its world leadership role. The curriculum worker must be a student of history, sociology, political science, economics, and current events to perceive the needs of the nation.

We should note that some writers hold that educational policy has been too closely tied to economics with its principles of efficiency and productivity. Critical of city, state, and national efforts at reform through governmental promotion of standards, assessment, and accountability, Ernest R. House, for example, contended that "national and state leaders formulate educational policies primarily in response to national or state economic concerns without sufficient understanding or appreciation of educational institutions."[13] House observed, "Frequently, policies dedicated to efficiency and productivity in education do not result in better education or improved productivity."[14]

STATE

States also have special needs. When the sale of automobiles declines, the state of Michigan experiences special difficulties. When the oil industry goes into recession,

---

[13]Ernest R. House, *Schools for Sale: Why Free Market Policies Won't Improve America's Schools and What Will* (New York: Teacher College Press, 1998), p. 8.

[14]Ibid., p. 10.

Texas suffers. When drought parches the wheat belt, the producers of wheat across the Great Plains feel pain. When floods swallow valuable farm land in the Midwest, the calamity strikes producers of corn and soybean. When frost injures the citrus crop, Florida's economy is hurt. When whole industries move from the cold and expensive Northeast to sunnier climes in the United States—and even to Mexico—where labor and other costs are lower, the abandoned states feel the loss.

The continuing movement of population from the North and Midwest to the South, Southwest, and West has brought with it an array of needs not only in the states that people are deserting but also in the states whose populations are growing. Migratory waves of citizens—including those from Puerto Rico—and of noncitizens from Cuba, Vietnam, Mexico, and Haiti have had a great impact on some states in particular and, of course, on the nation as a whole.

State needs become apparent when pupils in schools of some states consistently score below the median of national norms on standardized tests of achievement. Consequently, many states have begun to require students to pass tests of minimal competence for receipt of the high school diploma.

Job opportunities, needs for training of specialized workers, and types of schooling needed differ from state to state and pose areas of concern for curriculum workers.

COMMUNITY

Curriculum workers are more frequently able to identify the needs of a community because they are usually aware of significant changes in its major businesses and industries. They know very well, as a rule, whether the community's economy is stagnant, depressed, or booming. On the other hand, changes are sometimes so gradual that schools neglect to adapt their programs to changing community needs. For example, it is possible to find schools that offer programs in agriculture although their communities have shifted to small business and light industry long ago, or we find schools that train pupils for particular manufacturing occupations when the type of manufacturing in the area has changed or factories have been converted to automation. More subtle and more difficult to respond to are needs produced by the impersonality of large urban areas with, in too many cases, an accompanying deterioration in the quality of life. Urban dwellers need to break through the facade of impersonality and develop a sense of mutual respect. They also need to become aware of possible contributions they can make to improve life in the big city.

Shifts of population within a state create problems for communities. There may be, for example, a population movement from the city to the suburbs or further into the country, followed later by another population shift from the country or the suburbs back to the city. During the 1970s, as disenchanted city dwellers sought a higher quality of life in the country, rural areas experienced significant growth with its accompanying problems. The U.S. Census Bureau figures showed that in the 1980s many Americans became dissatisfied with the rural areas and once again gravitated to the metropolitan areas.[15] We are currently witnessing some regrouping even *within* the

---

[15]Donald E. Starsinic, *Patterns of Metropolitan Area and County Population Growth, 1980–1984,* Current Population Reports, Population Estimates and Projection Series P-25, No. 976, U.S. Department of Commerce, Bureau of the Census (Washington, D.C.: U.S. Government Printing Office, October 1985).

metropolitan areas, as, for example, the rejuvenation and restoration of deteriorating downtown and historic areas of cities. Some suburban dwellers have been returning to the central city where properties are depressed and therefore relatively cheap (at least early on). Renovation of old homes promises to make some formerly depressed central city locations once again choice, even expensive, places to inhabit. In contrast, responding to concerns about crime, some urban dwellers have created restricted refuges with walls, gates, alarm systems, and security personnel.

Shifts in population create problems for the schools just as the tax base, on which schools rely for partial support, affects the quality of education in a community. School staffs know full well the differences in communities' abilities to raise taxes to support public education. As the *Serrano v. Priest* decision of the California Supreme Court in 1971 and the *Edgewood v. Kirby* decision of the Texas Supreme Court in 1989 clearly demonstrated, wealthier communities with the ability to raise funds through taxes on property can provide a higher quality of education than can communities with a poorer tax base.[16] In this respect community need becomes a state need because education, through the Tenth Amendment to the U.S. Constitution, is a power reserved to the states.

Schools cannot, of course, solve these societal problems by themselves. Communities must turn primarily to their state legislatures for help in equalizing educational opportunities throughout the state. On the other hand, schools can make—and cannot avoid the obligation to make—an impact on the future citizens of the community whom they are educating by making them aware of the problems and equipping them with skills and knowledge that will help them resolve some of the problems.

NEIGHBORHOOD

Are there needs, the curriculum developer must ask, peculiar to the neighborhood served by the school? The answer is obvious in most urban areas. The people of the inner city have needs of which the people of the more comfortable suburbs are scarcely aware except through the press and television.

Crime and use of drugs are more common in some neighborhoods than in others. The needs of people in areas that house migrant workers are much different from those of people in areas where executives, physicians, and lawyers reside. Children in lower socioeconomic levels often achieve less in their neighborhood schools than more affluent children do in theirs. A notable and heartwarming exception is Jaime Escalante's success in teaching calculus to inner-city students at Garfield High School in Los Angeles.[17] As a rule, families of children in the more fortunate schools are able to afford cultural and educational experiences that children in the less fortunate schools seldom encounter.

The curriculum worker must be perceptive of changes in neighborhoods. For example, city dwellers who moved to suburbia in search of the good life are finding—after

---

[16]*Serrano v. Priest,* 5 Cal. 3rd 584, 487 P. 2nd 1241 (1971) and *Edgewood Independent School District et al. v. William Kirby et al.* S. W. Texas 777 S.S. 2d 391 (Tex. 1989).

[17]See the Warner Brothers movie *Stand and Deliver,* Burbank, Calif.: Warner Home Video, 1988, starring James Edward Olmos.

some years in a housing development, often a tract variety with a sameness of architectural design, and after countless hours of commuting—that the good life has eluded them. They have become disenchanted with wall-to-wall housing (which some sociologists predict as our future) and with block after block of shopping centers. Grass, trees, and unpolluted air have given way to the bulldozer, the cement mixer, and disconcerting traffic.

Some of the suburban settlements have joined the central city in experiencing blight, decay, crime, and the host of problems that they originally ascribed to the cities. Consequently, some suburbanites have reversed direction, willing to contend with urban problems and at the same time enjoy the cultural, educational, and recreational resources of the city.

Worth watching are housing developments designed to create a congenial small-town atmosphere in a suburban-type setting. These new planned communities employ the concept of a community center surrounded by a mixture of single-family and multi-family residences and apartments. Schools and commercial and recreational facilities are planned to be within walking distance of the homes. Mass transit will link suburbs and nearby urban centers, reducing dependence upon the automobile. Sites near Sacramento, California; Tacoma, Washington; Orlando and Tampa, Florida; and in Brevard County, Florida are locales testing the small-town center concept wherein schools, shops, jobs, and services can be found within walking distance of homes. Perhaps in the twenty-first century not all of America's population will be living in the beehive dwellings predicted by some futurists.

The curriculum specialist must develop plans that show an understanding of the needs of society on all of the foregoing levels.

NEEDS OF SOCIETY: TYPES

The curriculum planner must additionally look at the needs of society from the standpoint of types. For example, each of the following types of societal needs has implications for the curriculum:

- political
- social
- economic
- educational
- environmental
- defense
- health
- moral and spiritual

A curriculum council studying the needs of society would be well advised to try to generate its own system for classifying societal needs. It might then compare its classification system with some of those found in the literature. The Seven Cardinal Principles and the Ten Imperative Needs of Youth, mentioned in Chapter 3, were efforts to identify needs of students as a function of the needs of society.

SOCIAL PROCESSES

Numerous attempts have been made throughout the years to identify societal needs or demands under the rubrics of social processes, social functions, life activities, and social institutions. As we review several well-known efforts to specify these needs, we should recall the student-society duality of needs. "Making a home," for example, is both a societal and personal need. The person has a need for the skills of making a home while society has a need for persons who possess homemaking skills. Curriculum specialists who seek to delineate social processes or functions do so in order to identify individual needs that have social origins. It might be argued, parenthetically, that all personal needs (except purely biological ones) are social in origin.

Robert S. Zais credited Herbert Spencer for the beginning of the practice of studying society empirically.[18] In 1859 Spencer recommended that students be prepared for "the leading kinds of activity which constitute human life."[19] He classified these activities in order of importance as follows:

1. Those activities which directly minister to self-preservation
2. Those activities which, by securing the necessaries of life, indirectly minister to self-preservation
3. Those activities which have for their end the rearing and discipline of offspring
4. Those activities which are involved in the maintenance of proper social and political relations
5. Those miscellaneous activities which make up the leisure part of life, devoted to the gratification of the tastes and feelings[20]

The 1934 Virginia State Curriculum Program has been identified as one of the better known attempts to organize a curriculum around life processes.[21] O. I. Frederick and Lucile J. Farquear reported the following nine areas of human activity that the state of Virginia incorporated into the curriculum of the schools:

1. Protecting life and health
2. Getting a living
3. Making a home
4. Expressing religious impulses
5. Satisfying the desire for beauty
6. Securing education
7. Cooperating in social and civic action
8. Engaging in recreation
9. Improving material conditions.[22]

---

[18]Robert S. Zais, *Curriculum: Principles and Foundations* (New York: Harper & Row, 1976), p. 301.

[19]Herbert Spencer, "What Knowledge Is of Most Worth?" in *Education: Intellectual, Moral, and Physical* (New York: John B. Alden, 1885). Quotations are from 1963 ed. (Paterson, N.J.: Littlefield, Adams), p. 32.

[20]Ibid.

[21]Hilda Taba, *Curriculum Development: Theory and Practice* (New York: Harcourt Brace Jovanovich, 1962), p. 398.

[22]O. I. Frederick and Lucile J. Farquear, "Areas of Human Activity," *Journal of Educational Research* 30, no. 9 (May 1937): 672–679.

The Wisconsin State Department of Public Instruction's *Guide to Curriculum Building* has been highly regarded for its social functions approach. The Wisconsin State Department of Public Instruction listed the following social functions in its guide for a core curriculum at the junior high school level.[23]

- To keep the population healthy.
- To provide physical protection and guarantee against war.
- To conserve and wisely utilize natural resources.
- To provide opportunity for people to make a living.
- To rear and educate the young.
- To provide wholesome and adequate recreation.
- To enable the population to satisfy aesthetic and spiritual values.
- To provide sufficient social cement to guarantee social integration.
- To organize and govern in harmony with beliefs and aspirations.[24]

Florence B. Stratemeyer, Hamden L. Forkner, Margaret G. McKim, and A. Harry Passow proposed a plan for organizing curriculum experiences around activities of human beings, as shown in the following list:

Situations Calling for Growth in Individual Capacities:
Health
A. Satisfying physiological needs
B. Satisfying emotional and social needs
C. Avoiding and caring for illness and injury
Intellectual power
A. Making ideas clear
B. Understanding the ideas of others
C. Dealing with quantitative relationships
D. Using effective methods of work
Moral choices
A. Determining the nature and extent of individual freedom
B. Determining responsibility to self and others
Aesthetic expression and appreciation
A. Finding sources of aesthetic satisfaction in oneself
B. Achieving aesthetic satisfactions through the environment

Situations Calling for Growth in Social Participation:
Person-to-person relationships
A. Establishing effective social relations with others
B. Establishing effective working relationships with others
Group membership
A. Deciding when to join a group
B. Participating as a group member
C. Taking leadership responsibilities
Intergroup relationships

---

[23]For discussion of the core curriculum see Chapter 9.

[24]Wisconsin State Department of Public Instruction, *Guide to Curriculum Building*, Bulletin No. 8 (Madison, Wis: State Department of Public Instruction, January 1950), p. 74.

    A. Working with racial, religious, and national groups
    B. Working with socioeconomic groups
    C. Dealing with groups organized for specific action

*Situations Calling for Growth in Ability to Deal with Environmental
    Factors and Forces:*
Natural phenomena
    A. Dealing with physical phenomena
    B. Dealing with plant, animal, and insect life
    C. Using physical and chemical forces
Technological resources
    A. Using technological resources
    B. Contributing to technological advance
Economic-social-political structures and forces
    A. Earning a living
    B. Securing goods and services
    C. Providing for social welfare
    D. Molding public opinion
    E. Participating in local and national government[25]

Taba pointed out the strength of the Stratemeyer, Forkner, McKim, and Passow scheme:

> This . . . scheme seems to be an effort to correct one deficiency of the social-process approach, the disregard for the learner. In effect, this approach combines the concepts of common activities, needs, and life situations with an awareness of the learner as a factor in curriculum design and uses both to find a unifying scheme.[26]

In sum, the curriculum worker must analyze both the needs of learners and of society. The study of both "sources," as Ralph Tyler called them, provides clues for curricular implementation and organization.

NEEDS DERIVED FROM THE SUBJECT MATTER

One major source of curriculum objectives remains for us to consider—needs as derived from the subject matter or, as Jerome S. Bruner and others would say, from the "structure of a subject."[27] Bruner refers to the structure of a subject as the "basic ideas"[28] or "fundamental principles."[29] "Grasping the structure of a subject," said Bruner, "is understanding it in such a way that permits many other things to be related to it meaningfully. To learn structure, in short, is to learn how things are related."[30]

---

[25]Florence B. Stratemeyer, Hamden L. Forkner, Margaret G. McKim, and A. Harry Passow, Chapter 6, "The Scope of Persistent Life Situations and Ways in Which Learners Face Them," in *Developing a Curriculum for Modern Living*, 2nd ed. New York: Teachers College Press, 1957, pp. 146–172.

[26]Taba, *Curriculum Development*, p. 399.

[27]Jerome S. Bruner, *The Process of Education* (Cambridge, Mass.: Harvard University Press, 1960), p. 6.

[28]Ibid., pp. 12–13.

[29]Ibid., p. 25.

[30]Ibid., p. 7.

As examples of elements of the structure of disciplines, Bruner mentioned tropism in the field of biology; commutation, distribution, and association in mathematics; and linguistic patterns in the field of language.[31] Each subject contains certain essential areas or topics (the bases for determining the scope of a course) that, if the learner is to achieve mastery of the field, must be taught at certain times and in a certain prescribed order (sequence). The sequence could be determined by increasing complexity (as in mathematics, foreign languages, English grammar, science), by logic (as in social studies programs that begin with the child's immediate environment—the home and school—and expand to the community, state, nation, and world), or by psychological means (as in vocational education programs that start with immediate interests of learners and proceed to more remote ones).

CHANGES IN THE DISCIPLINES

The subject matter areas remained essentially the same (except for updating) until the 1950s with the advent of the "new math," the "new science," the "new linguistics," and the widespread development of the audio-lingual method of teaching foreign languages. The scholarly ferment of the 1950s, propelled by National Defense Education Act funds, produced such new definitions of the structures of the disciplines as the three versions of a course in biology (blue, green, and yellow) developed by the Biological Sciences Curriculum Study (BSCS). Each version presented principles of biology with a different central focus and organization. The structure of this field of science as prescribed in the green version, considered by many as the easiest of the three, centered around the topics of evolution and ecology. The blue version, considered by many as the most difficult, stressed biochemistry and physiology, and the yellow version concentrated on genetics and the development of organisms.

Two additional projects reflect the type of planning going on in the field of science in the mid-1950s and early 1960s. The Physical Sciences Study Committee(PSSC)—which began its work in 1956, just three years before the Biological Sciences Curriculum Study was initiated—unified a high school course in physics under the following four topics:

1. the universe, which includes time, space, matter,and motion
2. optics and waves, which involves a study of optical phenomena
3. mechanics, which concerns dynamics, momentum, energy, and the laws of conservation
4. electricity, which includes electricity, magnetism, and the structure of the atom[32]

In the early 1960s the Earth Science Curriculum Project developed an earth-science course with the following ten unifying themes:

1. Science as inquiry
2. Comprehnsion of scale
3. Prediction
4. Universality of change

---

[31]Ibid., pp. 7–8.
[32]Peter F. Oliva, *The Secondary School Today*, 2nd ed. (New York: Harper & Row, 1972), p. 151.

5. Flow of energy in the universe
6. Adjustment to environmental change
7. Conservation of mass and energy in the universe
8. Earth systems in time and space
9. Uniformity of process
10. Historical development and presentation[33]

While scientists were overhauling the curriculum of their specialties, the foreign language curriculum workers were breaking out of the mold of the old reading-translation objectives that dominated foreign language study for generations. Calling attention to the change in objectives of foreign language study, I wrote:

> The objectives, in order of priority, among foreign language teachers are: (a) aural comprehension, (b) speaking, (c) reading, and (d) writing. . . . The four above-mentioned linguistic objectives are integrated with the general cultural objectives, understanding of the foreign customs and foreign peoples.[34]

Foreign language study provides an excellent illustration of a sequenced structure because language students will learn a foreign language more readily when, for example, the concept of singular is presented before the concept of plural, when regular verbs are taught before irregular verbs, when the first person singular is mastered before other persons, when the present tense is perfected before other tenses, when simple tenses come before compound, and when the indicative mood is taught before the subjunctive.

PERFORMANCE OBJECTIVES/STANDARDS

Many state departments of education and/or local school districts have published syllabi, courses of study, and curriculum guides developed by teacher-specialists in particular fields.[35] These publications outline the structure of a subject, the appropriate grade level for each topic; the performance objectives, standards, skills, or minimal competencies to be accomplished; and often the order of presentation (sequence) of topics. Many cities and states and even the nation have been and continue to be engaged in the specification of performance objectives or standards in subject areas.[36]

Some education specialists criticize the movement toward adoption of performance objectives/standards. They raise objections not only to the standardizing effect but also the nature of standards that they view as imposed and contrary to pressing social needs. Although specification of subject-matter standards has been subjected to criticism, the movement during the past twenty years continues strong as we can see from the following examples from Chicago, Arizona, California, Florida, and Virginia.

Chicago.   In preparing its systemwide objectives and standards the Chicago Public Schools has integrated Illinois State Goals for Learning in the various disciplines.[37]

---

[33]Ibid., p. 152.

[34]Peter F. Oliva, *The Teaching of Foreign Languages* (Englewood Cliffs, N.J.: Prentice-Hall, 1969), p. 11.

[35]For discussion of curriculum products, see Chapter 15 of this text.

[36]See Chapter 14 for discussion of national standards.

[37]Chicago Public Schools, *Systemwide Objectives and Standards, Grades 9–12* (Chicago Board of Education, City of Chicago, 1990).

Chicago has used the state's seven goals for learning in mathematics and has created a list of performance objectives for each goal based on the state's sample learning objectives (SLO)[38] and standards of the National Council of Teachers of Mathematics (NCTM).[39]

To illustrate this integration, we will examine the fourth goal for learning in mathematics:

> As a result of their schooling, students will be able to identify, analyze, and solve problems using algebraic equations, inequalities, functions, and their graphs.[40]

To meet this state goal Chicago has identified the performance objectives below (See Box 7.1), which students are expected to master during their algebra courses.

Arizona.   Curriculum planners have traditionally conveyed the fundamentals of subject matter to the learners by outlining topics or identifying unifying themes. Often the structures of the disciplines are communicated to learners in terms of essential skills or minimal competencies written in the form of objectives to be accomplished at various grade levels and before high school graduation. The state of Arizona, for example, has developed an extensive list of eighth-and twelfth-grade skills in seven subject areas. Eighty-seven skills have been identified in the area of health for eighth-grade students. The first ten skills from this list may serve as examples:

1. Identifies personal care practices. Example: washing hands before eating.
2. Communicates symptoms of his/her physical illness.
3. Lists some of the ways communicable diseases are transmitted.
4. Identifies and describes a variety of foods.
5. States the importance of eating breakfast and describes a healthful breakfast.
6. Explains that medicines are never taken except when given by parents, guardians, doctors, or nurses.
7. Describes the dangers of taking unknown substances.
8. Names common safety hazards and rules for preventing home, school, and transportation accidents.
9. Identifies major body parts. Example: arms, legs, ears, eyes.
10. Describes how people in a community work together to keep the neighborhood clean.[41]

California.   The state of California through its Standards-Based Accountability System and Standardized Test and Reporting provides for specification of performance standards and annual testing. Started in the spring of 1998, the accountability system called for completion of standards in language arts and mathematics in 1999 and in history-social science and science in 2000. Illustrative of the California effort is an example from grade eight, language arts:

---

[38]Illinois State Board of Education, *State Goals for Learning and Sample Learning Objectives, Mathematics* (Springfield, Ill.: Illinois State Board of Education, n.d.).

[39]National Council of Teachers of Mathematics, *Curriculum and Evaluation Standards for School Mathematics* (Reston, Va.: The Council, 1989).

[40]Illinois State Board of Education, *State Goals*, as cited in Chicago Public Schools, *Systemwide Objectives*, p. 34.

[41]Arizona Department of Education, *Essential Skills List* (Phoenix: Arizona Department of Education, June 1984), p. 1.

BOX 7.1

OBJECTIVES

Apply the rules for order of operations to evaluate expressions involving integers and powers. (SLO)

Relate situations that involve variable quantities to expressions, equations, and inequalities. (NCTM)

Define and use function notation and terminology. (SLO)

Solve linear equations. (SLO)

Solve one-step inequalities. (SLO)

Interpret solutions to an equation or inequality in terms of the situation they represent. (SLO)

Solve equations and inequalities resulting from situations that occur in everyday life. (SLO)

Recognize all real numbers whose squares are given numbers. (SLO)

Compare different powers of the same number or same power of different numbers. (SLO)

Judge the appropriateness of particular values for a variable in a formula. (SLO)

Apply formulas with and without the use of a calculator. (SLO)

Recognize and determine equivalent forms of a formula. (SLO)

Determine values in a sequence when given a formula for the next term. (SLO)

Cite the rule by which the next term in a given sequence may be obtained. (SLO)

Model real-world phenomena by using a variety of functions. (NCTM)

Operate on expressions and solve equations and inequalities. (NCTM)

Use an equation or a rule and graph a simple function. (SLO)

Identify the slope of a line that is determined by two points. (SLO)

Use the graph of a function to interpret rates of change. (SLO)

Identify the solutions to a system of equations from a graph on a coordinate plane. (SLO)

Solve a simple system of equations in two variables by using graphing, algebraic technique, or technology. (SLO)

Test solutions to systems of equations. (SLO)

Compare values of two or more functions represented on a graph or in a table. (SLO)

Add and subtract polynomials. (SLO)

Factor common monomial factors out of algebraic expressions. (SLO)

Multiply binomials. (SLO)

Make a table of values for a simple polynomial function by using a given domain. (SLO)

Represent and analyze relationships by using tables, verbal rules, equations, and graphs. (NCTM)

Analyze a graph to determine when a function has a given value. (SLO)

Translate tabular, symbolic, and graphical representations of functions. (NCTM)

Analyze the effects of parameter changes on the graphs of functions. (NCTM)

Use tables and graphs as tools to analyze and interpret expressions, equations, and inequalities. (NCTM)

Read maximum and minimum values of a function from the graph of the function. (SLO)

SOURCE: Board of Education of the City of Chicago, *Systemwide objectives and standards, Grades 9–12, 1990* (Chicago: Board of Education, 1990), pp. 34–36. Reprinted with permission of the Board of Education of the City of Chicago.

1.0 Written and Oral English Language Conventions (Grade Eight)

Students write and speak with a command of standard English conventions appropriate to this grade level.

Sentence Structure (Grade Eight)

1.1 Use correct and varied sentence types and sentence openings to present a lively and effective personal style.

1.2 Identify and use parallelism, including similar grammatical forms, in all written discourse to present items in a series and items juxtaposed for emphasis.

1.3 Use subordination, coordination, apposition, and other devices to indicate clearly the relationship between ideas.

Grammar (Grade Eight)

1.4 Edit written manuscripts to ensure that correct grammar is used.

Punctuation and Capitalization (Grade Eight)

1.5 Use correct punctuation and capitalization.

Spelling (Grade Eight)
1.6 Use correct spelling conventions.[42]

Florida.   From 1985 to 1994 Florida schools were guided by the state's *Minimum Student Performance Standards for Florida Schools.* Demonstrating the axiom that curriculum development is a never-ending process, Florida initiated development of revised standards in 1994, completed in 1996, with administration of the Florida Comprehensive Assessment Test in 1998. *The Florida Curriculum Framework: Pre K–12 Sunshine State Standards and Instructional Practices* sets forth standards in seven areas at each grade level: language arts, mathematics, science, social studies, the arts, health and physical education, and foreign language. Let's look at one example from the Florida performance standards:

LANGUAGE ARTS 6–8

Reading
Standard 2 The student constructs meaning from a wide range of texts.

1. determines the main idea or essential message in a text and identifies relevant details and facts and patterns of organization.
2. identifies the author's purpose and/or point of view in a variety of texts and uses the information to construct meaning.
3. recognizes logical, ethical, and emotional appeals in texts.
4. uses a variety of reading materials to develop personal preferences in reading.

---

[42]From California Department of Education Web site http://www.cde.ca.gov/board/standards.html, accessed December 12, 1998.

5. locates, organizes, and interprets written information for a variety of purposes, including classroom research, collaborative decision making, and performing a school or real-world task.
6. uses a variety of reference materials, including indexes, magazines, newspapers, and journals, and tools, including card catalogs and computer catalogs, to gather information for research topics.
7. synthesizes and separates collected information into useful components using a variety of techniques, such as source cards, note cards, spreadsheets, and outlines.
8. checks the validity and accuracy of information obtained from research in such ways as differentiating fact and opinion, identifying strong vs. weak arguments, recognizing that personal values influence the conclusion an author draws.[43]

Virginia.   Approved by the Virginia Board of Education in June 1995, *Standards of Learning* comprised performance standards in mathematics, science, English/writing, history/social science, and computer technology with achievement to be demonstrated by statewide accountability tests. An example of Virginia's effort in standards' development is seen in Box 7.2, computer/technology standards to be accomplished by students by the end of grade five.

The purpose of the discussion of needs to this point is to direct the curriculum developers to consider three major sources of needs—the learner, the society, and the subject matter. Although Ralph Tyler discusses these three sets of needs as sources from which tentative general objectives are derived[44]—a sound procedure—they are examined and illustrated here as a preface to a systematic procedure for studying needs and identifying those not met by the school's curriculum. Such a procedure is usually referred to in the literature as a needs assessment.

CONDUCTING A NEEDS ASSESSMENT

In its simplest definition a *curriculum needs assessment* is a process for identifying programmatic needs that must be addressed by curriculum planners. Fenwick W. English and Roger A. Kaufman offered several interpretations of the term "needs assessment." This earlier work published by the Association for Supervision and Curriculum Development remains a thorough description of a process that school systems have been engaging in for many years. English and Kaufman described the process in the following ways:

Needs assessment is a process of defining the desired end (or outcome, product, or result) of a given sequence of curriculum development. . . .
Needs assessment is a process of making specific, in some intelligible manner, what schooling should be about and how it can be assessed. Needs assessment is not by itself a curricular innovation, it is a method for determining if innovation is necessary and/or desirable.

---

[43]From Florida Department of Education Web site: http://www.firn.edu/doe/curric/prek12/langart6.htm, accessed December 12, 1998.
[44]See Chapter 5.

BOX 7.2

STANDARDS BY THE END OF GRADE FIVE

C/T 5.1 The student will demonstrate a basic understanding of computer theory including bits, bytes, and binary logic.

C/T 5.2 The student will develop basic technology skills.
- Develop a basic technology vocabulary that includes cursor, software, memory, disk drive, hard drive, and CD-ROM.
- Select and use technology appropriate to tasks.
- Develop basic keyboarding skills.
- Operate peripheral devices.
- Apply technologies to strategies for problem solving and critical thinking.

C/T5.3 The student will process, store, retrieve, and transmit electronic information.
- Use search strategies to retrieve electronic information using databases, CD-ROMs, videodiscs, and telecommunications.
- Use electronic encyclopedias, almanacs, indexes, and catalogs.
- Use local and wide-area networks and modern-delivered services to access information from electronic databases.
- Describe advantages and disadvantages of various computer processing, storage, retrieval, and transmission techniques.

C/T5.4 The student will communicate through application software.
- Create a 1-2 page document using word processing skills, writing process steps, and publishing programs.
- Use simple computer graphics and integrate graphics into word-processed documents.
- Create simple databases and spreadsheets to manage information and create reports.
- Use local and worldwide network communication systems.

SOURCE: Virginia Department of Education: http://www.knowledge.state.va.us/frames/frames.htm, accessed December 12, 1998.

Needs assessment is an empirical process for defining the outcomes of education, and as such it is then a set of criteria by which curricula may be developed and compared. . . .

Needs assessment is a process for determining the validity of behavioral objectives and if standardized tests and/or criterion-referenced tests are appropriate and under what conditions.

Needs assessment is a logical problem-solving tool by which a variety of means may be selected and related to each other in the development of curriculum.

Needs assessment is a tool which formally harvests the gaps between current results (or outcomes, products) and required or desired results, places these gaps in priority order, and selects those gaps (needs) of the highest priority for action, usually through the implementation of a new or existing curriculum or management process.[45]

---

[45]Fenwick W. English and Roger A. Kaufman, *Needs Assessment: A Focus for Curriculum Development* (Alexandria, Va.: Association for Supervision and Curriculum Development, 1975), pp. 3–4.

The objectives of a needs assessment are twofold: (1) to identify needs of the learners not being met by the existing curriculum and (2) to form a basis for revising the curriculum in such a way as to fulfill as many unmet needs as possible. The conduct of a needs assessment is not a single, one-time operation but a continuing and periodic activity. Some curriculum workers perceive a needs assessment as a task to be accomplished at the beginning of an extensive study of the curriculum. Once the results are obtained from this initiatory needs assessment, these planners believe that further probing is unnecessary for a number of years.

Since the needs of students, society, and the subject matter change over the years and since no curriculum has reached a state of perfection in which it ministers to all the educational needs of young people, a thorough needs assessment should be conducted periodically—at least every five years—with at least minor updating annually.

A needs assessment is also not time-specific in that it takes place only at the beginning of a comprehensive study of the curriculum. A needs assessment is a continuing activity that takes place (a) before specification of curricular goals and objectives, (b) after identification of curricular goals and objectives, (c) after evaluation of instruction, and (d) after evaluation of the curriculum.[46] English and Kaufman pointed out that most school systems require six months to two years to complete a full-scale needs assessment.[47] Not all school systems, of course, conduct full-scale needs assessments. The scope of assessments varies from simple studies of perceived needs to thorough analyses using extensive data.

PERCEIVED NEEDS APPROACH

Some schools limit the process of assessing needs to a survey of the needs of learners as perceived by (1) teachers, (2) students, and (3) parents. Instead of turning to objective data, curriculum planners in these schools pose questions that seek opinions from one or more of these groups. Parents, for example, are asked questions like these:

- How well do you feel your child is doing in school?
- Is your child experiencing any difficulty in school? If so, please explain.
- What content or programs do you believe the school should offer that are not now being offered?
- What suggestions do you have for improving the school's programs?
- Are you satisfied with the programs that the school is offering your child? If you are dissatisfied with any program, please specify which ones and your reasons.

Teachers and students may be asked to respond to similar questions in order to gain their perceptions of the school's curriculum and of needed improvements. The perceived needs approach, however, is but the first stage of the process. It is advantageous in that it is a simple process, requires relatively little time and effort, and is relatively inexpensive to conduct. It also provides an opportunity for the various groups to express their views about what is needed in the curriculum. The perceived needs approach becomes an effective public relations device when it is used with parents; it

---

[46]See components of the suggested model for curriculum development, Figure 5.4.
[47]English and Kaufman, *Needs Assessment*, p. 14.

says, in effect, that the school cares to know what parents think about the school's programs and wants their suggestions. As a first step, the perceived needs approach is worthwhile.

On the other hand, the perceived needs approach is limited. By its very nature, it is concerned with perceptions rather than facts. Although the curriculum planner must learn the perceptions of various groups, he or she must also know what the facts are. The needs of learners as perceived by the various groups may be quite different from needs as shown by more objective data. Consequently, a needs assessment must be carried beyond the gathering of perception of needs.

DATA COLLECTION

Those charged with conducting a needs assessment should gather data about the school and its programs from whatever sources of data are available. Necessary data include background information about the community, the student body, and the staff. Curriculum planners will need information on programs offered and available facilities. They must have access to all test data on the achievement of students in the school. Data may be obtained from various sources, including student records; school district files; surveys of attitudes of students, teachers, and parents; classroom observations; and examination of instructional materials. English described a process for collecting data in a school through examination of appropriate documents and practices, which he referred to as a "curriculum audit."[48]

Adequate data are necessary for making decisions about the selection of fields and topics to be encountered by the students and for specifying the goals of the curriculum. The data will provide clues as to the necessity for curriculum change. All these data should be put together in a coherent fashion so that they can be analyzed and decisions can be made about revising the curriculum.[49]

A needs assessment is customarily carried out when pressure is felt by personnel in schools seeking accreditation by their regional accrediting associations. Schools desiring regional accreditation normally conduct a full-scale self-study and are visited by a full committee every ten years; they also conduct interim studies every five years. Schools applying for accreditation follow criteria established by their accrediting association, often in conjunction with materials produced by their state department of education and the National Study of School Evaluation (NSSE).

Schools in past years that used NSSE's *Evaluative Criteria* (which are no longer available) can now use NSSE's *School Improvement: Focusing on Student Performance* and their *Program Evaluation Series.* The *School Improvement* instruments call for development of a school improvement plan. The *Program Evaluation Series* enables schools to evaluate the academic disciplines, library media service, and technology systems.[50]

---

[48]Fenwick W. English, *Curriculum Auditing* (Lancaster, Penn.: Technomic Publishing Company, 1988), p. 33.

[49]See Jon Wiles and Joseph C. Bondi, *Curriculum Development: A Guide to Practice,* 5th ed. (Upper Saddle River, N.J.: Merrill, 1998), p. 173 for a suggested outline of needs assessment data.

[50]National Study of School Evaluation, 1699 East Woodfield Road, Suite 406, Schaumburg, IL 60173-4958.

STEPS IN CONDUCTING A NEEDS ASSESSMENT

English and Kaufman proposed one of the most detailed plans for conducting a needs assessment. Their plan included fourteen generic and seven post-needs-assessment steps.[51] Following each step is a brief explanation in my own words.

GENERIC STEPS OF NEEDS ASSESSMENT

1. *Planning to plan: charting means and ends*— Preparations need to be made for the needs assessment, including decisions about time allotted, resources available, who will be participating, and so on.
2. *Goal derivation*—Knowledgeable persons are asked to state outcomes of education that they feel to be desirable.
3. *Goal validation*—Face validity is determined by asking citizens, both educators and noneducators, whether the goals are appropriate.
4. *Goal prioritization*—A large sampling of citizens, including students, educators, and school board members, is asked to rank the goals in order of importance.
5. *Goal translation*—Statements of goals are converted into measureable performance standards.
6. *Validation of performance objectives*—The groups that validated the goals now validate the performance standards (objectives) as to the accuracy of translating the goals into performance objectives and as to whether all the necessary objectives have been specified.
7. *Goal reprioritization*—Goals are reconsidered in light of a second sampling of students, staff, and community that repeats step 2. Step 3 and following steps may also be repeated, if desired.
8. *Futuristic input in goal ranking*—Future-oriented objectives are included. The Delphi Technique, in which informed persons are asked to predict future directions (in this case for education), may be used to generate and validate educational goals from which performance objectives may then be derived.[52]
9. *Rerank goals*—Goals are reranked using research and predictive studies such as the Delphi Technique.
10. *Select testing instruments or evaluative strategies for assessing the current state*— Testing instruments are selected and administered to ascertain current levels of student performance, to learn whether student achievement meets the desired defined levels.
11. *Collate data gathered*—Collected data must be put into tables, charts, graphs, and the like. English and Kaufman reminded us that "a needs assessment is the process of formulating gaps or discrepancies between two sets of criteria, a list of future desired conditions and results, and a list of current, existing (not necessarily desired) conditions and results."[53] Thus in presenting the data "the most detailed in-

---

[51]English and Kaufman, *Needs Assessment*, pp. 12–48.

[52]For discussion of the Delphi Technique see Olaf Helmer, "Analysis of the Future: The Delphi Method," in James R. Bright, ed., *Technological Forecasting for Industry and Government: Methods and Applications* (Englewood Cliffs, N.J.: Prentice-Hall, 1968), pp. 116–122.

[53]English and Kaufman, *Needs Assessment*, p. 35.

formation should be provided to those by whom decisions must ultimately be made about what to do with the 'gaps' as the primary consideration."[54]

12. *Develop initial gap or "need statements"*—A list of needs—gaps in student performance between what is desired and what is performed—is drawn up.

13. *Prioritize gap statements according to step four*— Gaps are clustered around the educational goals to which they relate and are ranked by the degree of difference between desired levels of student achievement and actual performance.

14. *Publish list of gap statements*—At this point the needs assessment is complete.

POST-NEEDS-ASSESSMENT STEPS

1. *Interpolate gaps by program and level*—Needs that are identified—the gaps—are located by program and level.

2. *Conduct diagnostic/planning sessions to develop implementation strategies to meet identified needs*— The responsible curriculum group tries to find out the reasons for the gaps and makes plans for closing them.

3. *Budget for implementation strategies*—The cost of each implementation strategy is calculated and budgeted.

4. *Fund strategies*—Depending on availability of funds, all strategies or only top strategies are funded.

5. *Implement strategies*—Strategies are put into operation either in existing or new programs.

6. *Reassess gap via feedback*—Both formative and summative data are gathered and analyzed to see if the gaps have actually been closed.

7. *Repeat steps of needs assessment process*—English and Kaufman recommended that generic steps 1 through 9 be repeated periodically and generic steps 10 through 14 continually.[55]

The process recommended by English and Kaufman goes beyond a simple needs assessment, incorporating the generation of goals and performance objectives as well as implementation and evaluation phases.

We can see that a thorough needs assessment is more than a "quick-and-dirty" survey of perceived needs. When done properly, it is a time-consuming process that requires the commitment of human and material resources sufficient to accomplish the job. A systematic process for discovering unmet needs of learners is an essential step in curriculum improvement.

SUMMARY

Curriculum planners must attend to the needs of students and society. These needs may be classified as to level and type. Various attempts have been made to identify the social processes, functions, and institutions that have import for the curriculum.

---

[54]Ibid., p. 39.
[55]Ibid., p. 47.

Each discipline has its own unique set of elements or structure that affects decisions about scope and sequence. The structure of a subject is shown by exposition of the basic ideas, fundamental principles, broad generalizable topics, competencies, or performance objectives.

In addition to studying empirically the needs of students, society, and the disciplines, curriculum workers should conduct systematic needs assessments to identify gaps—discrepancies between desired and actual student performance. Identified unmet needs should play a major role in curriculum revision.

A curriculum needs assessment permits school systems to discover deficiencies in their curricula. In addition, it creates a vehicle for school and community cooperation, builds community understanding of the school's programs and support for the school's efforts to fill in the gaps, and forces decisions on priorities.

QUESTIONS FOR DISCUSSION

1. What is the relationship between (1) needs of learners, society, and subject matter and (2) a curriculum needs assessment?
2. What is the appropriate role of the community in a curriculum needs assessment?
3. What is the appropriate role of teachers in a curriculum needs assessment?
4. What is the appropriate role of administrators and supervisors in a curriculum needs assessment?
5. What is the appropriate role of students in a curriculum needs assessment?

SUPPLEMENTARY EXERCISES

1. Explain how you would go about identifying the needs of students.
2. Explain how you would go about identifying needs of society.
3. Identify several of the basic ideas (structure) of a discipline that you know well.
4. Explain how a curriculum needs assessment model could be implemented in your community.
5. Give an illustration of at least one need of students at the following levels:
   human
   national
   state or regional
   community
   school
   individual
6. Give an illustration of at least one student need of the following types:
   physical
   sociopsychological
   educational
7. Analyze Robert J. Havighurst's developmental tasks of middle childhood or adolescence (see bibliography) and judge whether you feel each task is still relevant. Give reasons for your position on each task that you feel is no longer relevant.
8. Contrast Jon Wiles' and Joseph Bondi's (see bibliography) description of developmental tasks with those of Robert Havighurst.

9. Confer with appropriate personnel in a school system you know well and see if the school system has conducted a curriculum needs assessment in recent years. Report on instrumentation and results if a needs assessment has been conducted.

10. Conduct a simple study using the Delphi Technique. (See Olaf Helmer reference in the bibliography).

11. Describe the process of goal validation as explained by English and Kaufman (see bibliography).

12. Examine the report of the school-and-community committee of a school that has undergone regional accreditation and summarize the data contained therein.

13. Identify needs that the following content is supposed to fill:

income tax
Jacksonian democracy
principle of leverage
Beowulf
adding mixed fractions
Latin declensions
building cabinets
typing

14. Report on ways in which schools are integrating academic and vocational education. Include in your report ways in which schools are easing the transition of students from school to work.

15. Read and report on Henry C. Morrison's description of social activities (see bibliography).

16. Create your own list of social processes or functions and compare this list with one found in the professional literature.

17. Read and report on Herbert Spencer's description of life activities (see bibliography).

BIBLIOGRAPHY

Bruner, Jerome S. *The Process of Education.* Cambridge, Mass.: Harvard University Press, 1960.

Combs, Arthur W., ed. *Perceiving, Behaving, Becoming,* 1962 Yearbook. Alexandria, Va.: Association for Supervision and Curriculum Development, 1962.

English, Fenwick W. *Curriculum Auditing.* Lancaster, Penn.: Technomic Publishing Company, 1988.

———. and Kaufman, Roger A. *Needs Assessment: A Focus for Curriculum Development.* Alexandria, Va.: Association for Supervision and Curriculum Development, 1975.

Frederick, O. I. and Farquear, Lucile J. "Areas of Human Activity." *Journal of Educational Research* 30 (May 1937): 672–679.

Goodlad, John I. *Curriculum Inquiry: The Study of Curriculum Practice.* New York: McGraw-Hill, 1979.

Gradler, Geoffrey G. and Schrammel, Kurt E., "The 1992–2005 Job Outlook in Brief," *Occupational Outlook Quarterly* 38, no. 1 (Spring 1994): 2–45.

Havighurst, Robert J. *Developmental Tasks and Education,* 3rd ed. New York: Longman, 1972.

Helmer, Olaf. "Analysis of the Future: The Delphi Method." In *Technological Forecasting for Industry and Government: Methods and Applications,* ed. James R. Bright, 116–122. Englewood Cliffs, N.J.: Prentice-Hall, 1968.

House, Ernest R. *Schools for Sale: Why Free Market Policies Won't Improve America's Schools and What Will.* New York: Teachers College Press, 1998.

Kaplan, B. A. *Needs Assessment for Education: A Planning Handbook for School Districts.* Trenton, N.J.: New Jersey Department of Education, Bureau of Planning, February 1974. ERIC: ED 089 405.

Kaufman, Roger A. "Needs Assessment." In Fenwick W. English, ed., *Fundamental Curriculum Decisions,* 1983 Yearbook. Alexandria, Va.: Association for Supervision and Curriculum Development, 1983.

———. *Planning Educational Systems.* Englewood Cliffs, N.J.: Prentice-Hall, 1988.

————. and English, Fenwick W. *Needs Assessment: Concept and Application.* Englewood Cliffs, N.J.: Educational Technology Publications, 1979.

————. *Needs Assessment: A Guide to Improve School District Management.* Arlington, Va.: American Association of School Administrators, 1976.

Kaufman, Roger and Stakenas, Robert G. "Needs Assessment and Holistic Planning." *Educational Leadership* 38, no. 8 (May 1981): 612–616.

Kelley. Earl C. "The Fully Functioning Self." In Arthur W. Combs, ed., *Perceiving, Behaving, Becoming,* 1962 Yearbook. Alexandria, Va.: Association for Supervision and Curriculum Development. 1962, pp. 9–20.

Morrison, George S. *Contemporary Curriculum K–8.* Boston: Allyn and Bacon, 1993.

Morrison, Henry C. *The Curriculum of the Common School.* Chicago: University of Chicago Press, 1940.

National Study of School Evaluation. *Elementary School Evaluative Criteria,* 2nd ed. Falls Church, Va.: National Study of School Evaluation, 1981.

————. *Evaluative Criteria,* 6th ed. Falls Church, Va.: National Study of School Evaluation, 1981.

————. *Middle School/Junior High School Evaluative Criteria.* Falls Church, Va.: National Study of School Evaluation, 1979.

National Study of School Evaluation. *Elementary School Improvement: Focusing on Student Performance.* Schaumburg, Ill.: National Study of School Evaluation, 1995.

————. *K–12 School Improvement: Focusing on Student Performance.* Schaumburg, Ill.: National Study of School Evaluation, 1995.

————. *Middle Level School Improvement: Focusing on Student Performance.* Schaumburg, Ill.: National Study of School Evaluation, 1995.

————. *School Improvement: Focusing on Student Performance.* Schaumburg, Ill.: National Study of School Evaluation, 1997.

————. *Senior High School Improvement: Focusing on Student Performance.* Schaumburg, Ill.: National Study of School Evaluation.

Oliva, Peter F. "Essential Understandings for the World Citizen." *Social Education* 23, no. 6 (October 1959): 266–268.

————. *The Secondary School Today,* 2nd ed. New York: Harper & Row, 1972.

————. *The Teaching of Foreign Languages.* Englewood Cliffs, N.J.: Prentice-Hall, 1969.

Smith, B. Othanel, Stanley, William O., and Shores, J. Harlan. *Fundamentals of Curriculum Development,* rev. ed. New York: Harcourt Brace Jovanovich, 1957.

Spencer, Herbert. *Education: Intellectual, Moral, and Physical.* New York: John B. Alden, 1885. Paterson, N.J.: Littlefield, Adams, 1963.

Stratemeyer, Florence B., Forkner, Hamden L., McKim, Margaret G., and Passow, A. Harry. *Developing a Curriculum for Modern Living,* 2nd ed. New York: Bureau of Publications, Teachers College Press, Columbia University, 1957.

Taba, Hilda. *Curriculum Development: Theory and Practice.* New York: Harcourt Brace Jovanovich, 1962.

Tyler, Ralph W. *Basic Principles of Curriculum and Instruction.* Chicago: University of Chicago Press, 1949.

Wiles, Jon and Bondi, Joseph C. *Curriculum Development: A Guide to Practice.* 5th ed. Upper Saddle River, N.J.: Merrill, 1998.

————. *The Essential Middle School,* 2nd ed. New York: Macmillan, 1993.

Willis, Scott. "Teaching Young Children: Educators Seek 'Developmental Appropriateness.'" *ASCD Curriculum Update* (November 1993): 1–8.

Witkin, B. R. *An Analysis of Needs Assessment Techniques for Educational Planning at State, Intermediate, and District Levels,* May 1975. ERIC: ED 108 370.

Zais, Robert S. *Curriculum: Principles and Foundations.* New York: Harper & Row, 1976.

Zenger, Weldon F. and Zenger, Sharon K. *Curriculum Planning: A Ten-Step Process.* Palo Alto, Calif.: R & E Research Associates, 1982.

AUDIOTAPE

Implementing a Developmentally Appropriate Early Childhood Program in a Public School Setting. 1995. (Linda Espinosa, Nedda Shafir, Judy Zimmerman, and Barbara Day). Association for Supervision and Curriculum Development, 1703 N. Beauregard St., Alexandria, Va. 22311-1714.

FEATURE FILM

Stand and Deliver. 103 min. 1988. Warner Bros., Jaime Escalante teaches calculus to inner-city students in Los Angeles.

VIDEOTAPE

Early Childhood Education. Color. 40 min. 1991. Part One: integrates developmental approaches with direct instruction through Learning Centers, Units of Study, and Skills Groups. Part Two: Typical day in K–1 class at Seawell Elementary School, Chapel Hill, N.C. Features Barbara Day, Kay Drake, and Markie Pringle. Facilitator's Manual. Association for Supervision and Curriculum Development, 1703 N. Beauregard St., Alexandria, Va. 22311-1714.

WEB SITE

National Study of School Evaluation: http://www.nsse.org

CHAPTER 8
CURRICULUM GOALS AND OBJECTIVES

After studying this chapter you should be able to:

1. **Distinguish between goals and objectives.**
2. **Distinguish between aims of education and curriculum goals and objectives.**
3. **Distinguish between curriculum goals and objectives and instructional goals and objectives.**
4. **Specify and write curriculum goals.**
5. **Specify and write curriculum objectives.**

HIERARCHY OF OUTCOMES

Following the model for curriculum improvement suggested in Chapter 5, let's see how far we have come. We have

- analyzed needs of students in general in society
- analyzed needs of American society
- reviewed aims of education and affirmed those with which we are in agreement
- written a philosophy of education
- initiated a needs assessment by surveying needs of students in the community and school and by surveying needs of the community
- conducted a needs assessment and identified unmet needs

All of these steps are a prelude to the next phase. They provide a framework; they set the stage. They furnish data that are vital to making curricular decisions. The planning of the curriculum is now about to begin.

In Chapter 6 you encountered the terms "aims of education," "curriculum goals," "curriculum objectives," "instructional goals," and "instructional objectives" as used in this text. We discussed a hierarchy of purposes of education from the broadest to the narrowest. Let's review that hierarchy; it is essential both to this chapter on

Figure 8.1 Hierarchy of outcomes

curriculum goals and objectives and to Chapter 10 on instructional goals and objectives. We might chart this hierarchy as shown in Figure 8.1.[1]

It sometimes seems that the educational literature is surfeited with discussions of goals and objectives. In spite of these many commentaries, I have included three chapters in this text (Chapters 6, 8, and 10) on aims, goals, and objectives for the following reasons:

1. They are essential components in a comprehensive model for curriculum improvement.
2. These various terms for 'purpose' are used loosely and interchangeably in the literature, leading to possible confusion.
3. Some of the recommendations in the literature on the writing of goals and objectives are helpful; other recommendations seem less helpful.

AIMS, GOALS, AND OBJECTIVES

Several problems can be found if we research the literature on aims, goals, and objectives. First, aims of education are often equated with goals, and in a lexical sense, of course, they are the same. Many years ago John W. Gardner in *Goals for Americans* was describing aims of education when he wrote:

> Our deepest convictions impel us to foster individual fulfillment. We wish each one to achieve the promise that is in him. We wish each one to be worthy of a free society, and capable of strengthening a free society. . . .
>
> Ultimately, education serves all of our purposes—liberty, justice, and all our other aims—but the one it serves most directly is equality of opportunity.

---

[1]For a different hierarchy of goals see Ronald S. Brandt and Ralph W. Tyler, in Fenwick W. English, ed., *Fundamental Curriculum Decisions,* 1983 Yearbook (Alexandria, Va.: Association for Supervision and Curriculum Development, 1983), pp. 40–52.

[The] . . . tasks of producing certain specially needed kinds of educated talent . . . should not crowd out the great basic goals of our educational system: to foster individual fulfillment and to nurture the free, rational and responsible men and women without whom our kind of society cannot endure. Our schools must prepare *all* young people, whatever their talents, for the serious business of being free men and women.[2]

In this case the problem of equating aims of education with goals is minor because Gardner communicates to the reader that he is consistently discussing broad goals or aims. The problem arises when discussions of aims, curriculum goals and objectives, and instructional goals and objectives are intermingled. There is little difficulty when a single meaning for a term is used in a single context or when an author clearly defines how he or she uses a term. That, however, does not always happen.

Second, the terms "educational goals" and "educational objectives" are used in the profession with varying meanings. Some use these terms in the same way other people speak of aims of education or educational aims. Some perceive educational goals as curriculum goals and educational objectives as curriculum objectives. Some substitute educational goals for instructional goals and educational objectives for instructional objectives.

Third, as we shall see in examples of school statements of goals and objectives, goals are equated with objectives, and the terms are used synonymously. However, if we believe what we read, there are two entities—one called goals and another, objectives—for numerous schools have prepared statements of both goals and objectives.

Some writers have used the terms "goals" and "objectives" interchangeably, as we can see from the writings of some early proponents of behavioral objectives. W. James Popham and Eva L. Baker wrote: "We have given considerable attention to the topic of instructional objectives because they represent one of the most important tools available to the teacher. . . . There is undoubtedly a positive relationship between a teacher's clarity of instructional goals and the quality of his teaching."[3] Robert F. Mager in his popular work on instructional objectives commented:

An instructor . . . must then select procedures, content, and methods that . . . measure or evaluate the student's performance according to the objectives or goals originally selected. . . . Another important reason for stating objectives sharply relates to the evaluation of the degree to which the learner is able to perform in the manner desired . . . . Unless goals are clearly and firmly fixed in the minds of both parties, tests are at best misleading.[4]

The widely followed taxonomies of educational objectives bear the subtitle *The Classification of Educational Goals.*[5] In some of the literature goals are objectives and vice versa. That is not the case in this textbook, as you will see.

---

[2]John W. Gardner, "National Goals in Education," in *Goals for Americans: Programs for Action in the Sixties,* Report of the President's Commission on National Goals, Henry W. Wriston, Chairman (New York: The American Assembly, Columbia University, 1960), pp. 81, 100.

[3]W. James Popham and Eva L. Baker, *Systematic Instruction* (Englewood Cliffs, N.J.: Prentice-Hall, 1970), p. 43.

[4]Robert F. Mager, *Preparing Instructional Objectives* (Belmont, Calif.: Fearon, 1962), pp. 1, 3–4.

[5]Benjamin S. Bloom, ed., *Taxonomy of Educational Objectives: The Classification of Educational Goals: Handbook I: Cognitive Domain* (New York: Longman, 1956) and David R. Krathwohl, Benjamin S. Bloom, and Bertram B. Masia, *Taxonomy of Educational Objectives: The Classification of Educational Goals: Handbook II: Affective Domain* (New York: Longman, 1964).

Fourth, some curriculum specialists do not distinguish curriculum goals and objectives from instructional goals and objectives, or they use these two sets of terms synonymously. If curriculum and instruction are two different entities—the position taken in this text—curriculum goals and objectives are different from instructional goals and objectives. Only if we choose a curriculum-instruction model in which the curriculum and instruction are mirror images can curriculum goals and objectives be identical to instructional goals and objectives. This text, however, presents the view that the two are separate but related entities.

These observations are not meant to criticize the positions, definitions, or approaches of other curriculum specialists nor to hold that the definitions given in this text are the "right" or only ones. As Decker F. Walker aptly stated in an enlightened discussion of writings on curriculum:

> Curriculum clearly is an iffy subject. It belongs to Aristotle's "region of the many and variable" where certain knowledge is not possible, only opinion—multiple and various, more or less considered, more or less adequate, but never clearly true or false.[6]

Mary M. McCaslin spoke in a similar vein when she said:

> We all live in glass houses. None of us can afford glib dismissal of alternative conceptions any more than we can afford to be noncritical or nonreflective about our own work.[7]

My remarks about the differences in the use of curriculum terms convey, as mentioned in Chapter 1, that the language of curriculum is somewhat imprecise and can lead to confusion. Curriculum specialists, unfortunately, do not agree among themselves on terminology. As a result, the practitioner who seeks to carry out curriculum development following principles established by the experts must first understand the contexts within which they appear.

In this text I have made distinctions between curriculum goals and objectives and instructional goals and objectives to help practitioners facilitate the natural flow of curriculum development from general aims of education to precise instructional objectives. Specifying curriculum goals and objectives, then, is viewed as an intermediate planning step between these two poles. First, let's define the terms curriculum goals and curriculum objectives, present some examples, and then develop some guidelines for writing them.

DEFINING GOALS AND OBJECTIVES

CURRICULUM GOALS

A *curriculum goal* is a purpose or end stated in general terms without criteria of achievement. Curriculum planners wish students to accomplish the goal as a result of

---

[6]Decker F. Walker, "A Brainstorming Tour of Writing on Curriculum," in Arthur W. Foshay, ed., *Considered Action for Curriculum Improvement,* 1980 Yearbook (Alexandria, Va.: Association for Supervision and Curriculum Development, 1980), p. 81.

[7]Mary M. McCaslin, "Commentary: Whole Language—Theory, Instruction, and Future Implementation," *The Elementary School Journal* 90, no. 2 (November 1989): 227.

exposure to segments or all of a program of a particular school or school system. For example, the following statement meets this definition of a curriculum goal: "Students will demonstrate responsible behavior as citizens of our school, community, state, nation, and world."

We have already seen examples of curriculum goals in Chapter 3. The Seven Cardinal Principles—health, command of fundamental processes, worthy home membership, vocation, citizenship, worthy use of leisure, and ethical character—are examples of curriculum goals, albeit in a form of shorthand.[8] The Commission on the Reorganization of Secondary Education could have expanded these principles into forms like the following:

- The school will promote the physical and mental health of the students.
- Students will achieve a command of the fundamental processes.
- A goal of the school is to foster worthy home membership.

The Ten Imperative Needs of Youth, listed by the Educational Policies Commission, is a set of curriculum goals that, as noted earlier, included such statements as these:

- All youth need to develop salable skills.
- All youth need to develop and maintain good health, physical fitness, and mental health.
- All youth need to grow in their ability to think rationally, to express their thoughts clearly, and to read and listen with understanding.[9]

At an earlier time the Educational Policies Commission pointed to four purposes or aims of education in American democracy. It identified these aims as self-realization, human relationships, economic efficiency, and civic responsibility.[10] These purposes might be modified by a particular school or school system and turned into curricular goals, stated in a variety of ways, for example:

- The school's program provides experiences leading to self-realization.
- Our school seeks to promote human relationships.
- A goal of the school is development of skills of learners that will lead to their country's and their own economic efficiency.
- Students will develop a sense of civic responsibility.

Many variations are used for expressing these four purposes. This chapter will later present a preferred form for writing goals and objectives. For now, these four goals are shown as examples of substance, not of form.

Aims of education can become curriculum goals when applied to a particular school or school system. The distinction drawn between aims of education and curriculum goals is one of generality (or looking at it from the other end of the telescope, specificity). "To transmit the cultural heritage" and "to overcome ignorance" are aims

---

[8]Commission on the Reorganization of Secondary Education, *Cardinal Principles of Secondary Education* (Washington, D.C.: United States Office of Education, Bulletin No. 35, 1918).

[9]Educational Policies Commission, *Education for All American Youth* (Washington, D.C.: National Education Association, 1938), pp. 225–226.

[10]Educational Policies Commission, *The Purposes of Education in American Democracy* (Washington, D.C.: National Education Association, 1938).

of all school programs. No single program or school can accomplish these extremely broad purposes. A school can, of course, contribute to transmitting the cultural heritage and to overcoming ignorance; stated with those qualifications, educational aims can become curriculum goals. The expression "to contribute to the physical development of the individual" can be both an educational aim of society and a curriculum goal of a particular school or school system.

CURRICULUM OBJECTIVES

Curriculum goals are derived from a statement of philosophy, defined aims of education, and assessment of needs. From curriculum goals, we derive curriculum objectives. We may define a curriculum objective in the following manner: A *curriculum objective* is a purpose or end stated in specific, measurable terms. Curriculum planners wish students to accomplish it as a result of exposure to segments or all of a program of the particular school or school system.

The following example of a curriculum goal has already been presented: "Students will demonstrate responsible behavior as citizens of our school, community, state, nation, and world." From that curriculum goal the following curriculum objectives are among those which could be derived:

- During the election of student government officers, ninety percent of the student body will cast ballots.
- One hundred percent of the students will make some kind of positive contribution to the community's clean-up campaign.
- Ninety percent of the students will be able to name the candidates running for the state senate and the state assembly from their district. They will be able to identify the candidates for the principal state executive offices. They will also identify the political party affiliation of the candidates.
- Ninety percent of the students will be able to identify their current U.S. senators and their representative to the U.S. House of Representatives. They will also identify the political parties of these officeholders.
- Ninety percent of the students will participate in some project that can increase international understanding, such as contributing coins to UNICEF, donating food or clothing to victims of some natural disaster abroad, writing to pen pals overseas, or taking part in other school or community projects of an international nature.

Note how the curriculum objectives refine the curriculum goal. Many curriculum objectives can emanate from the same curriculum goal. When we reach Chapter 10 you will see that some of the foregoing curriculum objectives referring to accomplishments of groups of students become instructional objectives referring to accomplishments of individual students, for example, identifying candidates for office.

LOCUS OF CURRICULUM GOALS AND OBJECTIVES

As the statements of the Seven Cardinal Principles and the Ten Imperative Needs of Youth demonstrated, curriculum goals are periodically written on a national basis by individuals and groups as proposals for consideration by schools throughout the country. However, curriculum objectives, as just defined, are too specific to emanate from national sources.

Curriculum goals and objectives are regularly written at the state, school-district, and individual school level with the expectation that they will be followed within the jurisdiction of the respective level. State pronouncements apply to all public schools in the state; school-district statements apply districtwide; and individual school specifications, schoolwide.

For the most part, curriculum goals and objectives developed at any level cut across disciplines. A school's statement of curriculum goals and objectives, for example, applies generally throughout the school. It is possible, however, for grades and departments to develop curriculum goals and objectives that do not apply generally throughout the school or subject area.

Let us suppose, by way of example, that the following statement is a curriculum goal of the school: "All children need to develop skill in working with numbers." The fourth-grade teachers could create a grade-level goal by simply reiterating the school goal as "Fourth graders need to develop skill in working with numbers." On the other hand, the fourth-grade teachers might choose to interpret the school's curriculum goal and create a grade-level curriculum objective, as follows: "This year's fourth graders will excel last year's by an average of five percentile points on the same standardized test of arithmetic."

Another example of a schoolwide curriculum goal is "Students will improve their scores on state assessment tests." One of the school's curriculum objectives derived from this goal might be "At least eighty-five percent of the students will achieve passing scores on the statewide assessment tests." The eleventh-grade faculty might set as its objective: "Ninety percent of the juniors will pass the state assessment test this year."

We encounter a similar case with a twelfth-grade faculty when the school seeks to accomplish the following curriculum goal: "Students will develop self-discipline and self-reliance." A twelfth-grade faculty might spell out the following curriculum goal: "Seniors will demonstrate skills of independent study." The twelfth-grade teachers might be more specific by following up this curriculum goal with a curriculum objective, as follows: "At least seventy percent of the seniors will seek to improve their self-discipline, self-reliance, and self-study techniques by engaging in independent research projects at least one period (fifty-five minutes) of the school day three times a week."

Teachers of foreign languages may furnish us with an example of curriculum goals and objectives found within a discipline. They might, for example, consider the school's curriculum goal: "Students will develop the ability to relate to ethnic and national groups different from their own." The foreign language teachers might also note one of the school's curriculum objectives, in this case applying to all the students in general but aimed at a particular field: "Seventy-five percent of the student body will elect a foreign language."

The foreign languages teachers might decide on the following curriculum goal: "Students will initiate a number of requests for advanced courses in a foreign language." They might identify as a curriculum objective: "Fifty percent of the students who are taking or who have taken a foreign language will enroll in a second foreign language."

In all cases, the grade or departmental and school's curriculum goals and objectives must be compatible with the district's and both an individual school's and the district's curriculum goals and objectives must be coordinated with those of the state.

STATE CURRICULUM GOALS AND OBJECTIVES

The state, through either its board or department of education, may exert curriculum leadership by promulgating a statement of curriculum goals and, in some cases, curriculum objectives for all its schools. The state of Florida, for example, furnishes an interesting illustration not only of state curriculum planning but also of the recognition of the need for continual change as needs of students and society change. In the late 1970s Florida identified seven goals of education: basic skills, general education, vocational competencies, professional competencies, advanced knowledge and skills, research and development, and recreation and leisure skills.[11] It offered one major curriculum objective: "On a statewide average, educational achievement in the State of Florida will equal that of the upper quartile of states within five years, as indicated by commonly accepted criteria of attainment."[12] In an earlier document the state of Florida offered some useful advice on how to conceptualize educational goals:

> The goals of education can be conceived in terms of the life activities of human adults in modern society. These activities may generally be placed in three categories: occupational, citizenship, and self-fulfillment. By constructing such a framework, it becomes possible to state the kinds of performance which should equip adults to function effectively in society—the *objectives* of education.[13]

The foregoing quotation recalls the method described in Chapter 7 of analyzing society's needs by spelling out social processes, functions, or life activities. This same document sought to help curriculum planners by summarizing the characteristics of goals as follows:

1. Goals are statements of ultimate desired outcomes; they specify conditions desired for the population in general.
2. Goals are timeless, in the sense that no time is specified by which the goals must be reached.
3. Goals do not specify criteria for achievement, but provide a direction for system improvement.
4. Goals are not permanent. Feedback from the entire evaluation/decision-making process is used to assess progress in the direction specified by the goals, and goals may be modified wherever necessary or desirable.
5. Goals are of equal importance.
6. Goals are stated broadly enough to be accepted at any level of the educational enterprise: state, district, or local school. They thus represent the conceptual framework upon which the education enterprise depends.[14]

---

[11]Ralph Turlington, *Focus on Education in Florida: The Annual Report of the Commissioner of Education* (Tallahassee, Fla.: State Department of Education, 1978). Goals 1–7, Florida State Board of Education, March 1975, amended May 6, 1980.

[12]Ibid., p. 16.

[13]Florida Department of Education, *Goals for Education in Florida* (Tallahassee, Fla.: State Department of Education, 1972), p. 4.

[14]Ibid., pp. 5–6.

The foregoing principles offer an illustration of an effort to describe the nature of curriculum goals. Some curriculum planners may take issue with some of the stated principles, particularly characteristics 2 and 5.

Reflecting changes in society—the global economy, the changing nature of the student clientele, the necessity for educational improvement, and national efforts like *America 2000* and *Goals 2000,* Florida launched a reform effort in 1991 with its *Blueprint 2000.* Amended in 1993, *Blueprint 2000* set forth seven education goals which are a combination of administrative, curricular, and instructional goals:

GOAL 1
Readiness to Start School
Communities and schools collaborate to prepare children and families for children's success in school.

GOAL 2
Graduation Rate and Readiness for Postsecondary Education and Employment
Students graduate and are prepared to enter the workforce and postsecondary education.

GOAL 3
Student Performance
Students successfully compete at the highest levels nationally and internationally and are prepared to make well-reasoned, thoughtful, and healthy lifelong decisions.

GOAL 4
Learning Environment
School boards provide a learning environment conducive to teaching and learning.

GOAL 5
School Safety and Environment
Communities provide an environment that is drug-free and protects students' health, safety, and civil rights.

GOAL 6
Teachers and Staff
The schools, districts, and state ensure professional teachers and staff.

GOAL 7
Adult Literacy
Adult Floridians are literate and have the knowledge and skills needed to compete in a global economy and exercise the rights and responsibilities of citizenship.

The state charged the individual schools with the responsibility of devising their own blueprints based on the seven goals.[15] An earmark of the Florida reform movement is the thrust to curtail some state restrictions on curriculum improvement and to empower local schools and communities to exercise a greater degree of control over how public education is carried out. Current moves nationally to site-based management and charter schools reinforce the practice of decentralization.[16]

Counterbalancing current efforts toward local autonomy and decentralization, the Florida Commission on Education Reform and Accountability in 1995 responded to

---

[15]Florida Department of Education, *Florida's System of School Improvement and Accountability September 1995 Blueprint 2000* (Tallahassee, Fla.: State Department of Education, 1995), p. i.

[16]See Chapter 14 for discussion of charter schools.

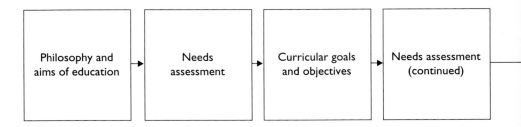

Figure 8.2 The sequence of goal specification and needs assessment

Blueprint 2000 by proposing statewide assessment of student achievement on prespecified curriculum objectives at every level and in every course, demonstrating once again that no direction in education ever runs in a straight line.

The early Florida document *Goals for Education* expressed clearly the value in stating curriculum goals and objectives: "While it is necessary to know current status in order to specify educational needs and to assign priorities for satisfaction of these needs, the statements of desired outcomes are logically a prerequisite to establishing needs."[17] In Chapter 7 I spoke to the timing of needs assessment and goal specification: "A needs assessment is a continuing activity that takes place (a) before specification of curricular goals and objectives, (b) after identification of curricular goals and objectives, (c) after evaluation of instruction, and (d) after evaluation of the curriculum."[18] To clarify the sequence of goal writing and needs assessment, we may refer to Figure 8.2.

Once curriculum goals and objectives have been spelled out, the needs assessment process proceeds to determine unmet needs. Once identified, these needs will result in the creation of more curriculum goals and objectives or a modification of those already specified.

In summary, a state may formulate both broad aims and curriculum goals (and also in some cases curriculum objectives, instructional goals, and instructional objectives as well—a depth of state planning and control decried by many curriculum workers) for all schools and all students in that state.

SCHOOL-DISTRICT CURRICULUM GOALS AND OBJECTIVES

In practice, school districts and individual schools may accept the state's formulation of goals and objectives verbatim or, if the state permits, may independently develop their own statements. In either case, however, the statements of the school districts and individual schools must be in harmony with the state's. Let's examine the statement of goals of the Dade County (Florida) Public Schools, a large urban school district with a multiethnic population. Borrowed from an earlier pronouncement of the state of Florida and amended slightly by the school district, this statement, "Goals for Student Development," is shown in Box 8.1.[19] Although first appearing in the mid 1970s, this statement is still retained in the district's board policies.

---

[17]Florida Department of Education, *Florida's System of School Improvement*, p. 5.
[18]See p. 224.
[19]Dade County Public Schools, *District Comprehensive Educational Plan, 1974–79* (Miami, Fla.: Dade County Public Schools, 1974), pp. 8–11.

```
┌──────────────────┐   ┌──────────────────┐   ┌──────────────────┐
│     Revised      │   │                  │   │                  │
│ curricular goals │ → │Instructional goals│ → │ Needs assessment │
│  and objectives  │   │  and objectives  │   │   (continued)    │
└──────────────────┘   └──────────────────┘   └──────────────────┘
```

INDIVIDUAL SCHOOL CURRICULUM GOALS AND OBJECTIVES

Not only do the states and school districts establish curriculum goals and objectives, but the individual schools also enter into the process by specifying their own philosophy, goals and objectives. Box 8.2 (excerpts from Handbook of Sequoia Middle School, Redding, California) furnishes an example of a middle school's statement of its vision, mission, priorities and expected competencies, and beliefs.

The statement of philosophy and goals (all of which in the context of this chapter would be identified as goals) of Miami (Florida) Palmetto Senior High School, shown in Box 8.3, reflects a relationship among the state's, the school district's, and the individual school's statement of goals and objectives.

Although the illustrations of curriculum goals and objectives cited in this chapter follow different formats, they serve as examples of the step in the planning process that calls for the specification of curriculum goals and objectives.

CONSTRUCTING STATEMENTS OF CURRICULUM GOALS

The examples of curriculum goals demonstrate a variety of forms of expression. Some schools phrase their goals in a way that stresses the role of the curriculum or of the school, like the following examples:

- To teach students to express themselves clearly and correctly in written and oral English.
- To teach students to work and live together through cooperative and inclusive practices.
- To develop the students' abilities to purchase goods and services wisely.
- To help students develop respect for cultures other than their own.
- To develop potentialities of all students through authentic learning experiences.
- To provide students with learning experiences that are developmentally appropriate.

Although an expression that stresses the role of the school is common, an alternate form that focuses on the students seems preferable for a number of reasons:

1. Philosophically, this form is more in keeping with progressive doctrine, which places the pupil at the center of learning—a sound principle.

BOX 8.1

GOALS FOR STUDENT DEVELOPMENT

Goal Area I:

Communication and Learning Skills. Students shall acquire, to the extent of their individual physical, mental, and emotional capacities, a mastery of the basic skills required in obtaining and expressing ideas through the effective use of words, numerals, and other symbols.

a. Students shall achieve a working knowledge of reading, writing, speaking, and arithmetic during the elementary school years, accompanied by gradual progress into the broader fields of mathematics, natural science, language arts, and the humanities.
b. Students shall develop and use skills in the logical processes of search, analysis, evaluation and problem-solving, in critical thinking, and in the use of symbolism.
c. Students shall develop competence and motivation for continuing self-evaluation, self-instruction, and adaptation to a changing environment.
d. Students shall have the opportunity during the elementary school years to develop and use the skills of speaking and understanding a foreign language in order to communicate effectively in the language for future personal or vocational achievements.

Goal Area II:

Citizenship Education. Students shall acquire and continually improve the habits and attitudes necessary for responsible citizenship.

a. Students shall acquire knowledge of various political systems with emphasis on democratic institutions, the heritage of the United States, the contributions of our diverse cultural backgrounds, and the responsibilities and privileges of citizenship.
b. Students shall develop the skills required for participation in the political processes of our country and for influencing decisions made by political organizations.
c. Students shall develop the competence and desire to become informed and critical participants in the electoral process of this county.
d. Students shall acquire those attributes necessary for functioning, on a daily basis, as good citizens in their own school and community settings.

Goal Area III:

Career and Occupational Education. Students shall acquire a knowledge and understanding of the opportunities open to them for preparing for a productive life, and shall develop those skills and abilities which will enable them to take full advantage of those opportunities—including a positive attitude toward work and respect for the dignity of all honorable occupations.

a. Students shall acquire knowledge of and develop an understanding of the fundamental structure and processes of America's economic system, together with an understanding of the opportunities and requirements for individual participation and success in this changing system.
b. Students shall develop occupational competencies, consistent with their interests, aptitudes, and abilities, which are necessary for entry and advancement in the economic system; they shall develop those academic competencies necessary for the acquisition of technical or professional skills through post–high school training.

(Continued)

Box 8.1 Continued

c. Students shall develop competence in the application of economic knowledge to practical economic functions: such as, planning and budgeting for the investment of personal income, calculating tax obligations, financing major purchases, and obtaining desirable employment.

d. Students shall develop an awareness of the relevance of the curriculum to the world of work and our social existence.

Goal Area IV:

Mental and Physical Health. Students shall acquire good health habits and an understanding of the conditions necessary for the maintenance of physical, emotional, and social well-being.

a. Students shall develop an understanding of the requirements of personal hygiene, adequate nutrition and leisure time activities essential to the maintenance of physical health, and a knowledge of the dangers to mental and physical health from addiction and other aversive practices.

b. Students shall develop skills in sports and other forms of recreation which will provide for life-long enjoyment of participation according to their own preferences and abilities.

c. Students shall develop competence in recognizing and preventing environmental health problems.

d. Students shall acquire a knowledge of basic psychological and sociological factors affecting human behavior and mental health, and shall develop competence for adjusting to changes in personal status and social patterns.

Goal Area V:

Home and Family Relationships. Students shall develop an appreciation of the family as a social institution.

a. Students shall develop an understanding of their roles and the roles of others as members of a family, together with a knowledge of the requirements for successful participation in family living.

b. Students shall develop an understanding of the role of the family as a basic unit in the society.

c. Students shall develop an awareness of the diversity of family patterns and the value of the contributions of the individuals to family and community living.

Goal Area VI:

Aesthetic and Cultural Appreciations. Students shall develop understanding and appreciation of human achievement in the natural sciences, the humanities and the arts.

a. Students shall acquire a knowledge of an appreciation for major arts, music, literary, and drama forms, and their place in the cultural heritage.

b. Students shall acquire a knowledge of the natural, physical and social sciences and their relationships to human and social development.

c. Students shall develop skills for creative use of leisure time and shall develop an interest in becoming active in one or more areas of creative endeavor.

d. Students shall develop discrimination skills in the critical evaluation of cultural offerings and opportunities.

Goal Area VII:

Human Relations. Students shall develop a concern for moral, ethical, and spiritual values and for the application of such values to life situations.

(Continued)

Box 8.1 Continued

a. Students shall acquire the greatest possible understanding and appreciation of themselves as well as of persons belonging to social, cultural, and ethnic groups different from their own, and of the worthiness of all persons as members of society.
b. Students shall develop those skills and attitudes necessary for positive interpersonal and group relationship and shall recognize the importance of and need for ethical and moral standards of behavior.
c. Students shall recognize the value of that level of group discipline and self-discipline that promotes a sense of worth of the individual while contributing to the collective benefit of all involved.

SOURCE: Dade County Public Schools, *District Comprehensive Educational Plan, 1974–79* (Miami, Fla.: Dade County Public Schools, 1974), pp. 8–11. Reprinted with permission.

2. It is in keeping with modern instructional design, which focuses on the achievements of the learner rather than on the performance of the teacher or school.
3. It parallels common practice, as we shall see in Chapter 10, in writing instructional goals and objectives. Thus, curriculum goals may be better understood and the process of curriculum development better integrated.
4. It is easier to design evaluation processes when we know what is expected in terms of student achievement.

Writing curriculum goals in a form that starts with the students, we might revise the preceding illustrations in the following manner:

- Students will express themselves clearly and correctly in written and oral English.
- Students will demonstrate the ability to purchase goods and services wisely.
- Students will show interest in and understanding of cultures other than their own.
- Students will demonstrate the ability to work productively with others.

CHARACTERISTICS OF CURRICULUM GOALS

The characteristics of curriculum goals as conceptualized in this text may be summarized as follows:

1. They relate to the educational aims and philosophy.
2. They are programmatic. Although they speak to one or more areas of the curriculum, they do not delineate the specific courses or specific items of content.
3. They refer to the accomplishment of groups (all students, students in general, most students) rather than the achievement of individual students.
4. They are broad enough to lead to specific curriculum objectives.

CONSTRUCTING STATEMENTS OF CURRICULUM OBJECTIVES

Like curriculum goals, curriculum objectives relate to the educational aims and philosophy of the school, are programmatic in nature, and refer to accomplishments of

BOX 8.2

EXCERPTS FROM HANDBOOK, SEQUOIA MIDDLE SCHOOL, REDDING, CALIFORNIA

VISION "A DREAM COME TRUE"

Sequoia Middle School is a *safe learning community* where every adolescent will be an intellectually reflective person; a person en route to a lifetime of meaningful work; a good citizen; a caring and ethical individual; and a healthy person.

SEQUOIA'S MISSION "WE CHOOSE TO ACCEPT"

Working together (parents, students, and staff), we will:
 create a community for learning;
 teach a core of common knowledge;
 ensure success for all students;
 empower staff, parents, and students;
 prepare teachers for the middle grades;
 improve academic performance through better health and fitness;
 re-engage families in the education of young adolescents; and
 connect schools with communities

PRIORITIES FOR 1999–2000 "WE CAN DO IT"

- **Safe Environment:**
 Provide and communicate a safe and positive learning environment.
 Maintain zero tolerance for racism, violence, gangs, drugs, and sexual harassment.
 Build positive relationships, especially through better communication.
 Implement "Character Counts" education

- **Student Achievement:**
 Develop the "Profile of a Scientist and Social Scientist" relative to each grade level.
 Implement content and performance standards and review purpose of homework in relation to what students need to know and be able to do.
 Implement Sequoia's 6–8 Reading and Algebra Programs.
 Integrate Health, Fitness, Safety, and Character Education

- **Parent-Family Involvement:**
 Identify mentors to assist students who need adult support away from school.

- **Technology:**
 Expand technological opportunities to students, family, and community beyond the traditional classroom day and year.
 Implement technology training with emphasis on full integration of technology in the classroom to expand students' knowledge of the world.

(Continued)

Box 8.2 Continued

- **Alternative Learning:**

    Explore options for students with severe behavior disorders.

    Design and implement intervention programs for students at risk, especially for students in danger of retention.

    Implement "School To Career" Grants—Portfolios and SCANS

- **Marketing:**

    Find community resources and link them in sustained partnerships with Sequoia.

EXPECTED STUDENT COMPETENCIES "THE POSSIBLE DREAM"

- **Basic Skills**—reading, writing, arithmetic, mathematics, listening, speaking
- **Thinking Skills**—creative, decision making, problem solving, visualization, reasoning, how to learn
- **Personal Qualities**—responsibility, self esteem, sociability, self management, accountability
- **Resourceful**—manages time, money, materials, facilities, and human resources, good work ethic
- **Interpersonal**—works as team member of diverse groups, teaches, service, leadership, negotiates
- **Information**—acquires, evaluates, organizes, maintains, interprets, communicates, uses computers
- **Technology**—selects and applies technology for tasks

BELIEF "LET'S WALK THE TALK"

- Positive relationships among students, teachers, and parents are essential for learning.
- All students can learn what is taught.
- Each of us makes a difference.
- Student growth and achievement are our primary challenges.
- Individually we are good; working together we are better.
- Students must have mastery of basic skills, have a positive work ethic, be problem solvers, work well with others, and communicate well.

SOURCE: Sequoia Middle School, Redding, California. Reprinted by permission.

groups. Unlike curriculum goals, curriculum objectives are stated in specific and measurable terms.

CHARACTERISTICS OF CURRICULUM OBJECTIVES

Curriculum objectives are refinements of the curriculum goals. They specify performance standards for the students for whom the curriculum is designed. We can turn a curriculum goal into a curriculum objective by adding the following three elements, which we will meet again when discussing instructional objectives:

- performance or behavioral terms—that is, those skills and knowledge the students are expected to be able to demonstrate
- the degree of mastery desired by the curriculum planners
- conditions under which the performance will take place, if not readily understood

BOX 8.3

PHILOSOPHY AND OBJECTIVES OF THE MIAMI PALMETTO SENIOR HIGH SCHOOL

Miami Palmetto Senior High School provides opportunities for all students to become mature, thinking, skilled young people, well equipped for education, career, personal, and life-long growth. The staff seeks to create an atmosphere conducive to the learning process and one which enables students to develop a positive self-image. These factors combine to enable students to develop as responsible citizens.

As educators, we are committed to the following philosophical principles:

1. To foster a knowledge of self and of the world in which the individual lives.
2. To encourage understanding and respect for the rights of others.
3. To stimulate critical, constructive, and creative thinking.
4. To assist in the development of a set of values meaningful to the individual and worthwhile to society.
5. To assist in the development of functional skills necessary for an individual to be a contributing member of society.
6. To provide experiences which will enrich career education and career choices.
7. To provide a positive and challenging experience for all students.

In order to fulfill the previous statements, the faculty seeks to meet the objectives stated below:

1. To offer a flexible curriculum ranging from instruction in basic through college-level courses.
2. To instruct students in learning processes which will provide them with methods of inquiry applicable to the future, as well as present, learning situations.
3. To encourage students to practice courtesy, friendliness, and cooperation as a way of life.
4. To motivate students in the development and maintenance of sound mental, emotional, and physical health.
5. To provide experiences which will enable students to develop an appreciation and an understanding of their own culture as well as the culture of others.
6. To provide students with instruction and materials which are appropriate to their ability and maturity level.
7. To guide students to think logically and creatively, to express ideas clearly in speaking and writing, and to listen and view critically.
8. To help students learn to discuss and to see the relationship between cause and effect.
9. To enable students to distinguish facts from unstated opinions, conclusions, and inferences.
10. To strengthen pupils' computational skills and to provide for those who operate at the concept level in mathematics.
11. To provide all students instruction in reading skills.
12. To encourage students to read widely both for their own intellectual growth and for their own enjoyment.

(Continued)

Box 8.3 Continued

13. To assist students in the discovery of scientific principles through the study of factual and experimental evidence.
14. To help students acquire an understanding of the principles and processes of the American free-enterprise system.
15. To involve students in school and community resources.
16. To promote in students an appreciation and understanding of those factors conducive to successful family living.
17. To orient students in the effective use of print and nonprint materials in the Media Center.
18. To provide opportunities for interested students to develop manual skills.
19. To provide students with vocational information and the opportunity to develop occupational skills.
20. To provide students with co-curricular activities which will develop interest, cooperativeness, pride, and satisfaction.
21. To foster a positive educational experience for the potential dropout.
22. To encourage female students to enroll in high level math and science courses.
23. To encourage minority students with potential to enroll in courses which will challenge their abilities.
24. To encourage students to maximize their potential by enrolling in courses which will challenge them.

SOURCE: Miami Palmetto Senior High School, Miami, Florida. Reprinted with permission.

Let's analyze the following curriculum objective for these three elements: "On completion of the first testing, seventy-five percent of the eleventh graders will have successfully passed the state's minimal competencies test; by completion of the second testing, ninety percent will have passed." Are all three elements present in this two-part objective? Yes, they are. The performance expected is successfully passing the state's minimal competencies test. The degrees of mastery desired are seventy-five and ninety percent. Completion of the first and second testing is the condition.

To accomplish the transition from curriculum goal to curriculum objective, you may find it helpful to jot down several indicators of student performance that will serve as guides for writing the objectives. Let's take another look at the illustrative curriculum goal mentioned earlier: "Students shall demonstrate responsible behavior as citizens of our school, community, state, nation, and world." What are some indicators of learner performance that would reveal evidence of students' accomplishment of this goal? We might look for such behaviors as the following:

- care of school building and grounds
- less fighting among students
- expressions of mutual respect among ethnic groups
- orderliness in school assemblies
- participation in community youth organizations such as church groups, scout groups, and the like

- refraining from littering the school and community
- serving on committees of the school
- observing highway speed limits
- cooperation among students in inclusive classes
- taking an interest in local, state, and national elections
- engaging in discussions on ways to reduce international tensions

We could turn the first performance indicator—care of school building and grounds—into a curriculum objective in the following manner: "By the end of April students will have demonstrated care of the building to the extent that there will be a ninety-five percent reduction in the number of graffiti on the walls." From the one curriculum goal on good citizenship we can generate many curriculum objectives, and from the first performance indicator alone we can create a number of objectives.

We should take note of the fact that Theodore R. Sizer presented a different approach toward specifying curriculum objectives. At Horace's fictitious school, the "Committee's Report" cast curriculum objectives [which the "Committee" called 'specific goals'] into an authentic assessment framework. Said the "Committee", "We believe that our school should be driven by specific goals in the form of Exhibitions through which the students can display their grasp and use of important ideas and skills. The school's program would be to the largest practical extent the preparation for these Exhibitions."[20]

Explanation of U.S. Supreme Court decisions, preparation of nutritious menus for the school cafeteria, preparation of a portfolio on a human emotion, completing an IRS Form 1040, drawing a map of the United States and placing a dozen states on it, and running a community service program are examples of Exhibitions possible at Horace's school.[21] In this context curriculum objectives are equated with Exhibitions, tasks by which students demonstrate achievement through performance.

Outcomes-based education, discussed in Chapter 14, is a current movement that specifies curriculum objectives in the form of expected outcomes to be achieved by the learners. The generation of curriculum goals and objectives is a highly creative exercise. Curriculum planners will approach the specification of curriculum goals and objectives in their own style, remembering that curriculum goals and objectives set the direction for the subsequent organization and development of the curriculum and that the curriculum goals and objectives determine the activities that will take place in the many classrooms of the school.

VALIDATING AND DETERMINING PRIORITY OF GOALS AND OBJECTIVES

As stated earlier, the assessment of curriculum needs is a continuing process that starts after a school formulates its philosophy and clarifies its aims of education. The needs of society; of students in general; and of the particular students, community, and sub-

[20]Theodore R. Sizer, *Horace's School: Redesigning the American High School* (Boston: Houghton Mifflin, 1992), p. 143.
[21]Ibid., pp. 8–9, 23, 48, 65, 80.

ject matter give rise to initial statements of curriculum goals and objectives. After these goals and objectives have been identified, the needs assessment process is continued to determine if any needs have not been met. When unmet needs are exposed, a revised list of curriculum goals and objectives is prepared. These goals and objectives require validation and placing in order of priority.

Validation is the process of determining whether the goals and objectives are accepted as appropriate or "right" for the school (or school system, if conducted on a systemwide level) proposing them. *Determining priority* is the placing of the goals and objectives in order of relative importance to the school. Groups concerned with the progress of the school should be enlisted to help identify suitable goals and objectives and to set priorities.

Some schools seek to validate both goals and objectives; others limit the process to validating goals on the presumption that once the goals are identified, a representative committee can handle the task of making the goals specific—that is, turning them into objectives.

FUNCTION OF CURRICULUM COMMITTEE

The validation process, whether carried out by the state, district, or school, assumes the formation of a curriculum committee or council charged with the task. The curriculum committee will submit the goals by means of a questionnaire or opinionnaire to groups who are concerned with the progress of the school(s).

Submitting curriculum goals and any already identified curriculum objectives to a broad sampling of groups—lay persons (including parents), students, teachers, administrators, and curriculum experts (on the staffs of public school systems or on the faculties of teacher education institutions)—is good practice. The effort should be made to learn whether there is widespread acceptance of the goals formulated by the curriculum planners and what the groups' priorities are. Curriculum objectives that are developed after a broad sampling of opinion has been gathered can be submitted to either a more limited sampling of the same groups or to the curriculum committee for validation and ranking.

Data should be gathered and interpreted, preferably by a curriculum committee representative of the various groups polled. Such a committee will be called on to make judgments that will tax its collective wisdom. It cannot treat the data in a simplistic fashion, tallying responses from all groups, and simply following the majority's opinions. It needs to analyze differences of opinion, if any, among the various groups surveyed and discuss the differences among themselves and with members of the various groups.

Weighing Opinions. As a general rule, the wishes of students, for example, should not hold the same priority as the beliefs of parents and other lay people. The opinions of groups small in number, like curriculum specialists or college professors, cannot be treated in the same light as the attitudes of large numbers of residents of the community. For that matter, the opinions of a few school administrators should not be given, simply because of their status, as great a weight as those of large numbers of teachers and parents.

Since the committee interpreting the data may not find consensus on goals and objectives among the various groups, it has the responsibility of reconciling differing positions and reaching consensus among its own members. Drawing on the opinions of the groups that have been polled, the curriculum committee must decide which goals are valid and which should be assigned priority. To set priorities is to say that some goals are more important than others and deserve more attention and emphasis in the curriculum.

It is clear that the goals of a state, district, or school should be submitted for validation and ranking by sizable numbers of educators and noneducators. It is debatable, however, whether curriculum goals and objectives of grades or departments need or should be submitted to persons beyond the school or school-district personnel. It would be somewhat impractical, redundant, expensive, and time-consuming for curriculum goals and objectives of the grades and departments to be submitted to significant numbers of the school system's constituents. The faculties of the grade and department levels may satisfy their responsibilities for validation and ranking of goals and objectives by submitting their statements to the curriculum committee and to experts in the field for review and endorsement.

The process of validation and determining priorities may be repeated as often as the curriculum committee finds necessary, with modifications and repeated rankings made as a result of each survey and prior to a subsequent survey. After the curriculum goals and objectives have been validated and placed in rank order, the curriculum planners turn to the next phase in the curriculum development process—putting the goals and objectives into operation.

SUMMARY

State school systems, school districts, and individual schools engage in the task of specifying curriculum goals and objectives. Curriculum goals and objectives are derived from the developers' philosophy and educational aims.

Curriculum goals are programmatic statements of expected outcomes without criteria of achievement. They apply to students as a group and are often interdisciplinary or multidisciplinary.

Curriculum objectives are specific, measurable, programmatic statements of outcomes to be achieved by students as a group in the school or school system.

Curriculum goals and objectives are essential for

1. conducting a complete needs assessment to identify unmet needs
2. carrying out subsequent phases of the suggested model for curriculum improvement
3. generating instructional goals and objectives
4. providing a basis for evaluating the curriculum
5. giving direction to the program

Curriculum goals and objectives should be phrased in terms of anticipated accomplishments of students. Curriculum objectives, which are more specific than curriculum goals, should stipulate expected degrees of mastery and the conditions under which students can master the desired behaviors. Curriculum goals and objectives should be validated and put in order of priority by the school's curriculum committee after review by representatives of the various constituencies that the school serves.

QUESTIONS FOR DISCUSSION

1. How do you go about specifying curriculum goals and objectives? Who does the specifying?
2. Which comes first: a curriculum needs assessment or the specification of curriculum goals and objectives? Why?
3. Can you have curriculum goals and objectives both across disciplines and within disciplines? If the answer is yes, give examples.
4. Can you have curriculum goals without curriculum objectives? Explain.
5. Can you have curriculum objectives without curriculum goals? Explain.

SUPPLEMENTARY EXERCISES

1. Define and give two examples of
   a. aims of education
   b. curriculum goals
   c. curriculum objectives
2. Following definitions in this text, explain both the relationship and difference between
   a. an aim of education and a curriculum goal
   b. a curriculum goal and a curriculum objective
3. Explain the relationship of curriculum goals and objectives to needs assessment.
4. Respond to the following questions, showing your position on each:
   a. Is it necessary to write an educational philosophy in order to specify curriculum goals and objectives?
   b. Is it necessary to list educational aims in order to specify curriculum goals and objectives?
5. Locate and report on illustrations of curriculum goals either in education textbooks or in curriculum materials of any school or school system in the United States.
6. Locate and report on illustrations of curriculum objectives either in education textbooks or in curriculum materials of any school or school system in the United States.
7. Obtain and, following principles advocated in this chapter, critique the statement of
   a. curriculum goals of a school that you know well
   b. curriculum objectives of a school that you know well
   c. curriculum goals and objectives of a school district that you know well
   d. curriculum goals and/or objectives of one of the 50 states

8. Write as many curriculum objectives as you can for each of the following curriculum goals:
   a. Students will maintain good health and physical fitness.
   b. Students will demonstrate skill in writing.
   c. Students will develop an appreciation for the free enterprise system.
   d. Students will exhibit positive attitudes toward each other regardless of differences in gender, religion, or ethnic origin.
   You may wish to divide the class into four small groups for this exercise.
9. Write a comparative analysis of the author's position on the separateness of curricular and instructional objectives and that of another curriculum specialist who takes a different position.
10. Describe the hierarchy of goals discussed by Ronald S. Brandt and Ralph W. Tyler (see bibliography) and give examples of each type.
11. Analyze the merits of equating Exhibitions of performance with curriculum objectives.

BIBLIOGRAPHY

Bloom, Benjamin S., ed. *Taxonomy of Educational Objectives: The Classification of Educational Goals: Handbook I: Cognitive Domain.* New York: Longman, 1956.

Brandt, Ronald S. and Tyler, Ralph W. "Goals and Objectives." In Fenwick W. English, ed. *Fundamentals of Curriculum Decisions.* 1983 Yearbook. Alexandria, Va.: Association for Supervision and Curriculum Development, 1983.

Commission on the Reorganization of Secondary Education. *Cardinal Principles of Secondary Education.* Washington, D.C.: United States Office of Education, Bulletin No. 35, 1918.

Dade County Public Schools, *District Comprehensive Educational Plan, 1974–79.* Miami, Fla.: Dade County Public Schools, 1974.

Doll, Ronald C. *Curriculum Improvement: Decision Making and Process,* 9th ed. Boston: Allyn and Bacon, 1996.

Educational Policies Commission. *Education for All American Youth.* Washington, D.C.: National Education Association, 1944.

———. *The Purposes of Education in American Democracy.* Washington, D.C.: National Education Association, 1938.

Florida Department of Education. *Goals for Education in Florida.* Tallahassee, Fla.: State Department of Education, 1972.

———. *Florida's System of School Improvement and Accountability September 1995 Blueprint 2000.* Tallahassee, Fla.: State Department of Education, 1995.

Gardner, John W. "National Goals of Education," in *Goals for Americans: Programs for Action in the Sixties,*

Report of the President's Commission on National Goals, Henry W. Wriston, Chairman. New York: The American Assembly, Columbia University, 1960.

Krathwohl, David R., Bloom, Benjamin S., and Masia, Bertram B. *Taxonomy of Educational Objectives: The Classification of Educational Goals: Handbook II: Affective Domain.* New York: Longman, 1964.

Mager, Robert F. *Preparing Instructional Objectives.* Belmont, Calif.: Fearon, 1962. 2nd ed., Belmont, Calif.: Pitman Learning, 1975.

McCaslin, Mary M. "Commentary: Whole Language-Theory, Instruction, and Future Implementation," *The Elementary School Journal* 90, no. 2 (November 1989): 227.

Popham, W. James and Baker, Eva L. *Establishing Instructional Goals.* Englewood Cliffs, N.J.: Prentice-Hall, 1970.

———. *Systematic Instruction.* Englewood Cliffs, N.J.: Prentice-Hall, 1970.

Sizer, Theodore R. *Horace's School: Redesigning the American High School.* Boston: Houghton Mifflin, 1992.

Tyler, Ralph W. *Basic Principles of Curriculum and Instruction.* Chicago: University of Chicago Press, 1949.

Walker, Decker F. "A Brainstorming Tour of Writing on Curriculum," in Arthur W. Foshay, ed., *Considered Action for Curriculum Improvement,* 1980 Yearbook. Alexandria, Va.: Association for Supervision and Curriculum Development, 1980.

Wiles, Jon and Bondi, Joseph C. *Curriculum Development: A Guide to Practice,* 5th ed. Upper Saddle River, N.J.: Merrill, 1998.

CHAPTER 9

ORGANIZING AND IMPLEMENTING THE CURRICULUM

After studying this chapter you should be able to:

1. Describe and state strengths and weaknesses of various plans and proposals for organizing and implementing the curriculum.
2. Relate each organizational arrangement discussed in this chapter to (a) the psychological and sociological circumstances of the public school and (b) the achievement of one or more aims of education or curriculum goals at each of the three school levels: elementary, middle, and senior high.
3. Specify several curriculum goals for the elementary, middle, or senior high school level; choose or design and defend a curriculum organization plan that you believe will most satisfactorily result in accomplishment of these goals.

NECESSARY DECISIONS

A HYPOTHETICAL SETTING

Imagine, if you will, a building complex of three schools—an elementary school of five grades plus kindergarten, a middle (formerly junior high) school of three grades, and a senior high school of four grades—constructed in the early days of Franklin D. Roosevelt's presidency and situated on a large tract of land. We could place this complex in a small town in any state where the three schools serve all the children of a particular school district, or we could locate it in a sector of a large urban area where the three schools are a part of the local school system.

Let's create in our own minds the administrative offices of the superintendent (or area superintendent) and school board across the street from this complex. From a second floor conference room we can look out on the children at play in the elementary school yard, we can see awkward teeny-boppers of the middle school up the street to our right, and we can observe the senior high school Harrys and Janes spinning out in their gasoline chariots from the parking lot in the background.

On a particular day in September a group of curriculum planners has gathered in the conference room. It is 4:00 P.M., and for the moment they stand at the window looking over the complex across the way. Activity at the elementary school has virtually ceased for the day, has just about tapered off at the middle school, and continues apace at the senior high school. Only two cars remain in the elementary school parking lot—the principal's and the custodian's.

Making up the curriculum group are the district supervisor (director of curriculum) and the chairpersons of the district curriculum steering committee and the curriculum councils of each of the three schools. In front of them—in finished form, neatly typed and packaged—are (1) the report of the needs assessment that revealed gaps in the school district's curricula and (2) a set of both district and individual school curriculum goals and objectives that they laboriously hammered out with the help of many faculty members, students, administrators, supervisors, and lay citizens.

HYPOTHETICAL STEPS

The task of this curriculum group now is to decide on next steps. What do they do with the curriculum goals and objectives now that they are specified? Shall they duplicate, distribute, and then forget them? Shall they take the position that the process of defining the goals and objectives was sufficient, or that the process should lead to further action? Shall they file the goals and objectives with the superintendent and principals, to be pulled out on special occasions such as visits of parent groups, accrediting committees, or others? How shall they meet the discrepancies shown by the needs assessment and the curriculum goals and objectives developed as a result of that assessment?

The curriculum planners of the district, whose leadership is represented by this committee, must decide how to put the goals and objectives into effect and how to organize the curriculum in such a way that the goals and objectives can be achieved. They must decide what structure will be most conducive to successfully accomplishing the goals and objectives and to fulfilling learner needs. They must ask themselves and their colleagues how best to go about implementing the curriculum decisions that they have made up to this point.

ASSESSING CURRICULUM ORGANIZATION

The question is often posed to curriculum workers: "How shall we go about organizing the curriculum?" The literature often appears to make one of two assumptions: (1) Curriculum planners regularly have the opportunity to initiate a curriculum in a brand new school (or perhaps in a deserted old school) for which no curriculum patterns yet exist; or (2) curriculum developers automatically have the freedom to discard that which now exists and replace it with patterns of their own choosing.

Both assumptions are likely to be erroneous. Curriculum planners do not frequently experience the responsibility for developing an original curriculum for a brand new school (or more accurately, for an upcoming new school, since planning must precede construction). It is true, of course, that new schools are built to meet growths and shifts in population and to replace decrepit structures, which, like old soldiers, slowly fade away. The development of a curriculum for a brand new school does provide the opportunity for curriculum planning from the ground floor, so to speak. But even that planning must be carried out within certain boundaries, including local traditions, state and district mandates, and the curricula of other schools of the district with which they must articulate. Curriculum planners cannot expect simply to substitute as they wish new patterns of curriculum organization for old. Again, we face certain parameters: student needs, teacher preferences, administrators' values, community sentiment, physical restrictions, and financial resources.

Our fictitious curriculum group is talking about possible ways of reorganizing the curriculum to meet pupil needs and to provide the best possible structure for attaining the district's and each school's curriculum goals and objectives. The group decides that one way of approaching this task is to consider the schools' past, present, and future ideas for curriculum organization. They will identify patterns that have been tried, those currently in operation, and those that might be feasible or successful in the immediate and distant future.

At this meeting the committee decides to clarify what they mean by curriculum organization. They agree to talk with their colleagues on their schools' curriculum councils and others and come to the next meeting of this group prepared to trace the historical development of the curricular organizations of the three schools. Each will provide an overview of the more significant patterns of curriculum organization that have been studied and implemented, studied and rejected, and considered for future implementation.

Before adjourning this meeting, the committee agrees on what they will include under the rubric of curriculum organization. They define curriculum organization as those patterns of both a curricular and administrative nature by which students encounter learning experiences and subject matter. Thus it includes not only broad plans for programmatic offerings, such as the subject matter curriculum, but also delivery systems, which possess an administrative dimension, such as team teaching.

Several weeks later when the committee reassembles, exhilarated by its research on the history of curriculum development in their schools, they express a newfound admiration for previous curriculum planners. Whereas the aging facades of the buildings might convey to the outside world, as the French say, that "the more things change, the more they stay the same," inside, innovation and change have been key words. The committee spends several sessions sharing their discoveries and studying what the experts say about the structures uncovered. The committee is sure that by examining past patterns, projecting future arrangements, and comparing both past practices and future possibilities with present structures, they can create more effective ways of implementing the curriculum.

This hypothetical committee's discoveries are significant enough to be shared with you. Our discussion will be organized into three major parts: the past (Where We've Been), the present (Where We Are), and the future (Where We're Going). For each period some major plans in school and curriculum organization at each of three levels—elementary, junior high/middle school, and senior high school—are described.

TABLE 9.1

DEVELOPMENTS AND RECOMMENDATIONS OF THE PAST, PRESENT, AND FUTURE*

LEVEL	WHERE WE'VE BEEN (PAST)	WHERE WE ARE (PRESENT)	WHERE WE'RE GOING (FUTURE)
Elementary	Graded school	Basic skills	Blending of traditional and nontraditional modes
	Activity curriculum	Teaching thinking skills	
	Nongraded elementary school		Changing status of public education
	Open education and open space	Provision for students with special needs, inclusion	
		Multicultural education	
		School choice	
		Home Schooling	
		Charter Schools	
		Bilingual education	
		Cooperative learning	
Junior high/ middle	The school in between: the junior high school	Whole language	Universality of the middle school
		Core knowledge	Integrated curriculum
	Conant's recommendations	Character education	Block/rotating schedules
		Year-round schools	
	ASCD proposals	Middle school	
	Core curriculum	Interdisciplinary teams	
Senior high	Subject matter curriculum	Comprehensive high school	Adoption of some of the recommendations of influential studies, including Mortimer J. Adler.
	Conant's proposals	Magnet schools	
	Broad fields curriculum	Higher requirements for graduation	Business Roundtable,
	Team teaching and differentiated staffing	Technological education	David P. Gardner (National Commission on Excellence in Education), Ernest L. Boyer,
	Flexible and modular scheduling	Community service	
		Health education	
	Nongraded high school	Outcomes-based education	John I. Goodlad,
	Ability grouping	National standards	Theodore R. Sizer
	Tracking	National assessment	
	Programmed instruction	Extended day and year	Technology in education
	Instructional television	Performance-based assessment	
		School-to-work programs	

*NOTE: Although developments on this chart are classified at one level to avoid duplication, many are applicable at more than one level. See also Chapter 14 for discussion of some of these developments.

Remember that Axiom 3 in Chapter 2 postulates that changes do not, as a rule, start and stop abruptly but overlap. Axiom 3 applies to our hypothetical community as it does elsewhere. Consequently, when I discuss the graded school, for example, as a place where we have been, I do not imply that it has necessarily disappeared from the present or that it will not exist in the future. When I discuss the middle school, I do not suggest that its predecessor, the junior high school, no longer exists.

Nor are curricular arrangements always confined to one level. The subject matter curriculum, the graded school, the nongraded school, team teaching, and flexible scheduling exist or have existed at more than one level. By placing a curricular arrangement at a particular level, I am not saying that it could not be found or could not have been found either at the same time or at another time at other levels even in the hypothetical community used for illustrative purposes.

However, you would tire if, for example, discussion of the subject matter curriculum were repeated at each of the three levels. Therefore, I have placed the arrangements, perhaps arbitrarily, at levels where the arrangements were particularly strong, significant, or common. Unless a curricular arrangement had particular significance for more than one level and possessed distinctive characteristics for each level, as in the case of the nongraded elementary school and the nongraded high school, a particular plan is discussed at only one level.

Table 9.1 shows various curricular and organizational developments and recommendations tried in the past or present and proposals for future change.

WHERE WE'VE BEEN: CURRICULUM PAST

THE ELEMENTARY SCHOOL

THE GRADED SCHOOL

Historians tell us that the concept of a graded school started in Prussia, a land famed for discipline and regimentation, and migrated across the ocean to the New World.[1] The Quincy Grammar School of Boston, which opened in 1848, is credited as the first school in the United States to become completely graded. With enough youngsters for several groups, it took not a quantum leap but a simple bit of ingenuity to reason that youngsters might be taught more efficiently if they were sorted and graded. Instead of being mixed, they could be divided largely on the basis of chronological age.

The graded school has become the standard model not only for the United States but for the world. As our country grew in population, expanded westward, and became industrialized, the number of grades provided for children by the numerous school districts of the nation increased in proportion.

---

[1]See William J. Shearer, *The Grading of Schools* (New York: H. P. Smith, 1898).

By the early twentieth century twelve grades were made available and were considered sufficient for most boys and girls. School systems grew, providing the opportunity for young people to receive not ten, not eleven, but twelve years of education at public expense. For one reason or another many children and youth in early days (and to a decreasing extent today) were not able to complete the twelves grades of elementary and secondary education even in communities that offered twelve grades. We could add in passing that both public and private community junior colleges and senior institutions have been established to offer youth opportunities for further learning, but that's another story in itself.

Twelve Years As Norm. Administrators, curriculum experts, teachers, and the public have accepted the twelve years as a norm for most of our young people and have adjusted the component levels as the situation seemed to demand. Thus, until rather recently the most common organizational plan for schools across the country was the eight-four plan (eight years of elementary school and four of secondary school). Under this plan grades seven and eight were considered parts of the elementary rather than the secondary school. As the junior high school began to emerge after the first decade of the twentieth century, the six-two-four plan (six elementary, two junior high, and four senior high grades) offered a variant to the eight-four.

Communities of moderate size showed a fondness for the six-six plan (six elementary and six secondary), which, although it clearly attaches junior high school to secondary education, also buries its identity in that of the senior high school. Larger communities expressed a preference for the six-three-three plan with three years of junior high school between the elementary and senior high school. The three-year junior high school combining grades seven, eight, and nine replicated the structure of the first junior high schools that came into existence in 1909 in Columbus, Ohio and in 1910 in Berkeley, California. Other variations have been suggested such as the six-three-five plan and the six-three-three-two plan, which would extend public secondary education through grades thirteen and fourteen. Those last two years, however, have clearly become identified with the college level. As it is, grades eleven and twelve are normally beyond the age of sixteen, the usual limit for compulsory school attendance. The rearrangement of the twelve years of public schooling has continued to the present, as we shall see later when we discuss the development of the middle school.

The concomitant outgrowth of the graded school was the self-contained classroom—a heterogeneous group of youngsters of approximately the same age, in multiples of twenty-five to thirty-five, under the direction of one teacher. Primary school teachers of the graded school were no longer required to master all disciplines of all grades like their counterparts in the one-room school but only to master all disciplines at the particular grade level. The group of children assigned to a teacher in a self-contained, graded elementary school spent the entire day under the watchful eye of that teacher. It has taken militant action of teacher organizations in recent years to pry loose some breathing time for elementary school teachers during the school day.

The concept of the graded school, aided by the measurement movement in education, has firmly established the principle that certain learnings should be accomplished by pupils not at certain periods of growth and development but by the end of certain grade levels. Syllabi, courses of study, and minimal competencies have been determined for each grade level.

In the graded school, material is tailored to fit the confines of fixed times during the customary ten months of the school year. Thus, by means of a standardized test of reading, for example, we can state that a third-grade child in April (the eighth month of the school year) whose test score placed him or her at the grade norm of 3.2 (second month of the third-grade year) was reading at a level six months below the norm for that grade.

When we speak of the self-contained classroom, we normally think of the elementary school. We sometimes forget that the self-contained classroom has been the prevailing pattern in the secondary school except for a brief period of popularity of core programs, which we shall discuss later.

Like the junior and senior high school, the elementary school adopted an organizational framework that stressed the mastery of subject matter. This framework, commonly referred to as the subject matter curriculum, will be examined shortly.

Typical Schedule.   A typical week in a self-contained, subject-oriented elementary school calls for separate subjects scheduled at specific and regular times during the day. Little or no effort is made to integrate these diverse areas. Some elementary schools, of course, have never departed from this model, whereas others departed for a time and then swung back in recent years.

In the late 1920s, through the 1930s, and into the 1940s, many elementary schools, warmed by the glow of the progressive movement that championed the child over subject matter, abandoned the subject matter curriculum for the activity or experience curriculum.

THE ACTIVITY CURRICULUM

The activity (or experience) curriculum was an attempt by educators to break away from the rigidity of the graded school. It is of historical interest that the activity curriculum was a contribution of two of the better known laboratory schools—the Laboratory School founded by John Dewey at the University of Chicago and the University Elementary School directed by J. L. Meriam at the University of Missouri. The activity curriculum came about as an effort to translate progressive beliefs into the curriculum. As such, it captured the imaginations of elementary school educators in the first quarter of the twentieth century.

Disenchanted with the subject matter curriculum promoted by the essentialist philosophers and curriculum makers, Dewey and others sought to free the learner from the confines of a subject-centered curriculum and to create an environment that catered to the learner needs and interests.

Human Impulses.   B. Othanel Smith, William O. Stanley. and J. Harlan Shores observed that Dewey's Laboratory School curriculum was based on the following four human impulses, which Dewey referred to as "uninvested capital":

> the *social impulse,* which is shown in the child's desire to share his experiences with the people around him; the *constructive impulse,* which is manifested at first in play, in rhythmic movement, in make-believe, and then in more advanced form in the shaping of raw materials into useful objects; the *impulse to investigate and experiment,* to find

out things, as revealed in the tendency of the child to do things just to see what will happen; and the *expressive or artistic impulse,* which seems to be a refinement and further expression of the communicative and constructive interests.[2]

Dewey's curriculum eschewed the usual subject organizers and focused on occupations in which all men and women engaged—carpentry, cooking, and sewing.

Human Activities.   The University Elementary School at the University of Missouri followed principles advocated by Junius L. Meriam and structured its program not around subjects but around human activities of observation, play, stories, and handiwork.[3] The California State Curriculum Commission outlined a daily program for an activity curriculum as shown in Table 9.2. As these two examples reveal, the content of the activity curriculum is centered on projects or experiences that are of immediate interest to the learners. The various subjects, including the basic skills, are used as a means of promoting learning rather than as ends or centers of learning for themselves.

Subject Matter from Child's World.   Here the curriculum is developed by the teacher in cooperation with the pupils. The subject matter evolves from the child's world rather than from the adult world. Although the teacher can suggest activities or problems to the learners, the children's interests become the dominant factor. William H. Kilpatrick advocated pupil activities that he referred to as projects (ergo, the "project method") and took the position that the child should do his or her own thinking and planning.[4]

Problem solving—Dewey's "reflective thinking"—is the activity curriculum's instructional method par excellence. Experience in the process of problem solving is perceived by those who espouse progressive thought as more important than attaining the solutions to the problems. A great effort is made to integrate subject matter, using any and all content as needed without regard to discipline boundaries, for the solution of problems or carrying out of projects.

By its very nature, the activity curriculum cannot be fully planned in advance. Consequently, the activity curriculum can be described only after it has been completed, for the teacher cannot be sure in advance where the interests of the students will lead them.

The unit method of organizing instruction (a unit of work centered on a single topic or problem) lends itself well to the goal of problem solving. Units are designed by the teacher in cooperation with the pupils to include a sufficient variety of activities to provide for individual differences among pupils. A series of units can provide a skeletal framework for a given grade level.

Drill, if needed, is carried out in meaningful terms, not in isolated rote fashion. With the social orientation of the progressivists, the activity curriculum calls for the socialization of the learners and the use of the community as a learning laboratory.

---

[2]B. Othanel Smith, William O. Stanley, and J. Harlan Shores, *Fundamentals of Curriculum Development,* rev. ed. (New York: Harcourt Brace Jovanovich, 1957), p. 265.

[3]See Junius L. Meriam, *Child Life and the Curriculum* (Yonkers, N.Y.: World Book Company, 1920), p. 382.

[4]See William H. Kilpatrick, "The Project Method," *Teachers College Record* 19, no. 4 (September 1918): 319–335.

TABLE 9.2

SCHEDULE FOR AN ACTIVITY CURRICULUM

TIME	MONDAY	TUESDAY	WEDNESDAY	THURSDAY	FRIDAY
9:00	Informal greetings, reports, observations, rhymes, music, events of current interest, informal activities designed to create a mental set conducive to a happy, profitable day.				

Arithmetical Enterprises

9:15	Playstores, banking activities, handling of school supplies, etc. Although rich in arithmetical content through which the child is trained in skills and abilities, such units also yield abundantly in group and individual situations which develop initiative, responsibility, and cooperation. The flexible period provides opportunity for individual instruction.				

Healthful Living Enterprises

10:00	Physical education enterprises, free play, the nutrition program, and adequate relief periods are provided for daily; units of work such as: "the study of milk," "a balanced meal," etc., provide enterprises which have healthful living as a center of interest but provide situations development of social and civic attitudes as well.				

Language Arts

10:50	Oral and written composition, spelling and writing develop from activities rich in opportunities for expression, as the writing of a play to be presented in the auditorium period, puppet shows, the school newspaper, etc. The period should provide opportunity for literary discrimination and original expression; the long period provides for concentration of effort and attention according to individual interest and need.				

12:00	Lunch, Rest and Directed Playground Activities				

Avocational Activities

1:00	Music; activities, music appreciation, rhythm, harmonica, band, orchestra, etc.	Nature Club, school museum, aquarium, gardens, terrarium.	Creative art and constructive activities in pottery, weaving, painting, drawing.	Use of auditorium for music, dancing, dramatics, projects, stagecraft, related to class activities.	Civics Club Committees responsible for various phases of school life.

1:50	Recreation and Rest				

Reading Groups: Library Activities

2:00	Group organization on the basis of reading ability provides opportunity for remedial work with children having reading deficiencies and library guidance to superior readers. The quiet reading period may contribute to the development of information needed in the class activities related to social science, avocational, or health or other interests.				

2:50	Recreation and Rest				

3:00	Social studies activities	Social studies activities	Free creative work period	Social studies activities	Shop enterprises

SOURCE: Ruth Manning Hockett, ed., *Teachers' Guide to Child Development: Manual for Kindergarten and Primary Teachers* (Sacramento, Calif.: California Department of Education, 1930), pp. 355–356. Reprinted by permission.

Scheduling is flexible with time allotments variable depending on the activities under way. Pupils are grouped according to interests and abilities, obviating the need for fixed grade levels. Some schools tossed out marks, report cards, and the assumption that certain learnings have to be mastered at each grade level.

The teacher of the activity curriculum finds his or her role not as subject matter specialist and expert-in-residence but rather as a guide and facilitator of learning. Key concepts that the progressivists wove into the activity curriculum are the active rather than the passive role of the learner and the sharing of students' experiences with the teacher and each other.

The activity curriculum, like progressive education itself, left its indelible imprint on American education. Flexible scheduling, unit teaching, problem solving, project method, nongraded schools, and open education owe a debt to the activity curriculum. Nevertheless, the activity curriculum lost popularity and died out as a viable organizational pattern for the public elementary school. There are a number of reasons for its demise.

With the activity curriculum the needs of society and the needs of the adult world took a back seat to the needs of immature youngsters. Progressive—that is, activity-oriented schools, projected an unfavorable image to the public who felt that subject-matter learning was being neglected and too much stress was being placed on the immediate interests of immature learners.

Excesses on the part of some progressive schools led to cynical jokes, such as the one in which the teacher asks, "Is the earth round or flat?" and the pupil answers, "I don't know; let's vote on it." Then there is the classic put-down of the progressive school: The teacher enters the room in the morning and asks the class, "O.K., kids, what do you want to learn today?" and the children complain, "Do we have to do what we want to do today?"

It was not commonly understood that teachers of the activity curriculum had to be more knowledgeable and *better* trained not only in subject matter but also in techniques of guiding learning. The activity curriculum also required for its success resources and facilities that exceeded those of the typical elementary school. Further, more flexible administrators and teachers were needed for successful operation of a program of this type. The secondary schools also complained when they received students, products of the activity curriculum, who had a great range of knowledge and skills but glaring gaps in their education.

THE NONGRADED ELEMENTARY SCHOOL

The nongraded elementary school, following plans that permit continuous progress, evolved as a an alternative to the graded school. The nongraded or continuous progress school was a reaction to increasing rigidity of the graded school, which was an innovation designed to provide a more efficient education for children.

Persons unfamiliar with the concept of the nongraded school are sometimes confused by the term and interpret it to signify a school without a formal marking system. When we speak of the nongraded school, we refer to schools that have abandoned grade-level designations rather than marks.

In a nongraded school, typical grade levels and standards for those levels are absent. Children are grouped for instruction according to their particular needs and progress through the program at their own speed. Effort is made to individualize—some say "personalize"—instruction. The nongraded concept has made its greatest headway at the elementary school level. However, as we shall see when we discuss developments in secondary education later in this chapter, nongradedness is possible in the high school as well.

John I. Goodlad and Robert H. Anderson, proponents of the nongraded elementary school, saw nongradedness as a reaction to the Procrustean bed of the graded school.[5] "The realities of child development defy the rigorous ordering of children's abilities and attainments into conventional graded structures," observed Goodlad and Anderson.[6]

Herbert I. Von Haden and Jean Marie King explained some of the principles underlying the nongraded school in the following way:

> Nongrading is a philosophy of teaching and learning which recognizes that children learn at different rates and in different ways and allows them to progress as individuals rather than as classes. Such designations as grade one and grade three are eliminated. Flexible groupings allow the pupil to proceed from one level of work to another whenever he is ready. Thus, the children's progress is not dependent upon that of others in the room. His own readiness, interest, and capacity set the pace for each pupil. . . . Flexible grouping permits each child to move ahead with other children of approximately the same level of ability. Groupings are different for each subject area and can be changed at any time. Failure, retention, and skipping of grades are replaced by continuous progress as the pupil proceeds at his own rate. Slower children are not forced to go on with the class group before they are ready. Faster workers are not compelled to wait for the others. Individualization and continuous progress are the key elements of nongrading.[7]

Growth of Nongraded Schools.   The nongraded movement began in earnest in the 1930s, grew in intensity through the 1940s and 1950s, and leveled off in the 1960s. Among the nongraded schools of the 1930s and 1940s were those in Western Springs, Illinois; Richmond, Virginia; Athens, Georgia; Youngstown, Ohio; and Milwaukee, Wisconsin.[8] In the 1950s and 1960s nongraded schools were started in Bellevue, Washington; Appleton, Wisconsin; Chicago, Illinois; and Southern Humboldt Unified School District, California.[9]

School personnel of Appleton, Wisconsin compared the graded school with the continuous progress school, as shown in Table 9.3. The nongraded school seeks to eliminate failures and retention by permitting children to proceed through the program at their own pace. Programs of the nongraded school are organized primarily around reading levels and to a lesser extent around mathematics levels rather than around the traditional chronological age-grade levels.

---

[5]John I. Goodlad and Robert H. Anderson, *The Nongraded Elementary School*, rev. ed. (New York: Teachers College Press, 1987), p. 1.

[6]Ibid., p. 3.

[7]Herbert I. Von Haden and Jean Marie King, *Educational Innovator's Guide* (Worthington, Ohio: Charles A. Jones, 1974), pp. 30–31.

[8]Ibid., p. 33. See also p. 38 for list of schools where nongraded plans were tried.

[9]David W. Beggs III and Edward G. Buffie, eds., *Nongraded Schools in Action: Bold New Venture* (Bloomington, Ind.: Indiana University Press, 1967).

TABLE 9.3

COMPARISON OF THE GRADED AND CONTINUOUS PROGRESS SCHOOLS

GRADED STRUCTURE	CONTINUOUS PROGRESS
1. It is assumed that all children of the same chronological age will develop to the same extent in a given period of time.	1. It is assumed that each child has his own pattern and rate of growth and that children of the same age will vary greatly in their ability and rate of growth.
2. A child who does not measure up to certain predetermined standards of what should be accomplished in nine months is called a failure.	2. No child is ever considered a failure. If he does not achieve in proportion to his ability, we study the cause and adjust his program to fit his needs and problems.
3. If a child fails, he is required to repeat the grade in which he did not meet the standards.	3. A child never repeats. He may progress more slowly than others in the group, but individual records of progress make it possible to keep his growth continuous.
4. A decision as to grade placement must be made after each nine months.	4. Decisions as to group placement can be made at any time during the three-year period (for social or emotional adjustment, an additional year if needed, etc.).
5. Grade placements are based too largely upon academic achievement.	5. Group placement is flexible, based upon physical, mental, social, and emotional maturity.
6. Fixed standards of achievement within a set time put pressures upon teachers and children which cause emotional tensions and inhibit learning.	6. Elimination of pressures produces a relaxed learning situation conducive to good mental health.

SOURCE: Royce E. Kurtz and James N. Reston, "Continuous Progress in Appleton, Wisconsin," in David W. Beggs III, and Edward G. Buffie, eds., *Nongraded Schools in Action: Bold New Venture* (Bloomington: Indiana University Press, 1967), p. 139. Reprinted by permission.

Reading is used as the nucleus for grouping of youngsters in the nongraded school Maurie H. Hillson explained:

> The present-day nongraded elementary schools, for the most part, rely on levels of accomplishment in reading as the bases for advancement and assignment in a program of vertical progression through the six years of the elementary school organization. Current nongraded plans, with some rare but exciting departures, accept the format of an attempted homogeneous grouping based on factors attendant to reading achievement.[10]

To form reading groups instructors pay attention to many factors, including intelligence, achievement, motivation, readiness, and maturity. Hillson elaborated on the salient features of nongraded plans:

---

[10]Maurie H. Hillson, "The Nongraded School: A Dynamic Concept," in David W. Beggs III and Edward G. Buffie, eds., *Nongraded Schools in Action: Bold New Venture* (Bloomington, Ind.: Indiana University Press, 1967), p. 34.

Briefly, then, many of the present nongraded schools are ones in which grades are replaced by levels which a child accomplishes at his own speed. No grade designators are used. These levels of experiences are clearly described and without the fear of retention or, conversely, without the fear of encroachment upon material reserved for a next higher grade, the child progresses through them as a competency is achieved. . . . The rapid learner may accomplish a three-year nongraded program in two years. . . . The slow learner may take four years to accomplish three.[11]

Problems Encountered.   Nongraded plans encountered problems that led to a tapering off in their popularity. Nongraded programs are much more complex than the traditional, graded organization. They require continuous flexibility, more time by the faculty, greater resources, and a style of teaching different from that in typical graded schools. Careful diagnosis must be made of the learners' needs.

Nongraded schools could become as inflexible as the graded school if teachers and administrators merely substituted reading levels for chronological grades. Continuous progress plans concentrated to a great degree on reading and to a much lesser degree on mathematics, generally leaving the other subjects in the curriculum much as they were before—traditionally organized without well-planned sequencing of levels.

Nongraded plans excelled in vertical organization of the reading curriculum and sometimes the mathematics curriculum but failed to work out relationships at any level among the various disciplines. Further, the transition from a continuous progress elementary school to a graded junior high school could be rather abrupt for the learners when the junior high school was less concerned with personalized learning.

That advocacy of the nongraded elementary school is still alive, even resurging, can be seen in the publication of the revised edition of Goodlad and Anderson and in the more recent work by Anderson and Barbara Nelson Pavan.[12] Contending that "views now in ascendance are far more compatible with nongradedness, and the prospects for its implementation are therefore much better," Anderson and Pavan commented, "the time is at last ripe for a serious onslaught on literally graded practice."[13]

OPEN EDUCATION AND OPEN SPACE

Several years ago the hypothetical elementary school created at the beginning of this chapter caught on to the tail end of a movement known as the open-space school. The interior walls between classrooms came tumbling down—or as many walls as possible in a building constructed as a graded school many years ago. The purpose in eliminating barriers between classes was to permit innovative approaches such as flexible grouping, individualized instruction, nongradedness, or, simply, the open school. In practice, the terms are often interchanged. An *open classroom,* for example, might signal a classroom operated according to principles of *open education.* At the same time, this classroom might be an *open area,* although open space is not a prerequisite to open education. An *open school* might be a school that implements the open-education concept, or it might be an open-space school in which all classrooms are without walls.

[11]Ibid., p. 45.

[12]Goodlad and Anderson, *The Nongraded Elementary School,* 1987; Robert H. Anderson and Barbara Nelson Pavan, *Nongradedness: Helping It to Happen* (Lancaster, Pa.: Technomic Publishing Co., 1993).

[13]Anderson and Pavan, *Nongradedness,* pp. 13, 10.

C. M. Charles and others commented: "Many people think that open space and open education are synonymous. They are not. In fact they can be (but don't have to be) quite opposite."[14] Charles and others defined an open school not as an open-space school but as a school with several classrooms following principles of open education.[15] Open-space schools normally subscribe to at least some of the principles of open education, whereas open schools, as defined by Charles and coauthors may or may not be open-space schools.

In the ensuing discussion I will use the terms "open school," "open classroom," and "open education" when speaking of the broad concept and "open space" or "open area" when talking about the architectural arrangement of classrooms without walls.[16]

Imported from Great Britain, the open-classroom concept was designed as a curriculum and organizational response to formal, traditional schools. Charles and others briefly described open education as follows:

> Open education refers to organizations and management that allow much student choice and self-direction. The teacher helps, but dominates neither the planning nor the learning activities. Instead, the teacher "facilitates" student learning. This facilitation is done through talking, exploring, suggesting options, helping find resources, and deciding on ways of working that suit the group. Emphasis falls continually on maintaining relationships, interacting positively with others, fostering a sense of personal and group worth, and providing for the development of individual potential.[17]

Louis Rubin described the philosophical basis for the open classroom as follows:

> The basic ideology is rooted in the notion that children have a natural interest and desire in learning. Thus, when there is a conducive environment, and when the learning structure does not inhibit individuality, good education invariably will occur. What we have come to call relevance, as a result, is built into the fundamental philosophy itself; the curriculum, in short, is derived almost entirely from student interests and needs.[18]

Rubin went on to contrast the traditional and open classrooms:

> The critical distinctions between open and traditional education are that the goals are different, their means of attainment vary, and different outputs are yielded by each. A traditional program, for example, requires that a prescribed course of study be followed, leaving little leeway for accommodation to individual student interests. Its chief virtue, therefore, is that we can determine in advance, to a very sizable extent, what the child will and will not learn. But in the open education climate precisely the opposite condition prevails; since the child's own intellectual interests serve as the educational

---

[14]From Charles, C.M. Gast, David K., Servey, Richard E., and Burnside, Houston M.: *Schooling, Teaching, and Learning: American Education*, p. 118. St. Louis, 1978. The C.V. Mosby Co.

[15]Ibid., pp. 118–119.

[16]To complicate the matter further, classrooms without walls are not the same as schools without walls. Schools without walls operate from their own school buildings, sending their students wherever they need to be sent in the area to receive the education they need. Thus the students may be studying in agencies of the community or may be enrolled in other schools.

[17]From Charles, C.M., Gast, David K., Servey, Richard E., and Burnside, Houston M.: *Schooling, Teaching, and Learning: American Education*, p. 119. St Louis, 1978. The C.V. Mosby Co.

[18]Louis Rubin, "Open Education: A Short Critique," in Louis Rubin, ed., *Curriculum Handbook: The Disciplines, Current Movements, and Instructional Methodology* (Boston: Allyn and Bacon, 1977), p. 375.

point of departure, predetermined objectives must defer to individual whim and specified learning outcomes cannot be guaranteed.[19]

Common sights in the open-area schools are large expanses of classroom space, groups of a hundred or more pupils spread out and engaged in a variety of activities at many stations within the areas, and teams of teachers working with individuals, small groups, and large groups of learners.

Beliefs Underlying Open-Space Schools.   Proponents of the open classroom stress active learning and the affective domain. "The primary advantage of open space," said John H. Proctor and Kathryn Smith, "is the increased communication and interaction of teacher to teacher, teacher to student, and student to student."[20] Significant features of the open-space concept are the flexibility of grouping and the use of concrete materials that appeal to the interests and maturity level of the learners. Whereas many open elementary schools were organized into clusters or teams of a single grade level (e.g., first grade), others were nongraded and organized into multiunits.

The open-education/open-space movements crested in the early 1980s and have since dwindled to the point where they are almost nonexistent. Schools that removed walls for an open-area model have reinstalled walls or partitions to recreate small, self-contained units. What happened to this seemingly promising movement in the short space of approximately a decade?

David Pratt offered one reason for difficulties incurred by the open-space school:

> The attempts to transplant the architectural aspect (of open-area schools in England) to North America has not been universally successful. Frequently, the innovation consisted of building schools with fewer interior walls, an environment into which teachers were introduced who had neither participated in, approved of, or been trained for the open environment. Continuing to teach in a conventional way, they found the absence of walls merely an audible and visible distraction. Bookcases, screens, and miniature palm trees were quickly turned into makeshift barriers between the teaching areas. Small wonder that the research evidence shows, at best, disappointing performance by students in open classrooms, not only in academic subjects but also in creativity, and an increased anxiety level.[21]

The audible and visual distractions have been, in my judgment, erroneously minimized. Visits to open classrooms rather consistently reveal a noise level that is not conducive to learning. Harried teachers must constantly elevate their voices to make themselves understood. When ardent proponents of the open classroom are questioned about the noise, their responses are often: "What noise?" or "Some noise is necessary for learning to take place." Perhaps we can attribute some of the fault for these distractions to the lack of fit between program and architecture.

Rubin pointed out that, contrary to the claims of some advocates of open education, traditional education is not necessarily as bad as some people painted it:

---

[19]Ibid., pp. 375–376.

[20]John H. Proctor and Kathryn Smith, "IGE and Open Education: Are They Compatible?" *Phi Delta Kappan* 55, no. 8 (April 1974): 565.

[21]David Pratt, *Curriculum: Design and Development* (New York: Harcourt Brace Jovanovich, 1980), p. 384.

In fairness, it must be acknowledged that the proponents of open education have some-times built their case upon a straw man. Traditional education—although formalized and structured—need not be depressing nor debilitating of the learner's spirit. In point of fact, there is abundant reason to believe that some learners thrive better in a tradi-tional setting than in an open one. To wit, children sometimes find a lack of structure uncomfortable and large doses of freedom anxiety provoking. Similarly, provisions for the affective components of education, for the emotional feelings of students, can be made in both a traditional and an open format. As a result, one cannot in good con-science claim that an unstructured, open curriculum is necessarily more "humanistic" than a structured, traditional one.

Nor, to extend the point further, can one claim that an open curriculum automati-cally teaches the child to think more than a traditional one, or that multiage grouping cannot exist in either situation, or that prescribed programs of instruction must, in-evitably, prohibit individualization. Put another way, a large number of benefits habit-ually claimed by champions of one approach or the other can, in reality, be used with equal effectiveness in both.[22]

In regard to the success of open-space and open-education plans, Charles and coauthors observed: "In many cases, open space has not produced the results that were hoped for. . . . There is little evidence, however, to support open education on the grounds of academic achievement."[23]

THE JUNIOR HIGH SCHOOL

THE SCHOOL IN-BETWEEN

Educators and behavioral scientists of the late nineteenth century and early twentieth century recognized the necessity for a type of educational program and institution that would provide special attention to the needs of youngsters between childhood and adolescence. Out of this concern grew the junior high school. From its inception the junior high school was an institution in search of an identity. The early junior high schools encompassed grades seven, eight, and nine. Prior to the separation of these grades to form their own institution, grades seven and eight were normally considered an integral part of the elementary school; grades nine through twelve formed the sec-ondary school. Early schools, if they did not house all grades in one classroom, grouped their pupils in self-contained seventh- and eighth-grade classrooms. Not until the advent of the junior high as an institution did departmentalization come to the schooling of the twelve- to fourteen-year-olds.

With the appearance of the junior high school, children entering adolescence found an institution created specifically for them. It bore the trappings of both the pri-mary school below it and the secondary school above it. Offering both a basic general education and exploratory experiences, the junior high school spread rapidly through

---

[22]Rubin, "Open Education," p. 376.

[23]From Charles, C.M., Gast, David K., Servey, Richard E., and Burnside, Houston M.: *Schooling, Teaching, and Learning: American Education,* pp. 118–119. St. Louis, 1978. The C.V. Mosby Co.

the first half of the twentieth century. School systems adopted either the seven-eight-nine pattern or a seven-eight model that maintained the ninth grade in the senior high school.

Educators' perceptions of the role of the junior high school have varied considerably. Is it an upward projection of the elementary school? Is it a downward extension of the senior high school? Is its purpose mainly exploratory, serving learners in a transition period between puberty and adolescence, or is it a preparatory school for the senior high? Should it be housed in the same building with the senior high school or located in a separate building?

In spite of varying perceptions of its role the junior high school serves as an example of the self-fulfilling prophecy. Established as a unique institution, the junior high school began to live up to its label "junior high." The junior high school quickly came to be identified as a part of secondary education, resulting in the kindergarten-six, seven-twelve dichotomy that to some extent still exists. Although at first it was somewhat experimental in nature with block-time scheduling and core curricula, as the years rolled by the junior high school became more and more like its higher-level companion with complete departmentalization of courses, senior-high scheduling patterns, and a subject matter curriculum.

Conant's Recommendations.   In Chapter 6 we discussed the studies of the junior and senior high school conducted by James B. Conant. Since Conant's recommendations were so favorably received, we should be remiss not to examine some and to discern their nature. Among Conant's fourteen recommendations for the junior high school were the following:

Required Subjects For All Pupils in Grades 7 and 8
The following subjects should be required of all pupils in grades 7 and 8: English (including heavy emphasis on reading skills and composition), social studies (including emphasis on history and geography), mathematics (arithmetic except as noted . . .) and science.

    In addition, all pupils should receive instruction in home economics and all boys instruction in industrial arts . . . .

New Developments in Mathematics and Foreign Languages
A small fraction of pupils should start algebra (or one of the new brands of mathematics) in grade 8. Some, if not all, pupils should start the study of a foreign language on a conversational basis with a bilingual teacher in grade 7.

Basic Skills
Instruction in the basic skills begun in the elementary school should be continued as long as pupils can gain from the instruction. This statement applies particularly to reading and arithmetic. Pupils with average ability should read at or above grade level; superior pupils considerably above grade level. By the end of grade 9 even the poorest readers (except the mentally retarded) should read at least at the sixth-grade level.

Block-Time and Departmentalization
Provisions should be made to assure a smooth transition for the young adolescent from the elementary to the secondary school.

Flexibility in Schedule
The daily class schedule should be sufficiently flexible to avoid the necessity for pupils to make choices between, for example, science and foreign languages.

Program in Grade 9
In the ninth grade, the curriculum should provide for the usual sequential elective program as well as the continuation of the required courses in general education.

Coordination of Subject-Matter Instruction
Whatever the organization of a school system, there should be careful coordination in each one of the subject areas in grades K-12.[24]

Many schools reviewed, reaffirmed, or modified their curricula in light of the Conant recommendations, and our hypothetical junior high school was no exception.

ASCD Proposals.   At about the same time Conant was recommending increased emphasis on the academics, the Commission on the Education of Adolescents of the Association for Supervision and Curriculum Development (ASCD) was presenting a different point of view on the function and programs of the junior high school.[25] Writing for the ASCD, Jean D. Grambs and others, acknowledging that the junior high school was under pressure, advocated variations in lengths of class periods, programs planned explicitly for the junior high school years, ungraded programs, and a block-of-time program offered each year for three years of junior high school. As we will see, a block-of-time program usually runs for two to three hours of a school day.

Whereas Conant's proposals for the school in the middle were more subject-centered, the ASCD proposals were more learner-centered. However, proponents of both points of view agree on the necessity for adequate facilities and resources, a professionally trained staff, a moderate and manageable size of school, and ample guidance.

THE CORE CURRICULUM

Basic education, common learnings, core curriculum, and general education are terms, like goals and objectives, that are tossed about rather loosely in the profession. These terms are used by educators to describe programs that are almost at opposite poles. To some, basic education, common learnings, and general education signal a set of courses or subjects that are required of all students—the earmark of the subject matter curriculum, grounded in essentialistic philosophy. In this vein, the Harvard Committee toward the end of World War II stated its interpretation of general education:

> Clearly, general education has somewhat the meaning of liberal education [p. 52] . . . , General education, we repeat, must consciously aim at these abilities: at effective thinking, communication, the making of relevant judgments, and the discrimination of values [p. 72]. . . . It therefore remains only to draw the scheme of general education that follows from these premises. At the center of it . . . would be the three inevitable areas of man's life and knowledge . . . : the physical world, man's corporate life, his inner visions and standards [p. 98]. . . . In school, in our opinion, general education in these

---

[24]James B. Conant, *Recommendations for Education in the Junior High School Years* (Princeton, N.J.: Educational Testing Service, 1960), pp. 16–33.

[25]Jean D. Grambs, Clarence G. Noyce, Franklin Patterson, and John Robertson, *The Junior High School We Need* (Alexandria, Va.: Association for Supervision and Curriculum Development, 1961).

three areas should form a continuing core for all, taking up at least half of a student's time [p. 99]. . . . Accepting the course-unit system as established at least for the present, despite its grave weaknesses dwelt on earlier, that would amount to some eight units, preferably spaced by means of half-courses over the four years of school rather than compressed into two or three. The common and desirable divisions within these eight units would probably be three in English, three in science and mathematics, and two in the social studies. But—and this is the important point—this half of the schoolwork to be spent on general education would seem the barest minimum, either for those not going on to college or for those who are [p. 100].[26]

James B. Conant, president of Harvard University at the time the Harvard Committee issued its report, took a similar position when he recommended general education programs consisting of required courses at both the junior and senior high school levels. In keeping with the spirit of the 1894 Report of the Committee of Ten, the 1945 Report of the Harvard Committee, and several national reports of the 1980s, high schools today designate a "core" or set of required subjects for graduation. However, in the section which follows I have used the terms "core" and "core curriculum" to describe a unique organizational structure in the secondary school, not required courses.

The essentialists championed—and still advocate—the set of required courses as their model for general education in the high school. At the other end of the spectrum, from the camps of the pragmatic and reconstructionist philosophers, come those who hold a quite different conception of general education. They frequently refer to their plans for common learnings or general education as a "core curriculum." Unlike the "continuing core for all" recommended by the Harvard Committee, the core curriculum at its inception was a radically new departure in curriculum organization. John H. Lounsbury and Gordon F. Vars noted that many curriculum specialists regarded core as a truly innovative development.[27]

What is the core curriculum? Lounsbury and Vars defined "core"—short for "core curriculum"—as follows: "Specifically, core is a form of curriculum organization, usually operating within an extended block of time in the daily schedule, in which learning experiences are focused directly on problems of significance to students."[28]

Unification of Subject Matter. The core curriculum gained momentum in the 1930s and 1940s, but its roots go back to the nineteenth century. In a presentation made by Emerson E. White to the National Department of Superintendents in 1896, White discussed one of the basic principles of core: the unification of subject matter.

Complete unification is the blending of all subjects and branches of study into one whole, and the teaching of the same in successive groups or lessons or sections. When this union is effected by making one group or branch of study in the course the center or core, and subordinating all other subjects to it, the process is properly called the concentration of studies.[29]

---

[26]Harvard Committee, *General Education a Free Society* (Cambridge, Mass.: Harvard University Press, 1945), pp. 52–100.

[27]See John H. Lounsbury and Gordon F. Vars, *A Curriculum for the Middle School Years* (New York: Harper & Row, 1978), p. 57.

[28]Ibid., p. 56.

[29]Emerson E. White, "Isolation and Unification as Bases of Courses of Study," *Second Yearbook of the National Herbart Society for the Scientific Study of Teaching* (now the National Society for the Study of Education) (Bloomington, Ind.: Pantograph Printing and Stationery Co., 1896), pp. 12–13.

Smith, Stanley, and Shores credited Ziller, founder of the Herbartian school at the University of Leipzig, and Colonel Francis W. Parker, superintendent of schools, Quincy, Massachusetts, in 1875 and later principal of the Cook County (Chicago) Normal School, as proponents of the principle of unification of subject matter.[30]

The core concept received a significant boost in the 1930s when the curriculum committees of a number of states sought to plan a curriculum around social functions of living and turned for assistance to Hollis L. Caswell, then of George Peabody College for Teachers and later of Teachers College, Columbia University. The Virginia State Curriculum Program pioneered in establishing the core curriculum—the content of which centered on societal functions.[31]

The core curriculum is in philosophy and intent the secondary school counterpart of the activity curriculum of the elementary school. Espoused as a concept for both the junior and senior high schools, the core curriculum made its greatest inroads at the junior high school level. The core concept was especially popular in the state of Maryland. However, Lounsbury and Vars pointed out that core, like many programs that are different, did not meet with universal acceptance even at the junior high school level.[32]

Characteristics of Core.   Although varying in structure and focus, core curricula. as described in this chapter, possess the following characteristics:

1. They constitute a portion of the curriculum that is required for all students.
2. They integrate, unify, or fuse subject matter, usually English and social studies.
3. Their content centers on problems that cut across the disciplines.
4. The primary method of learning is problem solving, using all applicable subject matter.
5. They are organized into blocks of time, usually two to three periods under a "core" teacher (with possible use of additional teachers and others as resource persons).
6. They encourage teachers to plan with students.
7. They provide pupil guidance.

Types of Core.   Harold B. Alberty and Elsie J. Alberty distinguished five types of core.[33] The first two are core in the sense that subjects are required of all; as such these two types fall into the classification of the subject-matter curriculum. Writing in 1962, Alberty and Alberty classified types of core as follows:

• Type 1: A set of subjects ("constants") is required for all students. Subjects are taught separately with little or no effort to relate them to each other. This type of organizational plan is predominant in high schools today.

---

[30]Smith, Stanley, and Shores, *Fundamentals of Curriculum Development*, pp. 312–313.

[31]State of Virginia, *Tentative Course of Study for the Core Curriculum of Virginia Secondary Schools* (Richmond, Va.: State Board of Education, 1934).

[32]Lounsbury and Vars, *Curriculum for Middle School*, p. 57.

[33]Harold B. Alberty and Elsie J. Alberty, *Reorganizing the High-School Curriculum*, 3rd ed.(New York: Macmillan, 1962), pp. 199–233. In previous editions Alberty and Alberty distinguished six types of core. They included a type of correlation related to Type 2, in which teachers of separate courses agreed on a joint theme to be taught in their respective courses.

- Type 2: Two or more subjects are correlated. Although subjects remain discrete and are taught separately, effort is made to relate one to the other. The history teacher, for example, may work with the English teacher to show students relationships between topics that they happen to be studying in the two courses.
- Type 3: Two or more subjects are fused. The majority of core programs in schools fall into this classification. English and social studies are fused or integrated and scheduled in a block of time, usually two to three periods. Not a complete departure from traditional subject matter organization, this type of core organizes content around contemporary social problems or around historic or cultural epochs. Several experimental schools of the Eight-Year Study of the Progressive Education Association used Types 2 and 3 cores.[34]
- Type 4: A block of time is established to study adolescent and/or social problems, such as school living, family life, economic problems, communication, multicultural relationships, health, international problems, conservation, and understanding the self. This type of core requires a complete departure from the typical subject matter curriculum and a thorough reorganization of the curriculum.
- Type 5: Learning activities are developed cooperatively by teachers and students, who are free to pursue whatever interests or problem areas they desire. This core program resembles the unstructured experience curriculum of the elementary school.

Core curricula tend to consume a block of time consisting of two to three periods of the school day. The remaining periods are devoted to specialized interests of students. "Block-time classes" is a term sometimes equated with "core." However, block-time classes may or may not be core classes.[35]

Reporting in 1958 on a survey of block-time classes and core programs in junior high schools, Grace S. Wright listed four types of programs in block-time classes as follows:

Type A—Each subject retains its identity in the block-time class, that is separate subjects are taught (1) with consciously planned correlation, (2) with no planned correlation.

Type B—Subjects included in the block-time class are unified or fused around a central theme or units of work or problems stemming from one or more of the subject fields in the block-time class.

Type C—Predetermined problem areas based upon the personal-social needs of adolescents—both needs that adolescents themselves have identified and needs as society sees them—determine the scope of the core program. Subject matter is brought in as needed in working on the problems. Pupils may or may not have a choice from among several of these problem areas; they will, however, have some responsibility for suggesting and choosing activities in developing units of study.

Type D—The scope of the core program is not predetermined. Pupils and teacher are free to select the problems upon which they wish to work. Subject matter content is brought in as needed to develop or to help solve the problems.[36]

---

[34]See Wilford M. Aikin, *The Story of the Eight-Year Study* (New York: Harper & Row, 1942).

[35]See William Van Til, Gordon F. Vars, and John H. Lounsbury, *Modern Education for the Junior High School Years*, 2nd ed. (Indianapolis: Bobbs-Merrill, 1967), pp. 181–182,

[36]Grace S. Wright, *Block-Time Classes and the Core Program in the Junior High School*, Bulletin 1958, no. 6 (Washington, D.C.: U.S, Office of Education, 1958), p. 9.

Note the points of agreement between the Wright and the Alberty and Alberty classifications.

Illustrative Schedule.[37]The organization of the core and its relationship to other subject areas are illustrated by the plan for grades seven through twelve shown in Figure 9.1. In a six-period day a block of four periods is devoted to core in the seventh grade, three periods in the eighth, and two periods each succeeding year.

Core programs have never been fully understood by the public. "What is core?" asks the average citizen. What does an "A" in core mean to parents and to college admissions officers? Informed persons will admit that the ripples caused by the Eight-Year Study, which allowed for innovative plans like the core, generally lost their force, and colleges went back to demanding high-school credit in subjects they understood.

Core teaching is a demanding task requiring skills that take special training. Teachers' colleges, by and large, neglected the preparation of core teachers. The perceived threat from the Soviet Union in 1957 renewed demand for the "hard" subjects—science, mathematics, and foreign languages—and brought about negative reactions to unusual programs like core.

Conant, who commanded a considerable audience, was less than ecstatic about core. He recommended that core be limited to a block of time (two to three periods) in grade seven only. Even in that block of time Conant took the position that instruction need not be integrated:

> To my mind, there should be a block of time set aside, at least in grade 7, in which one teacher has the same pupils for two or more periods, generally in English and social studies. Otherwise, grades 7, 8, and 9 should be departmentalized; that is to say, pupils should have specialist teachers in each of the subject-matter fields. . . . The block-time teaching I am discussing need not break down subject-matter lines.[38]

Tanner and Tanner observed that "The core idea never gained the widespread acceptance that was expected of it by progressive educators."[39]

Although core programs had largely disappeared from the scene, in recent years we have witnessed renewed interest in core-type programs. We find proposals for "integrating the curriculum" and plans in operation which emulate some of the earlier efforts at core: theme-centered instruction, block-time organization, and interdisciplinary teams.[40] Though proposals for integrated and interdiscipinary curricula are made for all levels, they are particularly in evidence at the middle-school level.

Referring to an integrated curriculum with thematic units and identifying the middle school as the "natural home of integrated curriculum," James Beane named Cross Keys Middle School (Florissant, Missouri) and Marquette Middle School (Madison,

---

[37]For a widely cited theoretical model of a senior high school schedule with a "common learnings" core, see Educational Policies Commission, *Education for All American Youth* (Washington, D.C.: National Education Association, 1944), p. 244.

[38]Conant, *Recommendations for Junior High*, pp. 22–23.

[39]Daniel Tanner and Laurel Tanner, *Curriculum Development: Theory into Practice,* 3rd ed. (New York: Merrill, 1995), p. 395.

[40]See themed issue "Integrating the Curriculum," *Educational Leadership* 49, no. 2 (October 1991). See chapter 13 of this text for further discussion of integration of the curriculum.

GENERAL EDUCATION BLOCK OF TIME

Includes work in language arts skills, literature, and social studies at all levels

7	8	9	10	11	12

Emphasis on geography and Florida history

Emphasis on American history

Theme: local, state, and regional social studies

Theme: national social studies

Theme: world social studies

Theme: contemporary problems of societies and individuals

Includes exploratory experiences in art, music, foreign languages, typing, speech, drama, and industrial arts

Includes science experiences

General science

An additional unit in mathematics and one in science must be included

Electives

Mathematics

Home economics

Physical education

Figure 9.1 Plan of a core curriculum. This plan existed for many years at the P. K. Yonge Laboratory School, University of Florida, Gainesville, Florida. Reprinted by permission.

Wisconsin) as examples of schools implementing what he called the "new curriculum vision."[41]

Gordon F. Vars cited as examples of core-type programs those in kindergarten to eighth grade at Martin Luther King Laboratory School (Evanston, Illinois) with its all-school themes; tenth grade at Horizon High School (Brighton, Colorado) where English, social studies, and science are organized around themes; and the seventh- and eighth-grade Common Learnings program at South Junior High School (Lawrence, Kansas) where language arts and social studies are taught in a two-hour block of time. Vars pointed out that "the popularity of core-type integrative programs waxes and wanes from year to year, as education shifts primary attention from student concerns to subject matter acquisition to social problems and back again."[42]

Continuing and renewed interest in the core curriculum is seen today not only in the numerous articles advocating integration of the curriculum and interdisciplinary learning but also in efforts of the National Association for Core Curriculum, its conferences, and its publication *Core Teacher,* to promote core programs.[43]

In the mid and late twentieth century, the junior high school underwent a metamorphosis, developing into a new institution designed to better meet the needs of the preadolescent. This innovative concept, the middle school, is discussed later in this chapter.

THE SENIOR HIGH SCHOOL

THE SUBJECT MATTER CURRICULUM

The subject matter curriculum has been the most prevalent form of curriculum organization at all levels of American education ever since the Boston Latin School, the first Latin Grammar School in the United States, opened in 1635. The subject matter curriculum remains the most common pattern of organization throughout most of the world. Although other forms of curriculum organization have asserted themselves in the United States from time to time, the subject matter curriculum has continued strong and has gained strength in recent years with the emphasis placed on the academics and basic skills. The subject matter curriculum has existed at all levels of schooling but has been particularly entrenched at the senior high and college levels.

Smith, Stanley, and Shores pointed out in the following passages that the subject matter curriculum dates back to antiquity:

The subject is the oldest and most widely accepted form of curriculum organization. Perhaps the earliest example of the organization is the Seven Liberal Arts, which were present in an incipient form in the schools of ancient Greece and Rome, and which were offered in a more advanced stage of development in the monastery and cathedral

[41]James Beane, "The Middle School: The Natural Home of Integrated Curriculum," *Educational Leadership* 49, no. 2 (October 1991): 9–13.

[42]Gordon F. Vars, "Integrated Curriculum in Historical Perspective," *Educational Leadership* 49, no. 2 (October 1991): 14–15.

[43]*Core Teacher,* Journal of the National Association for Core Curriculum, 1640 Franklin Ave., Ste. 104, Kent, Ohio 44240–4324, Gordon F. Vars, editor.

schools of the Middle Ages. The Seven Liberal Arts consisted of two divisions: the trivium, which was comprised of grammar, rhetoric, and dialectic (logic); and the quadrivium, which consisted of arithmetic, geometry, astronomy, and music. . . . In the modern period the trivium was further divided to include literature and history as distinct subjects; and the quadrivium, to include algebra, trigonometry, geography, botany, zoology, physics, and chemistry. In the last half century the number of subjects offered in the public schools increased by leaps and bounds, so that by 1930 there were over three hundred distinct subjects of instruction. Despite this enormous multiplication of subjects the Seven Liberal Arts are still the nucleus of the subject curriculum, as a casual survey of required courses will reveal.[44]

As the name implies, the subject matter curriculum is an organizational pattern that breaks the school's program into discrete subjects or disciplines. The seventeenth century Latin Grammar School stressed classical subjects, including Greek, Latin, Hebrew, mathematics, history, and the Bible. Notably absent from this early school were English and science, which were considered too functional or too frivolous for scholars of this period. With the opening of Benjamin Franklin's Academy and Charitable School in 1751, English, science, and modern languages were added to the curriculum. Today's secondary schools offer a potpourri—some say smorgasbord—of courses.

Essentialistic in outlook, the subject matter curriculum seeks to transmit the cultural heritage. The subjects or disciplines organize knowledge from the adult world in such a way that it can be transmitted to the immature learner.

As we saw in Chapter 6 when we discussed the philosophy of essentialism, the subject matter curriculum has not been at a loss for spokespersons. Max Rafferty left no doubt of his position regarding the subject matter curriculum when he said, "What is significant for the children—what the people want for their children and mean to get—is subject matter that is systematic, organized, and disciplined and that is taught effectively and interestingly as subject matter. . . . Stress subject matter, *all* subject matter."[45]

Although the subject matter curriculum is found at all school levels, it has had its greatest impact at the secondary level. Elementary and middle school faculties have been more prone to experiment and to try out new patterns of organization that depart from subject matter emphasis. Secondary school teachers and administrators have consistently tended to be more subject-centered than their counterparts at the elementary school level.

Advantages. The subject matter curriculum presents to its followers certain distinct advantages. It is the easiest organizational pattern to structure. On the elementary school level, it is simply a matter of allocating a certain number of minutes for each subject during the course of the day. On the secondary school level, subject matter is organized into "courses" that are designated as either required subjects or electives. Every subject of the secondary school is typically scheduled for the same amount of time. The recommendations of two well-known groups helped to imprint the model of equal time for each subject in the secondary school.

At the tail end of the nineteenth century the National Education Association's Committee of Ten proposed:

---

[44]Smith, Stanley, and Shores, *Fundamentals of Curriculum Development*, pp. 229–230.
[45]Max Rafferty, *What They Are Doing to Your Children* (New York: New American Library, 1964), pp. 43–44.

Every subject which is taught at all in a secondary school should be taught in the same way and to the same extent to every pupil so long as he pursues it, no matter what the probable destination of the pupil may be, or at what point his education is to cease. Thus, for all pupils who study Latin, or history, or algebra, for example, the allotment of time and the method of instruction in a given school should be the same year by year. Not that all pupils should pursue every subject for the same number of years, but so long as they do pursue it, they should all be treated alike.[46]

A few years later, in 1906, the Carnegie Foundation for the Advancement of Teaching created the Carnegie unit, which for purposes of college admission standardized the amount of time to be spent in each subject in high school. To most people today the concept is known simply as a "unit," the Carnegie modifier having been lost over time. The Carnegie Foundation for the Advancement of Teaching defined a unit as satisfactory completion of a subject that met five days per week, a minimum of forty minutes per period, and a minimum of 120 clock hours for the school year. In addition, the Carnegie Foundation stipulated that a secondary school pupil should amass a total of sixteen units for graduation. These two recommendations were universally adopted by American secondary schools and have continued in force with infrequent modifications up to the present. In today's educational environment, states have moved well past the Carnegie Foundation's recommendation of sixteen units for high school graduation, as we shall see later in this chapter.

The content of the subject matter curriculum, unlike that of the experience curriculum, is planned in advance by the teacher or, more accurately, by the writers of the textbooks or curriculum guides that the teacher follows. The needs and interests of learners play little part in the curriculum that is organized around disciplines.

Unlike the activity or experience curriculum and the core curriculum discussed earlier in this chapter, the subject matter curriculum is well understood by the public, students, and the profession and for the most part has met with general favor. The methodology followed in the subject matter curriculum is rather straightforward. The teacher is the expert in the field and is likely to pursue a set of procedures that some instructional specialists refer to as the "assign-study-recite-test" method. William H. Burton succinctly described these procedures:

The learning situation is organized around materials and experiences which are assigned by the teacher. The pupils then study in various ways. The results of their studying are presented and shared during a recitation period. Testing of results occurs at the conclusion of a series of assignments and may occur at stated times within the sequence.[47]

Writing in 1962, Burton stated, "The assign-study-recite-test formula will be used for many years to come."[48] What he might have said is that the assign-study-recite-test formula has been used for generations and is likely to continue for generations to

[46]National Education Association, *Report of the Committee of Ten on Secondary School Studies* (New York: American Book Company, 1894), p. 17.

[47]William H. Burton, *The Guidance of Learning Activities: A Summary of the Principles of Teaching Based on the Growth of the Learner,* 3rd ed.(Englewood Cliffs, N.J.: Prentice-Hall, 1962), p. 289.

[48]Ibid.

come. This approach is what many people both within and without the profession call "teaching."

Cognitive Emphasis. The subject matter curriculum, which in days of old was imbedded in faculty psychology or mental discipline, has found behavioristic psychology compatible with its objectives. Student achievement is rather easily assessed, since evaluation is limited to measuring cognitive objectives by teacher-made or standardized tests. Some effort is made to measure performance in the psychomotor domain, but the perceptual motor skills are treated more or less as appendages to the cognitive domain. For example, in high schools that have separate tracks of curricula—such as general, commercial, industrial, and college preparatory—the most cognitive, the college preparatory track, is usually regarded as the most prestigious.

In the subject matter curriculum little effort is made to gauge student performance in the affective domain. Not only is evaluation of feelings and values extremely difficult, but also proponents of the subject matter curriculum, essentialists as they are, do not accept the affective domain as a primary concern of the school. Robert L. Ebel expressed this position forcefully when he said:

> Feelings are essentially unteachable. . . . Nor do they need to be taught. . . . The kind of learning on which schools should concentrate most of their efforts is cognitive competence. . . . Affective dispositions are important products of the human experience, but they seldom are or should be the principal targets of our educational efforts.[49]

The approach to individual differences and needs of students in the subject matter curriculum lies more in the provision of elective or special interest subjects from among which the students may choose. The breadth or scope of the subject matter curriculum and its sequence are revealed in the textbooks that are adopted for use in the classroom.

Conant's Proposals. Conant's studies of both the American high and junior high schools strengthened advocates of the subject matter curriculum. So that you may sense the overall impact of the Conant report on the high school, which preceded the report on the junior high, let's look at several of his twenty-two recommendations.

One wonders if the titles of Conant's two reports have political significance as well as educational. His 1959 report on the high school was labeled "a first report to interested citizens," whereas his 1960 junior high school report was subtitled "a memorandum to school boards." Among Conant's proposals for the high school were the following:

REQUIRED PROGRAMS FOR ALL
A. General Education
The requirements for graduation for all students should be as follows: four years of English, three or four years of social studies—including two years of history (one of which should be American history) and a senior course in American problems or American government—one year of mathematics in the ninth grade (algebra or general mathematics), and at least one year of science in the ninth or tenth grade, which might well be biology or general physical science. By a year, I mean that a course is given five

---

[49]Robert L. Ebel, "What Are Schools For?" *Phi Delta Kappan* 54, no. 1 (September 1972): 4, 7.

periods a week throughout the academic year or an equivalent amount of time. This academic program of general education involves nine or ten courses with homework to be taken in four years and occupies more than half the time of most students, whatever their elective programs.

B. The Elective Program

The other requirements for graduation should be successful completion of at least seven more courses, not including physical education. *All students should be urged to include art and music in their elective programs.* All students should be advised to have as the central core of their elective programs significant sequences of courses, either those leading to the development of a marketable skill or those of an academic nature.

C. Standards for Pass and Failure

The teachers of the advanced *elective* courses-foreign languages, mathematics, and science—should be urged to maintain high standards. They should be told not to hesitate to fail a student who does not meet the minimum level of performance they judge necessary for mastery of the subject in question. . . . On the other hand, for the *required* courses another standard should be applied. Since these courses are required of all, irrespective of ability, a student may be given a passing grade if he has worked to full capacity whether or not a certain level of achievement has been reached. . . .

ABILITY GROUPING

In the required subjects and those elected by students with a wide range of ability, the students should be grouped according to ability, subject by subject. . . . This type of grouping is not to be confused with across-the-board grouping according to which a given student is placed in a particular section in *all* courses. . . .

ENGLISH COMPOSITION

The time devoted to English composition during the four years should occupy about half the total time devoted to the study of English. Each student should be required to write an average of one theme a week. Themes should be corrected by the teacher. . . . no English teacher should be responsible for more than one hundred pupils.

To test the ability of each student in English composition, a schoolwide composition test should be given in every grade; in the ninth and eleventh grades, these composition tests should be graded not only by the teacher but by a committee of the entire school. Those students who do not obtain a grade on the eleventh-grade composition test commensurate with their ability as measured by an aptitude test should be required to take a special course in English composition in the twelfth grade . . . .

DIVERSIFIED PROGRAMS FOR THE DEVELOPMENT OF MARKETABLE SKILLS

Programs should be available for girls interested in developing skills in typing, stenography, the use of clerical machines, home economics . . . . Distributive education should be available. . . . If the community is rural, vocational agriculture should be included. . . . For boys, depending on the community, trade and industrial programs should be available. Half a day is required in the eleventh and twelfth grades for this vocational work. . . .

SPECIAL CONSIDERATION FOR THE VERY SLOW READERS

Those in the ninth grade of the school who read at a level of the sixth grade or below should be given special consideration. These pupils should be instructed in English and the required social studies by special teachers. . . . Remedial reading should be part of the work, and special types of textbooks should be provided. The elective programs of these pupils should be directed toward simple vocational work. . . .

THE PROGRAMS OF THE ACADEMICALLY TALENTED

. . . the elective programs of academically talented boys and girls [the top 15 percent] should [include] . . . as a minimum:

Four years of mathematics, four years of one foreign language, three years of science, in addition to the required four years of English and three years of social studies, a total of eighteen courses with homework to be taken in four years. This program will require at least fifteen hours of homework each week. . . .

HIGHLY GIFTED PUPILS

For the highly gifted pupils [the top 3 percent] some type of special arrangement should be made. . . . If enough students are available to provide a special class, these students should take in the twelfth grade one or more courses which are part of the Advanced Placement Program.

ORGANIZATION OF THE SCHOOL DAY

The school day should be so organized that there are at least six periods in addition to the required physical education and driver education. . . . A seven- or eight-period day may be organized with periods as short as forty-five minutes. . . . laboratory periods as well as industrial arts should involve double periods. . . .[50]

The thrust of the Conant recommendations for the high school reaffirmed the subject matter curriculum and placed special emphasis on the needs of the academically talented. As such, albeit in more modern dress, it reinforced and expanded the Harvard Committee's report that had preceded it by almost fifteen years. Whereas many secondary schools rushed to implement some of Conant's recommendations, particularly those for the academically talented, they gave up on others. English teachers still wistfully hope for a maximum of one hundred pupils. School personnel still dream of a full-time counselor for every 250 to 300 pupils; the normal ratio is often one counselor to 500 or more. Finally, although the recommendation to group students by ability has been implemented widely in the past, its practice is generally frowned on today.

The subject matter curriculum has been popular with many curriculum planners because it lends itself well to a mechanical type of curriculum development: dropping, adding, or splitting courses, rearranging or extending sequences, updating topics, and changing textbooks. Current interest in integrating the curriculum at all levels, however, runs counter to separation of knowledge into discrete subjects. Deborah P. Britzman faulted the compartmentalization of knowledge into subjects saying:

Compartmentalization defines the limits of relevancy, it brackets our definitions of context and content, and imposes measures of credibility that determine what we accept and reject as true and as false.[51]

A curriculum organized around separate subjects "is fragmented into instructional activities reduced to discrete blocks of time, thereby isolating subject areas and teachers, abstracting knowledge from its socio-cultural roots and political consequences, and decontextualizing knowledge and skills from their practical existence."[52]

---

[50]James B. Conant, *The American High School Today* (New York: McGraw-Hill, 1959), pp. 47–65.

[51]Deborah P. Britzman, *Practice Makes Practice: A Critical Study of Learning to Teach* (Albany, N.Y.: State University of New York Press, 1991), p. 35.

[52]Ibid.

BROAD-FIELDS CURRICULUM

In the early part of the twentieth century a pattern of curriculum organization appeared that became—on the surface at least—a standard feature of both elementary and secondary schools. Called the broad-fields curriculum, this form of curriculum organization is a modification of the strict subject matter curriculum. Effort is made to unify and integrate content of related disciplines around broad themes or principles. For example, history A (ancient), history B (modern), and history C (American), as existed in the secondary school curriculum of New York State schools well into the 1930s, were converted into broad fields and designated simply tenth-grade social studies, eleventh-grade social studies, and twelfth-grade social studies.

"In the broad fields approach," said Tanner and Tanner, "the attempt is made to develop some degree of synthesis or unity for an entire branch of knowledge. . . . The broad fields approach may also encompass two or more branches of knowledge."[53] "Courses in the broad-fields curriculum," explained Smith, Stanley, and Shores, "have various appellations. . . . In the college, they are called 'survey' or 'comprehensive courses,' and sometimes 'general courses.' At the high school level they are called 'fusion courses' or 'general courses,' or else they are simply designated by course titles as in the elementary school."[54]

Thus we find the various elements of English (reading, writing, grammar, literature, speech, etc.) brought together under the rubric of language arts. The various social science fields (history, political science, government, economics, anthropology, sociology, etc.) were combined to become the social studies. Art, music, architecture, and literature became the humanities. Principles of physical and natural science were unified into a course in general science. The industrial arts tied together various aspects of vocational education. Physical education included health and safety. General mathematics offered knowledge and skills drawn from arithmetic, algebra, and geometry.

Robert S. Zais spoke about the advantages of the broad-field curriculum as follows:

> Two main advantages are claimed for the broad-fields design. First, because it is ultimately based on the separate subjects, it provides for an orderly and systematic exposure to the cultural heritage. This advantage it shares with the subject curriculum. But it also integrates separate subjects, thereby enabling learners to see relationships among various elements in the curriculum. This second advantage is the special strength that the broad-fields design claims over the subject curriculum.[55]

He warned, however, "With respect to the integration claimed for the broad-fields design, it is worth noting that in practice, combining subjects into a broad field often amounts to little more than the compression of several separate subjects into a single course with little actual unification taking place."[56]

In a true broad-fields approach, teachers select certain general themes or principles to be studied at each year of the sequence of a discipline, such as social studies. Obviously, not all curricula labeled broad fields are truly of that genre.

---

[53]Tanner and Tanner, *Curriculum Development*, p. 384.
[54]Smith, Stanley, and Shores, *Fundamentals of Curriculum Development*, p. 257.
[55]Robert S. Zais, *Curriculum: Principles and Foundations* (New York: Harper & Row, 1976), p. 407.
[56]See Zais, pp. 407–408, for criticisms of the broad-fields curriculum.

Common criticisms of the broad-fields curriculum focus on its lack of depth as opposed to breadth, its lack of appeal to student needs and interests, and its emphasis on covering content, which excludes other important goals of education.[57]

Proponents of the broad-fields curriculum would respond to these criticisms by saying that if the curriculum were properly planned and carried out, these deficiencies would be overcome. What appears to have happened in many schools is that the rubric of broad fields has been retained but the curricula themselves have reverted to the separate disciplines of the subject matter curriculum.

The majority of boys and girls in American schools, both elementary and secondary, have been and continue to be educated under some form of the subject matter curriculum. Admittedly, some modifications have been made, but by and large the subject matter curriculum has proved to be a comfortable plan that is widely accepted in the American culture. The subject matter curriculum at the senior high school level has been favored by college admissions officers and regional accrediting associations, for it is much easier to understand and evaluate than more experimental types of curricula. We must also add that the subject matter curriculum has met with considerable success.

TEAM TEACHING

While Conant was conducting his surveys of the American high and junior high schools, the National Association of Secondary School Principals (NASSP) in 1956 was seeking ways to cope with increased enrollments in the schools, a teacher shortage, and the introduction of new curricula in various disciplines. Under the leadership of J. Lloyd Trump, associate secretary of the NASSP, the Commission on Curriculum Planning and Development was launched to create a proposal for new ways of using staff through teaming of faculty.

Supported by the Ford Foundation's Fund for the Advancement of Education, team teaching enjoyed a brief flurry of popularity in secondary schools across the country from Newton, Massachusetts; to Evanston, Illinois; to San Diego, California. The NASSP proceeded to appoint the Commission on the Experimental Study of the Utilization of the Staff in the secondary school (with J. Lloyd Trump as its director) and to charge it with the task of promoting the cause of team teaching. Harvard University's Graduate School of Education and Claremont Graduate School (California) took a special interest in this innovative organizational plan.

J. Lloyd Trump and Delmas F. Miller defined team teaching as follows:

> The term "team teaching" applies to an arrangement in which two or more teachers and their assistants, taking advantage of their respective competencies, plan, instruct, and evaluate in one or more subject areas a group of elementary or secondary students equivalent to two or more conventional classes, using a variety of technical aids to teaching and learning through large-group instruction, small-group instruction, and independent study.[58]

---

[57]Ibid.

[58]J. Lloyd Trump and Delmas F. Miller, *Secondary School Curriculum Improvement: Meeting the Challenge of the Times*, 3rd ed. (Boston: Allyn and Bacon, 1979), p. 410.

Ira J. Singer described team teaching in this way:

Team teaching may be defined as an arrangement whereby two or more teachers, with or without teacher aides, cooperatively plan, instruct, and evaluate one or more class groups in an appropriate instructional space and given length of time, so as to take advantage of the special competencies of the team members.[59]

Singer pointed out that the major factors in a team teaching plan are

- cooperative planning, instruction, and evaluation
- student grouping for special purposes (large group instruction, small group discussion, and independent study)
- flexible daily schedule
- use of teacher aides
- recognition and utilization of individual teacher talents
- use of space and media appropriate to the purpose and content of instruction[60]

The purpose of team teaching was to capitalize on the strengths of teachers, using their varying expertise in different ways. Teams were organized within subject areas and across subject fields.

A particular variant of team teaching came to be known as the Trump Plan. J. Lloyd Trump and Dorsey Baynham postulated three ingredients for an effective organizational structure that would capitalize on teacher assets and provide better opportunities for the learners. The school week, according to Trump and Baynham, should provide opportunities for pupils to attend large-group instruction, to interact in small groups, and to carry out independent study. Prophesied Trump and Baynham:

The school of the future will schedule students in class groups an average of only 18 hours a week. The average student at the level of today's tenth grade will spend about 12 of the 18 hours in *large-group instruction and six in small-group discussion.*

In addition, students will spend, on the average, 12 hours each week in school in individual *independent study.*[61]

These figures convert to forty percent of a student's time in large-group instruction, twenty percent in small-group discussion, and forty percent in independent study.

Singer contrasted schedules of two history teachers under a conventional plan and under a team teaching plan that incorporates the three ingredients: large-group instruction (LG), small-group discussion (SG), and independent study (IS) (see Table 9.4).

Differentiated Staffing.   Team teaching offered a creative answer to the problem of using limited faculty and resources more effectively. More elaborate schoolwide staffing patterns were developed that incorporated the principle of differentiated assignment. In the early 1970s the North Miami Beach Senior High School (Florida), for example, developed a set of categories of personnel for its differentiated staffing

---

[59]Ira J. Singer, "What Team Teaching Really Is," in David W. Beggs III, ed., *Team Teaching: Bold New Venture* (Bloomington,: Indiana University Press, 1964), p. 16.

[60]Ibid.

[61]J. Lloyd Trump and Dorsey Baynham, *Focus on Change: Guide to Better Schools* (Chicago: Rand McNally, 1961), p. 41.

TABLE 9.4

COMPARISON OF TWO TYPES OF SCHEDULES

(A) CONVENTIONAL SCHEDULE

TIME	MONDAY	TUESDAY	WEDNESDAY	THURSDAY	FRIDAY
8:00– 8:50	Hist. 10A Hist. 10B	Hist. 10A Hist. 10B	Hist. 10A Hist. 10B	Hist. 10A Hist. 10B	Hist. 10A Hist. 10B

(B) SINGLE-DISCIPLINE TEAM SCHEDULE

TIME	MONDAY	TUESDAY	WEDNESDAY	THURSDAY	FRIDAY
8:00– 8:50	History 10AB (LG)	History 10AB1* (SG) History 10AB2 (SG) History 10AB3 (SG)	History 10AB (LG)	History 10AB* (SG) History 10AB2 (SG) History 10AB3 (SG)	History 10AB1 (IS) Project work in library, laboratory, music room, art studio, etc.

(60 students, 2 teachers, 1 instruction assistant)
*One History 10AB-SG can be supervised by an instruction assistant, student teacher, or student leader.
LG = large group, SG = small group, IS = independent study.
SOURCE: Ira J. Singer, "What Team Teaching Really Is," in David W. Beggs III, ed., *Team Teaching: Bold New Venture* (Bloomington: Indiana University Press, 1964), p. 17. Reprinted by permission.

plan.[62] These included in addition to a principal, vice-principal, and business manager the following positions:

- *Community Relations Specialist.* Coordinates activities involving school and community.
- *Human Relations Specialist.* Seeks to create harmonious climate within the school.
- *In-service Coordinator.* Coordinates the training and development program of the professional and paraprofessional staff.
- *Psychologist.* Counsels students on emotional problems.
- *School Social Worker.* Helps students to function adequately in school; a behavioral consultant.
- *Media Specialist.* Supervises and develops media program.
- *Media Technician.* Provides skilled technical assistance to staff and students.
- *Coordinating Librarian.* Supervises library resources.

---

[62]North Miami Beach Senior High School, Dade County, Florida Public Schools. Reprinted by permission.

- *Teaching Designer.* Assists teachers in improving instruction and evaluating effectiveness.
- *Teaching Prescriber.* Provides assessment, diagnosis, and prescription for each student's program through observation, testing, and individual and/or group conferences.
- *Resource Specialist.* Gathers, coordinates, and disseminates materials for helping solve specific learning situations.
- *Facilitating Teacher.* Guides students through learning; teaches specific courses.
- *Instructional Intern.* Assists a directing teacher, a college junior, senior, or graduate student who serves for a full school year in the high school.
- *Instructional Aide.* Assists by performing paraprofessional responsibilities.
- *Clerical Aide.* Performs clerical duties.

In recent years secondary schools have turned away from the concepts of team teaching and differentiated staffing. However, team teaching is a prominent feature of most plans for middle and open-space schools. Results were not always as anticipated. In some cases teachers found themselves incompatible, unable to cooperate effectively. Cooperative planning requires a high degree of interpersonal skill that some team members lacked.

Some administrators favored the large-group instruction aspect of team teaching for the convenience and economy of scheduling large numbers of students; they omitted the important companion features of small-group discussion and independent study. Large-group instruction by itself deprives students of interaction with the teacher and with each other. Large-group instruction, frequently coupled with instructional television, a strategy also attempted at this period, often resulted in students becoming inattentive and bored.

Schools experienced varying degrees of success with independent study. Plans for large-group instruction, small-group discussion, and independent study call for special facilities and resources that were missing in some schools that attempted this type of organization.

The very complexity of staffing and scheduling under team teaching patterns confused parents, teachers, and students. Tradition, therefore, caused them to prefer uniform blocks of time, completely supervised study, and individual assignments.

FLEXIBLE AND MODULAR SCHEDULING

With but a few significant departures from traditional practice, high schools have continued to schedule subjects in the conventional mode, one period per day, five days per week. The Carnegie unit, Conant's recommendations that each course meet five times a week for the academic year, and customary standards of the regional accrediting associations have added to the pressure to maintain traditional scheduling.

However, it is difficult to find a logical reason why all subjects must be taught for the same period of time. Some disciplines are by their very nature more difficult to teach than others and require more time for mastery. Some courses are most effectively taught when accompanied by a laboratory that requires extra time. Some subject matter is simply not as relevant as other subject matter and, therefore, should be accorded less time.

Nor is there a logical reason why equal amounts of time must be allotted to every subject every day of the week. Some days and some weeks more time is needed to explore a topic in depth. Some days it is apparent to the teacher that youngsters have not comprehended the lesson and need to spend more time on it or undergo remedial work.

There is also not sufficient reason why the instructional mode must be standardized every period of every day. Variation should be possible for lecture, mediated instruction, laboratories, seminars, field trips, independent study, and other modes.

Efforts were made in the 1960s to break out of the mold of the standard schedule. These efforts are subsumed in a movement referred to as flexible scheduling. Donald C. Manlove and David W. Beggs III described the concept of flexible scheduling as follows:

> The flexible schedule is an organization for instruction which:
> 1. calls for classes of varying size within and between courses. (Students sometimes may meet in large assembly classes, and at other times in small inquiry classes. In addition, part of the day will be spent in individual or independent study.)
> 2. provides for instructional groups which meet at varying frequencies for varying lengths. (Some classes may meet every day of the week, others will not. Some instructional sessions will be for a short duration, others for an extended period of time.)
> 3. makes team teaching possible in any content area or for any group of students in the school. (The use of a teaching team, two or more teachers working within a given group of students on a common instructional problem, is suggested in this model.)
> 4. requires countless professional decisions by teachers about students, content, and teaching methods.[63]

Types of Schedules.   Flexible schedules have taken varying forms; some are minor departures from traditional plans, others radical changes. Among the varieties of flexible scheduling are the following:

1. Two or more periods are simply combined, as in the case of core classes.
2. Subjects are scheduled for both double and single periods in the same week. For example, some classes may meet two periods on Monday and Thursday, other classes two periods on Tuesday and Friday, but all only one period on Wednesday. Teachers can thus use the larger blocks of time in ways not permitted by the constraints of the single-period schedule.
3. Classes are rotated during the week. Trump and Miller supplied diagrams of rotating schedules with standard periods and with periods of varying length (see Table 9.5).
4. Instead of typical forty-five minute periods, the schedule is broken into modules, which, by faculty agreement, may be multiples of 15, 20, 30, or more minutes. Modular scheduling can be described as follows:

> Modular scheduling, or flexible-modular scheduling, . . . requires complete abandonment of the division of the school schedule into equal amounts of time for each course. . . . Some subjects are scheduled for two or three modules (conceivably, even for a single module) per day. Those which require a great deal of time are scheduled in multiple modules. . . .

---

[63]Donald C. Manlove and David W. Beggs III, *Flexible Scheduling: Bold New Venture* (Bloomington, Ind.: Indiana University Press, 1965), pp. 22–23.

TABLE 9.5

ROTATING SCHEDULES

ROTATION OF CLASSES—STANDARD PERIODS				
TIME	MONDAY	TUESDAY	WEDNESDAY	THURSDAY	FRIDAY
---	---	---	---	---	---
8:00	1	1	1	1	2
9:00	2	2	2	3	3
10:00	3	3	4	4	4
11:00	4	5	5	5	5
12:00			Lunch		
12:30	6	6	6	6	7
1:30	7	7	7	Special	Special

ROTATION OF CLASSES—PERIODS VARY IN LENGTH				
TIME	MONDAY	TUESDAY	WEDNESDAY	THURSDAY	FRIDAY
---	---	---	---	---	---
8:55–10:26	1	2	4	5	6
10:36–11:26	2	4	5	6	1
11:30–12:26	3	3	3	3	3
12:26–1:04			Lunch		
1:04–2:30	4	5	6	1	2
2:34–3:30	5	6	1	2	4

NOTE: Numbers indicate different subjects.
SOURCE: J. Lloyd Trump and Delmas F. Miller, From *Secondary School Curriculum Improvement: Meeting the Challenges of the Times,* 3rd ed. (Boston: Allyn and Bacon, Inc. 1979), p. 400. Reprinted by permission of Allyn and Bacon, Inc.

The duration of the module is purely a matter for decision, ordinarily made by the faculty of the school at the time a modular schedule is introduced. Fifteen-minute modules are common. A school day based on fifteen-minute modules would encompass approximately twenty-five modules. Schools which follow the Stanford School Scheduling System use modules of twenty-two minutes; twenty modules make up the day. The Indiana Flexible Schedule uses fifteen modules per day of thirty minutes each. Ridgewood High School, Norridge-Harwood Heights, Illinois (as one example) has a school day made up of twenty modules of twenty minutes plus an additional ten-minute module for homeroom period.[64]

---

[64]Peter F. Oliva, *The Secondary School Today,* 2nd ed. (New York: Harper & Row, 1972), p. 196.

TABLE 9.6

FIFTEEN-MINUTE MODULES— SAME SCHEDULE EVERY DAY

TIME	SUBJECT
8:00	
8:15	
8:30	Mathematics
8:45	
9:00	Speech correction
9:15	
9:30	
9:45	Science
10:00	
10:15	
10:30	
10:45	Music
11:00	
11:15	Spanish
11:30	
11:45	Music practice
12:00	Lunch
etc.	

SOURCE: J. Lloyd Trump and Delmas F. Miller, From *Secondary School Curriculum Improvement: Meeting the Challenges of the Times,* 3rd ed. (Boston: Allyn and Bacon, Inc. 1979), p. 398. Reprinted by permission of Allyn & Bacon, Inc.

Trump and Miller provided an illustration of a modular schedule using fifteen-minute modules, as shown in Table 9.6.

5. Class schedules are set frequently, even daily. This "scheduling on demand" is the ultimate goal of flexible scheduling. As J. Lloyd Trump observed, it allows teachers and students the greatest possible latitude in determining their instruction and learning. Trump told how this process was accomplished at the Brookhurst Junior High School in Anaheim, California.

Individual members of teaching teams determine three days in advance what students they want to teach, in what size groups, for what length of time, in what places, and with what technological aids. Teacher job-specification forms containing this information are turned in to their team leaders. The team leaders then assemble to make a master schedule each day. The master schedule is then duplicated and made available to the students and their counselors. In a daily 20-minute meeting, with the advice and consent of their counselor (twenty minutes to a counselor), each student makes his schedule. A student noting, for example, that the schedule calls for large-group presentation on a given subject and deciding that he already knows that material, may elect rather to spend his time in independent study in the art room or library or some place else. The counselor either approves or rejects this decision. Then the student makes out his own schedule for the day in quadruplicate. One copy is for himself, one for the office, one for the counselor, and one for his parents.[65]

Traditional Versus Flexible Scheduling.   Flexible scheduling is an essential aspect of plans for curriculum organization such as team teaching, which calls for large-group instruction, small-group discussion, and independent study. Traditional schedules have forced teachers to use the same amounts of time for all activities.

Manlove and Beggs contrasted the traditional and the flexible schedule in Table 9.7. They summarized the advantages and disadvantages of flexible scheduling to teachers, making the comparisons shown in Table 9.8.

Trump and Miller also warned of a danger inherent in modular scheduling—or in any innovation, for that matter—"once a change is made, the new schedule can become almost as rigid as the one it replaced."[66] The complexity of operation; a structure that shifts from day to day; the high degree of planning required on the part of students, teachers, and administrators; and the decline in popularity of the team teaching concept have militated against flexible scheduling and caused some schools to return to more traditional and more commonly understood forms of scheduling.

Rotating schedules are not at all practices of the past. The Tuskawilla Middle School (Oviedo, Florida), for example, employs modified rotation with its seven-period days on a nine-week cycle. Table 9.9 shows its Quarterly Rotation Schedule. Periods 2, 3, 6 (55 minutes) and 7th (57 minutes) are rotated whereas periods 1 (10 minutes at the beginning of the day) and 4 and 5, affected by the lunch hour, remain constant. This system allows distribution of the majority of classes over the mornings and afternoons during the school year, thus averaging out the effect of the hour of the day on students' learning.

Lyman High School (Longwood, Florida) features a daily schedule broken into three blocks as shown by the vertical columns in Table 9.10. Days are classified as Blue and Gold. They meet 103 minutes on alternate days five times over a two-week period, thus satisfying Florida's requirement of 150 hours of instruction in each class. The schedule allows a seventh-period during which students may take an additional course (fourteen choices are available), attend a study hall, or go home. The schedule is modified somewhat on days when the school holds a pep rally.

THE NONGRADED HIGH SCHOOL

During the 1960s when the elementary schools were experimenting with continuous progress plans and eliminating grades as we know them, several high schools were attempting to develop ungraded patterns of organization. Prominent among these high

---

[65]J. Lloyd Trump, "Flexible Scheduling—Fad or Fundamental?" *Phi Delta Kappan* 44, no. 8 (May, 1963): 370.

[66]J. Lloyd Trump and Delmas F. Miller, *Secondary Curriculum Improvement: Meeting the Challenges of the Times,* 3rd ed. (Boston: Allyn and Bacon, 1979), p. 398.

TABLE 9.7

CHARACTERISTICS OF TRADITIONAL AND FLEXIBLE SCHEDULES

ELEMENT	TRADITIONAL SCHEDULE	FLEXIBLE SCHEDULE
Content	Assumes each course is equivalent in requirements for mastery to all others	Assumes requirements for mastery of content vary from course to course
Facilities	Use is set by schedule	Use is determined sometimes by student needs
Groups	All class groups are nearly equal size	Class groups differ in size depending on instructional task
Scheduling unit	The day; each day in the week has the same order as every other day	The week; each day in the week has a different order
Students	Students should be in a class group or supervised study	Students may be in a class group or working independently
Teachers	All have equal numbers of classes or assignments and demands on their time	Number of classes varies from teacher to teacher and demands on time vary
Time	Usually equal for all subjects	Usually different for various subjects

SOURCE: Donald C. Manlove and David W. Beggs III, *Flexible Scheduling: Bold New Venture* (Bloomington: Indiana University Press, 1965), p. 26. Reprinted by permission.

TABLE 9.8

ADVANTAGES AND DISADVANTAGES OF FLEXIBLE SCHEDULING

ADVANTAGES FOR TEACHERS	DISADVANTAGES FOR TEACHERS
1. Provides a mean for pacing the instruction to an individual student's needs	1. Danger of not giving enough time to one subject
2. Allows teachers to make decisions about the length and frequency of learning activities	2. Requires more time and cooperative effort of teachers in making the schedule
3. Gives teachers time to work with small groups and individuals	3. Possibility of too little identification of a student with his teachers
4. Takes unnecessary repetition out of the teacher's day	4. Is difficult to schedule
5. Places increased responsibility on students for learning	5. Requires teachers to change their teaching patterns
6. Provides the opportunity to use resource experts for a large group of students in an economical way for the resource person	6. Is not understood by the public or even by all teachers

SOURCE: Donald C. Manlove and David W. Beggs III, *Flexible Scheduling: Bold New Venture* (Bloomington: Indiana University Press, 1965), p. 67. Reprinted by permission.

TABLE 9.9

QUARTERLY SCHEDULE ROTATION, 1999–2000, TUSKAWILLA MIDDLE SCHOOL, OVIEDO, FLORIDA. REPRINTED BY PERMISSION.

	9:15 A.M.	9:28 A.M.	10:26 A.M.	STAGGERED	STAGGERED	1:53 P.M.	2:53 P.M.
August 9	1	2	3	4	5	6	7
October 14	1	7	2	4	5	3	6
January 4	1	6	7	4	5	2	3
March 20	1	3	6	4	5	7	2

TABLE 9.10

BELL SCHEDULE, LYMAN HIGH SCHOOL, LONGWOOD, FLORIDA, 1999–2000. REPRINTED BY PERMISSION.

BLUE		GOLD		ACTIVITIES	
1st 7:15–8:58		2nd 7:15–8:58		1st/2nd 7:15–8:48	
Break 8:58–9:08		Break 8:58–9:08		Break 8:48–8:58	
3rd 9:13–10:06	3rd 9:13–10:56	4th 9:13–10:06	4th 9:13–10:56	3rd/4th 9:03–9:56	3rd/4th 9:03–10:36
Lunch 10:06–10:36		Lunch 10:06–10:36		Lunch 9:56–10:56	
3rd 10:41–11:26	Lunch 10:56–11:26	4th 10:41–11:26	Lunch 10:56–11:26	3rd/4th 10:31–11:06	Lunch 10:36–11:06
5th 11:31–1:14		6th 11:31–1:14		5th/6th 11:11–12:44	
				Activity 12:44-1:14	

7th Period every day except Wednesday
1:19–2:22

schools were Nova High School (Broward County, Florida) and Melbourne High School (Brevard County, Florida).

In the mid-1960s Nova High School and Melbourne High School were the epitome of innovation. Nova High School was established amid what was at that time a semi-rural tract of land of now populous Broward County (Fort Lauderdale) as the first facility in a projected complex that eventually would include elementary schools, a junior high school, and a junior college as well as the high school—all publicly supported. A private institution of higher learning, Nova Southeastern University, is nearby.

Nova High School made use of teaching teams complete with clerical assistants and teacher aides. Organized on a trimester plan, Nova High School incorporated closed circuit television, a photographic laboratory, data processing equipment, and learning resource centers equipped with tape recorders, microfilm readers, and teaching machines.

A daily schedule was devised that consisted of five periods of eighty minutes each and an optional sixth period of one hour's duration. Speaking about the nongraded feature of Nova High School, Arthur B. Wolfe, Director of the K–12 Center at that time, set forth the Nova Plan in these terms:

> The Nova Plan will eliminate grade designation and will establish a far wider range of learning levels through which each student may progress at a rate commensurate with his interests and abilities. Each of the established levels will be only slightly advanced over the level below, thereby enabling the student to move from one level to the next at any given time during the school year. This process will be applicable to the program of each student and to each separate subject area, thereby placing a realistic evaluation on each student's progress on an individual basis, one not entirely related to the sum total of his progress. . . .
>
> Following the enrollment of new students, records will be examined and a series of tests will be administered. The faculty will place students in an achievement group that will provide a smooth transition to a new learning environment. This process will be followed for each of the subject areas in which students may be enrolled. It will be necessary in some cases to move students forward or back until an achievement level has been found in which they will feel comfortable.[67]

Melbourne, like Nova, sought to put into action some of the more significant innovations of the day. Situated in the stimulating setting of space-oriented Brevard County with Cape Canaveral practically in its backyard, Melbourne High School, under its principal, B. Frank Brown, achieved widespread recognition in both the professional and lay periodicals. As its stationery proclaimed, Melbourne High School was the school "where the library is bigger than the gymnasium." Melbourne High School was host to so many visitors from all over the country that at one time it set up monthly briefing sessions for visiting groups.

Like Nova High School, Melbourne High School ventured to try out many new ideas. Its emphasis on the academics was evidenced by its library with carrels, which

---

[67]Arthur B. Wolfe, *The Nova Plan for Instruction* (Fort Lauderdale, Fla.: Broward County Board of Public Instruction, 1962), pp. 14–15.

resembled a college library, by its six foreign languages (including Russian and Chinese), and by its stress on independent study, particularly for the academically talented. Melbourne's chief claim to fame, however, lay in its nongraded organizational plan. In the Melbourne Plan students are grouped not by ability as measured by tests of intelligence or scholastic aptitude but on the basis of achievement tests, subject by subject. A tenth-grade student, therefore, might be enrolled in Algebra I, Phase 2 and English II, Phase 3. Some subjects. such as typing and physical education, are neither graded nor phased. Melbourne's schedule of course offerings described each of its seven phases:

- Phase 1: Subjects are designed for students who need special assistance in small classes.
- Phase 2: Subjects are designed for students who need more emphasis on the basic skills.
- Phase 3: Courses are designed for students who have an average background of achievement.
- Phase 4: Subject matter is designed for extremely well prepared students desiring education in depth.
- Phase 5: Courses are available to students who are willing to assume responsibility for their own learning and pursue college level courses while still in high school.
- Phase Q: Students whose creative talents are well developed should give consideration to the Quest phase of the curriculum. This is an important dimension of the phased organization designed to give thrust in the direction of individual fulfillment. In this phase a student may research an area in which he is deeply and broadly curious either to develop creative powers or in quest of knowledge.
- Phase X: Subjects which do not accommodate student mobility; e.g., typing, physical education, are ungraded but unphased.[68]

Melbourne's phased schedule is illustrated in Table 9.11 which shows the schedule of mathematics courses for Fall 1999. The last digit of the eight-number designation denotes the phase level.

Brown referred to the ungraded concept implemented at Melbourne High School not only as the nongraded school[69] but also the multiphased school.[70] Brown gave particular attention to the independent study or quest phase of the program. He referred to the quest phase as both "Education by Appointment"[71] because students see their teachers by appointment in a tutorial fashion and "Education by Agreement" because he recommended that schools emulate the Dalton plan by drawing up an agreement form or contract specifying the independent study that a student plans to do.[72]

---

[68]Melbourne High School. Brevard County, Florida Public Schools.

[69]B. Frank Brown, *The Nongraded High School* (Englewood Cliffs, N.J.: Prentice-Hall, 1963).

[70]B. Frank Brown, *The Appropriate Placement School: A Sophisticated Nongraded Curriculum* (West Nyack, N.Y.: Parker, 1965).

[71]B. Frank Brown, *Education by Appointment: New Approaches to Independent Study* (West Nyack, N.Y.: Parker, 1968), p. 61.

[72]For information on the Dalton (Massachusetts) Plan see Helen Parkhurst, *Education on the Dalton Plan* (New York: E. P. Dutton, 1922).

TABLE 9.11

PARTIAL SCHEDULE, 1999–2000,
MELBOURNE HIGH SCHOOL, MELBOURNE, FLORIDA. REPRINTED BY PERMISSION.

	A	B	C	D	E	F	G	H
1	MELBOURNE HIGH SCHOOL—MASTER SCHEDULE—FALL 1999							8/20/99
2								
3	MATHEMATICS DEPARTMENT—MR. SKUFCA—CHAIRPERSON							
4	TEACHER	PERIOD 1	PERIOD 2	PERIOD 3	PERIOD 4	PERIOD 5	PERIOD 6	PERIOD 7
5	BILLINGS	INF. GEOMETRY	INF. GEOMETRY		ALG. I	ALG. I	ALG. I	
6		12,063,103			12,003,103	12,003,103	12,003,103	
7	R-848	1,206,300						
8	===
9	CATTELL	BCC ALG		BCC ALG	BCC ALG	ALG II (H)	ALG II (H)	
10	#22	MAC11045-01		MAC11045-03	MAC11045-04	12003405-05	12003405-06	
11	R-841	BCC PRE-CALC		BCC PRE-CALC	BCC PRE-CALC			
12		MAC11425-2001		MAC11425-2003	MAC11425-2004			
13			X					
14	===
15	CHIZEK	ALG II (H)	GEOM (H)		GEOM (H)	ALG II (H)	GEOM (H)	
16	#23	12003405-01	12063205-02		12063205-04	12003405-15	12063205-06	
17	R-844							
18								
19	===
20	EATON, L.	APP I	ALG I	APP I		APP I	APP I	
21	#45	1205400x-11	12003103-02	1205400x-03		1205400x-05	1205400x-06	
22	R-846							
23	===
24	HART	AP STAT	APP I	PRECALC	PRECALC	PRECALC		
25	#55	12103205-01	1205400x-02	12023405-03	12023405-04	12023405-05		
26	R-842						X	
27	===
28	HEISEL		GEOM	GEOM (H)	GEOM (H)	GEOM (H)	GEOM	
29	#58		12063103-12	12063205-03	12063205-14	12063205-15	12063103-16	
30	R-10-105	X						
31	===
32	HELLER	APP I	APP II	APP II	APP II	APP II		
33	#986	1205400x-01	1205410x-02	1205410x-03	1205410x-04	1205410x-05		
34	R-1D							
35	===
36	KARCHER	ALG II		GEOM	GEOM	ALG II	GEOM	
37	#70	12003303-01		12063103-03	12063103-04	12003303-05	12063103-06	
38	R-845		X					
39								
40	KING	ALG I		ALG II	ALG I	ALG I	ALG II	
41	#262	12003103-01		12003303-13	12003103-04	12003103-05	12003103-06	
42	R-10-120							
43								
44	===
45	LONG		ALG II	ALG II	ALG II	LIB ARTS	LIB ARTS	
46	#74		12003303-02	12003303-03	12003303-14	1208300x-05	1208300x-06	
47	R-801	X						
48	===
49	MACKENS	APP I		ALG II	ALG II (H)	APP I	ALG II	
50	#80	1205400x-51		12003303-23	12003405-14	1205400x-55	12003303-16	
51	R-10-132							
52	===
53								
54				Page 1 of 26				

Although a noble experiment in curriculum reorganization, nongradedness has not reached the goal that Brown predicted—namely, that within a few years after its inception—"every intellectually respectable high school will have some degree of non-graded education."[73]

Over the decades a number of curricular arrangements have been tried with varying degrees of success in both our hypothetical community and elsewhere. Some have been adopted; others, abandoned. May we stop to wonder what innovations so-highly touted today will be with us a decade, two decades, three decades from now.

WHERE WE ARE: CURRICULUM PRESENT[74]

THE ELEMENTARY SCHOOL

Following the so-called "Back-to-Basics" movement of the 1970s and 1980s, schools at all levels across the nation are still struggling to raise student achievement in the subject areas. Nowhere are these efforts more apparent than in the elementary school, where efforts continue to improve students' mastery of the basic skills.

Concerned about students' low achievement and public dissatisfaction, schools have taken strong and sometimes controversial measures for improving student achievement and restoring public confidence. Among the measures designed to raise student achievement during the past three decades are the following:

- Implementation of strategies based on the "effective schools" research documented by Ronald P. Edmonds, Wilbur Brookover, Lawrence Lezotte, and others.[75] This body of research has led teachers to such practices as keeping students on task, holding learners to high expectations, and monitoring pupil achievement.
- Implementation of research on instruction conducted by David C. Berliner, N. J. Gage, Donald M. Medley, Barak V. Rosenshine, and others, whose research attributed such factors as time on task (academic engaged time) and direct instruction to effective teaching.[76]
- Emphasis—what some people would call overemphasis—on testing. Student progress is monitored by a plethora of local, state, and national tests and is measured not only by local and state criterion—referenced tests but also by national norm-referenced tests.
- Detailed planning and demand for implementation of the curriculum on a districtwide and sometimes statewide basis, sometimes referred to as "curriculum

---

[73]Brown, *Nongraded High School*, p. 44.

[74]This section discusses curriculum developments that appear to be generally accepted. In addition to the programs and practices presented in this chapter we are witnessing a sizable number of rapidly spreading curriculum developments that have generated both followers and opponents. These developments are examined in other chapters, particularly in Chapter 14.

[75]See *Phi Delta Kappan* 64, no. 10 (June 1983): 679–702; bibliography, p. 694. Note articles both supportive and critical of the effective schools research.

[76]See Penelope L. Peterson and Herbert J. Walberg, eds., *Research on Teaching: Concepts, Findings, and Implications* (Berkeley, Calif.: McCutchan, 1979).

alignment." Curriculum coordinators and teachers strive for a degree of curriculum uniformity by specifying pupil performance objectives in targeted subject areas for every grade level. School personnel choose or prepare teaching materials, learning activities, and tests that fit the specified objectives. Those objectives that are tested by state and national examinations are included and coded by test. Some school systems specify objectives and administer tests for each marking period in the designated disciplines. Principals', teachers', and—ipso facto—the schools' successes are measured by pupils' mastery of the objectives. With increasing frequency today schools are reporting test results to their communities, a practice championed by many but decried by others.

• Supplementing (some people, perhaps, would prefer the word "supplanting") traditional testing techniques, many teachers are turning to authentic or performance-based assessment in the form of individualized portfolios and projects. We will return to the use of performance-based assessment in Chapter 12.

Driven by an awareness of less than laudable student academic achievement and competitive factors like parental choice of school, vouchers, charter schools, and home schooling, schools are continuing to seek ways to improve students' mastery of the basic skills and academics. The setting of high expectations of both academic achievement and conduct coupled with a degree of autonomy and teacher collaboration in a nurturing environment account at least in part for the success of students in schools such as Central Park East (East Harlem)[77] and Frederick Douglass Academy (Harlem).[78]

While struggling to fulfill essentialistic goals of subject matter achievement schools are at the same time applying progressive principles as seen in concern for enhancing the self-esteem of learners. In Chapter 14 we will explore some of the issues raised in developments designed to improve student success.

TEACHING THINKING SKILLS

More than forty years ago (1944) the Educational Policies Commission identified the ability to think as one of the Ten Imperative Needs of Youth.[79] Seventeen years later the Educational Policies Commission set forth the premise that the central purpose of American education was the development of the student's ability to think.[80] About the same time the influential National Committee of the National Education Association's Project on Instruction included among its priorities for improving the instructional program of the schools "ways of creative and disciplined thinking, including methods of inquiry and application of knowledge."[81]

---

[77]See Deborah Meier, *The Power of Their Ideas: Lessons for America from a Small School* in *Harlem* (Boston: Beacon Press, 1995).

[78]See Lorraine Monroe, *Nothing's Impossible: Leadership Lessons from Inside and Outside the Classroom* (New York: Times Books, 1997).

[79]See p. 83 of this text.

[80]Ibid.

[81]Dorothy M. Fraser, *Deciding What to Teach* (Washington, D.C.: Project on the Instructional Program of the Public Schools, National Education Association, 1963), p. 222.

In the 1980s we witnessed a resurgence of interest in the teaching of thinking skills. Prominent national organizations called for renewed and increased emphasis on the development of thinking skills. Among these associations are the National Council of Teachers of Mathematics;[82] the National Council of Teachers of English;[83] the National Science Board Commission of Pre-College Education in Mathematics, Science, and Technology;[84] and the Association for Supervision and Curriculum Development.[85]

A new body of literature defines thinking skills and suggests strategies for teaching those skills. Discussion has moved away from the general declared goal of teaching young people to think to identification of thinking skills and prescribed methods for achieving those skills.[86]

As with many other terms in education, we can find differing definitions of thinking skills. Barry K. Beyer pointed out that some people use the term "critical thinking" to signify all forms of thinking. Beyer maintained that it was a mistake to equate critical thinking with inquiry, decision making, problem solving, and other thinking skills. Said Beyer, "Critical thinking is, instead, the process of determining the authenticity, accuracy, and worth of information or knowledge claims."[87] Where the experts agree, however, is that thinking skills are fundamental, the most basic of the basic skills.

PROVISION FOR STUDENTS WITH SPECIAL NEEDS

Schools are struggling to meet the needs of many special groups—exceptionalities of all types of students, including the physically disabled, emotionally disturbed, mentally retarded, and those with behavior disorders. Bolstered by federal legislation and dollars and by state mandates and funding, special education is a fundamental part of today's curriculum. To care for the needs of many exceptionalities, special education teachers, psychometrists, and school psychologists have been in demand.

One of the groups with special needs—the so-called "students-at-risk"—has received considerable attention in recent years. Students-at-risk may be narrowly defined as those students most likely to drop out of school or broadly defined as those most likely to emerge from school with insufficient education, unprepared to play a productive role in society.

Students-at-risk tend to come from low-income environments and to perform poorly in the basic skills. Proposals for meeting the needs of students-at-risk suggest

---

[82]*An Agenda for Action* (Reston, Va.: National Council of Teachers of Mathematics, 1980).

[83]*Essentials of English* (Urbana, Ill.: National Council of Teachers of English, 1982).

[84]*Educating Americans for the 21st Century* (Washington, D.C.: National Science Board Commission on Pre-College Mathematics, Science, and Technology, 1983).

[85]Association for Supervision and Curriculum Development, "1984 Resolutions," ASCD *Update* 26, no. 4 (May 1984), insert.

[86]See Arthur L. Costa, ed., *Developing Minds: A Resource Book for Teaching Thinking* (Alexandria, Va.: Association for Supervision and Curriculum Development, 1985); Edward de Bono, "The Direct Teaching of Thinking As a Skill," *Phi Delta Kappan* 64, no. 10 (June 1983): 703–708; Jerry L. Brown, "On Teaching Thinking Skills in the Elementary and Middle School," *Phi Delta Kappan* 64, no. 10 (June 1983): 709–714; and Bruce Joyce, "Models for Teaching Thinking," *Educational Leadership* 42, no. 8 (May 1985): 4–7. See also Chapter 7 of this text.

[87]Barry K. Beyer, "Critical Thinking: What Is It?" *Social Education* 49, no. 4 (April 1985): 276.

modification of instructional strategies, such as offering compensatory education and increasing student motivation; staff development to enable teachers to understand the special needs of these students; increased use of positive disciplinary practices; encouraging participation in extraclass activities; working with parents; addressing community problems; and abandonment of the graded school structure.

Increasingly, a cyclically neglected group—the gifted—is receiving attention through classes and other means that are designed for their particular intellectual capacities. Bilingual education programs are provided for those pupils for whom English is not their native language. In Chapter 14 we will examine some of the issues involved in providing for educating speakers of languages other than English and for exceptionalities.

Concentration on pupils with special needs such as the learning disabled and the gifted has provoked some objections from parents and others who perceive the schools as neglecting "woodwork children", that is average students. Citing figures from the Economic Policy Council, *TIME* reported a dramatic drop in the percentage of the school budget allotted to "regular education" between 1967 and 1996.[88]

COOPERATIVE LEARNING

The strategy of organizing people into small instructional groups with the intended purpose of helping each other is discussed in Chapter 11.

THE MIDDLE SCHOOL

A NEWER INSTITUTION

Not too long ago our hypothetical school district maintained a traditional organizational plan for six years of senior high school. Dissatisfaction with that organizational structure had been brewing for a long time. As our school staff studied the literature and watched innovations at other school districts, they began to realize that the junior high school as they knew it was rapidly disappearing. A new institution—the middle school—was rising to the forefront, creating an organizational structure more suited to its time.

As it became clear to the personnel of our hypothetical school district that the needs of a special group of youngsters—early adolescents or, as Donald H. Eichhorn called them, "transescents"[89] were not being met by the existing junior high school structure, they implemented dramatic and substantial changes which had an impact on all levels of the educational ladder of that district. The elementary school lost a grade, and the senior high school regained a grade that it had lost years ago to the junior high school. The junior high school was transformed into a middle school that consisted of three grades (six through eight) for preadolescents—the children in the middle.

---

[88]Romesh Ratnesar, "Lost in the Middle," *TIME* 152, no. 11 (September 14, 1998): 60–62, 64.
[89]Donald H. Eichhorn, *The Middle School* (New York: Center for Applied Research in Education, 1966), p. 3.

Special Needs of Students.   Some other countries have recognized the needs of middle students for a long time, as in Germany with its *Mittelschule*. Boys and girls of the pre- and early adolescent years, ages ten to fourteen as a rule, are too mature to be treated as primary school children and too immature to be considered high schoolers. They evidence a host of physical, social, and emotional growth needs as well as educational demands. Their career and life interests are just beginning to take shape. They need time to explore, to adjust, and to socialize as well as to study.

As a result, the junior high school spun off from the other levels as a separate institution and mushroomed. From the two identified separate junior high schools with grades seven, eight, and nine in 1910, the junior highs grew to approximately six thousand.

Lounsbury and Vars characterized the junior high school as a significantly successful development in American education.[90] Although the seven-eight-nine pattern was the most common for the junior high school, other relatively common patterns were seven-eight, six-seven-eight, seven through ten, and eight through ten. Despite this variety, as the years passed dissatisfaction with the junior high school began to set in. It was argued that this intermediate school had become a carbon copy of the senior high school with all its trapping-interscholastic athletics, band, high school subjects, and so on.

Junior high school students were changing not only physically but also socially in response to new, unexpected social pressures and values. As a result of these changes and of society's new demands on adolescents, the program for these years was revised and updated. A new organizational pattern grouped grades five or six through eight into a middle school with its own unique program, and a four-four-four system or five-three-four system began to emerge. Although the ninth grade is generally considered as "belonging" to the high school, there is some uncertainty amongst middle-school specialists as to whether the fifth grade should be attached to the elementary school or to the middle school. Jon Wiles and Joseph Bondi defined this new institution as "a transitional school concerned with providing the most appropriate program to cope with the personal and educational needs of emerging adolescent learners."[91]

Phenomenal Growth.   The middle school has experienced phenomenal growth. In 1965 the Educational Research Service of the National Education Association conducted a nationwide survey and found 65 middle schools.[92] In a 1967–68 survey William M. Alexander reported 1,101 middle schools, and Mary Compton accounted for 3,723 middle schools in 1974.[93] Kenneth Brooks identified 4,060 middle schools operating in 1978.[94] By the mid-1980s figures showed close to 7,000 middle schools in existence.[95] A National Education Association publication in 1988 projected a figure

---

[90]See Lounsbury and Vars, *Curriculum for the Middle School,* p. 15.

[91]Jon Wiles and Joseph Bondi, *The Essential Middle School,* 2nd ed. (New York: Macmillan, 1993), p. 10.

[92]Lounsbury and Vars, *Curriculum for the Middle School,* pp. 22–23.

[93]Ibid.

[94]Kenneth Brooks, "The Middle Schools—A National Survey," *Middle School Journal 9,* no. 1 (February 1978): 6–7.

[95]Valena White Plisko and Joyce D. Stern, *The Condition of Education,* 1985 edition. Statistical Report of the National Center for Education Statistics (Washington, D.C.: U.S. Government Printing Office, 1985), p. 28.

of over 12,000 of these schools by 1992.[96] Although junior high schools still exist in some communities, confirming Axiom two that curriculum changes of earlier periods can coexist with newer curriculum changes, their number has drastically declined as they undergo the metamorphosis from junior high school to middle school. Paul S. George, Chris Stevenson, Julia Thomason, and James Beane predicted that "In some states, it is possible that the junior high school, as a grade-level entity, will completely disappear by the end of the century."[97]

William M. Alexander and others saw the middle school as an emerging institution and defined it in the following manner:

> To us, it is *a school providing a program planned for a range of older children, preadolescents, and early adolescents that builds upon the elementary school program for older childhood and in turn is built upon by the high school's program for adolescence.*[98]

They perceived the middle school as a distinct phase of schooling between elementary and secondary school levels.

Somewhat later Alexander in writing with Paul S. George offered the following definition:

> We define a middle school as a school *of some three to five years between elementary and high school focused on the educational needs of students in these in-between years and designed to promote continuous educational progress for all concerned.*[99]

Transformation of the junior high school into a middle school should not be perceived as a reorganization of but one level of the school system. Alexander and others observed that the change from junior high to middle school is a reorganization of the entire grade structure.[100]

Recommendations for the Middle School. Thomas E. Gatewood and Charles A. Dilg, speaking for the Association for Supervision and Curriculum Development's Working Group on the Emerging Adolescent Learner, made a series of recommendations for the middle school.[101] Let's examine a few. Speaking of the physical characteristics of transescents, they recommended:

> A program for the emerging adolescent that is adapted to the ever-changing physical needs of this learner. . . .
> Instruction related to growth of the body so that one can better understand changes in himself or herself and in others and be prepared for future changes and problems.[102]

---

[96]Sylvester Kohut, Jr., *The Middle School: A Bridge Between Elementary and High Schools,* 2nd ed. (Washington, D.C.: National Education Association, 1988), p. 7.

[97]Paul S. George, Chris Stevenson, Julia Thomason, and James Beane, *The Middle School—And Beyond* (Alexandria, Va.: Association for Supervision and Curriculum Development, 1992), p. 10.

[98]William M. Alexander, Emmett L. Williams, Mary Compton, Vynce A. Hines, and Dan Prescott, *The Emergent Middle School,* 2nd enl. ed. (New York: Holt, Rinehart and Winston, 1969), p. 5.

[99]William M. Alexander and Paul S. George, *The Exemplary Middle School* (New York: Holt, Rinehart and Winston, 1981), p. 3.

[100]Alexander et al., *Emergent Middle School,* p. 4.

[101]Thomas E. Gatewood and Charles A. Dilg, *The Middle School We Need* (Alexandria, Va.: Association for Supervision and Curriculum Development, 1975).

[102]Ibid., p. 8.

Speaking of mental and intellectual growth, Gatewood and Dilg made the following recommendations:

Learning experiences for transescents at their own intellectual levels, relating to immediate rather than remote academic goals.

A wide variety of cognitive learning experiences to account for the full range of students who are at many different levels of concrete and formal operations. . . .

Opportunities for the development of problem-solving skills, reflective-thinking processes, and awareness for the order of the student's environment.

Cognitive learning experiences so structured that students can progress in an individualized manner. However, within the structure of an individualized learning program, students can interact with one another. . . .

A common program in which areas of learning are combined and integrated to break down artificial and irrelevant divisions of curriculum content. . . .

Methods of instruction involving open and individually directed learning experiences. The role of the teacher should be more that of a personal guide and facilitator of learning than of a purveyor of knowledge.[103]

Speaking of personality development characteristics, Gatewood and Dilg recommended:

Administrative arrangements to ensure that personality development has continuity both in breadth and in depth. Thus continuous, cooperative curriculum planning is essential among elementary, middle, and secondary school personnel.

A comprehensive, integrated series of learning encounters to assist learners to develop a self which they realize, accept, and approve. . . .

Classroom instruction, counseling, and extra-class activities that take into account the social-emotional needs of transescents.

An approach in working with emerging adolescents that will have consistency with basic democratic principles.[104]

Gatewood and Dilg have called attention to the broad range of physical, intellectual, and personal characteristics of middle school students. In their recommendations they have presented guidelines for meeting various needs of the emerging adolescent.

Proposed Design.   Lounsbury and Vars proposed a curriculum design for the middle school that consists of three main components: core, continuous progress (nongraded learning experiences), and variable.[105]

Core in their conception is "a problem-centered block-time program."[106] The continuous progress (nongraded) component consists of "those skills and concepts that have a genuine sequential organization."[107] Science, for example, may overlap with the core along with its placement in the nongraded component. The variable component is comprised of "the activities and programs that have proven their worth in schools . . . neither so highly sequential as to be placed exclusively in the nongraded component

[103]Ibid., pp. 11–12.
[104]Ibid., p. 16.
[105]Lounsbury and Vars, *Curriculum for the Middle School*, pp. 45–48.
[106]Ibid., p. 46.
[107]Ibid., p. 47.

nor so essentially problem-centered as to fit entirely within the core."[108] The middle-school curriculum as proposed by Lounsbury and Vars is shown schematically in Figure 9-2.[109] Note that this proposal incorporates some earlier principles of the core curriculum and nongradedness.

Our hypothetical junior high school has changed to a pattern that has been in successful operation throughout the United States for some forty years. The middle school in our hypothetical school district is a significant development in education for the preadolescent years.

THE SENIOR HIGH SCHOOL

A COMPREHENSIVE HIGH SCHOOL

The academics? Students from this school regularly achieve high scores on national standardized tests of achievement in the subject areas; graduates are placed in college and universities without difficulty; students master computer skills; science students yearly win recognition at the science fairs; foreign language students bring home prizes from state competitions in their field; many students are enrolled in advanced placement courses; the student body as a whole is well above the norm in reading and mathematics.

Marching band? They can put on a razzle-dazzle spectacular at half-time and compete with the best. They have been invited to participate in parades of the major bowls in the United States.

Football? Basketball? Try baseball, golf, and tennis. The showcase in front of the principal's office is crammed with shiny trophies won by students of this school. School officials are moving rapidly to eliminate gender discrimination in athletics and proudly display trophies won by both the boys' and girls' teams.

Business education? Students are mastering the use of computers, electronic typewriters, and fax machines. Students in all programs are encouraged to develop skill in typing and word processing.

Art? Come to the annual art show put on by the school's art students to appreciate the excellence of their work.

Vocational education? Wood shop, metal shop, electricity, and auto mechanics are all available. Each shop has ample space and is well equipped.

What we are describing here is a high-quality, traditional, comprehensive high school. As such it meets the definition of a comprehensive high school given by James B. Conant, who saw it as "a high school whose programs correspond to the educational needs of *all* youth in the community."[110] Personnel of this school concur with the Association for Supervision and Curriculum Development and with Conant as to the objectives of the school. The ASCD maintained:

---

[108]Ibid.

[109]Gordon F. Vars, "New Knowledge of the Learner and His Cultural Milieu: Implications for Schooling in the Middle Years." Paper presented at the Conference on the Middle School Idea, College of Education, University of Toledo, November 1967, ERIC Document No. ED016267 CG 901400, p. 14. See also Lounsbury and Vars, *Curriculum for Middle School*, p. 45.

[110]Conant, *American High School*, p. 12.

Figure 9.2 A junior high/middle school program. Note that core classes are scheduled back-to-back in order to facilitate cross-graded grouping on a temporary basis wherever appropriate. From Gordon F. Vars, "New Knowledge of the Learner and His Cultural Milieu: Implications for Schooling in the Middle Years," Paper presented at the Conference on the Middle School Idea, College of Education, University of Toledo, November 1967. Reprinted by permission. ERIC Document No. ED016267CG901400, p. 14. See also John H. Lounsbury and Gordon F. Vars, *A Curriculum for the Middle School Years* (New York: Harper & Row, 1978), p. 45.

The secondary school should be a comprehensive school. If a major task of the public school in America is to develop the basic values of a free society, and mutual respect for the range of persons and groups within our diverse culture, students must have an opportunity to live and work together. The comprehensive secondary school is an essential element in the development of a common viewpoint sufficiently strong to hold our nation together.[111]

Conant cited three main objectives of a comprehensive high school:

First, to provide a general education for all the future citizens; *second,* to provide good elective programs for those who wish to use their acquired skills immediately on graduation; *third,* to provide satisfactory programs for those whose vocations will depend on their subsequent education in a college or university.[112]

This school performs well on criteria suggested by both Conant and the ASCD. Conant listed the following points to be considered in evaluating a comprehensive school:

A. Adequacy of general education for all as judged by:
1. Offerings in English and American literature and composition
2. Social studies, including American history
3. Ability grouping in required courses
B. Adequacy of nonacademic elective program as judged by:
4. The vocational programs for boys and commercial programs for girls
5. Opportunities for supervised work experience
6. Special provisions for very slow readers
C. Special arrangements for the academically talented students:
7. Special provisions for challenging the highly gifted
8. Special instruction in developing reading skills
9. Summer sessions from which able students may profit
10. Individualized programs (absence of tracks or rigid programs)
11. School day organized into seven or more instructional periods
D. Other features
12. Adequacy of the guidance services
13. Student morale
14. Well-organized homerooms
15. The success of the school in promoting an understanding between students with widely different academic abilities and vocational goals (effective social interaction among students)[113]

ASCD Recommendations.   Our hypothetical secondary school would meet not only the criteria set forth by Conant but also the standards recommended by the Association for Supervision and Curriculum Development. Writing for the ASCD's Commission on the Education of Adolescents, Kimball Wiles and Franklin Patterson made recommendations for the comprehensive high school, some of which are cited here:

---

[111]Kimball Wiles and Franklin Patterson, *The High School We Need* (Alexandria, Va.: Association for Supervision and Curriculum Development, 1959), pp. 5–6.

[112]Conant, *American High School,* p. 17.

[113]Ibid., pp. 19–20.

Certain types of growth must be promoted in all youth who attend the secondary school. Each youth should develop increased understanding of self and his responsibility in society, commitment to democratic values, economic understanding, political acumen, and ability to think. . . .

The program for each individual must contain general education and specialized education. . . . One-third to one-half of each student's program should be devoted to general education . . . the required courses and activities . . . essential for competent citizenship. . . . One-half to two-thirds of each student's program should be used to develop his talents and so further his personal goals within the framework that the community is willing and able to support. . . .

Choices among the various offerings of the curriculum should be made jointly by the pupil, parents, and staff members of the school in terms of the pupil's purposes, aptitude and level of achievement. . . .

Each student should have one staff member who guides him throughout his high school career. . . .

Each high school student should be a member of at least one home base group with which he has a continuing relationship. . . .

Students should be grouped in various ways in different phases of their high school experience. . . . the general education phase of an individual's schedule should be in classes that are heterogeneously grouped. . . . In the portion of the student's program that is elective, the grouping should be homogeneous in terms of two factors: the pupil's intensity of purpose and his level of achievement.[114]

When Conant came out with his follow-up study, officials of our hypothetical senior high school were pleased that their school compared favorably with the better comprehensive high schools. They surely enrolled more than 750 pupils; they graduated at least 100 pupils every year; they offered calculus and four years of a modern foreign language (two languages, to be exact); their ratio of counselors to students was within the recommended range of 250 to 300; their students were grouped homogeneously in the elective subjects and heterogeneously in the required courses; and they offered a full range of courses in the academic disciplines, business education, homemaking, and industrial arts.[115] This school met the tests of comprehensiveness well.

Some Alternatives

The comprehensive high school was conceived as a unique American response to the needs of youth. Every young person would find in this institution programs necessary to his or her present and future success in society. The comprehensive high school was a reaction to specialized high schools that cared for specific segments of the student population. This institution would accommodate boys and girls from every social stratum and ethnic group. Students would study, work, and play together, thus breaking down barriers between them. The comprehensive high school was a democratic response to education in a democratic society.

The comprehensive high school, however, has not been free of criticism. The National Panel on High Schools and Adolescent Education claimed that the comprehensive high school reinforced social-class and race stratification rather than diminished

---

[114]Wiles and Patterson, *High School We Need*, pp. 6–17.
[115]See James B. Conant, *The Comprehensive High School* (New York: McGraw-Hill, 1967).

it.[116] The comprehensive high school was criticized for a number of reasons. Some felt it deemphasized the academics; others felt the opposite and claimed it deemphasized the affective domain. Some believed it was too structured; others, that is was not structured enough. Some maintained it was taking on too many responsibilities; some, that it was not assuming enough. Some accused the comprehensive high school of slighting career education; others were not satisfied with the students' achievement in the cognitive domain.

Call for Reform.   Over the years we have heard repeated clarion calls for "reform" not only in secondary education but in public education at all levels. Larry Cuban noted that efforts at reforming education have been made "again, again, and again."[117] John Henry Martin, author of *The Education of Adolescents*—the report of the National Panel on High Schools and Adolescent Education of the United States Office of Education—expressed the belief that the Seven Cardinal Principles were too inclusive and were "inflated statements of purpose."[118] He argued that the Seven Cardinal Principles were much too broad, stating, "Among the unfortunate consequences of the sweeping language of the Seven Cardinal Principles has been our assumption that the schools could reform all of society's ills. Schools have undertaken burdens that they have neither the resources nor the talents to overcome."[119] The excessive offerings and services of some high schools have caused Arthur G. Powell, Eleanor Farrar, and David K. Cohen to apply the label, "Shopping Mall High School."[120]

Richard Mitchell challenged the Seven Cardinal Principles as anti-intellectual, labeling them, "The Seven Deadly Principles" proposed by "The Gang of Twenty-Seven." (i.e., the National Education Association's Commission on the Reorganization of Secondary Education appointed in 1913). Mitchell was favorably disposed toward the NEA's Committee of Ten, which was formed in 1892 and made "largely of scholars."[121]

Martin took the position that schools cannot be responsible for all aspects of life, that goals of the school (that is, the high school) must be redefined, and that aims more modest than those of the Seven Cardinal Principles must be set. Theodore R. Sizer, however, observed that Americans have agreed for decades on the goals set forth by the Seven Cardinal Principles.[122]

Martin perceived the community as sharing responsibility for the education of youth. He advised as follows:

---

[116]See John Henry Martin, *The Education of Adolescents*. Report of the National Panel on High Schools and Adolescent Education (Washington, D.C.: U.S. Office of Education, 1976).

[117]Larry Cuban, "Reforming Again, Again, and Again," *Educational Researcher* 19, no. 1 (January-February 1990): 3–13.

[118]John Henry Martin, "Reconsidering the Goals of High School Education," *Educational Leadership* 37, no. 4 (January 1980): 280.

[119]Ibid., p. 279.

[120]Arthur G. Powell, Eleanor Farrar, and David K. Cohen, The *Shopping Mall High School: Winners and Losers in the Educational Marketplace* (Boston: Houghton Mifflin, 1985).

[121]Richard Mitchell, *The Graves of Academe* (Boston: Little, Brown, 1981), pp. 69–70.

[122]Theodore R. Sizer, *Horace's Compromise: The Dilemma of the American High School* (Boston: Houghton Mifflin, 1984), p. 78.

Redefining the goals of schools and building new relationships between youth and adults requires that the comprehensive high school be replaced with a comprehensive program of community-based education. Such a design for the education of adolescents should delineate those purposes of education that would remain the primary responsibility of the high school, those that might better be shifted to other and new community agencies, and those that would be served by a cooperative sharing of resources.[123]

A. Harry Passow discussed proposals of five national groups looking at secondary education.[124] In addition to the reports of the National Panel on High Schools and Adolescent Education, the American public has received reports from the National Association of Secondary School Principals,[125] the National Commission on the Reform of Secondary Education (referred to as the Kettering Commission),[126] the Panel on Youth of the President's Science Advisory Committee,[127] and Educational Facilities Laboratories and IDEA.[128]

Among the proposals coming out of the national groups in the 1970s were calls for

- a reduced school day with more time being spent in work experience programs in the community
- educational options—that is, alternative forms of schooling to be selected by students and parents.
- a lowering of the age of compulsory attendance to fourteen years of age
- establishment of specialized high schools in the European tradition
- an emphasis on career education
- restriction of the function of the high school to cognitive learning

It is clear that if some of these proposals were seriously considered and adopted, the comprehensive high school which was designed to bring together young people from all walks of life and offer a wide range of programs would be greatly altered or might even disappear.

REFORM EFFORTS

Movements toward accountability, emphasis on cognitive skills and minimal competencies, expansion of content, an increase in academic engaged time, frequent testing, and the raising of marking standards have affected the high school as well as the levels

---

[123]Martin, "Reconsidering Goals," p. 281. See also "High School Goals: Responses to John Henry Martin," *Educational Leadership* 37, no. 4 (January 1980): 286–298.

[124]A. Harry Passow, "Reforming America's High Schools," *Phi Delta Kappan* 56, no. 9 (May 1975): 587–590.

[125]National Association of Secondary School Principals, National Committee on Secondary Education, *American Youth in the Mid-Seventies* (Reston, Va.: National Association of Secondary School Principals, 1972).

[126]National Commission on the Reform of Secondary Education, *The Reform of Secondary Education: A Report to the Public and the Profession* (New York: McGraw-Hill, 1973).

[127]James S. Coleman, chairman, Panel on Youth of the President's Science Advisory Committee, *Youth: Transition to Adulthood* (Washington, D.C.: Superintendent of Documents, U.S. Government Printing Office, 1973; Chicago: University of Chicago Press, 1974).

[128]Ruth Weinstock, *The Greening of the High School* (New York: Educational Facilities Laboratory, 1973).

below. During the 1980s and early 1990s the high school has been examined and reexamined in a series of reports that produced numerous recommendations.[129] Schools are engaged in testing some of the proposals found in the reports.

Among the many widely discussed reports during this period were the following:

- *The Paideia Proposal: An Educational Manifesto* by Mortimer Adler for the Paideia Group (1982)[130]
- *A Nation at Risk: The Imperative for Education Reform* by David P. Gardner for the National Commission on Excellence in Education (1983)[131]
- *High School: A Report on Secondary Education in America* by Ernest L. Boyer, president of the Carnegie Foundation for the Advancement of Teaching (1983)[132]
- *A Place Called School: Prospects for the Future* by John I. Goodlad (1984)[133]
- *Horace's Compromise: The Dilemma of the American High School* by Theodore R. Sizer (1984)[134]
- *Essential Components of a Successful Education System* by The Business Roundtable (1990).[135]
- *Horace's School: Redesigning the American High School* by Theodore R. Sizer (1992).[136]

Four of the studies (Adler, Business Roundtable, Gardner, and Goodlad) addressed schools at both the elementary and secondary levels. To help grasp the essence of these studies, we might chart their major curricular recommendations for the high school, as shown in Table 9.12.

Having reviewed past developments and evaluated present programs of the high school, our hypothetical curriculum committee—like those in other school systems throughout the country—is studying the many, sometimes conflicting recommendations for change in the high school.

Predicting the impact of these studies in the years ahead is difficult. The Conference Board reported that ten years after *A Nation at Risk,* business involvement in the schools had increased, new programs had been developed, broad-based coalitions had

---

[129]See "A Compilation of Brief Descriptions of Study Projects," *Wingspread* (Racine, Wis.: Johnson Foundation, November 1982); *Almanac of National Reports,* wall chart (Reston, Va.: National Association of Secondary School Principals, 1983); *An Analysis of Reports of the Status of Education in America,* (Tyler, Tex.: Tyler Independent School District, 1983); A. Harry Passow, "Tackling the Reform Reports of the 1980's," *Phi Delta Kappan* 65, no. 10 (June 1984): 674–683. See also David L. Clark and Terry A. Asuto, "Redirecting Reform: Challenges to Popular Assumptions About Teachers and Students," *Phi Delta Kappan* 75, no. 7 (March 1994): 512–520 and "School Reform: What We Have Learned," *Educational Leadership* 52, no. 5 (February 1995): 4–48.

[130]Mortimer J. Adler, *The Paideia Proposal: An Educational Manifesto* (New York: Macmillan, 1982).

[131]National Commission on Excellence in Education, David P. Gardner, chairman, *A Nation at Risk: The Imperative for Educational Reform* (Washington, D.C.: U.S. Government Printing Office, 1983).

[132]Ernest L. Boyer, *High School: A Report on Secondary Education in America* (New York: Harper & Row, 1983).

[133]John I. Goodlad, *A Place Called School: Prospects for the Future* (New York: McGraw-Hill, 1984).

[134]See Sizer, *Horace's Compromise.*

[135]The Business Roundtable, *Essential Components of a Successful Education System* (New York: The Business Roundtable, 1990).

[136]Theodore R. Sizer, *Horace's School: Redesigning the American High School* (Boston: Houghton Mifflin, 1992).

been formed, and the public's attention to education had been attracted and maintained. Nevertheless, business involvement "has not yet produced wide-scale improvement."[137]

Sizer sought to stimulate reform through the Coalition of Essential Schools, which was formed in 1984. Working with fifty-two schools Sizer attempted to combat the "shopping mall" concept of the high school by encouraging schools to reduce the amount of subject matter covered and to emphasize depth rather than breadth. Sizer's efforts encountered difficulties including financing; faculty resistance, cynicism, and inertia; parental concern over deemphasis of extracurricular activities within the context of the school day; and student objections to a more demanding, academically oriented curriculum.

Among early reported successes of the coalition schools (schools within schools) are improved reading scores, a rise in the number of graduates going on to college, and a decrease in the dropout rate. Emphasis on the academics for all students, a coaching model of instruction, smaller classes, and local faculty control are central to Sizer's efforts.[138]

To tackle school reform more effectively the Coalition of Essential Schools entered into an alliance with the Education Commission of the States "to encourage the reform effort 'from the schoolhouse to the statehouse,'" an initiative aided by Citibank and the Danforth Foundation, labeled 'Re: Learning.'[139] Horace's Franklin High School, Sizer's fictitious vehicle for conveying coalition principles, pictured an "adaptation of Essential School ideas."[140] Among recommendations of the fictitious committee of Horace's school were organization of the curriculum into three areas, two stages for all, a third voluntary stage, an integrated curriculum, demonstration of mastery by Exhibition, and focus on a limited number of competencies.

Sizer, speaking of subsequent reform efforts of some of the now over 200 members of the coalition, observed, "Each of these schools reports improved student academic performance, attendance, morale, and admission to college." He continued, however, " . . . comparative assessment of success or failure remains conjectural, but judgments from close observation are encouraging."[141]

Will school systems lean toward Adler's recommendations? Boyer's? The Business Roundtable's? Gardner's? Goodlad's? Sizer's? Will they go even further back to the Committee of Ten, the Commission on the Reorganization of Secondary Education, or the Educational Policies Commission? Will they adopt other proposals for reform and restructuring such as national standards, national assessment, privatized schools, schedule revision, and outcomes-based education which we examine in Chapter 14?

What we are most likely to see will be a synthesis of the many recommendations with variations determined by local school districts and the states. No single standardized model of secondary education—nor of elementary or middle schools, for that

---

[137]Leonard Lund and Cathleen Wild, *Ten Years After A Nation at Risk* (New York: The Conference Board, 1993), p. 1.

[138]See Thomas Toch and Matthew Cooper, "Lessons from the Trenches," *U.S. News and World Report* 108, no. 8 (February 26, 1990): 50–55.

[139]Sizer, *Horace's School*, p. 209.

[140]Ibid., p. 207.

[141]Ibid., pp. 209–210.

TABLE 9.12

MAJOR CURRICULAR RECOMMENDATIONS FOR THE HIGH SCHOOL

ADLER (1982)	BOYER (1983)	GARDNER (1983)*	GOODLAD (1984)
One track with same objectives for all	Centrality of language (English proficiency)	Five new basics to be required for graduation:	Five fingers of knowledge and experience:
No electives except in choice of foreign language	Required core (a half to a third of total units required for graduation):	Four years of English	Up to 18% literature and language (English and foreign)
No specialized training for jobs	Literature	Three years of math	Up to 18% mathematics and science
Areas of subject matter:	U.S. history (one year)	Three years of science	Up to 15% society and social studies
Acquisition of organized knowledge	Western civilization	Three years of social studies	Up to 15% the arts
Development of intellectual skills	Non-Western civilization (one semester)	Two years of foreign language for college-bound	Up to 15% the vocations
Enlarged understanding of ideas and values	Science and the natural world (two years)	Better use of time	Up to 10% physical education
	Technology	Longer school day or longer school year (seven-hour school day; 200- to 220-day school year)	No more than 90% from the above categories
	Mathematics (two years)		At least 10% electives, as high as 20% to pursue special interests
	Foreign language (two years for all students)		
	The arts		Common required core: common concepts, principles, skills, and ways of knowing, not common topics
	Civics		
	Health		
	Work (one semester)		About two-thirds of program in each of five domains of knowledge will be common to all students opposed to ability grouping and tracking
	Senior independent project		
	First two years devoted to the core		
	Last two years devoted to elective clusters		
	Requirement of one unit of service in the community or at school		

(Continued)

*For the National Commission on Excellence in Education

SIZER (1984)	BUSINESS ROUNDTABLE (1990)	SIZER (1992)
Skills:	Four operating assumptions:	Principles:
Reading	All children can learn at significantly higher levels	Use minds well
Writing		Competencies rather than conventional subjects
Speaking	We know how to teach all students successfully	
Listening		Depth rather than breadth
Measuring	Curriculum content to reflect high expectations; instructional time and strategies may vary	
Estimating		Practice tailored to needs of students
Calculating		Personalized teaching and learning
Seeing	Every child needs an advocate	
Knowledge:		Student as worker
No universal body of subject matter	Performance- or outcome-based system	Coaching
Vocational training		Remedial work in language and elementary math if needed
Start where the student is	Assessment strategies strong and rich	
Understanding:	Reward schools for success; assist to improve; penalties for failure	Diploma awarded on demonstration of mastery ("Exhibition")
Development of powers of discrimination and judgment		
	School staff has major role in making instructional decisions	No strict age grading
Discovery-values-character education:		No system of credit by time in class
Fairness	Major emphasis on staff development	
Generosity		
Tolerance	High-quality prekindergarten, at least for all disadvantaged children	
	Sufficient health and other social services to reduce learning barriers	
	Use of technology	

matter—is likely to be acceptable to all the school systems in the United States. Certainly, as the trend toward greater local autonomy over the school's program and toward the empowerment of teachers and parents gain momentum, diversity of models may be anticipated.

We have to take notice of the cyclical nature of curricular recommendations. The Committee of Ten (1894) recommended the same program for all high school students. Almost 100 years later the Paideia Group (1982) was proposing a single track for all students during their twelve years of schooling.[142] Conant (1959) recommended a year of calculus in high school, as did the Paideia Group (1982). In 1959 Conant advocated foreign languages for the academically talented (four years of one foreign language), in 1983 the National Commission on Excellence in Education recommended two years of a foreign language for the college-bound, and in that same year Boyer advocated beginning foreign language study in the elementary school and requiring two years of all high school pupils. Conant (1959) pointed to the need for more guidance counselors, as did Boyer (1983). Goodlad (1984) accepted the broad categories of human knowledge and organized experiences of the Harvard Committee on General Education (1945).

We can already see that that it has become more difficult for high school students to earn a diploma—a fact that may satisfy a long-held wish of both the public and the profession to make the high school diploma a symbol of a reasonable standard of academic achievement.

Once minimal competencies have been comfortably mastered by students, faculties will seek ways of enriching the program and responding to individual differences. Efforts to create voucher plans, proposals for tuition tax credits, and competition from private schools have contributed to forcing the public schools to reassess their programs. Although schools are now on a necessary cognitive swing, they are not likely to abandon the psychomotor domain nor eliminate affective learnings from the curriculum. Two generations of progressive doctrine, with its concern for the whole child instead of solely the intellect, cannot be—nor should it be—lightly discarded.

During the intensity of reform efforts over the years, gains in student achievement have been very limited. In a 1989 report, the Center for Policy Research in Education noted two waves of reform efforts. The first occurred from about 1982 to 1986 with state mandates for minimum competency standards. The second, beginning in 1986 and continuing into the present, saw efforts in some localities to restructure schooling at the local level. The Center observed that state policies were still more characteristic of first wave reform efforts than of the second wave's implementation of restructuring at the local level.[143]

Considerable relaxation of state mandating, however, has occurred in the past decade with the movements toward empowerment of teachers and laypeople and site-

---

[142]Do not confuse this proposal for single track, i.e., basically the same content for all students, with the single track of year-round schools, i.e, a scheduling practice. See scheduling revisions in Chapter 14.

[143]William A. Firestone, Susan H. Fuhrman, and Michael W. Kirst, *The Progress of Reform: An Appraisal of State Education Initiatives* (New Brunswick, N.J.: Center for Policy Research in Education, Eagleton Institute of Politics, Rutgers, The State University of New Jersey, 1989), p. 13.

based management. With the "downsizing" of state departments of education further relaxation may occur. Note once again that change is incremental, rarely wholesale, across-the-board.

Donald C. Orlich took a critical view of reform efforts in general when he observed:

> This nation has wasted billions of dollars on poorly conceived but politically popular reform movements that have sapped the energies of schoolpeople. We need a national moratorium on reforms so that educators and local policy makers can analyze their own problems. This could lead to a new concept: *local system analysis.* Each local school district would systematically study its own cultures—*yes,* cultures—*and* then implement a carefully researched, well-coordinated, and well-funded plan for specific improvements.[144]

Although state mandating had tapered off in the 1990s, reform efforts continue with the promulgation of national goals under the Bush and Clinton administrations, state and local spinoffs of *America 2000,* national efforts at developing standards, and individual and group recommendations. Like many efforts in education, the process of goal-setting and varying goal statements of the 1980s and 1990s has met with criticism. Kenneth A. Sirotnik found "the continual displays of lists of lofty educational goals a curious phenomenon."[145] Following the 1983 report of the National Commission on Excellence in Education (*A Nation at Risk*) George Leonard disagreed with recommendations to improve education at that time and termed them the "Great School Reform Hoax."[146] Several years later Lewis J. Perelman, took a sharply critical view of reform efforts like *America 2000,* citing them as a failure, and calling them a "hoax," advocated nothing less than substituting a privatized system of education which makes use of the latest technology in place of public schools as we know them.[147]

Ernest R. House saw reforms of the 1980s such as toughening of standards, testing, changes in school governance like decentralization and school choice as low-cost efforts designed to protect middle and upper class interests.[148]

School districts, the states, and the nation have continued pronounced efforts to improve the success and image of public education. Education held and continues to hold a top priority on the agenda of many state and national politicans of the late 1990s and early 2000s. Yet, reform efforts of the 1990s in modifying goals, raising standards, assessing achievement, and promoting accountability do not satisfy some

---

[144]Donald C. Orlich, "Educational Reforms: Mistakes, Misconceptions, Miscues,"*Phi Delta Kappan* 70, no. 7 (March 1989): 517.

[145]Kenneth A. Sirotnik, "What Goes on in Classrooms? Is This the Way We Want It?" in Landon E. Beyer and Michael W. Apple, *The Curriculum: Problems, Politics, and Possibilities,* 2nd ed. (Albany, N.Y.: State University of New York Press, 1998) p. 65.

[146]George Leonard, *Education and Ecstasy* with *The Great School Reform Hoax* (Berkeley, Calif.: Atlantic Books, 1987, pp. 241–263.

[147]Lewis J. Perelman, *School's Out: Hyperlearning, the New Technology, and the End of Education* (New York: William Morrow, 1992).

[148]Ernest R. House, *Schools for Sale: Why Free Market Policies Won't Improve America's Schools and What Will* (New York: Teachers College Press, 1998), p. 23.

advocates of a more complete restructuring of schools and their curricula. They view recent reform efforts as promoting the so-called industrial or factory model of schooling whose goal, using standardized programs, is to prepare students for work instead of for what they believe should be the primary goal—democratic citizenship. They perceive the current model of schooling as imposed on students and teachers; view it as perpetuating the dominance of white, male, European culture; and regard it as undemocratic.[149] Renata Nummela Caine and Geoffrey Caine faulted the factory model of education for what they see as its emphasis on separate subjects, covering subject matter, memorization of facts, and lack of connectedness, averring that the model does not address "relevant skills and attributes students need for this century and the next . . ."[150] Perhaps we should have added an eleventh axiom in Chapter 2: unanimous agreement on the curriculum among all constituencies of the school is an ever-elusive goal.

Alternative Schools.   Some of the current criticisms of public education have resulted in an increase in alternative schools at both the elementary and secondary levels. Alternative education is also known as education by choice or educational options.

Let's briefly consider the rationale for developing and supporting alternative public secondary education. Some young people, perhaps many, cannot profit from the established high school; they cannot learn effectively in a structured setting. The impact of agencies outside the school—the families, peer groups, churches, businesses, and industries—on learners is far greater than that of the school; these agencies should therefore be tapped. In a democratic society families should have a choice as to the type of education they wish their children to receive. Unless the public schools make changes from within, young people will either drop out physically, stay in and drop out mentally, or transfer to private schools.

What, we may ask, is an alternative school? The National Consortium for Options in Public Education described an alternative school as "any school (or minischool) within a community that provides alternative learning experiences to the conventional school program and is available by choice to every family within the community at no extra cost."[151]

Some school systems have established what are called "alternative schools" for young people with behavior problems who cannot function well in regular schools. However, these schools are not alternative schools in the sense described by the National Consortium because they are not available by choice. Students are assigned to

---

[149]See, for example, James A. Banks, ed., *Multicultural Education, Transformative Knowledge, and Action: Historical and Contemporary Perspectives* (New York: Teachers College Press, 1996); Landon E. Beyer and Michael W. Apple, eds., *The Curriculum: Problems, Politics, and Possibilities,* 2nd ed. (Albany, N.Y.: State University of New York Press, 1998); Deborah P. Britzman, *Practice Makes Practice: A Critical Study of Learning to Teach* (Albany, N.Y.: State University of New York Press, 1991); William F. Pinar, William M. Reynolds, Patrick Slattery, and Peter M. Taubman, *Understanding Curriculum: An Introduction to the Study of Historical and Contemporary Curriculum Discourses* (New York: Petert Lang, 1996); and James T. Sears and J. Dan Marshall, eds., *Teaching and Thinking About Curriculum: Critical Inquiries* (New York: Teachers College Press, 1990).

[150]Renate Nummela Caine and Geoffrey Caine, *Making Connections: Teaching and the Human Brain* (Alexandria, Va.: Association for Supervision and Curriculum Development, 1991), pp. 12–13.

[151]National Consortium for Options in Public Education, *The Directory of Alternative Public Schools,* ed. Robert D. Barr (Bloomington, Ind.: Educational Alternatives Project, Indiana University, 1975), p. 2. The 1975 directory is out of print and no longer available.

these schools by the school system and must remain until their behavior improves sufficiently for them to return to their regular schools. (In the case of some alternative schools, however, choice by parents and students must necessarily be restricted by admission requirements and examinations, especially when demand for enrollment exceeds the capacity of the school.)

Free schools, street academies, storefront schools, and schools without walls are examples of alternative education. Among the better known options are the Parkway Program in Philadelphia, which dates back to 1969, and Metro High School in Chicago, which began its program in 1970. In programs of this type, the community, in effect, becomes the school. The school system enlists the cooperation of business, cultural, educational, industrial, and social institutions to serve in the education of young people. The school system draws on the talents of knowledgeable and experienced persons in the community to serve as instructors.

However, education by choice is possible in the more typical school *with* walls. Parents may be accorded the option of placing their children in open-space schools, bilingual schools, or even traditional basic skills schools. In many communities, particularly in urban centers, parents may choose to send their children to a *magnet school,* an institution that offers high-quality specialized programs around a central theme designed to attract students from all parts of the school district. Developed as a means of fostering racial integration, magnet schools offer strong academic or vocational programs in specialties that appeal to young people from all ethnic groups and that are not adequately provided, if at all, in the traditional schools.

The Boston Latin School, Detroit's Cass Technical School, the Bronx High School of Science, New York's High School for the Performing Arts, Brooklyn Tech, Stuyvestant High School in New York City, Lane Technical School in Chicago, Central High School in Philadelphia, and Lowell High School in San Francisco are examples of specialized schools that were forerunners of today's magnet schools. Since attendance at a magnet school is by choice rather than by assignment according to neighborhood boundaries, magnet schools often produce higher student motivation and achievement.

Magnet schools have grown in number in recent years. Dallas, Texas furnishes an example of the rapid growth of magnet schools: since 1976 that community has established seven magnet schools in addition to the already existing Skyline Center: the Arts Magnet High School, the Business and Management Center, the Health Professions High School, the Human Services Center, the Law and Public Administration High School, the Transportation Institute, and the Multiple Careers for special education students. In the mid-1990s Orange County (Orlando, Florida) created magnet schools featuring the tourism industry at its Colonial High School and sports medicine and management at its Jones High School. During the same period Seminole County (Florida) offered a health services magnet program at its Seminole High School.

Extending the magnet school concept on a statewide basis, some states have considered or established residential public secondary schools. Opened in 1980, the prototype of such schools in the United States, the School of Science and Mathematics in Durham, North Carolina, admits juniors and seniors from around the state on a competitive basis and offers them a highly intensive program.

The concept of choice in education is certainly appealing and is in the best democratic tradition. Obviously, growth in alternative schools will have an inevitable impact on the neighborhood and comprehensive schools, illustrating once again the change process in operation.

The American public—concerned that children achieve the fundamentals, that they have access to higher education, and that economy of operation is maintained—is unlikely to support radical departures from the established forms of schooling. The public is not likely to heed proposals for deschooling, that is, surrendering education of the young to businesses and other agencies in the community[152] or for turning fourteen-year olds on the job market. On the other hand, it may well support reasonable alternatives within the existing framework. We will examine some of the more recent and controversial aspects of alternatives in education and school choice in Chapter 14.

REQUIREMENTS FOR GRADUATION

In the mid-1900s, sixteen Carnegie units were the minimum required for graduation from the four-year high school. Only the academically talented carried five or more units per year. Twenty or more units are commonly required throughout the United States, with ten or more "solid" subjects required for the regular diploma.

Idaho, for example, in 1988 increased its requirements for the regular diploma from forty semester credits (twenty units) to forty-two (twenty-one). Of the forty-two credits (twenty-one units), thirty (fifteen) are required. In 1986–1987, Kentucky increased its requirement from eighteen to twenty units, with thirteen units required. Missouri has set twenty-two units with twelve required. Oklahoma mandates twenty, requiring ten of them. Tennessee, too, places its requirement at twenty, with eleven subjects specified.

College-bound students exceed these minimal requirements. They are finding more of their high school program required and less elective as the number of subjects and credits that they must present for admission to college rises. States typically mandate a set (called a "core" by some people) of subjects that students must pass to earn the high school diploma. Some states have added the passing of a test to the requirements for the diploma. Tennessee, for example, administers a proficiency test consisting of four subtests on reading, language, spelling, and mathematics. Florida and Georgia require satisfactory performance on a test of basic skills.

The movement toward raising the requirements for graduation from high school is very much in line with repeated reports that have been issued over the years. The increase in requirements brings to fruition reports of the Committee of Ten (1894), the Harvard Committee (1945), James B. Conant (1959), and several reports of the 1970s and 1980s.

We may expect high schools of the future that have not already strengthened academic requirements to follow moves to increase the number of required courses, decrease the number of electives, raise the score considered passing in the various subjects, raise grades required for eligibility in sports, deemphasize extraclass activities, cover more content, make more effective use of instructional time, set passing of local

---

[152]For example, see Ivan Illich, *Deschooling Society* (New York: Harper & Row, 1971).

and/or state tests as a requirement for the diploma, and improve teaching techniques, including the use of computers and other forms of technology.

An Encouraging Note.   Amid the many studies of the high school in the 1980s (some of which are discussed in the following section of this chapter) is the study carried out by Sara Lawrence Lightfoot.[153] Lightfoot deliberately chose schools that teachers, lay people, and others considered "good." Unlike some studies, Lightfoot's work focused on the positive aspects of the schools rather than their deficiencies. Painting word "portraits" of six high schools, both public and private, she concentrated on the good features of each institution.

She found faculties and administrators who cared for their students, sought to motivate them, and took pride in their achievements. She discovered imperfect institutions struggling to achieve and making carefully considered changes. Though demonstrating quite different and contrasting styles, the leaders of these schools set the tone for the schools. Teachers played a central and dominant role; administrators treated them with respect as persons and professionals. In these schools, Lightfoot observed a high degree of rapport between teachers and students. Students and adults felt a sense of community arising from clear codes of behavior, a secure environment, and positive interrelationships.

Lightfoot's study demonstrated that, contrary to impressions some people hold of high schools, it is possible without much difficulty to find goodness in these institutions. Gerald W. Bracey, author of annual reports on the condition of public education, noting that "the high school graduation rate in the United States has swelled from 3 percent a century ago to 83 percent today," commented, "We cannot rest on any laurels, but we can be proud of that record even as we seek to improve it."[154]

OTHER MODES

As we travel today's educational scene we encounter educators and laypeople who are implementing newer administrative, organizational, and curricular modes that depart from the traditional such as outcome-based education, year-round schooling, and inclusion, which we will examine in Chapter 14.

To summarize Curriculum Present, we discern strong currents and countercurrents. We witness a constant tug-of-war between latter-day progressivist and essentialist educators and parents. We find champions of cooperative learning, integration of the curriculum, whole language, values education, interdisciplinary programs, inclusion and mainstreaming of exceptional children, nongradedness, multicultural education, and portfolio assessments arrayed against advocates of academic learning, separate courses, increased requirements for graduation, increased hours of the school day, increased days of the school year, phonics, traditional assessment, school choice, and national standards of achievement.

---

[153]Sara Lawrence Lightfoot, *The Good High School* (New York: Basic Books, 1983).

[154]Gerald W. Bracey, *Setting the Record Straight: Responses to Misconceptions About Public Education in the United States* (Alexandria, Va.: Association for Supervision and Curriculum Development, 1997), p. 197. See also annual Bracey reports in the *Phi Delta Kappan* starting October 1991 and every October except November 1995.

WHERE WE'RE GOING: CURRICULUM FUTURE

THE ELEMENTARY SCHOOL

Blending of Traditional and Nontraditional Modes

Today we find the elementary school maintaining its emphasis on the basic skills while at the same time addressing other educational, physical, social, and emotional needs of pupils. To the present time the public, through its state legislatures, has given its strong endorsement to programs of state assessment—the testing of youngsters in a number of subject areas, but especially in reading and mathematics. There is some evidence that reaction to testing is setting in. Although testing, both standardized and teacher-made, remains a feature of most schools, by parental and state support if not by educators, other forms of assessment are being incorporated into the curriculum. We will discuss newer techniques of assessment in Chapter 12.

Our hypothetical elementary school has long since restored the walls it removed in open-space days, reverting to the self-contained classroom model. The broad-fields approach will continue to predominate with more attention to integrating the curriculum through the use of units that cut across disciplines. Minimal competencies or outcomes in and across the various disciplines will be spelled out by the school, district, or state so that the direction of the school's program will be more evident. The elementary school will attempt to curb the flight of pupils to private, home, and parochial schools by striving to ensure academic progress in a nurturing environment.

Mastery of the minimal competencies will be expected of all. There is the real danger that those competencies that are labeled "minimal" will become maximal as well. Teachers may be so preoccupied with helping students to achieve minimal competencies and pass the tests that measure attainment of the competencies that they will allow little time to go beyond the minimum. Current pedagogy calls for both individualized and cooperative learning experiences.

The essentialist-progressive pendulum continues to swing. We can detect a move away from subject-centeredness toward child-centeredness. Once schools have satisfied the public's desire for higher test scores and once the schools have demonstrated that pupils have mastered basic and survival skills, they may pay greater attention to the affective domain with its concern for attitudes, feelings, and values. We may find greater interest in individual students, in their learning styles, and in their special learning capacities. A growing body of research that reveals differences in learning strategies of students will affect teaching strategies.[155] We will find greater efforts on the part of administrators to match teachers' instructional styles with pupils' learning styles.[156]

---

[155]See Ned Herrman, "The Creative Brain," *NASSP Bulletin* 66, no. 455 (September 1982): 31–46. See also "Learning Styles and the Brain," *Educational Leadership* 48, no. 2 (October 1990): 4–80.

[156]See Rita S. Dunn and Kenneth J. Dunn, *Teaching Students Through Their Individual Learning Styles: A Practical Approach* (Reston, Va.: Reston Publishing Company, 1978).

NEW DEVELOPMENTS

Innovations will, no doubt, continue to come down the pike. As an observer of curriculum developments for many years, I cannot help being awed at how rapidly some innovations flower into movements with a body of literature, recognized experts, a network of like-minded people, how-to textbooks and other media on the subject, and both preservice and in-service educational activities on the topic. Cooperative learning (discussed in Chapter 11) and whole language (discussed in Chapter 14) fit the pattern well.

The elementary school of the immediate future will be a sophisticated version of the school of the past, essentialistic in character but with progressive overtones. We will see continuing experimentation with varying programs and practices as, for example, current efforts at looping or multiyear grouping in which teachers stay with their students for two or more years.

THE MIDDLE SCHOOL

UNIVERSALITY OF THE MIDDLE SCHOOL

The junior high school has fast faded from the scene. George et al. noted "a new wave of middle schools has swept forth as a result of the national attention on education during the '80s and the comprehensive state legislation that accompanied a raft of critical reports. . . . whole states have endorsed the middle school concept and are encouraging their districts to move toward middle schools."[157]

Remaining junior high schools will continue to be converted into middle schools, in concept if not in name. Just as some senior high schools still cherish the historic name "academy," some newly converted middle schools may continue to call themselves "junior high schools." However, they will have all the characteristics of the modern middle school as described earlier in this chapter. New schools for transescents will be specifically built as middle schools and will be referred to as "middle schools" for "middle school students."

We can anticipate further resuscitation of the core curriculum concept in the form of integrated curricula. Middle schools will continue to use interdisciplinary teams and interdisciplinary instructional units. Schools will revive earlier attempts at block and rotating scheduling. In a period of confusion on moral values and ethical behavior we may look for renewed interest in promoting character education along with the academics.

You may very well take the position that before the middle school reaches universality it may evolve into another institution, as yet undefined. To support your position you can reiterate the axioms cited in Chapter 2: Change is both inevitable and necessary, for it is through change that life forms grow and develop; a school curriculum not only reflects but is a product of its time; and curriculum changes made at an

---

[157]George et al., *The Middle School—And Beyond*, pp. 8, 9.

earlier period of time can exist concurrently with newer curriculum changes at a later period of time.

THE SENIOR HIGH SCHOOL

PROGRAMS AND PRACTICES

Some of the present programs and practices discussed in this and later chapters will undoubtedly continue into the future, at least into the immediate future. Among these are constructivist practices and character/values education (Chapter 6), cooperative learning and recognition of multiple intelligences (Chapter 11), performance-based assessment (Chapter 12), integration of the curriculum (Chapter 13), alternative education, bilingual education, community service, cultural literacy, health education, inclusion, development and assessment of national standards, outcomes-based education, multicultural education, schedule revision, and whole language (Chapter 14). Schools may also become "full-service" institutions that seek to provide for intellectual, physical, vocational, cultural, and social needs of students.

If we were to fashion a mosaic of current innovative curriculum practices advocated by various groups and individuals, pupils would attend nongraded, full-service schools of choice; 220 days, year-round; following an outcomes-based, integrated, interdisciplinary curriculum; working cooperatively; using multicultural materials; pursuing individual goals; constructively creating their own knowledge; developing their multiple intelligences; demonstrating success by exhibiting authentic performance; learning language by a whole language approach; and deemphasizing or abandoning homework, grading, and testing as we now know it. Middle and secondary schools would feature block schedules. High schools would incorporate community service, and school-to-work programs in addition to many of the practices of the other levels.

Counter trends of national and state standards and national and state assessment make the preceding scenario somewhat unrealistic. If past is prologue, some of the current innovative practices will endure well into the twenty-first century; others will fall by the wayside. In an era of site-based management and empowerment of teachers and parents what we are likely to see is a multitude of institutions with varying programs responding to community needs and wishes.

Remembering Axiom 3, we can expect to find in the twenty-first century highly innovative schools (incorporating as yet-to-be-created innovations) on one hand and highly traditional schools on the other. Some of both genres will be termed effective; others, ineffective. More likely, we will find traditional schools that embody innovative practices or, put another way, innovative schools that have retained traditional practices.

TECHNOLOGY IN EDUCATION

Whereas today's schools strive to provide some degree of *technological education,* that is the development of skills using modern technology, *technology in education or technology literacy* as some people call it, will be an earmark of education at all levels. Schools have made strides in enabling their students to demonstrate computer literacy.

They have but scratched the surface of computer-assisted instruction and the use of the Internet as an instructional tool. Further, many schools have yet to be equipped with an adequate number of computers or to go online. We must take note, however, that accessibility to computers in public schools has increased remarkably between 1984–1985 which found 63.5 students per computer and 1996–1997 which recorded 7.3 students per computer.[158] The percentage of public schools with Internet access jumped from thirty-five percent in 1994 to seventy-eight percent in 1997.[159] The Technology Literacy Challenge initiated during the Clinton administration sought to assure that every public school would become connected to the Internet. Data from the National Center for Education Statistics, however, showed a lower rate of Internet access in public schools with a high percentage of low-income students, in public schools with a high percentage of minorities as well as in private schools.[160]

In the future with the aid of state, federal, and private funding we may expect the schools to continue to overcome the lack of hardware and software. When that happens instruction will take a more pronounced turn toward continuous use of technology. Technology will permeate the curriculum. Students will possess and make use of computer skills in studying a wide range of subjects. Through e-mail they will be put in contact with peers and experts in various fields throughout the world. Through the Internet they will have a world of learning at their fingertips.

Schools at all levels will continue to incorporate technological skills into the curriculum. They will give witness to the fact that computer skills have become one of the basic survival skills necessary in a technology-driven society as it enters the twenty-first century. The bewildering array of innovative and rapidly changing devices to be mastered mandates an emphasis on technology from preschool through graduate school and on into adult education. To help meet the challenge of creating technologically literate citizens the National Educational Technology Standards Project of the International Society for Technology in Education has developed a set of standards for prekindergarten through twelfth grade.[161]

LOOKING FURTHER AHEAD

A growing number of individuals both inside and outside of the academic world are identified by the rather ambiguous label of "futurist." One of the earlier and better known persons in this group is Alvin Toffler, whose books, *Future Shock* and *The Third Wave*, provoked many of us to contemplate problems of the future and to begin considering ways to solve them.[162] High on the agenda of any futurist are problems like population control, health needs, preservation of the environment, housing needs, adequate food supplies, demands for energy, and the use and abuse of technology.

[158]Source: Market Data Retrieval, Shelton, Conn., as cited in U.S. Bureau of the Census, *Statistical Abstract of the United States 1997* (Washington, D.C.: U.S. Government Printing Office, 1997), Table 263, p. 171.

[159]National Center for Education Statistics, "Internet Access in Public and Private Schools," *The Condition of Education, 1998,* (Washington, D.C. U.S. Department of Education, National Center for Education Statistics, 1998), p. 40.

[160]Ibid.

[161]For *NETS Standards for Students* see International Society for Technology in Education Web site: http://cents.iste.ðrg.

[162]Alvin Toffler, *Future Shock* (New York: Random House, 1970); *The Third Wave* (New York: William Morrow, 1980).

Some educational futurists view the new technology as aiding the teacher and administrator to provide a more effective education within the school setting. Others predict what amounts to a type of deschooling. Almost two decades ago Peter Sleight, for example, reported on the type of deschooling that might be effected by the computer age:

> It may be that children won't attend schools at all, but attend classes in their homes, taking lessons through the computer with the teacher talking to them through a video image.
>
> Through the same network, the teacher will know whether a student is tuned in and can take "attendance" in the old-fashioned sense.
>
> Homework for the children will also be changed. No longer will they be bringing home textbooks and doing assignments on paper. Instead, they may plug into the school data base to receive their assignments, execute them on the computer screen at home and "send" it to their teacher via the computer hook-up.[163]

In the relatively few years since Sleight's prophetic comments in 1980 the use of scanning, e-mail and faxing have become common in personal, business, and educational life. Through these techniques students can share the products of their work with each other and, in fact, with the world, if desired. Twelve years later Perelman moved beyond Sleight's predictions about deschooling and sought replacement of the traditional public school system with new techniques effected by technology, which he called "hyperlearning."[164]

As you will note in Chapter 14 where we discuss alternatives in education, some schools, particularly those in rural and less accessible areas, are already implementing "distance learning," instruction at home via computer networks. Computers can allow ill students to keep up with classwork and interact with their teachers and classmates. Members of World Community College, an association of colleges and universities, offer college courses via distance learning.

If the day comes when schools are eliminated and instruction proceeds through the medium of the computer, what will happen to the notion of face-to-face interaction between teacher and students and between student and student? We recognize the movement toward "interactive" learning by means of technology. Will interacting via a computer screen, fax, and printer enable learners to achieve the multiple goals of schooling? How will students learn to socialize with each other? What will happen to multicultural, multiethnic education? How will boys and girls learn to live in a pluralistic society? What will happen to cooperative learning? What disposition will be made of extraclass activities and athletics formerly under the aegis of the school?

Perhaps we might wish to conceptualize computerized schooling as consuming only a portion of the day, with other forms of education in the school or community filling the remaining portion. At any rate, you may be safe in postulating that the elementary, middle, and senior high school as we know them today and as we will know them in the immediate future may well evolve into decidedly different kinds of institutions in the distant future.

---

[163]Peter Sleight, "Information Services: Possibilities Are Endless," *Fort Lauderdale News and Sun-Sentinel,* July 27, 1980, Section H, p. 3.

[164]Perelman, School's Out.

PUBLIC AND PRIVATE ENROLLMENTS

It is not likely that we will return to the days when ninety percent of school-age children were enrolled in public education and ten percent in private. Private school enrollments have edged up to approximately thirteen percent. Recent figures of school enrollments showed 46.8 million pupils in public schools, projected to increase to 48.2 million by 2008 whereas private school enrollments numbered 5.9 million, expected to grow to 6.1 million by 2008.[165] We are more likely to see continued movements to a larger percentage of the public, if the economy permits, seeking alternatives to public education in the form of private schools, parochial schools, charter schools, and home-schooling. However, public education can survive, even flourish, given adequate funding, by refining its practices, making known its successes, and meeting the competition head-on.

SUMMARY

As curriculum planners proceed with their task of developing the curriculum, they must also decide on the organizational structure within which programs will be implemented. At the beginning of this chapter we visualized as illustrative examples three schools—elementary, middle, and senior high. Like their actual counterparts, our hypothetical schools have undergone numerous internal changes.

This chapter traced some of the past organizational patterns at each level, described current organizational structures, and discussed possible and probable future developments. On the elementary level we reviewed the graded school, the activity curriculum, continuous progress plans, and open-education/open-space plans. At the middle school level we looked at its predecessor, the junior high school, and at a variety of proposals for that level, including the core curriculum. We studied several organizational plans at the senior high school level, including the subject matter curriculum, the broad-fields curriculum, team teaching, differentiated staffing, flexible and modular scheduling, and the nongraded high school.

The elementary school currently emphasizes teaching basic and thinking skills and providing for students with special needs. Some schools are trying innovative departures from traditional practices. The middle school presently offers programs that have been adapted to meet the needs of preadolescents. A prevailing practice is the use of interdisciplinary teams. The senior high school is involved in efforts to establish a quality comprehensive model, to furnish a number of alternatives both within and outside the school system, and to reinforce higher requirements for graduation.

In the near future the elementary school, if it is to retain public support must continue emphasis on the basic skills, although it will intensify some of the fundamental overtones of child-centeredness. At this level we noted cooperative learning in practice. The middle school has generally become the universal model for the education of

---

[165]National Center for Education Statistics, "Elementary and Secondary School Enrollment," Indicator 42, *The Condition of Education 1998* (Washington, D.C.: U.S. Government Printing Office, 1998), Web site http://nces.gov/pubs98/condition98/c9842a01.html.

preadolescents. We may expect renewed efforts at integrating the curriculum, interdisciplinary teams, and block/rotating scheduling. The comprehensive high school will share the spotlight with magnet schools and other alternatives. The high school will meet demands for reform and restructuring by adopting some of the recommendations of national studies and organizations and by incorporating some of the innovative practices found in many schools.

We can expect the ubiquitous computer, videocassette recorder, laser videodisc, and other wonders of technology to literally revolutionize education at all levels. Curricula will need to respond substantively—and organizationally—to current and emerging social problems of growing concern to the American people.

QUESTIONS FOR DISCUSSION

1. What are some ways of organizing and implementing the curriculum that have been repeated through American educational history?
2. Why have the graded school and the subject matter curriculum been so enduring?
3. Which of the present curriculum programs and practices do you believe are only temporary and will disappear in the future? Why?
4. How can curriculum planners reconcile conflicting proposals for reform of the high school?
5. What programs and practices would you add to the second and third sections of this chapter, "Where We Are: Curriculum Present" and "Where We're Going: Curriculum Future"?

SUPPLEMENTARY EXERCISES

1. Explain what is meant by the activity curriculum. Critique this approach.
2. Describe advantages and disadvantages of the nongraded elementary school.
3. Look up the Eight-Year Study and write a report summarizing its methodology and findings.
4. Describe one or more core programs from either the professional literature or from a school with which you have firsthand experience.
5. Prepare a paper on the topic: "Shall We Group Pupils?" Whether the answer is yes or no, state reasons. If yes, explain how you would group.
6. Describe advantages and disadvantages of the nongraded elementary (continuous progress) school.
7. Describe advantages and disadvantages of the nongraded high school.
8. Describe one or more plans for team teaching and show its advantages and disadvantages.
9. Write a paper, citing at least three references, that accounts for the continuing emphasis on the basic skills.
10. Write a paper on the question of the placement of fifth grade in the educational system—in the elementary school or middle school?
11. Write a paper on the question of the placement of ninth grade in the educational system—in middle school or high school.

12. State pros and cons of specialized versus comprehensive high schools and show your position.
13. Explain what is meant by a broad-fields curriculum. Critique this approach.
14. Write a paper on the question "Why did the decade from 1955 to 1965 produce so many innovations?"
15. Read and summarize one of the national reports of the 1980s or 1990s on reform of the high school.
16. Read and summarize one of the national reports of the 1980s or 1990s on reform of the elementary school.
17. Evaluate movements for school reform in your state as to: process, substance, purpose, strengths, and weaknesses.
18. State whether you believe the school (choose any level) should limit itself to cognitive learning. Give reasons for the position taken.
19. Explain what is meant by differentiated staffing and show its advantages and disadvantages.
20. Distinguish between traditional, flexible, modular, and block scheduling and state the purposes of each.
21. Define "magnet school," state its purposes, and report on one successful example of such a school.
22. Find out if there is a residential public secondary school in your state. If there is, describe its program, its student body, its admission requirements, and its costs of operation.
23. Write a paper on the uses of computers in education.
24. Play the role of futurist and predict what may happen in curriculum organization and implementation ten years hence.

BIBLIOGRAPHY

Adler, Mortimer J. *Paideia: Problems and Possibilities.* New York: Macmillan, 1983.

———. *The Paideia Program: An Educational Syllabus.* New York: Macmillan, 1984.

———. *The Paideia Proposal: An Educational Manifesto.* New York: Macmillan, 1982.

Aikin, Wilford M. *The Story of the Eight-Year Study.* New York: Harper & Row, 1942.

Alberty, Harold B. and Alberty, Elsie J. *Reorganizing the High-School Curriculum,* 3rd ed. New York: Macmillan, 1962.

Alexander, William M. and George, Paul S. *The Exemplary Middle School.* New York: Holt, Rinehart and Winston, 1981.

———, Williams, Emmett L., Compton, Mary, Hines, Vynce A., and Prescott, Dan. *The Emergent Middle School,* 2nd., enl. ed. New York: Holt, Rinehart and Winston, 1969.

———. "Guidelines for the Middle School We Need Now." *The National Elementary School* Principal 51, no. 3 (November 1971): 79–89.

Anderson, Robert H. and Pavan, Barbara Nelson. *Nongradedness: Helping It to Happen.* Lancaster, Pa.: Technomic, 1993.

Association for Supervision and Curriculum Development. *Effective Schools and School Improvement.* Alexandria, Va.: Association for Supervision and Curriculum Development, 1989.

———. *Teaching Thinking.* Alexandria, Va.: Association for Supervision and Curriculum Development, 1989.

Banks, James A., ed. *Multicultural Education, Transformative Knowledge, and Action: Historical and Contemporary Perspectives.* New York: Teachers College Press, 1996.

Beane, James A. *A Middle School Curriculum: From Rhetoric to Reality.* Columbus, Ohio: National Middle School Association, 1990.

Beggs, David W., III, ed. *Team Teaching: Bold New Venture.* Bloomington: Indiana University Press, 1967.

——— and Buffie, Edward G., eds. *Nongraded Schools in Action: Bold New Venture.* Bloomington: Indiana University Press, 1967.

Bell, Terrel H. "Reflections One Decade After *A Nation at Risk*," *Phi Delta Kappan* 74, no. 8 (April 1993): 592–597.

Beyer, Barry K. "Critical Thinking: What Is It?" *Social Education* 49, no. 4 (April 1985): 276.

Beyer, Landon E. and Apple, Michael W., eds. *The Curriculum: Problems, Politics, and Possibilities*, 2nd ed. Albany, N.Y.: State University of New York Press, 1998.

Boyer, Ernest L. *High School: A Report on Secondary Education in America*. New York: Harper & Row, 1983.

Bracey, Gerald W. *Setting the Record Straight: Responses To Misconceptions About Public Education in the United States*. Alexandria, Va.: Association for Supervision and Curriculum Development, 1997.

Brandt, Ronald S., ed. *Content of the Curriculum*. 1988 Yearbook. Alexandria, Va.: Association for Supervision and Curriculum Development, 1988.

Britzman, Deborah P. *Practice Makes Practice: A Critical Study of Learning to Teach*. Albany, N.Y.: State University of New York Press, 1991.

Brooks, Kenneth, "The Middle Schools—A National Survey." *Middle School Journal* 9, no. 1 (February 1978): 6–7.

Brown, B. Frank. *The Appropriate Placement School: A Sophisticated Nongraded Curriculum*. West Nyack, N.Y.: Parker, 1965.

———. *Education by Appointment: New Approaches to Independent Study*. West Nyack, N.Y.: Parker, 1968.

———. *The Nongraded High School*. Englewood Cliffs, N.J.: Prentice-Hall, 1963.

Brown, Jerry L. "On Teaching Thinking Skills in Elementary and Middle School," *Phi Delta Kappan* 64, no. 10 (June 1983): 709–714.

Buffie, Edward G. and Jenkins, John M. *Curriculum Development in Nongraded Schools: Bold New Venture*. Bloomington: Indiana University Press, 1971.

Burton, William H. *The Guidance of Learning Activities: A Summary of the Principles of Teaching Based on the Growth of the Learner*, 3rd ed. Englewood Cliffs, N.J.: Prentice-Hall, 1962.

Bush, Robert N. and Allen, Dwight W. *A New Design for High School Education: Assuming a Flexible Schedule*. New York: McGraw-Hill, 1964.

Business Roundtable, The. *Essential Components of a Successful Education System*. New York: The Business Roundtable, 1990.

Caine, Renata Numela and Caine, Geoffrey. *Making Connections: Teaching and the Human Brain*. Alexandria, Va.: Association for Supervision and Curriculum Development, 1991.

Calvin, Allen D., ed. *Programmed Instruction: Bold New Venture*. Bloomington: Indiana University Press, 1969.

Chamberlin, L. J. and Girona, R. "Our Children Are Changing." *Educational Leadership* 33, no. 4 (January 1976): 301–305.

Charles, C. M., Gast, David K., Servey, Richard E., and Burnside, Houston M. *Schooling, Teaching, and Learning: American Education*. St. Louis: The C. V. Mosby Company, 1978.

Coleman, James S. chairman. Panel on Youth of the President's Science Advisory Committee. *Youth: Transition to Adulthood*. Washington, D.C.: Superintendent of Documents, U.S. Government Printing Office, 1973; Chicago: University of Chicago Press, 1974.

Commission on the Reorganization of Secondary Education. *Cardinal Principles of Secondary Education*. Bulletin 35. Washington, D.C.: U.S. Office of Education, 1918.

Conant, James B. *The American High School Today*. New York: McGraw-Hill, 1959.

———. *The Comprehensive High School*. New York: McGraw-Hill, 1967.

———. *Recommendations for Education in the Junior High School Years*. Princeton, N.J.: Educational Testing Service, 1960.

Conference Board, The. *Ten Years After A Nation at Risk*. New York: The Conference Board, 1993.

Costa, Arthur L., ed. *Developing Minds: A Resource Book for Teaching Thinking*. Alexandria, Va.: Association for Supervision and Curriculum Development, 1985.

——— and Lowery, Lawrence. *Techniques for Teaching Thinking*. Pacific Grove, Calif.: Midwest Publications Critical Thinking Press, 1990.

Cuban, Larry. "At-Risk Students: What Teachers and Principals Can Do." *Educational Leadership* 70, no. 6 (February 1989): 29–32.

———. "Reforming Again, Again, and Again." *Educational Researcher* 19, no. 1 (January–February 1990): 3–13.

"Curriculum Development in the U.S. and the World." *Educational Leadership* 44, no. 4 (December 1986–January 1987): 3–79.

deBono, Edward. "The Direct Teaching of Thinking As a Skill," *Phi Delta Kappan* 64, no. 10 (June 1983): 703–708.

Doyle, Denis and Levine, Marsha, "Magnet Schools: Choice and Quality in Public Education." *Phi Delta Kappan* 66, no. 4 (December 1984): 265–270.

Dunn, Rita S. and Dunn, Kenneth J. *Teaching Students Through Their Individual Learning Styles: A Practical Approach*. Reston, Va.: Reston Publishing Company, 1978.

Ebel, Robert L. "What Are Schools For?" *Phi Delta Kappan* 54, no. 1 (September 1972): 3–7.

Educational Policies Commission. *Education for All American Youth*. Washington, D.C.: National Education Association, 1944.

Eichhhorn, Donald H. *The Middle School*. New York: Center for Applied Research in Education, 1966.

Fantini, Mario, ed. *Alternative Education: A Source Book for Parents, Teachers, and Administrators*. Garden City, N.Y.: Anchor Books, 1976.

————. "Alternatives within Public Schools." *Phi Delta Kappan* 54, no. 7 (March 1973): 444–448.

————. *Public Schools of Choice: Alternatives in Education.* New York: Simon and Schuster, 1973.

————. "The What, Why, and Where of the Alternatives Movement." *The National Elementary School Principal* 52, no. 6 (April 1973): 14–22.

Faunce, Roland C. and Bossing, Nelson L. *Developing the Core Curriculum.* Englewood Cliffs, N.J.: Prentice-Hall, 1951.

Firestone, William A., Furhman, Susan H., and Kirst, Michael W. *The Progress of Reform: An Appraisal of State Education Initiatives.* New Brunswick, N.J.: Center for Policy Research in Education, Eagleton Institute of Politics, Rutgers, The State University of New Jersey, 1989.

Foshay, Arthur W. *Curriculum for the 70's: An Agenda for Invention.* Washington, D.C.: National Education Association, Center for the Study of Instruction, 1970.

Fraser, Dorothy M. *Deciding What to Teach.* Washington, D.C.: Project on the Instructional Program of the Public Schools, National Education Association, 1963.

Fry, Edward B. *Teaching Machines and Programmed Instruction: An Introduction.* New York: McGraw-Hill, 1963.

Frymier, Jack. *A Study of Students at Risk: Collaborating To Do Research.* Bloomington, Ind.: Phi Delta Kappa, 1989.

———— and Gansneder, Bruce. "The Phi Delta Kappa Study of Students at Risk." *Phi Delta Kappan* 71, no. 2 (October 1989): 142–146.

Gatewood, Thomas E. and Dilg, Charles A. *The Middle School We Need.* Alexandria, Va.: Association for Supervision and Curriculum Development. 1975.

George, Paul S. and Lawrence, Gordon. *Handbook for Middle School Teaching.* Glenview, Ill.: Scott, Foresman, 1982.

————, Stevenson, Chris, Thompson, Julia, and Beane, James. *The Middle School and Beyond.* Alexandria, Va.: Association for Supervision and Curriculum Development, 1992.

Glasser, William. *The Quality School: Managing Students Without Coercion,* 2nd ed. New York: HarperPerennial, 1992.

————. *Schools Without Failure.* New York: Harper & Row, 1969.

Goodlad, John I. *A Place Called Schools: Prospects for the Future.* New York: McGraw-Hill, 1984.

———— and Anderson, Robert H. *The Nongraded Elementary School,* rev. ed. New York: Teachers College Press, 1987.

Grambs, Jean D., Noyce, Clarence G., Patterson, Franklin, and Robertson, John. *The Junior High School We Need.* Alexandria, Va.: Association for Supervision and Curriculum Development, 1961.

Hansen, John H. and Hearn, Arthur C. *The Middle School Program.* Chicago: Rand McNally, 1971.

Harrison, Charles H. *Student Service: The New Carnegie Unit.* Princeton, N.J.: The Carnegie Foundation for the Advancement of Teaching, 1987.

Harvard Committee. *General Education in a Free Society.* Cambridge, Mass.: Harvard University Press, 1945.

Hass, Glen. *Curriculum Planning: A New Approach,* 5th ed. Boston: Allyn and Bacon, 1987.

Hassett, Joseph D. and Weisberg, Arline. *Open Education: Alternatives Within Our Tradition.* Englewood Cliffs, N.J.: Prentice-Hall, 1972.

Herrman, Ned. "The Creative Brain." *NASSP Bulletin* 66, no. 455 (September 1982): 31–46.

Hillson, Maurie H. "The Nongraded School: A Dynamic Concept," in David W. Beggs III and Edward G. Buffie, eds. *Nongraded Schools in Action: Bold New Venture.* Bloomington: Indiana University Press, 1967.

Hillson, Maurie and Bongo, Joseph. *Continuous-Progress Education: A Practical Approach.* Palo Alto, Calif.: Science Research Associates, 1971.

House, Ernest R. *Schools for Sale: Why Free Market Policies Won't Improve America's Schools and What Will.* New York: Teachers College Pres,s 1998.

Hunkins, Francis P. *Curriculum Development: Program Planning and Improvement.* Columbus, Ohio: Charles E. Merrill, 1980.

Illich, Ivan. *Deschooling Society.* New York: Harper & Row, 1971.

"Improving Learning Conditions for Students at Risk." *Educational Leadership* 44, no. 6 (March 1987): 3–80.

"Integrating the Curriculum." *Educational Leadership* 49, no. 2 (October 1991): 4–75.

"Integrating Technology Into the Curriculum." *Educational Leadership* 56, no. 5 (February 1999): 6–91.

Jackson, Philip W., ed. *Handbook of Research on Curriculum.* New York: Macmillan, 1992.

Jacobs, Heidi Hayes, ed. *Interdisciplinary Curriculum Design and Implementation.* Alexandria, Va.: Association for Supervision and Curriculum Development, 1989.

Joyce, Bruce. "Models for Teaching Thinking," *Educational Leadership* 42, no. 8 (May 1985): 4–7.

Kilpatrick, William H. *Foundations of Method: Informal Talks on Teaching.* New York: Macmillan, 1925.

————. "The Project Method." *Teachers College Record* 19, no. 4 (September 1918): 319–335.

Kindred, Leslie W., Wolotkiewicz, Rita J., Mickelson, John M., and Coplein, Leonard E. *The Middle School Curriculum,* 2nd ed. Boston: Allyn and Bacon, 1981.

Kohl, Herbert R. *The Open Classroom: A Practical Guide to a New Way of Teaching.* New York: New York Review, distributed by Random House, 1969.

Kohut, Sylvester, Jr. *The Middle School: A Bridge Between Elementary and High Schools,* 2nd ed. Washington, D.C.: National Education Association, 1988.

Koos, Leonard V. *Junior High School,* enl. ed. Boston: Ginn and Company, 1927.

————. *Junior High School Trends.* Westport, Conn.: Greenwood Press, 1955.

"Learning Styles and the Brain," *Educational Leadership* 48, no. 2 (October 1990): 4–80.

Leeper, Robert R., ed. *Middle School in the Making: Readings from Educational Leadership.* Washington, D.C.: Association for Supervision and Curriculum Development, 1974.

Leonard, George. *Education and Ecstasy* with *The Great School Reform Hoax.* Berkeley, Calif.: North Atlantic Books, 19897, pp. 241–263.

Lightfoot, Sara Lawrence. *The Good High School.* New York: Basic Books, 1985.

Lounsbury, John H. *Middle School Education as I See It.* Columbus, Ohio: Middle School Association, 1984.

———— and Vars, *Gordon F. A Curriculum for the Middle School Years.* New York: Harper & Row, 1978.

Lowery, Lawrence. *Thinking and Learning.* Pacific Grove, Calif.: Midwest Publications Critical Thinking Press, 1990.

Lund, Leonard and Wild, Cathleen. *Ten Years After A Nation at Risk.* New York: Conference Board, 1993.

Manlove, Donald C. and Beggs, David W., III. *Flexible Scheduling: Bold New Venture.* Bloomington: Indiana University Press, 1965.

Martin, John Henry. *The Education of Adolescents.* Report of the National Panel on High Schools and Adolescent Education. Washington, D.C.: United States Office of Education, 1976.

Marzano, Robert et al. *Dimensions of Thinking: A Framework for Curriculum and Instruction.* Alexandria, Va.: Association for Supervision and Curriculum Development, 1988.

Meier, Deborah. *The Power of Their Ideas: Lessons for America from a Small School in Harlem.* Boston: Beacon Press, 1995.

Meriam, Junius L. *Child Life and the Curriculum.* Yonkers, N.Y.: World Book Company, 1920.

Miller, John P. and Seller, Wayne. *Curriculum: Perspectives and Practice.* White Plains, N.Y.: Longman, 1985.

Miller, John W. "Ten Reform Reports That Can Change Your School." *Principal* 66, no. 2 (November 1986): 26–28.

Miller, Richard I., ed. *The Nongraded School: Analysis and Study.* New York: Harper & Row, 1967.

Mitchell, Richard. *The Graves of Academe.* Boston: Little, Brown, 1981.

Monro, Lorraine. *Nothing's Impossible: Leadership Lessons from Inside and Outside the Classroom.* New York: Times Books, 1997.

Morris, Robert C., ed. "At-Risk Youth." *Thresholds in Education* 16, no. 2 (May 1990): 1–33.

Morrison, George S. *Contemporary Curriculum K–8.* Boston: Allyn and Bacon, 1993.

Murray, Evelyn M. and Wilhour, Jane R. *The Flexible Elementary School: Practical Guidelines for Developing a Nongraded Program.* West Nyack, N.Y.: Parker, 1971.

National Association for Core Curriculum. *Core Today: Rationale and Implications.* Kent, Ohio: National Association for Core Curriculum, 1973.

National Center for Education Statistics. *The Condition of Education 1998.* Washington, D.C.: U.S. Department of Education, National Center for Education Statistics, 1998.

National Commission on Excellence in Education. David P. Gardner, Chairman. *A Nation at Risk: The Imperative for Educational Reform.* Washington, D.C.: U.S. Government Printing Office, 1983.

National Commission on the Reform of Secondary Education. *The Reform of Secondary Education: A Report to the Public and the Profession.* New York: McGraw-Hill, 1973.

National Education Association. *Report of the Committee of Ten on Secondary School Studies.* New York: American Book Company, 1894.

National Middle School Association. *Perspectives: Middle School Education, 1964–1984.* Columbus, Ohio: National Middle School Association, 1984.

Norris, Stephen and Ennis, Robert. *Evaluating Critical Thinking.* Pacific Grove, Calif.: Midwest Publications Critical Thinking Press, 1990.

Ogden, Evelyn and Germinario, Vito. *The At-Risk Student: Answers for Educators.* Lancaster, Pa.: Technomic Publishing Company, 1988.

Oliva, Peter F. *The Secondary School Today,* 2nd ed. New York: Harper & Row, 1972.

Orlich, Donald C. "Education Reforms: Mistakes, Misconceptions, Miscues." *Phi Delta Kappan* 70, no. 7 (March 1989): 512–517.

Parkhurst, Helen. *Education on the Dalton Plan.* New York: E. P. Dutton, 1922.

Passow, A. Harry, ed. *Curriculum Crossroads.* New York: Teachers College, Columbia University, 1962.

————. "Reforming America's High Schools." *Phi Delta Kappan* 56, no. 9 (May 1975): 587–596.

————. "Tackling the Reform Reports of the 1980s." *Phi Delta Kappan* 65, no. 10 (June 1984): 674–683.

Paul, Robert. *Critical Thinking: What Every Person Needs to Survive in a Rapidly Changing World.* Rohnert Park, Calif.: Center for Critical Thinking and Moral Critique. Sonoma State University, 1990.

Perelman, Lewis J. *School's Out: Hyperlearning, the New Technology, and the End of Education.* New York: William Morrow, 1992.

Peterson, Penelope L. and Walberg, Herbert J., eds. *Research on Teaching: Concepts, Findings, and Implications.* Berkeley, Calif.: McCutchan, 1979.

Phenix, Philip H. *Realms of Meaning: A Philosophy of the Curriculum for General Education.* New York: McGraw-Hill, 1964.

Pinar, William F., Reynolds, William M., Slattery, Patrick, and Taubman, Peter M. *Understanding Curriculum: An Introduction to the Study of Historical and Contemporary Curriculum Discourses.* New York: Peter Lang, 1996.

Popper, Samuel H. *The American Middle School: An Organizational Analysis.* Waltham, Mass.: Blaisdell, 1967.

Powell, Arthur G., Farrar, Eleanor, and Cohen, David K. *The Shopping Mall High School: Winners and Losers in the Educational Marketplace.* Boston: Houghton Mifflin, 1985.

Pratt, David. *Curriculum: Design and Development.* New York: Harcourt Brace Jovanovich, 1980.

Proctor, John H. and Smith, Kathryn. "IGE and Open Education: Are They Compatible?" *Phi Delta Kappan* 55, no. 8 (April 1974): 564–566.

"The Quest for Higher Standards." *Educational Leadership* 48, no. 5 (February 1991): 3–69.

Rafferty, Max. *What They Are Doing to Your Children.* New York: New American Library, 1964.

Ratnesar, Ramesh. "Lost in the Middle." *TIME* 152, no. 11 (September 14, 1998): 60–62.

Resnick, Lauren B. and Klopfer, Leopold E., eds. *Toward the Thinking Curriculum: Current Cognitive Research.* 1989 Yearbook. Alexandria, Va.: Association for Supervision and Curriculum Development, 1989.

"Restructuring Schools: What's Really Happening." *Educational Leadership* 48, no. 8 (May 1991): 3–76.

Roberts, Arthur D. and Cawelti, Gordon. *Redefining General Education in the American High School.* Alexandria, Va.: Association for Supervision and Curriculum Development, 1984.

Rollins, Sidney P. *Developing Nongraded Schools.* Itasca, Ill.: F. E. Peacock, 1968.

Rubin, Louis, ed. *Current Movements and Instructional Technology.* Boston: Allyn and Bacon, 1977.

———. *Curriculum Handbook: The Disciplines, Current Movements, and Instructional Methodology.* Boston: Allyn and Bacon, 1977.

———. "Open Education: A Short Critique," in Louis Rubin, ed., *Curriculum Handbook: The Disciplines, Current Movements, and Instructional Methodology.* Boson: Allyn and Bacon, 1977, p. 375.

"The School in the Middle." *NASSP Bulletin* 67, no. 463 (May 1983): 1–82.

"School Reform: What We Have Learned." *Educational Leadership* 52, no. 5 (February 1995): 4–48.

Sears, James T. and Marshall, J. an, eds. *Teaching Thinking About Curriculum: Critical Inquiries.* New York: Teachers College Press, 1990.

Shanker, Albert. "The End of the Traditional Model of Schooling—and a Proposal for Using Incentives to Restructure Our Public Schools." *Phi Delta Kappan* 71, no. 5 (January 1990): 344–357.

Shearer, William J. *The Grading of Schools.* New York: H. P. Smith, 1898.

Singer, Ira J. "What Team Teaching Really Is," in David W. Beggs III, ed., *Team Teaching: Bold New Venture.* Bloomington: Indiana University Press, 1964, p. 16.

Sirotnik, Kenneth A. "What Goes on in Classrooms? Is This the Way We Want It?" In Landon E. Beyer and Michael W. Apple, eds. *The Curriculum: Problems, Politics, and Possibilities,* 2nd ed. Albany, N.Y.: State University of New York Press, 1998.

Sizer, Theodore R. *Horace's Compromise: The Dilemma of the American High School.* Boston: Houghton Mifflin, 1984.

———. *Horace's School: Redesigning the American High School.* Boston: Houghton Mifflin, 1992.

Slavin, Robert E., Karweit, Nancy L., and Madden, Nancy A. *Effective Programs for Students at Risk.* Needham Heights, Mass.: Allyn and Bacon, 1989.

——— and Madden, Nancy A. "What Works for Students at Risk: A Research Synthesis." *Educational Leadership* 70, no. 6 (February 1989): 4–13.

Sleight, Peter. "Information Services: Possibilities Are Endless." *Fort Lauderdale News and Sun-Sentinel,* July 27, 1980, Section H, p. 3.

Smith, B. Othanel, Stanley, William O., and Shores, J. Harlan. *Fundamentals of Curriculum Development,* rev. ed. New York: Harcourt Brace Jovanovich, 1957.

A special section on middle schools. *Phi Delta Kappan* 72, no. 10 (June 1991): 738–773.

Stephens, Lillian S. *The Teacher's Guide to Open Education.* New York: Holt, Rinehart and Winston, 1974.

Stevenson, Chris and Carr, Judy F., eds. *Integrated Studies in the Middle Grades: Dancing Through Walls.* New York: Teachers College Press, 1993.

"Students At Risk." *Educational Leadership* 50, no. 4 (December 1992/January 1993): 4–63.

Swartz, Robert and Perkins, David. *Teaching Thinking: Issues and Approaches.* Pacific Grove, Calif.: Midwest Publications Critical Thinking Press, 1990.

Tanner, Daniel and Tanner, Laurel. *Curriculum Development: Theory into Practice,* 3rd ed. Englewood Cliffs, N.J.: Prentice-Hall, 1995.

"Teaching Thinking Skills in the Curriculum. *Educational Leadership* 39, no. 1 (October 1981): 6–54.

"Teaching Thinking Throughout the Curriculum." *Educational Leadership* 45, no. 7 (April 1988): 3–30.

"Thinking Skills in the Curriculum." *Educational Leadership* 42, no. 1 (September 1984): 3–87.

Timar, Thomas B. and Kirp, David L. "Education Reform in the 1980s: Lessons from the States." *Educational Leadership* 70, no. 7 (March 1989): 504–511.

Toch, Thomas. *In the Name of Excellence: The Struggle to Reform the Nation's Schools. Why It's Failing and What Should Be Done.* New York: Oxford University Press, 1991.

———— with Litton, Nancy and Cooper, Matthew. "Schools that Work." *U.S. News and World Report* 110, no. 20 (May 27, 1991): 58–66.

Toffler, Alvin. *Future Shock.* New York: Random House, 1970.

————. *The Third Wave.* New York: William Morrow, 1980.

Trump, J. Lloyd. "Flexible Scheduling—Fad or Fundamental?" *Phi Delta Kappan* 44, no. 8 (May 1963): 370.

———— and Baynham, Dorsey. *Focus on Change: Guide to Better Schools.* Chicago: Rand McNally, 1961.

———— and Miller, Delmas F. *Secondary School Curriculum Improvement: Meeting the Challenges of the Times,* 3rd ed. Boston: Allyn and Bacon, 1979.

Tyler, Ralph W. "Curriculum Development Since 1900." *Educational Leadership* 38, no. 8 (May 1981): 598–601.

Van Til, William, Vars, Gordon F., and Lounsbury, John H. *Modern Education for the Junior High School Years,* 2nd ed. Indianapolis, Ind.: Bobbs-Merrill, 1967.

Vars, Gordon F. "Integrated Curriculum in Historical Perspective." *Educational Leadership* 49, no. 2 (October 1991): 14–15.

————, Gordon F., ed. *Common Learnings: Core and Interdisciplinary Team Approaches.* Scranton, Pa.: International Textbook Company, 1969.

Virginia, State of. *Tentative Course of Study for the Core Curriculum of Virginia Secondary Schools.* Richmond Va.: State Board of Education, 1934.

Von Haden, Herbert I. and King, Jean Marie. *Educational Innovator's Guide.* Worthington, Ohio: Charles A. Jones, 1974.

Weeks, Ruth Mary. *A Correlated Curriculum: A Report of the Committee on Correlation of the National Council of Teachers of English.* New York: D. Appleton-Century, 1936.

Weinstock, Ruth. *The Greening of the High School.* New York: Educational Facilities Laboratories, 1973.

"When Teachers Tackle Thinking Skills." *Educational Leadership* 42, no. 3 (November 1984): 3–72.

White, Emerson E. "Isolation and Unification as Bases of Courses of Study," *Second Yearbook of the National Herbart Society for the Scientific Study of Teaching.* Bloomington, Ind.: Pentograph Printing and Stationery Co., 1986, pp. 12–13.

Wiles, Jon and Bondi, Joseph. *The Essential Middle School,* 2nd ed. New York: Macmillan, 1993.

Wiles, Kimball. *The Changing Curriculum of the American High School.* Englewood Cliffs, N.J.: Prentice-Hall, 1963.

———— and Patterson, Franklin. *The High School We Need.* Alexandria, Va.: Association for Supervision and Curriculum Development, 1959.

Wolfe, Arthur B. *The Nova Plan for Instruction.* Fort Lauderdale, Fla.: Broward County Board of Public Instruction, 1962.

Wright, Grace S. *Block-Time Classes and the Core Program in the Junior High School.* Bulletin 1958, no. 6. Washington, D.C.: U.S. Office of Education, 1958.

Zais, Robert S. *Curriculum: Principles and Foundations.* New York: Harper & Row, 1976.

ACSD EDUCATION BULLETIN

To subscribe to the Free Online *ASCD Education Bulletin* of the Association for Supervision and Curriculum Development e-mail listserv@listserv.ascd.org. The body of the message should contain the line: subscribe bulletin. There should be nothing in the subject area. The bulletin is sent every two or three weeks and contains items on K–12 education. The bulletin also contains links to useful Web sites on various topics.

AUDIOTAPES

The following are audiotapes from the Association for Supervision and Curriculum Development, 1703 N. Beauregard Street, Alexandria, Va. 22311–1714.

Assessment in the Nongraded/Multi-Age School. (Barbara Nelson Pavan, Robert Anderson, Marlene Dergousoff, and Cathy Braxdale)

Children in Crisis: The Learning Styles of At-Risk, Drop-Out, and Multicultural Underachievers—How to Increase Their Achievement. 1990. (Rita Dunn)

Curriculum Planning. (Athur Roberts)

Dimensions of Thinking: A New Framework for Curriculum and Instruction. (Robert Marzano et al.)

Districtwide Programs for At-Risk Youth. Five tapes. 1988.

   Curriculum in At-Risk Schools. (Larry Cuban)

   The Dropout and the Public Investment. (Richard Green).

   Dropouts in America. (Jacqueline Danzberger)

   Expanding Learning Opportunities for the Educationally Disadvantaged. (Floretta McKenzie)

   Meeting the Needs of Students at Risk in a Large School District. (Victor Herbert)

Hear Arthur Costa. Three one-hour audiotapes tapes:

   Classroom Conditions that Encourage Student Thinking. 1985.

   Teaching Thinking: Who's Really Doing It? 1988.

   What Human Beings Do When They Behave Intelligently. 1987.

Making the Middle School (Nancy Doda)

Restructuring Schools for Results. Seven audiotapes:
   Organizing Schools for Change Based on the Teacher's Role. (Albert Shanker)
   Reshaping the Teaching Profession Through Agency Cooperation. (Phyllis Schlechty).
   Restructuring High Schools. (Ted Sizer)
   Roles Administrators Play in Supporting and Initiating Restructuring. (Marian Leibowitz)
   School Illustrations of Restructuring. Two tapes (Robert McClure, Patricia Schaefer, David Wallace, and Gerald Dreyfuss)
   What Restructuring the Teaching Profession Means. (Ann Lieberman)
Rethinking the Curriculum for the Next Decade. Six one-hour audiotapes. 1990.
   Curriculum and Citizenship. (Maxine Greene)
   Curriculum Deliberations in Hard Times. (Walter Parker)
   Curriculum for the 1990s. (Graham Down)
   Direct Instruction Reconsidered. (Barak Rosenshine)
   Falling Between the Cracks. (Grant Wiggins)
   Where Have We Been and Where Are We Going? (Ralph Tyler)
Talks on Teaching Thinking. Ten audiotapes. 1984 and 1985.
   Practice Is Not Enough. (Barry Beyer)
   Survey of Thinking Skills. (Sandra Black)
   Approaches to Teaching Thinking. (Ron Brandt)
   Classroom Conditions That Encourage Student Thinking. (Arthur Costa)
   Teaching for Intelligent Behavior. (Arthur Costa)
   Thinking as a Skill. (Edward de Bono)
   Knowledge as Design. (David Perkins)
   Beyond the Three R's—Reasoning and Responsibility. (Jane Stallings)
   Teaching for Problem Solving in the Real World. (Robert Sternberg)
   Training Intellectual Skills—a Triarchic Model. (Robert Sternberg)
Teaching Thinking in Elementary Schools. Five audiotapes. 1987.
   Analyzing Approaches to Teaching Thinking. (Ron Brandt and David Perkins)
   Critical Thinking in Elementary School. (Richard Paul)
   The Development of Children's Thinking and Teaching. (Esther Fusco and John Barell)
   Planning a Thinking Skills Program. (Barry Beyer)
   What Human Beings Do When They Behave Intelligently. (Arthur Costa)

CD-ROM

Planning for Learning Through the Use of Technology. The Research on Technology for Learning.

Available from Association for Supervision and Curriculum Development, P. O. Box 796760, Baltimore, MD 21279-0760.

MULTIMEDIA

Tactics for Thinking. Association for Supervision and Curriculum Development, 1703 N. Beauregard Street, Alexandria, Va. 22311–1714. Includes eight hours of videotape identifying 22 tactics for thinking, a trainer's manual, a teacher's manual, and student activities blackline masters. Features Robert Marzano and Daisy Arredondo.

NEWSLETTER

Horace. Coalition of Essential Schools, Box 1969, Brown University, Providence, R.I. 02912.

PERIODICALS

Core Teacher. Publication of the National Association for Core Curriculum, 1640 Franklin Ave. , Ste. 104, Kent, Ohio 44240–4324.
The Futurist, publication of the World Future Society, 7910 Woodmont Ave., Ste. 450, Bethesda, Md. 20814.

VIDEOTAPES

Association for Supervision and Curriculum Development, 1703 N. Beauregard Street, Alexandria, Va. 22311-1714.
Improving the Quality of Student Thinking. 1986. 20 min. Illustrates ways teachers can improve student thinking skills.
Teacher and School Effectiveness. 1981. 21 min. Barak K. Rosenshine, Ronald Edmonds, and Peter Mortimore discuss ways of improving teacher and school effectiveness.
Teaching Skillful Thinking. 1986. 103 min. Four videotapes featuring Ernest Boyer, Arthur Costa, Matthew Lippman, David Perkins, and Robert Sternberg; leader's guide. Titles are:
   Issues in Teaching Thinking
   The Skillful Thinker
   Teaching for Thinking
   Teaching of and About Thinking
Center for Critical Thinking and Moral Critique, Sonoma State University, Rohnert Park, Calif. 94928:
Critical Thinking Forum 1990: Educational Reform for the Year 2000 and Beyond. A series of eight one-hour videotapes originally broadcast by the Adult Learning Satellite Service of PBS. Titles include:
   Critical Thinking and the Human Emotions
   Critical Thinking and Mathematical Problem Solving

Infusing Critical Thinking into Community College Instruction

Infusing Critical Thinking into Instruction at Four-Year Colleges and Universities

Critical Thinking: The Thinking that Masters the Content

Transforming Critical Thinking Principles into Teaching Strategies

Remodeling Lessons and Redesigning Instruction to Infuse Critical Thinking

The Greensboro Plan: Long-Term Critical Thinking: Staff Development in an Urban Multi-Racial School District

Web Sites

ArtsedNet: http://www.artsednet.getty.edu

Association for Supervision and Curriculum Development: http://www.ascd.org

Coalition of Essential Schools: http://www.essentialschools.org

Electronic School: http://www.electronic-school.com

Global Schoolhouse: http://www.gsh.org/wce

International Society for Technology in Education: http://www.iste.org

Link2Learn: http://L2L.org

Pathways to School Improvement: http://www.ncrel.org/sdrs/areas/te0cont.htm

Report on American Education: A State-by-State Analysis http://www.ALEC.org

Technology Education Lab: http://www.techedlab.com/k12.html

CHAPTER 10
INSTRUCTIONAL GOALS AND OBJECTIVES

After studying this chapter you should be able to:

1. Identify the three major domains of learning.
2. List the major categories of learnings from one taxonomy of each of the three domains.
3. Explain the relationships between curriculum goals and objectives and instructional goals and objectives.
4. Distinguish between curriculum goals and curriculum objectives.
5. Distinguish between instructional goals and instructional objectives.
6. Be able to identify and write curriculum goals in each of the three domains.
7. Be able to identify and write curriculum objectives in each of the three domains.
8. Be able to identify and write instructional goals in each of the three domains.
9. Be able to identify and write instructional objectives in each of the three domains.

PLANNING FOR INSTRUCTION

With the curriculum decisions made, the broad territory known as instruction looms before us. In some ways it is a familiar region whose landmarks—lesson plans, teaching strategies, and tests—are recognized by administrators, teachers, students, and parents. As we enter the area of instruction, decision making remains a major responsibility, only this time the responsibility falls directly on the classroom teacher. Up to this point persons identified as curriculum planners, among whose number are classroom teachers, have been engaged in making decisions of a programmatic nature. Now classroom teachers will become occupied with making decisions of a methodological nature. They will be answering questions like these:

- What are the objectives to be accomplished as a result of instruction?
- What topics will we cover?

VI–IX Planning phases
X–XI Operational phases

Figure 10.1 The instructional model

- What procedures are best for directing the learning?
- How do we evaluate instruction?

At this stage the teacher must decide whether to designate topics or specify competencies, whether to feature the teacher's objectives or the pupils', whether to seek mastery of content or simply exposure to the material, and whether to aim instruction at groups or at individuals.

Planning for instruction includes specifying instructional goals and objectives (discussed in this chapter), selecting instructional strategies and choosing techniques to evaluate instruction (treated in Chapter 12).

To put our next task in perspective, let's review the steps we have taken so far. We have

- surveyed needs of students in general
- surveyed needs of society
- clarified our philosophy of education and stated general aims
- identified curriculum goals and objectives
- determined needs of students in the school, needs of the community, and needs as shown by the subject matter
- reaffirmed plans for organizing the curriculum or selected and implemented plans for reorganizing the curriculum

Having completed these steps, we are ready to undertake planning, presenting, and evaluating instruction. The instructional phases of the curriculum-instruction continuum are shown as a subset of the model for curriculum development suggested in Chapter 5.[1] The subset consists of six components (VI, VII, VIII, IX A and B, X, XI), shown in Figure 10.1. In Chapter 5, we diagrammed these instructional components in such a way that they could be removed from the overall model for curriculum development. However, in Chapter 1 we posited an intimate relationship between curriculum and instruction, concluding that the two could be separated for purposes of analysis but that the existence of one could not be meaningful without the other.

---

[1]See Figure 5.4.

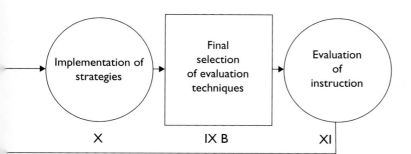

THE INSTRUCTIONAL MODEL

Figure 10.1 represents a model of instruction that, for simplicity, we will refer to as the Instructional Model. This Instructional Model is broken into two major phases: planning and operational. The operational phase is divided into two parts: the implementation or presentation of instruction and the evaluation of instruction.

The planning phase of the Instructional Model consists of four components: component VI—the identification of instructional goals; component VII—the specification of instructional objectives; component VIII—the teacher's plans for instructional strategies; and component IX—which consists of both a preliminary and a final phase of planning for the evaluation of instruction.

Then where and how does the teacher begin to plan for instruction? Let's look at several approaches to planning for instruction. Teacher A comes into the class without a preconceived notion of what he or she will cover and pulls a theme out of the air as the spirit moves him or her. Given the profession's penchant for turning rubrics into seeming substance, some might call this approach instantaneous planning. Others, less kind, might term it nonplanning.

Teacher B takes the textbook, divides the number of chapters by the number of weeks in the school year, lists the topics of each chapter by week, and from there takes any one of a number of directions. For each topic in its turn the teacher might

- jot down some questions for class discussion
- prepare notes for a lecture
- design individual and group assignments for clarifying points in the chapters

Teacher C selects topics for study during the year, using all kinds of materials related to each topic—including the textbook—and creates a succession of units of work for the class.

Teacher B's most likely course of action is the assign-study-recite-test approach, mentioned in the preceding chapter. Teacher C will follow what is commonly called the unit method of teaching, a problem-solving approach.

All three teachers may or may not relate their plans to the predetermined curriculum goals and objectives. All three may or may not specify the instructional goals and objectives that pupils are expected to accomplish. It is my position that both of these actions should be taken by teachers.

Of course, these three illustrations of types of teachers are exaggerated. These are but three examples of an almost infinite variety of teacher models, yet the illustrations are general enough to represent a significant number of teachers. The thesis of this chapter is that, regardless of the teacher's model or style of teaching, curriculum goals and objectives are more likely to be accomplished and students more likely to demonstrate mastery of learning if instructional goals and objectives are specified before starting instruction.

INSTRUCTIONAL GOALS AND OBJECTIVES DEFINED

Before we tackle the central mission of this chapter—selecting and writing instructional goals and objectives—let's see where instructional goals and objectives come in the curriculum development process. First, however, we should review the hierarchy of outcomes discussed in Chapter 8. At the top of the hierarchy are aims of education from which the school's curriculum goals and objectives are derived. In turn, the curriculum goals and objectives serve as sources of the instructional goals and objectives. Aims are stated by prominent individuals and groups for national, and sometimes even international, consideration. Curriculum goals and objectives are formulated by individual school and school system curriculum groups. Instructional goals and objectives are specified by the classroom teacher, who is sometimes assisted by other teachers and local curriculum groups.

To put these various aims, goals, and objectives in perspective, let's look at a simple example of outcomes in their hierarchical order (Box 10.1).

From the broad aim of education, we have moved to the specific instructional objective. Now let's examine instructional goals and objectives more closely.

An *instructional goal* is a statement of performance expected of each student in a class, phrased in general terms without criteria of achievement. The term "instructional goal" is used in this text like Norman E. Gronlund's *general instructional objective*[2] and Ralph W. Tyler's term *general objective*.[3] "The student will show an understanding of the stock market" is an example of an instructional goal. It indicates the performance expected of the learner, but the performance is not stated in such a fashion that its attainment can be readily measured. As a curriculum goal points the direction to curriculum objectives, so an instructional goal points the way to instructional objectives.

An *instructional objective* is a statement of performance to be demonstrated by each student in the class, derived from an instructional goal and phrased in measurable and observable terms. We may equate the term with Gronlund's *specific learning outcome* and Tyler's *behavioral objective*. The following statement is an example of an instructional objective: "The student will convert the following fractions to percentages

---

[2]Norman E. Gronlund, *Stating Objectives for Classroom Instruction,* 2nd ed. (New York: Macmillan, 1978).
[3]Ralph W. Tyler, *Basic Principles of Curriculum and Instruction* (Chicago: University of Chicago Press, 1949).

BOX 10.1

ILLUSTRATION OF THE HIERARCHY OF OUTCOMES

- *Aim:* Students will develop knowledge and skills necessary for living in a technological society.
- *Curriculum goal:* Students will recognize the influence of the computer on our lives.
- *Curriculum objective:* By the end of the senior year, at least 90 percent of the students will have taken a computer literacy course either in this school or elsewhere.
- *Instructional goal:* The student will become familiar with personal computers.
- *Instructional objective:* The student will demonstrate skills in word processing using his or her assigned computer by writing a one-page paper with 90 percent accuracy

---

with 100 percent accuracy: 1/4, 1/3, 1/2, 2/3, 3/4." Instructional objectives are also known as *behavioral objectives, performance objectives,* or *competencies.*

STATING OBJECTIVES

Tyler discussed four ways that instructors state objectives. Objectives are:

1. things that the instructor will do. Tyler gave as examples: "to present the theory of evolution," "to demonstrate the nature of inductive proof," "to present the Romantic poets," and "to introduce four-part harmony."
2. topics, concepts, generalizations, or other elements of content that are to be dealt with in the course or courses. Tyler's examples are "The Colonial Period," and "Matter Can be Neither Created nor Destroyed."
3. generalized patterns of behavior that fail to indicate more specifically the area of life or the content to which the behavior applies. Tyler identified illustrations of this type of objective: "to develop critical thinking," "to develop appreciation," and "to develop social attitudes."
4. terms that identify both the kind of behavior to be developed in the student and the content or area of life in which this behavior is to operate. Tyler's examples are: "to write clear and well-organized reports of social studies projects" and "to develop an appreciation of the modern novel."[4]

THE USE OF BEHAVIORAL OBJECTIVES

Whether to use behavioral objectives or not is a debate that has raged among educators for years. Supporters of behavioral objectives argue that this approach to instruction

- forces the teacher to be precise about what is to be accomplished
- enables the teacher to communicate to pupils what they must achieve

---

[4]Ibid., pp. 44–47.

- simplifies evaluation
- makes accountability possible
- makes sequencing easier

W. James Popham, in support of behavioral objectives, wrote:

Measurable instructional objectives are designed to counteract what is to me the most serious deficit in American education today, namely, a preoccupation with the process without assessment of consequences. . . . There are at least three realms in which measurable objectives have considerable potential dividends: in curriculum (what goals are selected); in instruction (how to accomplish those goals); and in evaluation (determining whether objectives of the instructional sequences have been realized). . . . It is perhaps because I am a convert to this position that I feel viscerally, as well as believe rationally, that measurable objectives have been the most significant advance in the past 10 years.[5]

The opponents of behavioral objectives hold that writing behavioral objectives

- is a waste of time
- is dehumanizing
- restricts creativity
- leads to trivial competencies

James D. Raths voiced his opposition to behavioral objectives as follows:

Consider the long range implications a teacher and his students must accept once it has been decided that all students are to acquire a specific instructional objective. The teacher's task becomes at once difficult and tedious. He must inform his students of the objectives to which they are expected to aspire; he must convince them of the relevance of this objective to their lives; he must give his students the opportunity to practice the behavior being taught; he must diagnose individual differences encountered by members of his group; he must make prescriptions of assignments based on his diagnosis and repeat the cycle again and again. . . . Yet even if all programs could be set up on the basis of behavioral objectives and even if strict training paradigms could be established to meet the objectives, who could argue that such a program would be other than tedious and ultimately stultifying.[6]

Among those who oppose the use of behavioral objectives are reconceptualists who view behavioral objectives as too mechanistic since they focus on observable behavior and ignore subjective behavior.[7] Some authorities have faulted the specification of instructional objectives as too narrow, too sequential, and too focused on specific, and inappropriate, content. They noted the debt of instructional objectives to behavioristic psychology and have looked instead to changes evoked by constructivist learning theories. John D. McNeil summarized these changes

. . . as a movement to (1) higher levels of thinking as opposed to the mastery of discrete tasks or skills; (2) a concern for coherence and relationship among ideas; (3) student-

[5]W. James Popham, "Practical Ways of Improving Curriculum via Measurable Objectives," *Bulletin of the National Association of Secondary School Principals* 55, no. 355 (May 1971): 76.

[6]James D. Raths, "Teaching Without Specific Objectives," *Educational Leadership* 28, no. 7 (April 1971): 715.

[7]See Peter S. Hlebowitsh, *Radical Curriculum Theory Reconsidered: A Historical Approach* (New York: Teachers College Press, 1993), pp. 11–12.

initiated activities and solutions instead of recitation and prespecified correct responses; and (4) students, as opposed to the teacher or the text, as the authority for knowing, constructing their own understanding as they work through problems and synthesize their ideas."[8]

Although some educators would reject the use of instructional objectives, examination of instructional materials not only in the education of the young but also in the training of people in business, industry, and government demonstrates continued widespread use of this technique.Conflicting views of the value of the use of instructional objectives cannot likely be resolved on the basis of research alone. McNeil noted that the research on instructional objectives is inconclusive. Said McNeil, "Some studies on the effect of objectives on learning, for example, have shown positive effects, but an equal number have not shown any significant differences."[9] McNeil added, however, "Objectives sometimes help and are almost never harmful."[10] As is the case in other issues in education decisions are often based more on philosophy than on results of research.

PROBLEMS WITH BEHAVIORAL OBJECTIVES

While the yea-sayers and naysayers argued with each other, the behavioral objectives camp itself added to the difficulty of convincing teachers to use behavioral objectives. Some, perhaps overenthusiastic about the behavioral objectives movement, turned off teachers by

1. assuming a rather dogmatic approach that seemed to rule out all other methods. Although I am favorably disposed toward the use of behavioral objectives and follow this approach myself, I would be hard-pressed to come up with solid experimental data to show that students exposed to a behavioral-objectives approach consistently show higher achievement than students whose instruction has been guided by other approaches.

    What some of the research reveals is that behavioral objectives can be useful in preinstructional strategies, that objectives work better if they pertain to the particular instructional task, that objectives are more effective with certain kinds of instruction than with others, that objectives are useful in accomplishing learning at higher levels of the cognitive domain, and that students of average ability, male students of high socioeconomic background, and both the more independent and less conscientious students benefit from behavioral objectives.[11]

2. resorting to formulas, which tended to make the writing of behavioral objectives mechanical rather than creative—for example, "Given the ＿＿＿＿＿＿＿＿, the student will ＿＿＿＿＿＿＿ in ＿＿＿＿＿＿＿ minutes with a score of ＿＿＿＿＿＿＿."

---

[8]John D. McNeil, *Curriculum: A Comprehensive Introduction,* 5th ed. (New York: HarperCollins College Publishers, 1996), p. 172.

[9]Ibid., p. 275.

[10]Ibid.

[11]See James Hartley and Ivor K. Davies, "Preinstructional Strategies: The Role of Pretests, Behavioral Objectives, Overviews, and Advance Organizers," *Review of Educational Research* 46, no. 2 (Spring 1976): 239–265.

3. downplaying affective objectives—a primary concern among opponents of behavioral objectives—and sometimes implying that it is as easy to write behavioral objectives in the affective domain as in the cognitive and psychomotor domains.

In spite of the hubbub over behavioral objectives, I believe that, with a reasoned approach, the practice of identifying and writing both instructional goals and objectives has considerable merit. Whether the regular classroom teacher specifies behavioral objectives or not, those who write individualized education programs (IEPs) for handicapped students must state both goals that students are to achieve by the end of the year and behavioral objectives for accomplishing the goals.

The writing of instructional objectives forces teachers to identify the outcomes they seek. The specification of instructional objectives simplifies the selection of instructional strategies and resources. When stated in behavioral terms, instructional objectives provide a basis for assessment, and they communicate to students, parents, and other professionals exactly what it is students are expected to demonstrate.[12] Outcome-based education of the 1990s is a direct descendant of competency- or performance-based education of the 1970s and 1980s, all three of which embody principles of behavioral objectives. We will return to outcome-based education in Chapter 14.

GUIDELINES FOR PREPARING INSTRUCTIONAL GOALS AND OBJECTIVES

To peruse the task of selecting and writing instructional goals and objectives, we will find it helpful to establish several guidelines to be followed. Instructional goals and objectives should

- relate to the already specified curriculum goals and objectives
- be specified for three domains of learning—the cognitive, affective, and psychomotor—whenever applicable
- be identified at both low and high levels of learning with greater emphasis on the higher
- follow a few simple rules for writing

Three current emphases in instruction should also guide teachers in the specification of behavioral objectives. These emphases are: (1) the developmemt of thinking skills,[13] (2) the integration of the curriculum through thematic interdisciplinary units,[14] and (3) recognition of intelligence as multiple, rather than global. The conception of intellectual ability is often limited to cognitive language and mathematical skills, often interpreted in terms of a single intelligence quotient score. We have had for many

---

[12]Leslie J. Briggs cited 21 reasons for writing instructional objectives in *Handbook of Procedures for the Design of Instruction* (Washington, D.C.: American Institute for Research, 1970), pp. 17–18.

[13]See Chapter 7 for discussion of thinking skills.

[14]See Chapter 13 for discussion of integrating the curriculum.

years, however, tests of differential aptitudes or primary mental abilities which yield scores in such areas as language usage, verbal reasoning, numerical ability, spatial relations, abstract reasoning, and memory.[15] Howard Gardner conceptualized the existence of seven intelligences: bodily-kinesthetic, interpersonal, intrapersonal, linguistic, logical-mathematical, musical, and spatial.[16] To the seven intelligences set forth in the 1980s, Gardner, in the 1990s, added the concept of naturalist intelligence, i.e., the ability to classify nature which Gardner described as "the ability to recognize and classify plants, minerals, and animals."[17]

We should add to Gardner's depiction of multiple intelligences the concepts of social intelligence as defined by Edward L. Thorndike[18] and emotional intelligence as perceived by Peter Salovey and John D. Mayer. Building on Thorndike's conception, Salovey and Mayer viewed emotional intelligence, now referred to by some people as EQ, "as a subset of social intelligence that involves the *ability to monitor one's own and others' feelings and emotions, to discriminate among them and to use this information to guide one's thinking and actions.*"[19] The concept of intelligences, in the plural, guides teachers to designing instruction that appeals to more than a single dimension of intelligence.

Relationship to Curriculum Goals and Objectives

Instructional goals and objectives should relate to curriculum goals and objectives. Unless the classroom teacher participated in drafting the curriculum goals and objectives, he or she must become familiar with them. The instructional goals and objectives are derived from the curriculum goals and objectives. Let's show this relationship by choosing a *curriculum goal* for the fifth grade: During the course of the year students will appreciably improve their skills in reading. From this general goal we may deduce the following *curriculum objectives:* (1) By the end of the eighth month, seventy-five percent of the students will have increased their ability to comprehend a selected set of English words by twenty-five percent, and (2) By the end of the academic year, all students will have met or exceeded the grade norm of 5.9 in reading comprehension.

The curriculum objectives are derived from the curriculum goals, are applied to the program and to groups of students, and are stated in measurable terms. The formulation of *instructional goals* follows and bears a direct relationship to the curriculum goals and objectives, as seen in the following examples: (1) The student will demonstrate ability to read new material silently without great difficulty, and (2) The student will demonstrate ability to read new material orally without difficulty.

---

[15]See, for example, *Differential Aptitudes Test,* 5th ed. (New York: The Psychological Corp., 1991).

[16]Howard Gardner, *Multiple Intelligences: The Theory in Practice* (New York: Basic Books, 1993). See also Gardner, *Frames of Mind: The Theory of Multiple Intelligences* (New York: Basic Books, 1983) and Thomas Armstrong, *Multiple Intelligences in the Classroom* (Alexandria, Va.: Association for Supervision and Curriculum Development, 1994).

[17]Kathy Checkley, "The First Seven . . . and the Eighth: A Conversation with Howard Gardner," *Educational Leadership* 55, no. 1 (September 1997): 8, 9.

[18]Edward L. Thondike, "Intelligence and Its Uses," *Harper's Magazine* 140 (1920): 227–235.

[19]Peter Salovey and John D. Mayer, "Emotional Intelligence," *Imagination, Cognition and Personality* 9, no. 3 (1989–90): 189. See also Daniel Goleman, *Emotional Intelligence* (New York: Bantam Books, 1995) and Peter Salovey and David J. Sluyter, eds. *Emotional Development and Emotional Intelligence: Educational Implications* (New York: Bantam Books, 1997).

Both of the foregoing statements are expectations of each pupil. The statements are couched in general terms and include no criterion of mastery. For each of the instructional goals we may create *instructional objectives*. To promote the goal of reading silently, for example, the teacher might design the following objectives: (1) The student will read silently a passage from the fifth-grade reader and then summarize orally without appreciable error in comprehension each of its four major points, and (2) The student will read silently a passage from the fifth-grade reader and then will write correct responses to eight out of ten written questions provided by the teacher.

To further the goal of reading orally, the teacher might identify the following objectives: (1) The student will read orally from a classroom library book and make no more than four mistakes in pronunciation in a passage of about 100 words, and (2) The student will read orally a passage from a classroom library book, and then orally summarize each of the three main points of the passage without appreciable error in comprehension.

Unless an instructional objective is differentiated for a particular subgroup of students—for example, bright, slow, or handicapped,—it is expected that every student will master the objective. When instructional objectives are aimed at all students in a given class, they may be called *minimal competencies*.

State testing programs are designed to assess students' mastery of the minimal competencies—for example, competencies to be achieved in all or selected disciplines at the end of, say, fourth, eighth, or eleventh grade.

Some confusion may exist between curriculum and instructional goals and objectives, for in one sense they both may be designed for all students. The curriculum goals and objectives are broader in nature, are aimed at all students as a group or groups, frequently jump across grade boundaries, often cut across disciplines, and many times are relevant to more than one teacher either within a discipline or among disciplines.

There are times, however, when a curriculum objective may be congruent with an instructional objective or, put another way, an instructional objective may repeat a curriculum objective. When we as curriculum planners designate as a curriculum objective improving the scores of all students on a standardized test in mathematics by ten percentile points, we will be pleased when the mathematics curriculum (program) is functioning to that degree. When we as classroom teachers stipulate that all of our pupils score ten percentile points higher on a standardized test of mathematics, we will be pleased with each student who functions that well and may refer to our own instruction as effective if many students achieve that objective.

Though we may state them slightly differently, curriculum and instructional goals and objectives may converge. One is the alter ego of the other, so to speak. Conversely, curriculum and instructional goals and objectives may diverge. When we as curriculum planners desire that eighty percent (even one hundred percent) of the seniors with quantitative aptitude test scores at the seventy-fifth percentile elect calculus, we are talking about program, not instruction.

The distinctions between curriculum and instructional goals and objectives matter only to the extent that neither of the two sets is overlooked. If an instructional objective repeats a curriculum objective, so be it; it is a perfect fit. On the other hand, instructional objectives by their very nature tend to be more specific than the curriculum goals and objectives, focus on what takes place in the classroom, and come to pass as a result of the individual instructor's efforts. Whatever the degree of congruence, there is a direct and natural progression from curriculum goal to instructional objective.

DOMAINS OF LEARNING

One way of viewing learnings exists in the concepts of three domains: the cognitive, affective, and psychomotor. Within each domain we find classification systems ranking objectives in a hierarchical structure from lowest to highest level. The instructional goals and objectives should be specified for three domains of learning—the cognitive, the affective, and the psychomotor—whenever applicable. Note these three illustrations of different types of learning:

- knowledge of the system of election primaries
- enjoyment in reading
- skill in laying bricks

These examples are illustrative of the three major areas (domains) of learning. Knowledge of the primary system falls into the cognitive domain, enjoyment in reading in the affective domain, and skill in laying bricks in the psychomotor domain.

Cognitive Domain.   Speaking for a committee of college and university examiners, Benjamin S. Bloom defined the cognitive domain as including objectives that "deal with the recall or recognition of knowledge and the development of intellectual abilities and skills."[20] Cognitive learnings, which involve the mental processes, range from memorization to the ability to think and solve problems.

Affective Domain.   David R. Krathwohl, Benjamin S. Bloom, and Bertram B. Masia defined the affective domain as including objectives that "emphasize a feeling tone, an emotion, or a degree of acceptance or rejection."[21]

Psychomotor Domain.   Robert J. Armstrong, Terry D. Cornell, Robert E. Kraner, and E. Wayne Roberson defined the psychomotor domain as including behaviors that "place primary emphasis on neuromuscular or physical skills and involve different degrees of physical dexterity."[22] Sometimes referred to as "perceptual-motor skills," psychomotor learnings include bodily movements and muscular coordination.

Ordinarily, schools assume responsibility for student achievement in all three broad areas. Although we might visualize the three horses—Cognitive, Affective, and Psychomotor—in the form of a Russian troika, racing three abreast, they are hitched more like a lead horse followed by two abreast. More often than not, Cognitive is in the forefront. On occasion, depending on the mood of the profession and the public, Cognitive is overtaken by Affective or Psychomotor.

---

[20]Benjamin S. Bloom, ed., *Taxonomy of Educational Objectives: The Classification of Educational Goals: Handbook I: Cognitive Domain* (White Plains, N.Y.: Longman, 1956), p. 7.

[21]David R. Krathwohl, Benjamin S. Bloom, and Bertram B. Masia, *Taxonomy of Educational Objectives: The Classification of Educational Goals: Handbook II: Affective Domain* (White Plains, N.Y.: Longman, 1964), p. 7.

[22]Robert J. Armstrong, Terry D. Cornell, Robert E. Kraner, and E. Wayne Roberson, *The Development and Evaluation of Behavioral Objectives* (Worthington, Ohio: Charles A. Jones, 1970), p. 22.

The battle over which domain is the most important has endured for many years. With the exception of work by people like Rousseau, Froebel, Pestalozzi, and Neil (Summerhill School, England), most of the rest of the world—if we may generalize on such a vast scale—marches to the beat of the cognitive drummer. Although many fine opportunities for vocational education are provided by many countries, the cognitive domain remains the prestige category and is the entrée to institutions of higher learning. If our horses were pitted in an international race, Affective would come in a poor third.

Judging from the popularity of books critical of public education, the accountability movement in education, the flight to private schools, the development of national standards in the fundamental disciplines, and national and state assessments of student achievement, we might conclude that the American public is partial to the cognitive domain.

Although we find strong preferences both within and outside the profession for stressing cognitive learnings, I would encourage each teacher to identify and write instructional goals and objectives in all three domains, making allowances for the nature of the subject matter.

Normally, the domains overlap; each possesses elements of the other, even when one is obviously dominant. Thus, it is often difficult to categorize learning as falling precisely into one domain. For example, we can identify learnings that are primarily psychomotor (running a football play) and secondarily cognitive and affective. We can give examples of learnings that are primarily cognitive (civil rights legislation) and secondarily affective. We can offer examples of learnings that are primarily affective (honesty) and secondarily cognitive. We can also identify learnings that are primarily cognitive (constructing an equilateral triangle) and secondarily affective and psychomotor.

Many learnings will obviously fall into single categories. If we discount the bit of affective pleasure a student may feel in knowing the right answer, the formula for finding the area of a triangle (1/2 base X height) is pretty much a cognitive experience. Doing sit-ups, a psychomotor exercise, requires very little cognition and may evoke either a positive or negative affective response. Faith in other human beings is primarily an affective goal, secondarily cognitive, and usually not psychomotor.

The classroom teacher should identify and write instructional goals and objectives in all three domains, if indeed all three are relevant. It might be asked. "From what cloth do we cut the instructional goals and objectives?" We might respond by saying, "From the same cloth from which we cut the curriculum goals and objectives—the three sources: the needs of students, of society, and of the subject matter—with the curriculum goals and objectives themselves serving as inspiration."

In recent years critics of the three taxonomies have maintained that learnings cannot and should not be separated into domains. Others, including this author, have found the widely-practiced classification of objectives into three domains a useful teaching strategy.

TAXONOMIC LEVELS

Instructional goals and objectives should be identified at both high and low levels of learning, with greater emphasis being placed on the higher levels. It is obvious that some learnings are more substantive, complex, and important than others. Note, for example, the following learning outcomes, all in the cognitive domain, to see the differences in complexity:

- The student will name the first president of the United States.
- The student will read Washington's first inaugural address and summarize the major points.
- The student will show how some of Washington's ideas apply or do not apply today.
- The student will analyze Washington's military tactics in the Battle of Yorktown.
- The student will write a biography of Washington.
- The student will evaluate Washington's role at the Continental Congress.

The knowledge and skills required for naming the first president of the United States are at a decidedly lower level than those for each of the subsequent objectives. Each succeeding item is progressively more difficult, requiring greater cognitive powers. What we have is a hierarchy of learning outcomes from lowest to highest.

Take the following illustrations from the affective domain:

- The student will listen while others express their points of view.
- The student will answer a call for volunteers to plant trees in a public park.
- The student will express appreciation for the contributions of ethnic groups other than his or her own to the development of our country.
- The student will choose nutritious food over junk food.
- The student will habitually abide by a set of legal and ethical standards.

As with examples in the cognitive domain, each objective is progressively more substantial than the preceding one.

Finally, let's look at a set of objectives from the psychomotor domain.

- The student will identify a woolen fabric by its feel.
- The student will demonstrate how to hold the reins of a horse while cantering.
- The student will imitate a right-about-face movement.
- The student will mix a batch of mortar and water.
- The student will operate a VCR.
- The student will arrange an attractive bulletin board.
- The student will create an original game requiring physical movements.

COGNITIVE TAXONOMY

Bloom and associates developed an extensive taxonomy for classifying educational objectives in the cognitive domain.[23] Of all classification systems the Bloom taxonomy of the cognitive domain is perhaps the best known and most widely followed. It categorizes the types of cognitive learning outcomes that are featured at all levels of the educational system. Bloom and his associates classified cognitive learnings in six major categories: knowledge, comprehension, application, analysis, synthesis, and evaluation. Let's take each of these categories, refer back to the examples previously given, and place them in the appropriate categories, as follows:

---

[23]Bloom, *Taxonomy: Cognitive Domain.*

- *Knowledge level:* The student will name the first president of the United States.
- *Comprehension level:* The student will read Washington's first inaugural address and summarize the major points.
- *Application level:* The student will show how some of Washington's ideas apply or do not apply today.
- *Analysis level:* The student will analyze Washington's military tactics in the Battle of Yorktown.
- *Synthesis level:* The student will write a biography of George Washington.
- *Evaluation level:* The student will evaluate Washington's role at the Continental Congress.

This taxonomy shows learning objectives as classified in a hierarchical fashion from the lowest (knowledge) to the highest (evaluation). A central premise of professional educators is that the higher levels of learning should be stressed. The ability to think, for example, is fostered not through low-level recall of knowledge alone but through application, analysis, synthesis, and evaluation.

Objectives in the cognitive domain are, of the three domains, the easiest to identify and simplest to evaluate. They are drawn primarily from the subject matter and are readily measurable, usually by written tests and exercises.

AFFECTIVE TAXOMONY

Shortly after the appearance of the cognitive taxonomy, Krathwohl and others, including Bloom, developed a taxonomy of objectives in the affective domain, which consists of five major categories.[24] We may categorize the affective examples given earlier in the following manner:

- *Receiving* (attending): The student will listen while others express their points of view.
- *Responding:* The student will answer a call for volunteers to plant a tree in a public park.
- *Valuing:* The student will express appreciation for the contributions of ethnic groups other than his or her own to the development of our country.
- *Organization:* The student will choose nutritious food over junk food.
- *Characterization by value or value complex:* The student will habitually abide by a set of legal and ethical standards.

The affective domain poses a serious problem for educators. Historically, parents and educators have viewed the school's primary mission as cognitive learning. Affective learning has typically held a lesser position. As mentioned elsewhere in this text, the affective domain is still not accepted by some educators as a legitimate focus of the school. On the other hand, some educators feel that affective outcomes are more important to the individual and society than other outcomes.

The perceptual psychologist, Arthur W. Combs, stated the case for affective education, tying it to the development of adequate personalities, as follows:

---

[24]Krathwohl et al., *Taxonomy: Affective Domain.*

For many generations education has done an excellent job of imparting information. . . . Our greatest failures are those connected with the problems of helping people
to behave differently as a result of the information we have provided them. . . . Adequate persons are, among other factors, the product of strong values. The implication
seems to be clear, then, that educators must be interested in and concerned with values.
Unfortunately, this is not the case in many schools and classrooms today. The emphasis is too often on the narrowly scientific and impersonally objective. . . . Education must
be concerned with the values, beliefs, convictions, and doubts of students. These realities as perceived by an individual are just as important, if not more so, as the so-called
objective facts.[25]

Bloom, J. Thomas Hasting, and George F. Madaus attested to the neglect of instruction for affective learning when they said:

Throughout the years American education has maintained that among its most important ideals is the development of such attributes as interests, desirable attitudes, appreciation, values, commitment, and will power. . . . the types of outcomes which in fact
receive the highest priorities in our schools, to the detriment of these affective goals,
are verbal-conceptual in nature.[26]

Bloom, Hastings, and Madaus identified these reasons for the neglect of affective
learning:

Our system of education is geared to producing people who can deal with the words,
concepts, and mathematical or scientific symbols so necessary for success in our technological society.[27]
  Standardized tests used by the schools...lay stress on intellectual tasks.[28]
  Characteristics of this kind, unlike achievement competencies, are considered to be
a private rather than a public matter.[29]

Some hold that affective outcomes are the province of the home and the church
and that instruction in the affective domain smacks of indoctrination. "One of the reasons for the failure to give instructional emphasis to affective outcomes is related to
the Orwellian overtones which attitudinal and value-oriented instruction often con-
jures up in the minds of teachers and the public," said Bloom and coauthors.[30]
  Whose values should be taught? Are white, Anglo-Saxon, Protestant, middle-class
values the ones to be promoted? Whence come the values to be selected? Although, as
noted in the preceding chapter, some people believe that values cannot or should not
be taught in school, others like Theodore R. Sizer held that values can and should be
taught.[31]

---

[25]Arthur W. Combs, ed., *Perceiving, Behaving, Becoming: A New Focus on Education,* 1962 Yearbook (Alexandria, Va.: Association for Supervision and Curriculum Development, 1962), p. 200.
  [26]From Benjamin S. Bloom, J. Thomas Hastings, and George F. Madaus, *Handbook on Formative and Summative Evaluation of Student Learning* (New York: McGraw-Hill, 1971), p. 225. Reproduced with permission of The McGraw-Hill Companies.
  [27]Ibid.
  [28]Ibid., p. 226.
  [29]Ibid., p. 227.
  [30]Ibid., p. 226.
  [31]Theodore R. Sizer, *Horace's Compromise: The Dilemma of the American High School* (Boston: Houghton Mifflin, 1984),
Chapter 6.

If affective learnings should be taught and values should be among those learnings, then identifying common values is an essential task for the curriculum planner. Robert S. Gilchrist and Bernice R. Roberts urged educators to include values in the educational program:

> Somehow the notion that everyone develops and formulates his own particular value system has resulted in the educator's choice of a do-nothing position. How can we continue with this stance when the provision of experiences for the development of a value system, possibly the most important, influencing task of the educator, is hierarchically the task of the schooling process?[32]

Affective objectives are both difficult to identify and extremely difficult—often impossible—to measure, and these difficulties constitute another reason why teachers tend to shy away from the affective domain. As noted in Chapter 6, however, character education, a product of the affective domain based on common moral, spiritual, and ethical values, has been and continues to be one of the important aims of American education. In Chapter 12 we will discuss some approaches to the evaluation of student performance in the affective domain.

PSYCHOMOTOR TAXONOMIES

For some reason difficult to fathom, the development and use of a taxonomy in the psychomotor domain have not been given as much emphasis as in the cognitive and affective domains. Taxonomies of the psychomotor domain do exist, but they seem not to be as widely known as the taxonomies of the other two domains. The examples from the psychomotor domain given earlier follow the classification system developed by Elizabeth Jane Simpson.[33] Following her taxonomy, we categorize these illustrations as follows:

- *Perception:* The student will identify a woolen fabric by its feel.
- *Set:* The student will demonstrate how to hold the reins of a horse when cantering.
- *Guided response:* The student will imitate a right-about-face movement.
- *Mechanism:* The student will mix a batch of mortar and water.
- *Complex overt response:* The student will operate a VCR.
- *Adaptation:* The student will arrange an attractive bulletin board display.
- *Origination:* The student will create an original game requiring physical movements.)

Anita J. Harrow provided a clarifying description for each of the categories of the Simpson taxonomy. She identified perception as interpreting, set as preparing, guided response as learning, mechanism as habituating, complex overt response as performing, adaptation as modifying, and origination as creating.[34] Harrow proposed her own

---

[32]Robert S. Gilchrist and Bernice R. Roberts, *Curriculum Development: A Humanized Systems Approach* (Belmont, Calif.: Lear Siegler/Fearon, 1974), p. 13.

[33]Elizabeth Jane Simpson, "The Classification of Educational Objectives in the Psychomotor Domain," *The Psychomotor Domain*, vol. 3 (Washington, D.C.: Gryphon House, 1972), pp. 43–56.

[34]Anita J. Harrow, *A Taxonomy of the Psychomotor Domain: A Guide for Developing Behavioral Objectives* (White Plains, N.Y.: Longman, 1972), p. 27.

taxonomy for classifying movement behaviors of learners. Her model consists of the following six classification levels.

1.00   Reflex Movements
     1.10   Segmental Reflexes
     1.20   Intersegmental Reflexes
     1.30   Suprasegmental Reflexes
2.00   Basic-Fundamental Movements
     2.10   Locomotor Movements
     2.20   Non-Locomotor Movements
     2.30   Manipulative Movements
3.00   Perceptual Abilities
     3.10   Kinesthetic Discrimination
     3.20   Visual Discrimination
     3.30   Auditory Discrimination
     3.40   Tactile Discrimination
     3.50   Coordinated Abilities
4.00   Physical Abilities
     4.10   Endurance
     4.20   Strength
     4.30   Flexibility
     4.40   Agility
5.00   Skilled Movements
     5.10   Simple Adaptive Skill
     5.20   Computed Adaptive Skill
     5.30   Complex Adaptive Skill
6.00   Non-Discursive Communication
     6.10   Expressive Movement
     6.20   Interpretive Movement[35]

The use of the taxonomies of the three domains as guidelines can lead to more effective instruction. The taxonomies direct attention to the three major domains of learning and to the subdivisions of each. Arranged in a hierarchical fashion, the taxonomies should serve to stimulate teachers to move their learners from the lower to the higher and more enduring levels of learning in each domain.

RULES FOR WRITING

Instructional goals and objectives should follow a few simple rules for writing. Early in this chapter we distinguished instructional goals from instructional objectives. Instructional goals defined student performance in general terms whereas instructional objectives defined it in more specific and measurable terms.

Instructional goals are often poorly stated instructional objectives. For example,"The student will know names of the first five presidents of the United States" is an

---

[35]Ibid., pp. 1–2.

instructional goal because it is not written in measurable and observable terms. We might change this instructional goal into an instructional objective by writing, "The student will name correctly and in order the first five presidents of the United States."

On the other hand, an instructional goal may serve the purpose of pointing out the direction that leads to instructional objectives. For example, the instructional goal, "The student will develop an awareness of energy needs" could lead to a multitude of instructional objectives—for example, "The student will identify the five leading oil-producing countries," "The student will identify three sources of energy that are alternatives to oil," "The student will determine how often the price of imported oil has fluctuated in the last ten years," and "The student will propose and describe three ways Americans can conserve energy."

An instructional goal may thus be written in rather broad, imprecise terms. On the other hand, it may be stated simply as a topic—for example, "The Organized Labor Movement." Implied in this topic is the instructional goal, "The student will develop an understanding of the organized labor movement."

Though variations in style of formulating instructional goals and objectives are certainly possible, there appears to be merit in starting instructional goals and objectives with "The student . . ." (in the singular) in order to (1) signal the meaning "each student" and (2) help distinguish curriculum goals and objectives from instructional goals and objectives by beginning the former with "Students . . ." (in the plural) to convey the meaning "students in general" or "groups of students." Although it is preferable for all plans to be committed to paper, it is possible for teachers to keep the instructional goals in mind and move directly to the writing of instructional objectives.

THREE ELEMENTS OF AN INSTRUCTIONAL OBJECTIVE

The literature generally recommends that three elements or components be included in an instructional (behavioral) objective:

1. the behavior expected of the student
2. the conditions under which the behavior is to be demonstrated
3. the degree of mastery required[36]

Specifying Behavior.   When specifying behavior, instructors should choose as often as possible, action verbs that are subject to measurement and observation. Action words in particular distinguish instructional objectives from instructional goals. The word "understanding," for example, is unsuitable in an instructional objective because it is neither measurable nor observable. Thus, "The student will understand his or her rights under the first ten amendments to the U.S. Constitution" is an instructional goal not an instructional objective. If "understand" is changed to a performance-oriented verb, we can create an instructional objective, such as "The student will write summaries of the first ten amendments to the U.S. Constitution." This cognitive objective can be raised from the comprehension level to the evaluation level by modifying the statement: "The student will write a paper listing the principal rights in the first ten amendments to the U.S. Constitution and will evaluate the importance of each right to

---

[36]For helpful discussion on writing instructional objectives, see Robert F. Mager, *Preparing Instructional Objectives*, 2nd ed. (Belmont, Calif.: Fearon, 1975).

TABLE 10.1

BEHAVIORALLY ORIENTED VERBS FOR THE DOMAINS OF LEARNING

COGNITIVE DOMAIN (BLOOM TAXONOMY)

LEVEL	VERBS
Knowledge	identify, specify, state
Comprehension	explain, restate, translate
Application	apply, solve, use
Analysis	analyze, compare, contrast
Synthesis	design, develop, plan
Evaluation	assess, evaluate, judge

AFFECTIVE DOMAIN (KRATHWOHL TAXONOMY)

LEVEL	VERBS
Receiving	accept, demonstrate awareness, listen
Responding	comply with, engage in, volunteer
Valuing	express a preference for, show appreciation by stating, show concern by stating
Organization	adhere to, defend, synthesize
Characterization by value or value complex	demonstrate empathy, express willingness to be ethical, modify behavior

PSYCHOMOTOR DOMAIN (SIMPSON TAXONOMY)

LEVEL	VERBS
Perception	distinguish, identify, select
Set	assume a position, demonstrate, show
Guided response	attempt, imitate, try
Mechanism	make habitual, practice, repeat
Complex overt response	carry out, operate, perform
Adaptation	adapt, change, revise
Origination	create, design, originate

NOTE: For a useful listing of verbs in the affective, cognitive, and psychomotor domains, see Gronlund, *Stating Objectives*, pp. 26–34, 69–72. For a useful listing of verbs and direct objects applicable to the Bloom and Krathwohl taxonomies, see Newton S. Metfessel, William B. Michael, and Donald A. Kirsner, "Instrumentation of Bloom's and Krathwohl's Taxonomies for the Writing of Educational Objectives," *Psychology in the Schools* 6, no. 3 (July 1969); 227–231.

us today." The instructional objective, therefore, must include behavior expected of the learner as a result of exposure to instruction.

To help with the writing of instructional objectives, the teacher may wish to develop lists of behaviorally-oriented verbs that can be used for each category of the three domains. Examples are shown in Table 10.1.

Specifying Conditions.   The condition under which the learner demonstrates the behavior should be specified, if necessary. In the objective, "Given a list of needs of this community, the student will rank them in order of priority." "Given a list of needs of this community" is the condition under which the behavior is performed. It is an essential part of the objective. As an additional illustration, in the objective, "On the classroom wall map the student will point out the People's Republic of China." "On the classroom wall map" is the necessary condition. However, if students are to point out several countries on the same wall map, it becomes redundant and therefore unnecessary to repeat "On the classroom wall map" for each instructional objective. What the instructor should do in this case is write: "On the classroom wall map the student will point out . . ." The instructor should then list all the geographical features to be pointed out.

To conserve the instructor's valuable time, obvious conditions need not be specified; they are simply understood. There is no need, for example, for the teacher to waste time placing before an objective "Given paper and pen" as in "Given paper and pen, the student will write an essay on the work of Joseph Conrad." Unless the use of paper and pen has some special significance and is not routine, it need not be specified. Adding routine and obvious conditions to instructional objectives can border on the ridiculous and can create an adverse reaction to the writing of instructional objectives at all. If we may exaggerate to stress the point, we do not wish to see the objective: "Given a tennis ball, a tennis racket, a tennis court, a net, a fair day, proper dress, and preferably an opponent also equipped with ball, racket, and proper dress, the student will demonstrate how to serve a tennis ball." "The student will demonstrate how to serve a tennis ball" is sufficient *ad diem,* as the lawyers say.

Specifying the Criterion.   The statement of the instructional objective should include the acceptable standard or criterion of mastery of the behavior if it is not obvious. For example, a French teacher might write the following statement: "The student will translate the following sentences." There is no need to write the condition, "from French to English"; the students know that. There is no need to specify the criterion "into good English" (which should be routinely expected behavior) or "with one hundred percent accuracy," or "with no errors." Unless a criterion is specified, it can be assumed that the teacher wishes students to achieve one hundred percent accuracy.

Some objectives require more elaborate criteria than others. For example, let's go back to the illustration, "The student will write an essay on the work of Joseph Conrad." We could embellish this objective with various criteria, some of which are essential, some, not. "In legible handwriting" or "free of typographical errors" should be normal expectations and, therefore, do not have to appear in every instructional objective. On the other hand, if the instructor desires an essay with no more than three spelling errors, with no more than three grammatical errors, and with all the footnotes and bibliographical entries in correct form, that information should be conveyed to the students. The criteria are particularly important if the objective is being used as a test item. It is a necessary and sound principle of evaluation that students be informed by what standards they will be evaluated.

Robert H. Davis, Lawrence T. Alexander, and Stephen L. Yelon listed six standards and gave examples of each, as follows:

1. When mere OCCURRENCE of the behavior is sufficient, describe the behavior. Example: The knot will be tied loosely as in the photograph.
2. When ACCURACY is important, provide a statement of acceptable range or deviation. Example: The answer must be correct to the nearest whole number.
3. If the number of ERRORS is important, state the number. Example: with a maximum of one error.
4. If TIME or SPEED is important, state the minimal level. Example: within five seconds; five units per minute.
5. If a KNOWN REFERENCE provides the standard, state the reference. Example: Perform the sequence of steps in the same order as given in the text.
6. If the CONSEQUENCES of the behavior are important, describe them or provide a model. Example: Conduct the class so that all students participate in the discussion.[37]

Novice instructors sometimes ask how the teacher decides on the criteria. How do you decide whether to permit three or four errors or whether a student should complete the task in ten rather than five minutes? These decisions are based on the teacher's past experience with students and on the teacher's professional and, if you will, arbitrary judgment. After a few years, the teacher begins to sense what is possible for students to accomplish and proceeds on that knowledge. Certain traditions may also guide the teacher. For example, seventy percent is considered by most students, teachers, and parents as so-so; eighty percent is considered not bad; ninety percent is considered good. Thus criteria in the seventy to one hundred percent range often show up in statements of instructional objectives.

Although it is relatively simple to specify objectives in the cognitive and psychomotor domains, specifying criteria in the affective domain is enough to tax one's soul. We shall wrestle with the problem of establishing criteria for affective objectives in Chapter 12. At this point, however, we should mention that it is usually impossible to specify criteria for objectives in the affective domain. What criteria, for example, should we append to this objective: "The student will express a sense of pride in his or her school"? Should the student's response be fervent? Passionate? The affective domain presents its unique instructional problems.

To the standards component, Davis, Alexander, and Yelon added a stability component—that is, the number of opportunities the student will be given and the number of times he or she must succeed in demonstrating the behavior.[38] We may illustrate the stability component with this example: "The student will word process fifty words per minute on each of three successive tries." Analyzing this objective shows that "to word process" is the behavior; the conditions, are understood (a central processing unit, a monitor, a keyboard, and, if printing is required, a printer, paper, ink cartridge); the performance criterion is "at least fifty words per minute"; and the stability component is "on each of three successive tries."

---

[37]From Robert H. Davis, Lawrence T. Alexander, and Stephen L. Yelon, *Learning System Design: An Approach to the Improvement of Instruction* (New York: McGraw-Hill, 1974), pp. 39–40. Reproduced with permission of The McGraw-Hill Companies.

[38]Ibid., p. 41.

Generally speaking, instructional objectives should consist of at least three components: the behavior (often called the terminal behavior); the conditions; and the criterion.

VALIDATING AND DETERMINING PRIORITY OF INSTRUCTIONAL GOALS AND OBJECTIVES

Instructional goals and objectives should be validated and put in order of priority. Teachers should know whether the instructional goals and objectives are appropriate and which are the more important.

In practice, it is far simpler to validate and rank instructional goals and objectives than curriculum goals and objectives. Instructional goals and objectives are not normally submitted with any regularity to lay groups or students for this process nor to administrators. Nor do they need to be, since instructional goals and objectives are content-specific. To make a judgment on their validity and to decide which are essential requires a foundation both in the subject matter being taught and in the methods for teaching that subject matter. The subject matter is often technical and beyond the knowledge and skills of lay persons and students. Instructional matters are the prerogative of persons trained in their fields of specialization.

As a result, far fewer persons need to be involved in validating and establishing priorities of instructional goals and objectives than is the case with curriculum goals and objectives.

Validating and ranking of instructional goals and objectives are usually accomplished by referring to the adopted textbooks, reference books, and curriculum guides. The authors of these materials serve as the persons who validate and set priorities. This method of validating and ordering of instructional goals and objectives is, by far, the most common.

The classroom teacher can also seek help in validating and ranking instructional goals and objectives from members of his or her team, grade level or department, other knowledgeable faculty members, curriculum consultants, and supervisors. Consultants and supervisors trained and experienced in special fields should also be able to help the classroom teacher decide which instructional goals and objectives are appropriate to the learners and which ones should be stressed. Finally, teachers may seek advice from acknowledged experts in the subject area outside the school system as well as from specialists in other school systems or in higher education institutions.

SUMMARY

Instructional goals and objectives are directly related to the previously specified curriculum goals and objectives. Instructional goals provide direction for specifying instructional objectives.

Learning outcomes may be identified in three major domains: the cognitive, the affective, and the psychomotor. The cognitive domain is the world of the intellect; the affective, the locale of emotions, beliefs, values, and attitudes; and the psychomotor, the territory of perceptual-motor skills.

Taxonomies of each domain classify objectives in a hierarchical fashion from the lowest to the highest level of learning. Taxonomies are useful in revealing the types of learning encompassed in each domain and in guiding instructors toward placing greater emphasis on learning at the higher levels.

Instructional goals are statements written in nonbehavioral terms without criteria of mastery. With the possible exception of outcomes in the affective domain, instructional objectives should be written in measurable and observable terms.

Whenever practical and necessary, instructional objectives should consist of three components: the behavior that learners will demonstrate, the conditions under which the behavior is to be demonstrated, and the criterion to show mastery of the behavior.

Instructors validate instructional goals and objectives and place them in order of priority by referring to text materials written by experts and by seeking the judgments of knowledgeable colleagues, supervisors, and consultants from both within and outside the school system.

QUESTIONS FOR DISCUSSION

1. In what ways do instructional goals and objectives differ from curriculum goals and objectives?
2. Is it necessary to specify both instructional goals and instructional objectives?
3. What are the purposes of writing instructional goals and objectives?
4. What are some alternatives to writing behavioral objectives?
5. Do instructional goals and objectives limit the creativity or artistry of the teacher? Explain.

SUPPLEMENTARY EXERCISES

1. Define "cognitive," "affective," and "psychomotor."
2. Define the word "taxonomy."
3. Distinguish between a nonbehavioral goal and a behavioral objective.
4. Consult the Bloom taxonomy of the cognitive domain and prepare a list of verbs that might be used for writing objectives in each category.
5. Consult the Krathwohl taxonomy of the affective domain and prepare a list of verbs that might be used for writing objectives in each category.
6. Consult the Simpson or Harrow taxonomies of the psychomotor domain and prepare a list of verbs that might be used for writing objectives in each category.
7. Write one instructional objective for each of the five major categories of the Bloom taxonomy of the cognitive domain.
8. Write one instructional objective for each of the five categories of the Krathwohl taxonomy of the affective domain.
9. Write one instructional objective for each of the major categories of either the Simpson or Harrow taxonomy of the psychomotor domain.

10. State the three components of an instructional objective.
11. List and give examples of six types of performance standards that may be included in an instructional objective.
12. Describe what is meant by "stability component" and give an example.
13. Consult a reference by Howard Gardner, Thomas Armstrong, or other author and describe each of the multiple intelligences.
14. Provide illustrations of the application of the multiple intelligences in the classroom.
15. Debate the concept: The specification of instructional objectives is a desirable teaching tool.
16. Poll a group of teachers on their feelings for and their extent of use of the technique of specifying instructional objectives.
17. Classify the following instructional objectives as to the principal domain and major category according to Bloom, Krathwohl, or Simpson. (Answers to this exercise follow). This exercise is taken from a workshop prepared for the Dade-Monroe County (Florida) Teacher Education Center.

    The student will

    a. solve ten multiplication problems in twenty minutes and achieve a score of eight correct.
    b. cut and splice a strip of film.
    c. spell fifteen words correctly.
    d. respond to a call to serve on an environmental clean-up committee.
    e. using the financial pages of the daily newspaper, study the closing prices of several common stocks on one day of a particular week and tell whether the value of the stocks has gone up or down or remained the same the next day of that week.
    f. using a wall map and pointer, trace the path of the Mississippi River from source to mouth.
    g. demonstrate an awareness that school spirit must be improved.
    h. write a paper of ten pages, typed, double-spaced, on the topic, "Traveling in Space." The paper must be scientifically accurate and in good English. It must contain at least two footnotes and a bibliography of at least five references.
    I. with a compass, draw a circle that has a two-inch diameter.
    j. express admiration for skills shown by a famous actor or actress.
    k. identify a living American author whose works he or she believes will become classics and, by referring to the author's works, support his or her choice of author.
    l. design and make a pair of earrings out of black coral.
    m. demonstrate the proper way to hold the bowling ball before beginning the approach.
    n. using a musical instrument, convert a classical theme to a rock or disco beat.
    o. regularly donate money or goods to a charity.
    p. explain reasons for his or her preference for a political party.
    q. apply epoxy glue to join two pieces of wood together following directions on the label.

    r. identify the smell of baking bread.

ANSWERS TO EXERCISE 17

    a. cognitive-application
    b. psychomotor-complex overt response
    c. cognitive-knowledge
    d. affective-responding
    e. cognitive-analysis
    f. cognitive-comprehension
    g. affective-receiving
    h. cognitive-synthesis
    I. psychomotor-mechanism
    j. affective-valuing
    k. cognitive-evaluation
    l. psychomotor-origination
    m. psychomotor-set
    n. psychomotor-adaptation
    o. affective-characterization by value or value complex
    p. affective-organization
    q. psychomotor-guided response
    r. psychomotor-perception

18. Choose one curriculum goal and write two curriculum objectives for it. Then write one instructional goal for one of the curriculum objectives and two instructional objectives for the instructional goal.

19. Using the appropriate format, explain the correct way of writing an individualized education program (IEP). In your explanation give examples of both annual goals and behavioral objectives derived from the goals.

20. In the following items, put a CG if you believe the item is a curriculum goal, CO for a curriculum objective, IG for an instructional goal, and IO for an instructional objective (answers follow):

    a. Students will develop an awareness of major social and economic problems of the community.
    b. Without using a calculator, the student will solve the following problem, carrying out the answer to two places: 6.859 divided by 27.
    c. Students will increase their use of the school library as evidenced by a ten percent rise in the circulation of library books over the previous year.
    d. The student will develop an appreciation for *Macbeth*.
    e. By the end of the year, all students will have engaged in at least one community service project.
    f. The student will understand why the United States entered the Vietnam War.
    g. The student will distinguish between the sounds of $\bar{a}$ and $\breve{a}$.
    h. Students will improve their skills in aesthetic expression.
    I. The student will know the functions of the executive, legislative, and judicial branches of the government.

j. Students will improve their skills in composition.

ANSWERS TO EXERCISE 20

a. CG	b. IO	c. CO	d. IG	e. CO
f. IG	g. IO	h. CG	i. IG	j. CG

BIBLIOGRAPHY

Armstrong, Robert J., Cornell, Terry D., Kramer, Robert E., and Roberson, E. Wayne. *The Development and Evaluation of Behavioral Objectives.* Worthington, Ohio: Charles A. Jones, 1970.

Armstrong, Thomas. *Multiple Intelligences in the Classroom.* Alexandria, Va.: Association for Supervision and Curriculum Development, 1994.

Bernhardt, Regis, Hedley, Carolyn N., Cattaro, Gerald, and Svolopoulos, Vasilios, eds. *Curriculum Leadership: Rethinking Schools for the 21st Century.* Cresskill, N.J.: Hampton Press, 1998.

Bloom, Benjamin S., ed. *Taxonomy of Educational Objectives: The Classification of Educational Goals: Handbook I: Cognitive Domain.* White Plains, N.Y.: Longman, 1956.

———, Hastings, J. Thomas, and Madaus, George F. *Handbook on Formative and Summative Evaluation of Student Learning.* New York: McGraw-Hill, 1971.

Brandt, Ronald S. and Tyler, Ralph W. "Goals and Objectives." In Fenwick W. English, ed. *Fundamental Curriculum Decisions.* l983 Yearbook, 40–52. Alexandria, Va.: Association for Supervision and Curriculum Development, 1983.

Briggs, Leslie J. *Handbook of Procedures for the Design of Instruction.* Washington, D.C.: American Institutes for Research, 1970.

Caine, Renate Nummela and Caine, Geoffrey. *Making Connections: Teaching and the Human Brain.* Alexandria, Va.: Association for Supervision and Curriculum Development, 1991.

Campbell, Linda and Campbell, Bruce. *Multiple Intelligences and Student Achievement: Success Stories from Six Schools.* Alexandria, Va.: Association for Supervision and Curriculum Development, 1999.

Campbell, Linda, Campbell, Bruce, and Dickinson, Dee. *Teaching and Learning Through Multiple Intelligences.* Needham Heights, Mass.: Allyn and Bacon, 1996.

Checkley, Kathy. "The First Seven . . . and the Eighth: A Conversation with Howard Gardner." *Educational Leadership 55,* no. 1 (September 1997): 8–13.

Combs, Arthur W., ed. *Perceiving, Behaving, Becoming: A New Focus for Education.* l962 Yearbook. Alexan-dria, Va.: Association for Supervision and Curriculum Development, 1962.

Davis, Robert H., Alexander, Lawrence T., and Yelon, Stephen L. *Learning System Design: An Approach to the Improvement of Instruction.* New York: McGraw-Hill, 1974.

Dick, Walter and Carey, Lou. *The Systematic Design of Instruction,* 2nd ed. Glenview, Ill.: Scott, Foresman, 1985.

Faculty of the New City School. *Celebrating Multiple Intelligences: Teaching for Success: A Practical Guide Created by the Faculty of The New City School.* St. Louis, Mo.: The New City School, Inc., 1994.

Gagné, Robert M. and Briggs, Leslie J. *Principles of Instructional Design.* New York: Holt, Rinehart and Winston, 1974.

Gardner, Howard. *Frames of Mind: The Theory of Multiple Intelligences.* New York: Basic Books, 1983.

——— *Multiple Intelligences: The Theory in Practice.* New York: Basic Books, 1993.

Goleman, Daniel. *Emotional Intelligence.* New York: Bantam Books, 1995.

Gronlund, Norman E. *Stating Objectives for Classroom Instruction,* 2nd ed. New York: Macmillan, 1978.

Harrow, Anita J. *A Taxonomy of the Psychomotor Domain: A Guide for Developing Behavioral Objectives.* White Plains, N.Y.: Longman, 1972.

Hartley, James and Davies, Ivor K. "Preinstructional Strategies: The Role of Pretests, Behavioral Objectives, Overviews, and Advance Organizers." *Review of Educational Research* 46, no. 2 (Spring 1976): 239–265.

Hlebowitsh, Peter S. *Radical Curriculum Theory Reconsidered: A Historical Approach.* New York: Teachers College Press, 1993.

Kibler, Robert J., Barker, Larry L., and Miles, David T. *Behavioral Objectives for Instruction and Evaluation.* Boston: Allyn and Bacon, 1974.

Kim, Eugene C. and Kellough, Richard D. *A Resource Guide for Secondary School Teaching: Planning for Competence,* 6th ed. Englewood Cliffs, N.J.: Merrill, 1995.

Krathwohl, David E., Bloom, Benjamin S., and Masia, Bertram B. *Taxonomy of Educational Objectives: The*

Classification of Educational Goals: Handbook II: Affective Domain. White Plains, N.Y.: Longman, 1964.

McAshan, H. H.: *Competency-Based Education and Behavioral Objectives.* Englewood Cliffs, N.J.: Educational Technology Publications, 1979.

McNeil, John D. *Curriculum: A Comprehensive Introduction,* 5th ed. New York: HarperCollins College Publishers, 1996.

Mager, Robert F. *Preparing* Instructional Objectives, 2nd ed. Belmont, Calif.: Fearon, 1975.

Nelson, Annabelle. *Curriculum Design Techniques.* Dubuque, Iowa: William C. Brown, 1990.

Popham, W. James. "Practical Ways of Improving Curriculum via Measurable Objectives." *Bulletin of the National Association of Secondary School Principals* 55, no. 355 (May 1971): 76–90.

——— *Systematic Instruction.* Englewood Cliffs, N.J.: Prentice-Hall, 1970.

——— and Baker, Eva L. *Establishing Instructional Goals.* Englewood, N.J.: Prentice-Hall, 1970.

Raths, James D. "Teaching Without Specific Objectives." *Educational Leadership* 28, no. 7 (April 1971): 714–720.

Salovey, Peter and Mayer, John D. "Emotional Intelligence." *Imagination, Cognition and Personality* 9, no. 3 (1989-90): 185–211.

Salovey, Peter and Sluyter, David J., eds. *Emotional Development and Emotional Intelligence: Educational Implications.* New York: Bantam Books, 1997.

Simpson, Elizabeth Jane. "The Classification of Educational Objectives in the Psychomotor Domain." In *The Psychomotor Domain,* vol. 3, 43–56. Washington, D.C.: Gryphon House, 1972.

"Teaching for Multiple Intelligences." *Educational Leadership* 55, no. 1 (September 1997): 8–74.

Thorndike, Edward L. "Intelligence and Its Uses." *Harper's Magazine* 140 (1920): 227–235.

Tyler, Ralph W. *Basic Principles of Curriculum and Instruction.* Chicago: University of Chicago Press, 1949.

AUDIOTAPE

Multiple Intelligences and Education. Features Howard Gardner. Association for Supervision and Curriculum Development, 1703 N. Beauregard St., Alexandria, Va. 22311-1714.

CD-ROM

Exploring Our Multiple Intelligences. Concept and application of the theory of multiple intelligences. Association for Supervision and Curriculum Development, P.O. Box 79760, Baltimore, MD 21279-0760.

PROFESSIONAL INQUIRY KIT

Emotional Intelligence. Video clips, activities, reading. 1997. Pam Robbins and Jane Scott, developers. Association for Supervision and Curriculum Development, 1703 N. Beauregard St., Alexandria, Va. 22311-1714.

VIDEOTAPES

Association for Supervision and Curriculum Development, 1703 N. Beauregard St., Alexandria, Va. 22311-1714.

Multiple Intelligences Series. 1995. 3 tapes: *Understanding Multiple Intelligences* (33 min.), *Classroom Applications* (36 min.), *and Creating the School of the Future* (20 min.). Three *Facilitator's Guides,* by Bruce and Linda Campbell. Book, *Multiple Intelligences in the Classroom* by Thomas Armstrong.

CHAPTER 11

SELECTING AND IMPLEMENTING STRATEGIES OF INSTRUCTION

After studying this chapter you should be able to:

1. Define style, model, method, and skills of teaching and state how each relates to the selection of instructional strategies.
2. Distinguish between generic and specific teaching skills.
3. Present a rationale for using a unit plan.
4. Relate daily lesson planning to long-range planning.

DECIDING ON INSTRUCTIONAL STRATEGIES

It's the planning period. The twelfth-grade American history teacher just left the teachers' lounge where she consumed a cup of coffee and chatted with her friends. She is seated now at a carrel in the teachers' workroom, curriculum guide and history textbook before her. The topic to be studied by the students is World War II—the European Theater. Conscientious planner that she is, she asks herself, "What is the best way to go about teaching this topic?" "What methods shall I use?" "What strategies are possible? suitable?" "How do I put together plans for instruction?" "Which suggestions from the curriculum guide should I adopt?" She jots down a number of approaches that she might use in creating a learning unit on the topic:

- Have the students read the appropriate chapters and come to class prepared to discuss them.
- Devise some key questions to give the class and let them find the answers as they read the chapter.
- Lecture to the class, adding points not covered in the text.
- Have each student write a paper on selected aspects of the war, such as the invasion of Normandy, the Battle of the Bulge, the crossing of the Rhine, and so on.

- Have each student select a related but different topic—for example, the opposing military leaders—and present an oral report to the class.
- Show the film *The Longest Day* or *Saving Private Ryan* on the invasion of Normandy, then follow it up with small group discussion and independent study on topics of interest to the students.
- Have students draw charts of the tactics of both sides in selected major battles.
- Have students read chapters in the textbook and give them quizzes in class the next day.
- Using a large classroom wall map of Europe or a small map with an opaque projector, point out the most significant geographical features of the area.
- Write a number of objective test items that will be incorporated in the end-of-unit test and drill the students on the answers as the topic is discussed.
- Invite a combat veteran of World War II to recount his experiences.
- Have students choose books on the topic from the school or public library, read them, and present oral reports to the class, comparing what they have read in the library books with accounts in the textbook.
- Make comparisons between World War I and World War II as to causes, numbers of combatants, numbers of casualties, battle tactics, and aftermaths.

The teacher must decide how many days she will devote to the topic, whether she will use any or all of the approaches considered, which approach she will use first, and how she will put the selected approaches together.

If you refer to Figure 10.1 in the previous chapter, you will note that selecting strategies is the next step called for in the Instructional Model. In this text, "strategy" broadly encompasses the methods, procedures, and techniques the teacher uses to present the subject matter to the students and to bring about desired outcomes. A strategy ordinarily includes multiple procedures or techniques. Lecturing, for example, can include procedures such as handing out charts and calling for evaluations at the end of the lecture. It may also include techniques like set induction and closure, which are generic teaching skills.

Among the common instructional strategies are the lecture, small group discussion, independent study, library research, mediated instruction (including computer-assisted instruction), repetitive drill, and laboratory work. To this list we can add coaching, tutoring, testing, and going on field trips. We could include the inquiry or discovery, inductive, and deductive methods. We could add programmed instruction, problem-solving, and oral questioning. Suffice it to say that the teacher has at his or her disposal a great variety of strategies for implementing instruction.

How does the teacher decide which strategy or strategies to use? The teacher may find a curriculum guide that will detail not only strategies to be used but also objectives, suggested resources, and suggested evaluation techniques.

Unfortunately, curriculum guides do not always exist for topics that the teacher wishes to emphasize, and often when they do exist and are accessible, they do not fit the teacher's and students' purposes. Consequently, the teacher must exercise professional judgment and choose the strategies to be employed. Selecting strategies becomes a less difficult problem when the teacher recognizes that instructional strategies are derived from five major sources. Before examining each of these sources we should emphasize a point that sometimes seems to be obscured in discussions of pedagogy, particularly in days of teacher shortages when teachers are assigned out of field. Paulo Freire hit on this point when he said, "The fact, however, that teachers learn how to teach a particular content must not in any way mean that they should venture into teaching without the necessary competence to do it. It does not give teachers a license to teach what they do not know."[1]

SOURCES OF STRATEGIES

OBJECTIVES AS SOURCE

The choice of strategies is limited at the onset by the specified instructional objectives. Although an almost infinite number of techniques for carrying out instruction may exist, only a finite number apply to any particular objective. For example, how many alternatives does the teacher have to teach the number fact that $2 \times 2 = 4$? He or she may tell the students or give a chalk talk using the blackboard; have the students repeat again and again the $2\times$ table, or use flash cards for drill purposes; have students practice using a workbook, an abacus, or a slide rule; or let pupils use a calculator or a printed multiplication table. Of course, not all of the possible courses of action will be suitable or acceptable to the teacher or the students, which limits the range of possibilities even more.

How many techniques suggest themselves for accomplishing the following objectives? The student will

- purify water by boiling
- write an editorial
- sew a zipper into a garment
- demonstrate a high jump
- help keep his or her school clean

Sometimes the strategy is obvious. There is no practical alternative; in essence, as "the medium is the message" (to use Marshall McLuhan's words), the objective is the strategy. The student will demonstrate high jump, for example, by performing that act. No amount of "teaching about" high jumping will permit the students to demonstrate that they can perform the high jump.

SUBJECT MATTER AS SOURCE

Subject matter provides a source of instructional strategies. With some subject matter selecting strategies is relatively simple. If we are teaching a course in television repair, certain operations must be mastered, such as checking the circuits, replacing the picture tube, replacing the solid state components, and adjusting the color.

The teacher must zero in on the subject matter and determine what principal facts, understandings, attitudes, appreciations, and skills must be mastered by the learners. Whereas some subject areas have a reputation for being harder to *learn*—for example, calculus, chemistry, and physics—others are more difficult to *teach*. Although learners

---

[1]Paulo Freire, *Teachers as Cultural Workers: Letters to Those Who Dare Teach* (Boulder, Col.: Westview Press, 1998), p. 17.

may have difficulty balancing chemical equations, the strategies for teaching this content are fairly straightforward: lecture-demonstration, followed by testing. Less apparent, however, are strategies for teaching the dictum "Thou shall not cheat." What would be the most effective method for inculcating an attitude of disapproval of cheating? How would the teacher test for mastery of this affective outcome?

Teaching about a subject as opposed to *teaching* a subject is an approach that even experienced teachers must guard against. We have alluded to this practice in the instance of teaching students to high jump. We can find other illustrations as well. For example, teachers who require students to commit grammar rules to memory often test only a knowledge of these rules rather than the students' ability to apply them. Rather than use the library, students are sometimes confined to studying the Library of Congress cataloging system only in the English classroom. Again, students are permitted to verbalize what a balanced meal is but are not required to select or prepare one.

It is easy to be trapped into teaching about desired outcomes in the affective domain. Students read about democracy as a way of life but are not given the opportunity—sometimes inadvertently, sometimes deliberately—to practice democracy in the school. Students are lectured on the importance of self-discipline but are not allowed an opportunity to demonstrate it.

Teaching about content can lead to verbalism—the ability to describe a behavior but not necessarily the ability to carry it out. Verbalism is more likely to result when students are placed in a passive mode. Whenever possible, the learners should be actively involved in the instructional process; they should be placed in real situations or, barring that, in simulated ones.

These comments are not meant to rule out vicarious learning. We would be lost without it and life would be much bleaker. Pupils cannot, of course, always be involved in real situations. History for example, must be learned vicariously. Until the day when the science fiction writer's dreams become reality, we cannot project ourselves backward in time, propel ourselves physically into the future, nor project ourselves spatially into a coexistent present. For example, most of us can sail up the Amazon River only through words and pictures of someone who has performed that feat and written and photographed his or her exploits for publications like *The National Geographic Magazine* or for television. We can experience directly the here and now in our own little corner of the universe.

Vicarious experience is more efficient in cases too simple for direct experiencing by every student. Valuable time would be wasted, for example, by having each student in an automotive program demonstrate the changing of an automobile's air filter. A presentation by the instructor should suffice for learning this uncomplicated skill. Vicarious experience is the only option, however, when (1) resources are lacking, as in the case of learning to use the latest version of Windows when only earlier versions are available; (2) facilities are lacking, as in learning to inspect an automobile's brakes when a school does not have appropriate space or equipment; and (3) the experience is too complicated or expensive, as in preparing a gourmet meal of bouillabaisse, coq au vin, or moo goo gai pan.

Textbooks as Source of Subject Matter.   We can find repeated criticisms in the literature of reliance on textbooks per se. Michael W. Apple called attention to "the ubiquitous character of the textbook" when he wrote:

Whether we like it or not, the curriculum in most American schools is not defined by courses of study or suggested programs, but by one particular artifact, the standardized, grade-level-specific text...While the text dominates curricula at the elementary, secondary, and even college levels, very little attention has been paid to the ideological, political, economic sources of its production, distribution, and reception.[2]

Freire put what some might term a constructivist spin on his concern about the way textooks are used:

Unfortunately, in general what has been done in schools lately is to lead students to become passive before the text. . . . Using their imagination is almost forbidden, a kind of sin. . . . They are invited neither to imaginatively relive the story told in the book nor to gradually appropriate the significance of the text.[3]

Obviously, with the wealth of knowledge surrounding learners today through print, tangible learning aids, and on-line data reliance on a single textbook, passively absorbed, is ineffective pedagogy.

To conclude, whether personal or vicarious in nature, instructional strategies may emerge from a variety of subject-matter sources.

STUDENT AS SOURCE

Instructional strategies must be appropriate for the students. The teacher will not send the average third grader to the media center to select one of Shakespeare's plays for leisure reading. Conversely, the teacher will not attempt to engage junior or senior high school boys and girls in a rousing game of London Bridge or Ring-Around-the-Rosie. Elementary Spanish is inappropriate for students ready for the intermediate level. Highly abstract verbal approaches to content do not fit the needs of the mentally retarded or slow learners. Independent study is applicable only to those with enough self-discipline and determination to profit from it.

Teachers need to capitalize on the special aptitudes or intelligences of learners. In the preceding chapters we mentioned Howard Gardner's concept of multiple intelligences. An adequate school curriculum would offer experiences to develop not only linguistic and logical-mathematical intelligence but also bodily-kinesthetic, interpersonal, intrapersonal, musical, and spatial as well.[4]

Teachers who underestimate the ability of learners and talk down to them or who overestimate the aptitude of learners and talk over their heads follow approaches that do not recognize the pupil as a source of strategy. Unless the teacher is careful, one source of strategy may conflict with another. A particular methodology may relate perfectly to the objectives, and may be right on target as to the subject matter, but may be completely inappropriate from the standpoint of the learner. We may generalize, therefore, that any particular strategy must not run counter to any of the sources of strategies.

---

[2]Michael W. Apple, "The Culture and Commerce of the Textbook," in Landon E. Beyer and Michael W. Apple, ed. *The Curriculum: Problems, Politics, and Possibilities*, 2nd ed. (Albany, N.Y.: State University of New York Press, 1998), p. 159.

[3]Freire, *Teachers as Cultural Workers*, p. 31.

[4]Howard Gardner, *Multiple Intelligences: The Theory in Practice* (New York: Basic Books, 1993).

The teacher should enlist the aid of students in both long-range and short-range planning for instruction. The teacher cannot assume, for example, that his or her purposes are identical to the students' purposes in studying a subject; he or she must therefore make an effort to discover student purposes.

When initiating a topic, the teacher should help students identify their personal reasons, if any, for studying the material. Students should be asked to state their objectives in their own words. For example, the teacher may wish students to study the Vietnam War so (1) they can complete a section of the textbook, (2) they can fulfill a requirement of a course in history, (3) they can become familiar with that segment of our history, and (4) they might become interested enough in history to continue studying it in college. The student, on the other hand, may wish to study the Vietnam War in order to (1) understand books, television programs, and films concerned with this topic, (2) learn what friends and relatives experienced there, and (3) find out what got us into the war, why there was so much student protest, and how we can avoid getting into such a situation again.

Students may effectively participate in planning by (1) choosing among equally acceptable topics, (2) helping to identify the instructional objectives, (3) suggesting appropriate strategies, (4) choosing individual and group assignments, (5) selecting materials, and (6) structuring learning activities.

COMMUNITY AS SOURCE

The desires of parents, the type of community, tradition, and convention all play a part in determining classroom strategies. Sexuality education, for example, alarms parents in many communities. Some oppose the school's venturing into this area on religious grounds; others feel it is the prerogative of the home. Consequently, examining various contraceptives might be considered by many in the community as inappropriate at any level.

A survey of drug habits among youth of a community might be rejected by some citizens who feel a negative image of the community might be the result. Counseling techniques that probe into a pupil's family life, psychological and personality tests, and values clarification may disturb parents.

Learning activities that stimulate excessive competition among students in the classroom and on the athletic field may meet with community disapproval. The use of outdated methodologies like the overuse of memorization can disturb parents as can procedures that call for behaviors either beyond the pupils' capacities or below their abilities.

Community efforts to censor materials and methods occur frequently in some localities. Although teachers may experience some difficulties with the community over their choice of techniques or content, they need not abandon a course of action for this reason alone. However, as discussed earlier in this text, involving members of the community in the process of curriculum development is desirable. Learning about community needs, beliefs, values, and mores may be necessary before the teacher can gain support for using techniques he or she believes are most effective. Through advisory committees, parent volunteer aides, parent-school organizations, and civic groups, community opinions about the school and its curricula can be gathered.

TEACHER AS SOURCE

Instructional strategies must conform to (1) the teacher's personal style of teaching and (2) the model or models of instructing the teacher follows. Large-group discussion, for example, will not appeal to the teacher who prefers to work closely with students. A teacher who regularly follows an inductive model of teaching is not likely to be content with using a deductive model. Teachers should analyze the particular style of teaching they project and the models they find most suitable for their particular styles. They should seek to expand their repertoires by developing more than a single model of teaching.

GUIDELINES FOR SELECTING STRATEGIES

To help choose instructional strategies, you may wish to consider the following guidelines, which suggest that a strategy must be right for

- the learners. It must meet their needs and interests and must be in keeping with their learning styles.
- the teacher. The strategy must work for the individual teacher.
- the subject matter. Artificial respiration, for example, is taught more effectively by demonstration and practice than by lecturing.
- the time available. For example, a scientific experiment requiring an extended period of several days is not possible if sufficient time is not available.
- the resources available. Reference materials, for example, must be available if students are required to carry out research projects that necessitate their use.
- the facilities. Dividing a class into small groups for discussion purposes, for example, may be impractical if the room is small, if acoustics are poor, and if the furniture is not movable.
- the objectives. The strategy must be chosen to fulfill the instructional objectives.[5]

STYLES OF TEACHING

A style of teaching is a set of personal characteristics and traits that clearly identify the individual as a unique teacher. Personal factors that make one teacher different from another include:

- dress
- language/speech
- voice
- gestures
- energy level
- facial expressions
- motivation
- interest in people
- dramatic talent

---

[5]Peter F. Oliva and George E. Pawlas, *Supervision for Today's Schools,* 5th ed. (New York: Longman, 1997), pp. 139–144.

- intellect
- scholarship

Teachers consciously or unconsciously adopt certain styles. The teacher as helper, disciplinarian, actor, friend, father or mother image, autocrat, artist, big brother or sister, or expounder of subject matter are examples of teaching styles. Barbara Bree Fischer and Louis Fischer defined teaching style as "a persuasive quality in the behavior of an individual, *a quality that persists though the content may change.*"[6] They observed that teachers differ in teaching style in much the same way that U.S. presidents varied in speaking style, famous painters differed in artistic style, or well-known tennis players demonstrated unique playing styles.

The teacher with a high, thin voice had best not rely heavily on lecture as a method. The teacher who is formal and proper in dress and manner will probably rule noisy games out of his or her repertoire. The teacher who lacks confidence in his or her management skills may not feel comfortable with a free-wheeling, open-ended discussion. If a teacher of low energy level or low motivation refuses to carefully read students' assigned essays or term papers, there is little point in using such strategies.

The teacher with a penchant for scholarship will likely include among his or her methods various forms of research. The teacher with an interest in people will choose procedures in which he or she and the students are interacting not only with each other but also with people both inside and outside the school.

The teacher who is confident about his or her work will invite visitors to the classroom, use resource persons, and permit audio—and video-taping of classroom activities. The teacher who is democratically oriented will design activities that permit students to participate in decision making. Unflappable individuals will be more inclined to try out innovative techniques that might result in failure whereas less intrepid individuals will tend to stick to the tried-and-true.

Some teachers reject the use of audiovisual techniques because they do not feel competent enough to use the equipment or they harbor the attitude that the use of media is somehow a waste of valuable time. In the judgment of these teachers, Guttenberg provided the definitive answer to instructional media—the printed page.

Fischer and Fischer identified a number of styles of teaching, including:

The Task-Oriented—These teachers prescribe materials to be learned and demand specific performance on the part of the students. Learning to be accomplished may be specified on an individual basis, and an explicit system of accounting keeps track of how well each student meets the stated expectations.

The Cooperative Planner—These teachers plan the means and ends of instruction with student cooperation. . . . Opinions of the learners are not only listened to, but are respected. These teachers encourage and support student participation at all levels.

The Child-Centered—This teacher provides a structure for students to pursue whatever they want to do or whatever interests them. . . . This style is not only extremely rare, it is almost impossible to imagine in its pure form because the classroom, with its adult-child ratio and adult-responsible environment, automatically encourages some interests and discourages others.

---

[6]Barbara Bree Fischer and Louis Fischer, "Styles in Teaching and Learning," *Educational Leadership* 36, no. 4 (January 1979): 245.

The Subject-Centered—These teachers focus on organized content to the near exclusion of the learner. By "covering the subject," they satisfy their consciences even if little learning takes place.

The Learning-Centered—These teachers have equal concern for the students and for the curricular objectives, the materials to be learned. They reject the over-emphasis of both the "child-centered" and "subject-centered" styles and instead help students, whatever their abilities or disabilities, develop toward substantive goals as well as in their autonomy in learning.

The Emotionally Exciting and Its Counterpart—These teachers show their own intensive emotional involvement in teaching. They enter the teaching-learning process with zeal and usually produce a classroom atmosphere of excitement and high emotion.[7]

You and I no doubt find some teaching styles more appealing and more acceptable than others. We might identify some styles as negative (e.g., undemocratic behavior) and some as positive (e.g., concern for students). Human beings that we are, we will probably give our approval to styles of teaching that emulate our own. Fischer and Fischer made their position clear:

> We do not consider all styles of teaching and learning to be equally valid. All too often, indefensible practices are justified with the claim, "Well, that's my style. I have mine, you have yours, and each is as good as the other."...Since the very idea of style is based on a commitment to individualization of instruction and the development of learner autonomy, styles that encourage undue conformity and dependence are not acceptable to us.[8]

Deborah P. Britzman took issue with the view that teaching style is "self-constructed product, mediated only by personal choice."[9] Britzman explained, "Teaching style, then, turns out to be not so much an individually determined product as a dialogic movement between the teacher, the students, the curriculum, the knowledge produced in exchange, and the discursive practices that make pedagogy intelligible."[10]

STYLES OF LEARNING

The teacher's style obviously bears some relationship to the pupils' styles of learning. Some pupils are

- eager beavers
- mules
- self-starters
- plodders
- shining stars
- skeptics

---

[7]Ibid., p. 251.

[8]Ibid., p. 246.

[9]Deborah P. Britzman, *Practice Makes Practice: A Critical Study of Learning to Teach* (Albany, N.Y.: State University of New York Press, 1991), p. 232.

[10]Ibid.

Some would add "survivors." Britzman noted that "those [students] who are most "successful" [sic] actively read the text of the teacher—her or his moods, behaviors, values, judgments, discourse strategies, and classroom expectations."[11]

Some learners can work under pressure; others cannot. Some need much direction; others, little. Some express themselves better orally than in written form. Some can deal with abstractions; others can learn only with concrete materials. Some learn more effectively from aural and visual techniques than through reading.

Recent research on the brain reaffirms the complexity of the functioning of the brain and at the same time reinforces differences in learners' styles, suggesting as Renata Nummela Caine and Geoffrey Caine wrote, the need for teachers "to select from the vast array of methods and approaches that are available."[12]

Perhaps an oversimplification, but nevertheless, a useful conception of functioning of the brain, postulates dominance in either the left hemisphere or the right hemisphere of the brain, although both hemispheres interact. Following this conception left-hemisphere dominance appears to favor logical processes, right-hemisphere, creative. The school curriculum traditionally caters to left-hemisphere characteristics.[13] Caine and Caine cautioned that the research on hemisphericity is inconclusive.[14]

The application of recent research on the brain to teaching and learning, however, according to Eric Jensen, places us on "the verge of a revolution" that "will change school start times, discipline policies, assessment methods, teaching strategies, budget priorities, classroom environments, use of technology, and even the way we think of the arts and physical education."[15] Pupils are as different in learning styles as teachers are in teaching styles.[16] In fact, they are more different since there are more of them. Teachers must be aware that their teaching styles can at times be at cross-purposes to their pupils'.

A teaching style cannot be selected in the same way an instructional strategy can. Style is not something that can be readily switched on and off. It is not simple to change from a task-oriented to a child-centered approach. Only with considerable difficulty, if at all, can a nonemotionally exciting teacher become an emotionally exciting one. Two questions must be asked about teaching styles: Can a teacher change his or her style? Should a teacher change his or her style?

Given a willingness to change, appropriate training, counseling or therapy, if need be, a teacher can change his or her style. Contrary to ancient beliefs about the impossibility of changing a person's behavior, human beings can and do change. Sometimes personality change is modeled on the behavior of another person who is in some way

---

[11]Ibid., p. 3.

[12]Renata Nummela Caine and Geoffrey Caine,"Understanding a Brain-Based Approach to Learning and Teaching," *Educational Leadership* 48, no. 2 (October 1990): 66–70.

[13]Regarding oversimplification of this theory see Susan Dobbs, "Some Second Thoughts on the Application of Left Brain/Right Brain Research," *Roeper Review* 12 (December 1989): 121.

[14]Renate Nummela Caine and Geoffrey Caine, *Making Connections: Teaching and the Human Brain* (Alexandria, Va.: Association for Supervision and Curriculum Development, 1991), p. 34.

[15]Eric Jensen, *Teaching with the Brain in Mind* (Alexandria, Va.: Association for Supervision and Curriculum Development, 1998), p. 1.

[16]For analysis of students' learning styles see Rita Dunn and Kenneth Dunn, *Teaching Students Through Their Individual Learning Styles: A Practical Approach* (Reston, Va.: Reston Publishing Company, 1978). See also Pat Burke Guild and Stephen Garger, *Marching to Different Drummers* (Alexandria, Va.: Association for Supervision and Curriculum Development, 1985) and "Learning Styles and the Brain," *Educational Leadership* 48, no. 2 (October 1990): 3–80.

important to an individual. Sometimes a crisis or trauma effects personality change. All religions share the basic premise that individuals can change their behavior. Thus change is possible, though it may not be easy.

Perhaps a larger question is whether a teacher *should* change his or her style. Three answers are given to this question, one of which presupposes a teacher's ability to change style. First, one school of thought holds that a teacher's learning style should match the pupils'. Consequently, we would attempt to analyze the styles of the teacher and pupils respectively, then group pupils and teachers with compatible styles. The pupils and teachers would then follow their own styles.

At first glance, ignoring the complexities of analyzing styles and grouping the pupils with compatible teachers, this position seems to be very sound and logical. Rapport between teacher and pupils would most likely be high, and the classroom climate would be conducive to learning. Herbert A. Thelen supported the concept of matching teachers and students: "We remain convinced that any grouping which does not in some way attempt to 'fit' students and teachers together can have only accidental success."[17]

According to a second school of thought, there is some merit in exposing students to a great variety of personal styles during their schooling so they will learn how to interact with different types of people. Although some students might prefer the less structured, informal, relaxed approach while they are in school, a legion of high school graduates compliment their task-oriented, subject-centered teachers for having "held their feet to the fire," thereby helping them to succeed after graduation in spite of themselves.

Richard L. Turner took this second position when he commented:

> A key feature of virtually all school organizations is that little effort is made to control the variability of teaching styles and learning styles. Schools rarely attempt to match the styles of learners to the styles of teachers. Therein lies much of the strength and durability of the school as a social entity.
>
> Among any group of students, some will adapt more readily to the style of a particular teacher than others will. The strength of the school as a collective lies in the fact that over long periods of time students are exposed to many different teaching styles. By virtue of this variation, all but a few students are exposed to several teaching styles to which they readily adapt, and to some with which they must struggle.[18]

A third response to the question of whether a teacher should change his or her style holds that a teacher should be flexible, using more than one style with the same group of students or with differing groups of students. This answer combines features of both the first and second responses. Teachers vary their styles, if they can, for particular groups of learners, and by the same token, the pupils are exposed to a variety of styles. Whatever the strategy chosen, it must conform to the teacher's inimitable style. That is why it is so important for teachers to know who they are, what they are, and what they believe. Rita S. Dunn and Kenneth J. Dunn spoke about the effect of the teacher's attitudes and beliefs on teaching style.

---

[17]Herbert A. Thelen, *Classroom Grouping for Teachability* (New York: John Wiley & Sons, 1967), p. 186.

[18]Richard L. Turner, "The Value of Variety in Teaching Styles," *Educational Leadership* 36, no 4 (January 1979): 257–258.

The attitudes teachers hold toward various instructional programs, methods, and resources as well as the kinds of youngsters they prefer working with constitute part of their "teaching style." It is true, however that some teachers believe in specific forms of instruction that they do not practice (administrative constraints, inexperience, lack of resources, or insecurity) and that others practice methods in which they do not believe (administrative or community mandates, inability to change or to withstand pressure). It is also true that teachers may prefer students different from those they are actually teaching.[19]

"Style" and "method" are used rather loosely—and often interchangeably—in the professional literature. Fischer and Fischer cautioned, "Style is not to be identified with method, for people will infuse different methods with their own styles. For example, lecturing is not a style, in our conception, for people with distinctive styles will infuse their respective lectures with their own unique qualities."[20]

MODELS OF TEACHING

Whereas style of teaching is a personalized set of teacher behaviors, a model of teaching is a generalized set of behaviors that emphasizes a particular strategy or set of strategies. Lecturing, for example, is an instructional strategy or method. One whose predominant strategy is lecturing is fulfilling the model of lecturer. The contrast between model and style can readily be seen by a person who attends presentations given by two different lecturers.

Bruce Joyce and Marsha Weil defined a model of teaching this way: "A model for teaching is a plan or pattern that can be used to shape curriculums (long-term courses of studies) to design instructional materials, and to guide instruction in the classroom and other settings"; in the fourth edition of their book Joyce and Weil with Beverly Showers noted, "Models of teaching are really models of *learning*."[21] The model or instructional role that the teacher displays guides the teacher's choice of strategies. In one sense, the model or role is the method or strategy. For example, when the teacher plays the role of questioner, questioning is the instructional strategy or method. If the teacher directs students in using computer software in a particular subject, computer-assisted instruction is the method. On the other hand, if the teacher acts as a facilitator—a much broader role—a number of instructional strategies or methods may be employed. Students may choose their own materials, make up their own questions, and critique their own work, all under the general facilitating supervision of the teacher.

Susan S. Ellis clarified the meaning of a model of teaching when she wrote:

Models of teaching are strategies based on the theories (and often the research) of educators, psychologists, philosophers, and others who question how individuals learn. Each model consists of a rationale, a series of steps (actions, behaviors) to be taken by

---

[19]Rita S. Dunn and Kenneth J. Dunn, "Learning Styles/Teaching Styles: Should They . . . Can They . . . Be Matched?" *Educational Leadership* 36, no. 4 (January 1979): 241

[20]Fischer and Fischer, "Styles," p. 245.

[21]Bruce Joyce and Marsha Weil, *Models of Teaching*, 2nd ed. (Englewood Cliffs, N.J.: Prentice-Hall, 1980), p. 1. 4th ed. with Beverly Showers (Boston: Allyn and Bacon, 1992), p. 1.

the teacher and the learner, a description of necessary support systems, and a method for evaluating the learner's progress. Some models are designed to help students grow in self-awareness or creativity; some foster the development of self-discipline or responsible participation in a group; some models stimulate inductive reasoning or theory-building; and others provide for mastery of subject matter.[22]

In preservice teacher education, students usually gain familiarity and some limited experience with several of the more common models of teaching, including expository teaching, group discussion, role playing, demonstration, simulation, discovery, learning laboratories, programmed instruction, tutoring, problem solving, computer-assisted instruction, and mediated instruction. The assumption teacher education institutions make is that students will gain proficiency in one or more of the models (methods) and identify those with which they will feel most comfortable. Given the limited time at their disposal, teacher education institutions can only introduce students to the many instructional models, encourage students to identify their favorites, and help students to develop a degree of skill in carrying out various models.

Bruce Joyce identified twenty-five models of teaching.[23] Joyce and Weil with Beverly Showers described sixteen models grouped under four categories or families: (1) the social family, (2) the information-processing family, (3) the personal family, and (4) the behavioral systems family.[24] Mary Alice Gunter, Thomas H. Estes, and Jan Schwab explained a models approach to instruction when they described some nineteen models.[25]

When we speak of models rather than methods of teaching, we convey the concept that a model is a generalized pattern of behavior that can be learned and imitated. Although teachers may develop their own enduring personal styles (which they may not be able to change easily or desire to change), they may develop skills inherent in a variety of models. Thus we might ask the same questions about models that we asked about styles: Can teachers change their models of teaching? Should they change them?

To the first question the answer must be yes. Were this not so, a significant portion of preservice and in-service teacher education would be useless. To the second question, a change of model is desirable if the teacher's stock-in-trade is limited to one particular model, no matter how successfully the teacher carries it out. Teachers should be masters of several models of teaching. Different models are necessary to reach different goals of instruction.

NEED FOR VARIETY

Variety of modeling is essential to successful teaching. Constant exposure to a single model can lead to restlessness and boredom on the part of students. Let us fabricate a very unlikely situation. A teacher develops a successful model that his colleagues ad-

---

[22]Susan S. Ellis, "Models of Teaching: A Solution to the Teaching Style/Learning Style Dilemma," *Educational Leadership* 36, no. 4 (January 1979): 275.

[23]Bruce Joyce, *Selecting Learning Experiences: Linking Theory and Practice* (Alexandria, Va.: Association for Supervision and Curriculum Development, 1978).

[24]Joyce and Weil with Showers, *Models of Teaching*, 4th ed.

[25]Mary Alice Gunter, Thomas H. Estes, and Jan Schwab, *Instruction: A Models Approach*, 3rd ed. (Boston: Allyn and Bacon, 1999), pp. 65–315.

mire. In their search for the "right" and "best" method, they emulate their colleague to the point where every teacher in the school adopts his model. Can you imagine what school would be like if every teacher were enthusiastic about the discovery method, for example, and attempted to use it to the exclusion of other models? Life could be extremely dull for students and teachers alike.

Of course, the use of a single, consistent model by all teachers is not sound pedagogy; a model must be compatible with both the teacher's style and the students' styles of learning. Deductive thinking—in which a rule is given first, then many opportunities for applying it—is less time-consuming and more efficient with some learners than inductive thinking, in which the applications are given first and the learners determine the rule from them.

Fortunately, the use of a uniform model by all teachers is unlikely. However, we can detect sentiment among some educators that there is both a "best" style and a "best" model of teaching. Grasping for surefire solutions to instructional problems, school districts throughout the country have frequently conducted in-service education programs designed to promote a particular, supposedly universal, model of teaching.

Joyce and Weil viewed the search for the best model of teaching as a fallacy and noted that the research does not champion one model over another.[26] You will, of course, discover differences of opinion on the propriety of certain models. Some experts reject models that cast the teacher in the role of subject-matter authority and information-giver. Caine and Caine, drawing on research on the brain, championed the model of teacher as facilitator.[27] Ernest R. House would supplant the model of teacher as information-presenter with that of teacher as tutor.[28]

Proficiency in a variety of models would seem to be in order for there are times when direct presentation models may be more productive than more indirect. Carl D. Glickman counseled:

> There is value in some traditional elements of schooling. For example, there is merit in reconsidering whether exchanging pencils for word processors or relying on pocket calculators instead of mental calculation have improved education. There are clear benefits to directly teaching students particular content, insisting on clear penmanship, and having students memorize certain material. Therefore, there are traditions to be retained at the same time that different configurations of time, space, methods, tools, and technology are incorporated.[29]

That teaching is complex is affirmed by the comment of Elizabeth Ellsworth, ". . . pedagogy is a much messier and more inconclusive affair than the vast majority of our educational theories and practices make it out to be...pedagogy poses problems and dilemmas that can never be settled or resolved once and for all."[30]

---

[26]Joyce and Weil, *Models,* 2nd ed., p. 1; see also 3rd ed., pp. 4–5.

[27]Caine and Caine, *Making Connections,* p. 22.

[28]Ernest R. House, *Schools for Sale: Why Free Market Policies Won't Improve America's Schools and What Will* (New York: Teachers College Press, 1998), p. 3.

[29]Carl D. Glickman, *Revolutionizing America's Schools* (San Francisco: Jossey-Bass, 1998), p. 39.

[30]Elizabeth Ellsworth, *Teaching Positions: Difference, Pedagogy, and the Power of Address* (New York: Teachers College Press, 1997), p. 8.

TEACHING SKILLS

Up to this point we have been discussing styles and models of teaching, both of which are germane to selecting particular strategies or methods. We will now add a third dimension that bears upon selecting instructional strategies—teaching skills. A word is needed to signify the interrelationship between style, model, and skill of teaching. "Method" would be a tempting word to use if it did not already convey the meanings of both "strategy" and "model"—for example, the strategy of lecturing equals the model of lecturing. For want of a better term, the coining of which we will leave to others, we will use the ambiguous word "approach" to signify the interrelationship among the triumvirate of style, model, and skills. We might chart this relationship in the form of a simple diagram, shown in Figure 11.1, in which the shaded area represents the teacher's approach.

Let's take a simple illustration of this relationship. The teacher who consistently plays the role of facilitator (model) is likely to be a person who is student-centered, friendly, and relaxed, and has skill in advising, counseling, and serving as resource persons (skills). At the risk of redundancy, we might say that facilitator is the teacher's model and facilitation of learning is the teacher's instructional strategy (method).

What skills are pertinent to a particular approach? For example, what skills are required for lecturing—a method used at some time or other by most teachers? We might list the following:

- ability to enunciate
- ability to project one's voice
- ability to use proper grammar and sentence structure
- ability to "read" students' facial expressions
- ability to sustain interest
- ability to relate content to past and future experiences of learners
- ability to speak to level of audience
- ability to deal with individuals causing distractions
- ability to stimulate thinking
- ability to organize thoughts

All of these abilities are generic teaching skills. We may define generic teaching skills as those instructional skills or competencies that are general in nature and can be employed by teachers in any field and at any level. The converse, special teaching skills, are specific abilities that must be demonstrated by teachers in a particular field or level. The foreign language teacher, for example, must be skilled in the generic competency of varying stimuli, while also being adept at projecting specific stimuli unique to the language being taught. Skill in translating one language into another is a special skill of a foreign language teacher, not a talent that must be evidenced by every teacher.

GENERIC COMPETENCIES

For many years educators have taken an interest in identifying generic teaching skills or competencies. Dwight Allen and Kevin Ryan compiled a well-known list of generic

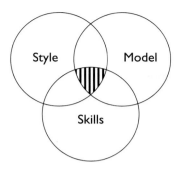

Figure 11.1   The teacher's approach

teaching skills.[31] Madeline Hunter and Douglas Russell listed seven steps—in effect, teaching skills—of planning for effective instruction.[32]

The state of Florida has identified generic teaching competencies that all its teachers should possess. These competencies, which provide the basis for the Professional Education portion of the Florida Teacher Certification Examination, are reproduced in Box 11.1. All persons seeking Florida teacher certification must pass not only the Professional Education Examination but also tests in a subject area (teaching field) and in college-level academic skills. Since 1975, Florida has altered the list of generic competencies from twenty-three to thirty-five in 1984, to twenty-seven in 1989, and to thirty in 1999.

Applicants for a teaching certificate in Texas must pass the criterion-referenced examination for the certification of educators in Texas (ExCET), which assesses subject-matter and professional knowledge required of entry-level educators. Competencies are stated and described under specified domains. Texas assesses performance on fifteen professional development competencies in three domains. The domains and statements of the competencies (without the descriptive statements) are shown in Box 11.2.

With appropriate training teachers can learn to master the generic teaching skills. Although generic teaching skills may be employed by all teachers at all levels, it does not follow that any teacher at any level or in any field can use any particular generic skills in just any given situation. Although every teacher should be able to ask probing questions, for example, each teacher will need to decide whether the nature of the content and the learning styles of the pupils will make probing questions appropriate.

Whether the skills are generic or specific, teachers must demonstrate a variety of instructional skills that can be adapted to their own styles and models. Research on teacher behaviors suggests that teaching skills can be imitated, learned, modified, and adopted.

The teachers' personal style, the models they follow, and the teaching skills they have mastered all affect their design for instruction. For example, teachers select strategies that match their personal styles. They follow models to which they are receptive and choose strategies for which they have the requisite teaching skills. The effective teacher implements a variety of teaching strategies as well as assessment strategies which are discussed in the following chapter.

---

[31]Dwight Allen and Kevin Ryan, *Microteaching* (Reading, Mass.: Addison-Wesley, 1969).

[32]Madeline Hunter and Douglas Russell, "How Can I Plan More Effective Lessons?" *Instructor* 87, no. 2 (September 1977): 74–75, 88.

BOX 11.1

FLORIDA'S GENERIC COMPETENCIES

1. Applies knowledge of physical, social, and academic developmental patterns and of individual differences, to meet the instructional needs of all students in the classroom and to advise students about those needs.
2. Enhances students' feelings of dignity and self-worth and the worth of other people including those from other ethnic, cultural, linguistic and economic groups.
3. Arranges and manages the physical environment to facilitate instruction and ensure student safety.
4. Recognizes overt signs of severe emotional distress in students and demonstrates awareness of appropriate intervention and referral procedures.
5. Recognizes signs of alcohol and drug abuse in students and demonstrates awareness of appropriate intervention and referral procedures.
6. Recognizes the overt physical and behavioral indicators of child abuse and neglect, knows the rights and responsibilities regarding reporting and how to interact appropriately with a child after a report has been made.
7. Formulates a standard for student behavior in the classroom.
8. Deals with misconduct, interruptions, intrusions, and digressions in ways that promote instructional momentum.
9. Determines the entry level knowledge and/or skills of students for a given set of instructional objectives using diagnostic tests, teacher observations, and student records.
10. Identifies long-range goals for a given subject area.
11. Constructs and sequences related short-range objectives for a given subject area.
12. Selects, adapts, and/or develops instructional materials for a given set of instructional objectives and student learning needs.
13. Selects/develops and sequences learning activities that are appropriate to instructional objectives and student needs.
14. Uses class time efficiently.
15. Communicates effectively using verbal and non-verbal skills.
16. Creates and maintains academic focus by using verbal, non-verbal and/or visual motivational devices.
17. Presents forms of knowledge such as concepts, laws and law-like principles, academic rules, and value knowledge.
18. Presents directions appropriate for carrying out an instructional activity.
19. Stimulates and directs student thinking, and checks student comprehension through appropriate questioning techniques.
20. Provides appropriate practice to promote learning and retention.
21. Relates to students' verbal communications in ways that encourage participation and maintain academic focus.
22. Uses feedback procedures that give information to students about the appropriateness of their response(s).
23. Conducts reviews of subject matter.

(Continued)

> **Box 11.1 Continued**
>
> 24. Constructs or assembles classroom tests and tasks to measure student achievement of objectives.
> 25. Establishes a testing environment in which students can validly demonstrate their knowledge and/or skill, and receive adequate information about the quality of their test performance.
> 26. Utilizes an effective system for maintaining records of students and class progress.
> 27. Uses computers in education.
>
> SOURCE: Florida Department of Education, *Study Guide for the Florida Teacher Certification Examination: Professional Education* (Tallahassee, Fla.: Florida Department of Education, 1989) and *Competencies and Skills Required for Teacher Certification in Florida,* 6th ed. (Tallahassee, Fla.: Florida Department of Education, 1999), pp. 00-2 to 00-12. Reprinted by permission.

TEACHING: ART OR SCIENCE?

The question whether teaching is an art or science has been debated almost from the time a person with the label "teacher"—from the Anglo-Saxon language—met with one or more disciples for the purpose of imparting some aspect of knowledge or belief. Foremost among those who view teaching as an art is Elliot W. Eisner whose widely known work, *The Educational Imagination: On the Design and Evaluation of School Programs,"* perceived the teacher as artist attuned to the qualities of life in the classroom and demonstrating "connoisseurship".[33]

David Levine proposed the use of the expression "teacher as artist" to replace "teacher as technician," and "school as an experiment in democracy" in place of school as factory."[34] Levine held that teaching for democracy "is a complex undertaking beyond the ability of teacher as technician."[35] Henry A. Giroux painted a larger role for teachers when he stated, "What classroom teachers can and must do is work in their respective roles to develop pedagogical theories and methods that link self-reflection and understanding with a commitment to change the nature of the larger society."[36]

On the other hand, those who lean toward the identification of generic teaching skills, the specification of instructional objectives, sequencing of content, national and state standards of achievement, and typical assessments would view teacher as scientist.

Successful teaching probably falls somewhere between the two poles.

ORGANIZING FOR INSTRUCTION

Planning for instruction involves selecting the following components:

- goals
- objectives

---

[33]Elliot W. Eisner, *The Educational Imagination: On the Design and Evaluation of School Programs,* 2nd ed. (New York: Macmillan, 1985), p. 219.

[34]David Levine, "Building a Vision of Curriculum Reform," in David Levine, Robert Lowe, Bob Peterson, and Rita Tenorio, eds., *Rethinking Schools: An Agenda for Change* (New York: The New Press, 1995), p. 53.

[35]Ibid, p. 54.

[36]Henry A. Giroux, *Pedagogy and the Politics of Hope: Theory, Culture, and Schooling: A Critical Reader* (Boulder, Col.: Westview Press, 1997), p. 28.

BOX 11.2

TEST FRAMEWORK FOR PROFESSIONAL DEVELOPMENT
(FIELDS 02—ELEMENTARY AND 03—SECONDARY)

Domain I—Understanding Learners
  (5 competencies = approximately 33% of test)
Domain II—Enhancing Student Achievement
  (6 competencies = approximately 40% of test)
Domain III—Understanding the Teaching Environment
  (4 competencies = approximately 27% of test)

DOMAIN I—UNDERSTANDING LEARNERS

Competency 001

The teacher uses an understanding of human developmental processes to nurture student growth through developmentally appropriate instruction.

Competency 002

The teacher considers environmental factors that may affect learning in designing a supportive and responsive classroom community that promotes all students' learning and self-esteem.

Competency 003

The teacher appreciates human diversity, recognizing how diversity in the classroom and the community may affect learning and creating a classroom environment in which both the diversity of groups and the uniqueness of individuals are recognized and celebrated.

Competency 004

The teacher understands how learning occurs and can apply this understanding to design and implement effective instruction.

Competency 005

The teacher understands how motivation affects group and individual behavior and learning and can apply this understanding to promote student learning.

DOMAIN II—ENHANCING STUDENT ACHIEVEMENT

Competency 006

The teacher uses planning processes to design outcome-oriented learning experiences that foster understanding and encourage self-directed thinking and learning in both individual and collaborative settings.

Competency 007

The teacher uses effective verbal, nonverbal, and media communication techniques to shape the classroom into a community of learners engaged in active inquiry, collaborative exploration, and supportive interactions. *(Continued)*

Box 11.2 Continued

Competency 008

The teacher uses a variety of instructional strategies and roles to facilitate learning and to help students become independent thinkers and problem solvers who use higher-order thinking in the classroom and the real world.

Competency 009

The teacher uses a variety of instructional materials and resources (including human and technological resources) to support individual and group learning.

Competency 010

The teacher uses processes of informal and formal assessment to understand individual learners, monitor instructional effectiveness, and shape instruction.

Competency 011

The teacher structures and manages the learning environment to maintain a classroom climate that promotes the lifelong pursuit of learning and encourages cooperation, leadership, and mutual respect.

DOMAIN III—UNDERSTANDING THE TEACHING ENVIRONMENT

Competency 012

The teacher is a reflective practitioner who knows how to promote his or her own professional growth and can work cooperatively with other professionals in the system to create a school culture that enhances learning and encourages positive change.

Competency 013

The teacher knows how to foster strong school–home relationships that support student achievement of desired learning outcomes.

Competency 014

The teacher understands how the school relates to the larger community and knows strategies for making interactions between school and community mutually supportive and beneficial.

Competency 015

The teacher understands requirements, expectations, and constraints associated with teaching in Texas, and can apply this understanding in a variety of contexts.

SOURCE: National Evaluation Systems, *ExCet: Examination for the Certification of Educators in Texas: Preparation Manual: Professional Development 02 Elementary 03 Secondary,* 1993, pp. 5–10. Reprinted with permission of the State Board of Educator Certification, Texas Education Agency.

- strategies
- learning resources
- evaluation techniques

We discussed selecting instructional goals and objectives in Chapter 10 and considered selecting strategies and, indirectly, the resources needed to carry them out in this chapter. Choosing evaluation techniques is the subject of Chapter 12.

Somehow the teacher must bring all the separate components together into a cohesive plan. Both long-range and short-range planning are required. Long-range plans will be examined in Chapter 15. Let's look now at the more immediate types of plans: the short-range unit plan and the even shorter range-daily plan.

UNIT PLANS

The unit plan—also called a "learning unit," "teaching unit," or simply, "unit"—is a means of organizing the instructional components for teaching a particular topic or theme. Many years ago William H. Burton provided a still-serviceable definition of a unit as follows: "A unit is any combination of subject-matter content and outcomes, and thought processes, into learning experiences suited to the maturity and needs (personal and social) of the learners, all combined into a whole with internal integrity determined by immediate and ultimate goals."[37]

Although units may be written narrowly within the confines of a particular field, for example, "Changing Decimals to Fractions," current efforts to integrate the curriculum promote the creation of units that cut across the disciplines. Even with a seemingly narrow theme like "Changing Decimals to Fractions" by selecting appropriate strategies the teacher can incorporate other learnings including linguistic, scientific, civic, vocational, artistic, and domestic.

The unit plan ordinarily covers a period from several days to several weeks. A series of units might actually constitute a particular course. The daily plan organizes the instructional components of the day's lesson(s). A unit serves as a source of a number of daily plans. Ordinarily, instructional planning progresses from course to unit to daily plans.

The writing of unit and daily lesson plans is a key skill that teacher education institutions seek to develop in preservice teachers. Some institutions insist on a degree of meticulousness and thoroughness in writing plans that is rarely seen in practice in the classroom.

You will find considerable variation in the structure of unit plans. Burton offered a detailed outline for a unit plan, as follows:

- *Title*. Attractive, brief, and unambiguous.
- *The Overview*. Brief statement of the nature and scope of the unit.
- *The Teacher's Objectives*. Understandings (generalizations), attitudes, appreciations, special abilities, skills, behavior patterns, facts.
- *The Approach*. A brief account of the most probable introduction.

---

[37]William H. Burton, *The Guidance of Learning Activities: A Summary of the Principles of Teaching Based on the Growth of the Learner,* 3rd ed.(Englewood Cliffs, N.J.: Prentice-Hall, Inc., 1962), p. 329.

- *The Pupil's Aim or Objective.* The major objective which it is hoped the learners will develop or accept.
- *The Planning and Working Period.* Learning activities with desired outcomes for each activity.
- *Evaluation Techniques.* How evidence will be gathered showing that the objectives of the unit have been developed.
- *Bibliographies.* Books useful to the teacher and books useful to the learners.
- *Audio-Visual Materials and Other Instructional Aids with Sources.*[38]

Analysis of various unit outlines shows that a unit plan should contain the title, the level or course for which it is intended, and the amount of time to be devoted to the following minimum essentials:

- instructional goals
- instructional objectives (cognitive, affective, psychomotor)
- instructional procedures (learning activities)
- evaluation techniques (preassessment, formative, summative)
- resources (human and material)

Units are written to be used, they are living documents and should be followed where helpful, and augmented, reduced, revised, and discarded when inappropriate. Box 11.3 provides an illustration of a unit plan.

LESSON PLANS

Lesson plans chart the daily instruction. Conceivably, lesson plans could (and sometimes are) written without reference to any written unit plan. However, on strictly logical grounds, lesson plans that are higher in quality, better organized, and more complete are achieved more often with unit plans than without them. Creating units is essential to holistic planning.

Like unit planning, lesson planning is an individual exercise. According to Laurence J. Peter, "A lesson plan is simply an outline prepared in advance of teaching, so that time and materials will be used efficiently."[39] Peter pointed out that "various types of lessons require different kinds of lesson plans."[40] We might add, on a philosophical level, "Various types of teachers, various types of learners, and various types of subject matter require different types of lesson plans." On a practical level, "Various types of administrators and supervisors require different types of lesson plans."

A six-part outline for a lesson plan that can be followed subject to modification for special situations contains six components:

A. Objectives
B. Activities
C. Assignment

---

[38]Ibid., pp. 372–374.

[39]Laurence J. Peter, *Competencies for Teaching: Classroom Instruction* (Belmont, Calif.: Wadsworth, 1975), p. 194.

[40]Ibid.

BOX 11.3

ILLUSTRATIVE UNIT PLAN

Title: Financing Our Community's Public Schools
Level: Senior High School—Problems of American Democracy
Time: Five Days

A. Instructional Goals
   1. The student will understand that quality education is costly.
   2. The student will understand that ignorance is more costly than education.
   3. The student will become aware of sources of funding for the schools.
   4. The student will become familiar with problems of financing education in our community.
B. Instructional Objectives

COGNITIVE
   1. The student will describe the role and extent of local involvement in financing the schools.
   2. The student will describe the role and extent of state involvement in financing the schools.
   3. The student will describe the role and extent of federal involvement in financing the schools.
   4. The student will explain the process by which public moneys are expended for the schools.
   5. The student will explain what our public moneys buy for the schools.
   6. The student will compare salaries of teachers in our community's schools with salaries paid outside of teaching.

AFFECTIVE
   1. The student will take a position on the property tax: necessary, too high, too low? Reasons must be stated for the position taken.
   2. The student will take a position on the statement: Teachers are underpaid. Reasons must be stated for the position taken.
   3. The student will take a position on federal aid to education: pro or con? Reasons must be stated for the position taken.
   4. The student will take a position on the statements: The schools cost too much. There are too many frills in education. Reasons must be stated for the position taken.

PSYCHOMOTOR
   None
C. Instructional Procedures
   1. Read the district superintendent's annual report and discuss the revenues and expenditures.
   2. Read this year's school budget and compare with proposed budget for next year. Account for changes in the total amounts each year.
   3. Draw a chart of the percentages of money spent by the locality, state, and federal government for support of the community's schools.
   4. Prepare a bar graph showing the total number of dollars expended this past year by the locality, state, and federal government for the community's schools.
   5. Report on your family's school tax and show how it was calculated.

(Continued)

Box 11.3 Continued

6. Invite a school principal to class and interview him or her about expenditures and revenues for his or her school.

7. Invite the superintendent, a member of the superintendent's staff, or a member of the school board to class and interview him or her about expenditures and revenues for the school district.

8. Report on the costs of one federally supported program in our community's schools.

9. Consult and discuss publications of the state department of education on financing schools in the state.

10. Compare amounts of money raised throughout the state by property taxes and by sales, income, and other taxes.

11. Compare salaries of teachers in our community with salaries of (1) teachers in other communities in the state, (2) teachers in other states, and (3) persons outside of teaching.

12. Account for variations in amounts of money raised for the support of education by localities of the state and in the total amounts of money available to these localities.

13. Account for variations in amounts of money raised for the support of education by the various states.

14. Compile a list of average annual costs of selected items for which schools must pay, including instructional supplies, equipment, heat, lights, water, salaries of all personnel, insurance, and maintenance.

15. Compute the costs of vandalism in our community's schools for a one-year period.

16. Write a report advocating either greater or lesser funding for our community's schools. In your report show what is to be added or cut.

17. Suggest improved ways of funding the schools.

D. Evaluation Techniques

1. Preassessment

Construct and administer a pretest to assess students' entry knowledge and skills. Sample questions might include:

   a. Estimate the total amount of money spent for the public schools of our community this past year.

   b. How is the property tax determined?

   c. Which spends more money on our community's schools: the locality, the state, or the federal government?

2. Formative evaluation

   a. Daily oral questioning of the students by the teacher on the more difficult aspects of the lessons.

   b. Daily summaries by students and teacher at the end of each lesson.

   c. Teacher's evaluation of student products, as charts, graphs, etc.

3. Summative evaluation

   a. Quiz on the day following conclusion of the unit. Sample test items may include questions similar to those of the pretest plus additional items. A combination of objective and essay test items may be used. Sample test items might include:

     (1) Essay: Explain the process by which our community raises money locally for the schools.

(Continued)

Box 11.3 continued

(2)   Objective: In reference to taxation, a mill is written as:
   (a) 01
   (b) 1.0
   (c) .001
   (d) .0001

E.   Resources

HUMAN

- School principal.
- School superintendent, member of the superintendent's staff, or member of the school board.

MATERIAL

- Publications of the local school board.
- Publications of the state department of education.
- Publications of the U.S. Department of Education, including:

   The Condition of Education: Statistical Report. Washington, D.C.: U.S. Department of Education, Center for Education Statistics, annually.
   Digest of Education Statistics. Washington, D.C.: U.S. Department of Education, Center for Education Statistics, annually.

- *Standard Education Almanac.* Chicago: Marquis Who's Who, annually.
- Bureau of the Census. *Statistical Abstract of the United States.* Washington, D.C.: Superintendent of Documents, U.S. Government Printing Office, annually.
- *The World Almanac and Book of Facts.* Mahwah, N.J.: PRIMEDIA Reference Inc., annually.

NOTE: This illustrative learning unit is based on the illustrative resource unit shown in Chapter 15.

D. Evaluation Techniques
E. Bibliography
F. Instructional Aids and Sources[41]

A sample lesson plan based on the illustrative unit plan is shown in Box 11.4.

The less experience a teacher has, the more complete that teacher's unit and lesson plans should be. It is desirable for both experienced and inexperienced teachers to prepare rather complete unit plans to fully communicate their ideas. Experienced teachers, however, will discover ways to simplify and shorten lesson plans. Once the unit and lesson plans have been made, the teacher can pay attention to matters of teaching style, model, and skills.

---

[41]Peter F. Oliva, *The Secondary School Today,* 2nd ed. (New York: Harper & Row, 1972), p. 313.

BOX 11.4

ILLUSTRATIVE LESSON PLAN

First Day
Unit: Financing Our Community's Schools
Fifty minutes

A. Objectives

COGNITIVE
   1. The student will list three sources of funding for the schools.
   2. The student will describe the source(s) of local funding for the schools.
   3. The student will define "property tax," "assessed valuation," and "mill."

AFFECTIVE
   1. The student will take positions, giving reasons whether the property tax is equitable, too high, or too low.
   2. The student will express an opinion and give reasons as to whether he or she believes expenditures for schools in the community are more than adequate, adequate, or inadequate.

B. Activities
   1. Set induction: Students will listen to the teacher read a recent editorial from the local newspaper on the needs of local schools. The class will discuss its perceptions of the editorial's accuracy (eight minutes).
   2. Using an overhead projector, the teacher will show transparencies of charts selected from the district superintendent's annual report to the school board. Students will respond to teacher's questions about interpretation of the charts (ten minutes).
   3. Using the same data, students will prepare original charts and/or graphs showing sources and amounts of funds for the community's schools this past year. Copies of the superintendent's report will also be available for students' use (ten minutes).
   4. Students will listen to teacher's description of sources of local funding. Key points: property tax, assessed evaluation, tax assessor, exemptions, and millage (ten minutes).
   5. Students will calculate amount of school tax to be paid on the following properties (five minutes):
        a.   A house assessed at $60,000; no exemptions; millage rate of 8.5 mills.
        b.   A house assessed at $50,000; homestead exemption of $5,000; millage rate of 6.52 mills.
        c.   A house assessed at $75,000; homestead exemption of $5,000 plus senior citizen exemption of $5,000; millage rate of 7.15 mills.
   6. Closure: Teacher will ask students such questions as: Which level of government spends most on the education of young people in the community? Approximately how much money was raised locally for schools last year? What percentage of funding came from the state? What percentage of funding came from the federal government? What is the current millage rate? (five minutes).

C. Assignment (two minutes)
   1. See if you can find any articles in the local newspapers about costs of education in the community, state, or nation.
   (Continued)

Box 11.4 continued

    2. Ask your parents how much school tax they paid last year and, if they do not object, report to the class how much it was and how it was calculated. Also ask your parents whether they believe the property tax is too high, too low, or about right.

D. Evaluation Techniques

    1. Spot-check students' in-class work on charts and calculations of property tax.

    2. Ask students to respond to teacher's oral questions at the end of the lesson.

E. Bibliography

    1. Copies of the district superintendent's annual report to the school board.

    2. Editorial from local newspaper.

F. Instructional Aids and Sources

    Overhead projector and transparencies.

PRESENTATION OF INSTRUCTION

After planning and organizing for instruction, the teacher proceeds to direct the students' learning experiences in the classroom. Entire volumes have been written on effective means of presenting instruction. Britzman commented: "Teaching is fundamentally a dialogic relation, characterized by mutual dependency, social interaction and engagement, and attention to the multiple exigencies of the unknown and the unknowable."[42]

Since this text focuses on curriculum development rather than instructional methodology, a discussion of methods of teaching will not be attempted in any detail. Instead, I would like to make a few general observations about presentation of instruction and direct you to a few sources for further study.

Research on effective teaching in the 1970s and 1980s supported commonsense principles to the effect that students learn more if teachers expect them to learn, focus on the content to be covered, keep them on task, provide adequate practice, monitor their performance, and care about whether they succeed. There is some evidence that for certain types of learnings and for certain types of students, direct instruction of the total group by the teacher is more effective than other strategies such as small grouping, inquiry, and Socratic techniques.

Evidence also shows that coaching is an appropriate technique for some types of learnings and students. Teacher training should make prospective teachers aware of the wide range of instructional strategies possible and help them develop proficiency in the use of those strategies.

For studies on the effective teaching research you may wish to consult some of the references in the bibliography at the end of this chapter, namely works by David C. Berliner et al.; Wilbur B. Brookover et al.; Jere E. Brophy and C. M. Evertson; Jere Brophy and Thomas L. Good; Ronald R. Edmonds; N. L. Gage; Bruce Joyce and Beverly Showers; Lawrence W. Lezotte and Beverly A. Bancroft; Donald M. Medley; Barak V. Rosenshine; David A. Squires, William G. Huitt, and John K. Segars, eds.;

---

[42]Britzman, *Practice Makes Practice*, p. 237.

Jane Stallings; Herbert J. Walberg; and Merlin C. Wittrock, ed. *Handbook of Research on Teaching,* 3rd ed. (New York: Macmillan, 1986), 35 chapters on research on teaching.

Two excellent references on teaching strategies are James M. Cooper, ed. *Classroom Teaching Skills,* 4th ed. and Eugene C. Kim and Richard D. Kellough, *A Resource Guide for Secondary School Teaching: Planning for Competence,* 6th ed. The complexity of teaching is readily evident in the roles expected of the teacher. D. John McIntyre and Mary John O'Hair, for example, viewed the teacher as an organizer, communicator, motivator, manager, innovator, counselor, and ethicist as well as fulfilling professional, political, and legal roles.[43]

Although many, perhaps most, educators accept the validity of the effective teaching research on generic teaching skills, some see the generalizations on effective teaching as limited. Current research on teaching has moved in the direction of case studies of teacher performance as opposed to the "process-product" orientation of the earlier studies. Newer foci include more astute recognition of the knowledge learners bring with them to the classroom, learners' use of knowledge to construct new knowledge (constructivism), more emphasis on social aspects of learning (e.g., cooperative learning, school as a community of learners), and realistic ("authentic") learning and performance-based ("authentic") assessment in place of standardized testing.[44]

INDIVIDUALIZED VERSUS GROUP INSTRUCTION

Controversy swirls around the respective efficacy of individualized versus group approaches to instruction. Proponents of individualization maintain that instruction must be geared toward the needs of the individual learners. Thus, we have seen strategies of programmed instruction, self-pacing, independent study, tutorials, guided independent study, and computer-assisted instruction in many classrooms. Proponents of group instruction point out that for some purposes, teaching entire groups is more efficient and practical in our mass educational system than attempting to individualize instruction. Consequently, teaching groups or subgroups in the classroom, be they heterogeneous or homogeneous, has been the time-honored approach to schooling. Research on teacher effectiveness has supported direct instruction of whole groups, at least for certain purposes.[45]

Interactive Video.   A newer direction in individualization is interactive video which builds onto the technology of computer-assisted instruction and combines it with features of video presentations. Gary W. Orwig and Donna J. Baumbach provided a simple definition of interactive video when they wrote: "Interactive video is a video message controlled by a computer program."[46]

---

[43]D. John McIntyre and Mary John O'Hair, *The Reflective Roles of the Classroom Teacher* (Belmont, Calif.: Wadsworth, 1996).

[44]See "Beyond Effective Teaching," *Educational Leadership* 49, no. 7 (April 1992): 4–73.

[45]See Barak V. Rosenshine, "Academic Engaged Time, Content Covered, and Direct Instruction," *Journal of Education* 160, no. 3 (August 1978): 38–66.

[46]Gary W. Orwig and Donna J. Baumbach., *What Every Educator Needs to Know About the New Technologies: Interactive Video 1* (Orlando, Fla.: UCF/DOE Instructional Computing Resource Center, University of Central Florida, 1989).

Whereas typical video presentations place the learner in a passive role, interactive video permits the student to assume an active part by responding to its presentations. Orwig and Baumbach described three levels of interactive video, albeit the first level uses no computer: (1) video disc player without a computer, the least expensive setup, capable of the least interaction on the part of the student; (2) video disc player with internal computer; and (3) video disc player controlled by an external desktop computer, the most expensive arrangement, possessing the greatest capability for interaction.[47] Orwig and Baumbach saw interactive video as "a powerful instructional medium, and it has the potential to change the way people learn."[48] They commented further:

> As interactive video becomes established, it will probably have a greater impact upon individualized instruction than all the self-paced workbooks, programmed instruction, drill and practice, lap-packs, computer assisted instruction, and other "individualized" techniques combined.[49]

In the years to come, we may expect to see increased use of the new technologies brought forth by computers, laser video discs, and interactive video. In many cases the electronic strategies will be incorporated into the existing curricula; in others, they will become alternatives to traditional textbook-oriented instruction.

Traditional means of grouping include tracking of students into varying groups and sectioning them by ability, practices we discuss in chapter 14 when we take a look at providing for exceptionalities. In place of (or perhaps in some cases, in spite of) these traditional practices has come the strategy of cooperative learning.

Cooperative Learning.   New versions of group instruction as well as individualized instruction have arisen. A considerable amount of research and experimentation transpired in the 1980s on presentation of instruction through cooperative learning, which is sometimes referred to as collaborative learning. Robert E. Slavin acknowledged that the concept of cooperative learning was an old idea and went on to define it in the following manner:

> Cooperative learning is a form of classroom organization in which students work in small groups to help one another learn academic material.[50]

In advancing his noncoercive lead-management control theory in the classroom William Glasser clearly supported cooperative learning, observing that "it is hard to visualize any quality school that is not deeply involved in this method of instruction."[51]

Slavin noted a key element of cooperative learning—group performance—when he said, "The term refers to classroom techniques in which students work on learning activities in small groups and receive rewards as recognition based on their group's per-

---

[47]Gary W. Orwig and Donna J. Baumbach, *What Every Educator Needs to Know About the New Technologies: Interactive Video 2* (Orlando, Fla: UCF/DOE Instructional Computing Resource Center, University of Central Florida, 1989).

[48]Orwig and Baumbach, *Interactive Video 1.*

[49]Ibid.

[50]Robert E. Slavin, "Cooperative Learning and Student Achievement," in Robert E. Slavin, ed. *School and Classroom Organization* (Hillsdale, N.J.: Lawrence Erlbaum, 1989), p. 129

[51]William Glasser, *The Quality School: Managing Students Without Coercion*, 2nd ed. (New York: HarperPerennial, 1992), p. 163.

formance."[52] Fran Lehr commented on the composition of groups, defining cooperative learning as "an instructional system that allows students of all achievement levels and backgrounds to work in teams to achieve a common goal."[53]

Cooperative learning research brings to the forefront old arguments about the relative merits of competition, cooperation, and individualization in the classroom. Competition among individuals for the teacher's approval, praise, smiling faces, grades, awards, and other forms of recognition has been a time-honored practice in our schools. We know that competition among pupils can produce negative effects, such as stifling motivation, especially when students cannot compete on an equal basis. David W. Johnson and Roger T. Johnson called attention to more than three hundred and twenty-three studies conducted in the past ninety years on the effects of cooperation, competition, and individualized instruction in student achievement and concluded that:

> . . . generally achievement is higher in cooperative situations than in competitive or individualistic ones and the cooperative efforts result in more frequent use of higher-level reasoning strategies, more frequent process gain and collective induction, and higher performance on subsequent tests taken individually . . .[54]

Cooperative learning, as currently defined, emphasizes the positive aspects of heterogeneously-grouped pupils working together to help each other. As such, it is distinguished from other cooperative methods of instruction such as small group discussion, group mastery learning, and peer tutoring, and from individualized methods such as programmed instruction, individualized mastery learning, interactive video, and independent study which retain individual achievement as the major goal. With cooperative learning, individuals are responsible to their group for the group's progress.

Cooperative learning techniques that are in practice place four to six pupils in groups, depending on the project under way. Groups are deliberately structured by the teacher to include a balance between high and low achievers, boys and girls, and ethnic backgrounds. You can easily infer that the goals of cooperative learning include but go beyond subject matter achievement.

Students in learning teams take responsibility for particular portions of the task, and they must share what they learn with their group in such a way that group members will comprehend. Groups may be restructured from time to time depending on the tasks to be accomplished. The teacher may assign grades both for the group as a whole and for individual members of the group. In some variations of grading under cooperative learning practices, grades represent the amount of progress made by individual members of the group. Group members' dependence upon each other serves as a motivator; in effect, it creates a positive form of peer pressure. Competition among teams provides a healthier climate than competition among individuals.

In your reading or observations you will encounter specific adaptations of cooperative learning developed by some of those who have conducted research on this mode

---

[52]Robert E. Slavin, "Cooperative Learning," *Review of Educational Research* 50, no. 2 (Summer 1980): 315.

[53]Fran Lehr, "Cooperative Learning," *Journal of Reading* 27, no. 5 (February 1984): 458.

[54]David W. Johnson and Roger T. Johnson, "Cooperative Learning and Achievement," in Shlomo Sharan, ed. *Cooperative Learning: Theory and Research* (New York: Praeger, 1990), p. 33.

of learning. Among these are Learning Together or Circles of Learning (David W. Johnson and Roger T. Johnson), Jigsaw (Elliott Aronson et al.), Student Teams-Achievement Division or STAD (Robert E. Slavin), Team-Assisted Individualization or TAI (Robert E. Slavin et al.), and Group Investigation (Shlomo Sharan et al.).[55]

Concerning the research on cooperative learning, Slavin drew the following implications from the results of research:

> Presently, the research on cooperative learning in classrooms justifies the following conclusions:
> 1. For academic achievement, cooperative learning techniques are no worse than traditional techniques, and in most cases they are significantly better.
> 2. For low level learning outcomes, such as knowledge, calculation, and application of principles, cooperative learning techniques appear to be more effective than traditional techniques to the degree that they use:
>   (a) A structured, focused, schedule of instruction;
>   (b) Individual accountability for performance among team members;
>   (c) A well-defined group reward system, including rewards or recognition for successful groups.
> 3. For high level cognitive learning outcomes, such as identifying concepts, analysis of problems, judgment, and evaluation, less structured cooperative techniques that involve high student autonomy and participation in decision-making may be more effective than traditional individualistic techniques.
> 4. Cooperative learning techniques have strong and consistent positive effects on relationships between black, white, and Mexican-American students.
> 5. Cooperative learning techniques have fairly consistent effects on mutual concern among students regardless of the specific structure used.
> 6. There is some indication that cooperative learning techniques can improve students' self-esteem.
> 7. Students in classes using cooperative learning generally report greater liking of school than do traditionally taught students.[56]

Slavin did note, however:

> What these results indicate is that cooperative learning techniques can achieve both cognitive and affective goals, but that there is still much to be discovered about when they do so—for which kinds of students, under what conditions, in which subjects, and for which techniques or components of techniques are positive effects likely to be observed.[57]

In planning, implementing, and evaluating a cooperative learning strategy teachers must take into consideration whether the facilities are conducive (or can be made conducive) to cooperative activity; whether students possess the ability to work together,

---

[55]For a brief description of these techniques, see George P. Knight and Elaine Morton Bohlmeyer, "Cooperative Learning and Achievement: Methods for Assessing Causal Mechanisms," in Sharan, *Cooperative Learning,* pp. 1–7. See also Slavin, *School and Classroom Organization,* pp. 129–156 (includes extensive bibliography, pp. 151–156).

[56]Slavin, "Cooperative Learning," *Review of Educational Research,* pp. 337–338.

[57]Ibid., p. 338.

sharing responsibility for the group's endeavors; or whether some training in group processes is required.

Increased emphasis today is placed on active involvement of students in their learning process not only by enabling them to work together but also by providing them with opportunities to choose learning activities and to evaluate their own performance.

SUMMARY

Selecting instructional strategies is one of the final steps in planning for instruction. Instructional strategies are derived from a number of sources, including the objectives, the subject matter, the pupil, the community, and the teacher.

Teachers vary in their styles, models, and skills. By style we mean the unique, personal qualities that a teacher develops over the years to distinguish himself or herself from all other teachers. Mr. Chips of *Goodbye, Mr. Chips* and Henry Higgins of *Pygmalion*, for example, have distinct, memorable styles.

When we speak of models of teaching, we mean a generalized role—a pattern of methods—such as discussion leader, television instructor, or foreign language informant. The so-called Socratic method of stimulating thinking is a model. Jesus, for example, used both a model (preacher) and a method (sermonizing).

Skills of teaching are those generic and specific competencies necessary to design and carry out instruction. Lesson planning, for example, is a generic skill; that is, it is pertinent to all teachers at all levels. The ability to teach pupils to perform the division of whole numbers is an example of a specific skill. Both the models and skills must be compatible with the teacher's style. Instructional strategies must be appropriate to the teacher's style, model, and skill.

Instructional strategies, styles of teaching, and teaching skills are all selected, adopted, and implemented to successfully fulfill instructional goals and objectives. The ultimate purpose of all strategies, styles, models, and skills is the fostering of student achievement.

The various instructional components should be organized into, among other types of plans, short-term units and daily lesson plans. Although teachers may design their own formats for unit and lesson plans, generic outlines are suggested in this chapter. As teachers gain experience, less detail in planning is possible. However, some planning is always necessary. The reader is referred to selections from the now large body of research on effective presentation of instruction.

The chapter concluded with discussions of new strategies for presentation of instruction, called "delivery systems" by some people. The technology of interactive video furnishes a newer approach to individualized instruction; cooperative learning is a newer variation of group instruction.

QUESTIONS FOR DISCUSSION

1. How do strategies, models, and styles of teaching differ from each other?
2. How would you go about matching a teacher's style and the learners' styles?

3. How do generic teaching skills differ from specific teaching skills? Give examples.
4. How do you account for the fact that specifications of generic teaching skills differ from state to state?
5. Which do you believe is most effective in promoting student achievement: individualization, competition, or cooperation?

SUPPLEMENTARY EXERCISES

1. Select an instructional objective and design at least three strategies for accomplishing it.
2. Observe several teachers, describe their styles, and tell what makes each teacher unique.
3. Describe with examples how a teacher's style affects selection of instructional strategies.
4. Select one of the models of teaching described by Bruce Joyce and Marsha Weil (see bibliography) and describe it to the class.
5. Select one of the models of teaching described by Mary Alice Gunter, Thomas H. Estes, and Jan Schwab (see bibliography) and describe it in class.
6. Prepare a report on the Comparison of Teaching Models in Caine and Caine, *Making Connections* (see bibliography), p. 124.
7. Debate the issue: Teaching as an Art vs. Teaching as a Science.
8. Observe several teachers and try to identify the models they are using.
9. Select one of the generic skills described by Dwight Allen and Kevin Ryan (see bibliography); demonstrate it in class or videotape your demonstration of the skill and critique it in class.
10. Select one of the generic skills discussed by Madeline Hunter and Douglas Russell (see bibliography); demonstrate it in class or videotape your demonstration of the skill and critique it in class.
11. Search the literature on instruction, find several outlines for unit plans, compare them, and select or create an outline you would use, stating reasons.
12. Search the literature on instruction, find several outlines of lesson plans, compare them, and select or create an outline you would use, stating reasons.
13. List several specific teaching skills for a teaching field you know well.
14. Write an essay with appropriate references in support of or opposed to training in generic skills for all teachers.
15. Critique Florida's twenty-seven generic competencies and decide whether you agree they are essential competencies for every teacher.
16. Critique the professional development competencies required by Texas for elementary and secondary school teachers and decide whether you agree they are essential competencies for every teacher.
17. If your state has a required or recommended set of generic competencies, critique those competencies and decide whether you agree they are essential skills for every teacher.
18. Take a position, stating reasons, for state testing of teacher competency.

19. State your views on on-the-job assessment of beginning teachers for state certification.
20. Tell whether you believe there should be some process for national certification of teachers based on national standards. State your reasons and tell whether you believe the process should be required or voluntary.
21. Design a five-to ten-day-long unit plan appropriate for teaching toward a specific instructional goal.
22. Design a lesson plan (a daily plan) based on the unit plan that you prepared for Exercise 21.
23. Report on some of the research on effective teaching, particularly studies of time on task (academic engaged time) and direct instruction.
24. Report on the applicability and effectiveness of coaching as an instructional technique.
25. Group exercise: You are a state task force. Your task is to draw up a set of defensible generic competencies that all teachers in your state would be required to master.
26. Locate and evaluate several articles that critique the effective teaching research. (See, for example, "Beyond Effective Teaching" in the bibliography.).
27. Prepare an oral or written report on one of the following:
    a. Mastery learning
    b. Peer tutoring
28. Conduct a demonstration of one of the following technologies adapted for classroom instruction:
    a. Computer-assisted instruction
    b. Interactive video
29. Prepare an oral or written report on one of the following adaptations of the concept of cooperative learning:
    a. Cooperative Integrated Reading and Comprehension (Nancy A. Madden et al.)
    b. Group Investigation (Shlomo Sharan)
    c. Jigsaw (Elliott Aronson et al.)
    d. Jigsaw II (Robert E. Slavin)
    e. Jigsaw III (A. Gonzalez and M. Guerrero)
    f. Learning Together or Circles of Learning (David W. Johnson and Roger T. Johnson)
    g. Student Teams—Achievement Division (Robert E. Slavin)
    h. Team-Assisted Individualization (Robert E. Slavin et al.)
    i. Teams-Games-Tournament (David DeVries and Robert E. Slavin)

BIBLIOGRAPHY

Allen, Dwight and Ryan, Kevin. *Microteaching.* Reading, Mass.: Addison-Wesley, 1969.

Apple, Michael W. "The Culture and Commerce of the Textbook," in Landon E. Beyer and Michael W. Apple, eds. *The Curriculum: Problems, Politics, and Possibilities,* 2nd ed. Albany, N.Y.: State University Press of New York, 1998.

Armstrong, Thomas. *Multiple Intelligences in the Classroom.* Alexandria, Va.: Association for Supervision and Curriculum Development, 1994.

"Authentic Learning," *Educational Leadership* 50, no. 7 (April 1993): 4–84.

Banks, James A. *Teaching Strategies for Ethnic Studies,* 5th ed. Boston: Allyn and Bacon, 1991.

Berenson, David H., Berenson, Sally R., and Carkhuff, Robert B. *The Skills of Teaching: Content Development Skills.* Amherst, Mass.: Human Resource Development Press, 1978.

———. *The Skills of Teaching: Lesson Planning Skills.* Amherst, Mass.: Human Resource Development Press, 1978.

Berenson, Sally R., Berenson, David H., and Carkhuff, Robert R. *The Skills of Teaching: Teaching Delivery Skills.* Amherst, Mass.: Human Resource Development Press, 1979.

Berliner, David C., ed. *Phase III of the Beginning Teacher Effectiveness Study.* San Francisco: Far West Laboratory for Educational Research and Development, 1976.

Beyer, Landon E. and Apple, Michael W. *The Curriculum: Problems, Politics, and Possibilities,* 2nd ed. Albany, N.Y.: State University of New York Press, 1998.

"Beyond Effective Teaching," *Educational Leadership* 49, no. 7 (April 1992): 4–73.

Britzman, Deborah P. *Lost Subjects, Contended Objects: Toward a Psychoanalytic Analysis of Learning.* Albany, N.Y.: State University of New York Press, 1998.

———. *Practice Makes Practice: A Critical Study of Learning to Teach.* New York: State University of New York Press, 1991.

Brookover, Wilbur B. et al. *A Study of Elementary School Social Systems and School Outcomes.* East Lansing: Michigan State University, Center for Urban Affairs, 1977.

Brooks, Douglas M. "Ethnographic Analysis of Instructional Method." *Theory into Practice* 19, no. 2 (Spring 1980): 144–147.

Brooks, Jacqueline Greenon and Brooks, Martin G. *In Search of Understanding: The Case for Constructivist Classrooms.* Alexandria, Va.: Association for Supervision and Curriculum Development, 1993.

Brophy, Jere E. and Evertson, C. M. *Process-Product Correlation in the Texas Teacher Effectiveness Study.* Austin: University of Texas, 1974.

Brophy, Jere E. and Good, Thomas L. "Teacher Behavior and Student Achievement." In Merlin C. Wittrock, ed. *Handbook of Research on Teaching,* 3rd ed. New York: Macmillan, 1986, pp. 328–375.

Brown's Directories of Instructional Programs, 1995–96. Alexandria, Va.: Association for Supervision and Curriculum Development, 1995.

Bruer, John T. "In Search of . . . Brain-Based Education." *Phi Delta Kappan* 80, no. 9 (May 1999): 648–657.

Caine, Renate Nummela and Caine, Geoffrey. *Education on the Edge of Possibility.* Alexandria, Va.: Association for Supervision and Curriculum Development, 1997.

———. *Making Connections: Teaching and the Human Brain.* Reading, Mass.: Addison-Wesley, 1991.

———. "Understanding a Brain-Based Approach to Learning and Teaching," *Educational Leadership* 48, no. 2 (October 1990): 66–70.

———. *Unleashing the Power of Perceptual Change: The Potential of Brain-Based Teaching.* Alexandria, Va.: Association for Supervision and Curriculum Development, 1997.

Carkhuff, Robert R. *The Art of Helping III.* Amherst Mass.: Human Resource Development Press, 1977.

———, Berenson, David H., and Pierce, Richard M. *The Skills of Teaching: Interpersonal Skills.* Amherst, Mass.: Human Resource Development Press, 1977.

Cohen, David, McLaughlin Milbrey, and Talbert, Joan. *Teaching for Understanding: Challenges for Policy and Practice.* San Francisco: Jossey-Bass, 1993.

"Collegial Learning.": *Educational Leadership* 45, no. 3 (November 1987): 3–75.

Cooper, James M., ed. *Classroom Teaching Skills,* 4th ed. Lexington, Mass.: D. C. Heath, 1990.

"Cooperative Learning." *Educational Leadership* 47, no. 4 (December 1989/January l990): 3–66.

Dobbs, Susan. "Some Second Thoughts on the Application of Left Brain/Right Brain Research." *Roeper Review* 12 (December 1989): 119–121.

Dunn, Rita S. and Dunn, Kenneth J. "Learning Styles/Teaching Styles: Should They . . . Can They . . . Be Matched?" *Educational Leadership* 36, no. 4 (January 1979): 238–244.

———. *Teaching Students Through Their Individual Learning Styles: A Practical Approach.* Reston, Va.: Reston Publishing Company, 1978.

Eisner, Elliot W. *The Educational Imagination: On the Design and Evaluation of School Programs,* 2nd ed. New York: Macmillan, 1989.

Ellis, Susan S. "Models of Teaching: A Solution to the Teaching Style/Learning Style Dilemma." *Educational Leadership* 36, no. 4 (January 1979): 274–277.

Ellsworth, Elizabeth. *Teaching Positions: Difference, Pedagogy, and the Power of Address.* New York: Teachers College Press, 1997.

Fischer, Barbara Bree and Fischer, Louis. "Styles in Teaching and Learning." *Educational Leadership* 36, no. 4 (January 1979): 245–254.

Floyd, Steve and Floyd, Beth with Hon, David, McEntee, Patrick, O'Bryan, Kenneth G., and Schwarz, Michael. *Handbook of Interactive Video.* White Plains, N.Y.: Knowledge Industry Publications, 1982.

Freire, Paulo. *Teachers as Cultural Workers: Letters to Those Who Dare to Teach.* Boulder, Col.: Westview Press, 1998.

Gage, N. L. *The Psychology of Teaching Methods.* 75th Yearbook of the National Society for the Study of Education, Part I. Chicago: University of Chicago Press, 1976.

————. *The Scientific Basis of the Art of Teaching.* New York: Teachers College Press, 1978.

Gardner, Howard. *Frames of Mind: The Theory of Multiple Intelligences.* New York: Basic Books, 1983.

————. *Multiple Intelligences: The Theory in Practice.* New York: Basic Books, 1993.

Giroux, Henry A. *Pedagogy and the Politics of Hope: A Critical Reader.* Boulder, Col.: Westview Press, 1997.

————. *Teachers as Intellectuals: Toward a Critical Pedagogy of Learning.* Granby, Mass.: Bergin & Garvey, 1988.

Glasser, William. *Control Theory in the Classroom.* New York: Perennial Library, 1986.

————. "The Quality School," *Phi Delta Kappan* 71, no. 6 (February 1990): 424–435.

————. *The Quality School: Managing Students Without Coercion,* 2nd ed. New York: HarperPerennial, 1992.

Glickman, Carl D. *Revolutionizing America's Schools.* San Francisco: Jossey-Bass, 1998.

Good, Thomas L. and Brophy, Jere. *Looking in Classrooms,* 3rd ed. New York: Harper & Row, 1984.

Guild, Pat Burke and Garger, Stephen. *Marching to Different Drummers.* Alexandria, Va.: Association for Supervision and Curriculum Development, 1985.

Gunter, Mary Alice, Estes, Thomas H., and Schwab, Jan. *Instruction: A Models Approach,* 3rd ed. Boston: Allyn and Bacon, 1999.

Harmin, Merrill. *Inspiring Active Learning: A Handbook for Teachers.* Alexandria, Va.: Association for Supervision and Curriculum Development, 1994.

Henson, Kenneth T. *Methods and Strategies for Teaching in Secondary and Middle Schools,* 2nd ed. White Plains, N.Y.: Longman, 1993.

Hilke, Eileen Veronica. *Cooperative Learning.* Fastback 299. Bloomington, Ind.: Phi Delta Kappa, 1990.

House, Ernest R. *Schools for Sale: Why Free Market Policies Won't Improve America's Schools and What Will.* New York: Teachers College Press, 1998.

"How the Brain Learns." *Educational Leadership* 56, no. 3 (November 1998): 8–73.

Hunter, Madeline and Russell, Douglas. "How Can I Plan More Effective Lessons?" *Instructor* 87, no. 2 (September 1977): 74–75, 88.

Hyman, Ronald T. *Strategic Questioning.* Englewood Cliffs, N.J.: Prentice-Hall, 1979.

Jensen, Eric. *Teaching with the Brain in Mind.* Alexandria, Va.: Association for Supervision and Curriculum Development, 1998.

Johnson, David W. and Johnson, Roger T. "Cooperative Learning and Achievement," in Shlomo Sharan, ed., *Cooperative Learning: Theory and Research.*" New York: Praeger, 1990, p. 33.

————. and Holubec, Edythe Johnson. *Cooperative Learning in the Classroom.* Alexandria, Va.: Association for Supervision and Curriculum Development, 1994.

————. *The New Circles of Learning: Cooperation in the Classroom and School.* Alexandria, Va.: Association for Supervision and Curriculum Development, 1994.

Jones, Beau, Palincsar, Annemarie, Ogle, Donna, and Carr, Eileen. *Strategic Teaching and Learning: Cognitive Instruction in the Content Areas.* Alexandria, Va.: Association for Supervision and Curriculum Development, 1988.

Joyce, Bruce. *Selecting Learning Experiences: Linking Theory and Practice.* Alexandria, Va.: Association for Supervision and Curriculum Development, 1978.

————. and Showers, Beverly. "The Coaching of Teaching." *Educational Leadership* 40, no. 1 (October 1982): 4–10.

Joyce, Bruce and Weil, Marsha with Showers, Beverly. *Models of Teaching,* 4th ed. Boston: Allyn and Bacon, 1992.

Kim, Eugene C. and Kellough, Richard D. *A Resource Guide for Secondary School Teaching: Planning for Competence,* 6th ed. Englewood Cliffs, N.J.: Merrill, l995.

Knight, George P. and Bohlmeyer, Elaine Morton, "Cooperative Learning and Achievement Methods for Assessing Causal Mechanisms," in Shlomo Sharan, ed., *Cooperative Learning: Theory and Research.* New York: Praeger, 1990, pp. 1–7.

Kowalski, Theodore J., Weaver, Roy A., and Henson, Kenneth T. *Case Studies in Teaching.* White Plains, N.Y.: Longman, 1990.

"Learning Styles and the Brain." *Educational Leadership* 48, no. 2 (October 1990): 3–80.

Lehr, Fran. "Cooperative Learning." *Journal of Reading* 27, no. 5 (February 1984): 458.

Levine, David, Lowe, Robert, Peterson, Bob, and Tenorio, Rita, eds. *Rethinking Schools: An Agenda for Change.* New York: The New Press, 1995.

Lezotte, Larence W. and Bancroft, Beverly A. "Growing Use of the Effective Schools Model for School Improvement." *Educational Leadership* 42, no. 6 (March 1985): 23–27.

McIntyre, D. John and O'Hair, Mary John. *The Reflective Roles of the Classroom Teacher.* Belmont, Calif.: Wadsworth, 1996.

McNeil, John and Wiles, Jon. *Essentials of Teaching Decisions, Plans, Methods.* New York: Macmillan, 1989.

Marzano, Robert J. *A Different Kind of Classroom: Teaching with Dimensions of Learning.* Alexandria, Va.: Association for Supervision and Curriculum Development, 1994.

Medley, Donald M. "The Effectiveness of Teachers." In Penelope L. Peterson and Herbert J. Walberg, eds., *Research on Teaching: Concepts, Findings, and Implications.* Berkeley, Calif.: McCutchan, 1979, pp. 1–27.

Oakes, Jeannie. *Keeping Track: How Schools Structure Inequality.* New Haven, Conn.: Yale University Press, 1985.

Oliva, Peter F. *The Secondary School Today,* 2nd ed. New York: Harper & Row, 1972.

———. and Pawlas, George E. *Supervision for Today's Schools,* 5th ed. New York: Longman, 1997.

Orlich, Donald C. et al. *Teaching Strategies: A Guide to Better Instruction.* Lexington, Mass.: D. C. Heath, 1980.

Ornstein, Allan C. and Behar, Linda S., eds. *Contemporary Issues in Curriculum.* Boston: Allyn and Bacon, 1995.

Orwig, Gary W. and Baumbach, Donna J. *What Every Educator Needs to Know About the New Technologies: Interactive Video 1.* Orlando, Fla.: UCF/DOE Instructional Computing Resource Center, University of Central Florida, 1989.

———. *What Every Educator Needs to Know About the New Technologies: Interactive Video 2.* Orlando, Fla.: UCF/DOE Instructional Computing Center, University of Central Florida, 1989.

Peter, Laurence J. *Competencies for Teaching: Classroom Instruction.* Belmont, Calif.: Wadsworth, 1975.

Peterson, Penelope L. and Walberg, Herbert J., eds. *Research on Teaching: Concepts, Findings, and Implications.* Berkeley, Calif.: McCutchan, 1979.

Rosenshine, Barak V. "Content, Time, and Direct Instruction." In Penelope L. Peterson and Herbert J. Walberg, eds. *Research On Teaching: Concepts, Findings, and Implications,* Berkeley, Calif.: McCutchan, 1979, pp. 28–56.

Sharan, Shlomo. "Cooperative Learning in Small Groups: Recent Methods and Effects on Achievement, Attitudes, and Ethnic Relations." *Review of Educational Research* 50, no. 2 (Summer 1980): 241–271.

———, ed. *Cooperative Learning: Theory and Research.* New York: Praeger, 1990.

Slavin, Robert E. *Cooperative Learning.* White Plains, N.Y.: Longman, 1983.

———."Cooperative Learning." *Review of Educational Research* 50, no. 2 (Summer l980): 315–342.

———. *Cooperative Learning: Student Teams,* 2nd ed. Washington, D.C.: National Education Association, 1987.

———. *Cooperative Learning: Theory, Research, and Practice.* Englewood Cliffs, N.J.: Prentice-Hall, 1990.

———, ed. *School and Classroom Organization.* Hillsdale, N.J.: Lawrence Erlbaum Associates, 1989.

———. *Student Team Learning: An Overview and Practical Guide.* Washington, D.C.: National Education Association, 1988.

———. "Synthesis of Research on Cooperative Learning." *Educational Leadership* 48, no. 5 (February 1991): 71–77.

——— et al., eds. *Learning to Cooperate, Cooperating to Learn.* New York: Plenum, 1985.

"Special Feature on Cooperative Learning." *Educational Leadership* 48, no. 5 (February 1991): 71–94.

Sprenger, Marilee. *Learning & Memory: The Brain in Action.* Alexandria, Va.: Association for Supervision and Curriculum Development, 1999.

Springer, Sally P. and Deutsch, Georg. *Left Brain, Right Brain,* 4th ed. New York: W. H. Freeman, 1993.

Squires, David A., Huitt, William G., and Segars, John K., eds. *Effective Schools and Classrooms: A Research-Based Perspective.* Alexandria, Va.: Association for Supervision and Curriculum Development, 1983.

Stallings, Jane. "A Study of the Implementation of Madeline Hunter's Model and Its Effects on Students." *Journal of Educational Research* 78, no. 6 (July/August 1985): 325–337.

Sylwester, Robert. *A Celebration of Neurons: Educator's Guide to the Human Brain.* Alexandria, Va.: Association for Supervision and Curriculum Development, 1995.

Thelen, Herbert A. *Classroom Grouping for Teachability.* New York: John Wiley & Sons, 1967.

Tomlinson, Carol Ann. *The Differentiated Classroom: Responding to the Needs of All Learners.* Alexandria, Va.: Association for Supervision and Curriculum Development, 1999.

———. *How to Differentiate Instruction in Mixed-Ability Classrooms.* Alexandria, Va.: Association for Supervision and Curriculum Development, 1995.

Turner, Richard L. "The Value of Variety in Teaching Styles." *Educational Leadership* 36, no. 4 (January 1979): 257–258.

Walberg, Herbert J. "Synthesis of Research on Teaching." In Merlin C. Wittrock, ed. *Handbook of Research on Teaching,* 3rd ed. New York: Macmillan, pp. 214–229.

Weil, Marsha and Joyce, Bruce. *Information Processing Models of Teaching: Expanding Your Teaching Repertoire.* Englewood Cliffs, N.J.: Prentice-Hall, 1978.

———. *Social Models of Teaching: Expanding Your Teaching Repertoire.* Englewood Cliffs, N.J.: Prentice-Hall, 1978.

——— and Kluwin, Bridget. *Personal Models of Teaching: Expanding Your Teaching Repertoire.* Englewood Cliffs, N.J.: Prentice-Hall, 1978.

Willis, Scott. "Cooperative Learning Fallout?" *ASCD Update* 32, no. 8 (October 1990): 6, 8.

Wittrock, Merlin C., ed. *Handbook of Research on Teaching,* 3rd ed. New York: Macmillan, 1986.

AUDIOTAPES

Association for Supervision and Curriculum Development, 1703 N. Beauregard St., Alexandria, Va. 22311-1714.

The Brain, the Mind, and the Classroom. Two audiocassettes. Marian Diamond, Eric Jensen, et al. 1997.

Direct Instruction Reconsidered. Barak V. Rosenshine, presenter. 1990.

On Multiple Intelligences and Education. 45 min. Howard Gardner, 1995.

Translating Brain Research into Classroom Practice. 90 min. Pat Wolfe. 1995.

CD-ROM

Exploring Multiple Intelligences. Association for Supervision and Curriculum Development, P. O. Box 79760, Baltimore, Md. 21279-1760.

PROFESSIONAL INQUIRY KIT

Learning Styles. Video clips, activities, readings. 1998. Pat Guild and Kathi Hand, developers. Association for Supervision and Curriculum Development, 1703 N. Beauregard St., Alexandria, Va. 22311-1714.

VIDEOTAPES

Agency for Instructional Technology, Bloomington, Indiana.

Quality Schools. 28 min. 1991. Featuring William Glasser on quality schools. Host: Lowell Rose.

Association for Supervision and Curriculum Development, 1703 N. Beauregard St., Alexandria, Va. 22311-1714.

The Brain and Learning. Four 20–30 min. videotapes. *Facilitator's Guide,* workshop outlines, handouts, overheads. Presenters: Geoffrey Caine, Marian Diamond, Eric Jensen, Robert Sylwester, and Pat Wolfe.

Cooperative Learning. Five videotapes. 20 min. to 42 min. 1990. Series features David Johnson, Roger Johnson, Robert Slavin, and Britt Tatman Vasquez showing how teachers implement cooperative learning in elementary, middle, and secondary school classrooms.

Effective Schools for Children at Risk. 25 min. 1991. Discusses the work of Ronald Edmonds on effective schools. Explains characteristics of effective schools. Richard Andrews, James Comer, Lawrence Lezotte, and Robert Slavin, presenters. Includes *Leader's Guide and Readings from Educational Leadership: Effective Schools and School Improvement.*

Multiple Intelligence Series. 3 tapes. *Understanding Multiple Intelligences,* 33 min. *Classroom Applications,* 36 min. *Creating the School of the Future,* 20 min. 1995. Features Howard Gardner. *Facilitator's Guides* by Bruce and Linda Campbell. Book, *Multiple Intelligences in the Classroom* by Thomas Armstrong, 1994.

CHAPTER 12
EVALUATING INSTRUCTION

After studying this chapter you should be able to:

1. Define preassessment, formative evaluation, and summative evaluation, and describe the purposes of each.
2. Explain the differences between norm-referenced and criterion-referenced measurement and state the purposes for which each is intended.
3. Design test/evaluation questions in the major categories of each of the three domains of learning.
4. Define and give examples of performance-based assessment.
5. Contrast traditional assessment with performance-based assessment.

ASSESSING INSTRUCTION

ASSESSING STUDENT ACHIEVEMENT

She holds her head in her hands, eyes transfixed on the top of the desk. She looks with displeasure at the pile of examinations in front of her, each filled with red marks indicating errors. She has administered the acid test—the examination on the unit on elections: local, state, and federal. Four weeks' work wasted! On a scale of one to one hundred and a passing grade of seventy, only twelve out of thirty-six pupils achieved the passing mark. Why? she asks herself. What went wrong? A stream of reasons floods her brain:

- The students are all blithering idiots who would flunk any test no matter how simple.
- They did not pay attention when she was going over the material.
- They do not study; they are more interested in drugs and sex than in the electoral process.

- They are too careless in answering the questions.
- Their parents do not force them to do their homework.

After several moments of indulging in recrimination and blaming the poor results on the students, she begins to take a look at the situation more rationally. What are some hypotheses, she asks herself, for such a high percentage of failures? After some serious reflection, she begins to wonder:

- Were the objectives appropriate? Were they pertinent to the subject matter? Were they within the learning abilities of the pupils? Were they relevant to the students?
- Did the pupils possess the prerequisite competencies before we began the unit in which they did so poorly? How do I know?
- Did I use the right instructional techniques? Did the strategies I chose fit the learning styles of the students?
- Did I make periodic checks along the way? What did they reveal?
- Did I alert them to the type of exam?
- Did the exam questions relate to the objectives? Were they clear?
- Did the pupils have sufficient time to respond to all the questions? Were the classroom conditions suitable for exam taking?
- Were the pupils at fault for their failures? Did I fail the pupils in my role as instructor? Or was there a blending of responsibilities for the low scores?
- Did I really find out what the students did or did not learn?
- And what do I do now? How shall I treat the exam results? What effect should their scores have on the next report card? How will I explain low scores to the principal, to the pupils, to the parents?
- Did I even use the right evaluation technique?

The term "evaluation of instruction" could be expanded to read "evaluation of instruction through the assessment of student achievement." In one sense, evaluation of instruction is evaluation of the effectiveness of the instructor. For example, does the teacher choose the right delivery system? Are the instructional objectives clear? Do test items relate to objectives? Does the teacher present the material clearly? These are types of questions a supervisor asks in evaluating teacher performance. Although this book does not examine the complex and important topic of teacher performance, you will find many helpful references on this topic in the professional literature on supervision.[1] This chapter focuses on the assessment of student performance.

In another sense, evaluation of instruction is evaluation of the curriculum. It reveals the success of one dimension—how well students achieve in areas that are assessed. It may also indicate whether the content has been adequately covered. Evaluation of instruction does not answer curricular concerns such as whether the subject matter was the right choice to begin with, whether its content is relevant, whether it meets student or societal needs, whether the profession and public are satisfied with it,

---

[1] For discussion of teacher evaluation see Peter F. Oliva and George E. Pawlas, *Supervision for Today's Schools,* 6th ed. (New York: John Wiley & Sons, 2001.), Chapters 10, 12, and 13.

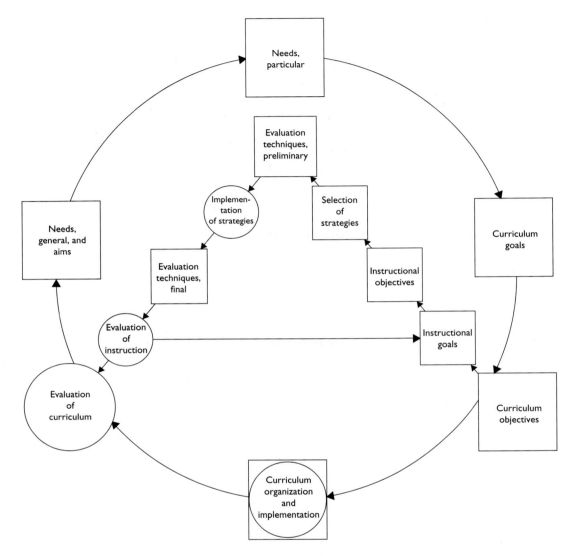

Figure 12.1   The instruction and curriculum cycles

whether it meets the school's philosophy and aims, or whether the content has been selected wisely. These are curricular dimensions that must be evaluated in addition to assessment of student achievement. We will look at the evaluation of curriculum in the next chapter. It is easy to see, however, that evaluation of instruction, evaluation of teacher performance, and evaluation of the curriculum are all intimately interrelated.

CYCLE WITHIN A CYCLE

Instruction in the model for curriculum development followed in this text is a cycle within the curriculum cycle (see Figure 12.1).

Let's once again pull out the instructional chain that makes up the instructional model. It is a submodel of the model for curriculum development presented in Chapter 5 (see Figure 12.2).

To keep the model for curriculum development uncluttered, the feedback line for this submodel was depicted simply. It proceeds from the terminal component of the instructional chain—the Evaluation of instruction—directly to the beginning of the instructional model—the Specification of instructional goals.

Note that the feedback line from the Evaluation of instruction to Instructional Goals demonstrates a cycle and indicates that modification in the system can be made in sequence. However, this figure would be more accurate if it showed the feedback lines to each component because evaluation results may reveal needed modifications in components anywhere in the system. The instructional submodel with all feedback lines is shown in Figure 12.3.

As we have seen, the instructional chain begins with specifying the goals. This cycle is not complete until we learn whether or not the instructional goals and objectives have been achieved. The problem before us now is one of evaluating the instruction that has taken place.

AN ERA OF ASSESSMENT

Evaluation. Assessment. Measurement. Testing. Accountability. These words are heard with great frequency today in both public and professional circles. Specialists in measurement and evaluation are in great demand, for we are now in an era of assessment. Although this era began some time ago, its tempo began to increase considerably in the mid-1970s. In the past few years, the movement's emphasis and the sources of its impetus have changed somewhat. We are all familiar with the phenomenon of mass testing that has dominated America ever since Edward L. Thorndike conceptualized the first standardized tests. The standardized SAT and GRE tests are household words in the United States in much the same way the nonstandardized baccalaureate tests are in France.

William H. Whyte, Jr., Martin Gross, and Banesh Hoffman were pointing to the dangers of mass testing in the late 1950s and early 1960s. Whyte and Gross were particularly concerned about personality testing, and Hoffman was critical of typical standardized multiple-choice tests.[2] In 1981, Andrew J. Strenio, Jr., cautioned us about "the testing trap."[3]

The terms evaluation, assessment, measurement, testing, and accountability evoke strong feelings; some, pro and some, con. Some educators would banish the use of tests, both standardized and nonstandardized, because they feel the tests set an imposed, predetermined curriculum. Some view tests as measuring insignificant learnings and destructive to students' self-concepts. Renate Nummela Caine and Geoffrey Caine saw "a majority of teachers teaching to simplistic tests, teaching for memorization, and thereby limiting what else students can learn and the connections they can

---

[2]William H. Whyte, Jr., *The Organization Man* (New York: Simon and Schuster, 1956); Martin L. Gross, *The Brain Watchers* (New York: Random House, 1962); Banesh Hoffman, *The Tyranny of Testing* (New York: Crowell-Collier, 1962).

[3]Andrew J. Strenio, Jr., *The Testing Trap* (New York: Rawson, Wade, 1981).

Figure 12.2 Instructional model with one feedback line

Figure 12.3 Instructional model with all feedback lines

make."[4] Faulting efforts like *America 2000,* which promotes testing of student achievement, Henry A. Giroux wrote:

> Testing has become the new ideological weapon in developing standardized curricula; a weapon that ignores how schools can serve populations of students that differ vastly with respect to cultural diversity, academic and economic resources, and classroom opportunities.[5]

If legislation effected by state and national representatives reflect the public's views, we might conclude that the public supports continuing efforts at assessment and accountability.

DEFINITION OF TERMS

At this point, let's clarify the meaning of the main terms used in this chapter. These are *evaluation, assessment, measurement,* and *testing.* "Evaluation," said Robert H. Davis, Lawrence T. Alexander, and Stephen L. Yelon, "is a continuous process of col-

---

[4]Renate Nummela Caine and Geoffrey Caine, *Making Connections: Teaching and the Human Brain* (Alexandria, Va.: Association for Supervision and Curriculum Development, 1991), p. 155.

[5]Henry A. Giroux, *Living Dangerously: Multiculturalism and the Politics of Difference* (New York: Peter Lang, 1993), p. 16.

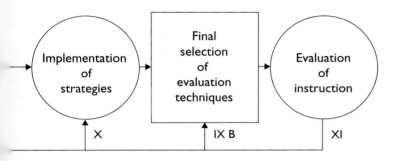

lecting and interpreting information in order to assess decisions made in designing a learning system."[6] *Evaluation and assessment* are used interchangeably in this text to denote the general process of appraisal. *Measurement and testing* are subsumed under the general classifications of evaluation and assessment.

Measurement is the means of determining the degree of achievement of a particular competency. *Testing* is the use of instruments for measuring achievement. Thus, measurement and testing are ways of gathering evaluation and assessment data. However, we have means other than testing to evaluate student performance. When we speak of evaluating a student's performance of a competency, we may or may not measure that performance. Measurement implies a degree of precision and observable behavior.

In this chapter, we will not fully explore measurement, evaluation, testing techniques, and the by-products of evaluating instruction—marking and reporting.[7] We will seek instead to develop some basic understandings about evaluating instruction, including a limited number of principles of measurement and testing.

---

[6]*From Learning System Design: An Approach to the Improvement of Instruction,* p. 81, by Robert H. Davis, Lawrence T. Alexander, and Stephen L. Yelon. Copyright c 1974 by McGraw-Hill. Reproduced with the permission of The McGraw-Hill Companies.

[7]*See L. R. Gay, Educational Evaluation and Measurement: Competencies for Analysis and Application,* 2nd ed. (Paramus, N.J.: Prentice-Hall, 1990).

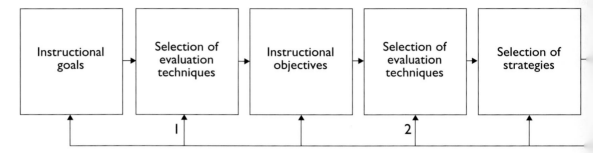

Figure 12.4   Stages of planning for evaluation

STAGES OF PLANNING FOR EVALUATION

You will note, in referring to the proposed model for curriculum development,[8] that component IX on the selection of evaluation techniques is divided into two parts: IX A, Preliminary selection of evaluation techniques, and IX B, Final selection of evaluation techniques. This separation is made in order to convey the understanding that planning of evaluation techniques takes place both before and after instruction. However, this dual separation is an oversimplification. To be more precise, we should show planning for evaluation techniques interspersed at each stage of the Instructional Model. An expanded diagram of instruction showing the many stages of planning for evaluation is presented in Figure 12.4.

EXPANDED MODEL OF INSTRUCTION

What the expanded model indicates is that the selection of evaluation techniques, including test items, is a continuous process. This concept of planning for evaluation differs from the practice of many teachers who wait until the end of the instruction, then prepare and administer a test. Evaluation techniques should be jotted down at each of the five stages shown in the expanded model. Three of these stages are prior to instruction; one midinstruction; and one postinstruction. Test items should be recorded when they occur to the teacher while the content is fresh in mind. Continuous accumulation of test items and choice of other evaluation techniques can simplify end-of-instruction evaluation.

THREE PHASES OF EVALUATION

The teacher needs to be able to demonstrate skill in three phases of evaluation:

---

[8]See Figure 5.4.

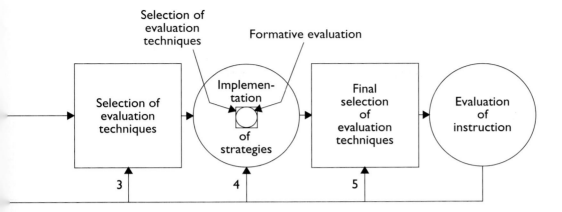

- preassessment
- formative evaluation
- summative evaluation

These terms are technical words to connote evaluation that takes place *before* instruction (preassessment), *during* instruction (formative), and *after* instruction (summative).

Preassessment.   *Preassessment* possesses a dual nature. Walter Dick and Lou Carey described two types of tests that precede instruction.[9] These two types are an entry-behaviors test and a pretest. The *entry-behaviors test* is "a criterion-referenced test designed to measure skills which have been identified as being critical to beginning instruction."[10] This type of preassessment is conducted to determine whether students possess the prerequisite knowledge that will enable them to proceed with the new treatment. The *pretest* is "criterion-referenced to the objectives the designer intends to teach."[11] "Criterion-referenced" tests, discussed later in this chapter, measure students' achievement not by how well they compare with their classmates but by how well they master predetermined instructional objectives.

The entry-behaviors (or entry-skills) test covers preceding (prerequisite) learnings, whereas the pretest covers subject matter to be learned. A pretest alone is not sufficient, for if students do poorly on a pretest (as they should, if future instruction is really new to them), the instructor cannot tell whether the students did poorly because they did not know the material to come (acceptable) or did not have the prerequisite knowledge or skills (not acceptable). Some means of judging possession of prerequisite skills is essential. Lack of prerequisite skills calls for remedial instruction and repetition of instruction before proceeding to new content.

---

[9]Walter Dick and Lou Carey, *The Systematic Design of Instruction,* 2nd ed. (Glenview, Ill.: Scott, Foresman, 1985), p. 109.
[10]Ibid. Reprinted with permission.
[11]Ibid.

Formative Evaluation.   *Formative evaluation* consists of the formal and informal techniques, including testing, that are used during the period of instruction. Progress tests are an illustration of formative evaluation. Benjamin S. Bloom, J. Thomas Hastings, and George F. Madaus advised instructors to "break a course or subject into smaller units of learning" and to administer "brief diagnostic progress tests."[12] Dick and Carey described an "embedded test," which consists of test items that "are included as part of the instructional strategy, and may appear every few pages, or after a major sequence of instruction."[13]

Through formative evaluation, teachers may diagnose and take remedial action to help students overcome difficulties before they are confronted with the *terminal (summative) evaluation.* Formative evaluation enables teachers to monitor their instruction so that they may keep it on course.

Summative Evaluation.   *Summative evaluation* is the assessment that takes place at the end of a course or unit. A final written examination (*posttest*) is the most frequently used means of summative evaluation of instruction. Its major purpose is to find out whether the students have mastered the preceding instruction.

Summative evaluation reveals whether or not prespecified outcomes of instruction have been achieved. In some cases, summative assessment of outcomes, particularly those in the affective and psychomotor domains, is achieved by the learner's actual demonstration of the outcomes rather than by paper-and-pencil tests which are designed primarily for cognitive learning. Recall, however, that cognitive learning remains the primary focus of schooling.

The astute teacher uses results of summative evaluation to revise his or her program and methods for subsequent groups.

NORM-REFERENCED MEASUREMENT AND CRITERION-REFERENCED MEASUREMENT

NORM-REFERENCED MEASUREMENT

Two divergent concepts of measurement compete for the attention and loyalty of instructors. *Norm-referenced measurement* is the classic approach to assessment in which a student's performance on a test is compared to the performance of other students who took the test. Following this principle, standardized tests of achievement are administered and norms—standards of performance—are calculated for various groups who took the tests. The scores made by students who subsequently take the tests are compared to those made by the population on whom the test was standardized.

Classroom teachers follow the same principle whenever they measure the achievement of one student against or in relationship to that of other students in class. As a gross example of this approach to measurement, the teacher will administer a test, cal-

---

[12]*From Handbook on Formative and Summative Evaluation of Student Learning*, p. 53, by Benjamin S. Bloom, J. Thomas Hastings, and George F. Madaus. Copyright c 1971 by McGraw-Hill. Reproduced with permission of The McGraw-Hill Companies. See also Benjamin S. Bloom, George F. Madaus, and J. Thomas Hastings, *Evaluation to Improve Learning* (New York: McGraw-Hill, 1981), a revision of Part I of the *Handbook.*

[13]Dick and Carey, *Systematic Design*, p. 109.

culate the scores, rank the score from highest to lowest, find the middle score (which becomes a C grade), then grade all other tests in relationship to that middle grade. In this nonstandardized situation, students are rated in relationship to performance of that particular group on that particular test.

CRITERION-REFERENCED MEASUREMENT

Since the norm-referenced approach to measurement is so common and so universally practiced, it might be asked, "What other approach is there?" *Criterion-referenced measurement* is the alternative to norm-referenced measurement. In this approach, the performance of students on a test is compared to criteria that were established in the instructional objectives. A student's success on a criterion-referenced test depends on demonstrated mastery of the objectives and not on his or her performance as related to others in the class.

Because of its long history of usage, the norm-referenced approach is reasonably well understood by teachers, students, and parents. Further, imbued with a sense of competition, many parents invite the kinds of comparisons that are made under a norm-referenced system.

Among the proponents of norm-referenced testing are standardized test makers, those who advocate competitive grading, those who have a need to screen or select persons (for example, college admissions officers), those who draw up honor rolls, admission committees of honorary societies, and those who award scholarships. Norm-referenced testing is necessary when a limited number of places are to be filled from a pool of applicants in excess of the number of places and when only a limited number of awards are to be distributed among a group of aspirants. Among the practitioners of criterion-referenced measurement are the instructional-design specialists and the district, state, and national assessment people. These persons desire to know whether students achieve mastery of specified objectives. If I may use the analogy of the smiling or frowning face, the norm-referenced tester frowns when all students pass an exam because it does not discriminate between high and low achievers. The criterion-referenced tester wears a broad smile when all students pass an exam, since students have mastered the objectives on which they were tested.

Concerning criterion-referenced measurement, Dick and Carey observed:

> As more and more emphasis has been placed on statements of explicit behaviors that students must demonstrate, it has been increasingly obvious that a fair and equitable evaluation system is one that measures those specific behaviors. After students have been told what they have to do to be successful on a learning unit, they should be tested accordingly.[14]

COMPARISON OF THE TWO TYPES OF MEASUREMENT

Mary-Jeanette Smythe, Robert J. Kibler, and Patricia W. Hutchings have made a comparison of general characteristics of norm-referenced and criterion-referenced measurement systems, as shown in Table 12.1.

---

[14]Ibid., pp. 107–108.

TABLE 12.1

COMPARISON OF NORM-REFERENCED AND CRITERION-REFERENCED MEASUREMENT

NORM-REFERENCED MEASUREMENT	CRITERION-REFERENCED MEASUREMENT
1. The main function of norm-referenced measurement is to ascertain the student's relative position within a normative group.	1. The main function of criterion-referenced measurement is to assess whether the student has mastered a specific criterion or performance standard.
2. Either general conceptual outcomes (usually done) or precise objectives may be specified when constructing norm-referenced measurement.	2. Complete behavioral objectives (i.e., planning objectives) are specified when constructing criterion-referenced measurement.
3. The criterion for mastery is not usually specified when using norm-referenced measurement.	3. The criterion for mastery must be stated (i.e., planning objectives) for use in criterion-referenced measurement.
4. Test items for norm-referenced measurement are constructed to discriminate among students.	4. Test items for criterion-referenced measurement are constructed to measure a predetermined level of proficiency.
5. Variability of scores is desirable as an aid to meaningful interpretation.	5. Variability is irrelevant; it is not a necessary condition for a satisfactory criterion-referenced measurement.
6. The test results from norm-referenced measurement are amenable to transposition to the traditional grading system (A, B, C, D, F).	6. The test results from criterion-referenced measurement suggest the use of a binary system (i.e., satisfactory–unsatisfactory; pass–fail). However, criterion-referenced measurement test results can be transposed into the traditional grading system by following a set of specifically constructed rules.

SOURCE: Mary-Jeanette Smythe, Robert J. Kibler, and Patricia W. Hutchings, "A Comparison of Norm-Referenced and Criterion-Referenced Measurement with Implications for Communication Instruction," *The Speech Teacher* 22, no. 1 (January 1973): 4. Reprinted by permission.

Robert J. Kibler, Donald J. Cegala, David T. Miles, and Larry L. Barker list the following four ways that criterion-referenced tests may be used:

- for preassessment purposes
- for formative testing . . . that is, testing that is used concurrently with instruction for the purpose of checking the progress of students so that assistance may be provided when necessary
- to determine whether components of the instructional model . . . need modification
- to determine whether students have achieved the criterion levels of objectives[15]

W. James Popham described a major distinction between the purposes of norm-referenced and criterion-referenced measurement when he explained:

---

[15]Robert J. Kibler, Donald J. Cegala, David T. Miles, and Larry L. Barker, *Objectives for Instruction and Evaluation* (Boston: Allyn and Bacon, 1974), p. 116.

Since norm-referenced measures permit comparisons among people, their primary purpose is to make decisions about individuals. Which pupils should be counseled to pursue higher education? Which pupils should be advised to attain vocational skills? . . .

Criterion-referenced tests make decisions both about individuals and treatments. In decisions regarding individuals, we might use a criterion-referenced test to determine whether a learner had mastered a criterion skill considered prerequisite to a new training program. In decisions regarding treatments, we might design a criterion-referenced measure which reflected a set of instructional objectives supposedly achieved by a replicable instructional sequence. By administering the criterion-referenced measure to appropriate learners who had completed the instructional sequence, we could decide the effectiveness of the sequence.[16]

On the surface, norm-referenced tests look no different from criterion-referenced tests. However, in the first edition of their book Dick and Carey spoke of differences in construction of the two types of measures as follows:

Criterion-referenced tests include only test items that are based on specified behavioral objectives. Each item requires students to demonstrate the performance stated in an objective. Standards for acceptable performance on the test are based upon criteria stated in the objectives.

Norm-referenced tests are constructed differently. It is usually unnecessary for the exact performance desired to be described in behavioral terms prior to item or test construction. Test items are not necessarily based on instruction students receive or on skills or behaviors that are identified as relevant for student learning. Items that are developed from a given domain for norm-referenced tests are administered to a variety of students from the target population. Those items that cause the greatest spread or range in students' responses are selected for inclusion on a norm-referenced test. The range of scores is usually expected to resemble a normal or bell-shaped curve, hence the name "norm-referenced."[17]

Popham saw differences in the construction of items for the two types of tests as a matter of "set":

The basic differences between item construction in a norm-referenced framework and item construction in a criterion-referenced framework is a matter of "set" on the part of the item writer. . . . When an individual constructs items for a norm-referenced test, he tries to produce variant scores so that individual performances can be contrasted. . . . He disdains items which are "too easy" or "too hard." He avoids multiple choice items with few alternative responses. He tries to increase the allure of wrong answer options. He does all of this to develop a test which will produce different scores for different people. . . .

The criterion-referenced item designer is guided by a different principle. His chief purpose is to make sure the item accurately reflects the criterion behavior. Difficult or easy, discriminating or indiscriminate, the item has to represent the class of behaviors delimited by the criterion.[18]

.[16]W. James Popham, *Evaluating Instruction* (Englewood Cliffs, N.J.: Prentice-Hall, Inc., 1973), pp. 25–26. Reprinted by permission of Prentice-Hall, Inc., Englewood Cliffs, New Jersey.

[17]Dick and Carey, *Systematic Design*, lst ed. (1978), p. 88. Reprinted with permission.

[18]Popham, *Evaluating Instruction*, p. 30. Reprinted by permission of Prentice-Hall, Inc., Englewood Cliffs, New Jersey.

We should take note that the tests developed by the states to assess achievements of both students and teachers are by and large criterion-referenced.

The Instructional Model suggested in this text places the specification of instructional objectives in a central position and, therefore, leans toward a criterion-referenced approach to classroom testing. This point of view, however, does not eliminate the use of standardized tests in the school or the use of norm-referenced teacher-made tests for purposes they can fulfill. It does eliminate the use of a norm-centered approach to classroom testing that permits teachers to adopt the philosophy of the normal curve and to generate scores that result in a normal distribution of grades ranging from A through F on every test. Such a practice violates the philosophy of the normal curve, which holds that traits are distributed at random throughout the general population. No single class is a random sample of the general population. Therefore, to hold As to a mere handful, to condemn some students automatically to Fs, to grant a certain percentage of Bs and Ds, and to assign about two-thirds of a class to the so-called average or C grade is not a defensible practice.

EVALUATION IN THREE DOMAINS

Objectives, as we have noted in Chapter 10, have been classified into three domains—the cognitive, the affective, and the psychomotor. Although an objective may possess elements of more than one domain, ordinarily it will exhibit the primary characteristics of one of the three domains. The fact that objectives may not fall neatly into a single domain should not dissuade teachers from assessing pupils' performance in the various domains. Teachers may choose any of the numerous types of tests: actual performance, essay, or one or more objective tests—multiple choice, alternate response, completion, matching, or rearrangement.[19]

Each domain presents its unique evaluation problems. Let's look at some illustrations of test items for the major categories of each domain.

PSYCHOMOTOR DOMAIN

Objectives in the psychomotor domain are best evaluated by actual performance of the skill being taught. For example, if we wish students to be able to swim 100 yards without stopping, we require that they hop into the water and show us that they can do it. The students fail, we might say, if they sink to the bottom. We may wish to qualify the performance by requiring students to swim 100 yards in x number of minutes. To pass the test, students would have to satisfy that criterion.

The teacher has to make some judgmental calls when students are asked to demonstrate perceptual-motor skills. Form and grace might be considered in the 100-yard swim as well as completion or speed of completion. Evaluative judgments are

---

[19]For discussion of types of tests and test items, see Peter F. Oliva, *The Secondary School Today*, 2nd ed. (New York: Harper & Row, 1972), Chapter 19.

made when students are asked to demonstrate the ability to make a mobile in art class, to build a bookcase in woodshop, to create a blouse in home economics, to drive a golf ball in physical education class, or to administer artificial respiration in the first aid course.

Beyond the simple dichotomy—performance or nonperformance (pass-fail, satisfactory-unsatisfactory)—of a skill lie such factors as speed, originality, and quality. The teacher may choose to include these criteria as part of the assessment process. When judgmental criteria are to be used, they should be communicated to the students in advance. The teacher will find it helpful to identify as many indicators of the criteria as possible. For example, in the case of the mobile made in art class, indicators of quality might be durability, precision of construction, neatness, and detail.

There are times when teachers settle for a cognitive recounting of how the student would demonstrate a perceptual-motor skill. Ideally, psychomotor skills should be tested by actual performance. Because of lack of time or facilities, however, it is not always possible for every pupil to demonstrate every skill. For example, a group of students in home economics working together may have baked bread. A final examination question might be, "List the steps you would take in making white bread." Although not altogether satisfactory from a pedagogical point of view—most of us can talk a better game than we can play—this technique may be used. We suspect, of course, that many a forlorn loaf of bread will be turned out by the inexperienced bakers before the skill is perfected.

Test Items of the Psychomotor Domain.
Here are examples of test items for each of the seven major categories of the Simpson taxonomy of the psychomotor domain:

1. *Perception:* Distinguish between an *s* and a *z* sound.
2. *Set:* Demonstrate how to hold a fishing pole.
3. *Guided response:* Make computer-generated mailing labels, following the teacher's explanation.
4. *Mechanism:* Saw a six-foot two-by-four into three pieces of equal size.
5. *Complex overt response:* Perform an auto tune-up.
6. *Adaptation:* Sketch a new arrangement for the furniture of a living room.
7. *Origination:* Paint an original landscape in watercolors.

All of these test items call for actual *performance*. Observe that all seven could equally be instructional objectives. We, therefore, have a perfect match between the objectives and the test items. On the other hand, let's take the following psychomotor objective. Is this objective at the same time a test item?

Objective for high school physical education: The pupil will demonstrate skill in swimming. This objective is broad, complex, and is without a stipulated degree of mastery. Although it is an objective desired by the physical education instructor, it is difficult to convert into a test item as it currently stands. Establishing a series of subobjectives from which we could derive the test items would help. For example, the student will demonstrate how to

- dive into the pool
- tread water
- float face down
- float face up
- do the breaststroke
- do the crawl
- swim underwater the width of the pool

The instructor might limit appraisal of the pupils' performance in these skills to "satisfactory" or "unsatisfactory."

COGNITIVE DOMAIN

Achievement in the cognitive domain is ordinarily demonstrated in school by pupil performance on written tests administered to a group—usually, but not always, an entire class. To administer individual written or oral tests on a regular basis would require an excessive amount of time. The teacher should seek to evaluate, when appropriate, student achievement in all six levels of the Bloom taxonomy of the cognitive domain, using both essay and objective test items.

Test Items of the Cognitive Domain.   Whereas objective items sample knowledge of content on a broad scale, essay tests sample limited content and provide information about the student's ability to organize his or her thoughts, write coherently, and use English properly. The following test items show several ways objectives in the cognitive domain can be evaluated:

1. Knowledge
   Essay: Explain how Samuel Clemens got the name Mark Twain.
   True-False: A whale is a warm-blooded mammal.
   Completion: The United States, Russia, Great Britain, France, and _____ hold permanent seats on the UN Security Council.

2. Comprehension
   Essay: What is meant when a person says, "Now you've opened Pandora's box"?
   Multiple Choice: A catamaran is a
   a. lynx
   b. boat
   c. fish
   d. tool

3. Application
   Essay: Describe, giving at least three current illustrations, how the law of supply and demand works.
   Multiple-Choice: 4 divided by 1/2 =
   a. 2
   b. 4
   c. 6
   d. 8

4. Analysis

   Essay: Analyze the school board's annual budget as to categories of funds, needs of the schools, and sources of funds.

   Multiple-Choice: A survey of parents showed 90 percent believe schools are too lax in discipline; 5 percent too strict; and 5 percent undecided. We might conclude that these parents
   a. favor looser discipline
   b. favor smaller classes
   c. favor stricter teachers
   d. favor higher taxes
   e. favor all of the above

5. Synthesis

   Essay: Describe the origin and significance of the Thanksgiving Day holiday.

   (Since synthesis and the highest category of the cognitive domain—evaluation—require extensive narration, they are best evaluated through use of essay test items.)

6. Evaluation

   Essay: Read the following planks from the platform of the Democratic or Republican Party and tell whether you believe the planks fulfill current needs in the country and state your reasons. Provide evidence to support your reasons.

The types of test items selected depend on the teacher's purpose and the amount of time that can be devoted to the test. As a general rule, a combination of test items provides variety and thereby stimulates interest. If essay items are used either alone or in conjunction with objective items, sufficient time needs to be provided for students to organize their answers and to respond fully to the essay questions. The passing score should always be communicated to the learners before they take a test.

Cognitive objectives, like those for psychomotor skills, are often suitable test items. For example, if we choose the objective, "The student will be able to list the steps by which a federal bill becomes a law," the teacher has a ready-made test item, "List the steps by which a federal bill becomes a law." However, if the objective is a general competency such as "The student will be able to divide whole numbers by fractions," the teacher must create specific test items that permit students to demonstrate the competency.

Affective Domain

We should refrain from using the terms "testing" and "measurement" in reference to the affective domain. As stated earlier, student achievement in the affective domain is difficult and sometimes impossible to assess. Attitudes, values, and feelings can be deliberately concealed; learners have the right to hide personal feelings and beliefs, if they so choose. Affective learnings may not be visible in the school situation at all.

The achievement of objectives in the affective domain, therefore—though important in our educational system—cannot be measured or observed like objectives in the cognitive and psychomotor domains. For that reason, students should not be graded on an A through F or percentage system for their lack or possession of affective attributes. Except for a few affective objectives like conduct (provided it can be defined and observed), these types of learning should probably not be graded at all, even with different symbols.

We attempt to evaluate affective outcomes when we encourage students to express their feelings, attitudes, and values about the topics discussed in class. We can observe students and may find obvious evidence of some affective learnings. For example, a child who cheats has not mastered the value of honesty. The bully who picks on smaller children has not learned concern for other people. The child who expresses a desire to suppress freedom of speech has not learned what democracy means. The normal child who habitually feels that he or she cannot do the work has developed a low self-concept.

Thus some affective behaviors are apparent. Teachers can spot them and through group or individual counseling can perhaps bring about a change in behavior. On the other hand, children are at school only six or seven hours a day. They are constantly demonstrating affective behaviors—positive and negative—outside of school, where the teacher will never have occasion to observe them. Are the students helpful at home? Are they law-abiding in the community? Do they protect the environment? Do they respect other people? Who can tell for sure without observing the behavior? Students may profess to behave in certain ways to please the teacher or others and then turn around and behave far differently outside the classroom.

Following the Krathwohl taxonomy of the affective domain, let's look at some affective objectives that contain ways for evaluating their achievement.

1. Receiving
   The student expresses in class an awareness of friction among ethnic groups in the school.
2. Responding
   The student volunteers to serve on a human relations committee in the school.
3. Valuing
   The student expresses a desire to achieve a positive school climate.
4. Organization
   The student controls his or her temper when driving.
5. Characterization by value or value complex
   The student expresses and exemplifies in his or her behavior a positive outlook on life.

Assessment Items of the Affective Domain.   In its evaluation of the Eight-Year Study, the Progressive Education Association assessed students' preference for newspaper reading (an objective within the affective category Receiving) by presenting them with a list of sections of the newspaper and asking them to mark each section with a U if they usually read it, an O if they read it occasionally, and an R if they read it rarely.[20] Whether students found pleasure in science activities (Responding) was evaluated by the Progressive Education Association by a list of scientific activities for each of which

---

[20]David R. Krathwohl, Benjamin S. Bloom, and Bertram B. Masia, *Taxonomy of Educational Objectives: The Classification of Educational Goals: Handbook II: Affective Domain* (White Plains, N.Y.: Longman, 1964), p. 116.

BOX 12.1

ITEMS FOR AFFECTIVE CATEGORY OF ORGANIZATION

Gordon W. Allport, Philip E. Vernon, and Gardner Lindzey created the following items that fall in the affective category organization
>   Category: Organization
>   Subcategory: Organization of a value system
>   Objective: Begins to develop dominant values
>   Item:

Directions: Each of the following situations or questions is followed by four possible attitudes or answers. Arrange these answers in the order of your personal preference by writing, in the appropriate box at the right, a score of 4, 3, 2, or 1. To the statement you prefer most give 4, to the statement that is second most attractive 3, and so on.

In your opinion, can a man who works in business all week best spend Sunday in
a. trying to educate himself by reading serious books?
b. trying to win at golf, or racing?
c. going to an orchestral concert?
d. hearing a really good sermon?

Viewing Leonardo da Vinci's painting "The Last Supper," would you tend to think of it
a. as expressing the highest spiritual aspirations and emotions?
b. as one of the most priceless and irreplaceable pictures ever painted?
c. in relation to Leonardo's versatility and its place in history?
d. the quintessence of harmony and design?

SOURCE: From Gordon W. Allport, Philip E. Vernon, and Gardner Lindzey, *Study of Values,* 3rd ed. (Boston: Houghton Mifflin, 1960), pp. 8, 10. In Krathwohl, Bloom, and Masia, pp. 163–164. Copyright © 1960. Reprinted with permission of the publisher, The Riverside Publishing Company, 8420 W. Bryn Mawr Avenue, Chicago, IL 60631. All rights reserved.

---

the students indicated satisfaction, uncertainty of their reaction, or dissatisfaction. In addition, students were asked if they had ever performed the activity.[21]

To assess the appreciation of economic factors in people's lives (Valuing), the Progressive Education Association created descriptions of economic problems. For each problem, a number of courses of action were presented for students to indicate approval, disapproval, or uncertainty.[22]

Boxes 12.1 and 12.2 illustrate assessment items for the affective categories of *Organization* and *Characterization by value or value complex.*

Observe that some instruments are titled "tests" by their makers. The agree-disagree attitude inventory is a frequent means used to determine achievement of affective

---

[21]Ibid., p. 138.
[22]Ibid., p. 144.

BOX 12.2

ITEMS FOR AFFECTIVE CATEGORY OF CHARACTERIZATION BY VALUE OR VALUE COMPLEX

Paul L. Dresser and Lewis B. Mayhew showed examples of items which assess objectives at the highest level of the affective domain: characterization by value or value complex.

> Category: Characterization by value or value complex
> Subcategory: Generalized set
> Objective: Respect for the worth and dignity of human beings

Item:

1. Tom and Bob who know each other only slightly were double-dating two girls who were roommates. A sudden storm made it impossible to go to the beach as planned. Tom suggested going to a movie. After making the suggestion, he realized that Bob was without funds. As Tom, what would you do?
   a. Pay for the party.
   b. Lend Bob money.
   c. Leave it up to the girls.
   d. Get Bob to suggest something.
   e. Apologize to Bob for making the suggestion.

2. Your social organization has pledged a student who is not liked by some of the members. One of your friends threatens to leave the social organization if this person is initiated. What would you do?
   a. Talk to your friend.
   b. Do not initiate the prospective member.
   c. Get more members to support the prospective member.
   d. Vote on the prospective member.
   e. Postpone the vote until the matter works itself out.

SOURCE: From *Problems in Human Relations Test*. Cited by Paul L. Dresser and Lewis B. Mayhew, *General Education: Explorations in Evaluation* (Washington, D.C.: American Council on Education, 1954), p. 233. In Krathwohl, Bloom, and Masia, p. 170. Reprinted with permission of the American Council on Education.

---

objectives. These types of questions reveal a basic problem in teaching for affective learning. If the teacher or test maker has preconceived notions of the "correct" responses, he or she is operating in a twilight zone between achievement of affective outcomes and indoctrination. Further, remember that students can and do respond to attitudinal questions as they believe the teacher or test maker wishes them to respond rather than as they actually feel.

The attainment of affective objectives is discerned by instruments such as opinionnaires or attitude inventories, by observation of the behavior of students, and by essay questions that ask pupils to state their beliefs, attitudes, and feelings about a given topic. Perhaps, instead of thinking of using instruments that seek to discover students' attitudes and values through an accumulation of items administered test-fashion, we should think more of asking frequent value-laden questions and listening to students' responses. Instead of leveling a continuous barrage of factual questions, teachers can interject questions like: How do you feel about . . . ? What do you believe about . . . ? Would you be interested in . . . ? Are you in agreement with . . . ?

OTHER MEANS OF EVALUATION

Although we normally equate the word "test" with "examination" and usually think of a test in a summative context at the end of the instruction, we should remember that it is really an attempt to demonstrate mastery of objectives in whatever domain. Students can demonstrate achievement both during and at the end of instruction through means other than typical examinations. For example, synthesis in the cognitive domain can be tested by means of essay items. Competency in synthesizing can also be tested by written reports during the period of instruction or by term papers at the end of instruction. A skilled instructor can tell a good deal about pupils' success just by observing their classroom performance. Individual and group oral reports may be assigned for a variety of purposes, including testing ability to speak, knowledge of the subject, and, in the case of group activities, the ability to work together. Alternative techniques of evaluation other than examinations include student logs, reports, essays, notebooks, simulations, demonstrations, construction activities, self-evaluation, and portfolios.

Employed by many teachers are practices collectively known as performance-based assessment, basically a personalized approach to demonstration of pre-specified outcomes.[23] A concomitant dimension of performance-based assessment is demonstration of performance in a realistic ("authentic") context. Performance-based measures are *authentic,* explained Thomas R. Guskey, "because they are valuable activities in themselves and involve the performance of tasks that are directly related to real-world problems."[24] Horace's School (via Theodore R. Sizer) would require demonstrated "Exhibitions" of performance to earn a high school diploma.[25]

Some advocates of performance-based assessment would substitute authentic measures for typical teacher-made and standardized tests. Others would supplement traditional testing with alternative techniques.

Alternative Assessments.   Disenchantment with standardized testing has led to the movement toward so-called authentic alternative assessments. Describing "most traditional standardized tests" as "poor predictors of how students will perform in other settings" and "unable to provide information about why students score as they do," Linda Darling-Hammond criticized standardized tests for not providing "information about how children tackle different tasks or what abilities they rely on in their problem solving."[26] Authentic alternative assessments allow students to demonstrate achievement as in the form of portfolios or exhibitions judged more frequently by qualitative rather than quantitative means.

---

[23]See discussion of outcomes-based education in Chapter 14.

[24]Thomas R. Guskey, "What You Assess May Not Be What You Get," *Education Leadership* 51, no. 6 (March 1994): 51.

[25]Theodore R. Sizer, *Horace's School: Redesigning the American High School* (Boston: Houghton Mifflin, 1992).

[26]Linda Darling-Hammond, Jacqueline Ancess, and Beverly Falk, *Authentic Assessment in Action: Studies of Schools and Students at Work* (New York: Teachers College Press, 1995), p. 7

Popular on the current scene is the use of *portfolios* as an alternative assessment measure. To create a portfolio students assemble samples of their work that, in essence, show evidence of their accomplishments. Portfolios may contain creative writings, tests, artwork, exercises, reflective essays, notes on topics, and whatever other materials portray achievement. Portfolios containing a generous sampling of students' work can reduce the pressure from testing and marking.

Like all products that reflect achievement, standards or criteria for portfolios should be set. They may include completeness, effort, neatness, and creativity. Whatever the criteria they should be conveyed to the students.

Portfolios offer a means of informing parents of some of the accomplishments of their students. Further, they can evince a feeling of pride on the part of students whose portfolios are well done.

Alternative assessment measures may include practices that could reduce or eliminate homework and change marking practices. William Glasser, for example, joined teachers in noting that students dislike homework and often fail to complete it. Labeling compulsory homework as a coercive technique, Glasser recommended reducing required homework and allowing students to do the work in class assisted by the teacher and by their classmates.[27]

Holistic assessment, often called qualitative or subjective, has appealed to many instructors in recent years. Teachers who assess students' creative efforts, like essays and portfolios, look at the product in its entirety, gaining impressions of quality, eschewing analytical treatment of grammar, style, spelling, syntax, and sentence structure. Teachers who assess holistically feel that analytical treatment of a student's work discourages further effort on the student's part.[28]

Performance-based principles of assessment may affect not only homework and grading of student work but also the marking system itself. Glasser would not place Cs, Ds, or Fs on a student's permanent transcript, in effect, eliminating symbols of failure. A+, A, and B would attest quality performance. Students who do less than quality work, designated by a temporary C, would be given the opportunity to raise the quality of their work and therefore their grades.[29]

The presence of alternative assessment measures is testimony to conflicting conceptions of evaluation, indeed, of schooling. Heated debate over testing, coupled with controversy over setting of standards, centers around the issue of whether to continue to use quantifiable means of student achievement. "Why," Maxine Greene asked, "the preoccupation in a day of whole language and portfolio assessment with quantifiable measures?"[30] As noted earlier, Giroux labeled testing as an ideological weapon.[31] Critical of present methods of evaluation Caine and Caine called attention to the effect of

---

[27]William Glasser, *The Quality School: Managing Students Without Coercion,* 2nd ed. (New York: HarperPerennial, 1992), pp. 115–117.

[28]For discussion of holistic assessment see Elizabeth Daly, ed. *Monitoring Children's Language Development: Holistic Assessment in the Classroom* (Portsmouth, N.H.: Heinemann, 1991). See also Richard J. Marchesani, *Using Portfolios for More Authentic Assessment of Writing Ability.* ERIC document ED 347555. 1992.

[29]Glasser, *Quality School,* pp. 104–111.

[30]Maxine Greene, *Releasing the Imagination: essays on Education, the Arts, and Social Change* (San Francisco: Jossey-Bass, 1995), p. 170.

[31]See p. 404.

evaluation on student self-concept.[32] Running counter to challenges leveled at testing was the observation of E. D. Hirsch, Jr. who wrote, "The final irony of the antitesting movement is that in the name of social fairness it opposes using high-stakes tests as gatekeepers, monitors, and incentives-functions that are essential to social fairness."[33]

Alternative assessments may supplement and reduce the use of some of the more traditional forms of classroom assessment. They are not likely for the foreseeble future at least to replace completely the use of standardized and teacher-made tests of student achievement.

Teachers should seek to develop competency in the use of a wide range of evaluative techniques.[34]

FEEDBACK

Evaluation yields data that provide feedback about student achievement and the instructional program. It is not sufficient for evaluative data to be used solely for the purpose of measuring pupil achievement. If pupils do poorly, teachers need to find out what caused the poor showing. Teachers need to ask themselves what they must do so that subsequent groups of students—or even the same group, if repetition of the instruction appears necessary—will not encounter the same difficulties. Teachers must know what needs to be changed, and the evaluation results provide them with this evidence.

Even if pupils do extremely well, teachers should use the data to reexamine the process. The instructional goals and objectives may have been too simple; students may have been capable of achieving higher objectives. If a test was administered, the test itself may not have been valid. The questions may have been too simple, they may not have measured all the objectives. At the implementation stage, the instructor may have omitted some crucial points and thereby left some objectives unachieved. The results of evaluation provide evidence for making changes in the instructional process.

ASSESSMENT INITIATIVES FROM BEYOND THE CLASSROOM

DISTRICT ASSESSMENTS

Up to this point the focus of this chapter has been on assessment of student achievement through techniques (largely testing) designed by the classroom teacher for his or her own pupils. We should not leave the topic of evaluation of instruction without giving some attention to assessment on a broader scale than the individual classroom, assessments that are of special importance to curriculum workers. Since the 1960s, an almost unbelievable amount of assessing student achievement has been going on (and continues) at the district, state, national, and international levels.

---

[32]Caine and Caine, *Making Connections,* p. 157.

[33]E. D. Hirsch, Jr., *The Schools We Need : Why We Don't Have Them* (New York: Doubleday, 1996), p. 214.

[34]For discussion of means of evaluation other than testing, see Oliva and Pawlas, *Supervision for Today's Schools,* Chapter 6. See also Association for Supervision and Curriculum Development, *Redesigning Assessment: Facilitator's Guide* and videotape, (Alexandria, Va.: Association for Supervision and Curriculum Development, 1991). See also F. Leon Paulson, Pearl R. Paulson, and Carol A Meyer, "What Makes Portfolio a Portfolio?" *Educational Leadership* 48, no. 5 (February 1991): 60–63.

Confronted with mounting criticism over both real and perceived deficiencies as evidenced by state, national, and international test scores, many school districts in the 1980s restructured both their curricula and instructional methods. In so doing, they also restructured or introduced for the first time assessments of districtwide student achievement. They employed a practice known as *curriculum alignment*. For each subject field, districts created plans that detailed objectives, activities, and resources. At the end of each nine-week marking period, students took tests developed to match the objectives in each field. District wide assessment has been one response to public demand for accountability.

STATE ASSESSMENTS

In the past two decades the assessment spotlight has focused on the state level. More than thirty-six states, responding to reports such as *A Nation at Risk*,[35] have set minimum competencies for student achievement at various grade levels and for graduation from high school. Several factors motivated state legislators and departments of education to establish minimum standards of performance on tests. They were disappointed by the results of national and international assessments; they felt dissatisfied with the "products" their schools were turning out; and they heard the public clamor for concentration on subject matter and for accountability of teachers and administrators for their pupils' achievement. Assessment tests, therefore, were deemed necessary for determining whether students had achieved the competencies.

Assessment is, of course, an expected and necessary part of the curriculum-instructional process. Schools must determine the extent to which pupils have attained the objectives. The intensity of assessment, especially at the state level, was relatively new to the educational scene. The emphasis on assessment saw states mandating the development and administration of criterion-reference tests to measure student achievement. For a period of fifteen to twenty years during the height of the reform movements, states took more seriously than ever their role as authority over the public educational system of their state. Assessment is but one phase in the exercise of that authority. In recent years we have seen some relaxation of that authority with the movement toward decentralization. As noted in Chapter 7 in the discussion of standards of student achievement states have continued to develop and administer assessment programs in order to determine whether their standards are being met.

NATIONAL AND INTERNATIONAL ASSESSMENTS

SAT and ACT Scores.   American public education has been under repeated attack in the recent past for the poor performance of students as reflected by scores on standardized tests of achievement. For whatever reasons—some say low standards in schools, social promotions, too much time off-task, poor instruction, and irrelevant content and activities—pupils' scores on certain standardized tests of verbal and quantitative reasoning skills declined between the 1950s and 1980s. The public and the critics of education took special note of the drop in the scores on the Scholastic Aptitude

[35]National Commission on Excellence in Education, David P. Gardner, chairman. *A Nation at Risk: The Imperative for Educational Reform* (Washington, D.C.: U.S. Government Printing Office, 1983).

Test (SAT, now called the Scholastic Assessment Test) and the American College Testing Program (ACT). For example, SAT scores on the verbal portion dropped fifty points between 1952 and 1982[36] and stabilized between 1982 and 1995.[37]

Scores on the mathematics portion declined about twenty-seven points during that same period. The decline in test scores may be attributed in part to a rise in the percentage of high-school graduates taking the test, which reduces the selectivity among students. The proportion of students who took the SAT between 1972 and 1995, for example, rose from thirty-four percent to forty-two percent.[38]

Between 1970 and 1982, the ACT scores suffered a slightly downward trend.[39] ACT scores rose between 1984 and 1986, reversing their downward trend, and except for a slight dip in 1989 have remained relatively stable. Between 1991 and 1995 scores on the SAT have risen slightly and scores on the ACT have remained at about the same level.[40] Boys continue to outperform girls overall on both the SAT and ACT although girls are closing the disparity between scores as they take more math and science courses.[41]

Since spring 1995 the College Entrance Examination Board has "recentered" scoring, "recalibrating" upward scoring of the test to compensate for the downward change in scores achieved by the average student between 1941 and the present. The average score on the test in early years was 500; recent scores have been in the 400s. Recentering boosts the average score once again to 500. Recent SATs have incorporated fewer multiple-choice questions.

National Assessment of Educational Progress.   Since 1969 when the National Assessment of Educational Progress (NAEP), known as "The Nation's Report Card," came into existence, it has operated with federal funding. Supported by a grant from the National Center for Education Statistics of the Office of Educational Research and Improvement within the U.S. Department of Education, Educational Testing Service currently administers this project.

In 1964, with the backing of the Carnegie Corporation, Ralph W. Tyler and the Committee on Assessing the Progress of Education began to develop criterion-referenced tests for nationwide assessment, Testing began in 1969 and encompassed ten areas:

- art
- career and occupational development
- citizenship
- literature
- mathematics
- music

[36]Ernest L. Boyer, *High School: A Report on Secondary Education in America* (New York: Harper & Row, 1983), pp. 22–26.

[37]U.S. Department of Education, National Center for Education Statistics, *The Condition of Education 1996*, NCES 96–304, by Thomas M. Smith (Washington, D.C.: U.S. Government Printing Office, 1996), p. 86.

[38]Ibid., p. 239.

[39]Boyer, *High School,* pp. 22–26.

[40]*Condition of Education 1996*, p.86.

[41]Ibid.

- reading
- science
- social studies
- writing

Reassessments are conducted periodically, and a "report card" showing patterns and trends is issued to the public after each assessment. Data for the areas tested have been collected from samples of children, ages 9, 13, and 17, and from young adults, ages 26 to 35. The data have been reported by geographical region, size and type of community, educational level of parents, gender, and race/ethnicity.

In 1985–86 NAEP undertook the first national assessment of third-, seventh-, and eleventh-grade students in their knowledge and skills in using the computer.[42] With a grant from the National Endowment for the Humanities, NAEP cooperated in 1986 with Diane Ravitch and Chester E. Finn's Educational Excellence Network in assessing about 8,000 high school juniors' knowledge of U.S. history and literature. Directed by Ravitch and Finn, this study emanated as part of their Foundations of Literacy project.[43] NAEP conducted a follow-up sampling in 1988 to determine changes that might have taken place in students' factual knowledge of U.S. history.[44] In 1988, NAEP turned its attention to geography, testing more than 3,000 high school seniors on their geography learning.[45] The sheer number of American pupils tested by NAEP is astonishing. In academic year 1987–88, approximately 130,000 elementary, middle, and secondary school students were assessed in some 1500 schools. Since its inception in 1969, NAEP has tested literally millions of students in a variety of subject fields.

Scores on the NAEP assessments have been inconsistent since NAEP began testing in 1969, sometimes up, sometimes down, sometimes stable. Progress has been made but improvements are still in order. Gaps between scores made by whites and by other racial/ethnic groups have narrowed over the past twenty years but more remains to be done to close the gaps.

A sampling of findings from some of the NAEP reports between 1984 and 1998 include:

- Students generally had difficulty answering questions about computer applications and programming.[46]

---

[42]Michael E. Martinez and Nancy A. Mead, *Computer Competence: The First National Asssessment* (Princeton, N.J.: National Assessment of Educational Progress, Educational Testing Service, 1988).

[43]Diane Ravitch and Chester E. Finn, Jr., *What Do Our 17–Year-Olds Know? A Report on the First National Assessment of History and Literature* (New York: Harper & Row, 1987). See also Arthur N. Applebee, Judith A. Langer, and Ina V. S. Mullis, *Literature and U.S. History: The Instructional Experience and Factual Knowledge of High-School Juniors* (Princeton, N.J.: National Assessment of Educational Progress, Educational Testing Service, 1987). See Chapter 14 for reference to NAEP's 1994 history assessment.

[44]David C. Hammack et al., *The U.S. History Report Card: The Achievement of Fourth-, Eighth-, and Twelfth-Grade Students in 1988 and Trends from 1986 to 1988 in the Factual Knowledge of High-School Juniors* (Princeton, N.J.: National Assessment of Educational Progress, Educational Testing Service, 1990).

[45]Russell Allen et al., *The Geography Learning of High School Seniors* (Princeton, N.J.: National Assessment of Educational Progress, Educational Testing Service, 1990).

[46]Martinez and Mead, *Computer Competence*, p. 5.

- Fewer than half the high school seniors assessed on knowledge of U.S. history were familiar with the U.S. Constitution and the Bill of Rights.[47] Student performance on the history assessment showed "a much lower level of attainment than has been seen in other subjects assessed by NAEP. . . . Male students outperformed female students only at grade 12 on the U.S. history composite scale." [48]

- On a geography assessment, most high school seniors could locate major countries of the world but had difficulty locating cities and physical land features and lacked understanding of physical and cultural geography. About a third of the students were unfamiliar with the concepts of latitude and longitude.[49] "On the overall geography scale male students performed better than female students . . . "[50] Approximately seventy percent of the students demonstrated basic-level knowledge of geography.[51]

- On 262 cognitive items in a national test of history and literature, Ravitch and Finn found that the average of the almost eight thousand juniors who were assessed was 54.5 percent correct on the history test and 51.8 percent correct on the literature test, which Ravitch and Finn judged to be the equivalent of failing marks.[52] Reporting on a 1987-89 study funded by the Lynde and Harry Bradley Foundation, the Bradley Commission on History in Schools also spoke to the weaknesses in the history curriculum.[53]

- "Overall, reading proficiency for 9-year-olds improved between 1971 and 1980, declined between 1980 and 1990, and was stable between 1990 and 1996. Little change occurred from 1971 to 1996 at ages 13 and 17, although scores for 17-year-olds increased slightly between 1971 and 1984. Females outscored males in reading proficiency across all age groups."[54] NAEP's 1998 Reading Report Card revealed average reading scores for students in grades 4, 8, and 12, the grades tested, increased somewhat although increases were not found for all students at all three levels. Females continued to exceed male in average reading scale scores at all levels.[55]

- "Average writing proficiency remained relatively stable for 4th-grade students between 1984 and 1996. Eighth-grade writing scale scores declined between 1984

[47]Hammack et al., *The U.S. History Report Card*, p. 28.

[48]Alexandra S. Beatty, Clyde M. Reese, Hilary R. Persky, and Peggy Carr, *NAEP 1994 U.S. Report Card: Findings from the National Assessment of Educational Progress*, National Center for Education Statistics, U.S. Department of Education (Washington, D.C.: U.S. Government Printing Office, 1996), p. 75.

[49]Allen et al., *Geography Learning*, 1990, pp. 7–8.

[50]Hilary R. Persky, Clyde M. Rees, Christine Y. O'Sullivan, Stephen Lazer, Jerry Moore, and Sharif Shrakami, *NAEP 1994 Geography Report Card: Findings from the National Assessment of Educational Progress*, National Center for Education Statistics, U.S. Department of Education (Washington, D.C.: U.S. Government Printing Office, 1996), p. xii.

[51]Ibid., p. 37.

[52]Ravitch and Finn, *What Do Our 17–Year-Olds Know?*, p. 1.

[53]See Paul Gagnon, ed., and the Bradley Commission on History in Schools, *Historical Literacy: The Case for History in American Education* (New York: Macmillan, 1989).

[54]U.S. Department of Education, National Center for Education Statistics, *The Condition of Education 1998*, NCES 98–013 by John Wirt, Tom Snyder, Jennifer Sable, Susan P. Choy, Yupin Bae, Janis Stennett, Allison Gruner, and Marianne Perie (Washington, D.C.: U.S. Government Printing Office, 1998), p. 68.

[55]Patricia L. Donohue, Kristin E. Voelkl, Jay R. Campbell, and John Mazzeo, *NAEP 1998 Reading Report Card* (Washington, D.C.: National Center for Education Statistics, Office of Educational Research and Improvement, 1999).

and 1990, but returned to about their original level by 1996. Eleventh-grade scores were slightly lower in 1996 than in 1984. Females have outscored males in writing proficiency at all grade levels since 1988."[56]

- "Average mathematics proficiency improved between 1978 and 1996 for all age groups, with 9-year-olds making the largest improvements."[57]
- Another mathematics assessment, one that reflects recent curricular emphasis and mathematics standards developed by the National Council of Teachers of Mathematics, showed that scores for 4th, 8th, and 12th-graders increased between 1990 and 1996.[58] Scores of 9-, 13-, and 17-year-olds in mathematics proficiency were only slightly higher for males than for females.
- "Average science achievement scores rose for all three age levels [9, 13, and 17] between 1982 and 1996. However, when compared to scores from the 1970s, the 1996 average scores were higher at age 9, about the same at age 13, and lower at age 17."[59] Scores of males led those of females by a slight margin.[60]
- Of special interest to curriculum workers are NAEP's reports summarizing twenty years of assessments. In spite of all the calls for educational reform in the 1970s and 1980s the summary shows that student achievement as a whole remains relatively low and stable since 1969.[61] Between 1970 and 1992 scores in reading writing, science, and mathematics at first decreased or stayed the same as in the 1970s, then increased slightly in the 1980s and early 1990s. . . . Said the National Center for Education Statistics, ". . . overall scores have not changed much over the last two decades. . . ." However, the Center pointed out that the gap between whites and minorities had narrowed substantially.[62]
- Assessments in four art fields: dance, music, theater, and visual arts, at the eighth-grade level, showed variations in students' performance in Creating, Performing, and Responding to the arts and differences in the availability of instruction in the arts in schools. Females outperformed males in these aspects of the curriculum.[63]

From analysis of these national studies, curriculum workers can make comparisons of their local and state assessment data against national norms and can make inferences about areas in need of remediation.

When NAEP was under formation, some educators expressed great concern that the data would identify and possibly embarrass specific schools. NAEP has allayed those concerns, reporting data only for groups and not identifying schools. On the

---

[56]Ibid., p. 70.

[57]Ibid., p. 72.

[58]Ibid.

[59]Ibid., p. 74.

[60]Ibid.

[61]Ina V. S. Mullis, Eugene H. Owen, and Gary W. Phillips. *America's Challenge: Accelerating Academic Achievement,* (Princeton, N.J.: National Assessment of Educational Progress, Educational Testing Service, 1990).

[62]National Center for Education Statistics, *The Condition of Education 1994,* p. 48.

[63]Hilary R. Persky, Brent A. Sandene, and Janice M. Askew, *The NAEP 1997 Arts Report Card: Eighth-Grade Findings from the National Assessment of Educational Progress* (Washington, D.C.: National Center for Education Statistics, Office of Educational Research and Improvement, 1998).

other hand, localities and states often release the assessment data that they have gathered on individual schools so that the public and profession can make comparisons among schools within the district and state.

New national examinations that will reveal achievement of both students and schools are under development and trial. Dissatisfaction with our educational system runs so deep that educators, business people, parents, and others are voicing a desire for national assessment, an undertaking which would run counter to historic objections to a national curriculum and to revealing test scores of individuals and schools. As noted in Chapter 6, one of the six national goals set forth by President George Bush and the National Governors' Association in 1989 was student demonstration of competency in English, mathematics, science, history, and geography. Students would demonstrate this competency on voluntary national examinations taken at the fourth-, eighth-, and twelfth-grade levels. Tests in various fields are at various stages of development. The 26th Annual Phi Delta Kappa/Gallup Poll of the public's attitudes toward the public schools found strong public support for a standardized national curriculum (eighty-three percent), and standardized national examinations that students must pass for promotion and graduation (seventy-three percent).[64]

Though emphasis on assessment has focused on the state level in recent years, as noted in this chapter and Chapter 14, the spotlight may well shift in the near future from the state to the national level. Advocates of national assessment, such as the President's Education Policy Advisory Committee, argue that the national testing will require schools throughout the nation to examine their instructional techniques and curricula (particularly the basic disciplines) and to take action to correct deficiencies revealed by the tests. Those who oppose national assessment, such as the National Education Association, argue that national testing will result in a national, common curriculum that cannot adequately provide for differences that exist among schools and among students in various communities. We will return to the issues of national curriculum and national standards in Chapter 14.

International Assessments.   Funded by the U.S. Office of Education and the Ford Foundation, the International Association for the Evaluation of Educational Achievement (IEA) has conducted cross-national studies of student achievement in mathematics, science, literature, reading comprehension, foreign languages (English and French), and civic education.[65] Carried out on a grand scale, the study surveyed some 250,000 students and 50,000 teachers in twenty-two countries. In 1964, the First International

---

[64]Stanley M. Elam, Lowell C. Rose, and Alec M. Gallup, "The 26th Annual Phi Delta Kappa/Gallup Poll of the Public's Attitudes Toward the Public Schools, *Phi Delta Kappan* 76, no. 1 (September 1994): 48.

[65]See T. Neville Posthlethwaite, "International Educational Surveys," *Contemporary Education* 42, no. 2 (November 1970): 61–68. Joseph Featherstone, "Measuring What Schools Achieve: Learning and Testing," *The New Republic* 169, no. 2 (December 6, 1973): 19–21. "International Study Brings Coleman Report into Question," *Phi Delta Kappan* 55, no. 5 (January 1974): 358. See also L. C. Comber and John P. Keeves, *Science Education in Nineteen Countries* (New York: John Wiley & Sons, 1973); Alan C. Purves, *Literature Education in Ten Countries* (New York: John Wiley & Sons, 1973); Robert L. Thorndike, *Reading Comprehension Education in Fifteen Countries* (New York: John Wiley & Sons, 1973); International Association for the Evaluation of Educational Achievement, *Science Achievement in Seventeen Countries: A Preliminary Report* (Oxford, England: Pergamon, 1988).

Mathematics Study alone surveyed more than 130,000 students taught by over 13,000 teachers in more than 5,000 schools in twelve countries.[66] The Second International Mathematics Study, funded by the National Science Foundation and the U.S. Department of Education in 1981–82, followed up the First International Mathematics Study by assessing and comparing achievement of 12,000 eighth- and twelfth-grade students enrolled in college-preparatory mathematics classes in some twenty countries.[67]

Benefitting from its experience directing the National Assessment of Educational Progress, the Educational Testing Service—with funding from the U.S. Department of Education and the National Science Foundation—cooperated with representatives of five countries in 1988 to initiate the first International Assessment of Educational Progress (IAEP). IAEP assessed mathematics and science proficiency of thirteen-year-olds in five countries (Ireland, Korea, Spain, the United Kingdom, and the United States) and four Canadian provinces (British Columbia, New Brunswick, Ontario, and Quebec). The U.S. average was below others in both mathematics and science.[68] Scores of U.S. students on international assessments reinforce scores made on national assessments, demonstrating that the achievement of our students remains less than desirable.

In IAEP's second international assessment, conducted in 1991, fourteen countries assessed science and mathematics achievement of nine-year olds and twenty countries assessed the achievement of thirteen-year olds. In both science and mathematics Korea and Taiwan rated at the top of the larger countries with the U.S. coming in third for nine-year olds and seventh for thirteen-year olds, a not too dismal picture.[69]

If perceptions of college instructors are valid indicators, a Carnegie Foundation for the Advancement of Teaching survey of some 20,000 college faculty members in thirteen countries plus Hong Kong revealed that only fifteen percent of the American instructors felt that their high-school graduates were adequately prepared in mathematics; only twenty percent, in writing and speaking. Hong Kong faculty topped the math survey (forty percent satisfied). South Korea faculty headed the writing and speaking list (sixty percent satisfied).[70]

Funded by the National Center for Education Statistics of the U.S. Department of Education, the National Science Foundation, the International Association for the Evaluation of Educational Achievement, and the participating countries, The Third International Mathematics and Science Study (TIMSS), the most comprehensive study of its kind, conducted in 1995, tested over a half million students in forty-one countries, including some 33,000 in public and private schools in the United States at the fourth-,

---

[66]See Torsten Husén, ed., *International Study of Achievement in Mathematics,* vols. 1 and 2 (New York: John Wiley & Sons, 1967).

[67]See Curtis C. McKnight et al., *The Underachieving Curriculum: Assessing U.S. School Mathematics from an International Perspective* (Champaigne, Ill.: Stipes Publishing Company, 1987). See also National Center for Education Statistics, *Second International Mathematics Study: Summary Report for the United States* (Washington, D.C.: National Center for Education Statistics, 1985).

[68]See Archie E. Lapointe, Nancy A. Mead, and Gary W. Phillips, *A World of Difference: An International Assessment of Mathematics and Science* (Princeton, N.J.: Center for the Assessment of Educational Progress, Educational Testing Service, 1989).

[69]Educational Testing Service, International Assessment of Educational Progress, 1992, as reported in National Center for Education Statistics, *The Condition of Education 1994,* 1994, p. 62.

[70]Ernest L. Boyer, Philip G. Altbach, and Mary Jean Whitlaw, *The Academic Profession: An International Perspective* (Princeton, N.J.: The Carnegie Foundation for the Advancement of Teaching, 1994), pp. 40–41.

eighth-, and twelfth-grade levels. The study compared scores made by students in mathematics and science.[71]

Interpretation of test scores is always a problem, especially so with transnational studies. Those who interpret the data can fault the philosophy, the process, and the findings. They can single out positive or negative aspects to emphasize. In spite of difficulties in interpreting the data we are, of course, interested in how well American students do on international assessments, particularly in the light of the previously proclaimed national goal of having our students rank first in the world in mathematics and science by the year 2000.

To cite a few of the findings of TIMSS:

> "U.S. fourth graders score above the international average in science and are outperformed only by students in Korea. U.S. fourth graders score above the international average in mathematics."[72]
> "U.S. eighth graders score above the international average in science. U.S. eighth graders score below the international average in mathematics. U.S. eighth graders are outperformed in *both* subjects by Austria, Bulgaria, Czech Republic, Hungary, Japan, Korea, Netherlands, Singapore, and Slovenia."[73]
> "U.S. twelfth graders scored below the international average and among the lowest of the 21 TIMSS nations in both mathematics and science general knowledge in the final year of secondary school."[74]

Some American students did well on the tests; others, poorly. The only safe generalization we can make is that judging by the results found by the study's assessment instruments the U.S. did not reach its national goal of becoming first in the world in mathematics and science by the year 2000.

Diane Ravitch summarized the data on national and international assessment:

> Overall, a review of student achievement on the SAT, NAEP, and international assessments as well as course-taking patterns, suggests that test scores declined in the late 1960s and throughout the 1970s; that the decline ended around 1980; that average achievement improved during the 1980s, probably because of higher graduation requirements . . . that the achievement gap between majority and minority students is narrowing. The changes observed during the past generation indicate that student achievement goes up or down in response to expectations and standards.[75]

Some Positive Notes.   A 1993 report of the Organization for Economic Cooperation and Development, with headquarters in Paris, reported that American students were only slightly behind students in other countries in mathematics and science and above

---

[71]U.S. Department of Education, *Attaining Excellence: A TIMSS Resource Kit* (Washington, D.C.: Office of Reform and Dissemination, Office of Educational Research and Improvement, 1997), p. 11. ERIC document 410 122. See also National Center for Education Statistics, *The Condition of Education 1998*, op. cit. and references to three reports *Pursuing Excellence* in bibliography.

[72]*Attaining Excellence*, p. 56.

[73]Ibid., p. 52.

[74]Sayuri Takahira, Patrick Gonzalez, Mary Frase, and Laura Hersh Salganik, *Pursuing Excellence: A Study of U.S. Twelfth-Grade Mathematics and Science Achievement in International Context: Initial Findings from the Third International Mathematics and Science Study* (Washington, D.C.: National Center for Education Statistics, 1997), p. 28. ERIC document 419 717.

[75]Diane Ravitch, *National Standards in American Education: A Citizen's Guide* (Washington, D.C.: The Brookings Institution, 1995), p. 97.

average in reading comprehension. The study of twenty-four countries noted that the U.S. has one of the highest percentages of college graduates in the world and spends more per student in higher education than any other country.[76]

U.S. nine-year olds rated at the top of the list of larger countries on the International Association for the Evaluation of Educational Achievement (IEA) study during the school year 1991–92 on Reading Literacy in thirty-two countries. U.S. fourteen-year olds came in second, just below France.[77]

Six U.S. high school students out of more than 360 from 69 countries at the 35th (1994) International Mathematical Olympiad in Hong Kong attained perfect scores on a two-day, nine-hour math exam. (China and Russia took second and third place).[78] Unofficial ranking of the seventy-six countries participating in the 1998 International Mathematical Olympiad hosted by Taipei showed the U.S. contestants at fourth place behind first-place Iran, second-place Bulgaria, and third-place Hungary.[79]

The U.S. team participating in the 1999 (Fourth) International Geography Olympiad, held in Toronto achieved top ranking among the ten countries entered in the competition, followed by Canada in second place and Russia, third.[80]

Eight out of ten Nobel prize winners in 1993 were Americans.[81]

In a series of annual articles in *Phi Delta Kappan* and in a book Gerald W. Bracey has placed a positive spin on American public education. In his first report on the condition of public education Bracey spoke of "the big lie about public education"[82] Bracey commented, "[international] comparisons have generated much heat, but very little light."[83] Critical of comparisons of the end-of-secondary-school test results of TIMSS Bracey commented, "When people make such comparisons, they are engaging in a political exercise, not an intellectual one."[84]

International assessments reveal how difficult it is to make comparisons of student achievement across cultures and to account for variations. Differences among nations that may affect scores include curricula, instructional strategies, political and social conditions, length of school year, time allocated to studies in school and at home, proportion of young people in school, number of pupils per teacher, motivation of students, dedication of parents to education, and traditions.[85]

---

[76]*New York Times,* December 9, 1993.

[77]International Association for the Evaluation of Educational Achievement, Study of Reading Literacy, *How in the World Do Students Read?, 1992* as cited in National Center for Education Statistics, *The Condition of Education 1994,* p. 58.

[78]Press report, July 20, 1994.

[79]International Mathematical Olympiad, Web site http://east.camel.math.ca/IMO, accessed September 29, 1999.

[80]Press report, *The Orlando Sentinel,* August 12, 1999.

[81]For discussion of the "hoaxes and myths that mar the public perception of American education" see Gerald W. Bracey, "The Fourth Bracey Report on the Condition of Public Education," *Phi Delta Kappan* 76, no. 2 (October 1994): 115–127. See also first three Bracey reports, *Phi Delta Kappan,* October 1991, 1992, 1993.

[82]Gerald W. Bracey, "Why Can't We Be Like We Were?" *Phi Delta Kappan* 73, no. 2 (October 1991): 104–117.

[83]Ibid., p. 113.

[84]Gerald W. Bracey, "Tinkering with TIMSS," *Phi Delta Kappan* 80, no. 1 (September 1998): 36. See also Gerald W. Bracey, *Setting the Record Straight: Responses to Misconceptions About Public Education in the United States* (Alexandria, Va.: Association for Supervision and Curriculum Development, 1997), 75–111.

[85]For differing interpretations of the ranking of American students on international assessments see Lawrence C. Stedman, "The New Mythology About the Status of U.S. Schools," *Educational Leadership* 52, no. 5 (February 1995): 80–85; Gerald W. Bracey, "Stedman's Myths Miss the Mark," *Educational Leadership* 52, no. 6 (March 1995): 75–80; and Lawrence C. Stedman, "Let's Look Again at the Evidence," *Educational Leadership* 52, no. 6 (March 1995): 78–79.

Whether from international or other assessments, test scores do signal strengths and weaknesses. Low test scores demand that curriculum workers determine whether the subject matter tested is essential and, if so, what measures must be taken for students to achieve mastery.

SUMMARY

Although evaluating instruction is generally perceived as an activity taking place at the end of the instructional process, teachers should begin selecting evaluation techniques as soon as they identify their instructional goals. Two types of preassessment are suggested: one to evaluate the pupils' possession of prerequisite knowledge and/or skills to begin study of the new subject matter, the other to determine whether pupils have already mastered the subject matter to be presented.

Evaluation that takes place during the process of instruction is referred to as formative evaluation and is necessary to monitor both pupil progress and the ongoing success of the instructional program. Summative evaluation is evaluation that comes at the end of instruction, as represented in a final examination.

Distinction is made between norm-referenced measurement in which a student's achievement on tests is compared to other students' achievement and criterion-referenced measurement in which a student's achievement is compared to a predetermined criterion of mastery. Norm-referenced tests are used when selection must be made from among a group of persons. Criterion-referenced tests are used to determine whether students achieved the objectives specified in advance.

The major purpose of evaluating instruction is to determine whether or not students accomplished the objectives. Instructors should design means of evaluating pupil performance in the three domains of learning—cognitive, psychomotor, and affective—whenever possible. Tests in the cognitive domain are normally written essay or objective tests administered to an entire class. Discovery of psychomotor outcomes is best carried out by means of actual performance tests of the skill being taught. Although we may speak of measurement and testing in the cognitive and psychomotor domains, we should use the more general term evaluation in reference to the affective domain. Though evaluating affective achievement is difficult and normally imprecise, teachers should engage in this activity. At times, evaluation of affective objectives will not be apparent at all. Nevertheless, affective learning is an important dimension of education, and instructors should strive to determine the best way they can the extent to which students have achieved the desired objectives.

Instructors should keep in mind that there are numerous techniques other than testing for evaluating pupil performance. Good pedagogy calls for a diversity of evaluation techniques, as appropriate.

Feedback is an important feature of the Instructional Model. On the basis of evaluative data, instructors revise the preceding components of the model for subsequent instruction. Evaluation is perceived as a continuous, cyclical process.

A great deal of assessment of student achievement is planned and administered by educators and measurement specialists from outside the individual classroom. District- and state-level assessments are designed and carried out to spot both strengths and deficiencies in the curricula of the schools. National and international assessments lend a broader perspective to student achievement. Among the many national assessments are the SATs and ACTs and the continuing assessments of the National Assessment of Educational Progress. The International Association for the Evaluation of Educational Achievement and the International Assessment of Educational Progress furnish us with cross-cultural data, comparing achievement of students in various countries and disciplines.

QUESTIONS FOR DISCUSSION

1. Are schools overemphasizing testing? Explain.
2. Are schools overemphasizing the use of objective tests? Explain.
3. Should schools use more norm-referenced tests or more criterion-referenced tests?
4. How would you recommend evaluating accomplishment of affective objectives? Give examples.
5. What strengths and weaknesses do you see in national assessments? International assessments?

SUPPLEMENTARY EXERCISES

1. Distinguish between evaluation, measurement, and testing.
2. Select a unit you will teach and prepare a pretest for it.
3. Search the literature on tests and measurement and prepare a set of guidelines for writing (a) essay, (b) multiple-choice, (c) alternate-response, (d) matching, (e) rearrangement, (f) completion items.
4. State the purposes for which essay test items are designed; state the purposes for objective test items.
5. Write a report on the use of test results.
6. Write an essay-test item and an objective-test item for each of the major categories of the cognitive domain.
7. Write a test item for each of the major categories of one of the taxonomies of the psychomotor domain.
8. Design some techniques for evaluating objectives in each of the major categories of the affective domain.
9. Deliver an oral report to the class on whether affective objectives can and should be evaluated.
10. Define formative evaluation and give some examples for a unit you are teaching or will teach.
11. Define summative evaluation and describe how you will conduct the summative evaluation for a unit that you are teaching or will teach.
12. Distinguish between quantitative and qualitative assessment.
13. Describe procedures you would use to evaluate
    a. oral reports
    b. group work

      c. products created by students (give examples)

      d. term papers

      e. dramatic presentations

14. Write a paper on the strengths and limitations of performance-based assessment.

15. Provide examples of authentic assessment in any subject field.

16. Read Theodore R. Sizer's book *Horace's School* (see bibliography), define, and cite examples of "Exhibitions."

17. Give an example of holistic assessment.

18. Debate the issue: Teachers should eliminate homework.

19. Debate the issue: Failing grades should be eliminated from a marking system.

20. Report to the class on changes in SAT and ACT scores in the last ten years.

21. Report on the district-level plan for assessing student achievement in a school district that you know well.

22. Report on results of a recent school district assessment in a particular subject area.

23. Report on your state's or another state's plans for assessing student achievement.

24. Report on results of a recent state assessment in a particular subject area.

25. Choose one of the areas in which the National Assessment of Educational Progress has conducted periodic assessments and describe trends.

26. Prepare an oral or written analysis of one of the following works (see bibliography):

      a. Paul Gagnon, ed. and the Bradley Commission on History in Schools. *Historical Literacy: The Case for History in American Education.*

      b. Diane Ravitch and Chester E. Finn, Jr., *What Do Our 17-Year-Olds Know? A Report on the First National Assessment of History and Literature.*

27. Prepare a position paper on national assessment, national academic standards, and national curriculum.

28. Describe findings of a recent international study of student achievement involving American students.

BIBLIOGRAPHY

Alexander, Lamar. *The Nation's Report Card: Improving the Assessment of Student Achievement.* Cambridge, Mass.: National Academy of Education, 1987.

Allen, Russell et al. *The Geography Learning of High-School Seniors.* Princeton, N.J.: National Assessment of Educational Progress, Educational Testing Service, 1990.

Applebee, Arthur N., Langer, Judith A., and Mullis, Ina V. S. Crossroads in *American Education: A Summary of Findings.* Princeton, N.J.: National Assessment of Educational Progress, Educational Testing Service, 1989.

————. *Literature and History: The Instructional Experience and Factual Knowledge of High-School Juniors.* Princeton, N.J.: National Assessment of Educational Progress, Educational Testing Service, 1987.

————. *The Writing Report Card: Writing Achievement in American Schools.* Princeton, N.J.: National Assessment of Educational Progress, Educational Testing Service, 1986.

————. *Writing Trends Across the Decade 1974–1984.* Princeton, N.J.: National Assessment of Educational Progress, Educational Testing Service, 1986.

Applebee, Arthur N., Langer, Judith A., Jenkins, Lynn B., Mullis, Ina V. S., and Foertsch, Mary A. *Learning to Write in Our Nation's Schools: Instruction and Achievement in 1988 at Grades 4, 8, and 12.* Princeton, N.J.: National Assessment of Educational Progress, Educational Testing Service, 1990.

Beatty, Alexandra S. *NEAP 1994 U.S. History Report Card: Findings from the National Assessment of Educational Progress.* Washington, D.C.: U.S. Department of Education, Office of Educational Research and Improvement, 1996.

Beyer, Barry. *How to Conduct a Formative Evaluation.* Alexandria, Va.: Association for Supervision and Curriculum Development, 1995.

Bloom, Benjamin S., ed. *Taxonomy of Educational Objectives: The Classification of Educational Goals: Handbook I: Cognitive Domain.* White Plains, N.Y.: Longman, 1956.

Bloom, Benjamin S., Hastings, J. Thomas, and Madaus, George F. *Handbook of Formative and Summative Evaluation of Student Learning.* New York: McGraw-Hill, 1971.

————, Madaus, George F., and Hastings, J. Thomas. *Evaluation to Improve Instruction.* New York: McGraw-Hill, 1981.

Boyer, Ernest L. *High School: A Report on Secondary Education in America.* New York: Harper & Row, 1983.

————, Altbach, Philip G., and Whitlaw, Mary Jean. *The Academic Profession: An International Perspective.* Princeton, N.J.: The Carnegie Foundation for the Advancement of Teaching, 1994.

Bracey, Gerald W. "American Students Hold Their Own." *Educational Leadership* 50, no. 5 (February 1993): 66–67.

————. "The Eighth Bracey Report on the Condition of Public Education." *Phi Delta Kappan* 80, no. 2 (October 1998): 112–131.

————. "The Fifth Bracey Report on the Condition of Public Education. *Phi Delta Kappan* 77, no. 2 (November 1995): 149–160.

————. "The Fourth Bracey Report on the Condition of Public Education." *Phi Delta Kappan* 76, no. 2 (October 1994): 115–127.

————. "The Second Bracey Report on the Condition of Public Education." *Phi Delta Kappan* 74, no. 2 (October 1992): 104–117.

————. *Setting the Record Straight: Responses to Misconceptions About Public Education.* Alexandria, Va.: Association for Supervision and Curriculum Development, 1997.

————. "The Sixth Bracey Report on the Condition of Public Education." *Phi Delta Kappan* 78, no. 2 (October 1996): 127–138.

————. "The Seventh Bracey Report on the Condition of Public Education." *Phi Delta Kappan* 79, no. 2 (October 1997): 120–136.

————. "Stedman's Myths Miss the Mark." *Educational Leadership* 52, no. 6 (March 1995): 75–80.

————. "The Third Bracey Report on The Condition of Public Education." *Phi Delta Kappan* 75, no. 2 (October 1993): 104–117.

————. "TIMSS: The Message and the Myths." *Principal* 77, no. 3 (June 1998): 18–22.

————. "Why Can't They Be Like We Were?." *Phi Delta Kappan* 73, no. 2 (October 1991): 104–117.

Caine, Renate Nummela and Caine, Geoffrey. *Making Connections: Teaching and the Human Brain.* Alexandria, Va.: Association for Supervision and Curriculum Development, 1991.

Comber, L. C. and Keeves, John P. *Science Education in Nineteen Countries.* New York: John Wiley & Sons, 1973.

Daly, Elizabeth, ed. *Monitoring Children's Language Development: Holistic Assessment in the Classroom.* Portsmouth, N.H.: Heinemann, 1991.

Darling-Hammond, Linda, Ancess, Jacqueline, and Falk, Beverly. *Authentic Assessment in Action: Studies of Schools and Students at Work.* New York: Teachers College Press, 1995.

Davis, Robert H., Alexander, Lawrence T., and Yelon, Stephen L. *Learning System Design.* New York: McGraw-Hill, 1974.

Dick, Walter and Carey, Lou. *The Systematic Design of Instruction,* 2nd ed. Glenview, Ill.: Scott, Foresman, 1985.

Donohue, Patricia L., Voelkl, Kristin E., Campbell, Jay R., and Mazzeo, John. *NAEP 1998 Reading Report Card for the Nation.* Washington, D.C.: National Center for Education Statistics, Office of Educational Research and Improvement, 1999.

Dossey, John A. et al. *The Mathematics Report Card: Are We Measuring Up? Trends and Achievement Based on the 1986 National Assessment.* Princeton, N.J.: National Assessment of Educational Progress, Educational Testing Service, 1988.

Elam, Stanley M., Rose, Lowell C., and Gallup, Alec M. "The 23rd Annual Gallup Poll of the Public's Attitudes Toward the Public Schools." *Phi Delta Kappan* 73, no. 1 (September 1991): 41–56.

————. "The 26th Annual Phi Delta Kappa/Gallup Poll of the Public's Attitudes Toward the Public Schools." *Phi Delta Kappan* 76, no. 1 (September 1994): 41–56.

Elley, Warwick B. *How in the World Do Students Read?* IEA Study of Reading Literacy. Hamburg: International Association for the Evaluation of Educational Achievement, 1992.

Featherstone, Joseph. "Measuring What Schools Achieve: Learning and Testing," *The New Republic* 169, no. 2 (November 1970): 19–21.

Frase, Mary. *Pursuing Excellence: A Study of U.S. Fourth-Grade Mathematics and Science Teaching, Learning, Curriculum, and Achievement in International Context: Initial Findings from the Third International Mathematics and Science Study.* Washington, D.C.: U.S. Department of Education, National Center for Education Statistics, 1997.

Gagnon, Paul, ed. and the Bradley Commission on History in Schools. *Historical Literacy: The Case for History in American Education.* New York: Macmillan, 1989.

Gay, L. R. *Educational Evaluation and Measurement: Competencies for Analysis and Application,* 2nd ed. Columbus, Ohio: Charles E. Merrill, 1985.

Giroux, Henry A. *Living Dangerously: Multiculturalism and the Politics of Difference.* New York: Peter Lang, 1993.

Glasser, William. *The Quality School: Managing Students Without Coercion,* 2nd ed. New York: HarperPerennial, 1992.

Goodlad, John I. *A Place Called School: Prospects for the Future.* New York: McGraw-Hill, 1984.

Greene, Maxine. *Releasing the Imagination: Essays on Education, the Arts, and Social Change.* San Francisco: Jossey-Bass, 1995.

Gronlund, Norman E. *How to Construct Achievement Tests,* 4th ed. Englewood Cliffs, N.J.: Prentice-Hall, 1988.

Gross, Martin L. *The Brain Watchers.* New York: Random House, 1962.

Guskey, Thomas R. "What You Assess May *Not* Be What You Get." *Educational Leadership* 51, no. 6 (March 1994): 51–54.

Hammack, David C. et al. *The U.S. History Report Card: The Achievement of Fourth-, Eighth-, and Twelfth-Grade Students in 1988 and Trends from 1986 to 1988 in the Factual Knowledge of High-School Juniors.* Princeton, N.J.: National Assessment of Educational Progress, Educational Testing Service, 1990.

Harrow, Anita J. *A Taxonomy of the Psychomotor Domain: A Guide for Developing Behavioral Objectives.* White Plains, N.Y.: Longman, 1972.

Herman, Joan, Aschbacher, Pamela, and Winters, Lynn. *A Practical Guide to Alternative Assessment.* Alexandria, Va.: Association for Supervision and Curriculum Development, 1992.

Hill, Clifford and Larsen, Eric. *Testing and Assessment in Secondary Education: A Critical Review of Emerging Practice.* ERIC document ED353445, 1992.

Hirsch, E. D., Jr. *The Schools We Need: Why We Don't Have Them.* New York: Doubleday, 1996.

Hoffman, Banesh. *The Tyranny of Testing.* New York: Crowell-Collier, 1962.

Husén, Torsten, ed. *International Study of Achievement in Mathematics,* vols. 1 and 2. New York: John Wiley & Sons, 1967.

International Association for the Evaluation of Educational Achievement. *Science Achievement in Seventeen Countries: A Preliminary Report.* Oxford, England: Pergamon, 1988.

Jaeger, Richard M. "World Class Standards, Choice, and Privatization: Weak Measurement Serving Presumptive Policy," *Phi Delta Kappan* 74, no. 2 (October 1992): 118–128.

Kibler, Robert J., Cegala, Donald J., Miles, David T., and Barker, Larry L. *Objectives for Instruction and Evaluation.* Boston: Allyn and Bacon, 1974.

Krathwohl, David R., Bloom, Benjamin S., and Masia, Bertram B. *Taxonomy of Educational Objectives: The Classification of Educational Goals: Handbook II: Affective Domain.* White Plains, N.Y.: Longman, 1964.

Langer, Judith A., Applebee, Arthur N., Mullis, Ina V. S., and Foertsch, Mary A. *Learning to Read in Our Nation's Schools.* Princeton, N.J.: National Assessment of Educational Progress, Educational Testing Service, 1990.

Lapointe, Archie E., Mead, Nancy A., and Phillips, Gary W. *A World of Differences: An International Assessment of Mathematics and Science.* Princeton, N.J.: Center for the Assessment of Educational Progress, Educational Testing Service, 1989.

Linn, Robert L. and Dunbar, Stephen B., "The Nation's Report Card Goes Home: Good News and Bad About Trends in Achievement." *Phi Delta Kappan* 72, no. 2 (October 1990): 127–133.

McDonald, Joseph, Barton, Eileen, Smith, Sidney, Turner, Dorothy, and Finney, Maria. *Graduation by Exhibition: Assessing Genuine Achievement.* Alexandria, Va.: Association for Supervision and Curriculum Development, 1993.

McKnight, Curtis C. et al. *The Underachieving Curriculum: Assessing U.S. School Mathematics from an International Perspective.* Champaign, Ill.: Stipes Publishing Company, 1987.

Mager, Robert F. *Preparing Instructional Objectives,* 2nd ed. Belmont, Calif.: Fearon, 1975.

Marchesani, Robert J. *Using Portfolios for More Authentic Assessment of Writing Ability.* ERIC document ED347555, 1992.

Martinez, Michael E. and Mead, Nancy A. *Computer Competence: The First National Assessment.* Princeton, N.J.: National Assessment of Educational Progress, Educational Testing Service, 1988.

Marzano, Robert J., Pickering, Debra, and McTighe, Jay. *Assessing Student Outcomes: Performance Assessment Using the Dimension of Learning Model.* Alexandria, Va.: Association for Supervision and Curriculum Development, 1993.

Mullis, Ina V. S. and Jenkins, Lynn B. *The Reading Report Card 1971–88: Trends from the Nation's Report Card.* Princeton, N.J.: National Assessment of Educational Progress, Educational Testing Service, 1990.

————. *The Science Report Card: Elements of Risk and Recovery—Trends and Achievement Based on the 1986 National Assessment.* Princeton, N.J.: National Assessment of Educational Progress, Educational Testing Service, 1988.

————, Jenkins, Lynn B., Owen, Eugene H., and Phillips, Gary W. *America's Challenge: Accelerating Acad-*

emic Achievement. Princeton, N.J.: National Assessment of Educational Progress, Educational Testing Service, 1990.

————, Martin, Michael O., Beaton, Albert E., Gonzalez, Eugenio J., Kelly, Dana L., and Smith Teresa A. *Mathematics and Science Achievement in IEA's Third International Mathematics and Science Study (TIMSS),* Chestnut Hill, Mass.: Center for the Study of Testing, Evaluating, and Educational Policy, School of Education, Boston College, 1998.

National Alliance of Business. *Achieving World Class Standards in Math and Science.* Washington, D.C.: National Alliance of Busines, 1997.

National Assessment of Educational Progress. *The 1990 Science Report Card.* Princeton, N.J.: Educational Testing Service, 1992.

————. *Trends in Academic Progress.* Princeton, N.J.: Educational Testing Service, 1992.

National Center for Education Statistics. *The Condition of Education 1994.* Washington, D.C.: U.S. Department of Education, Office of Educational Research and Improvement, 1994.

————. *The Condition of Education 1995.* Washington, D.C.: U.S. Department of Education, Office of Educational Research and Improvement, 1995.

————. *The Condition of Education 1996,* Smith, Thomas M., ed. Washington, D.C.: U.S. Department of Education, Office of Educational Research and Improvement, 1996.

————. *The Condition of Education 1997.* Washington, D.C.: U.S. Department of Education, Office of Educational Research and Improvement, 1997.

National Commission on Excellence in Education, David P. Gardner, chairman. *A Nation at Risk: The Imperative for Educational Reform.* Washington, D.C.: U.S. Government Printing Office, 1983.

O'Connell, Pat, Peak, Lois, Dorfman, Cynthis Hern, Azzam, Rima, Chacon, Ruth, and colleagues. *Introduction to TIMSS: The Third International Mathematics and Science Study.* Washington, D.C.: U.S. Department of Education, Office of Educational Research and Improvement, 1997.

Ogle, Laurence T. and Alsalam, Nabeel. *The Condition of Education 1990.* vol. 1, *Elementary and Secondary Education.* Washington, D.C.: U.S. Department of Education, 1990.

Oliva, Peter F. *The Secondary School Today,* 2nd ed. New York: Harper & Row, 1972.

———— and Pawlas, George E. *Supervision for Today's Schools.* 6th ed. New York: John Wiley & Sons, 2001.

Paulson, F. Leon, Paulson, Pearl R., and Meyer, Carol A. "What Makes a Portfolio a Portfolio?" *Educational Leadership* 48, no. 5 (February 1991): 60–63.

Peak, Lois. *Pursuing Excellence: A Study of U.S. Eighth-Grade Mathematics and Science Teaching, Learning, Curriculum, and Achievement in International Context: Initial Findings from the Third International Mathe-*

matics and Science Study. Washington, D.C.: U.S. Department of Education, National Center for Education Statistics, 1996.

Persky, Hilary R., Rees, Clyde M., O'Sullivan, Christine Y., Lazer, Stephen, Moore, Jerry, and Shrakami, Sharif. *NAEP 1994 U.S. Geography Report Card: Findings from the National Assessment of Educational Progress.* Washington, D.C.: U.S. Department of Education, Office of Educational Research and Improvement, 1996.

————, Sandene, Brent A., and Askew, Janice M. *The NAEP 1997 Arts Report Card: Eighth-Grade Findings from the National Assessment of Educational Progress.* Washington, D.C.: National Center for Education Statistics, Office of Educational Research and Improvement, 1998.

Plisko, Valena White and Stern, Joyce D. *The Condition of Education 1985.* Washington, D.C.: U.S. Department of Education, National Center for Education Statistics, 1985.

Popham, W. James. *Evaluating Instruction.* Englewood Cliffs, N.J.: Prentice-Hall, 1973.

Posthlethwaite, T. Neville. "International Educational Surveys. *Contemporary Education* 42, no. 2 (November 1970): 61–68.

Purves, Alan C. *Literature Education in Ten Countries.* New York: John Wiley & Sons, 1973.

Ravitch, Diane. *National Standards in American Education: A Citizen's Guide.* Washington, D.C.: The Brookings Institution, 1995.

———— and Finn, Chester E. Jr. *What Do Our 17-Year-Olds Know? A Report on the First National Assessment of History and Literature.* New York: Harper & Row, 1987.

Simpson, Elizabeth Jane. "The Classification of Educational Objectives in the Psychomotor Domain." In *The Psychomotor Domain,* vol. 3, 43–56. Washington, D.C.: Gryphon House, 1972.

Sizer, Theodore R. *Horace's School: Redesigning the American High School.* Boston: Houghton Mifflin, 1992.

Smith, Thomas M. *The Condition of Education 1996.* Washington, D.C.: U.S. Department of Education, National Center for Education Statistics, 1996.

Smythe, Mary-Jeanette, Kibler, Robert J., and Hutchings, Patricia W. "A Comparison of Norm-Referenced and Criterion-Referenced Measurement with Implications for Communication Instruction." *The Speech Teacher* 22, no. 1 (January 1973): 1–17.

Stedman, Lawrence C. "Let's Look Again at the Evidence," *Educational Leadership* 52, no. 6 (March 1995): 78–79.

————. "The New Mythology About the Status of U.S. Schools." *Educational Leadership* 52, no. 5 (February 1995): 80–85.

Stevenson, Harold W. "Why Asian Students Still Outdistance Americans." *Educational Leadership* 50, no. 5 (February 1993): 63–65.

Strenio, Andrew, Jr. *The Testing Trap.* New York: Rawson, Wade, 1981.

Takahira, Sayuri, Gonzalez, Patrick, Frase, Mary, and Salganik, Laura Hersh. *Pursuing Excellence: A Study of U.S. Twelfth-Grade Mathematics and Study: Initial Findings from the Third International Mathematics and Science Study.* Washington, D.C.: U.S. Department of Education, National Center for Education Statistics, 1998.

Thorndike, Robert L. *Reading Comprehension Education in Fifteen Countries.* New York: John Wiley & Sons, 1973.

"What Schools Can Do About What Students Don't Know." *Educational Leadership* 47, no. 3 (November 1989): 3–91.

Whyte, William H., Jr. *The Organization Man.* New York: Simon and Schuster, 1956.

Wiggins, Grant. "Teaching to the (Authentic) Test," *Educational Leadership* 46, no. 7 (April 1989): 41–47.

Wirt, John, Snyder, Tom, Sable, Jennifer, Choy, Susan P., Bae, Yupin, Stennett, Janis, Gruner, Allison, and Perie, Marianne. *The Condition of Education 1998.* Washington, D.C.: U.S. Department of Education, National Center for Education Statistics, 1998.

Worthen, Blaine R. and Spandel, Vicki. "Putting the Standardized Test Debate in Perspective." *Educational Leadership* 48, no. 5 (February 1991): 65–69.

AUDIOTAPES

Association for Supervision and Curriculum Development, 1703 N. Beauregard St., Alexandria, Va. 22311-1714.

Assessing Student Outcomes. 3 tapes. 40 to 60 min. ea. 1995.

Assessing *Process, Not People, Teaching/Learning Practices that Work for All. (Barry Raebeck).*

Assessment in the Nongraded/Multi-Age School (Barbara Nelson Pavan, Robert Anderson, Marlene Dergousoff, and Cathy Braxdale).

Assessing Student Outcomes with the Dimensions of Learning (Robert J. Marzano and Debra Pickering).

Conversations About Children's Learning: Portfolios and the Culture of Learning (Elizabeth Hebert, Mary Mumbrue, and Carolyn Schoeller).

Designing Performance-Based Assessment Using Dimensions of Learning. 90 min. 1995. Presenters; Jay McTighe and Debra Pickering.

PROFESSIONAL INQUIRY KIT

Assessing Student Performance. Video clips, activities, readings. 1996. Judy Arter, developer. Association for Supervision and Curriculum Development, 1703 N. Beauregard St., Alexandria, Va. 22311-1714.

REPORTS

Reports of the International Assessment of Educational Progress may be obtained from the Center for the Assessment of Educational Progress, Educational Testing Service, Rosedale Road, Princeton, New Jersey 08541-0001.

Reports of the National Assessment of Educational Progress may be obtained from the National Assessment of Educational Progress, Educational Testing Service, Rosedale Road, Princeton, New Jersey 08541-0001.

RESOURCE KIT

Attaining Excellence: A TIMSS Resource Kit. Report ORAD-97-1010. An overview of TIMSS. 4 modules: Education, Student achievement, Teaching, and Curricula. Reports of findings, videotapes, presentation overheads, checklists, leaflets, and flyers. U.S. Department of Education, Office of Reform Assistance and Dissemination, Washington, D.C., 1997.

VIDEOTAPES

Association for Supervision and Curriculum Development, 1703 N. Beauregard St., Alexandria, Va.: 22311-1714.

Developing Performance Assessments. 60-min. videotape. *Facilitator's Guide.* Jay McTighe, Grant Wiggins, and K. Michael Hibbard, presenters.

What's New in School: A Parent's Guide to Performance Assessment, 1995. One of a series of four tapes: introduction, cooperative learning, curriculum integration, and performance assessment.

WEB SITES

Educational Testing Service: http://www.ets.org

International Association for the Evaluation of Educational Achievement: http://www.ccsso.org/IEA.html

National Center for Education Statistics: http://www.nces.ed.gov

National Assessment of Educational Progress: http://nces.ed.gov/nationsreportcard

Office of Educational Research and Improvement: http://www.ed.gov/offices/OERI

CHAPTER 13
EVALUATING THE CURRICULUM

After studying this chapter you should be able to:

1. Describe several processes for evaluating the curriculum.
2. Explain the major features of at least two models of curriculum evaluation.
3. Describe how one or more models of curriculum evaluation can be used by curriculum planners.
4. Select and apply a model of curriculum evaluation.
5. Describe eight principles of curriculum construction and explain their significance to curriculum planners.

PURPOSES AND PROBLEMS OF CURRICULUM EVALUATION

Years ago in a college foreign language class, the instructor lured his students into a grammatical frame of mind by promising to reveal to them "the secrets of the subjunctive." In this chapter some of the secrets of curriculum evaluation will be disclosed. I'll make this revelation right now. The secrets of evaluation are

- to ask questions
- to ask the *right* questions
- to ask the *right* questions of the *right* people

Depending on the problems, questions might be addressed to teachers, administrators, pupils, lay people, parents, other school personnel, or experts in various fields, including curriculum.

As is often necessary in pedagogical discourse, we must first clarify terms before we can talk about them. We find numerous articles and textbooks on educational, instructional, and curriculum evaluation. The broadest of these terms—educational evaluation—is used in this text to encompass all kinds of evaluations that come under the aegis of the school. It includes evaluation not only of curriculum and instruction but also of the grounds, buildings, administration, supervision, personnel, transportation, and so on.

Instructional evaluation, discussed in the preceding chapter, is an assessment of (1) pupils' achievement, (2) the instructor's performance, and (3) the effectiveness of a particular approach or methodology. *Curriculum evaluation* includes instructional evaluation. Recall that the Instructional Model is a submodel of the comprehensive curriculum development model. Curriculum evaluation also goes well beyond the purposes of instructional evaluation into assessment of the program and related areas. Albert I. Oliver listed five areas of concern that call for evaluation. "The five Ps," as he termed them, are program, provisions, procedures, products, and processes.[1]

The axiom that change is inevitable not only in education but also outside of education was advanced early in this text. As curriculum planners, we wish changes in education to take place for the better. Because the creations of mortals are always less than perfect, we can always seek improvement. Evaluation is the means for determining what needs improvement and for providing a basis for effecting that improvement.

You have already encountered in Chapter 7 one dimension of curriculum evaluation—the needs assessment, a process by which you can identify gaps in the curriculum. In this chapter we are concerned with the evaluation of curricula that are or have been in operation.

PROBLEMS IN EVALUATION

Many concede that one place where we are vulnerable in education is in evaluating the programs we have instituted. Our evaluation is often spotty and frequently inconclusive. We should be able to demonstrate, for example, whether

- Interdisciplinary teamwork results in higher student achievement than the self-contained classroom.
- Integrated curricula result in higher student achievement than discrete disciplines.
- The learning of a second language helps in learning one's native language.
- Nongraded schools are more effective than graded.
- Modern materials to teach reading are better tools than *The McGuffey Reader.*
- The specification of minimal competencies improves student performance.
- One series of biology texts results in greater student achievement in biology than another series.
- An inductive or deductive approach is more effective in teaching grammar.
- Cooperative learning is more effective than either didactic or individualized learning.
- Class size makes a difference in pupil achievement.
- A whole language approach to teaching language arts is more effective than a phonics approach.

---

[1]Albert I. Oliver, *Curriculum Improvement: A Guide to Problems, Principles, and Process,* 2nd ed.(New York: Harper & Row, 1965), p. 306.

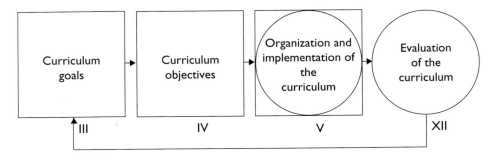

Figure 13.1 Curriculum model with one feedback line

Many of the conclusions reached about the success of educational innovations have been based on very limited evidence. The lack of systematic evaluation may be attributed to a number of causes. Careful evaluation can be very complicated. It requires know-how on the part of the evaluators, and, therefore, training in evaluation. Further, it is time- and energy-consuming and often expensive. We could say that schools generally do not do a thorough job of evaluation and what they do is often not too helpful.

Daniel L. Stufflebeam and others observed that evaluation was ill and suffered from the following symptoms:

1. The avoidance symptom. Because evaluation seems to be a painful process, everyone avoids it unless absolutely necessary. . . .
2. The anxiety symptom. . . . Anxiety stems primarily from the ambiguities of the evaluation process. . . .
3. The immobilization symptom. . . . Schools have not responded to evaluation in any meaningful way. . . .
4. The skepticism symptom. . . . Many persons seem to argue that there is little point in planning for evaluation because "it can't be done anyway." . . .
5. The lack-of-guidelines symptom. . . . Among professional evaluators . . . is the notable lack of meaningful and operational guidelines. . . .
6. The misadvice symptom. Evaluation consultants, many of whom are methodological specialists in educational research, continue to give bad advice to practitioners. . . .
7. The no-significant-difference symptom. . . . Evaluation . . . is so often incapable of uncovering any significant information. . . .
8. The missing-elements symptom. [There] is a lack of certain crucial elements needed if evaluation is to make significant forward strides. The most obvious missing element is the lack of adequate theory. . . . [2]

Revising the Curriculum Model.   As in our analysis of evaluating instruction, we will develop some general understandings about curriculum evaluation and will discuss a limited number of evaluation procedures. Let's begin by taking a look at the Curriculum Model shown in Figure 13.1, which is a submodel of the proposed model for curriculum improvement.

---

[2]Daniel L. Stufflebeam, et al., *Educational Evaluation and Decision Making* (Itasca, Ill.: F. E. Peacock, 1971), pp. 4–9. Reprinted with permission.

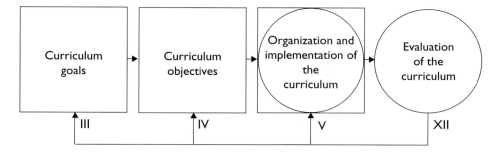

Figure 13.2 *Curriculum model with all feedback lines*

The Curriculum Model is conceptualized as consisting of four components—Curriculum goals, Curriculum objectives, Organization and implementation of the curriculum, and Evaluation of the curriculum. A feedback line connects the Evaluation component with the Goals component, making the model cyclical in nature. We should redefine the Curriculum Model in two ways. First, as with the Instructional Model, we should show the feedback line as affecting more than just the Curriculum goals. Although the impact on Curriculum goals is felt through all subsequent components, evaluative data should feed back to each of the components of the Curriculum Model. A more precise rendering of the feedback concept would show lines from Evaluation of the curriculum not only to Curriculum goals but also to Curriculum objectives and to Organization and implementation of the curriculum, as shown in Figure 13.2.

Second, let's make clear that evaluation of the curriculum is not something done solely at the end of a program's implementation but is an operation that takes place before, during, and at the end of the implementation. Figure 13.3 shows the continuous nature of curriculum evaluation in a manner similar to the way in which the continuous nature of instructional evaluation was shown. Circles within the squares of Figure 13.3 indicate that curriculum evaluation is going on while evaluation procedures are being planned.

DELIMITING EVALUATION

DIFFERENCES BETWEEN INSTRUCTIONAL AND CURRICULUM EVALUATION

Some instructors and curriculum planners believe that assessing the achievement of *instructional* objectives constitutes *curriculum* evaluation. Thus, if students achieve the cognitive, affective, and psychomotor learnings, the curriculum is considered effective. To follow that line of reasoning, we would add all the evaluations of instruction together in a one-plus-one fashion presumably to determine the success of the curriculum. This position makes the mistake of equating curriculum with instruction. If this were the case, separate components for the Evaluation of instruction and Evaluation of the curriculum would not be shown in the Curriculum Development Model (Figure 5.5).

However, instruction and curriculum are not the same. The instructional process may be very effective whereas the curriculum, like the times, may be out of joint. In Aldous Huxley's *Brave New World,* the society runs very efficiently, but few would opt

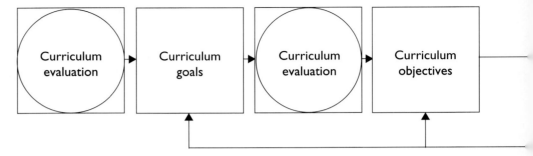

Figure 13.3 Continuous nature of curriculum evaluation

to live there. Instructional evaluation may reveal that pupils are achieving the instructional objectives. On the other hand, unless we evaluate the curriculum—the programs—we may be effectively teaching all the wrong things. If I may exaggerate to make this point, we could do a beautiful job of teaching young people that:

- The earth is flat.
- The earth is the center of the solar system.
- One ethnic group is inherently superior to another.
- All children can be doctors and lawyers.
- White-collar workers always earn more money than blue-collar workers.
- There will always be plenty of cheap energy.
- All scientific advancements are the result of American ingenuity.
- Illnesses are caused by the evil eye.

The primary purpose of curriculum evaluation is, of course, to determine whether the curriculum goals and objectives are being carried out. However, we want to answer other questions as well. We want to know if the goals and objectives are right to begin with. We want to learn whether the curriculum is functioning while in operation. We want to find out if we are using the best materials and following the best methods. We must learn whether the products of our schools are successful in higher education and in jobs, whether they can function in daily life and contribute to society. We must also determine whether our programs are cost-effective—whether we are getting the most for our money.

DIFFERENCE BETWEEN EVALUATION AND RESEARCH

Discussion of evaluation inevitably leads us into the area of research. Evaluation is the process of making judgments, research is the process of gathering data to make those judgments. Whenever we gather data to answer problems, we are engaged in research. However, the complexity and quality of research differ from problem to problem. We may engage in research ranging from simple descriptive research to complex experimental research. As an example of the former: How many library books does the school library possess per child? As an example in the latter: Do children with learning disabilities perform more effectively when they are in segregated classes or when they are mainstreamed? Most ambitious of all—and very rare—are longitudinal studies like the Eight-Year Study that compared the success in college of

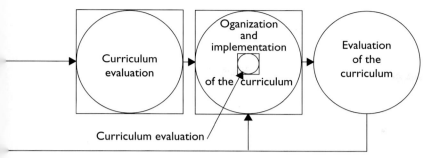

graduates from traditional high schools to that of graduates from experimental high schools.[3]

The field of evaluation often calls for the services of specialists in evaluation and research. Some large school systems are able to employ personnel to direct, conduct, and supervise curriculum evaluation for their school systems. These people bring to the task a degree of expertise not shared by most teachers and curriculum planners. Some school systems, which do not hire their own evaluation personnel, invite in outside consultants to help with particular curriculum problems and research. However, most evaluative studies must be and are conducted by the local curriculum planners and the teachers. The shortage of trained personnel and the costs of employing specialists are prohibitive for many school systems. Even in large systems that employ curriculum evaluators, many curriculum evaluation tasks are performed by teachers and curriculum planners.

EVALUATION MODELS

Models have been developed showing types of evaluation that schools should carry out and the processes they should follow.[4] As in the case of models of instruction and of curriculum development, evaluation models differ in detail and the points which their creators choose to include.

For our purposes let's look first at two rather simple approaches to curriculum evaluation that we will label *Limited Models.* Then let's turn to two well-known, frequently-cited *Comprehensive Models*—that of J. Galen Saylor, William M. Alexander, and Arthur J. Lewis,[5] a rather easily understood model that shows the scope and na-

---

[3]For an account of the Eight-Year Study see Wilford M. Aikin, *The Story of the Eight-Year Study* (New York: Harper & Row, 1942).

[4]See, for example, the following models:

Center for the Study of Evaluation, *Evaluation Workshop I: An Orientation* (Del Monte Research Park, Monterey, Calif.: CTB/McGraw-Hill, 1971).

Malcolm Provus, *Discrepancy Evaluation for Educational Program Improvement and Assessment* (Berkeley, Calif.: McCutchan, 1971).

Robert E. Stake, "Language, Rationality, and Assessment," in *Improving Educational Assessment and an Inventory of Measures of Affective Behavior,* ed. Walcott H. Beatty (Alexandria, Va.: Association for Supervision and Curriculum Development, 1969).

[5]See J. Galen Saylor, William M. Alexander, and Arthur J. Lewis, *Curriculum Planning for Better Teaching and Learning,* 4th ed. (New York: Holt, Rinehart and Winston, 1981).

ture of curriculum evaluation and the model of the Phi Delta Kappa National Study Committee on Evaluation, a more complex model written in rather technical terms.[6]

LIMITED MODELS

Evaluation of Curriculum Objectives. Recall that chapter eight described curriculum goals and objectives and distinguished them from instructional goals and objectives. Recall also that we defined curriculum objectives as "specific, measurable, programmatic statements of outcomes to be achieved by students as a group in the school or school system."[7]

We ascribed the following characteristics to curriculum objectives, paralleling characteristics of instructional objectives:

- they specify performance or behavior to be demonstrated
- they include a degree of mastery
- they state conditions under which the performance will take place, if not readily understood.

Drawing on previously specified nonmeasurable curriculum goals, curriculum objectives pertain to programs, not specific content and refer to accomplishments of groups of students (all students, students in general, most students, groups of students) rather than the achievement of individual students. Curriculum evaluation assesses programs directly and individual student performance indirectly. Instructional evaluation assesses individual students directly and programs indirectly.

The most fundamental approach to curriculum evaluation—one that must be taken regardless of other supporting approaches—is the assessment of achievement of the specified curriculum objectives. Observation surveys, portfolios, and test results are all means by which to gather evaluative data. Let's take a few examples of curriculum objectives for a given year and mention a corresponding technique for evaluating.

- The number of incidents of conflict among members of diverse ethnic groups will be reduced by fifty percent (statistics).
- All students will demonstrate proficiency in performing without error a selected number of computer skills (samples of work, observation).
- The high-school dropout rate will be decreased by ten percent (statistics).
- Pupils will increase their leisure-time reading by ten percent (book reports, school library circulation figures).
- Eighth-graders will raise their scores on a standardized test of mathematics by ten percentile points (test results).
- An increased twenty percent of both boys and girls will elect participation in interscholastic, intramural, or individualized athletic activities (statistics).
- Ten percent more high-school students will enroll in elective music or art courses (statistics).

---

[6]See Stufflebeam et al., *Educational Evaluation.*
[7]See Chapter 8

- All students will demonstrate knowledge of the seriousness and facts of AIDS and what they must do to protect themselves from the disease (class discussions, counseling, portfolios, quizzes).
- Students will evidence responsible citizenship by demonstrating knowledge of our political system (class discussion, portfolios, quizzes).
- Students will describe ethical behavior in a given number of problem situations (class discussions, reflective papers, observation).

Curriculum planners must determine whether the programmatic, (i.e., curricular) objectives have been achieved. If the curriculum objectives have been reached, planners would then identify next steps by specifying new curriculum objectives and establishing new priorities. If the curriculum objectives have not been met, planners must decide whether the objectives still merit pursuing and if so, what measures must be taken to achieve them.

Evaluation of Principles of Curriculum Construction and Organization. Certain principles are inherent in constructing and organizing the curriculum. In one sense these principles are characteristics of curriculum construction and organization. In another sense they are continuing problems for curriculum developers.

Supplementing assessment of the curriculum objectives, curriculum workers should assess the degree to which they implement basic principles of curriculum construction and organization. In this chapter we will describe eight perennial problems of curriculum construction and organization: scope, relevance, balance, integration, sequence, continuity, articulation, and transferability.

An evaluation process cognizant of these problems would provide answers to such questions as:

- Is the scope of the curriculum adequate? Realistic?
- Is the curriculum relevant?
- Is there balance in the curriculum?
- Is curriculum integration desirable?
- Is the curriculum properly sequenced?
- Is there continuity of programs?
- Are curricula well articulated between levels?
- Are learnings transferable?

To answer questions like these curriculum planners must understand the nature of the principles. The assessing of principles of curriculum construction and evaluation not only calls for gathering of considerable data but also for intelligent reflexion on the part of the evaluators.

GUIDING PRINCIPLES

Although a model for curriculum improvement may show us a process, it does not reveal the whole picture. It does not show us, for example, how we go about choosing from competing content, what we do about conflicting philosophies, how we assure articulation between levels, how we learn to live with change, how dependent we are upon effective leadership, what incentives motivate people to try out new ideas, how to go about finding the information we need to make intelligent decisions, and how we release human and material resources to do the job.

We already examined in Chapter 4 several major problems of curriculum development, including effecting change, group dynamics, interpersonal relationships, decision making, curriculum leadership, and communication skills. The eight guiding factors to be discussed are not only perennial problems for curriculum developers but, in essence, are also concepts that lead to the formulation of principles of curriculum development. The creation of a well-functioning sequence, for example, is a continuing problem for the curriculum developer. At the same time, the curriculum planner must understand the concept of sequencing, which is essential to an effective curriculum. Bringing the two elements, curriculum and sequencing, together we formulate the principle: An effective curriculum is one that is properly sequenced. We will, therefore, refer to these eight guiding factors as problems, concepts, or, by inference, principles.

All eight concepts are interrelated. We shall first examine four concepts closely related to each other: scope, relevance, balance, and integration. The last three are dimensions of scope; all four relate to the choice of goals and objectives. We shall then consider three other closely interrelated concepts: sequence (or sequencing), continuity, and articulation. The last two are dimensions of sequencing. Finally, we shall look at the concept of transferability.

Scope

Scope is usually defined as "the breadth" of the curriculum. The content of any course or grade level—identified as topics, learning experiences, activities, organizing threads or elements,[8] integrative threads,[9] or organizing centers,[10]—constitutes the scope of the curriculum for that course or grade level. The summed content of the several courses or grade levels makes up the scope of the school curriculum. J. Galen Saylor and William M. Alexander in an earlier work defined scope in the following way: "By scope is meant the breadth, variety, and types of educational experiences that are to be provided pupils as they progress through the school program. Scope represents the latitudinal axis for selecting curriculum experiences."[11]

When teachers select the content that will be dealt with during the year, they are making decisions on scope. When curriculum planners at the district or state level set the minimum requirements for graduation from high school, they are responding to the question of scope.

We encounter a problem when we equate the activities or learning experiences with scope. It is true that the sum of all activities or learning experiences reveals the scope of the curriculum. However, the activities or learning experiences are the opera-

---

[8]Ralph W. Tyler, *Basic Principles of Curriculum and Instruction* (Chicago: University of Chicago Press, 1949), p. 86.

[9]Benjamin S. Bloom, "Ideas, Problems, and Methods of Inquiry," in *The Integration of Educational Experiences,* 57th Yearbook, National Society for the Study of Education, Part 3 (Chicago: University of Chicago Press, 1958), pp. 84–85.

[10]John I. Goodlad, *Planning and Organizing for Teaching* (Washington, D.C.: National Education Association, 1963), Chapter 2.

[11]J. Galen Saylor and William M. Alexander, *Curriculum Planning for Better Teaching and Learning* (New York: Holt, Rinehart and Winston, Inc., 1954), p. 284.

tional phases of the topics. For example, to present the topic of the Renaissance, we can design many activities or learning experiences to teach that topic, including viewing photographs of works of art of the period, writing biographies of famous artists, reading novels about the period, reading histories of the period, writing reports on the roles of the church and state during this time, and so on.

Organizing Centers or Threads.   John I. Goodlad defined the elements of scope as "the actual focal points for learning through which the school's objectives are to be attained."[12] He wanted to convey the meaning of these elements as one term for the following reason:

> Nowhere in the educational literature is there a term that conveys satisfactorily what is intended in these focal points. The words *activities and learning experiences* are used most frequently but are somewhat misleading. Under the circumstances there is virtue in using the technical term *organizing centers.* Although somewhat awkward, the term does permit the inclusion of such widely divergent focal points for learning as units of work, cultural epochs, historical events, a poem, a film on soil erosion, and a trip to the zoo. The *organizing center* for teaching and learning may be as specific as a book on trees or as general as press censorship in the twentieth century. *Organizing centers determine the essential character of the curriculum.*[13]

In a similar vein, Tyler advised those who are organizing the curriculum to identify the organizing threads or elements—that is, the basic concepts and skills to be taught.[14] Thus, curriculum planners must choose the focal points, the basic concepts and skills, and the knowledge that will be included in the curriculum. A central problem of this horizontal organization that we call scope is the delimitation of the concepts, skills, knowledge, and attitudes to be included.

Explosion of Knowledge.   Teachers must continuously wrestle with the problem of limiting subject matter. Knowledge, spurred on by constantly evolving technology, increases at a fantastic—and often alarming—rate. Humankind has no sooner begun to live more or less comfortably with the computer than it has become involved in cloning, in vitro fertilization, and splicing genes to create new life forms. Humankind has journeyed through space but now worries about the debris floating around in our solar system. Humankind has harnessed the atom but has not learned to dispose of radioactive waste safely.

As long ago as 1970 Alvin Toffler spoke about the phenomenal increase in knowledge in this way:

> The rate at which man has been storing up useful knowledge about himself and the universe has been spiraling upward for 10,000 years. The rate took a sharp upward leap with the invention of writing. . . . The next great leap forward in knowledge-acquisition did not occur until the invention of movable type in the fifteenth century. . . . Prior to 1500, by the most optimistic estimates, Europe was producing books at the rate of 1000 titles per year. . . . By the mid-sixties, the output of books on a world scale, Europe included, approached the prodigious figure of 1000 titles per day. . . .

---

[12]Goodlad, *Planning and Organizing, p. 28.*
[13]Ibid.
[14]Tyler, *Basic Principles, p. 86.*

Today the United States government alone generates 100,000 reports each year plus 450,000 articles, books and papers. On a worldwide basis, scientific and technical literature mounts at a rate of some 60,000,000 pages a year. The computer has raised the rate of knowledge-acquisition to dumbfounding speeds.[15]

Have you tried to keep up with the mind-boggling amount of information on the Internet? Clearly, the problem of limiting knowledge will only intensify in the future.

Aims Procedure.   Somehow, someway, curriculum workers must select the concepts, skills, and knowledge to be incorporated into the curriculum. Many years ago Hollis L. Caswell and Doak S. Campbell suggested a procedure for determining the scope of the curriculum. Referring to the process as the "aims procedure," they outlined the steps as follows:

First, a general all-inclusive aim of education is stated. Second, this all-inclusive statement is broken up into a small number of highly generalized statements. Third, the statement of a small number of aims is divided to suit the administrative organization of the school [for the elementary, junior high, or senior high school divisions]. . . . Fourth, the aims of each division are further broken up by stating the objectives to be achieved by each subject. Fifth, the general objectives for the subjects in each division are analyzed into specific objectives for the several grades; that is, statements in as specific terms as possible are made of the part of the subject objectives to be achieved in each grade. The specific objectives for all the subjects in each grade represent the work to be carried forward in the respective grades and indicate the scope of work for the grades.[16]

Caswell and Campbell perceived the specific objectives—not learning experiences, focal points, topics, or organizing threads—as indicating the scope of the curriculum.

Necessary Decisions.   With time so precious and the content burden so great, every organizing center included in the curriculum must be demonstrably superior to those not included. Decisions as to the superiority of the selected elements are reached by group consensus, by expertise, or by both. Curriculum planners must answer questions to which there are no easy answers, like these:

- What do young people need to succeed in our society?
- What are the needs of our locality, state, nation, and world?
- What are the essentials of each discipline?

Albert I. Oliver highlighted the levels at which decisions on scope must be made, as follows:

Scope operates [on] at least four levels. First, there must be decisions as to what to include in the curriculum as a whole, in the major areas within which the curriculum operates. Should we concern ourselves with sex education? Shall we offer driver education? German? Geometry? . . .

Within this total pattern of elements selected to achieve the school's projected goals there is a second level—the scope of an area. Whether this be called a subject field, an interdiscipline or a domain, it is a subject within the total scope. What from

---

[15]Alvin Toffler, *Future Shock* (New York: Random House, 1970), pp. 30–31. Reprinted with permission.
[16]Hollis L. Caswell and Doak K. Campbell, *Curriculum Development* (New York: American Book Company, 1935), p. 152.

the discipline of mathematics is appropriate for an elementary school, for a secondary school? . . .

The third level of scope determination concerns the individual teacher within the broad framework of the curriculum. What theorems shall the teacher of geometry include? . . .

The fourth level relates to an individual lesson.[17]

As we see in Oliver's comments, decisions on the scope of the curriculum are multiple and relate to the curriculum as a whole, the various disciplines, courses or content within the disciplines, and the individual lesson. We might add an additional level before the individual lesson: the unit plan.

Curriculum workers must make decisions on scope not only within each of the three domains but also from among the domains. Within the domains they must raise questions such as the following:

- Shall we include a course in geology as well as biology (cognitive)?
- Shall we include development of charity as a value as well as the attitude of cooperation (affective)?
- Shall we teach auto mechanics as well as word-processing (psychomotor)?

Curriculum planners and teachers may find the determination of scope within a domain, albeit taxing, easier to resolve than making decisions between domains. Which domain, it must be asked, is most important? This question resurrects philosophical arguments about the nature of knowledge, the nature and needs of learners and of society. The question brings us back to Herbert Spencer's classic query, "What knowledge is of most worth?"[18] Arno Bellack addressed the same question and concluded that schools should enable teachers to develop students' knowledge in the major disciplines.[19]

Others have stressed the domain of knowledge—the cognitive domain. Jerome S. Bruner wrote: "The structure of knowledge—its connectedness and its derivations that make one idea follow another—is the proper emphasis in education";[20] Robert L. Ebel championed cognitive learning;[21] and Philip H. Phenix said: "My thesis, briefly, is that all curriculum content should be drawn from the disciplines, or to put it another way, that only knowledge contained in the disciplines is appropriate to the curriculum."[22]

Arthur W. Combs, Abraham H. Maslow, and others, on the other hand, looked beyond the realm of knowledge to the development of values and the self-concept as central to the educational process.[23] We shall not reopen the great debate between cognitive and affective learning, but we should point out that the issue looms large in determining the scope of the curriculum.

---

[17]Albert I. Oliver, *Curriculum Improvement: A Guide to Problems, Principles, and Process,* 2nd ed.(New York: Harper & Row, 1965), pp. 188–189..

[18]See p. 214 of this text.

[19]See Arno A. Bellack, "What Knowledge Is of Most Worth?" *The High School Journal* 48 (February 1965): 318–322.

[20]Jerome S. Bruner, *On Knowing* (Cambridge, Mass.: Harvard University Press, 1962), p. 120.

[21]See Robert L. Ebel, "What Schools Are For," *Phi Delta Kappan* 54, no. 1 (September 1972): 3–7.

[22]Philip H. Phenix, "The Disciplines as Curriculum Content," in *Curriculum Crossroads,* ed. A. Harry Passow (New York: Teachers College Press, Columbia University, 1962), p. 57.

[23]See Arthur W. Combs, ed. *Perceiving, Behaving, Becoming,* 1962 Yearbook (Alexandria, Va.: Association for Supervision and Curriculum Development, 1962).

Many teachers and curriculum planners, refusing to rely on their own judgment, leave decisions on scope to others—to curriculum consultants, to writers of curriculum guides, and to the authors and publishers of textbooks. Thus the scope consists, for example, of many pages of one or more texts, and the determination is made simply by dividing the number of pages by the number of days' schooling or by dividing the number of topics and learning activities in a course of study by the number of days or weeks. Although this simplistic planning is better than none, the curriculum would be far more pertinent if, through a systematic, cooperative process, planners exercised their own combined professional judgment and selected from the entire field only those concepts, skills, and knowledge they deemed appropriate to their school, learners, society, state, region, and country.

RELEVANCE

To assert that the curriculum must be relevant is to champion mom's blueberry pie. For who can disagree that mom's blueberry pie is one of the tastiest dishes ever concocted and is in the great American tradition? No one will stand up and argue for an irrelevant curriculum. However, the repeated demand for relevance in the curriculum—unless it is a strawman—must indicate a lack of this essential characteristic in the curriculum.

Varying Interpretations.   The difficulty of determining relevance lies in the multitude of interpretations of the word. What is considered relevant education for suburbia may not be for the inner city. What is considered relevant for the Anglo may not be for the Hispanic. What is relevant to the essentialists may not be to the progressivists. Relevance, like beauty, is in the eyes of the beholder. "Like the words 'relation' and 'relating,'" said Harry S. Broudy, "'relevance' excludes virtually nothing, for everything mentionable is relevant in some sense to everything else that is mentionable."[24]

We should stress the word *considered* in "what is considered relevant." Whether the curriculum is relevant or not may be beside the point. The consumers of curriculum—the constituents and patrons of the school—will form attitudes toward relevance. Curriculum planners must deal first with perceptions of relevance before they can deal with the question of relevance itself. William Glasser attributed students' perceptions of their lessons as "boring" to the fact that they could not relate what they were studying to their lives.[25]

Arguments about relevance swirl around immediate (as opposed to remote) needs and interests of learners. College and work, for examples, are psychologically if not chronologically far into the future for most children. They feel a need for certain knowledge *now*. Like Scarlett O'Hara, they'll worry about remote needs tomorrow.

Disagreements arise over contemporary as opposed to historic content. There is some question as to how many students would enroll in history courses—with the possible exception of American history—if the classes were not required. History teachers

---

[24]Harry S. Broudy, *The Real World of the Public Schools,* (New York: Harcourt Brace Jovanovich, 1972), p. 179.

[25]William Glasser, *The Quality School: Managing Students Without Coercion,* 2nd ed. (New York: HarperPerennial, 1992), p. 7.

constantly have trouble showing young people the value of history, and the more ancient the history, the more difficulty they have.

Conflicts come about between the academic studies and the vocational curriculum. Preparation for careers is of extreme importance to young people. They can see the value in skill courses but often do not realize that the academic areas may (1) provide a grounding needed in every curriculum and (2) open new vistas toward other careers. English teachers, for example, must feel an increasing despair that, in spite of their best efforts, the American population—arguably a more or less literate public in one of the most highly developed countries on earth—is not really a reading public. Furthermore, what is read is not of the highest quality. We can attribute the lack of reading in part to difficulties young people experience when learning to read in school. Children acquire early an aversion to reading.

We can also attribute the lack of reading to the American frontier mentality that equated reading with effete living and not with the macho men and pioneer women who tamed the West. Finally, television has delivered a significant blow to the printed word. Watching television is easier and more enjoyable to many, though perhaps less imaginative than reading. Will the computer, perhaps, by combining the printed word and technology, lead to increased reading, if not of great literature (who wants to sit at a monitor and read Shakespeare's plays?), then of the plethora of material careering down the information superhighway?

Disagreements over relevance arise from conceptions of what exists in society and what should be. The question becomes: Should curriculum planners educate young people for life as it is or as they think it should be? Should the curriculum develop the desire of citizens to read nonfiction, to subscribe to scholarly journals, to listen to classical music, and to frequent art galleries? Should the curriculum encourage young people to make money, to prefer pop fiction, to enjoy rock music, and to artistically liven up their own homes? Should the curriculum remain neutral and abstain from all such value-laden content, or, conversely, should it expose the learners to both "highbrow" and "lowbrow" content?

Arguments arise over the relative merits of the concrete versus the abstract. Some prefer to concentrate on content that can be experienced with the senses whereas others prefer to concentrate on developing the intellect through high-level generalizations.

An Explanation of Relevance.   B. Othanel Smith clearly explained relevance when he wrote:

> The teacher is constantly asked "Why should I learn that?" "What is the use of studying history?" "Why should I be required to take biology?" If the intent of these questions is to ask what use can one make of them in everyday activities, only general answers are possible. We can and do talk about the relevance of subject matter to the decisions and activities that pupils will have to make. We know, among other things, that they must:
>
> - choose and follow a vocation,
> - exercise the tasks of citizenship,
> - engage in personal relationships,
> - take part in culture-carrying activities . . .

. . . the question of relevance boils down to the question of what is most assuredly useful.[26]

Smith admitted that it is difficult to show the utility of abstract subject matter:

> Unfortunately, the utility of this form of subject matter is much more difficult to demonstrate. . . . Perhaps the chief reason utility of abstract knowledge cannot be demonstrated to the skeptic is that a great deal of it functions as a second-order utility. A first-order utility is illustrated in the skills that we use in everyday behavior such as handwriting and reading. The second-order utility consists of a learning that shapes behavior, but which is not itself directly observable in behavior.[27]

Uses of Knowledge.   Smith classified the uses of knowledge that are not directly observable as associative, interpretive, and applicative.[28] By associative Smith meant the learner's ability to relate knowledge freely, sometimes bringing about solutions to problems. Abstract knowledge helps individuals to interpret their environment, which they cannot do without fundamental knowledge. Abstract subject matter enables learners to apply concepts to solve new problems.

Curriculum workers must, with considerable help from students and others, decide what is meant by relevance and then proceed to make the curriculum as relevant as possible.

BALANCE

Balance is an unusual curriculum concept that on the surface seems obvious but with some probing becomes somewhat cloudy. Nailing down a precise definition of balance is difficult. Many—perhaps most—educators feel that somehow the curriculum is in a state of imbalance. Observed Paul M. Halverson, "Curriculum balance will probably always be lacking because institutions of all kinds are slow in adapting to new needs and demands of the culture except when social change is rapid and urgent in its implications for these institutions."[29]

Balance, then, is something that schools may not have but apparently should. How would we know a balanced curriculum if we saw one? This is the key question for us to examine.

The search for a definition is complicated by differing interpretations of the word "balance" as it applies to the curriculum. Halverson spoke of balancing ends and means, as follows: "A balanced curriculum implies structure and order in its scope and sequence (means) leading to the achievement of educational objectives (ends)."[30]

Goodlad would bring the learner-centered curriculum and the subject-centered curriculum into balance, commenting:

---

[26]B. Othanel Smith et al., *Teachers for the Real World* (Washington, D.C.: American Association of Colleges for Teacher Education, 1969), pp. 130–131. Reprinted with permission. See also Harry S. Broudy, B. Othanel Smith, and Joe R. Burnett. *Democracy and Excellence in American Secondary Education* (Chicago: Rand McNally, 1964). Chapter 3. Broudy, Smith, and Burnett discuss four uses of knowledge: replicative (repetition of a skill), associative, applicative, and interpretive.

[27]Smith et al., *Teachers,* p. 131.

[28]Ibid, pp. 131–133.

[29]Paul M. Halverson, "The Meaning of Balance," *Balance in the Curriculum,* 1961 Yearbook (Alexandria, Va.: Association for Supervision and Curriculum Development, 1961), p. 7

[30]Ibid., p. 4.

Much recent and current controversy over the curriculum centers on the question of what kind and how much attention to give learners and subject matter, respectively. The prospect of stressing one to the exclusion of the other appears scarcely worthy of consideration. Nonetheless, the interested observer has little difficulty finding school practices emphasizing one component to the impoverishment of the other.[31]

Ronald C. Doll looked at balance from the learner's standpoint and described it as follows:

A balanced curriculum for a given learner at a given time would completely fit the learner in terms of his or her particular educational needs at that time. It would contain just enough of each kind of subject matter to serve the individual's purposes and to speed his or her development. General balance in the curriculum can be partly achieved, in the sense that certain kinds of experiences can be planned for large groups of learners according to what we know about them and about the subject matter they might learn. . . . Perhaps the best that can be done in working toward balance is to be clearer about what is valued for the growth of individual learners and then to apply these values in selecting curriculum content, grouping pupils for instruction, providing for articulation, and furthering guidance programs.[32]

In the foregoing comments Goodlad stressed the need for balance between the learner and the subject-centered curriculum whereas Doll emphasized the need for a curriculum that fits individuals through a judicious balance of group and individual experiences.

Sets of Variables.   We can apply the principle of balance in a number of ways. Given the typical elementary school, middle or junior high school, and a comprehensive senior high school, curriculum planners should seek balance between the following sets of variables. You will note below that some of the sets of variables call for proportions or splits other than a fifty-fifty distribution. When we speak of proportions, we distort the mathematical concept of balance as equilibrium. In reference to the curriculum, however, we cannot and probably should not always seek to achieve a fifty-fifty balance. There are times when a "balance" of one-third/two-thirds is defensible.

1. The child-centered and the subject-centered curriculum. This variable presupposes a balance between the conflicting philosophies of progressivism and essentialism.
2. The needs of society and of the learner. The curriculum must be not only socially but also personally oriented.
3. General and specialized education. Electives at the high school level should provide opportunities for learners in specialized areas. The Commission on the Education of Adolescents of the Association for Supervision and Curriculum Development advocated that one-third to one-half of each student's program in high school consist of general education and one-half to two-thirds consist of elective education.[33] Schools may still specialize, however, as in the case of New York City's Bronx

---

[31]Goodlad, *Planning and Organizing*, p 29. Reprinted with permission.

[32]Ronald C. Doll, *Curriculum Improvement: Decision Making and Process*, 9th Edition (Boston: Allyn and Bacon, 1996), pp. 186–187.

[33]Kimball Wiles and Franklin Patterson, *The High School We Need* (Alexandria, Va.: Association for Supervision and Curriculum Development, 1959), pp. 9–10.

High School of Science or Cooks' and Bakers' School. Balance can be achieved across a school system by having both general and specialized high schools. But there must be balance in schools that claim to be comprehensive in nature.

4. Breadth and depth. The curriculum can be so broad as to be superficial or conversely so profound as to limit learning. In either extreme learning is restricted.

5. The three domains, if we may create a three-way balance. We cannot ignore either the cognitive, affective, or psychomotor domain. Each has its importance in the life of the individual. Youngsters cannot find their own balance when learning is limited to one domain.

6. Individualization and mass education. We must find some way to provide for individual differences, to individualize or personalize instruction within the context of a mass educational system. Many recommendations have been made to achieve individualization—from programmed instruction to individually prescribed instruction to diagnostic-prescriptive teaching to independent study. However, of necessity, education remains largely a group process.

7. Individualization and group instruction. We must discover effective ways of combining grouping techniques like cooperative learning, subgroupings both small and large, and instruction of the total class with personalized techniques.

8. Innovation and tradition. Innovation cannot be incorporated at the drop of a hat. Tradition provides for stability and finds favor with the public. Constant innovation, often for its own sake, keeps faculties, students, and parents in a state of perpetual turmoil. We must pace innovations as to frequency and quantity in order to digest and evaluate changes taking place.

9. The logical and psychological. These variables are equated in a philosophical context with the differences between essentialism and progressivism. Some content must be organized according to the logic of the subject matter; some to the logic of the learner.

10. The needs of the exceptional and the nonexceptional child. If intelligence is distributed at random among the population, some two-thirds of the students are in the "average" range. Romesh Ratnesar, writing for *TIME*, reported on the disproportionate amount of attention and funding going to students with special needs to the neglect of average students who are sometimes referred to as "woodwork children."[34] Curriculum planners must be careful that attention to the needs of special groups does not far outstrip attention to the needs of the more numerous average student.

11. The needs of the academically talented or gifted and the slow. In recent times if we have stressed either group, we have catered to the needs of slow learners. Perhaps we assumed that the academically talented and the gifted will teach themselves in spite of school. Or perhaps we were guided by statistics; there are more slower students than academically talented (the top fifteen percent) and gifted (the top three percent). Awareness of the needs of the gifted is coming into vogue once again.

12. Methods, experiences, and strategies. Teachers should use a mixture of techniques, including audio and visual media. Some schools rely almost exclusively on

---

[34]Romesh Ratnesar, "Lost in the Middle," *Time* 152, no. 11 (September 14, 1998): 60–64.

the printed word, which runs counter to the population's addiction to mediated learning—films, tapes, television, and the computer. Educators are pointing out the need for computer literacy, for example, and urging training in the use of the computer.

13. The immediate and the remote in both time and space. Some people would omit the study of ancient history (too remote) or the study of the non-Western world (too distant) and design only sparkling, new, contemporary, "with-it" curricula.

14. Work and play. At all levels youngsters need some balance, though certainly not fifty-fifty, between academic work and leisure or physical activities. Play in the form of games, sports, and personal pursuits not only helps alleviate incipient boredom but can be an education in itself. Some of the avocations pursued by young people may become vocations or lifelong interests.

15. The school and the community as educational forces. Teachers sometimes forget that there is much to be learned outside the walls of the classroom. In fact, in many important areas of life more is learned of both a positive and negative nature outside of school than in school. Curriculum planners should build ways of using the community as an educational laboratory. If the world can be one's oyster, the community can be one's pearl.

16. Between disciplines. Disciplines, especially elective ones in the secondary school, vie with each other for student enrollment. Occasionally, a school becomes known for an exceptionally strong department in some discipline. Although excellence is to be encouraged, this situation may imply less than excellence in other disciplines. Curriculum planners should seek to foster excellence in all fields.

17. Between programs. The college preparatory program of the secondary school often dwarfs other curricula. Curriculum planners must ensure that the general, vocational, business, home economics, and other curricula have their place in the sun as well as the college preparatory curriculum.

18. Within disciplines. The natural and social sciences, as examples, should offer a mixture of didactics and inquiry learning. The foreign language curriculum should seek achievement in comprehension, speaking, and writing as well as reading. No single phase of a particular discipline should be permitted to crowd out other important phases.

Striving for balance in the curriculum is an essential responsibility of the curriculu planner.

INTEGRATION

Curriculum workers should concern themselves with the problem of integrating subject matter. Integration, in the context of a curriculum construction concept, means the blending, fusion, or unification of disciplines, a concept visited in chapter 9 when we discussed the activity and core curricula. A fully integrated curriculum tears down barriers between disciplines and fuses disciplines under overarching themes or topics. Unlike determination of scope and sequence, which must be accomplished, the integration of disciplines is an optional and controversial undertaking. Whether to integrate the curriculum is an issue which divides educators.

Whether curriculum planners choose to integrate subject matter hinges upon their philosophy of the nature of knowledge, the nature of learners, and the purposes of education. Many educators support the integration of subject matter based on their analyses of studies pointing to successes with interdisciplinary curricular plans. Tyler defined integration as "the horizontal relationship of curriculum experiences" and went on to say, "The organization of these experiences should be such that they help the student increasingly to get a unified view and to unify his behavior in relation to the elements dealt with."[35] Hilda Taba commented, "It is recognized that learning is more effective when facts and principles from one field can be related to another, especially when applying this knowledge."[36]

However, our schools have typically and traditionally behaved as if the integration of subject matter were not too important or even detrimental to student achievement. The tenacity of the subject matter curriculum, which organizes subject matter into discrete disciplines, has been shaken only briefly by experiments like the activity curriculum and the core curriculum. The activity curriculum on the elementary school level and the core curriculum on the secondary school level sought to break down the disciplinary barriers and to organize education around problems to be solved, using whatever subject matter was applicable. The popularity of integrated curricula has waxed and waned over the years. We are witnessing a renewed interest in curriculum integration, particularly at the middle school level where interdisciplinary programs are a common feature.

Subject matter may be organized on the basis of separate disciplines with their own time blocks. Another approach is to integrate it either on a schoolwide basis (as with the core curriculum) or on the classroom level (as with certain types of unit plans) without regard for disciplines.

Not all educators, of course, are advocates of integrating subject matter. Some believe that the various disciplines should be taught separately. Thus they reject the broad-fields approach to curriculum organization and recommend that teachers and students concentrate on the separate disciplines.

The progressives feel with considerable logic that understanding is enhanced when the artificial barriers between disciplines are removed. It is true that human beings solve their problems by judiciously selecting whatever subject matter is needed. However, whether a program to educate the immature learner must consist of integrated disciplines is debatable. Two responses have been made over the years to reduce the separateness of disciplines. Subject matter has been both correlated and integrated. Curriculum planners have positioned themselves somewhere on a continuum that appears as follows:

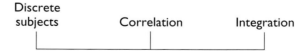

Correlation of Subject Matter.   Correlation is the relating of subjects to one another while still maintaining their separateness. Relationships between subjects taught at a

[35]Tyler, *Basic Principles*, p. 85.
[36]Hilda Taba, *Curriculum Improvement: Theory and Practice* (New York: Harcourt Brace Jovanovich, 1962), p. 298.

particular school level are shown to pupils, as in the cases of history and literature; math and science; art, music, and literature.

Subjects may be correlated horizontally across one grade level or vertically across two or more. As an example of the latter, ancient history, taught in the sophomore or junior year of high school, may be correlated with Latin, taught in the junior or senior year. The study of Latin is therefore enriched by this progression. If the courses are taken concurrently, the study of both disciplines is enhanced.

Correlation becomes integration when the subjects lose their identities. In the cultural-epoch core approach to curriculum organization, epochs of humankind's history provide the framework; the subjects—English, social studies, science, mathematics, art, music—illuminate the cultural epochs. In the case of either correlation or integration, cooperative planning by all teachers affected is necessary.

Two Views of Curriculum Integration.   Taba offered two views of curriculum integration. The first view is the one we have been discussing: the horizontal relationship of subjects. In addition, said Taba, "Integration is also defined as something that happens to an individual."[37] If we follow the second view, "The problem, then, is that of developing ways of helping individuals in this process of creating a unity of knowledge. This interpretation of integration throws the emphasis from integrating subjects to locating the integrative threads."[38]

Regardless of whether the subject matter is presented to the learner in an integrated fashion by the teacher, the learner must integrate the knowledge into his or her own behavior. The distinction between an educated and an erudite person lies in the degree to which knowledge is integrated in the person.

Taba remarked:

> Unification of subjects has been a theme in education ever since the Herbartians. By far the greatest number of experimental curriculum schemes have revolved around the problem of unifying learning. At the same time we are far from achieving unification, partly because of fear of loss of disciplined learning if the study of specialized subjects is discarded, and partly because as yet no effective basis has been found for unifying school subjects.[39]

You have seen and will see a number of references to interdisciplinary/multidisciplinary integrated curricula in this text. Although many schools seek to employ an interdisciplinary approach to curriculum and instruction at more than one level, integration of the curriculum was, in the days of the core curriculum, found more frequently in the junior high school and is at present a noticeable feature of most middle schools.

Integrated curricula challenge the time-honored organization of curricula into separate disciplines. James A. Beane pointed to the difficulty of implementing an integrated curriculum when he said, "To resist the powerful push for a prescribed, separate subject curriculum and related tests is no easy thing to do."[40] Curriculum planners

---

[37]Ibid., p. 299.

[38]Ibid.

[39]Ibid., pp. 298–299.

[40]James A. Beane, in Chris Stevenson and Judy F. Carr, eds., *Integrated Studies in the Middle Grades: Dancing Through Walls* (New York: Teachers College Press, 1993), p. x. The Stevenson and Carr book describes the experiences of Vermont teachers who created and implemented integrated teaching plans.

must decide whether they will make a conscious effort either to correlate or to integrate subject matter and, if they plan to do either, what organizational structure they will create to do so.[41] Scope, relevance, balance, and integration are interrelated principles to which curriculum workers must give attention.

SEQUENCE

Sequence is the order in which the organizing elements or centers are arranged by the curriculum planners. Whereas scope is referred to as "the what" of curriculum organization, sequence is referred to as "the when." Sequence answers the questions of when and where the focal points will be placed. Some time ago Saylor and Alexander defined sequence as

> the order in which educational experiences are developed with pupils. Sequence refers to the "when" in curriculum planning. Determination of the sequence of educational experiences is a decision as to the most propitious time in which to develop those educational experiences suggested by the scope. If we think of scope as the latitudinal aspect of curriculum planning, sequence becomes the longitudinal axis.[42]

Once we identify the scope of the curriculum, we must put the elements into some kind of meaningful order. Let's take a simplified illustration from the reading curriculum. Suppose as reading teachers we wish students to be able to

- read novels
- read words
- read paragraphs
- read sentences
- recognize letters of the alphabet

Is there some particular order in which pupils learn those elements? The answer is obvious here. The student should recognize letters of the alphabet first, then proceed to reading words, sentences, paragraphs, and novels. Unless one is a Mozart-like prodigy, one does not normally begin to demonstrate reading skills by reading adult tomes.

But take the following organizational threads in economics:

- insurance
- real estate
- banking
- stock market
- inflation
- recession
- foreign exchange

---

[41]For discussion of types of integrated curricula see Gordon F. Vars, ed. *Common Learnings: Core and Interdisciplinary Team Approaches* (Scranton, Pa.: International Textbook Company, 1969).

[42] J. Galen Saylor and William M. Alexander, *Curriculum Planning for Better Teaching and Learning* (New York: Holt, Rinehart and Winston, 1954), p. 249.

What is the sequence in this case? Is there a preferred sequence? What makes it preferred? As another example, in what order should we study the American Revolution, the War of 1812, the Korean War, World War I, the Civil War, the Vietnam War, World War II, the Persian Gulf War, and the Spanish-American War? The answer in this case is simple, you say. Simply place the wars in chronological order. But could there be any other defensible way of sequencing these items?

The problem of sequencing produces questions about

- the maturity of the learners
- the interests of the learners
- the readiness of the learners
- the relative difficulty of the items to be learned
- the relationship between items
- the prerequisite skills needed in each case

Ways of Sequencing.   How do curriculum workers decide which content comes first? Sequencing is accomplished in a variety of ways, including arranging the content.

1. From the simplest to the most complex. We must deal with tens, for example, before we work with hundreds.
2. In chronological order. History is most often taught in this fashion.
3. In reverse chronological order. Occasionally, a history teacher will start with the most recent events and work backward to the most ancient under the assumption that pupils' attention can be grasped quicker with more recent and therefore more familiar events. Themes that exist in the present may be seen repeated as they go backward in time.
4. From the geographically near to the geographically far. Some argue that it makes more sense to study phenomena and conditions close to home and to gradually expand the learner's horizons ultimately to the world and even the universe.
5. From the far to the near. This procedure focuses on distant lands and reserves study of the home environment—the pièce de résistance—until the end.
6. From the concrete to the abstract. The pupil learns to count blocks by first manipulating them physically and only later manipulating them mentally.
7. From the general to the particular. This approach starts with the principle and proceeds to examples.
8. From the particular to the general. This approach starts with examples and proceeds to the principle.

When we are determining sequencing, we will find that there are times when the order of the units of content does not matter. When we are studying the works of twentieth-century American authors, we might want to group writers of drama, short stories, novels, and nonfiction, but it is not likely to make a great deal of difference which grouping or which author within the grouping we study first.

There are times when we will deliberately violate a sequence. The class may be studying the political structure of ancient Rome, for example, when a landmark case affecting the country's political and social system is decided by the U.S. Supreme Court. This immediate and significant case is permitted to alter the planned sequence.

Prerequisite Skills.   Frequently, pupils cannot engage in a unit of content until they master a preceding unit. The student of algebra is hard pressed unless he or she has mastered arithmetic skills. The student cannot succeed in a second-year foreign language class without mastering the skills developed in the first year. For this reason the assessment of prerequisite skills is sound pedagogy. Teachers must know whether the students have mastered the skills needed to proceed with the tasks before them.

Dubious Sequencing.   Some curriculum planners in the past, following their own notions of what constitutes prerequisite skills, have instituted sequencing that is hard to defend on any solid grounds. For years, high school students were required, for example, to take general science, biology, chemistry, and physics in that order. Actually, none is necessarily dependent upon the other. Each science depends more upon mastery of reading and mathematics than upon mastery of other sciences. In fact, proposals were surfacing in early 1999 for reversing the age-old biology-chemistry-physics sequencing in high schools on the grounds that advancement in scientific knowledge has made biology a much more difficult subject better understood after physics and chemistry or perhaps concurrently with its companion sciences.[43] We can find evidence of dubious sequencing in mathematics with the prescribed order of algebra I, geometry, algebra II, trigonometry, and calculus. Although it may be wise planning to start with algebra I and hold calculus for the end, there is little reason to hold algebra II until after the completion of geometry. Why is *Macbeth* invariably taught after *Julius Caesar*? Why does American history often come after world history? From a chauvinist point of view, we could argue that American history ought to come first in the senior high school sequence.

Conceptions of Sequencing.   Donald E. Orlosky and B. Othanel Smith discussed three conceptions of sequencing: (1) sequencing according to need, (2) macrosequencing, and (3) microsequencing. According to the first conception,

> the learner orders his own learning as he deals with a situation from moment to moment. He selects what he wants to know as the need arises. If he makes a mistake in the selection he simply goes through the process again until he finds that which satisfies his present need. This is an opportunistic notion of sequencing but those who advocate it maintain that it is psychologically sound.[44]

This perception of sequencing fits the views of some progressive educators and proponents of open education.

Macrosequencing follows principles of child development expounded by persons like Arnold Gesell, Frances L. Ilg, and Jean Piaget. Macrosequencing, said Orlosky and Smith, is

> the organization of knowledge and the formulation of instruction to coincide with the different stages of the individual's development. For a long time teachers have arranged the knowledge of instruction roughly in accordance with the development of the child.

---

[43]See *New York Times*, Section 1, page 1, January 24, 1999.

[44]Donald E. Orlosky and B. Othanel Smith, *Curriculum Development: Issues and Insights* (Chicago: Rand McNally College Publishing Company, 1978), p. 267.

Examining the existing program of studies of almost any school proves that it corresponds roughly to the child's development.[45]

Microsequencing is the ordering of subject matter according to the prerequisite knowledge required of each unit of content. "This assumes," said Orlosky and Smith, "that for any learning task there is a hierarchy extending from the very simple to the more abstract and complex elements which lead to the attainment of a specified objective."[46]

Curriculum planners are called upon to make decisions on placement of content at the appropriate grade levels. Using the terms "sequence" and "grade placement" together, B. Othanel Smith, William O. Stanley, and J. Harlan Shores observed:

There are only two possible approaches to the solution of problems of grade placement and sequence. *The first* accepts the child as he is and adjusts the experience to his level of development while holding the instructional goals constant. . . . *The second approach* assumes curriculum experiences to be located at a given grade level and provides learnings to adjust the child to these experiences—that is, to get him ready for the learning.[47]

Where to Begin.   Disagreements over the process of sequencing center on whether curriculum planners should start with learners or subject matter. The first demands choosing emphases in keeping with the learners' actual growth and development, or, when learning experiences are, in current terminology, "developmentally appropriate"; the second, placing subject matter at the grade level at which it is assumed learners will be able to master it. The latter approach to sequencing has been the historic approach.

Smith, Stanley, and Shores advocated a blending of the two approaches:

To accept wholeheartedly the first approach, which emphasizes the nature of the child and regards the curriculum as always flexible enough at each grade level to be bent to the child's needs, is probably unrealistic. And just as unrealistic is the inflexibility of the second approach, which allows objectives and content to be so fixed at any one grade that lower grade experiences must always prepare for this hurdle and later experiences always build upon it. Probably neither of these approaches will be used without consideration for the other.[48]

They counseled curriculum workers to take into account the maturation, experiential background, mental age, and interests of the learners and the usefulness and difficulty of the subject matter when developing a sequence.[49] The ordering of the organizing elements of the curriculum is one of the major tasks of the curriculum developer.

---

[45]Ibid., p. 251.

[46]Ibid., p. 267.

[47]B. Othanel Smith, William O. Stanley, and J. Harlan Shores, *Fundamentals of Curriculum Development,* Revised Edition (New York: Harcourt Brace Jovanovich, 1957), p. 171.

[48]Ibid.

[49]Ibid., pp. 174–186.

CONTINUITY

Continuity is the planned repetition of content at successive levels, each time at an increased level of complexity. Tyler described continuity as follows:

> Continuity refers to the vertical reiteration of major curriculum elements. For example, if in the social studies the development of skills in reading social studies is an important objective, it is necessary to see that there is recurring and continuing opportunity for these skills to be practiced and developed. This means that over time the same kinds of skills will be brought into continuing operation. In similar fashion, if an objective in science is to develop a meaningful concept of energy, it is important that this concept be dealt with again and again in various parts of the science course. Continuity is thus seen to be a major factor in effective vertical organization.[50]

Spiral Curriculum.   The principle of continuity is represented in what has been called the spiral curriculum.[51] Concepts, skills, and knowledge are introduced and reintroduced—for example, the repetition of addition, study of democracy, writing, personal health, and conservation, each reintroduction enhancing the earlier exposures.

Expertise Needed.   Planning a curriculum for continuity requires a high degree of expertise, which demands both knowledge of the subject field and of the learners. For example, to plan a mathematics sequence for twelve grades with appropriate scope, sequence, and continuity requires the combined skills of subject matter specialists and teachers. Continuity is not simply repetition of content but repetition with increasing levels of complexity and sophistication. Whereas elementary school youngsters, for example, may learn that democracy means government of the people, by the people, and for the people, secondary students may wrestle with controversial and unresolved problems of democracy.

Experience will reveal to curriculum developers which units of content must be reintroduced and at what point. Preassessment, if only of the most rudimentary kind, is essential before each new organizing element is broached. Preassessment will uncover whether the learners are ready for (1) new content based on prior content and (2) prior content that will be repeated at a more complex level.

ARTICULATION

If we view continuity as the spiraling of content upward through the grades of a particular school, we should view articulation as the meshing of organizing elements across school levels—that is, across elementary and middle or junior high schools, across junior high or middle and senior high schools, and across senior high school and college. Like continuity, articulation is a dimension of sequencing.

Horizontal and Vertical.   Oliver used the term "articulation" synonymously with "horizontal articulation" or "correlation." He equated the concept of "continuity" with "vertical articulation."[52] Regarding correlation as a halfway move toward inte-

---

[50]Tyler, *Basic Principles*, pp. 84–85.

[51]See Jerome S. Bruner, *The Process of Education* (Cambridge, Mass.: Harvard University Press, 1960), pp. 13, 52–54.

[52]Oliver, *Curriculum Improvement*, p. 222. Some authors also refer to scope as a horizontal dimension of curriculum organization and sequence as a vertical dimension.

gration, I would agree with calling correlation horizontal articulation. Sequence, continuity, and articulation are all interrelated. I would separate continuity from vertical articulation and define continuity as a reintroduction of content at progressively more complex levels and articulation as the meshing of the curriculum of the various levels of the educational ladder to provide for smooth transition on the part of the learners. This meshing may or may not involve reintroduction of units of content, progressively more difficult. When speaking of articulation, I am addressing the problem of vertical articulation.

Unfortunately, efforts at articulation between levels are in many cases feeble and ineffective. Cooperative efforts are necessary among curriculum workers if articulated sequences are to be planned from kindergarten through twelfth grade and beyond.

We find considerable unplanned repetition of content among levels. This is neither articulation nor continuity but a laissez-faire attitude that permits curriculum workers to develop their own programs without knowledge of what instructors at preceding and succeeding levels are teaching.

With our decentralized system of education, lack of articulation occurs frequently. Articulation is particularly difficult in some states where separate school districts managing different levels of schooling exist side by side under separate administrators and separate school boards. Even when all levels of schooling are centralized under a single administrator and school board, articulation remains a problem.

Gaps Between Levels.   We often find great gaps between levels. The seventh-grade teacher (failing or refusing to preassess) assumes certain levels of mastery of knowledge when children enter from the elementary school; the senior high school teacher expects certain entry skills from youngsters who are promoted from the middle or junior high school.

Personal Articulation.   There is not only a need for planned articulation of subject matter but also for pupils' personal articulation. Schools look for ways to respond to students' varied capabilities. Some junior high/middle school pupils, for example, are able to tackle senior high school subjects. Some senior high school pupils can perform ably in advanced placement courses given in the high school and in junior or senior college courses in their area of residence. Some students can skip a year of high school and enter college early or can skip the lower division of college and enroll in the upper division.

Improved articulation eases the movement of pupils from one level to the next, which can be a traumatic experience for most young people. With all the problems of social adjustment as they enter a higher level, they have little need for suffering either needless repetition, exposure to subject matter that is too easy for them, or, worse yet, grasping for learnings beyond their abilities and skills. Thus curriculum planners cannot avoid the problem of articulation.

Let's recap what has been said about sequencing, continuity, and articulation. Continuity and articulation are dimensions of sequencing. Sequencing is the logical or psychological arrangement of units of content within lessons, units, courses, and grades. Continuity is the planned introduction and reintroduction of the same units of content through the grades of a school system at ever-increasing levels of complexity. Articulation is the planned sequencing of units of content across grade levels—that is, from one grade level to the next to ensure that the next grade level takes up where the previous grade level left off.

The three principles—sequence, continuity, and articulation—are interrelated and complement each other. Material must be appropriately sequenced at whatever level. Articulation must be observed to ensure that there are no gaps in a sequence from one grade level to the next, whereas continuity must be sought to permit students to achieve greater depth in a subject.

Although this text presents sequencing and related principles in a favorable light as useful concepts in planning, organizing and evaluating the curriculum, as we have noted many times in this text, views on many concepts and practices in education differ. The concepts of sequencing and the spiral curriculum are no exception. Holding that "there is little interest today in sequencing," John D. McNeil wrote, "Current research casts doubt on rigid conceptions of skill hierarchies and spiraled curriculum. Although there may be some valid skill hierarchies such as teaching addition before multiplication, little evidence supports hierarchies such as those in Bloom's taxonomy." [53] He did add, however, "some people believe that increasing the complexity of the content and tasks, increasing the diversity of applications, and providing adequate support for learning, gradually transferring responsibility from teacher to student (scaffolding) may be helpful." [54]

TRANSFERABILITY

Whatever is taught in school should in some way possess transfer value, that is, learning in school should have applicability in either a broad or narrow sense outside of school and after school years. Education for education's sake—the mark of the learned person—is simply not sufficient as a goal of education. Education should in some way enrich the life of the individual.

The transfer of learning or transfer of training, as it is sometimes called, has been discussed at some length in the literature of educational psychology. [55] Transfer gives a permanence to learning beyond the moment of its first introduction into the classroom.

Vocational education possesses a built-in one-upmanship in transferability. You can see the transfer; it's apparent. Skills learned in industrial arts and vocational education classes can be transferred to life situations. Teachers of psychomotor skills are particularly fortunate because pupils have no difficulty seeing the transfer value of these areas of study. Students can and will use the skills they learn in such areas as music, art, physical education, typing, word processing, and home economics. Transfer is paramount with most teachers of perceptual-motor skills. Physical educators tout the carry-over value of their activities—that is, transfer.

Transfer in the affective and cognitive areas is more difficult to discern. Of course, we wish students to carry over ethical values and positive attitudes into their daily liv-

---

[53]John D. McNeil, *Curriculum: A Comprehensive Introduction*, 5th ed. (New York: HarperCollins, 1996, p. 440.
[54]Ibid.
[55]See Edward L. Thorndike, "Mental Discipline in High School Studies," *Journal of Educational Psychology* 15, no. 1 (January 1924): 1–22; continued in 15, no. 2 (February 1924): 83–98. See also Edward L. Thorndike, *The Principles of Teaching* (New York: Seiler, 1906) and Sidney L. Pressey and Francis P. Robinson, *Psychology and the New Education,* rev. ed. (New York: Harper & Row, 1944).

ing. We would like a student who demonstrates democratic principles in the classroom to retain that behavior all his or her life. Transfer of cognitive learning is most often visible in student performance on assessment and standardized tests, in admission to and success in college, and in the evaluations employers give of the intellectual competence of their employees.

Proponents of faculty psychology (mental or formal discipline) maintained that rigorous subjects disciplined the mind; thus such education was generally transferable. Some of the essentialists have held that education is the storing of data—computer-fashion—for use at a later date when the occasion arises. Unfortunately, disuse sets in; we forget, and when we need to retrieve the supposedly stored data, we find that they have slipped away.

It has generally been believed by many—a holdover of the formal discipline days—that certain subjects lead to transfer more than other subjects. After an exhaustive study of more than 8,000 students, Thorndike concluded:

> The expectation of any large difference in general improvement of the mind from one study rather than another seems doomed to disappointment. The chief reason why good thinkers seem superficially to have been made such by having taken certain school studies is that good thinkers have taken such studies, becoming better by the inherent tendency of the good to gain more than the poor from any study.[56]

Daniel Tanner and Laurel N. Tanner pointed out that the Eight-Year Study disproved the notion that certain subjects lead to transfer:

> But probably the most stunning attack (aside from Thorndike's 1924 study) on the idea that certain subjects have superior transfer to intelligence was delivered by the Progressive Education Association's Eight-Year Study (1933–1941). . . . the study proved that success in college is not dependent on credits earned in high school in prescribed subjects.[57]

Taba, however, explained the more current view on transfer as follows: "The recent ideas on transfer have returned to earlier assumptions of the possibility of fairly wide transfer, depending on the level of generalizing that takes place regarding either the content or the method of approach."[58] Thus, if teachers wish to encourage transfer, they must stress general principles.

Current Beliefs.   Let's summarize some of the current beliefs about transfer.

- Transfer is at the heart of education: it is a—if not the—goal of education.
- Transfer is possible.
- The closer the classroom situation is to the out-of-classroom situations, the greater is the transfer.
- Transfer can be increased and improved if teachers consciously teach for transfer.
- Transfer is greater when teachers help pupils to derive underlying generalizations and to make applications of those generalizations.

---

[56]Thorndike, "Mental Discipline," (February 1924), p. 98.

[57]Daniel Tanner and Laurel Tanner, *Curriculum Development: Theory into Practice,* 3rd ed. (New York: Merrill, 1995), p. 68.

[58]Hilda Taba, *Curriculum Development: Theory and Practice* (New York: Harcourt Brace Jovanovich, 1962), p. 124.

• Generally speaking, when the learner discovers knowledge for himself or herself, transfer is enhanced.

Bruner provided an example of children in a fifth-grade class learning "a way of thinking about geography" as opposed to being dished out selected, unconnected geographical facts.[59] Bruner encouraged teachers to use a discovery approach, justifying it on the grounds of "increased intellectual potency, intrinsic rewards, useful learning techniques, and better memory processes."[60]

Guided Discovery. The jury is still out on the question of the extent of use of inquiry or discovery methods. David Ausubel pointed out that some discovery techniques can be an inefficient use of time.[61] Renate Nummela Caine and Geoffrey Caine were critical of discovery learning when they said, "Unfortunately, even this often fails to work because discovery learning is used as a trick or device to get students to remember the facts that the teacher wants them to remember."[62] Some authorities prefer to speak of guided discovery rather than discovery per se. Whatever the process used—discovery or other—enhancement of meaning during the process of instruction should increase the degree of transfer.

Transferability is a principle of both instruction and the curriculum. When we talk about methods of teaching for transferability, we are referring to the instructional process. When we analyze what the learner has transferred, we are in the area of curriculum. Curriculum developers should specify objectives, select content, and choose instructional strategies that will lead to maximum transfer. Furthermore, plans for evaluating the curriculum should include means of judging the degree of the transfer of the many segments of the curriculum.

IMPLICATIONS OF THE CONTINUING CURRICULUM PROBLEMS

Given the range and the many facets of curriculum problems covered, it is useful to briefly redefine them in the light of the curriculum worker's responsibilities. Curriculum workers attend to the problem of

- *scope* when they select topics to be studied and specify the instructional objectives
- *relevance* when they "effect a congruence between the entire school system and the social order in which the young of today will spend their adult lives"[63]
- *balance* when they maintain certain sets of elements proportionately
- *integration* when they make an effort to unify subject matter
- *sequence* when they determine the order in which subject matter will be made available to the students

---

[59]Jerome S. Bruner, "Structures in Learning," *Today's Education* 52, no. 3 (March 1963): 26.
[60]Ibid., p. 27.
[61]See David P. Ausubel, *Educational Psychology: A Cognitive View* (New York: Holt, Rinehart and Winston, 1968).
[62]Renate Nummela Caine and Geoffrey Caine, *Making Connections: Teaching and the Human Brain* (Alexandria, Va.: Association for Supervision and Curriculum Development, 1991), p. 47.
[63]Broudy, *Real World*, p. 193.

- *continuity* when they examine the curriculum of each course and grade level to discover where units of content may fruitfully be repeated at increased levels of complexity
- *articulation* when they examine the curriculum of each discipline at each grade level to be sure the subject matter flows sequentially across grade level boundaries
- *transferability* when they seek ways to achieve maximum transfer of learning

In identifying the eight guiding principles of curriculum development, we give structure to a philosophy of curriculum development, saying that we believe a functional curriculum is one that attends to scope, relevance, balance, integration, sequence, continuity, articulation, and transferability.

COMPREHENSIVE MODELS

The foregoing limited models focus on specific aspects of the curriculum: accomplishment of the curriculum objectives and the presence or absence of selected guiding factors in curriculum construction. Let's examine now two models which ask us to evaluate the entire curriculum development process.

The Saylor, Alexander, and Lewis Model.   Figure 13.4 shows how J. Galen Saylor, William M. Alexander, and Arthur J. Lewis charted a model of curriculum evaluation.[64] The Saylor, Alexander, and Lewis model calls for evaluating five components:

1. the goals, subgoals, and objectives
2. the program of education as a totality
3. the specific segments of the education program
4. instruction
5. evaluation program

The first, third, and fourth components contribute to the second—evaluating the program of education as a totality—by, among other ways, providing data that bear on the total program. In the figure, these relationships are shown by the three arrows between the boxes, which point toward the second component. By including the fifth component—evaluation program—in their model, Saylor, Alexander, and Lewis suggested that it is necessary to evaluate the evaluation program itself. No arrow is shown from the box labeled "evaluation program" because the evaluation of the evaluation program is perceived as an independent operation that has implications for the entire evaluation process. Perhaps we could embellish the Saylor, Alexander, and Lewis model by drawing four curved arrows leading out of the right-hand side of the Evaluation Program box to the right-hand side of each of the four boxes above it.

Once again, as we look at the model, we encounter the terms "formative evaluation" (evaluation that takes place during a component) and "summative evaluation"

---

[64]J. Galen Saylor, William M. Alexander, and Arthur J. Lewis, *Curriculum Planning for Better Teaching and Learning,* 4th ed., (New York: Holt, Rinehart and Winston, Inc., 1981), p. 334.

Figure 13.4   The Saylor, Alexander, and Lewis evaluation model. From J. Galen Saylor, William M. Alexander, and Arthur J. Lewis, *Curriculum Planning for Better Teaching and Learning,* 4th ed. (New York: Holt, Rinehart and Winston, 1981) p. 334. Reproduced by permission of the publisher.

(evaluation that takes place at the end of a component). Saylor, Alexander, and Lewis's model calls attention to both formative and summative aspects of evaluation of each component.

Evaluation of Goals, Subgoals, and Objectives.

Goals, subgoals, and objectives are evaluated (validated) in their formative stages by

1. analysis of the needs of society
2. analysis of the needs of the individual
3. referring the goals, subgoals, and objectives to various groups
4. referring the goals, subgoals, and objectives to subject matter specialists
5. use of previous summative data

Curriculum planners must make their own analyses of whether a given goal, subgoal, or objective meets the needs of society and of the learners. They should seek the judgments of students (if they are mature enough), teachers, parents, and other lay people and should further consult subject matter specialists to determine whether a given goal, subgoal, or objective is appropriate to the particular discipline. Data gained from previous tryouts of the program should be used to revise goals, subgoals, and objectives prior to the next trial. For practical purposes, instead of referring every goal, subgoal, and objective to all the groups mentioned, the curriculum planner may elect to refer the goals for validation to all groups and the subgoals and objectives for validation to just the teachers, subject matter specialists, and other curriculum specialists.

To clarify this validation process, let's take as an example the prosaic objective mentioned in Chapter 12—the baking of bread in homemaking class. Although we can certainly teach young people to bake bread and can evaluate their performance in this psychomotor skill, a more fundamental question must be answered: Should the baking of bread be included in the homemaking curriculum?

The question is not so simple to answer as it might first appear. A number of questions must be raised before this particular item of content can be validated. Some of these questions are as follows:

- Does society (the community, the home, the family) have any need for bread bakers?
- Is the skill of baking bread necessary or helpful to the individual?
- Does teaching the skill make sense in the light of comparison of costs of the home-baked bread versus store-bought bread?
- Does it require more energy to bake a loaf of bread at home or for commercial bakers to produce loaves for sale?
- Is there some overriding aesthetic or personal satisfaction in baking bread as opposed to purchasing it?
- Is home-baked bread more nutritious than store-bought bread?
- If baking bread is a content item, what other items were left out of the curriculum so that it could be included? Which items are the most important?
- Would experts in home economics assert that this content item is essential to the home economics curriculum?
- What percentage of families today bake their own bread?

- Is this skill something that can and should be taught in the home rather than in school?
- What has the success or failure of previous groups of students been in respect to this particular skill?

As we have seen, goals, subgoals, and objectives are established for the total program of the school. They are also established for specific program segments and for instruction. The accomplishment of curricular goals, subgoals, and objectives is revealed through an evaluation of the total program, the specific segments, and instruction.

Although Saylor, Alexander, and Lewis make the evaluation of the program of education as a totality the second component of their model of curriculum development, I would prefer to vary the sequence. Let's comment first on the two other components that impinge on the total educational program—the evaluation of instruction and of the specific segments of the program. We will return to the evaluation of the total program in a moment.

Evaluation of Instruction. We examined procedures for evaluating instruction in Chapter 12. Saylor, Alexander, and Lewis recommended that after instructional goals and objectives are specified and validated as part of the formative evaluation process, the antecedent conditions should be examined—a process referred to by some evaluators as context evaluation. The learners' total educational environment, the characteristics of the learners and the teachers, classroom interaction, and the curriculum design are all evaluated and may affect the choice of instructional goals and objectives.[65] The use of criterion-referenced and norm-referenced tests and other evaluative techniques provide formative and summative data on the success of instruction.

Evaluation of Specific Segments. The specific segments of the program require evaluation. Saylor, Alexander, and Lewis included within their concept of specific segments the following: "the plan for organizing curriculum domains, the design or designs of the curriculum for each domain, courses offered, other kinds of sets of learning opportunities provided, extrainstructional activities sponsored, services provided students, and the kinds of informal relations that characterize the institutional climate."[66]

Assessment data from district, state, and national sources should be gathered by the curriculum planners for purposes of formative evaluation of the specific program segments. At this stage data from the National Assessment of Educational Progress, for instance, can prove helpful. If, for example, the NAEP data revealed that nine-year-old children in urban areas of the southeast United States are more deficient in reading skills than children in comparable urban areas elsewhere in the country, intensive examination of the reading program of the particular school system is essential. SAT and ACT scores will provide clues. Assessments made by the International Association for the Evaluation of Educational Achievement (IEA) and the International Assessment of Educational Progress (IAEP) may also provide helpful data.[67] State and district assessments, focusing as they do on children of the state and locality, may be even more meaningful in this respect.

---

[65]Ibid., pp. 350–352.
[66]Ibid., p. 344.
[67]See Chapter 12 for discussion of NAEP, IEA, and IAEP.

Evaluative Instruments.   At this stage, too, the evaluation instruments of the National Study of School Evaluation (NSSE) may be used to gather empirical data about specific areas of study and other segments of the program.[68] This particular set of standards is often used by schools as part of a self-study process for accreditation. These instruments permit faculties to analyze the principles related to the particular program, the evaluation techniques used, plans for improvement, and the current status.

English proposed a way of looking at specific segments of the curriculum through a technique referred to as "curriculum mapping."[69] Following this technique teachers can analyze the content that they present and the amount of time spent on each topic.

Curriculum planners must design summative measures to determine whether the curriculum goals and objectives of the specific segments have been achieved. If it was desired, for example, that seventy-five percent of the students in a senior high school be involved in at least one extraclass activity, a simple head count would reveal whether this objective has been realized. As is the case when evaluating instruction, sometimes the objective itself is the evaluation item. On the other hand, if it is desired to know whether a fourth-grade class whose members average two months below grade level in mathematics at the beginning of the year raised its scores to grade level by the end of the year, pretesting and posttesting will be necessary.

Evaluation of the Total Program.   The functioning of the curriculum as a whole must be evaluated. The curriculum planners want to learn whether the goals and objectives of the total curriculum have been realized.

The aforementioned National Study of School Evaluation enables schools to gather opinions of constituencies of the school by making available inventories for teachers, students, and parents to register their perceptions about the school and its programs. English adapted the concept of a management audit to curriculum evaluation, defining an audit as "an objective, external review of a record, event, process, product, act, belief, or motivation to commit an act."[70] English went on to describe a curriculum audit as "a process of examining documents and practices that exist within a peculiar institution normally called a 'school' in a given time, culture, and society."[71] From documents, interviews, and on-site visits, the auditor, sometimes an external agent, seeks to determine how well programs are functioning and whether they are cost-effective. English pointed out that the curriculum audit is both a process and a product in that the auditor engages in collecting and analyzing data and prepares a report delineating the results. Standards applied by English to a school district's curriculum audit include district control over its people, program, and resources; clear program objectives; documentation about its programs; use of district assessments; and program improvements.[72]

Studies of the needs of society and of young people speak to the question of the school's total program. Unless one limits the school's program to purely cognitive

---

[68]See Chapter 7 of this text re NSSE instruments.

[69]Fenwick W. English, "Curriculum Mapping," *Educational Leadership* 37, no. 7 (April 1980): 558–559. See also Donald F. Weinstein, *Administrator's Guide to Curriculum Mapping: A Step-by-Step Manual* (Englewood Cliffs, N.J.: Prentice-Hall, 1988).

[70]Fenwick W. English, *Curriculum Auditing* (Lancaster, Pa.: Technomic Publishing Company, 1988), p. 3.

[71]Ibid., p. 33.

[72]Ibid., pp. 33–34.

goals, some response should be made to some of the pressing problems of the day. These studies provide formative data for the curriculum planners. Surely problems like abuse of the environment, waste of natural resources, discrimination of all types, and the misuse of chemical substances should be examined by young people.

Saylor, Alexander, and Lewis recommended formative evaluation of the program of education as a totality by means of "judgments of competent persons, research data on human needs, recommendations of study groups." They recommended summative evaluation of the educational program through "surveys; follow-up studies; judgments of scholars, citizens, and students; test data."[73]

Summative evaluation of the total program is conducted in several ways. Empirical data are gathered to determine if curriculum objectives have been accomplished. Schoolwide test data are analyzed. Follow-up studies reveal the success or lack of success of young people after leaving the school. Finally, surveys ask teachers, parents, students, and others to evaluate the school's program.

Evaluation of the Evaluation Program.   The program for evaluating the curriculum should be continuously assessed. Judgments about how evaluation will be conducted should be made before an innovation or change is put into practice. The techniques for ongoing evaluation and final evaluation must be carefully planned and followed.

Sometimes it is beneficial to enlist the services of an evaluation specialist to review the evaluation techniques proposed by the curriculum planners. Questions must be answered as to whether the instruments to be used are reliable and valid; whether the evaluation program is comprehensive, covering all the dimensions of the curriculum to be evaluated; and whether the procedures are appropriate and possible. Reactions and suggestions about the evaluation procedures should be obtained from those who are most intimately exposed to them—the students and teachers.

If research studies are to be conducted, specialists inside or outside the system should review the proposed research techniques to determine whether they meet the standards of acceptable research.

When data are ultimately gathered, the planners may feel the need to request the help of evaluation specialists to treat and interpret the data. It must now be determined whether all the variables have been considered and appropriately controlled and whether the evaluation measures are designed to assess the appropriate objectives. For example, a cognitive test of American history will not assess student performance of citizenship skills. The ability to recite rules of grammar does not guarantee skill in writing.

When flaws are discovered in the evaluation program, changes should be made. Conclusions reached as a result of research and evaluation are often attacked, not on their substance, but on the evaluation processes by which they were reached.

For example, why is it that we can find skeptics for almost every curricular innovation ever tried? You name it—core curriculum; competency-based education; open education; team teaching; nongradedness; the once new, now old math; and so on—and we can find criticisms of it. Some who object do so because they are not convinced that the evaluation techniques purported to have been used actually proved the superi-

---

[73]Saylor, Alexander, and Lewis, *Curriculum Planning for Better Teaching and Learning*, 4th ed., p. 334.

ority of an innovation. Students of curriculum might well examine the processes for evaluating almost any program, change of program, or innovation in their school system—past or present—and at any level to find out if curricula were evaluated rigorously. Students are also likely to discover many innovations evaluated on the basis of perceived opinion of success (without adequate data), participants' feelings about the program (like/dislike), change of pace (variety as a spice), pleasure of being involved (Hawthorne effect), administrative assertion ("I say it works"), cost (if it was an expensive undertaking, it has to be good), public relations ("Look what we've done for your/our young people"), and perceived leadership ("We're in the vanguard," also known as "on the cutting edge").

To conclude, Saylor, Alexander, and Lewis have illuminated the major evaluation components that confront curriculum planners in the process of curriculum development. Less technical than some models, the Saylor, Alexander, and Lewis model offers a comprehensive view of curriculum evaluation.

The CIPP Model.   The Phi Delta Kappa National Study Committee on Evaluation, chaired by Daniel L. Stufflebeam, produced and disseminated a widely cited model of evaluation known as the CIPP (context, input, process, product) model.[74] Reference has already been made in Chapter 4 to two of the major features of the CIPP model: stages of decision making and types of decisions required in education.[75]

Comprehensive in nature, the model reveals types of evaluation, of decision-making settings, of decisions, and of change. In shaping their model, Stufflebeam and his associates defined evaluation in the following way: "Evaluation is the process of delineating, obtaining, and providing useful information for judging decision alternatives."[76]

Stufflebeam clarified what was meant by each of the parts of the definition as follows:

1. *Process.* A particular, continuing and cyclical activity subsuming many methods and involving a number of steps or operations.
2. *Delineating.* Focusing information requirements to be served by evaluation through such steps as specifying, defining, and explicating.
3. *Obtaining.* Making available through such processes as collecting, organizing, and analyzing, and through such formal means as statistics and measurement.
4. *Providing.* Fitting together into systems or subsystems that best serve the needs or purposes of the evaluation.
5. *Useful.* Appropriate to predetermined criteria evolved through the interaction of the evaluator and the client.
6. *Information.* Descriptive or interpretive data about entities (tangible or intangible) and their relationships.

[74]Stufflebeam et al., *Educational Evaluation*, pp. 218–235.

[75]See p. 114 of this text.

[76]Daniel L. Stufflebeam, an address given at the Eleventh Annual Phi Delta Kappa Symposium on Educational Research, Ohio State University, June 24, 1970. Quoted in Blaine R. Worthen and James R. Sanders, *Educational Evaluation: Theory and Practice* (Worthington, Ohio: Charles A. Jones, 1971), p. 129.

7. *Judging.* Assigning weights in accordance with a specified value framework, criteria derived therefrom, and information which relates criteria to each entity being judged.

8. *Decision Alternatives.* A set of optional responses to a specified decision question.[77]

"The evaluation process," said Stufflebeam, "includes the three main steps of delineating, obtaining, and providing. These steps provide the basis for a methodology of evaluation."[78] Before we begin to examine the various elements of the CIPP model, let's look at a figure of the entire model, shown in Figure 13.5.

In flow-chart form, the model consists of rectangles (with small loops attached), hexagons, ovals, a circle, a fancy *E*, solid and broken lines with arrows, and three types of shading. Shaded dark, the hexagons show types of decisions; hatched, the ovals, the circle, and the big *E* depict activities performed; and lightly shaded, the rectangles stand for types of evaluation.

Four Types of Evaluation.   The Phi Delta Kappa Committee pointed to four types of evaluation—context, input, process, and product—hence the name of the model CIPP. Context evaluation is "the most basic kind of evaluation," said Stufflebeam. "Its purpose is to provide a rationale for determination of objectives."[79] At this point in the model, curriculum planner-evaluators define the environment of the curriculum and determine unmet needs and reasons why the needs are not being met. Goals and objectives are specified on the basis of context evaluation.

Input evaluation has as its purpose "to provide information for determining how to utilize resources to achieve project objectives."[80] The resources of the school and various designs for carrying out the curriculum are considered. At this stage, the planner-evaluators decide on procedures to be used. Stufflebeam observed, "Methods for input evaluation are lacking in education. The prevalent practices include committee deliberations, appeal to the professional literature, the employment of consultants, and pilot experimental projects."[81]

Process evaluation is the provision of periodic feedback while the curriculum is being implemented. Stufflebeam noted, "Process evaluation has three main objectives—the first is to detect or predict defects in the procedural design or its implementation during the implementation stages, the second is to provide information for programmed decisions, and the third is to maintain a record of the procedure as it occurs."[82]

Product evaluation, the final type, has as its purpose

> . . . to measure and interpret attainments not only at the end of a project cycle, but as often as necessary during the project term. The general method of product evaluation includes devising operational definitions of objectives, measuring criteria associated with the objectives of the activity, comparing these measurements with predetermined

---

[77]Ibid.

[78]Ibid.

[79] Stufflebeam, in Worthen and Sanders, *Educational Evaluation*, p. 136.

[80]Ibid.

[81]Ibid., p. 137.

[82]Ibid.

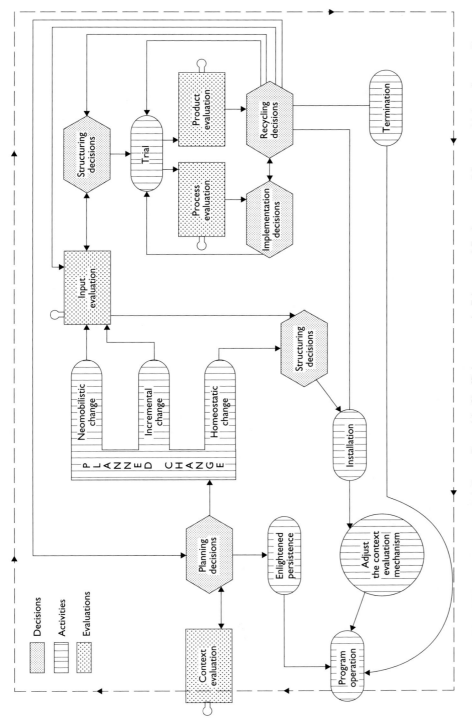

Figure 13.5 The CIPP evaluation model. From Daniel L. Shufflebeam et al., *Educational Evaluation and Decision Making* (Itasca, Ill.: F. E. Peacock, 1971), p. 236. Reprinted by permission.

absolute or relative standards, and making rational interpretations of the outcomes using the recorded context, input, and process information.[83]

Stufflebeam outlined the types of evaluation in respect to objectives, methods, and in relation to decision making in the change process as shown in Table 13.1.

Four Types of Decisions.   The hexagons in Figure 13.5 represent four types of decisions, which were mentioned in Chapter 4: Planning, Structuring, Implementing, and Recycling. Note in the figure that the hexagon Planning decisions follows Context evaluation; Structuring decisions follows Input evaluation; Implementation decisions follows Process evaluation; and Recycling decisions follows Product evaluation.[84]

Decision making, according to the Phi Delta Kappa Committee, occurs in four different settings:[85]

a. small change with high information
b. small change with low information
c. large change with high information
d. large change with low information

Four Types of Changes.   In these settings, four types of changes may result: neomobilistic, incremental, homeostatic, and metamorphic. *Neomobilistic change* occurs in a setting in which a large change is sought on the basis of low information. These changes are innovative solutions based on little evidence. *Incremental changes* are series of small changes based on low information. *Homeostatic change,* which is the most common in education, is a small change based on high information. Finally, *metamorphic change,* a large change based on high information, is so rare that it is not shown on the CIPP model.

The model plots the sequence of evaluation and decision making from context evaluation to recycling decisions. The committee has touched up the model with small loops that look like light bulbs on the evaluation blocks to indicate that the general process of delineating, obtaining, and providing information is cyclical and applies to each type of evaluation.

The ovals, the circle, and the *E* in the model represent types of activities, types of change, and adjustment as a result of the evaluations made and decisions taken. The CIPP model presents a comprehensive view of the evaluation process. Like Saylor, Alexander, and Lewis, Stufflebeam and his associates also called for evaluation of the evaluation program. Said the Phi Delta Kappa Committee: "To maximize the effectiveness and efficiency of evaluation, evaluation itself should be evaluated. . . . The criteria for this include internal validity, external validity, reliability, objectivity, relevance, importance, credibility, scope, pervasiveness, timeliness, and efficiency."[86]

MODEL WITH TYPES OF EVALUATION

To refine our concept of the necessary types of evaluation and to show what types are carried out at specific stages, I have rediagrammed the Curriculum Model in

---

[83]Ibid., p. 138.
[84]Stufflebeam et al., *Educational Evaluation,* pp. 79–84.
[85]Ibid., pp. 61–69.
[86]Ibid., p. 239.

TABLE 13.1

FOUR TYPES OF EVALUATION

	CONTEXT EVALUATION	INPUT EVALUATION	PROCESS EVALUATION	PRODUCT EVALUATION
OBJECTIVE	To define the *operating context*, to identify and assess *needs* and *opportunities* in the context, and to diagnose *problems* underlying the *needs* and *opportunities*.	To identify and assess *system capabilities*, available input *strategies*, and designs for implementing the strategies.	To identify or predict, in process, *defects* in the procedural design or its implementation, to provide information for the preprogrammed decisions, and to maintain a record of *procedural events* and activities.	To relate *outcome information* to objectives and to context, input, and process information.
METHOD	By describing the context; by comparing actual and intended inputs and outputs; by comparing probable and possible system performance; and by analyzing possible causes of discrepancies between actualities and intentions.	By describing and analyzing available human and material resources, solution strategies, and procedural designs for relevance, feasibility and economy in the course of action to be taken.	By monitoring the activity's potential procedural barriers and remaining alert to unanticipated ones, by obtaining specified information for programmed decisions, and describing the actual process.	By defining operationally and measuring criteria associated with the objectives, by comparing these measurements with predetermined standards or comparative bases, and by interpreting the outcomes in terms of recorded context, input and process information.
RELATION TO DECISION MAKING IN THE CHANGE PROCESS	For deciding upon the *setting* to be served, the *goal* associated with meeting needs or using opportunities, and the *objectives* associated with solving problems, i.e., for *planning* needed changes.	For electing *sources of support*, solution strategies, and procedural designs, i.e., for *structuring* change activities.	For *implementing* and *refining the program design and procedure*, i.e., for effecting process control.	For deciding to *continue, terminate, modify,* or *refocus* a change activity, and for linking the activity to other major phases of the change process, i.e., for recycling change activities.

SOURCE: Daniel L. Stufflebeam, an address given at the Eleventh Annual Phi Delta Kappa Symposium on Educational Research, Ohio State University, June 24, 1970. Quoted in Blaine R. Worthen and James R. Sanders, *Educational Evaluation: Theory and Practice* (Worthington, Ohio: Charles A. Jones, 1973), p. 139. Reprinted by permission.

Figure 13.6   Sequence and types of evaluation

Figure 13.6. In this submodel of the model for curriculum development, the types of evaluation are now numbered for easy reference.
Let's review each of the numbered elements:

1. As a part of context evaluation, needs are assessed.
2. Curriculum goals are validated.
3. Curriculum objectives are validated.
4. Context evaluation begins with the needs assessment and continues up to the implementation stage.
5. Input evaluation takes place between specification of curriculum objectives and implementation of the curriculum.
6. Process evaluation is carried out during the implementation stage. Michael Scriven described three types of process research: noninferential studies, investigations of causal claims about the process, and formative evaluation.[87]
   Noninferential studies are those observations and investigations of what is actually happening in the classroom. Investigation of causal claims is referred to by some educators as "action research." This type of research is a less than rigorous attempt to establish whether one teaching technique is better than another. Formative evaluation is assessment during the course of a study or program. To these three types of process research we might add the term "descriptive research," of which noninferential studies of teacher and student classroom behavior represent one form. The use of survey instruments and the application of the instrument standards also fall into the category of descriptive research.
7. Product evaluation is summative evaluation of the entire process. This type of evaluation is sometimes referred to as outcome evaluation or program evaluation. Program evaluation, however, is used not only in the sense of summative evaluation but also as a synonym for the entire process of curriculum evaluation. Thus, a model for curriculum evaluation might also be called a model for program evaluation.

[87]See Michael Scriven, "The Methodology of Evaluation," *Perspectives of Curriculum Evaluation*, AERA Monograph Series on Curriculum Evaluation No. 1 (Chicago: Rand McNally, 1967), pp. 49–51.

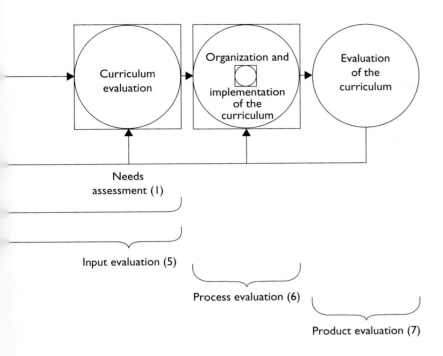

The Saylor, Alexander, and Lewis and CIPP models provide us with two different ways of viewing the process of curriculum evaluation. The models are similar to the extent that they urge a comprehensive approach to evaluation. They are different in the terminology they use and the level of detail they depict. The Saylor, Alexander, and Lewis model is somewhat less complex than the CIPP model and may perhaps be more readily understood by curriculum workers in general. The CIPP model may be more appealing to specialists in curriculum evaluation. Some dissatisfaction has been expressed for so-called process-product research. McNeil discussed what he perceived as the continuing methodological and theoretical problems of this form of research. He cautioned of over emphasis on generalization of results.[88]

STANDARDS FOR EVALUATION

The use of any evaluation model will be more effective and proper if the evaluators follow some agreed-upon standards. The Joint Committee on Standards for Educational Evaluation, chaired by James R. Sanders, identified four attributes of an evaluation: utility, feasibility, propriety, and accuracy.[89] This committee proposed seven utility standards "to ensure that an evaluation will serve the information needs of intended users."[90] They offered three feasibility standards "to ensure that an evaluation will be

---

[88]McNeil, *Curriculum*, pp. 441–442.

[89]The Joint Committee on Standards for Educational Evaluation, James R. Sanders, Chair, *The Program Evaluation Standards: How to Assess Evaluations of Educational Programs*, 2nd ed.(Thousand Oaks, Calif.: Sage Publications, 1994). See also The Joint Committee on Standards for Educational Evaluation, Daniel L. Stufflebeam, Chair, *Standards for Evaluations of Educational Programs, Projects, and Materials* (New York: McGraw-Hill, 1981), pp. 19, 51, 63, 97.

[90]The Joint Committee, *The Program Evaluation Standards*, p. 23.

realistic, prudent, diplomatic, and frugal."[91] Eight propriety standards were advanced "to ensure that an evaluation will be conducted legally, ethically, and with due regard for the welfare of those involved in the evaluation, as well as those affected by its results."[92] Twelve accuracy standards were suggested "to ensure that an evaluation will reveal and convey technically adequate information about the features that determine worth or merit of the program being evaluated."[93]

With evaluation of the curriculum, we conclude the model for curriculum development proposed in this text. However, I must stress that there is really no fixed end to the model; it is cyclical. Results of evaluation produce data for modifying earlier components. Without evaluation there can be no considered modifications and, therefore, little likelihood in improvement.

SUMMARY

Evaluation is a continuous process by which data are gathered and judgments made for the purpose of improving a system. Thorough evaluation is essential to curriculum development. Evaluation is perceived as a process of making judgments, whereas research is perceived as the process of gathering data as bases for judgments.

Eight perennial or continuing problems were considered. Each was presented as a principle to which curriculum workers must give attention.

Scope is the breadth of the curriculum—the "what." The major task in planning the scope of the curriculum is selection of content, organizing elements, organizing centers, or integrative threads from the wealth of possible choices.

Relevance is the usefulness of content to the learner. What makes determining the relevance of a curriculum difficult is the variety of perceptions of what is relevant. A consensus of the opinions of the various constituencies and patrons of the school should be sought by curriculum workers to determine what is of sufficient relevance to be included in the curriculum.

Curriculum planners should strive for balance among a number of variables. When a curriculum gives excessive attention to one dimension or to one group and ignores or minimizes attention to others, the curriculum may be said to be out of balance and in need of being brought into balance.

Integration is the unification of disciplines—the weakening or abandoning of boundaries between discrete subjects. Many educators feel that integrated content helps students in the task of problem solving. Relevance, balance, and integration are perceived as dimensions of scope.

Sequence is the "when"—the ordering of the units of content. Attention must be paid to prerequisite learning requirements.

Continuity is the planned introduction and reintroduction of content at subsequent grade levels and at ever-increasing levels of complexity. This concept is at the heart of the "spiral curriculum."

[91]Ibid., p. 63.
[92]Ibid., p. 81.
[93]Ibid., p. 125.

Articulation is the meshing of subject matter and skills between successive levels of schooling to provide a smooth transition for boys and girls from a lower to higher level. Sequence, continuity, and articulation are all related concepts. Continuity and articulation are perceived as dimensions of sequencing.

Transferability is that characteristic of learning which when realized in one setting permits it to be carried over into another setting. Although there is no proof that certain subjects per se enhance the transfer of learning, there is some evidence to support the thesis that teaching basic principles of a discipline and stressing their application increases transfer. Transfer is a much-desired goal of education.

Curriculum planners engage in various types of evaluation and research. Among the types of evaluation are context, input, process, and product. Among the types of research are action, descriptive, historical, and experimental. In another vein, curriculum planners engage in both formative (process or progress) evaluation and in summative (outcome or product) evaluation.

Two models of curriculum evaluation were reviewed in this chapter. The Saylor, Alexander, and Lewis model seeks evaluation of five components: the goals, subgoals, and objectives; the program of education as a totality; the specific segments of the education program; instruction; and the evaluation program. The CIPP model was designed by the Phi Delta Kappa National Study Committee on Evaluation, which was chaired by Daniel L. Stufflebeam. It is more complex and technical than the Saylor, Alexander, and Lewis model. The CIPP model combines "three major steps in the evaluation process (delineating, obtaining, and providing), . . . three classes of change settings (homeostasis, incrementalism, and neomobilism), . . . four types of evaluation (context, input, process, and product), and . . . four types of decisions (planning, structuring, implementing, and recycling)."[94] The creators of both these models also urge an evaluation of the evaluation program. The limited and comprehensive models may be used independently or in conjunction with each other.

Curriculum evaluators from both inside and outside are employed by school systems. Much of the burden for curriculum evaluation falls on teachers as they work in the area of curriculum development. Following a set of agreed-upon standards improves the evaluation process. Attention should be given to utility, feasibility, propriety, and accuracy standards.

Evaluation of the curriculum is the culmination of the proposed model for curriculum improvement. Though placed at the end of the diagrammed model, evaluation connotes the end of one cycle and the beginning of the next. Improvements in the following cycle are made as a result of evaluation.

QUESTIONS FOR DISCUSSION

1. How do you know if a curriculum works?
2. If you evaluate instruction, is there any need to evaluate the curriculum? Explain.
3. Why is it that curriculum evaluation is often omitted or carried out ineffectively?

---

[94]Stufflebeam et al., *Educational Evaluation*, p. 238.

4. What effect should curriculum evaluation have on other components of the model for curriculum development presented by the author of this text?

5. Does the Hawthorne Effect enter into curriculum evaluation? How?

SUPPLEMENTARY EXERCISES

1. Outline the scope of a course you have taught or plan to teach.

2. Poll a number of teachers, students, and parents to find out what they feel is relevant in the curriculum and what relevant topics they think have been left out.

3. Determine in what ways a curriculum you know well appears to be in or out of balance. If you believe that the curriculum is out of balance, recommend ways to bring it into balance.

4. Report on any planned efforts you can find to correlate or integrate subject matter.

5. Outline and explain the rationale of the sequence of the topics or elements of a course you have taught or plan to teach.

6. Determine whether a school you know well has planned the curriculum keeping in mind the principle of continuity. Recommend improvements in continuity, if necessary.

7. Determine whether a school system you know well has planned the curriculum keeping in mind the principle of articulation. Recommend improvements in articulation, if necessary.

8. Show the transfer value of a discipline that you are certified or becoming certified to teach.

9. Write an analysis of J. Richard Suchman's Inquiry Training Model (see bibliography).

10. Write an analysis of David P. Ausubel's Advance Organizer Model (see bibliography).

11. Locate and summarize the content of at least one article or chapter of a book on one of the eight continuing curriculum problems discussed in this chapter.

12. Define context, input, process, and product evaluation.

13. Report on evidence of any of the types of evaluation in exercise 12 carried out in a school system you know well.

14. Search the literature on evaluation, and locate and report on a model of evaluation different from either of the two models described in this chapter. Contrast the model you discover to the two presented. (See footnote 4 and bibliography of this chapter for suggested models.)

15. Look up and explain to the class what is meant by internal validity, external validity, reliability, objectivity, relevance, importance, credibility, scope, pervasiveness, timeliness, and efficiency as they relate to the evaluation of evaluation programs.

16. Distinguish between instructional and curriculum evaluation.

17. Define empirical data, descriptive research, action research, historical research, experimental research, and dynamic hypotheses.

18. Locate and present to the class a school system's job description for a curriculum evaluator.

19. Draw up a list of skills needed by a curriculum evaluator.

20. Write a position paper, using appropriate references, on the topic: When should outside consultants on evaluation be used by school systems?
21. Show with appropriate evidence that a school system you know well has used evaluative data to modify a curriculum.
22. Examine and critique the final evaluation (audit) of any state or federal program in a school system you know well.
23. Determine and provide evidence as to whether curriculum evaluation in a school system you know well suffers from any of the eight symptoms listed by the Phi Delta Kappa National Study Committee on Evaluation.
24. Explain the difference between goal-based evaluation and goal-free evaluation. Compare these two approaches and state under what conditions each is appropriate.
25. This assignment is for four students. Refer to the publication of the Joint Committee of Standards for Educational Evaluation (see bibliography). Each student should select one of the four attributes (utility, feasibility, propriety, and accuracy) of an evaluation and describe to the class the standards suggested for it. Critique the standards as to applicability and appropriateness.
26. Describe any curriculum changes that have come about as a result of district or state assessments.
27. Read a study of one of the following and derive any implications for a school or school district which you know best:
    a. SAT or ACT scores
    b. National Assessment of Educational Progress
    c. International Association for the Evaluation of Educational Achievement
    d. International Assessment of Educational Progress
28. Report on the process and product of a curriculum audit conducted in any school system you know or reported in the literature. (See the Fenwick W. English reference on curriculum auditing for case studies.)
29. For those currently teaching: Carry out a curriculum mapping in the grade or course you teach.
30. Explain how J. Galen Saylor, William M. Alexander, and Arthur J. Lewis (see bibliography) defined sequence, continuity, and integration.

BIBLIOGRAPHY

Aikin, Wilford M. *The Story of the Eight-Year Study.* New York: Harper & Row, 1942.

Apple, Michael W., Subkoviak, Michael J., and Luffler, Henry S., Jr., eds. *Educational Evaluation: Analysis and Responsibility.* Berkeley, Calif.: McCutchan, 1974.

Armstrong, David G. *Developing and Documenting the Curriculum.* Boston: Allyn and Bacon, 1989.

Association for Supervision and Curriculum Development. *Balance in the Curriculum.* 1961 Yearbook. Alexandria, Va.: Association for Supervision and Curriculum Development, 1961.

Beane, James A. "Foreword: Teachers of Uncommon Courage," in Chrisa Stevenson and Judy F. Carr, eds. *Inte-*grated Studies in the Middle Grades: Dancing Through Walls. New York: Teachers College Press, 1993.

———, Toepfer, Conrad F., Jr., and Alessi, Samuel J., Jr. *Curriculum Planning and Development.* Boston: Allyn and Bacon, 1986.

Bellack, Arno, "What Knowledge Is of Most Worth?" *High School Journal* 48, no. 5 (February 1965): 318–332.

Bellon, Jerry J. and Handler, Janet R. *Curriculum Development and Evaluation: A Design for Improvement.* Dubuque, Iowa: Kendall/Hunt, 1982.

Bloom, Benjamin S. "Ideas, Problems, and Methods of Inquiry." In *The Integration of Educational Experiences.* 57th Yearbook. National Society for the Study of Education, Part 3, pp. 84–85. Chicago: University of Chicago Press, 1958.

Broudy, Harry S. *The Real World of the Public Schools*. New York: Harcourt Brace Jovanovich, 1972.

Bruner, Jerome S. *On Knowing: Essays for the Left Hand*. Cambridge, Mass.: Harvard University Press, 1962.

———. *The Process of Education*. Cambridge, Mass.: Harvard University Press, 1960.

———. *The Relevance of Education*. New York: Norton, 1973.

———. "Structures in Learning." *Today's Education* 52, no. 3 (March 1963): 26–27.

Caine, Renate Nummela and Caine, Geoffrey. *Making Connections: Teaching and the Human Brain*. Alexandria, Va.: Association for Supervision and Curriculum Development, 1991.

Caswell, Hollis L. and Campbell, Doak S. *Curriculum Development*. New York: American Book Company, 1935.

Center for the Study of Evaluation. *Evaluation Workshop I: An Orientation*. Del Monte Research Park, Monterey, Calif.: CTB/McGraw-Hill, 1971. Participant's Notebook and Leader's Manual.

Combs, Arthur W., ed. *Perceiving, Behaving, Becoming*. 1962 Yearbook. Alexandria, Va.: Association for Supervision and Curriculum Development, 1962.

"Curriculum Evaluation: Uses, Misuses, and Nonuses." *Educational Leadership* 35, no. 4 (January 1978): 243–297.

Doll, Ronald C. *Curriculum Improvement: Decision Making and Process*, 9th ed. Boston: Allyn and Bacon, 1996.

Drake, Susan. *Planning Integrated Curriculum: The Call to Adventure*. Alexandria, Va.: Association for Supervision and Curriculum Development, 1993.

Ebel, Robert L. "What Schools Are For." *Phi Delta Kappan* 54, no. 1 (September 1972): 3–7.

Eisner, Elliot W. *The Educational Imagination: On the Design and Evaluation of School Programs*, 2nd ed. New York: Macmillan, 1985.

———. "Educational Connoisseurship and Criticism: Their Form and Functions in Educational Evaluation." *Journal of Aesthetic Education* 10, numbers 3–4 (July–October, 1976): 135–150.

English, Fenwick W. *Curriculum Auditing*. Lancaster, Pa.: Technomic Publishing Company, 1988.

———. "Curriculum Mapping." *Educational Leadership* 37, no. 7 (April 1980): 558–559.

Glasser, William. *The Quality School: Managing Students Without Coercion*, 2nd ed. New York: HarperPerennial, 1992.

Goodlad, John I. *Planning and Organizing for Teaching*. Washington, D.C.: National Education Association, 1963.

Guba, Egon, and Lincoln, Yvonna S. *Effective Evaluation: Improving the Usefulness of Evaluation Results Through Responsive and Naturalistic Approaches*. San Francisco: Jossey-Bass, 1981.

Halverson, Paul M. "The Meaning of Balance." In *Balance in the Curriculum*. 1961 Yearbook, 3–16. Alexandria, Va.: Association for Supervision and Curriculum Development, 1961.

Johnson, Mauritz, Jr. *Intentionality in Education: A Conceptual Model of Curricular and Instructional Planning and Evaluation*. Albany, N.Y.: Center for Curriculum Research and Services, 1977.

"Integrating the Curriculum." *Educational Leadership* 49, no. 2 (October 1991): 4–75.

Jacobs, Heidi Hayes, ed. *Interdisciplinary Curriculum: Design and Implementation*. Alexandria, Va.: Association for Supervision and Curriculum Development, 1989.

Joint Committee on Standards for Educational Evaluation, James R. Sanders, Chair. *The Program Evaluation Standards: How to Assess Evaluations of Educational Programs*, 2nd ed. Thousand Oaks, Calif.: Sage Publications, 1994.

———, Daniel L. Stufflebeam, Chair. *Standards for Evaluations of Educational Programs, Projects, and Materials*. New York: McGraw-Hill, 1981.

Lindvall, C. M., and Cox, Richard C., with Bolvin, John O. *Evaluation as a Tool in Curriculum Development: The IPI Evaluation Program*. American Educational Research Association Monograph, no. 5. Chicago: Rand McNally, 1970.

McNeil, John D. *Curriculum: A Comprehensive Introduction*, 5th ed. New York: HarperCollins, 1996.

National Study of School Evaluation. *Elementary School Improvement: Focusing on Student Performance*. Schaumburg, Ill.: National Study of School Evaluation, 1995.

———. *K–12 School Improvement: Focusing on Student Performance*. Schaumburg, Ill.: National Study of School Evaluation, 1995.

———. *Middle Level School Improvement: Focusing on Student Performance*. Schaumburg, Ill.: National Study of School Evaluation, 1995.

———. *School Improvement: Focusing on Student Performance*. Schaumburg, Ill.: National Study of School Evaluation, 1997.

———. *Senior High School Improvement; Focusing on Student Performance*. Schaumburg, Ill.: National Study of School Evaluation, 1995.

Oliver, Albert I. *Curriculum Improvement: A Guide to Problems, Principles, and Processes*, 2nd ed. New York: Harper & Row, 1977.

Orlosky, Donald and Smith, B. Othanel, eds. *Curriculum Development: Issues and Insights*. Chicago: Rand McNally, 1978, Part 5.

Phenix, Philip H. "The Disciplines as Curriculum Content." In *Curriculum Crossroads*, ed. A. Harry Passow, 57–65. New York: Teachers College Press, Columbia University, 1962.

The Phi Delta Kappa/Gallup Polls of the Public's Attitudes Toward the Public Schools. *Phi Delta Kappan.* Annually, usually September.

Plakos, Marie, Plakos, John, and Babcock, Robert. *Workbook on Program Evaluation,* 2nd ed. Princeton, N.J.: Educational Testing Service, 1978.

Popham, W. James, *Educational Evaluation.* Englewood Cliffs, N.J.: Prentice-Hall, 1975.

Pressey, Sidney L. and Robinson, Francis P. *Psychology and the New Education,* rev. ed. New York: Harper & Row, 1944.

Provus, Malcolm. *Discrepancy Evaluation for Educational Program Improvement and Assessment.* Berkeley, Calif.: McCutchan, 1971.

Ratnesar, Romesh. "Lost in the Middle." *Time* 152, no. 11 (September 14, 1998): 60–64.

Rogers, Frederick A. "Curriculum Research and Evaluation." In Fenwick W. English, ed., *Fundamental Curriculum Decisions,* 1983 Yearbook, 142–153. Alexandria, Va.: Association for Supervision and Curriculum Development, 1983.

Saylor, J. Galen and Alexander, William M. *Curriculum Planning for Better Teaching and Learning.* New York: Holt, Rinehart and Winston, 1954.

Saylor, J. Galen, Alexander, William M., and Lewis, Arthur J. *Curirculum Planning for Better Teaching and Learning,* 4th ed. New York: Holt, Rinehart and Winston, 1981.

Schubert, William H. *Curriculum: Perspective, Paradigm, and Possibility.* New York: Macmillan, 1986.

Scriven, Michael. "The Methodology of Evaluation." *Perspectives of Curriculum Evaluation.* AERA Monograph Series on Curriculum Evaluation, no. 1, 39–83. Chicago: Rand McNally, 1967.

Smith, B. Othanel et al. *Teachers for the Real World.* Washington, D.C.: American Association of Colleges for Teacher Education, 1969.

Smith, B. Othanel, Stanley, William O., and Shores, J. Harlan. *Fundamentals of Curriculum Development,* Revised edition. New York: Harcourt Brace Jovanovich, 1957.

Stake, Robert E. "Language, Rationality, and Assessment." In *Improving Educational Assessment and an Inventory of Measures of Affective Behavior,* ed. Walcott H. Beatty. Alexandria, Va.: Commission on Assessment of Educational Outcomes, Association for Supervision and Curriculum Development, 1969.

Stevenson, Chris and Carr. Judy F., eds. *Integrated Studies in the Middle Grades: Dancing Through Walls.* New York: Teachers College Press, 1993.

Stufflebeam, Daniel L. "Educational Evaluation and Decision Making," an address to the 11th Annual Phi Delta Kappa Symposium on Educational Research. Ohio State University, June 24, 1970.

Stufflebeam, Daniel L. et al. *Educational Evaluation and Decision Making.* Itasca, Ill.: F. E. Peacock, 1971.

Taba, Hilda. *Curriculum Development: Theory and Practice.* New York: Harcourt Brace Jovanovich, 1962.

Tanner, Daniel and Tanner, Laurel. *Curriculum Development: Theory into Practice,* 3rd ed. New York: Merrill, 1995.

Thorndike, Edward L. "Mental Discipline in High School Studies." *Journal of Educational Psychology* 15, no. 1 (January 1924): 1–22, continued in vol. l5, no. 2 (February 1924): 83–98.

Toffler, Alvin. *Future Shock.* New York: Random House, 1970.

Tyler, Ralph W. *Basic Principles of Curriculum and Instruction.* Chicago: University of Chicago Press, 1949.

———— ed. *Educational Evaluation: New Roles, New Means,* 68th Yearbook of the National Society for the Study of Education. Chicago: University of Chicago Press, 1969.

Tyler, Ralph W., Gagné, Robert M., and Scriven, Michael. *Perspectives of Curriculum Evaluation.* AERA Monograph Series on Curriculum Evaluation, no. 1. Chicago: Rand McNally, 1967.

Vars, Gordon F., ed. *Common Learnings: Core and Interdisciplinary Team Approaches.* Scranton, Pa.: International Textbook Company, 1969.

————. "Integrated Curriculum in Historical Perspective." *Educational Leadership* 49, no. 2 (October 1991): 14–15.

Weinstein, Donald F. *Administrator's Guide to Curriculum Mapping: A Step-by-Step Manual.* Englewood Cliffs, N.J.: Prentice-Hall, 1988.

Wiles, Kimball and Patterson, Franklin. *The High School We Need.* Alexandria, Va.: Association for Supervision and Curriculum Development, 1959.

Worthen, Blaine R. and Sanders, James R. *Educational Evaluation: Alternative Approaches and Practical Guidelines.* White Plains, N.Y.: Longman, 1987.

————. *Educational Evaluation: Theory and Practice.* Worthington, Ohio: Charles A. Jones, 1973.

Worthen, Blaine R., Sanders, James R., and White, Karl R. *Evaluating Educational and Social Programs: Guidelines for Proposal Review, Onsite Evaluation, Evaluation Contracts, and Technical Assistance.* Boston: Kluwer-Nijhoff Publishing, 1987.

Wulf, Kathleen M. and Schave, Barbara. *Curriculum Design: A Handbook for Educators.* Glenview, Ill.: Scott, Foresman, 1984.

Zais, Robert S. *Curriculum Principles and Foundations.* New York: Harper & Row, 1976.

Audiotape

On Action Research. 90 min. 1995. Features Carl Glickman. Association for Supervision and Curriculum Development, 1703 N. Beauregard St., Alexandria, Va. 22311–1714.

On Curriculum Integration. 90 min. 1995. Features Heidi Hayes Jacobs. Association for Supervision and Curriculum Development, 1703 N. Beauregard St., Alexandria, Va. 22311–1714.

ERIC MATERIALS

Current Index to Journals in Education. Monthly. Oryx Press, 2214 North Central at Encanto, Phoenix, Arizona 85004.

Resources in Education. Monthly. Washington, D.C.: Superintendent of Documents, U.S. Government Printing Office, Washington, D.C. 20402. Semiannual indexes available from the U.S. Government Printing Office. Annual cumulations: abstracts (2 volumes) and index (1 volume) available from Oryx Press. *Resources in Education* replaced *Research in Education* in January 1975.

Thesaurus of ERIC Descriptors, Oryx Press, 2214 North Central at Encanto, Phoenix, Arizona, 1995.

PROFESSIONAL INQUIRY KIT

Curriculum Integration. Video clips, activities, readings. 1998. Carol Cummings, developer. Association for Supervision and Curriculum Development, 1703 N. Beauregard St., Alexandria, Va. 22311–1714.

REPORTS

Reports of the International Assessment of Educational Progress may be obtained from the Center for the Assessment of Educational Progress, Educational Testing Service, Rosedale Road, Princeton, New Jersey 08541-0001.

Reports of the National Assessment of Educational Progress may be obtained from the National Assessment of Educational Progress, Educational Testing Service, Rosedale Road, Princeton, New Jersey 08541-0001.

VIDEOTAPE

Curriculum Mapping: Charting the Course for Content. Two 30–minute videotapes and Facilitator's Guide. Heidi Hayes Jacobs, consultant. Association for Supervision and Curriculum Development, 1703 N. Beauregard St, Alexandria, Va. 22311-1714.

Integrating the Curriculum. 2 tapes. Over 1 hour. Program on linking content from the various disciplines. Describes six design options. Scenes from schools in Howard County, Md. and Jefferson County, Kentucky. Features Heidi Hayes Jacobs, Marilyn Hohmann, and Joan Palmer. Facilitator's Guide and book, Interdisciplinary Curriculum: Design and Implementation, Heidi Hayes Jacobs, ed.. Association for Supervision and Curriculum Development, 1703 N. Beauregard St., Alexandria, Va. 22311-1714.

Planning Integrated Units: A Concept-Based Approach. 65–min. videotape and Facilitator's Guide. 1997. Association for Supervision and Curriculum Development, 1703 N. Beauregard St., Alexandria, Va. 22311-1714.

WEB SITE

National Study of School Evaluation:
http://www.nsse.org

PART IV

CURRICULUM DEVELOPMENT: PROBLEMS AND PRODUCTS

CHAPTER 14

PROBLEMS IN CURRICULUM DEVELOPMENT

After studying this chapter you should be able to:

1. Identify current and continuing curriculum problems that are brought about by social and political forces and explain their significance for curriculum development.
2. Identify professional problems that make an impact on the curriculum and explain their significance to curriculum planners.

CURRENT CURRICULUM PROBLEMS

A number of curricular developments, that is, programs and practices, on the current scene have gained both followers and critics. As such, they have become issues around which there swirls considerable debate. Controversial in nature, they pose challenges to curriculum developers. Borrowing the rubric of Chapter 9 where we examined a number of curricular innovations and programs by periods of history, ending with *Curriculum Future,* Chapter 14 returns to *Curriculum Present.* We have reserved for this chapter discussion of a number of the more significant current programs and practices, some of which have been in operation for some time; others, relatively new.

Curriculum planners are buffeted by strong educational, social, and political forces affecting the curricular decisions they must make. Movements have emanated from networks of like-minded professional educators, from the public in general, and from individuals and pressure groups from outside the teacher education profession.

Some of the desires of both pressure groups and the public generally and, even on occasion, of professional educators, have been enacted into state or federal law. No law, however, has mandated strong movements of cooperative learning, discussed elsewhere, and whole language, discussed in this chapter. Those nonmandated movements that have become practices in the schools have done so by gathering enough voluntary support among the *teacher education* and *public school professionals* to translate them into action.

Among the significant contemporary curricular problems facing curriculum workers are (1) alternative schooling, (2) bilingual education, (3) censorship, (4) community service, (5) cultural literacy, (6) educational management organizations (7) gender discrimination, (8) health education, (9) multiculturalism, (10) national standards, (11) outcomes-based education, (12) provision for exceptionalities, (13) religion in the schools, (14) schedule revisions, and (15) whole language. All of the foregoing have been problems for some time and remain so. In fact, as we enter the twenty-first century some of them are even more of an issue than in the past.

Many of these movements are manifestations of reform in curriculum and instruction and restructuring of school administrative practices. Controversy swirls around each of these movements. You will note that many of the problems identified are intertwined.

ALTERNATIVE SCHOOLING

Options in Education.   In the 1960s and 1970s school districts were engaged in efforts to accommodate students who could not fare well in the established public schools by offering options either within or outside the school. Among the more common alternatives outside the established schools were the so-called free schools, storefront schools, and schools without walls in which individuals, organizations, and businesses in the community participated in the education of youth. School systems took advantage of the human and material resources available in the community and offered students practical instruction in a setting less structured than the established school. A common plan was the assignment of students to these learning stations for a portion of the day with the remainder of the day spent at the established school. This type of alternative, posing numerous problems of quality of instruction, administration, and accountability has diminished in popularity to the point where we rarely hear of this kind of experimental offering.

Still popular, however, are alternatives within the school systems themselves, particularly magnet schools and schools to which students posing behavior problems are assigned for varying periods of time. In calling these structures options we should mention that choice of magnet school is to a large extent, depending on availability, the decision of the student and parents. Assignment to the alternative school for students with behavior problems is at the option of school personnel.

Most of the foregoing types of alternative schools have been perceived as strengthening the public school system. Far more threatening to public education are the growing opportunities either in place or under consideration for parents to select (1) public or private schools that their children may attend and (2) home schools. Even more threatening is the rapid development of the phenomenon of privatization which may include the element of parental choice.(Educational Management Organizations below).

Parental Choice.   In recent years, pressure has been building for the state to support parental choice of schools whether public or private. The Association for Supervision and Curriculum Development reported that by 1991 schools-of-choice programs existed in some thirty states.[1] Customarily, parents who have children in the public school system must send them to schools within their assigned subdistricts of the local school district. Parents may send their children to schools outside their assigned subdistricts only in special cases such as magnet schools or other programs that are not available within that assigned subdistrict. Parents have encountered even greater difficulty when they wished to send their children to public schools across school-district lines; this type of move, if permitted, may require the parents to pay tuition to the school district of choice.

In the fall of 1998 Seattle ceased arbitrary assignment of students to schools and permitted parents to select the public school they would like their children to attend. Choice of school within the public system, although resisted by many administrators and school boards, is less contentious than the larger issue of provision of public funding for parental choice of school from among public, private, and parochial schools.

Ever since the U.S. Supreme Court rendered its decision in the case of *Pierce v. Society of Sisters* in 1925, parents have had the choice of sending their children to private schools, at their own expense, of course.[2] Only in recent years, however, have some states reinforced this right by issuing vouchers for payment of tuition or allowing tax credits for families whose children are being educated in the private schools. Dissatisfied with the public schools, parents have made headway in gaining the right to choose their children's schools and, in so doing, receive financial support from their state and local governments.

Since 1985 Minnesota's School District Enrollment Options Program (Open Enrollment) has allowed parents to choose a public school or program outside the district in which they live. Minnesota further allows a deduction from parents' gross income for expenses incurred in sending their children to public, private, or parochial schools.

Wisconsin in 1990 became the first state to offer to pay parents in low-income brackets up to $2500 per pupil so that their children might attend Milwaukee private/nonsectarian schools. Wisconsin law offers vouchers to pupils in families with income at 1.75 times the established poverty level. In December 1990 the Bush administration created a Center for Choice in Education within the U.S. Department of Education; the center provided information about open enrollments in public schools throughout the country and about tax credits and voucher plans for private schools. By 1992 legislatures of twelve states had already passed legislation granting parents the right to choose the schools their children would attend. In Milwaukee some 6,000 low-income students in 1998 received vouchers in the amount of $4,900 to enable them to attend private or religious schools. Responding to the challenge of Milwaukee's voucher system the U.S. Supreme Court in the fall of 1998 sanctioned Wisconsin's law permitting the practice.

In 1993 New York City extended choice of schools to elementary and junior high schools students, a procedure already extended to high school students. In 1995 Berkeley, California divided its district into three zones and permitted choice of elementary school within a resident's zone. Plans cannot, of course, guarantee that parents and students will receive their first choice. Factors such as demand, facilities, and racial balance will determine whether choices can be honored.

---

[1]Gordon Cawelti, "Will Competition Accelerate School Reform?" *ASCD Curriculum Update* 33, no. 2 (February 1991): 2.
[2]*Pierce v. Society of Sisters*, 268 U.S. 510 (1925).

Advocates of voucher systems argue that provision of choice will in the long run strengthen the public schools by forcing them for economic reasons to overcome those problems that have provoked parental dissatisfaction. Some ambivalence on this issue is seen in comparing survey results to other indicators. For example, voucher systems have been rejected by the electorate in California, Colorado, and Pennsylvania. A plan to permit tax deductions for sending children to public or private schools in Oregon went down to defeat in 1990. The 23rd Annual Phi Delta Kappa/Gallup Poll of the Public's Attitudes Toward the Public Schools (1991) discovered that fifty percent of the public supported vouchers permitting children to attend public, private, or parochial school of their choice.[3] However, three years later the 26th Annual Poll found that fifty-four percent of the respondents opposed choice programs that would allow the government to pay all or part of nonpublic school tuition.[4] Although the National Education Association, the American Civil Liberties Union, and People for the American Way have opposed voucher systems, public sentiment has shifted in the direction of support for the use of vouchers. The 30th Annual Phi Delta Kappa/Gallup Poll (1998) revealed a majority of fifty-one percent of the public in favor of vouchers that pay all or part of a student's tuition at nonpublic schools, which is a reversal of the findings in 1996 when fifty-four percent of the public opposed.[5]

However, a year later when the 31st Annual Phi Delta Kappa/Gallup Poll of the Public's Attitudes Toward the Public Schools presented an either-or choice, the American public overwhelmingly (seventy percent) expressed a preference for improving existing public schools instead of providing vouchers for use in private and/or parochial schools.[6]

Cleveland, Ohio has awarded tax-funded vouchers for use in secular or religious private schools. The majority of Cleveland's students on vouchers have been enrolled in religious Protestant, Catholic, and Islamic schools, raising the issue of separation of church and state. In the spring of 1999 Florida with its Republican governor and legislative majority became the first state to enact a statewide voucher system. Governor Jeb Bush's "A-Plus" education reform called for grading of schools on an A–F system, issuance of vouchers to students in schools graded "F" two years out of four, assessment of achievement through statewide tests, higher teacher standards, and elimination of social promotion. Florida's vouchers, issued in the name of parents of eligible students, may be used at private, including religious, schools that meet certain requirements. In March 2000 a Florida circuit court judge ruled this voucher plan contrary to the Florida Constitution. At the time of writing of this text an appeal from the state is expected with the issue likely to go to the Florida Supreme Court. While governmental agencies and the public debated the wisdom of providing vouchers, in the spring of

---

[3]Stanley M. Elam, Lowell C. Rose, and Alec M. Gallup, "The 23rd Annual Gallup Poll of the Public's Attitudes Toward the Public Schools, *Phi Delta Kappan,* 73, no. 1 (September 1991): 47.

[4]Stanley M. Elam, Lowell C. Rose, and Alec M. Gallup, "The 26th Annual Phi Delta Kappa/Gallup Poll," *Phi Delta Kappan* 76, no. 1 (September 1994): 48–49.

[5]Lowell C. Rose and Alec M. Gallup, "The 30th Annual Phi Delta Kappa/Gallup Poll," *Phi Delta Kappan* 80, no. 1 (September 1998): 44.

[6]Lowell C. Rose and Alec M. Gallup, "The 31st Annual Phi Delta Kappa/Gallup Poll of the Public's Attitudes Toward the Public Schools," *Phi Delta Kappan* 81, no. 1 (September 1999): 44.

1999 the Children's Scholarship Fund, underwritten by Ted Forstmann and John Walton, awarded through lottery some 40,000 scholarships for use by low-income students in private or parochial schools.[7]

Pending a decision by the Sixth U.S. Circuit Court of Appeals on the constitutionality of the Cleveland voucher plan, the U.S. Supreme Court in November 1999 temporarily blocked a decision by the district court which would have prevented extension of Cleveland's voucher plan while the district court judge ruled on its constitutionality.

Ambivalence toward vouchers was also seen in deliberations of the U.S. House of Representatives which in late 1999 called for higher standards and accountability but rejected the provision of vouchers for use in private schools.

Parental choice, with or without vouchers or tax credits, faces strong opposition from public school administrators and teachers who are not anxious for competition among schools and who might face the loss of revenue-generating enrollments. Teachers unions in Puerto Rico, for example, called for a strike to protest legislation in 1993 authorizing grants of $1,500 per child (in grades two through twelve) for families earning $18,000 or less to permit parents to send students to a public or private school of their choice.

School personnel argue that parental choice of schools is not the answer to the social ills that impede learning. In fact, *School Choice*, a report of the Carnegie Foundation for the Advancement of Teaching, questions the purported benefits from school choice.[8]

Charter Schools.   Rapidly developing in the late 1990s and continuing into the 2000s is the growth of charter schools which adds another dimension to the issue of parental choice. Based on a free-market concept, charter schools, supported by tax moneys, are freed of some of the local school district's and the state's regulations. They may be housed within a school system or operated outside of the school system. They may or may not use public school personnel. They may be run for profit or without profit.

Minnesota is credited with establishing the first American charter school in 1991. Charter schools have grown exponentially since that date. Arizona, California, and Michigan have led the nation in the development of charter schools. U.S. Charter reported that as of 1998 thirty-two states, the District of Columbia, and Puerto Rico had passed legislation for the creation of charter schools.[9] The U.S. Department of Education found close to 1500 charter schools operating in 31 states and the District of Columbia serving over 250,000 students as of September 1999.[10] President Bill Clinton joined in support for a sharp increase in the number of charter schools throughout the country.

Charter schools gain their status through the issuing of a charter by the local school board or the state department of education. Teachers, laypeople, and organizations may apply for charters which will grant them "waivers exempting them from the

---

[7]See Children's Scholarship Fund web site: http://www.scholarshipfund.org.

[8]Carnegie Foundation for the Advancement of Teaching, *School Choice* (Princeton, N.J.: Carnegie Foundation for the Advancement of Teaching, 1993).

[9]U.S. Charter web site, http://www.uscharterschools.org, January 26, 1999.

[10]U.S. Department of Education, *The State of Charter Schools 2000—Fourth-Year Report, January 2000, Executive Summary,* Web site: http://www.ed.gov/pubs/charter4thyear/es.html, accessed March 4, 2000.

state education code, local school board policies, and provisions of the union contract,"[11] leaving in place provisions pertaining to disclosure of finances, health, safety, and civil rights.

States vary in their procedures for granting a charter. Michigan, for example, allows local school boards, boards of intermediate service districts, and boards of community and senior colleges and universities to grant charters.[12] Massachusetts permits businesses and museums to apply for charters in addition to teachers, parents, colleges and universities. Whereas charters in Massachusetts are issued by its state department of education, charters in Georgia must be approved by both the local school board and the state department of education.

Paralleling Britain's grant-maintained schools,[13] U.S. charter schools are supported by tax moneys. They put into practice principles of site-based management, placing responsibility for student success squarely on the shoulders of the schools' personnel. Unlike contractual schools managed by corporations with a profit motive, charter schools may be operated by either for-profit business organizations or by individuals or groups not for profit.

Charter schools come in all shapes and sizes. Some operate making use of school personnel although management rests in the hands of the founders of the school, not the local school board. Harrington-Lueker commented that "no single definition of a charter school applies."[14] Michigan sets no limit to the number of charter schools. California limits the number of charter schools in each school district with a state cap. Massachusetts and Colorado limit the number of charter schools in the state. California allows existing schools as well as new schools established by individuals and groups to apply for a charter. Fifty percent of the teachers at an existing school must favor a charter before it can be granted. California grants charters to home schools whereas Colorado does not. Arizona permits religious schools to hold a charter if their program is not sectarian. Legislation in Florida would prohibit charters to religious institutions. Charters may run from a minimum of three years in Minnesota to ninety-nine years in Michigan.

What of the programs of the charter schools? Examples of some of the charter schools in some of the states are traditional basic skills (Colorado), home schooling (California, Michigan), storefront program (Los Angeles), students-at-risk (Colorado, Los Angeles), deaf students (Minnesota), state wards (Massachusetts), gifted (Colorado), civic education (Massachusetts), home-school enabling communication with teachers and other students via computers (California), and "distance-learning" via computers for a rural home-school network (Michigan).

Some fifty-four percent of the public in 1994 felt positive about charter schools.[15] Supporters see charter schools as the means of reforming public education. Teachers unions object to the use of tax moneys for particular schools and to the creation of

[11]Donna Harrington-Lueker, "Charter Schools," *The American School Board Journal* 181, no. 9 (September 1994): 22.

[12]Donna Harrington-Lueker, "Charter 'Profit,'"*The American School Board Journal* 181, no. 9 (September 1994): 27–28.

[13]See Priscilla Wohlstetter and Lesley Anderson, "What Can U.S. Charter Schools Learn from England's Grant-Maintained Schools?" *Phi Delta Kappan* 75, no. 6 (February 1994): 486–491.

[14]Harrington-Lueker, *Charter Schools,* p. 25. Subsequent data on charter schools in various states from Harrington-Lueker, "Charter Schools," pp. 22–26 and "Charter Profit," pp. 27–28.

[15]Stanley M. Elam, Lowell C. Rose, and Alec M. Gallup, "The 26th Annual Phi Delta Kappa/Gallup Poll of the Public's Attitudes Toward the Public Schools," *Phi Delta Kappan* 76, no. 1 (September 1994): 53–54.

new bureaucracies. Financial support for the charter schools ordinarily is kept at the same level as other schools although Colorado limits support for its charter schools to eighty percent of the amount spent on its other schools.

Charter schools manifest the problems of church-state relations when public tax moneys flow to sectarian schools. Proponents of vouchers for religious schools argue that there is no inherent violation of the principle of separation of church and state inasmuch as the funds go to the student, not to the school.

Charter schools can contribute to racial and ethnic divisiveness when the charter schools enroll only members of a single ethnic group which emphasizes its own customs. Thomas Toch noted that the Sankofa School in Lansing, Michigan, for example, celebrates holidays like African Independence Day in place of such holidays as Thanksgiving and the 4th of July.[16]

Although some charter schools are established for students who are experiencing difficulty in the public schools, (e.g., those with learning diabilies, those at risk, and those demonstrating behavior problems), others possess the luxuries of selecting their students and rejecting those who cannot abide by the schools' rules and regulations pertaining to academics, conduct, and dress, luxuries not for the most part available to the public schools. Like public schools, generally, success of charter schools varies from school to school. We can find charter schools meeting parental expectations. We can find charter schools that have opened with fanfare and have folded for one reason or another, often financial. Parents do, however, appreciate the smaller classes of the charter schools and the relatively more secure environment. At the beginning of the twenty-first century the movements to voucher systems and charter schools remain strong.

The practice of rendering public support to private and parochial schools is often referred to as *privatization*. For an additional dimension of privatization see the section below on Educational Management Organizations.

Dissatisfaction with the public schools and the call for parental choice have led to the movement toward charter schools. Failure to fulfill expectations will result in non-renewal of charters. Existing public schools are attempting to counteract demands for charter schools by restructuring their programs, by working more closely with parents and community advisory groups, and by offering appealing in-system alternatives such as magnet schools, and, of course, by evaluating the success of charter schools. Further, they have themselves established charter-like schools, that is, schools that remain an integral part of the school system but have been granted a degree of autonomy by the school board.

In addition to charter *schools* we may see the concept of chartering applied to the school district level. Three county school systems in Florida, for example, in late 1999 secured dispensation from some state regulations in order to create pilot charter *districts*.

Home Schools.   A growing phenomenon that also discomforts public school personnel is the increasing popularity of home schooling as an alternative to public education. The Congressional Subcommittee on Oversight and Investigations of the Committee on Education and the Work Force in the United States estimated the number of

---

[16]Thomas Toch, "The New Education Bazaar," *U.S. News & World Report* 124, no. 16 (April 27, 1998): p. 46.

students being home schooled in 1998 at 1.5 million.[17] J. John Harris II and Richard E. Fields observed, "Alternative education of the 1960s and 1970s is still with us, but now its impact is being felt outside the public school classroom."[18] Whereas in earlier years public schools sought to provide alternative education under their supervision and control, home schools seek to provide alternative education outside of the control of public school administrators and faculty.

The education of children in the home dates back to the "dame" or "kitchen" schools of colonial days where parents or other educated adults would tutor individuals or instruct small groups in private homes. John Holt, one of the leading exponents of home schooling, has encouraged parents to take their children out of the public schools and provide for their education at home.[19] John Naisbitt perceived the rise in home schooling as part of a nationwide self-help movement in which community groups form to solve problems not only concerning education but also crime, distribution of food for the needy, and health. Naisbitt commented:

> Self-help is the blossoming of America's entrepreneurial movement, which rejects large corporations in favor of self-employment and small business. In the schools, it is increased parental activism along with questioning of the public school system—and in some cases the rejecting of it for private schools or (more radically) home education.[20]

Home schooling has threatened the time-honored tradition of compulsory education. In the early 1980s Mississippi was reportedly the only state in the nation that gave legal sanction to home schooling. Today, however, home schooling is permitted in all fifty states. One of the more serious blows against state compulsory attendance laws was the U.S. Supreme Court's decision in *Wisconsin v. Yoder,* the First Amendment religious liberty case in which the Supreme Court ruled that Amish parents could not be required to send their children to school beyond the eighth grade.[21] Florida's 1985 law permitting home schooling came about only after litigation by families charged with truancy. Requirements placed on home schools vary from state to state. Florida, for example requires home schools to register with the school district and to use standardized tests of student achievement.

J. Gary Knowles observed that advocates of home school may be found among conservatives on the right and liberals on the left.[22] The same disillusionment with the public schools that led parents to established private and parochial schools has also led to the increase in home education. Parents may choose home schooling for their chil-

---

[17]Subcommitte on Oversight and Investigations of the Committee on Education and the Work Force in the United States, *Education at a Crossroads: What Works and What's Wanted Today* (Washington, D.C.: U.S. Government Printing Office, 1998), p. 41.

[18]J. John Harris III and Richard E. Fields, "Outlaw Generation: A Legal Analysis of the Home-Instruction Movement," *Educational Horizons* 61, no. 1 (Fall 1982), p. 31.

[19]John Holt, *Teach Your Own: A Hopeful Path for Education* (New York: Delacorte Press/Seymour Lawrence, 1981). See also John Holt, *How Children Fail* (New York: Dell, 1964).

[20]John Naisbitt, *Megatrends: Ten New Directions Transforming Our Lives* (New York: Warner Books, 1982), p. 133. Reprinted with permission.

[21]*Wisconsin v. Yoder,* 406 U.S. 205 (1972).

[22]J. Gary Knowles, ed., "Understanding Home Schools Emerging Research and Reactions," *Education and Urban Society* 21, no. 1 (November 1988): 3–113.

dren because they are dissatisfied with, among other factors, the secular orientation of the public schools, poor academic achievement, lack of safety in the schools, drug use among students, lack of discipline, large classes, "assembly-line" teaching, and the forced socialization of their children with others whom they deem undesirable.

The statistics of home schooling are imprecise and difficult to obtain, in part because of the nebulous definition of home school. In some cases, a home school consists of parents instructing only their own children in their own home. In other cases groups of parents band together to form a school for their children in someone's home, in their church, or at another location. Out of some 40 million students, 1.5 million may not seem to be a significant figure. However, because most of the children schooled at home are under the age of twelve, it would be more accurate to compare the figures for home schooling to the figure of 29 million elementary school children. The spread of these schools has been rapid since the 1970s when estimates ranged from 10,000 students to 10,000 families with children in home schooling.[23] In 1990 Campbell reported about 5,000 households registered as home schools in Florida and noted that some 1,000 families per year have taken the home-school option since 1985 when Florida legalized home schooling.[24]

Restrictions on home schools vary from state to state. Iowa, Michigan, and North Dakota require home-school instructors to be certified teachers.[25] Some states require home schools to obtain approval of their curricula and to accept varying degrees of monitoring by the boards of education of their local school districts. For example, home-school instructors may have to furnish to the local school board copies of their curriculum materials, lists of textbooks, information on number of days and hours of instruction, attendance data, and test results. Some groups of home schoolers have bypassed local school districts by conducting their programs under the aegis of an established private school.

Advocates of home schools will most likely continue to challenge both the constitutionality of compulsory attendance laws per se and the state restrictions on home schooling. The U.S. Congress took note of the popularity of homeschooling by exempting home schools from provisions of the 1994 reauthorization of the Elementary and Secondary Education Act concerning the licensing of home-school teachers.

Speaking of the various forms of alternative education, David S. Hurst observed:

> Like it or not, the ultimate adoption of some of these alternatives appears inevitable. . . . Schools in the United States will not become victims of any single alternative to traditional structures; instead we will wind up with levels of alternatives, ranging from our most traditional schools today to avant-garde institutions on the fringes of society.[26]

Success of pupils in home schooling is difficult to measure. Monitoring of home schooling is spotty. Results vary from school to school. The Subcommittee on Over-

---

[23]Gregory J. Cizek, "Applying Standardized Testing to Home-Based Education Programs: Reasonable or Customary?" *Educational Measurement Issues and Practice* 7, no. 5 (Fall 1988), p. 13; Naisbitt, p. 144.

[24]Ramsey Campbell, "Home Schooling: The Quiet Revolution in Education," *The Orlando Sentinel* (June 3, 1990), p. A-1.

[25]Sarah Banks Zakariya, "Home Schooling Litigation Tests State Compulsory Education Laws," *The American School Board Journal* 175, no. 5 (May 1988), p. 45.

[26]David S. Hurst, "We Cannot Ignore the Alternatives," *Educational Leadership* 52, no. 1 (September 1994): 78.

sight claimed that students in home schools were doing well, citing ACT scores of the 1997 graduating class who posted an average of 22.5 (out of a possible 36) as opposed to the national average of 21.[27] Although secular public schools can never satisfy those who prefer a sectarian education, renewed academic excellence in the public schools—a result of restructuring and reform—may make the public school more attractive to some of those now involved in home schooling.[28]

BILINGUAL EDUCATION

As ethnic groups whose first language is other than English grow in size and power, more and more curriculum workers find themselves charged with the task of developing bilingual education programs. In 1967 Amendments to the Elementary and Secondary Education Act, the U.S. Congress provided support for bilingual education programs. Although bilingual education programs are offered in more than seventy languages and dialects, the largest number of students in bilingual programs are Hispanic.

Second-language instruction is not limited to the most widely spoken languages. As a result of state legislation requiring second-language studies in the public schools, some children of Native Americans in Oklahoma starting in 1993–94 were learning Cherokee, Chickasaw, Choctaw, Creek, and Seminole languages.

The U.S. Supreme Court's decision in the *Lau v. Nichols* case in 1974, which required San Francisco to provide English language instruction for the Chinese-speaking students, advanced the cause of bilingual education. The efforts of Hispanic groups (Hispanics, predicted to become the largest minority within a decade, now number about nine percent of the U.S. population) have largely brought about the current emphasis on bilingual (and, in addition, bicultural) education.

Bilingual education is an educational, linguistic, social, cultural, political, and economic issue. As such, it has become highlycontroversial.[29] Dade County (Florida) provides an example of continuing public discord over this issue. In April 1973, after a large number of Spanish-speaking refugees had immigrated from Cuba, Dade County was declared a bilingual community. Many "Anglos" took issue with the designation of the county as bilingual. This sentiment came to a head in 1980 when county voters approved an ordinance prohibiting the conduct of government business in any language other than English except in the cases of emergencies and elections. Thirteen years later with almost fifty percent of the population of Dade County Hispanic and with more than fifty percent speaking languages other than Engish the Dade County Commission repealed the English-only ordinance. In 1994 the Third District Court of Appeals rejected a challenge to the authority of the county commission to repeal the English-only ordinance and upheld the commission's right to do so.

The English only/Spanish only argument flared again the summer of 1999 in Texas. With most of its population speaking Spanish, the small town of El Cenizo at-

---

[27]Subcommittee on Oversight, *Education at a Crossroads*, p. 41.

[28]For a thoughtful analysis of educational choice, vouchers, and home schooling see Myron Lieberman, *Privatization and Educational Choice* (New York: St. Martin's Press, 1989).

[29]For pros and cons of bilingual education see Rudolph C. Troike, "Bilingual-Si!" *Principal* 62, no. 3 (January 1983): 46–50 and Muriel Paskin Carrison, "Bilingual-No!" *Principal* 62, no. 3 (January 1983): 41–44.

tracted attention and controversy by passing an ordinance to conduct local government business in Spanish, with provision for translation in English.

English-only legislation at the state level has met with mixed results. In the spring of 1990, Alabama voters overwhelmingly adopted an amendment to their state constitution recognizing English as the official language of their state government. In the spring of 1991 Puerto Rico passed a law that designated Spanish as the only official language of the commonwealth, rescinding a 1902 law that had designated both Spanish and English as official languages. In 1995 Puerto Rico passed and the governor signed the English-also law declaring both English and Spanish as official languages. The language issue has heated up periodically in Puerto Rico. One of the reasons for Puerto Ricans rejecting statehood has been the effort of some members of the U.S. Congress to make English the official language if Puerto Rico becomes a state and of some governing officials of Puerto Rico itself who recommended adoption of English-language textbooks in some subjects in Puerto Rican schools in order to develop bilingual skills.

In the 1980s Arizona, California, and Florida amended their constitutions making English the states' official language. Arizona and California provide cases that demonstrate the divisiveness of the issue. Arizona adopted its constitutional amendment in 1998. Eight years later the federal district court declared the law unconstitutional. An advocacy group, Arizonans for Official English, appealed the district court decision. The Ninth Circuit Court of Appeals upheld the decision of the federal district court. The case worked its way to the Arizona Supreme Court that in 1997 agreed with the district and appeals courts that the law was unconstitutional. In 1998 the U.S. Supreme Court reaffirmed the decision of the Arizona Supreme Court.

Since the late 1960s California with its polyglot population has offered programs of bilingual education in its schools. In June of 1998 California voters overwhelmingly endorsed Proposition 227 that scuttled bilingual education and in its place mandated an English-language immersion program for students of limited language ability. Although some school districts have threatened not to abide by the law, a federal judge ruled that the law did not violate the rights of minorities. Proposition 227 left some wiggle-room for schools to offer English-language instruction part of the time and for parents through waivers to continue their children in bilingual education programs. Although bilingual education is championed by language minorities, many members of minority groups supported the banning of bilingual education programs because they perceived fluency in English as essential for career oportunities for their children.

Some twenty-five states from as far back as 1811 and as recently as 1998 have passed a law or constitutional amendment that designates English as the official language of their state governments.[30] Hawaii has designated both English and Hawaiian as official languages of the state and teaches both English and Hawaiian in its schools.

The controversy over bilingual education brings into sharp focus the opposing philosophies of acculturation versus pluralism.[31] The resurgence of the melting-pot

---

[30]See U.S. English web site http://www.us-english.org/states.htm for map that clearly shows states that have official English laws.

[31]Promoting the cause of bilingual education is the National Association for Bilingual Education, 1220 L St., N.W., Suite 605, Washington, D.C. 20005–4018. Promoting the cause of English as the official language of the United States is U.S. English, 818 Connecticut Ave., N.W., Suite 200, Washington, D.C. 20006. The Center for Equal Opportunity, 815 15th Street, Suite 928, Washington, D.C. 20005 opposes both bilingual education and affirmative action.

concept, with its emphasis on blending has challenged the salad-bowl concept of pluralism. Proposals from both Democrats and Republicans to establish English as the official language of the federal government have surfaced in both the Senate and the House of Representatives. In 1990 the House Judiciary Committee referred to a subcommittee a recurring proposal for an amendment to the U.S. Constitution that would make English the official language of the government.

Those who support making English the official language note that throughout our nation's history immigrants have learned English. Proponents of bilingual education, however, believe that curtailment of bilingual education and designation of English as the official language is discriminatory. They maintain that an English-only instructional approach impedes the learning of children who are not native speakers of English. Critics, on the other hand, argue that bilingual education segregates students, exascerbates problems posed by diversity, and has proved ineffective.

Results of Proposition 227 at the end of its first year have proved inconclusive. Test data, though not conclusive, provided some indications of improvement. Responding to Proposition 227 Oceanside, California ceased all non-English instruction. Oceanside reported in the summer of 1999 that its English-immersion program resulted in significant improvement by non-English-speaking students in English and other subjects. The administration and interpretation of the data have been challenged.

Compounding the problem, beginning in the school year 1997-98 California required students to take statewide tests which some people declared unfair to limited-English-speaking students. The mandate has met strong opposition with San Francisco's school district, for example, refusing to administer the test to limited-English-speaking students. The President's Advisory Commisison on Educational Excellence for Hispanic Americans in the fall of 1999 voiced opposition to English-only tests.

Curriculum planners as well as the public are also divided as to the exact definitions of "bilingual" and "bicultural." To some, bilingual education may simply mean setting up English classes for students who are not native speakers of English. Others often extend bilingual education to include additional dimensions, including teaching courses in the native language. In describing a proposal for bilingual education that was introduced in the U.S. Senate in 1967 by Ralph Yarborough from Texas, Francesco Cordasco made clear the multifaceted scope of the Bilingual Education Act:

> At long last the Congress had before it legislation which would legitimize the cultivation of individual differences in our schools.
>
> The bill recognized that Mexican-American children had been neglected by American schools. It proposed 1) bilingual education programs; 2) the teaching of Spanish as the native language; 3) the teaching of English as the second language; 4) programs designed to impart to Spanish-speaking students a knowledge of and pride in their ancestral culture and language; 5) efforts to attract and retain as teachers promising individuals of Mexican or Puerto Rican descent; and 6) efforts to establish closer cooperation between the school and the home.[32]

The Bilingual Education Act passed in 1968 and renewed several times since has provided federal funding for programs for students whose native language is

---

[32]Francesco Corasco, "The Bilingual Education Act," *Phi Delta Kappan* 52, no. 2 (October 1969): 75. Reprinted with permission.

other than English. Educators are in disagreement as to whether programs designed to promote mastery of English should allow for instruction of students in their native language until they achieve English language skills or should immerse students in English from the start. The U.S. Department of Education has usually required schools that wished to receive bilingual education funds to provide instruction in the native language. When the U.S. Department of Education sought to force Fairfax County, Virginia, to offer instruction to all students in their native language, Fairfax County brought suit on the grounds that its program of intensive English for speakers of other languages was successful as shown by their test scores. In late 1980, the U.S. Department of Education, on the strength of the success of Fairfax County students decided not to force Fairfax County to provide instruction in the native language.

The U.S. House of Representatives has jumped into the fray on more than one occasion since passage of the 1968 Bilingual Education Act, as, for examples, its proposals for an English-Language Empowerment Act (1996) and its English Language Fluency Act (1998) that would offer funding to the states in the form of block grants and set a maximum of three years for student participation in federally-funded bilingual education programs. The scope of the language problem is seen in the fact that some 32 million residents speak a language other than English in their homes. However, the 25th Annual Phi Delta Kappa/Gallup Poll of the Public's Attitudes Toward the Public Schools found that only twenty-seven percent of those surveyed believed that the public schools should provide instruction in the students' native languages while they were learning English; seventy-one percent felt students should learn English either before enrolling in public schools (twenty-five percent) or in the public schools (forty-six percent) *before* receiving instruction in other subjects.[33]

An early term for an instructional program known as "English as a second language" has encountered strong objections on the part of champions of English who misinterpret the term to imply relegating English to second place. "English for Speakers of Other Languages," referred to as ESOL, has reduced the misunderstanding.

William J. Bennett, former U.S. Secretary of Education, took note of the needs of children whose first language is other than English. He commented, however, that English-language proficiency is "crucial to social and economic achievement in America."[34] He took the position that schools should be free to adopt whatever methods they wish and need in order to achieve the goal of English-language literacy.[35]

Holding that bilingual education should not be controversial, Secretary of Educatino Richard Riley in March 2000 proposed increasing dual-language schools to 1,000 in number.[36] Bilingual education, however, remains a sensitive and controversial issue. Related issues of racial/ethnic integration and cultural diversity are discussed later in this chapter.

[33]Elam et al., "The 25th Annual Phi Delta Kappa/Gallup Poll," p. 146.

[34]William J. Bennett, *Our Children and Our Country: Improving America's Schools and Affirming the Common Culture* (New York: Simon and Schuster, 1988), p. 187.

[35]Ibid., pp. 186–187.

[36]Web site http://www.ed.gov/Speeches/03-2000/000315.html, accessed March 15, 2000. For reports on bilingual education and language policy see Language Policy Web Site and Emporium, http://ourworld.compuserve.com/homepages/JWCRAWFORD and "The Debate Over English Only" at the National Education Association web site, http://www.nea.org/society/engonly.html.

CENSORSHIP

Schools in many communities throughout the United States find themselves enmeshed in a seemingly endless struggle with individuals and groups in the community who seek to censor textbooks and library books and to prohibit certain types of instruction or, conversely, to promote certain types of instruction. Attempts to remove library books, textbooks, and other teaching materials from the schools are frequent and widespread. Dissension over this issue and over religion, as we shall see again later in this chapter, stem from differing interpretations of the First Amendment to the U.S. Constitution which says:

> Congress shall make no law respecting an establishment of religion, or prohibiting the free exercise thereof; or abridging the freedom of speech, or of the press; or the right of the people peaceably to assemble, and to petition the government for a redress of grievances.

The Office of Intellectual Freedom of the American Library Association (ALA) listed 164 books challenged, that is requests to ban books, most of which were not successful attempts, or banned between March 1994 and March 1995.[37] The ALA counted close to 600 challenges in 1997.[38] People for the American Way recorded 458 challenges to curriculum materials in 1994–95. A near-record 338 of these challenges consisted of attempts to remove or restrict materials. Fifty percent of these censorship attempts were reported as successful.[39] A year later the count was down slightly to a still high 300.[40] Edward B. Jenkinson in an earlier study observed that estimates of unreported incidents range from twenty-five to fifty per reported incident.[41]

Protest over schoolbooks has been a big problem in some communities. One of the more publicized and heated controversies over textbooks took place in 1974 in Kanawha County, West Virginia.[42] The conflict over a list of 325 English/language arts textbooks recommended by a committee of teachers resulted in violence, closing of schools, workers staying away from their jobs in the mines in support of the protesters, attacks on the books by ministers of some of the churches, and the resignation of the superintendent of schools. Though the books were ultimately permitted in the classroom, a set of guidelines was drawn up that required the establishment of teacher-parent committees to screen books to be adopted and retained by the school system.

---

[37]American Library Association, *Books Challenged or Banned in 1994–95* (Chicago: Office of Intellectual Freedom, American Library Association, 1995. See also Fact Sheet, (Chicago: Public Information Office, American Library Association, June 1995).

[38]American Library Association Web site, http://www.ala.org, accessed February 1, 1999. The American Library Association compiles an annual list of the most frequently challenged books and sponsors an annual Banned Books Week in the fall.

[39]People for the American Way, *Attacks on the Freedom to Learn* (Washington, D.C.: People for the American Way, 1995).

[40]People for the American Way web site, http://www.pfaw.org, accessed February 1, 1999.

[41]Edward B. Jenkinson, *The Schoolbook Protest Movement: 40 Questions and Answers* (Bloomington, Ind.: Phi Delta Kappa, 1986), p. 16.

[42]Franklin Parker, *The Battle of the Books: Kanawha County* (Bloomington, Ind.: Phi Delta Kappa Educational Foundation, 1975). See also James C. Hefley, *Textbooks on Trial* (Wheaton, Ill.: Victor Books, 1976); Edward B. Jenkinson, *Censors in the Classroom: The Mind Benders* (Carbondale, Ill.: Southern Illinois University Press, 1979), Chapter 2; and articles in *Principal* 61, no. 3 (January 1982): 4–36.

Schoolbook protestors have made their appearance in communities from one end of the United States to the other.[43] Jenkinson made a conservative estimate of 200 as the number of local, state, and national organizations that protest schoolbooks.[44] There is no reason to believe there are fewer such organizations today. Protests against certain schoolbooks include charges that they

- portray too much sex or violence
- use profanity
- use poor English
- promote "secular humanism," are irreligious, anti- Christian
- are un-American, lacking in patriotism
- promote one-worldism and globalization
- are racist
- depict the "wrong" values
- teach the theory of evolution instead of scientific creationism
- are too graphic

Efforts to censor topics of public discussion, reading matter, films, tapes, drama, television, and art works recur in the schools—and in society at large—with great frequency, testing First Amendment rights to free speech and press. In recent years, charges of obscenity, for example, have produced vigorous challenges to art exhibitions, novels, films, and lyrics to musical compositions. Michelangelo's *David* would have been banned in 1996 from a Florida school that covered a statute of a nude man, created by an art student, and placed in a school lobby.

The definition of obscenity has proved to be elusive. The U.S. Supreme Court has let local communities determine what printed and visual matter violates their community standards and possesses "no redeeming value." Many people consider the sufficient standard to be U.S. Supreme Court Justice Potter Stewart's famous statement about obscenity, "I know it when I see it."

Schools have both engaged in self-censorship and responded to pressures for censorship from outside forces. A sampling of targets of those who protest their use reveals a wide range. Some of the works attacked in various parts of the country between 1990 and 1998 (not necessarily the first time they were targeted) and the purported reasons claimed by those objecting were:

Little Red Riding Hood, violence (1990–91)
My Friend Flicka by Mary O'Hara, certain words (1990–91)
Snow White, violence (1992)
The Dead Zone and *The Tommyknockers* by Stephen King, rape and language (1992)
Daddy's Roommate by Michael Willhoite, homosexuality (1992)
A Light in the Attic, by Shel Silverstein, manipulation of parents by children (1993)
The Autobiography of Malcolm X, antiwhite, pro-Islam (1994)
Peter Pan, portrayal of Native Americans (1994)
Roselily by Alice Walker, antireligious and *Am I Blue?* antimeat-eating (1994)

---

[43]Jenkinson, *Schoolbook Protest,* pp. 43–46.
[44]Ibid., p. 70.

An American Childhood by Anne Dillard, violent snowball fight (1994)
Tex by S.E. Hinton, language (1995)
The Light in the Forest by Conrad Richter, too graphic (1996)
It's Perfectly Normal by Robie Harris, sex education (1997)
Beloved by Toni Morrison, racial content (1998)

Frequent candidates for banning are J. D. Salinger's *Catcher in the Rye* and Mark Twain's *The Adventures of Huckleberry Finn;* John Steinbeck's *The Grapes of Wrath* and *Of Mice and Men;* Maya Angelou's *I Know Why the Caged Bird Sings;* Katherine Paterson's *A Bridge to Terebithia;* Judy Blume's *Forever;* Maurice Sendak's *In the Night Kitchen.* Hans Christian Anderson's *The Little Mermaid,* and the Grimm brothers' *Fairy Tales* appear on some lists. Richard Wright's *Black Boy* and *Native Son* have both evoked challenges.

Books dealing with racial themes whether written by a white author (Twain) or black (Morrison, Wright) can provoke controversy.

Efforts have been made to remove or revise textbooks in the field of health because of material on sexuality education and in historical treatments of Columbus' discovery of the New World and contributions of European Western civilization. You will note that efforts to censor materials comes from both the right (*My Friend Flicka, Catcher in the Rye*) and the left (*Peter Pan, Huckleberry Finn*). That school boards readily respond to many attacks of books affirms the fact that school administrators and boards are extremely sensitive to criticism and public pressure. In 1998, for example, a third-grade teacher in Brooklyn, New York was threatened by a parent and temporarily removed from her classroom for using the book *Nappy Hair* by black author Carolivia Herron on the grounds that the book was racially insensitive.

Any work dealing with homosexuality stirs considerable protests as in the case of Michael Willhoite's *Daddy's Roommate.* In 1998 efforts were made to revoke a California fifth-grade teacher's license because she had permitted a discussion of the episode on the television show *Ellen* in which Ellen admitted that she was gay. The formation of the Gay-Straight Alliance in a Salt Lake City high school in 1996 resulted in the school board's banning of all clubs except those related to academics. Shortly after the school board's action the Utah state legislature passed a law barring gay student clubs in Utah high schools.

The teaching of values has come under attack by protesters who hold that some of the schoolbooks undermine traditional American values. Protesters have taken special exception to the book *Values Clarification,* ostensibly because the program that it proposes allows students to express their own views on personal problems.[45]

The teaching of the Darwinian theory of the evolution of humankind has long been a cause of concern to the scientific creationists, who champion the biblical account of creation in *Genesis.* The Scopes trial in Tennessee in the 1920s reflected the sentiments of the creationists.[46] In 1968 in the case of *Epperson v. Arkansas* the U.S.

---

[45]Sidney B. Simon, Leland W. Howe, and Howard Kirschenbaum, *Values Clarification* (New York: Hart, 1972). For a grammarian's criticism of values clarification, see Richard Mitchell. *Less than Words Can Say* (Boston: Little, Brown, 1979), pp. 79–95.

[46]See p.78 of this text.

Supreme Court ruled that the theory of evolution may be taught;[47] however, challenges have continued up to the present and may be anticipated in the future.

Examples of the evolution versus creationism dispute are not difficult to find. In 1982 the federal district court holding that scientific creationism was a religious doctrine, struck down an Alabama statute that would have required instruction in scientific creationism in addition to the theory of evolution. In June 1987 the U.S. Supreme Court ruled unconstitutional Louisiana's Balanced Treatment for Creation Science and Evolution Science Act of 1981, which would have required that scientific creationism be given equal instructional time with the theory of evolution. In 1982 Arkansas' attempt to introduce Creationism into the curriculum met with rejection by the courts on the grounds that the law promoted religion and was, therefore, unconstitutional. In October 1990, more than twenty years after Epperson, the Texas Education Agency's approval of state-adopted textbooks that taught the theory of evolution made national news. Sentiment for teaching scientific creationism either in place of or in addition to evolution theory remains strong as evidenced in 1999, for example, in Kansas.

Scarcely five months before the start of the millenium, in the summer of 1999, Kansas joined the opponents of evolution. The powerful State Board of Education by a 6-4 vote banned the treatment of evolution as a scientific principle (i.e., humankind descended from the apes) in science classes, a decision provoking strong criticism from educators, legislators, and the governor. The Board permitted continuation of study of evolution but rejected it as a requirement or as an item on state-approved tests. On the other hand, in October 1999 the New Mexico State Board of Education barred the study of Creationism in the public school science curriculum while retaining the study of the theory of evolution. Illinois lent yet another dimension to the issue when also in October 1999 its state Board of Education eliminated the word "evolution" from its state standards, using the expression "change in time."

Often, protests over schoolbooks are not intended to force the schools to eliminate certain material but to adopt textbooks that incorporate particular topics, such as scientific creationism. Although the Supreme Court has ruled that reading the Bible and prayers for devotional purposes in the school are unconstitutional, many groups are still attempting to reintroduce or introduce these sectarian practices into the public schools' curriculum.

Of concern to teachers, administrators, and curriculum workers is the judicial decision rendered in Tennessee in the fall of 1986. In 1983 the Hawkins County schools adopted the widely used Holt, Rinehart and Winston Basic Reader Series for kindergarten through eighth grade. Christian fundamentalist families objected to the readers on the grounds that the books violated their religious beliefs and that, by requiring their children to read these books, the schools deprived them of their First Amendment rights. They demanded that their children be allowed to use alternative textbooks, which the school board permitted for a brief period of time. However, the board soon disallowed this practice and resumed requiring the adopted textbooks.

When parents forbade their children to attend classes that used the controversial textbooks, school officials suspended the children. Seven families of Church Hill, Tennessee, though they did not seek complete removal of the readers from the schools, did

---

[47]*Epperson v. Arkansas*, 393 U.S. 97 (1968).

file suit demanding the right for their own children to use alternative textbooks. Tried in July 1986, the case attracted as much or more attention than the famous Scopes trial.

On October 24, 1986, U.S. District Judge Thomas G. Hull found for the plaintiffs, ruling that the school board could not force children to use textbooks that went against their religious beliefs and that the school board had violated the parents' rights to freedom of religion. By the same token the judge declared that the children had a right to a public education and that the school district must permit them to use alternative textbooks. He placed responsibility for finding the alternative texts on the parents. In addition, the judge ruled that the families could seek monetary damages from the school board for the violation of their rights. In December 1986 the judge awarded the parents more than $50,000, which included the cost of tuition for their children at private school.

Some saw in the Tennessee decision potential disaster for the public schools if other sects demanded textbooks of their own choosing and insisted that their children be permitted to opt out of instruction when textbooks that they found objectionable were used. Others felt that, in actuality, few parents would object to the use of local- and state-adopted textbooks. However, the Hawkins County school board appealed the decision to the Sixth U.S. Circuit Court of Appeals. In August 1987 the Circuit Court of Appeals ruled that the First Amendment rights of the family had not been violated by the school system. In February 1988 the U.S. Supreme Court refused to hear the case, letting the appellate court's decision stand.

The Tennessee case is not an isolated episode; while the district judge was making his ruling in Tennessee, parents in Alabama were suing the Alabama board of education for the removal of state-adopted textbooks in social studies, history, and home economics because of the books' purported liberal bias toward "secular humanism." On March 4, 1987, U.S. District Court Judge W. Brevard Hand (the same judge who in *Wallace v. Jaffree* upheld the Alabama statute providing for silent meditation or prayer) banned more than forty textbooks from use as primary textbooks or primary sources in elementary and secondary schools of Alabama. Thirteen days later Judge Hand modified his order and allowed use of portions of the home economics books and use of the history and social studies books if they were appropriately supplemented. In August 1987 the Eleventh U.S. Circuit Court of Appeals reversed Judge Hands' ruling.

Underlying some of the protests over textbooks is the perennial conflict of differing secular and religious values in a pluralistic society and the interpretation of the Jeffersonian doctrine of separation of church and state, an issue explored later in this chapter.

First amendment cases have cropped up in the arena of student expression. Schools, establishing dress codes, have sought to ban T-shirts which they deemed to carry offensive, vulgar, profane, or lewd language. Two teenagers in Massachusetts, for example, challenged as unconstitutional the school's decision in 1994 to ban their T-shirts that read, "Coed Naked: Do It In Rythmn." That same year a high school girl brought suit against the Los Angeles school board on First Amendment grounds for preventing her from wearing in school packaged condoms attached to her clothes as a means of advocating safe sex practices. In the face of a possible lawsuit, the Roswell, New Mexico school board in the fall of 1999 rescinded a decision banning student display of pentagrams, a symbol of the Wiccan religion.

The student press has run afoul of internal censorship by school administrators who frequently or regularly review and restrict student articles, stories, and photographs prior to publication. Administrators tend to expunge materials that are critical of the school, appear racist, offensive, or obscene.

The U.S. Supreme Court in a 5-3 decision in *Hazelwood v. Kuhlmeier* (1988) affirmed school officials' authority to censor student publications. Reversing an appellate court decision, the Supreme Court ruled that school officials may exercise prior review and restraint of student publications if such action serves any valid educational purpose.[48] *Hazelwood* erupted in 1983 when the principal of a high school suppressed articles in the school newspaper on student pregnancy and divorce. The Supreme Court decision permits administrators to censor various forms of student expression, although nondisruptive expression as determined in *Tinker v. Des Moines Independent Community School District* (1969) still stands. In the latter case the Supreme Court ruled that students had the right to protest the Vietnam War by wearing black armbands.[49]

Hazelwood, in effect, permits censoring of articles that may reflect unfavorably on the school, as in the case of articles on religion, sex, drugs, alcohol, even partisan political statements. Administrators have chastised teachers directing class writing projects and those serving as sponsors of student newspapers and yearbooks when they have allowed text and photographs to be printed that officials felt objectionable. Although administrative decisions to censor student publications are not frequently challenged, especially in the light of *Hazelwood*, that was not the case in New Jersey in 1993 when a state court of appeals held that a junior high school should not have refused to print in the school newspaper a student's reviews of *Rain Man* and *Mississippi Burning* which the principal felt would encourage underage children to go see the movies.

Ironically, directing attention to works considered by some as undesirable often has the opposite effect from that desired, stimulating curiosity and increasing interest in the banned works, especially on the part of those who wish to make their own decisions about a work.

To respond to various social and political pressures, curriculum planners need not only professional knowledge and skills but also skills in public relations and working with community groups. When dealing with controversial issues in the curriculum, they should have channels through which they may determine the seriousness of problems, the strength of community feelings, and the ways in which issues might be resolved before they become magnified and disproportionate. They need established procedures by which parents can register objections to materials and at the same time secure broad-based review of those objections. Some objections may prove valid, necessitating removal of the materials; some may prove valid at certain levels; some may prove invalid. Community mores, state and national law, national educational needs, learners' maturity level, and children's right to learn must all be taken into consideration when making decisions on suppressing or, conversely, including, materials. School officials must avoid the extremes of everything goes on one hand and nothing controversial may be published on the other hand.[50]

---

[48]*Hazelwood School District v. Kuhlmeier*, No. 86–836 (1994).
[49]*Tinker v. Des Moines Independent Community School District*, 393 (U.S. 503), 89 Sup. Ct. 733 (1969).
[50]For an additional source on censorship see National Coalition Against Censorship web site, http://www.ncac.org.

COMMUNITY SERVICE

A relatively new curricular development is the movement toward unpaid community service as a requirement for high school graduation. The National Service-Learning Clearinghouse quoted the definition of service learning as set forth in the National and Community Service Trust Act of 1993:

> Service-learning is a method whereby students learn and develop through active participation in thoughtfully organized service that is conducted in and meets the needs of communities.[51]

Service to the community, a concept promoted by the Carnegie Foundation for the Advancement of Teaching as "The New Carnegie Unit," has gained in popularity throughout the nation's schools. A Carnegie study in 1987 reported youth service as becoming a trend in our schools.[52] The study found that, out of 1,000 public schools responding to its survey, seventy percent offered community service programs, and twenty percent of these schools had made community service a requirement.

Maryland requires community service of all its public school graduates. Atlanta, Detroit, and Washington, D.C. provide examples of this trend in the secondary school curriculum. The Atlanta public schools offer a course, "Duties to the Community," that requires students to perform seventy-five hours of unpaid volunteer work and to write a follow-up report on their experiences. Through this service students can earn half a credit toward graduation. The Detroit public schools provide ten hours of credit toward graduation for "Outside of Class Learning Experiences," which requires each pupil to work 200 clock hours of paid or voluntary service. Banneker High School, a magnet school in Washington, D.C. requires completion of a community laboratory project. During all four years students spend one afternoon a week performing voluntary service. For this experience they earn one and a half units of credit.

Community service requirements continued to blossom through the mid-1990s. Bishop Moore High School, a Catholic school in Orlando, Florida, requires freshmen to complete ten hours of community service; sophomores, twenty hours; juniors, thirty hours; and seniors, forty hours. The state of Florida has created a voluntary system offering a half unit of social studies and a half unit elective for seventy-five hours of community service. Since 1998 students who wish to participate in the Florida Academic Scholars Program which subsidizes education at a Florida college or university fulfill seventy-five hours of community service. The National Center for Education Statistics reported forty-nine percent of students in grades six through twelve in 1996 participated in some form of regular or occasional community service.[53]

Proponents of community service believe this feature of the curriculum allows students to connect with the community, to learn altruism, and to make use of the community as an educational resource. In keeping with society's demands for high school graduates who can demonstrate civic competence, programs that enable students to

---

[51]National Service-Learning Clearinghouse, http://www.nicsdl.coled.umn.edu, accessed February 6, 1999.

[52]Charles H. Harris, *Student Service: The New Carnegie Unit* (Princeton, N.J.: The Carnegie Foundation for the Advancement of Teaching, 1987).

[53]National Center for Education Statistics, *The Condition of Education, 1998* (Washington, D.C.: U.S Department of Education, Office of Educational Research and Improvement, 1998), p. 86.

serve the community can help them develop positive social attitudes. At the same time, students can acquire interpersonal skills and vocational skills that can lead to a career. Seventy percent of the American public is ready for instituting a community service requirement for graduation from the public schools.[54]

Community service can be of positive educational value to the student not only in the form of knowledge to be gained outside the classroom but also in the development of character and of the individual's sense of responsibility for improving his or her community. At the same time the community benefits by having some of its service needs fulfilled, what we might call a win-win situation.

It is, perhaps, a tautology, however, to speak of required community service as voluntary. Critics of the community service requirement for school youth are quick to point out this inconsistency. Although they may or may not agree with community service programs that are voluntary, critics distinguish between volunteerism, an activity publicly championed by retired General Colin Powell, and mandatory requirements for graduation from either school or college.

Opponents see required and unpaid community service as involuntary servitude. As is the case with many curricular provisions the requirement of community service has landed in the courts. Students challenged the requirement of sixty hours of community service, instituted in 1990 by the Bethlehem, Pennsylvania school board, on the grounds that work without pay violated the Thirteenth Amendment and amounted to slavery. The federal court of appeals, however, in 1993 disagreed and supported the school board. The following year the U.S. District Court had before it a complaint against the requirement of forty hours of community service set in 1992 by the Rye Neck High School, New York, averring that the requirement violated the antislavery provisions of the Thirteenth Amendment and the due process clauses of the Fourteenth Amendment. Those who object to required community service programs argue that some activities are a nonproductive waste of time, that community service takes away valuable classroom time, and can involve the schools in litigation in the event of something unforeseen happening to the student while participating at the direction of the school.

We should not be surprised in spite of objections to see altruistic unpaid community service continuing to appear as a requirement or elective offering in the curricula not only of schools, particularly at the secondary level, but also of institutions of higher learning.

CULTURAL LITERACY (CORE KNOWLEDGE)

Ever since schools were first created, literacy—the ability to read and write—has been the primary goal of instruction, yet, even today our educational system fails to reach that goal. An estimated third of the American population is illiterate—completely lacking the skills of reading and writing—or functionally illiterate—demonstrating severe deficiency in those skills.

Derived from the Latin word *littera* ("letter"), literacy in its purest sense pertains merely to reading and writing. Today, both professional and popular literature address

---

[54]Elam et al., "The 25th Annual Phi Delta Kappa/Gallup Poll", p. 146.

computer literacy, economic literacy, geographic literacy, historical literacy, scientific literacy, and other literacies. Unfortunately, American students as a whole excel in none of these. Results of tests administered by the National Assessment of Educational Progress, the International Association for the Evaluation of Educational Achievement, and the International Assessment of Educational Progress repeatedly reveal that American students trail European and Asian students in most grades or disciplines.

To that roster of deficiencies critics of the schools have recently added the concept of *cultural literacy*. American children and adults, they say, do not have a sufficiently broad background of general knowledge for communicating intelligently with each other. Diane Ravitch and Chester E. Finn, Jr. reported the results of a 1986 survey of approximately 8,000 high-school juniors concerning their knowledge of history and literature.[55] This assessment, funded by the National Endowment for the Humanities and conducted by the National Assessment of Educational Progress, disclosed that the students demonstrated a disheartening lack of knowledge in the two disciplines.

A 1994 history assessment conducted by the National Assessment of Educational Progress confirmed students' deficiencies in this core area. For the 1994 history assessment NAEP developed three performance levels: Basic, Proficient, and Advanced. Sampling aproximately 22,500 public and nonpublic students in grades four, eight, and twelve, NAEP found that thirty-six percent of the fourth graders, thirty-nine percent of the eighth graders, and fifty-seven percent of the twelfth graders performed below the *Basic* level. Fewer than one-fifth of the students in any grade reached *Proficient* ("solid academic performance") level. Two percent of the fourth graders and one percent of the eighth and twelfth graders reached the *Advanced* level.[56]

It is ironic that, although the public school system is presently dominated by the essentialistic philosophy, achievement of the major goal of that philosophy—transmission of the cultural heritage—has eluded far too many of our public schools' students.

In the 1980s educators and laypeople entered into serious discussion of the sometimes controversial idea that cultural literacy should be a major goal of schooling. E. D. Hirsch, Jr., professor of English at the University of Virginia, popularized the term cultural literacy (more recently referred to as "core knowledge," first in an article for *The American Scholar* in 1983 and later in a book that was widely circulated and discussed.[57]

Cultural literacy, according to Hirsch, is a broad, general knowledge that ideally should be possessed by all members of our democratic society. Hirsch sought to rem-

---

[55]Diane Ravitch and Chester E. Finn, Jr., *What Do Our 17–Year Olds Know?: A Report on the First National Assessment of History and Literature* (New York: Harper & Row, 1987).

[56]Paul Williams, Stephen Lazer, Clyde M. Reese, and Peggy Carr, *NAEP 1994 U.S. History: A First Look: Findings from the National Assessment of Educational Progress* (Washington, D.C.: Office of Educational Research and Improvement, U.S. Department of Education, 1995), p. 19.

[57]E. D. Hirsch, Jr., "Cultural Literacy," *The American Scholar 52, no. 2 (Spring 1963): 159–169* and E. D. Hirsch, Jr., *Cultural Literacy: What Every American Needs to Know* (Boston: Houghton Mifflin, 1987).

For a critical view of Hirsch's ideas on cultural literacy, see Thomas H. Estes, Carol J. Gutman, and Elise K. Harrison, "Cultural Literacy: What Every Educator Needs to Know," *Educational Leadership* 46, no. 1 (September 1988): 14–17. See also Hirsch's response to Estes, Gutman, and Harrison, "Hirsch Responds: The Best Answer to a Caricature is a Practical Program," *Educational Leadership* 46, no. 1 (September 1988): 18–19.

edy what he felt to be "the deep aversion to and contempt for factual knowledge that pervade the thinking of American educators."[58] Said Hirsch, "Part of the essential American educational doctrine has consisted of the disparagement of so-called 'traditional' education."[59] Although elements of this knowledge may change from time to time, most items remain the same or change slowly. A culturally literate person is one who possesses this background of knowledge. The advocates of cultural literacy state that possession of this knowledge enables a person to read with understanding, to communicate thoughts to others within our society, to contribute to the development of our society, and to open doors that lead to success in American society.

A cultural literacy curriculum would start in the elementary schools and would impart that knowledge deemed by scholars, educators, and laypeople to be important information about American culture. Hirsch pointed out that writers assume their readers possess certain cultural information. Thus, to read with understanding and to write to be understood, citizens of our society must possess a store of knowledge about the culture—people, places, facts, vocabulary, and historic and current events from our own and world cultures.

Cultural literacy rejects the concept of pluralism, in which aspects of all subcultures in the nation are studied with equal concentration. Instead, it gives precedence to a national, overriding culture and to the English language. Supporters of cultural literacy posit an American culture. They view the fragmentation of the culture and the populace's lack of commonly shared information as serious problems that schools face in their attempts to develop literate citizens.

Advocates of cultural literacy oppose the teaching of reading and writing through a culture-free skills approach. In agreement with whole language theorists and practitioners, they would use authentic materials, perhaps with more emphasis on factual materials. Cultural literacy proponents do not subscribe to efforts at teaching critical thinking as though it were a cultural-neutral skill or set of skills.

Hirsch conceptualized a two-part curriculum: the "extensive curriculum" that "constitutes the part of the curriculum that has to be known by every child and must be common to all the schools of the nation"[60] and the "intensive curriculum" that permits students to gain an in-depth knowledge of content related to student and teacher needs. Hirsch would let local schools determine how and when students will become acquainted with the specifics of the extensive curriculum; neither the extensive nor the intensive curriculum are standardized programs and methods.

Hirsch called for knowledgeable persons to develop a list of cultural items sufficiently important for incorporating in the curriculum, especially at the elementary school level. Hirsch, Joseph Kett, and James Trefil began the task by compiling a preliminary list of *What Literate Americans Know*.[61] A suitable list, Hirsch maintained, would be finite and limited in scope and would not be as formidable to assemble as some might think. He further observed that, although some items would change over

[58]E. D. Hirsch, Jr., *The Schools We Need : Why We Don't Have Them* (New York: Doubleday, 1996): 54.

[59]Ibid., p. 69

[60]E. D. Hirsch, Jr. *Cultural Literacy: What Every American Needs to Know* (Boston: Houghton Mifflin Co., 1987), p. 128.

[61]Ibid., pp. 146–215.

time, most of the items on the list were historic and therefore would remain the same. Cultural literacy would not require in-depth knowledge of all items; in some cases an imprecise, even superficial knowledge—enough for a reader or listener to understand what a writer or speaker means—would suffice. For example, one doesn't need detailed knowledge of genes to understand the concept of Mendel's laws. Through the early 1990s Hirsch edited a Core Knowledge Series of books that outline what pupils at various grade levels should know.[62]

Hirsch's ideas have met with criticism. Those who espouse the teaching of reading through decoding, phonics, and word recognition object to the culture-laden approach through the use of factual material. Hirsch's acceptance of memorization (he pointed out that various cultures depend on memorization for perpetuation of their traditions) caused critics to claim that the cultural literacy movement would reduce learning to rote memorization without true understanding.

Hirsch's position that students might need only vague understanding about some cultural items has led critics to decry the cultural literacy approach as superficial and a deterrent to teaching critical thinking. On the other hand, a proponent of cultural literacy would counter that a person does not need to know all the details about nuclear fission, for example, to understand a reference to that term in a book, magazine, or newspaper article written for the general reader.

Some critics of cultural literacy feel that it is presumptuous for any individual or group to deign to draw up a list of items that all pupils in America must know. However, Hirsch and his colleagues who proposed a tentative list, urged study and review of the list by others, and made clear that their list was *descriptive*—not *prescriptive*—of information possessed by culturally literate Americans.[63] Hirsch's views of progressive education methods and his references to research supporting his position in his 1996 work, *The Schools We Need and Why We Don't Have Them*,[64] have been sharply challenged by Linda Darling-Hammond.[65]

Cultural pluralists who reject the melting-pot concept of American culture feel that Hirsch's specification of cultural items is elitist and a barrier to minorities and the disadvantaged. Hirsch attributed lower scores reported for black children on certain standardized achievement tests not to an elitist curriculum but to the schools' failure to impart the informational background needed by their students.[66] Regarding the disadvantaged, Hirsch commented:

> To be culturally literate is to possess the basic information needed to thrive in the modern world. . . . Cultural literacy constitutes the only sure avenue of opportunity for disadvantaged children, the only reliable way of combating the social determinism that now condemns them to remain in the same social and educational condition as their parents. That children from poor and illiterate homes tend to remain poor and illiterate is an unacceptable failure of our schools, one which has occurred not because our

---

[62]See bibliography.

[63]Hirsch, Jr., *Cultural Literacy*, p, xiv.

[64]E. D. Hirsch, Jr., *The Schools We Need and Why We Don't Have Them.*, op. cit.

[65]Linda Darling-Hammond, *The Right to Learn: A Blueprint for Creating Schools That Work* (San Francisco: Jossey-Bass, 1997), pp. 8–10.

[66]Hirsch, Jr., *Cultural Literacy*, p. 111.

teachers are inept but chiefly because they are compelled to teach a fragmented curriculum based on faulty educational theories.[67]

Hirsch noted the general decline in verbal abilities as evidenced by SAT scores and the National Assessment of Educational Progress,[68] and he proposed tests of general knowledge to assess cultural literacy. Some critics fear that, if these proposed tests are established, teachers will structure lessons around the tests, additional testing will cause further national standardization of the curriculum, and the tests would promote rote memorization and thereby perpetuate superficiality. Some would reject the intrusion of any more tests and would claim with some justification that there is already a surfeit of assessments. However, were cultural literacy to become a goal, there would have to be some type of assessment of students' accomplishment of that goal.

Some critics have perceived lists of cultural items as trivia that can be looked up rather than stored in the brain. They feel it is impossible to draw up a list of items that should be knowledge shared by all citizens of our society for the welfare of both the individual and the nation.

There have been objections to the preponderance of items derived from British traditions on the list of cultural items developed by Hirsch and his collegues. Hirsch explained:

> By accident of history, American cultural literacy has a bias toward English literate traditions. Short of revolutionary political upheaval, there is absolutely nothing that can be done about this. It is not a weakness of our literate culture that it has its origins in English traditions, for, like all other literate traditions connected with great national languages, the English tradition is broad and heterogeneous and grows ever more so. . . .
>
> After more than two hundred years of national life, the main elements of our vocabulary have transcended the sphere of contention and dispute. . . . No matter how value-laden or partisan some of these common elements were in their origins long ago, they now exist as common materials of public discourse, the instruments through which we are able to communicate our views to one another and make decisions in a democratic way.[69]

That Hirsch's proposals have proved appealing to many curriculum planners is evidenced by the rapid growth of Core Knowledge Schools. Hirsch cited some fifty core knowledge schools throughout the country as of 1992 with Three Oaks Elementary School in Fort Myers, Florida and P.S. 67, South Bronx credited as the first and second schools of this type.[70] The Core Knowledge Foundation created by Hirsch in 1986 works with a Core Knowledge Network to implement the Core Knowledge Sequence that specifies content for each grade level. In 1999 the Core Knowledge Foundation listed several hundred public, private, and parochial schools in forty-four states and the District of Columbia committed to using the Core Knowledge Sequence.[71] We may expect to see continued experimentation with models emphasizing this approach to

---

[67]Ibid., p. xiii..
[68]Ibid., p. 4.
[69]Ibid., pp. 106–107.
[70]E. D. Hirsch, Jr, "Core Knowledge," *Newsweek* 120, no. 12 (September 21, 1992): A8–9.
[71]Core Knowledge Foundation, http://www.coreknowledge.org, accessed Februay 2, 1999.

curriculum implementation. *Cultural literacy* should be distinguished from *information literacy,* a movement fostered by the National Forum on Information Literacy. The latter seeks development of research-based skills of researching, interpreting, and communicating information.[72]

EDUCATIONAL MANAGEMENT ORGANIZATIONS

Coming on strong at the end of the twentieth century and the beginning of the twenty-first is the movement referred to as *privatization,* the involvement of individuals, groups, foundations, and corporations in the management of the public schools. Privatization has taken two forms: (1) chartering, which we discussed above, (2) contracting, that is, educational management of already established schools, and (3) for-profit educational management of charter schools. Already privatized, of course, are the non-profit and for-profit private schools some of which are operated on contract with educational managers and others, created and managed as investments.

Joseph Murphy reviewed a number of definitions of the relatively new term *privatization,* which in essence means the transfer of public control to private.[73] Privatization rests on the concepts of efficiency and school choice. The presumption is made that educational managers, following sound business and educational principles, freed of restrictions imposed by state and locality, can be more successful in terms of student achievement than the present system of school administration and supervision. Further, educational management organizations, which some refer to as EMOs, are a response to the public's desire for school choice. Dissatisfaction with public schools, disenchantment with government generally, calls for educational reform, and adherence to a business philosophy have fostered the movement toward privatization.

Contracting.   Reminiscent of performance contracting in the late 1960s as exemplified by the Texarkana, Texas schools,[74] public schools in the 1990s began turning noticeably to private organizations to manage their schools. Allen Berger pointed out that the concept of schools' contracting with private entities dates back a hundred years.[75]

Dade County (Florida) and Baltimore, among other communities in the early 1990s, experimented with private educational management by contracting with Educational Alternatives, Inc. (now known as the Tesseract Group) which viewed its arrangement with schools as a "public-private partnership" rather than privatization.[76] Education Alternatives offered an instructional program called "Tesseract," en-

---

[72]Association for Supervision and Curriculum Development, "Developing Information Literacy," *Education Update* 37, no. 2 (February 1995): 1, 3, 8. See also Patricia Senn Breivik and J. A. Senn, *Information Literacy: Educating Children for the 21st Century* (New York: Scholastic, 1994).

[73]Josephy Murphy, *The Privatization of Schooling: Problems and Possibilities* (Thousand Oaks, Calif.: Corwin Press, 1996): 9–34.

[74]See "Performance Contracting as Catalyst for Reform," *Educational Technology* 9, no. 8 (August 1969): 5–9. See also Charles Blaschke, "Performance Contracting Costs, Management Reform and John Q. Citizen," *Phi Delta Kappan* 53, no. 4 (December 1971): 245–247.

[75]Allen Berger, "Performance Contracting and Educational Accountability," *Elements: Theory Into Practice* 3, no. 8 (April 1972): 4–8.

[76]Scott Willis, "Public Schools, Private Managers," *ASCD Update* 36, no. 3 (Match 1994): 1.

compassing a number of practices, including a constructivist approach to learning, whole language, use of technology, and inservice training of teachers.[77] Although contracts with Baltimore; Dade County; and Hartford, Connecticut have been terminated, the Tesseract Group now operates charter schools in several states among which are Arizona, Indiana, Minnesota, and New Jersey.[78]

In the management arena also is the Whittle Communications' Edison Project which began operation with four schools in 1995. As of 1998 the Edison Project was administering fifty-one partnership schools in twelve states.[79] Other organizations in educational management are the Leona Group, National Heritage Academies, and SABIS Educational Systems.

Contractual plans normally call for management of existing schools with existing faculty with ultimate control retained by the school board. Contractual schools, unlike many charter schools remain public schools albeit with private management whereas independent for-profit charter schools of the EMOs hire their own faculty and provide their own curricula. Furtwengler estimated that for-profit EMOs in 1998 were managing about ten percent of established charter schools.[80]

Private enterpreneurs maintain that they can offer more efficient administration and improve student achievement at less cost than under public school management. John E. Chubb and Terry M. Moe would apply a marketplace concept that encourages creation of private schools to compete with public schools, parental choice of public or private school, and governmentally funded vouchers.[81] Chubb and Moe strongly decried restrictions imposed on schools by their bureaucratic structure.[82] Comparing control of public schools with that of privately-run schools, Chubb and Moe noted, "Public schools are subject to direct control through politics, private schools are subject to indirect control through markets."[83] This means that if educationally managed schools are to thrive they must produce results acceptable to the public.

Private operation of public schools has reaped both praise and criticism. Teachers have praised those schools where student achievement has risen and where teachers have experienced advantages of training in new techniques and help in the form of materials, equipment, and aides. Criticism has emanated from teachers, including their unions who fault use of tax moneys in for-profit operations and differentials in funding. Controversy centers around results of student achievement; costs of operation; quality of facilities and teaching staff; and quality and quantity of materials and supplies.[84]

[77]Ibid., pp. 2–3.

[78]Carol B. Furtwengler, "Heads Up! The EMOs Are Coming," *Educational Leadership* 56, no. 2 (October 1998): 45.

[79]The Edison Project: http://www.edisonproject.com, accessed February 9, 1999.

[80]Ibid.

[81]John E. Chubb and Terry M. Moe, *Politics, Markets, and America's Schools* (Washington, D.C.: The Brookings Institution, 1990).

[82]Ibid., p. 187.

[83]Ibid., p. 189.

[84]For description of ways school systems are involved in privatization of some of their functions see Karen Powe, *Private Options for Public Schools: Ways Public Schools Are Exploring Privatization* (Alexandria, Va.: National School Boards Association, 1995). For critical view of privatization see Carol Ascher, Norm Fruchter, and Robert Berne, *Hard Lessons: Public Schools and Privatization* (New York: The Twentieth Century Fund, 1996). For analysis of privatization see also Myron Lieberman, *Privatization and Educational Choice,* (New York: St. Martin's Press, 1989).

Whether student achievement is enhanced under private management and to what extent and whether contracting is cost-effective must be demonstrated if this relationship with private enterprise is to continue. Accountability will play a fundamental role in the cases of both the contractual and charter schools. Private management must translate their goals into reality if it is to obtain and retain contracts or charters.

In passing we should note that many school systems have already privatized food, custodial, and transportation services.

GENDER DISCRIMINATION

Madeleine R. Grumet highlighted the significance of gender not only in education but universally when she wrote, "what is most fundamental to our lives as men and women sharing a moment on this planet is the process and experience of reproducing ourselves."[85] Gender discrimination or sexism has been a perennial problem in education. Title IX of the Educational Amendments of 1972 passed by the U.S. Congress caused school personnel to examine programs and to remove practices that discriminate between the sexes. Restricting home economics to girls and industrial arts to boys, for example, are sexist practices. Funding of interscholastic athletics, with the lion's share traditionally going to boy's athletics, has been challenged as sexist. The integration of females into male athletic teams and males into female teams has stirred controversy within the profession and outside.

We can find considerable argument as to what degree, if any, sex stereotypes and gender discrimination in school actually exist. In the mid 1980s Myra and David Sadker studied over 100 fourth, sixth, and eighth graders in four states and the District of Columbia, observing language arts, English, mathematics, and science classes. The Sadkers concluded that, regardless of the subject or grade level, boys dominated classroom interaction and received more attention from the teacher than did girls.[86]

A 1992 study commissioned by the American Association of University Women (AAUW) and researched by the Wellesley College Center for Research on Women, reported data on gender discrimination and concluded that schools were shortchanging girls.[87] In the winter of 1994 the American Civil Liberties Union filed a complaint against the U.S. Department of Education on behalf of the National Center for Fair and Open Testing (FairTest) charging gender discrimination on standardized tests, citing the fact that approximately sixty percent of the National Merit Scholarship semifinalists and winners are male.

For years the theme has prevailed that our educational system discriminates against girls. Diane Ravitch in a commentary to *The Washington Post* rebutted arguments of gender discrimination in the schools. She cited as evidence that although boys tend to achieve higher grades in mathematics and science and higher SAT scores (some studies show the differences in math scores as negligible or girls' scores higher than

---

[85]Madeleine Grumet, *Bitter Milk: Women and Teaching* (Amherst, Mass.: The University of Massachusetts Press, 1988), p. 4.

[86]Myra and David Sadker, "Sexism in the Schoolroom of the '80s," *Psychology Today* 19, no. 3 (March 1985): 54–57.

[87]American Association of University Women and Wellesley College Center for Research on Women, *How Schools Short-change Girls: The AAUW Report: A Study of Major Findings on Girls and Education* (Washington, D.C.: AAUW Educational Foundation and National Education Association, 1992. Trade edition: New York: Marlowe & Co., 1995).

boys'), girls excel boys in the language arts; more boys are retained in grade than girls; a higher percentage of girls go on to college and attain bachelor's degrees than boys.[88]

At the beginning of this new century more voices are being heard that, contrary to older beliefs, girls, often more acceptant, more attentive to their studies, and less aggressive than boys, are favored in school. While Janice Weinman described barriers girls face in school Judith Kleinfeld noted the bias that exists in against boys, especially those of minority groups.[89] Although boys continue to excel girls in mathematics, science, engineering, and technology, girls demonstrate higher achievement in other fields and the gap between girls and boys in traditional male areas has narrowed. Boys drop out of high school at a greater rate than do girls, ostensibly because school does not meet their needs and appealing opportunities exist in the market place. With exception of a few well-known colleges and universities, the percentage of girls enrolled in college exceeds enrollment of boys.[90]

The AAUW in a 1998 follow-up study conducted for them by the American Institutes for Research reflected the progress made by females in education, noting, however, males' continued dominance in technology.[91] The Horatio Alger Association provided further evidence that girls' attention to studies, academic achievement, and career goals surpass those of boys.[92]

Children's attitudes about gender roles are shaped early and, like many attitudes and values, are strongly influenced by the children's significant others—parents, relatives, close friends, teachers, coaches, role models, and other persons whom they respect. A study by Jacquelynne S. Eccles and Rena D. Harold at the University of Michigan found that "already by the first grade, girls have a more negative assessment of their general athletic ability than do boys."[93] Athletic skills at early ages are virtually comparable regardless of gender. Not until puberty can physiological differences between boys and girls account for differences in athletic abilities. Sex roles are to a large extent culturally determined; the school often perpetuates those social determiners, either through the intentional or the hidden curriculum. One has only to look at the subordinate role in which females are cast and the superordinate role accorded males by some societies on this globe to provide evidence of the impact of culture in shaping male and female behavior. If culture is a determining factor as most people believe we should perhaps be concerned about some of the changes in the culture itself since, on the flip side, girls are beginning to exhibit some of the lesser admired traits demonstrated more often by males such as aggressive antisocial behavior and use of tobacco, alcohol, and drugs.[94] Although we can cite countless cases of discrimination

---

[88]Diane Ravitch, "Girls Are Not Victims of Discrimination in School, "Special to *The Washington Post, reported in The Orlando Sentinel,* November 28, 1993, p. G-1.

[89]Janice Weinman and Judith Kleinfeld, "Do Public Schools Shortchange Girls on Educational Opportunities?", *Insight* 14, no. 4 (December 14, 1998). See also Judith Kleinfeld, "Student Performance: Males versus Females," *The Public Interest 134* (1999).

[90]See Brendan I. Koerner, "Where the Boys Aren't," *U.S. News & World Report* 126, no. 5 (February 8, 1999): 46–55.

[91]American Association of University Women and American Institutes for Research, *Gender Gaps: Where Schools Fail Our Children* (New York: Marlowe & Co., 1999).

[92]Horatio Alger Association, *The State of Our Nation's Youth* (Alexandria, Va.: Horatio Alger Association, 1997).

[93]Jacquelynne S. Eccles and Rena D. Harold, *Gender Differences in Sport Involvement: Applying the Eccles' Expectancy-Value Model* (Ann Arbor, Mich.: University Press, n.d.), pp. 28–29.

[94]Lynn Phillips, *The Girls Report* (New York: National Council for Research on Women, 1998).

against girls, the rash of schoolhouse shootings in the late 1990s carried out by boys; boys' higher dropout rate; the fact that boys are subjected to torment and bullying more often than girls; and the percentage of boys who commit suicide suggest that boys may now be the neglected gender.

As mentioned earlier in this text, as recently as 1972 Robert J. Havighurst perceived the achievement of a masculine or feminine social role as one of the developmental tasks of adolescence.[95] The accomplishment of these roles is no longer simple, if it ever was. Though traditional attitudes toward the roles of men and women are still held by sizable segments of the public—especially among certain ethnic groups and nationalities, in certain areas of the country, and by certain religious groups—the distinctions in roles have been changing rapidly. Cultural and family attitudes may well shape perceptions of sex roles and contribute to gender discrimination to a much greater extent than schools. What once appeared to be male occupations, like truck driving, construction work, firefighting, police work, and fighter pilot are no longer the exclusive province of the male. With females now assigned to naval vessels we may expect the term *seaman* to go into oblivion along with *mankind, mailman,* and *Dear Sirs.* Conversely, a "house-husband" is no longer unheard of, and the female can be the family "breadwinner." Men can pursue careers and avocations that were formerly considered only for women, such as nursing, elementary school teaching, and secretarial work. Schools today are counseling girls to take science, mathematics, and industrial arts, courses formerly viewed as more appropriate for boys. On the other hand, boys are advised to elect the fine arts and home economics subjects often considered particularly suitable for girls. The unisex philosophy has shaken, if not toppled, some of the stereotypes of men and women.

In response to changing attitudes about gender-based stereotypes, authors have had to "de-sex" their textbooks. They may no longer use the single generic pronoun "he" to refer to both sexes. Just as authors may no longer portray all persons in their textbooks as Caucasian, so also they may no longer depict males and females as performing only socially or culturally predetermined occupations.

There is an awareness that women have been discriminated against in the workplace. Such discrimination includes fewer opportunities for women to gain executive positions in some occupations, and the fact that women continue to earn lower salaries than men do in comparable positions.

Efforts are being made to eradicate vestiges of gender discrimination and to equalize opportunity between males and females. Senate Bill 1463, for example, introduced in 1993 by Senator Barbara Mikulski as amendments to the Elementary and Secondary Education Act of 1965, comprising two titles: Gender Equity in Mathematics and Science and Elimination of Sexual Harrassment and Abuse, became the Gender Equity in Education Act in 1994.

School systems themselves have sought to answer criticisms of gender discrimination through careful attention to curriculum and instruction, counseling, and staff development. Borrowing a leaf from private schools and the concept of all-male black schools, some school systems have attempted classes and schools segregated by gender. California has established a number of all-girl schools. Others have cropped up in

---

[95]See Havighurst, footnote, p. 206 of this text.

New York City and in Iowa, although in the latter case the state of Iowa required the discontinuance of the practice of segregating students by gender.

That the issue of gender (as well as racial) discrimination remains a sensitive one can be seen by the actions of the New Jersey legislature in the fall of 1999. New Jersey's General Assembly passed a bill, subsequently killed by its Senate, to the effect that before the Pledge of Allegiance school children would be required to recite the passage from the preamble of the Declaration of Independence which begins "We hold these truths to be self-evident, that all men are created equal . . ." Opponents of the bill branded the Declaration not only as a document employing sexist language ("all men") but also racist and, with its references to the Creator, contrary to the principle of separation of church and state.

Like racism, sexist stereotypes and discriminatory practices when found are difficult to eradicate. Nevertheless, curriculum workers must proceed to design curricula that will help to eliminate bias, based not only on race, creed, and national origin, but also on gender.

HEALTH EDUCATION

No better example of the convergence of needs of students and needs of society can be found than the health-related problems experienced by today's young people. In addition to offering long-standing programs of physical fitness, hygiene, and nutrition education, the schools are confronted with a number of health problems—"crises" might be a better word—that demand the close and immediate attention of curriculum planners. Specifically, the schools are seeking ways to respond to the use and abuse of alcohol, drugs, and tobacco, to the high incidence of teen pregnancies, and to the prevalence of sexually transmitted diseases, including acquired immune deficiency syndrome (AIDS).

Let's briefly look at the dimensions of these problems and schools' responses to them.

Drugs, Alcohol, Tobacco.   Since 1975 the Institute for Social Research at the University of Michigan, with funds from the National Institute on Drug Abuse, has conducted annual surveys on the use of drugs, alcohol, and tobacco by high school seniors, college students, and young adults. In 1991 the Institute for Social Research added data from eighth and tenth graders.

Monitoring the Future: A Continuing Study of the Lifestyles and Values of Youth, formerly known as The National High School Senior Survey, in 1998 sampled approximately 50,000 seniors in 422 public and private high schools in the continental United States, about 18,700 eighth graders in 149 schools, about 15,400 tenth graders in 129 schools, and about 15,800 twelfth graders in 144 schools.[96]

The 1998 study brought forth encouraging news. After six years of increases, the use of illicit drugs by teenagers had started either a modest decline or had leveled off

---

[96]L. D. Johnston, P. M. O'Malley, J. G. Bachman (Dec. 1998). *Drug Use by American Young People Begins to Turn Downward.* [Online]. Web site: www.isr.umich.edu/src/mtf, accessed February 21, 1999. See also Lloyd D. Johnston, Jerald G. Bachman, and Patrick M. O'Malley, *Monitoring the Future,* press release, The University of Michigan News and Information Services, Ann Arbor, December 17, 1999.

from the year before. Though not statistically significant in several instances, the results showed a gradual downward trend in the use of marijuana, inhalants, hallucinogens, stimulants, alcohol, and tobacco. Heroine use had leveled off among eighth and tenth graders and decreased among twelfth graders. Trouble spots included an upturn in the use of cocaine, an increase in the number of eighth graders who had been drunk in the past thirty days, and an increase in the use of steroids by eighth and twelfth graders.[97]

Both the 1998 National Household Sruvey on Drug Abuse released by the Department of Health and Human Services in 1999[98] and the 12th Annual National Survey of Student Drug Use conducted by the Parents' Resource Institute for Drug Education (PRIDE),[99] released in September 1999, offered further evidence of the decrease in illicit drug use by teenagers. The use of alcohol and tobacco remained steady.

Encouraging too are the negative attitudes teenagers are manifesting about the use of drugs, alcohol, and tobacco. The concerted effort of parents, schools, media, and government to combat drug use may be credited for the turnaround.

The University of Michigan studies show that although a clear majority of teenagers disapprove of the use of drugs and abuse of alcohol, too many students still do not perceive the risks involved in use of drugs, alcohol, and tobacco. Obviously, the struggle against use of illicit drugs, consumption of alcohol, and addiction to tobacco is far from over.

The public is obviously concerned about the drug problem. Drugs and violence in the schools ranked at the top of the list of school problems considered serious by the public in a 1994 study by Public Agenda.[100] The 30th and 31st Annual Phi Delta Kappa/Gallup Polls of the Public's Attitudes Toward the Public Schools revealed that the public continues to rank the abuse of drugs as a serious; (number four in both 1998[101] and 1999[102]) problem in the schools today. Lack of discipline, which headed the Phi Delta Kappa/Gallup poll lists for many years, held second place behind violence in the 1998 poll and rose again to first place in 1999. Lack of proper financial support came in third in both polls.

Teenage Pregnancies, Live Births, and Abortions. Along with the decline in the use of illicit drugs, alcohol, and tobacco the frequency with which teenagers engage in sexual activity, teenage pregnancies, births, and abortions between 1992 and 1995 showed a steady drop.[103] Data gathered in 1996 and 1998 by the National Center for

---

[97]Ibid. See also Lloyd D. Johnston, Patrick M. O'Malley, and Jerald G. Bachman, *National Survey Results on Drug Use from the Monitoring the Future Study, 1975–1998. Volume 1: Secondary School Students* (Rockville, Md.: National Institute on Drug Abuse, 1998).

[98]Department of Health and Human Services, "Annual National Drug Survey Results Released," Web site: http:www.samhas.gov/PRESS/99/990818nr.htm, accessed September 29, 1999.

[99]Parents' Resource Institute for Drug Education, "News from PRIDE Surveys," Web site: http://www.pride.org/press99/9899drug.htm, accessed September 29, 1999.

[100]Jean Johnson and John Immerwahr, *First Things First: What Americans Expect from the Public Schools* (New York: Public Agenda, 1994), p. 41.

[101]Lowell C. Rose and Alec M. Gallup, "The 30th Annual Phi Delta Kappa/Gallup Poll of the Public's Attitudes Toward the Public Schools," *Phi Delta Kappan* 80, no. 1 (September 1998): 51.

[102]Lowell C. Rose and Alec M. Gallup, "The 31st Annual Phi Delta Kappa/Gallup Poll of the Public's Arttitudes Toward the Public Schools," *Phi Delta Kappan* 81, no. 1 (September 1999): 47.

[103]See Centers for Disease Control, *Morbidity and Mortality Weekly Report* 47, no. 24 (June 26, 1998): 497–498.

Health Statistics of the Centers for Disease Control and Prevention confirmed the national decline in teenage birthrates.[104] The Alan Guttmacher Institute's 1997 study acknowledged a continuing drop in teenage pregnancies, birthrates, and abortions although the rate of teenage pregnancy in the United States surpasses rates in France, Germany, and Japan.[105] Still, four out of ten teenage girls become pregnant before the age of 20.[106] The 1999 Anne E. Casey Foundation's KIDS COUNT Special Report, "When Teens Have Sex: Issues and Trends," reported the fact that teen pregnancies, though down, hover around one million per year for women ages fifteen to nineteen with nearly 500,000 births resulting.[107]

Legal abortions in the United States in 1996 numbered approximately 1,220,000.[108] Abortions which had been hovering around 1.6 million per year for the decade 1980 to 1990 were placed by the Alan Guttmacher Institute at 1,364,000 in 1995.[109] As disturbing as the figures on teenage pregnancies, births, and abortions are, of particular interest is the change in attitudes among teenagers. In spite of the omnipresence of sexual stimuli through movies, television, and the Internet as well as much-publicized pecadillos of public figures, the Centers for Disease Control and Prevention noted that several studies have shown that the proportion of teenagers who are sexually experienced declined in the 1990s and the use of condoms has increased.[110] Apparently, a fortuitous combination of factors has led to a reversal of student attitudes.

Sexual intercourse is not always the in-thing at the turn of the century. Programs calling for abstinence; fear of AIDS and other sexually-transmitted diseases; distribution of sexuality information and condoms; provision of organized after-school recreation; willingness of more and more parents to discuss sexual topics with their children and to support sexuality education programs in the schools; and efforts by teachers, churches, social agencies, government, and foundations have combined to reverse attitudes of the permissive so-called sexual revolution of the sixties through the eighties. In fact, *Newsweek* noted the recent formation of "virgin clubs," whose members go on record to refrain from sexual activity.[111]

TIME, although noting the decrease in sexually-transmitted diseases and teenage pregnancies and the increase in use of condoms, painted American children as in the middle of their own sexual revolution. Without doubt teenagers are struggling to come to terms with their sexuality in a world rife with sexual images.[112]

---

[104]The National Center for Health Statistics, Center for Disease Control and Prevention, *Teenage Birth Rates Down in a Majority of States,* 1998, Web site: http://www.cdc.gov/nchswww/releases/96facts/96sheets/teenbirth.htm, accessed May 5, 1999. See Child Trends, press release, Washington, D.C., January 19, 2000.

[105]The Alan Guttmacher Institute, *Teenage Pregnancy: Overall Trends and State-by-State Information, 1999,* web site: http://www.agi-usa.org, accessed May 5, 1999 and *Family Planning Perspectives 2000; 32:* 14–23.

[106]See Anne E. Casey Foundation, *When Teens Have Sex: Issues and Trends* a KIDS COUNT Special Report (Baltimore, Md.: Anne E. Casey Foundation, 1999).

[107]Ibid.

[108]Ibid.

[109]See S. K. Henshaw and J. Van Vort, eds. *Abortion Factbook: 1992 Edition: Readings, Trends, and State and Local Data to 1988* (New York: The Alan Guttmacher Institute, 1992).

[110]Centers for Disease Control and Prevention, "Decline in Sexual Activity and Increase in Condom Use," Web site: http://www.cdc.gov/nchswww/data/nvs47_12.pdf, accessed October 2, 1999.

[111]Pat Wingert, "The Battle Over Falling Birthrates," *Newsweek* 131, no. 19 (May 11, 1998): 40.

[112]Ron Stodghill II, "Where Did You Learn That?" *TIME* 151, no. 23 (June 15, 1998): 52–59.

Sexually Transmitted Diseases.   How to reduce the lower, but continuing high, incidence of sexually-transmitted diseases (STDs) is of paramount concern not only to public health workers but also to curriculum planners. How serious is the problem can be seen from the figures for notifiable diseases. The National Center of Allergy and Infectious Diseases estimated more than twenty types of STDs affect more than 13 million men and women in the United States per year.[113] Two-thirds of these cases occur in people under twenty-five years of age.[114] Figures for 1997 from the Centers for Disease Control and Prevention showed 323,307 cases of gonorrhea of which 185,933 were young people fifteen to twenty-four years of age and 8,540 cases of primary and secondary syphilis, which included 2,091 in the fifteen to twenty-four-year-old group. The lesser known STD, chlamydia tops the list with 520,164 cases, the vast majority of which, 374,295, were in the fifteen to twenty-four age group.[115] Running a close second in number of cases is genital herpes with some 500,000 new cases per year and an estimated 60,000,000 Americans infected with this malady.[116]

Although the number of cases of gonorrhea and syphilis was down considerably since 1989, the incidence of acquired immunodeficiency syndrome (AIDS) continues at a high level. Historically, the pace of AIDS has been startling. Between 1981, when AIDS was first reported in the United States, and 1985, some 11,000 cases had been diagnosed. The number of cases had climbed to an estimated 40,000 by the end of 1986.[117] By December 31, 1988 the number of cases was more than 82,000 (over 74,000 males, more than 6,900 females, and some 1,300 children under age thirteen).[118] The Centers for Disease Control counted an astounding 103,691 cases of AIDS in 1993; 487 of these cases were in the fifteen to nineteen group.[119] By 1997 the number of reported AIDS cases had dropped to 58,492 with 2,099 of these in the fifteen to twenty-four age group.[120] Nevertheless, an estimated 900,000 people in the United States are infected with the AIDS virus.[121]

The Centers for Disease Control estimated some 40,000 deaths among persons with AIDS between about 1991 and 1996, 39,200 in 1996 alone.[122] The 39,200 estimated deaths from AIDS in 1996 represented a significant drop from the estimated 50,700 deaths in 1995.[123] HIV infection (AIDS) remains the leading cause of death of men ages twenty-five to forty-four and the third ranking cause of death of women in

---

[113]National Institute of Allergy and Infectious Diseases, National Institutes of Health, Web site: http://www.niaid.nih.gov/factsheets/stdinfo.htm, accessed February 28, 1999.

[114]Ibid.

[115]Centers for Disease Control and Prevention, "Summary of Notifiable Diseases, 1997," *Morbidity and Mortality Weekly Report* 46, no. 54 (November 20, 1998): 10.

[116]National Institute of Allergy and Infectious Diseases. op. cit.

[117]James H. Price, "AIDS, the Schools, and Policy Issues," *Journal of School Health* 56, no. 4 (April 1986): 137.

[118]Leads from the Morbidity and Mortality Weekly Report: Update: Acquired Immunodeficiency Syndrome–United States, *JAMA, The Journal of the American Medical Association* 261, no. 18 (May 12, 1989): 2609ff.

[119]Centers for Disease Control, "Summary of Notifiable Diseases, United States, 1993," *Morbidity and Mortality Weekly Report* 42, no. 53 (October 20, 1994): 3, 10.

[120]Centers for Disease Control and Prevention, "Summary of Notifiable Diseases, 1997," p. 10.

[121]National Institute of Allergy and Infectious Diseases, op. cit.

[122]U.S. Bureau of the Census, *Statistical Abstract of the United States,* 1998, (Washington, D.C.: U.S. Government Printing Office, 1998) p. 106.

[123]Ibid.

this same age group.[124] Estimates of those infected with the immunodeficiency virus (HIV) number around a million with cases worldwide in the millions.

Schools, churches, social agencies, and parents all have roles to play in combatting teenage pregnancies and sexually-transmitted diseases.

Sexuality Education and School Clinics.   Health-related problems pose the classic question to curriculum planners. To what extent must the schools respond to problems of society? What can the schools do about these overwhelming problems? If educators agree that the schools can make some response, how will that response be made?

The public appears to be in rather general agreement about the school's responses to the use of alcohol, drugs, (both prescription and nonprescription), and tobacco. State legislatures, reflecting public opinion, have in some cases, mandated instruction on the use and abuse of these substances. In spite of the school's concerted attack on the use of alcohol, drugs, and tobacco, usage among young people remains high. Figures show that much remains to be done in reducing the use of these substances. The public, however. generally supports the school's efforts to educate young people about the hazards of these products, especially the use of drugs.

In the area of sexuality education, however, parents and other citizens of the community are in sharp disagreement. Attitudes range from support for strong sexuality education programs in the schools to avoidance of the topic. Attitudes of the various religious and ethnic groups differ considerably on responses schools should take toward sexual problems. Since sexuality education is value-laden, some people believe the school's program should be confined to the academics, leaving moral education to the home and church.

A 1993 study carried out by the Sex Information and Education Council of the United States (SIECUS) surveyed the extent of sexuality education in the fifty states, District of Columbia, Puerto Rico, and American Samoa and reviewed curricular materials used in sexuality education programs. Acknowledging the seriousness of the AIDS problem and early sexual activity on the part of teenagers, state legislators have listened to the advocates of sexuality education. SIECUS found:

- Forty-seven states either recommend or require sexuality education through state law or policy.
- Thirty-five states have developed guidelines for sexuality education and seventeen have developed curricula, usually within the framework of health education.
- Fewer than one-third of state guides include any sexual behavior topic other than abstinence.[125]

Table 14.1 details the sexuality topics covered at the various grade levels in the states whose curricula were examined.

You will note that the topics most frequently covered were: families, decision making, STD/HIV, abstinence, puberty, values, reproductive anatomy and physiology,

---

[124]Ibid., p. 103.

[125]Sex Information and Education Council of the United States, *Unfinished Business: A SIECUS Assessment of State Sexuality Education Programs, 1993* (New York: Sex Information and Education Council of the United States, 1993), pp. 5–7.

TABLE 14.1

Number of States Covering Sexuality Topics at Grade Levels

SEXUALITY TOPICS	K–3	4–6	7–9	10–12	OVERALL
HUMAN DEVELOPMENT					
Puberty	8	18	14	*	26
Reproductive Anatomy and Physiology	8	18	16	11	25
Reproduction	8	14	13	14	24
Body Image	14	15	13	12	23
Sexual Identity and Orientation	0	0	7	8	13
RELATIONSHIPS					
Families	16	17	14	12	28
Parenting	2	6	11	17	24
Friendship	10	10	12	9	22
Marriage & Lifetime Commitments	0	0	2	11	21
Love	6	8	13	*	19
Dating	1	4	10	11	19
PERSONAL SKILLS					
Decision-making	11	15	16	13	28
Values	6	7	15	9	26
Communication	–	14	13	11	25
Assertiveness	7	9	11	7	23
Negotiation	*	*	15	10	20
Finding Help	9	12	15	14	25
SEXUAL BEHAVIOR					
Abstinence	0	4	12	7	27
Sexuality Throughout Life	2	8	12	9	20
Masturbation	0	4	3	2	10
Shared Sexual Behavior	0	0	3	4	9
Human Sexual Response	0	0	1	2	4
Fantasy	*	*	0	1	1
Sexual Dysfunction	*	*	1	0	1
SEXUAL HEALTH					
STD/HIV	4	13	16	17	28
Sexual Abuse	11	12	10	12	22
Reproductive Health	0	5	9	13	22
Contraception	0	1	10	10	21
Abortion	0	1	5	5	11

(Continued)

Table 14.1 Continued

SEXUALITY TOPICS	K–3	4–6	7–9	10–12	OVERALL
SEXUALITY AND SOCIETY					
Gender Roles	8	12	12	9	21
Diversity	9	6	6	*	18
Sexuality and Society	*	*	7	5	14
Sexuality and the Media	4	6	8	*	13
Sexuality and the Law	*	*	2	5	12
Sexuality and the Arts	*	*	3	3	4
Sexuality and Religion	0	1	1	2	4

*Guidelines do not include topic coverage for these grade levels.

SOURCE: The Sex Information and Education Council of the United Stated, *Unfinished Business: A SIECUS Assessment of State Sexuality Education Programs* (New York: The Sex Information and Education Council of the United States, 1993), p. 19. Reprinted with permission.

and communication. Topics least covered were sexual identity and orientation, abortion, masturbation, shared sexual behavior, human sexual response, sexuality and the arts, sexuality and religion, fantasy, and sexual dysfunction.[126]

Responding in 1986 to the AIDS crisis, C. Everett Koop, former Surgeon General of the United States, strongly endorsed sex education, recommending that it begin in the third grade. Koop has been severely criticized for his positions on sex education, AIDS education, use of condoms, and abortion.[127] In July 1989 after eight years as Surgeon General Koop resigned. Attitudes toward sexual issues brought down a second Surgeon General, Joycelyn Elders. Appointed by President Clinton in 1992, Elders, a pediatrician from Arkansas, was asked to resign in December 1994, just two years after her appointment reportedly as a result of announced positions she had taken publicly on sexuality topics such as distribution of condoms, abortion, and, masturbation. Individuals and groups like the American Coalition for Traditional Values called for her resignation after she responded to a question at the United Nations World AIDS Day to the effect that masturbation is a part of human sexuality and perhaps should be a topic of study. You will note that the SIECUS study found ten states which do include study of masturbation in their sexuality curricula.

Critics of sexuality education believe that exposure of young people to sex education leads to promiscuity and threatens traditional family values. They are concerned about the lack of well-trained instructors. Perhaps they have a right to be concerned about lack of trained teachers; the 1993 SIECUS study found that fewer than half of the states provide training in sexuality education.[128] Opponents are worried that the current curricula stress the physical aspects rather than the moral issues of sexuality

---

[126]SIECUS, *Unfinished Business*, pp. 19–20.

[127]See, for example, "Disowning the Surgeon General," *Harper's Magazine* 275, no. 1647 (August 1987): 16–17.

[128]SIECUS, *Unfinished Business*, p. 8.

education. They claim that sexuality education has not been able to solve the problem of teenage pregnancies and sexually transmitted diseases. They argue instead for a sexuality education curriculum that promotes abstinence. This point of view accounts for the increased number of abstince-only curricula.

As early as the start of the 1990s seventy-two percent of over 1500 adults interviewed for the 22nd Annual Gallup Poll of the Public's Attitudes Toward the Public Schools favored making sexuality education courses a requirement.[129] Although some critics argue that education about sex should be the parents' responsibility, repeated polls confirm that a sizable majority of the public look to the schools for imparting both sexuality information and values to American children and young adults.

Curriculum planners are likely to encounter controversy whatever position they take with regard to sexuality education. If they put sexuality education in the schools, some communities will object to its presence in the curriculum. If they ignore sexuality education, critics say the schools are neglecting their responsibilities and not meeting the needs of learners or society. If they establish a purely biological approach to sexuality education or try to teach sexual content in a value-free context, criticism arises because the school has omitted the moral aspects of the subject, and many people contend that the moral dimension is more important than the biological. If they introduce moral education—that is, values—which values will be taught? For example, shall the school condemn, condone, or ignore artificial birth control measures? The debate over sexuality education in the schools is comparable to the old Middle Eastern anecdote of the little boy, the old man, and the mule. If the old man leads the mule while the boy rides, the boy is criticized for making the old man walk. If the boy leads the mule while the old man rides, the old man is blamed for mistreating the boy. If neither ride the mule, they are both called stupid. Or, if both ride the mule, they are accused of abusing the animal.

Examples of controversies over school health services exist in the presence of school-based health clinics and distribution of condoms. Joy G. Dryfoos viewed school-based primary health centers as "one of the building blocks of full-service schools." Dryfoos defined a full-service school in terms of law in Florida which pioneered the concept as a school that "integrates education, medical, social, and/or human services that are beneficial to meeting the needs of children and youth." Dryfoos noted that whereas only ten school-based clinics were in existence in 1983, by 1993 there were over 500.[130] Making the Grade, an organization supported by a grant from the Robert Wood Johnson Foundation and monitored by the George Washington Univeristy, to encourage state-community partnerships whose objective is the creation of comprehensive school-based health centers, found 1,154 such centers in 1998, mostly in urban districts, almost double the number in 1994.[131] Not all of these, however, distribute condoms or advise students on sexuality problems.

Part-time and full-time physicians and other health personnel provide physical examinations and much-needed information and counseling about health problems and

---

[129]Stanley M. Elam, "The 22nd Annual Gallup Poll of the Public's Attitudes Toward the Public Schools," *Phi Delta Kappan* 72, no. 1 (September 1990): 50.

[130]Joy G. Dryfoos, "Full-Service Schools: What They Are and How To Get to Be One," *NASSP Bulletin* 77, no. 557 (December 1993): 1–3.

[131]Making the Grade, Web site: http://www.gwu.edu/~mtg, accessed February 28, 1999.

family planning. Clinics have been established at elementary, middle, and secondary school levels. A particular point of conflict between the school and community is the dispensing of contraceptives or prescriptions for contraceptives and pertinent counseling to middle and high school students. Some religious, political, and ethnic groups have strongly protested contraceptive services. The National Conference of Catholic Bishops, for example, has repeatedly protested the distribution of contraceptives in the public schools and against abortion.

School systems in the United States and Canada have provided both contraceptives and counseling through their school clinics. In the winter of 1999 the French government authorized school nurses to distribute morning-after pills to teenage girls. In the fall of 1990 Baltimore became one of the first cities in the United States to distribute both birth control pills and condoms in its middle and high schools. In the spring of 1991, the New York City Board of Education, in spite of objections from religious groups, approved a plan to distribute condoms in its high schools beginning in the fall of 1991. The Philadelphia school board took a similar action in the summer of 1991. Among some forty urban school systems which make condoms available to youth are Chicago, Los Angeles, Miami, and Washington. The New York Supreme Court may have set a precedent for other areas in its decision that students did not have to obtain parental consent to receive condoms.[132] The U.S. Supreme Court in early 1996 upheld the decision of the Massachusetts Judicial Court that rejected parental objections to the distribution of condoms, a voluntary program for junior and senior high school students in Falmouth, Massachusetts.

In spite of the controversial nature of condom distribution forty-one percent of the public surveyed by the 25th Annual Phi Delta Kappa/Gallup Poll supported distribution of condoms to all students who want them while another nineteen percent approved distribution with parental consent.[133] Through preliminary and follow-up studies of high school students who had access to condoms in a Los Angeles County high school Mark A. Schuster and others concluded that making condoms available to students resulted in improvement in condom use by boys but no increase in sexual activity.[134]

Educators and the public, by and large, agree that the school has some responsibility for helping young people develop the knowledge and attitudes necessary to preserve and improve their own and the nation's health. Thus, exemplifying the principle of adaptation of the curriculum to the needs of the learners, society, the times, and the subject matter, schools have modified their curricula of health education, science, and the social studies to incorporate study of critical health and social problems.

Curriculum planners can make a convincing argument that the preservation of the health and well-being of the American people (and therefore, the nation) is the most basic survival skill of all. In urgency, it surpasses thinking skills, reading, writing, and

---

[132]584 N.Y.S. 2d (N.Y. Sup. Ct, 1992). See also Michael J. Forbes, "Legality of a High School Condom Distribution Program to Prevent HIV Infection: *Alfonso v. Fernandez,*" *Journal of Law & Education* 22, no. 1 (Winter 1993): 134–138.

[133]Elam et al.,"The 25th Annual Phi Delta Kappa/Gallup Poll," p. 152. See also Johnson and Immerwahr, *First Things First,* pp. 50–51 on the public's attitudes toward sex education proposals.

[134]Marl A. Schuster, Robert M. Bell, Sandra H. Berry, and David E. Kanouse, "Impact of High School Condom Availability on Sexual Attitudes and Behaviors," *Family Planning Perspectives* 30, no. 6 (March/April 1998): 67–72 & 88, Web site: http://www.edc.gov/nchswww/releases/97news/97news/nsfgteen.htm, accessed October 2, 1999.

arithmetic. In spite of challenges sexuality education has become a staple of today's curriculum. One strategy in handling complaints by parents about the sexuality curriculum is to allow students to opt out of the course or the part of the course that deals with sexual topics.

Deborah P. Britzman posed a thoughtful question about sexuality education: "Shall we admit that nothing about sex education is easy and that, if the direction is to make a curriculum that both forgets the difficulty of knowledge and does not incite curiosity, sex education will continue to signify 'our passion for ignorance'?"[135]

MULTICULTURALISM

Racial/Ethnic Integration. Ever since the decision in the case of *Brown v. Board of Education of Topeka, Kansas*[136] in which the U.S. Supreme Court ruled segregation of the races unconstitutional, efforts have been under way to eliminate vestiges of racial discrimination in the schools. Problem areas have included curriculum materials that were slanted toward white, middle-class culture to teaching methods, testing, and administrative practices such as busing, desegregation of faculties, and methods of discipline.

James S. Coleman, sociologist, surveyed some 4,000 elementary and secondary schools, 60,000 teachers, and 600,000 students to determine the extent and sources of inequality of educational opportunity among ethnic groups.[137] Authorized by the 1964 Civil Rights Act, the Coleman Report, which was issued in 1966, supported the desegregation of schools. Coleman concluded that achievement of students is influenced first by their social environment (families and peers); second, by their teachers; and third, by nonpersonal resources such as per pupil expenditures on education. A dozen years later, after observing the operation of schools that had been integrated, Coleman concluded that integration per se does not necessarily increase the achievement of black students.[138] He remained committed to integration but maintained that parents should choose whether black students attend integrated schools.

That not all black parents have been satisfied with progress made by their children in the public schools is evidenced by the suit brought in 1986 by eight families, including Linda Brown Smith (of the 1954 Brown v. Board of Education decision), once again against the board of education of Topeka, Kansas. At issue was the contention by the black families that Topeka had not done enough to desegregate its schools. U.S. District Court Judge Richard D. Rogers ruled in the spring of 1987 against the plaintiffs, a decision that was reversed by a three-judge panel of the Tenth U.S. Circuit Court of Appeals in December 1989, in effect holding that segregation still existed in the Topeka schools. With federal courts beginning to release school districts from federal desegregation orders, as in the 1992 U.S. Supreme Court's Dekalb County, Geor-

---

[135]Deborah P. Britzman, *Lost Subjects, Contested Objects: Toward a Psychoanalytical Inquiry of Learning* (Albany, N.Y.: State University of New York Press, 1998), p. 76.

[136]*Brown v. Board of Education of Topeka, Kansas* 347 U.S. 483, 74 Sup. Ct. 686 (1954).

[137]See James S. Coleman et al. *Equality of Educational Opportunity* (Washington, D.C.: U.S. Office of Education, 1966).

[138]See the *Miami Herald,* September 24, 1978, p. 19-A.

gia decision, the Supreme Court in the spring of 1992 directed the Tenth Circuit Court of Appeals to reconsider its ruling.

Other school systems are still grappling with the problem of integrating the schools. A 1993 report by the Harvard Project on School Desegregation found that segregation of blacks and Hispanics in predominantly minority schools, primarily in poor, large urban areas, has been on the increase. The report indicated that integration occurred more often in rural, small, and medium-sized communities.[139]

The magnet school, which was discussed in Chapter 9, has provided a partial solution to the problem of multicultural student bodies in urban settings. Busing, primarily of black children to predominantly white schools, has been a frequent court-ordered remedy since the U.S. Supreme Court's decision in the case of *Swann v. Charlotte-Mecklenburg Board of Education,* which required desegregation "with all deliberate speed."[140] The laudable concept of the magnet school has itself been attacked for splitting the community.

Oklahoma City may well have become a pivotal case in deciding the length of time that school systems must continue busing for the purpose of integration. Like many other school systems prior to *Brown,* Oklahoma City had maintained a de jure segregated system. Under court order Oklahoma City instituted in 1972 a busing plan designed to correct racial imbalances in the public schools. In 1984 the U.S. District Court ruled that Oklahoma City's schools were now integrated and court supervision could terminate. In 1985 Oklahoma City ceased busing of pupils in kindergarten and the first three grades and permitted parents to send their children to neighborhood elementary schools.

Because many neighborhoods in Oklahoma City were segregated de facto, the schools in those neighborhoods again became racially imbalanced once busing ceased. Black parents argued that the school system must continue busing as long as it is necessary in order to maintain racial balance. In 1989 the Tenth U.S. Circuit Court of Appeals agreed with their position and reversed the district court's decision. The case then proceeded to the U.S. Supreme Court. In January 1991 the Supreme Court took issue with the ruling of the appeals court and directed federal judges to discontinue their supervision once the court-ordered plans had successfully desegregated the schools.

Another important and closely watched case began in Kansas City, Missouri, in 1978. In this legal action, black parents in urban Kansas City sought admission of their children to suburban school districts, a desegregation measure that was permitted by the U.S. Supreme Court in an October 1990 decision. Litigation brought by the state of Missouri in 1997 sought to free Kansas City from continuing crosstown busing as no longer necessary.

In various parts of the country members of all racial and ethnic groups are raising the question of whether allowing parents to send their children to the school of their choice and/or near to their homes might not be a better solution to racial discrepancies in education than busing. Questions have been raised in recent years about the validity

---

[139]See Gary Orfield et al.,"The Growth of Segregation in American Schools: Changing Patterns of Segregation and Poverty Since 1968," *Equity and Excellence in Education* 27, no. 1 (April l994): 5–8.

[140]*Swann v. Charlotte-Mecklenburg Board of Education,* 402 U.S. 1 (1971).

of the practice of integration.[141] Critics note that even in some cases where physical integration has been achieved segregation by curriculum, that is, the placement of black students in remedial and less demanding classes with lowered expectation of achievement, continues. Perhaps Nashville, Tennessee's experience provides clues toward solution of the segregation-integration dilemma. In the fall of 1998 the courts permitted Nashville schools to cease court-ordered busing with the stipulation that Nashville would provide renovated or new school centers nearer pupils' homes.

At the time of publication of this text, the trend is clearly away from court-ordered busing for purposes of integrating the schools. Busing plans to desegregate have been or are being ended in communities across the country from Jacksonville, Florida to Seattle, including Boston, a center of angry protest over the desegregation plan mandated by the U.S. District Court in 1974.

More than forty years after the original *Brown v. Board of Education* ruling, problems related to racial integration of the schools have not been completely resolved as seen in widely-reported cases, for examples: When an Alabama white high school principal had sought to cancel the 1994 school prom if interracial couples attended, controversy erupted in the community, resulting in the principal's reversing himself, his suspension, reinstatement, reassignment, and national attention. Hernando High School, Mississippi made the headlines in 1997 when a white female student challenged time-honored practices including dual principals, one white, one black and co-class presidents, one white, one black; other offices and honors divided racially.

Adding fuel to the fire, a controversial book, *The Bell Curve* by Richard J. Herrnstein and Charles A. Murray,[142] resurrected the issue of the connection between intelligence and heredity, a thesis which has been widely challenged. Critics charged the book as racist and challenged the validity of IQ tests as a measure of intelligence. Psychologists have long questioned to what degree an IQ score is affected by heredity or environment. The concept of differentiated intelligences counters the concept of a global intelligence quotient. James A. Banks noted that *The Bell Curve* was "consistent with the conservative political agenda for the 1990s."[143] He commented, "A basic thesis of *The Bell Curve* is that people are poor because of their genetic characteristics, not because of the lack of social and economic opportunities in U.S. society."[144]

Symptomatic of impediments on the road to multiculturalism are the objections raised by some Native Americans (in Los Angeles in 1997 and in Asheville, North Carolina in 1999) to the propriety of the longtime practice of using American Indian names such as Braves, Redskins, and Seminoles for high school and college teams and their mascots. The need to eliminate racial and ethnic tensions and to design curricula that meet the needs of children and youth of all ethnic groups in America's multicultural population is a continuing problem for curriculum planners.

To reduce racial conflict and prevent racial problems from arising, many school systems have established multiracial committees whose task it is to recommend solu-

---

[141]See, for examples, James S. Kunen, "The End of Integration," *TIME* 147, no. 18 (April 29, 1996): 39–45 and "Has Integration Failed?" *Modern Maturity* 37, no. 2 (April-May 1994): 24–34.

[142]Richard J. Herrnstein and Charles A. Murray, *The Bell Curve: Intelligence and Class Structure in American Life* (New York: Free Press, 1994).

[143]James A. Banks, ed., *Multicultural Education, Transformative Knowledge and Action: Historical and Contemporary Practices* (New York: Teachers College Press, 1996), p. 79.

[144]Ibid.

tions to tensions and incidents of conflict among racial groups. Multiracial committees and entire faculties find that, in order to eliminate negative attitudes and conflicts, they must analyze all aspects of the school, including the "hidden curriculum"—the school climate, social relationships among individuals and groups, values and attitudes held by both student and faculty, presses on student conduct, unspoken expectations, and unwritten codes of conduct.

New Curriculum Responses.   Responses to the issue of providing a suitable education for minorities have evoked considerable controversy. The first of these developments is a proposal to desegregate the curriculum; the second is the creation of all-male, predominantly black schools.

Curriculum Desegregation.   The thrust of desegregation efforts is shifting from the physical movement of pupils to securing racial balance in the schools to reconstruction of the curriculum. Demands are increasing for the institution of "Afrocentric" curricula that would feature contributions made by early African civilizations before colonial powers expanded into the continent. Proponents of Afrocentric programs feel that the schools have placed too much emphasis on European achievements and culture. They point to Africa as the birthplace of humankind, cite African achievements in the fine arts, mathematics, and science, and take the position that the school curriculum ignores or minimizes the contributions of African civilizations.

Like bilingual education, other-centric curricula—which some people call a "curriculum of inclusion"—is an issue that goes to the heart of the debate over cultural pluralism versus the melting pot of acculturation. Should the curriculum reflect and equate all cultures, maintaining their separate identities and creating a mosaic or fruit salad as some people term it, or should schools seek to develop citizens who manifest values of a common, national American culture? For example, the Portland, Oregon, school system promotes multiculturalism through its *African-American Baseline Essays,* which present contributions attributed to African civilizations.[145] Black and white educators are found on both the supporting and the opposing sides of the debate over ethnocentric curricula. An ostensible purpose of Afrocentric curricula is to enhance black students' pride in their ethnic origins. Questions have been raised, however, about the historical interpretation of some of the content presented in some of the Afrocentric curricula. In addition, some educators are concerned about the extent to which ethnocentric curricula will further fragment the curriculum. Will there need to be Latino-centric, Asian-centric, Islamic-centric, and many additional other-centric curricula to reflect every culture represented in the public schools?

Cultural Diversity.   Like so many concepts in education multiculturalism can be and is interpreted in a variety ways from a simplistic level of familiarizing ethnic groups with samplings of each other's culture to the title of Christine E. Sleeter's book *Multicultural Education as Social Activism*[146] or, as Banks put it, "a vehicle to facilitate the

---

[145]Portland Public Schools, *African-American Baseline Essays* (Portland, Ore.: Portland Public Schools, 1989). See also Portland Public Schools, *Multicultural/Multiethnic Education in Portland Public Schools* (Portland, Ore.: Portland Public Schools, 1988).

[146]Christine E. Sleeter, *Multicultural Education as Social Activism* (Albany, N.Y.: State University of New York Press, 1996).

transformation of the nation's educational institutions and the structural inclusion of the nation's diverse groups into U.S. society."[147]

The core issue in multiculturalism or cultural diversity is the predominance of a culture that blends various subcultures into a "melting pot" versus the maintenance of separate and distinct subcultures within an overall framework. Those who champion a melting pot concept point to the eventual assimilation of early immigrant groups—the Irish, the Italians, the Poles, the Germans, the Scandinavians, Asians, and others—into the American culture. Lilian and Oscar Handlin viewed the social reforms of the Great Society of the 1960s as resulting in supplanting equality of opportunity with equality of results, a breakdown in traditional family and social values, a splintering of homogeneity in America into numerous subgroups, the rejection of responsibility for one's actions and the portrayal of self as victim, the identification of success in terms of group-affiliation instead of individual achievement, and the reinterpretation of American history.[148] Speaking of multiculturalism the Handlins said:

> By denigrating the very core of traditional American middle-class education, in favor of the mores of the social margins, multiculturists effectively robbed students of the few tools useful for their future that schools could impart."[149]

Negative criticism has greeted Paul Boyer's new multiculturized version of Lewis Paul Todd and Merle Curti's history textbook, *The American Nation,* for portraying in John Leo's words "a balkanized view of America.[150]

Less acceptant of the melting pot concept are Hispanics and blacks. Typical of challenges to the melting pot concept is the comment by Hugh B. Price:

> The trouble is that the meltingpot works only at the margins and only in some aspects of life. It seldom works socially and has succeeded in education and the labor market only under duress. It took decades of political, judicial, and legislative pressure to include some, and only some, minorities and women in the melting pot.[151]

Jeannie Oakes saw melting as "almost entirely in one direction—" Americanization of immigrants "in the sense of conformity to white Anglo-Saxon mores." [152]

Advocates of cultural diversity feel multicultural education should permeate the curriculum, not just in English and social studies, the more common fields for study of diverse cultures. Some look for ways of culturally diversifying mathematics and science as well. Reminiscent of the brief flurry over the Korean mathematics approach known as chisenbop, suggestions have been made, for example, to teach the mathematical system of the ancient Mayas.

Most educators concede that the public schools have done a poor job of teaching about the contributions of ethnic groups. Educators generally endorse and promote inclusion of information about the contributions of males and females of all races,

---

[147]Banks, *Multicultural Education,* p. 336.

[148]Lilian and Oscar Handlin, "America and Its Discontents: A Great Society Legacy," *The American Scholar* 64, no. 1 (Winter 1995): 15–37.

[149]Ibid., p.36.

[150]John Leo, "Multicultural History Book Trips, Stumbles and Falls," *The Orlando Sentinel,* March 23, 1994, p. A-15. See Paul Boyer, *Todd and Curti: The American Nation* (Austin, Tex.: Holt, Rinehart and Winston, 1995).

[151]Hugh B. Price, "Multiculturalism: Myths and Realities," *Phi Delta Kappan* 74, no. 3 (November 1992): 212.

[152]Jeannie Oakes, *Keeping Track: How Schools Structure Inequality* (New Haven: Yale University Press, 1985), p. 26.

creeds, ethnic groups, and national origins. However, some educators state that just adding ethnocentric and multicultural content to achieve this purpose is not sufficient because it simply superimposes this content on a traditional, white, male, Anglo, middle-class curriculum structure.

Addressing selection of content in the schools, Deborah P. Britzman concluded:

> The liberal arts canon, or the body of knowledge deemed "sacred and great," valorizes the worldviews of white male writers to the extent of significantly excluding all other views. The presentation of European and North American white male authors as the faithful transmitters of universal experience obscures their cultural specificity, sociohistorical context, and political interests served and perpetuated by the canon's selective biases.[153]

Geneva Gay advocated curriculum desegregation as a means of achieving educational equality.[154] Gay classified efforts to construct curricula for culturally diverse populations as first-, second-, and third-generation curriculum desegregation. According to Gay's classification, the first generation introduced the study of the contributions of ethnic personalities, revision of textbooks to eliminate bias against and stereotypes of minorities and women, and programs such as compensatory education, Head Start, Upward Bound, and cultural enrichment. The second generation incorporated bilingual education, multicultural education, provisions for the handicapped, and efforts to eliminate sex discrimination. Gay noted that neither the first- nor the second-generation curriculum desegregation efforts changed the basic structure of the curriculum. The third and current generation of curriculum desegregation must, according to Gay, subscribe to the principle that "a pluralistic ideology must replace an assimilationist orientation" and work toward the goal of "ultimately making American society more genuinely egalitarian."[155] Gay set forth a difficult task for the schools:

> anything short of total instructional reform is likely to be ineffective . . . educational equality for diverse learners cannot be achieved within the existing curriculum structures and with present assumptions about what are valuable educational outcomes. At their very core these structures and assumptions are ethnocentric and discriminatory . . . the foundations of curriculum . . . must become culturally pluralistic . . . information taught about various cultures and groups must be presented as having equal value and . . . expected outcomes must be deliberately taught. Knowledge of facts about cultural pluralism, values that promote human diversity, and skills in social activism to combat oppression and create a more egalitarian society and world should all be included in efforts to achieve curriculum desegregation.

> Multiculturalism should be the driving force of subsequent efforts to desegregate school curricula. It is a reconstructive and transformative principle. Its application necessitates changing the fundamental value assumptions, substantive content, operational strategies, and evaluation procedures of all instructional programs that are planned and implemented for all students.[156]

---

[153]Deborah P. Britzman, *Practice Makes Practice: A Critical Study of Learning to Teach* (Albany, N.Y.: State University of New York Press, 1991), p. 41.

[154]Geneva Gay, "Achieving Educational Equality Through Curriculum Desegregation," *Phi Delta Kappan* 72, no. 1 (September 1990): 56–62.

[155]Ibid., p. 60.

[156]Ibid., p. 62.

Schools have moved toward multicultural curricula. Florida, for example, in 1994 passed legislation requiring incorporating in the curriculum study of contributions of African-Americans and history of the Holocaust in addition to studying the content of the Declaration of Independence, the essentials of the U.S. Constitution, and flag education.[157] Ironically, while the state of Florida was broadening implementation of aspects of a multicultural curriculum, conservatives on the Lake County, Florida school board made national news in the spring of 1994 with a 3-2 vote requiring teachers to teach their students that American culture is superior to other cultures. American superiority according to the Lake County policy encompassed capitalism, republican form of government, patriotism, free enterprise, family values, and religious freedom. The local teachers union strongly opposed the policy as unnecessary on the grounds that patriotic values are already being taught and such a requirement is parochial in outlook. Elections that fall swept three new board members, all opponents of the policy, into office sealing its doom and preventing it from being put into practice.

The implementation of multicultural curricula has not always come easily as evidenced by New York City's experience with the initial draft of its *Children of the Rainbow* curriculum guides, the first of which appeared in 1990. Opponents charged that multicultural curricula conflicted with parental rights, featured unacceptable lifestyles, inappropriately dealt with social issues, and departed from the basic skills.[158] In a much different vein the Oakland, California school board created a furor at the tail end of the 1990s with its decision to declare Black English, otherwise known as Ebonics, as a second language, a move widely condemned by both prominent blacks and whites as an impediment to black students' learning standard English. Language specialists have held Black English to be a dialect of American English and not a foreign language. The Oakland board clarified the intent of its decision as creation of a path toward learning standard English, not incorporation of Black English into the curriculum as a foreign language to be taught and learned. Hawaii, too, faces its own linguistic difficulties as it wrestles with the use of Pidgin English which some hold as detrimental to learning standard English.

Rejecting an either/or approach, the public endorsed by a substantial margin (seventy-five percent) a curriculum that promotes both one common tradition and diverse traditions of different populations. Fifty-three percent would put equal emphasis on both.[159]

All-Male, Primarily Black Schools. Alternative education took on a new aspect in 1990 with Milwaukee's plans to create within the public school system two African-American Immersion Schools (one elementary and one middle school). New York City drew up plans for the Ujamaa Institute, which would also focus on programs for black male students. To counter objections to the planned schools, proponents argued that the schools, located in the inner city, already have an entirely African-American student body. Opponents point out that the schools may still violate Title IX of the Educational Amendments of 1972, which outlawed discrimination based on gender. In fact,

---

[157]Florida Statute 233.061, effective July 1, 1994.
[158]Leslie Agard-Jones, "Implementing Multicultural Education," *Multicultural Education* 1, no. 1 (Summer 1993): 13–15, 38.
[159]Elam et al., *The 26th Annual Phi Delta Kappa/Gallup Poll*, pp. 52–53.

Detroit had planned to open in the fall of 1991 three schools, open to males of all races, with an African-American curricular emphasis. The American Civil Liberties Union (ACLU) and the National Organization for Women (NOW) brought suit, objecting to the exclusion of girls. In August 1991 U.S. District Court Judge George Woods ruled that the schools could not open unless females were also admitted. So that the schools might open, the Detroit school board agreed to admit girls.

Dealing with Cultural Diversity.   Determining what responses the schools should make to the cultural diversity of our population is one of the greatest challenges for curriculum workers. The issue of multiculturalism and plural values versus cultural mainstreaming and common values has grown in intensity on both public school and college campuses.[160] The issue is entangled in a myriad of social, political, economic, educational, philosophical, secular, and religious values. Banks advocated the creation of an "authentic [in contrast to imposed] unum," a society that "actualizes the concept of *e pluribus unum,* out of many, one."[161]

On the positive side, all the recent efforts to empower ethnic minorities and women prove that educators are searching for ways to educate all children and raise the achievement level of those individuals and groups who are not now succeeding in the schools. Banks observed, "The United States has done better than most other nations in creating a society that actualizes a just and authentic *unum.*"[162]

Citing George Washington's concept of *e pluribus unum,* that is, the creation of a unified people through assimilation of immigrants in American customs, Arthur M. Schlesinger, Jr. observed:

> "Our task is to combine due appreciation of the splendid diversity of the nation with due emphasis on the great unifying Western ideas of individual freedom, political democracy, and human rights."[163]

Commented Schlesinger, "If the republic now turns away from Washington's old goal of 'one people,' what is its future?—disintegration of the national community, apartheid, Balkanization, tribalization?"[164]

Banks would have the school teach about both American ideals and American realities, saying, "In a democratic curriculum, students need to be taught about and have opportunities to acquire American democratic values at the same time learning about American realities that challenge these ideals, such as discrimination based on race, gender, and social class."[165]

---

[160]See William A. Henry, III, "Upside Down in the Groves of Academe," *Time* 137, no. 23 (April 1, 1991): 66–68. See also Paul Gray, "Whose America?" *Time* 138, no. 1 (July 8, 1991): 12–17. See also Arthur Schlesinger, Jr., "The Cult of Ethnicity, Good and Bad," *Time* 138, no. 1 (July 8, 1991)): 21 and Schlesinger, Jr., *The Disuniting of America* (Knoxville, Tenn.: Whittle Direct Books, 1991). See also articles on Afrocentrism in *Newsweek* 118, no. 13 (September 23, 1991): 42–50.

[161]Banks, ed., *Multicultural Education,* p. 335.

[162]Ibid., p. 336.

[163]Arthur M. Schlesinger, Jr., *The Disuniting of America: Reflections on a Multicultural Society* (New York: W. W. North, 1992), p. 138.

[164]Ibid., p. 118.

[165]Banks, James A., *Educating Citizens in a Multicultural Society* (New York: Teachers College Press, 1997), p. 9.

NATIONAL STANDARDS

Without a doubt as we enter the third millenium the movement toward setting standards, making schools and teachers accountable, and assessing student achievement continues strong and is intensifying. As we noted elsewhere in this text some dissenters object to the entire direction education has taken to specify uniform standards and assessment, whether national or state, whether voluntary or mandated, holding that schools should be more concerned about curricula that foster student self-esteem and bringing about improvements in American society. Critical of the adoption of content-standards as a means of reform, Ernest R. House wrote: "Such an approach overestimates the degree to which teachers will adopt standards and miscalculates how teachers will react if their students' test scores are made public. The history of such attempts is rampant with teachers' teaching the test items under conditions of strong accountability and manipulating or distorting the scores (opportunism)."[166] The effects of "tougher standards," in the view of Alfie Kohn are to make testing centers of our schools and to impair creative teaching.[167]

John S. Kendall and Robert J. Marzano[168] placed the impetus for setting national standards on *A Nation at Risk,*[169] (1983) whereas Diane Ravitch[170] attributed the beginning of the movement toward national standards and assessment to the promulgation of *America 2000,*[171] the national educational goals proposed by President George Bush and the state governors. In spite of dissatisfactions with public education that evoked the standards movement, Marzano and Kendall concluded that "The alleged decline in the knowledge and basic skills of American students—as well as the decline in SAT scores—are not matters of fact."[172] Included in their citation of "well-regarded researchers who have challenged the notion that American Education is failing" are the works of David Berliner and Bruce Biddle and Gerald W. Bracey.[173]

Although objections have been leveled at the standards-movement, the specification of state and national standards remains popular with the public and with those whom the public has elected to office. In the early 1990s key features of the Kentucky

[166]Ernest R. House, *Schools for Sale: Why Free Market Policies Won't Improve America's Schools and What Will* (New York: Teachers College Press, 1998), p. 91.

[167]Alfie Kohn, *Rescuing Our Schools From "Tougher Standards,"* web site: http://www.alfiekohn.org/teaching/standards.htm, accessed May 5, 1999.

[168]John S. Kendall and Robert J. Marzano, *Content Knowledge: A Compendium of Standards and Benchmarks for K–12 Education,* 2nd ed. (Aurora, Col.: Mid-Continent Regional Educational Laboratory, 1997 and Alexandria, Va.: Association for Supervision and Curriculm Development, 1997), p. 1.

[169]See Chapter 2 of this text.

[170]Diane Ravitch, *National Standards in American Education: A Citizen's Guide* (Washington, D.C.: The Brookings Institution, 1995), p. 2.

[171]See Chapter 6 of this text.

[172]Robert J. Marzano and John S. Kendall, *Essential Knowledge: The Debate Over What American Students Should Know,* Advance Briefing: www.mcrel.org/standards/articles/advbriefing.asp, p. 2, accessed March 31, 1999. See also Robert J. Marzano and John S. Kendall, *Essential Knowledge: The Debate Over what American Students Should Know* (Aurora, Col.: McRel Institute, 1999).

[173]Ibid., p. 3. See David Berliner and Bruce Biddle, *The Manufactured Crisis: Myths, Fraud, and the Attack on America's Public Schools* (Reading, Mass.: Addison-Wesley-Longman, 1996). See also Gerald W. Bracey, *Setting the Record Straight: Reponses to Misconceptions About Public Education in the United States* (Alexandria, Va.: Association for Supervision and Curriculum Development, 1997). See also annual reports on the condition of public education by Bracey since 1992 in fall issues (usually October) of *Phi Delta Kappan.*

reform movement, for example, included "the development of a state authentic assessment system"[174] and "new high-level standards."[175] While President Clinton in the spring of 1999 was calling on the Congress to enact new national educational standards, the governor and legislature of Florida were enacting an educational reform package which included grading schools from A to F, tougher standards for students and teachers, statewide assessment of student achievement in grades three through ten, and the end of social promotion. Ending social promotions is predicted to result in a significant increase in numbers of pupils held-back.

Individuals and groups have engaged in the specification of standards. Hirsch, as noted earlier in this chapter, has set forth core knowledge standards. Marzano and Kendall labeled the standards recommended by Hirsch as arbitrary, flawed, and inconsistent.[176] They subscribed to the belief that standards should be established by "those who have a thorough grounding in their discipline and who can see the future of their areas with enough clarity and understanding that they are equipped to make reasonable judgments about the information and skills that are basic to understanding."[177] Not only are decisions on specifying standards a problem but Terry J. Foriska pointed out that decisions on types of standards must be made.[178] To demonstrate the extent of standards development Marzano and Kendall listed professional organizations and coalitions that have produced standards documents (see Table 14.2).[179]

More acute even than the establishment of state standards is the creation of national standards. Among those who espouse state standards, subscribing to the belief of the state's responsibility for education, are those who oppose national standards, a national curriculum, and national assessment. In spite of objections to national efforts in this direction, however, in actuality we already have elements of national standards, curriculum, and assessment.

The current debate over the issues of a national curriculum, national standards, and national assessment is reminiscent of the argument over the creation of the National Assessment of Educational Progress (NAEP) in the 1960s when educators predicted dire results if NAEP were allowed to conduct nationwide tests. Some forty years have passed and NAEP has taken a valued place in the educational spectrum not only because of its technical competence but also because it has zealously guarded results so individuals and schools could not be identified. Its results are reported for regions, age groups, and ethnic groups which lessens its impact on the curriculum of individual schools.

A national curriculum would mean some uniformity of standards across the country. In effect, we already have earmarks of a rather loose national curriculum at the moment. The same textbooks are adopted in many states, bringing a semblance of uniformity at least to content. Professional associations have produced and disseminated curriculum materials widely, further standardizing the curriculum. What is different

[174]Betty E. Steffy, *The Kentucky Education Reform* (Lancaster, Pa.: Technomic Publishing Co., 1993), p. 57.

[175]Ibid., p. 262.

[176]Marzano and Kendall, *Essential Knowledge*, pp. 3, 4.

[177]Ibid., p. 5.

[178]Terry J. Foriska, *Restructuring Around Standards: A Practitioner's Guide to Design and Implementation* (Thousand Oaks, Calif.: Corwin Press, 1998), p. 2.

[179]For a detailed listing of standards see Kendall and Marzano, *Content Knowledge,* op cit.

TABLE 14.2

STANDARDS DOCUMENTS
PRODUCED BY PROFESSIONAL ORGANIZATIONS AND COALITIONS

SUBJECT AREA	DOCUMENT(S)
Science	National Research Council (1996). *National Science Education Standards.* Washington, DC: National Academy Press.
Foreign Language	National Standards in Foreign Language Education Project (1996). *Standards for Foreign Language Learning: Preparing for the 21st Century.* Lawrence, KS: Allen Press.
Language Arts	National Council of Teachers of English and the International Reading Association (1996). *Standards for the English Language Arts.* Urbana, IL: National Council of Teachers of English.
History	National Center for History in the Schools. (1994). *National Standards for History for Grades K–4: Expanding Children's World in Time and Space.* Los Angeles: Author.
	National Center for History in the Schools (1994). *National Standards for United States History: Exploring the American Experience.* Los Angeles: Author.
	National Center for History in the Schools (1994). *National Standards for World History: Exploring Paths to the Present.* Los Angeles: Author.
	National Center for History in the Schools (1996). *National Standards for History: Basic Edition.* Los Angeles: Author.
Arts	Consortium of National Arts Education Associations (1994). *National Standards for Arts Education: What Every Young American Should Know and Be Able to Do in the Arts.* Reston, VA: Music Educators National Conference.
Health	Joint Committee on National Health Education Standards (1995). *National Health Education Standards: Achieving Health Literacy.* Reston, VA: Association for the Advancement of Health Education.
Civics	Center for Civic Education (1994). *National Standards for Civics and Goverment.* Calabasas, CA: Author.
Economics	National Council on Economic Education (1997). *Voluntary National Content Standards in Economics.* New York: Author.
Geography	Geography Education Standards Project (1994). *Geography for Life: National Geography Standards.* Washington, DC: National Geographic Research and Exploration.
Physical Education	National Association for Sport and Physical Education (1995). *Moving Into the Future, National Standards for Physical Education: A Guide to Content and Assessment.* St. Louis: Mosby.
Mathematics	National Council of Teachers of Mathematics (1989). *Curriculum and Evaluation Standards for School Mathematics.* Reston, VA: Author.
Social Studies	National Council for the Social Studies (1994). *Expectations of Excellence: Curriculum Standards for Social Studies.* Washington, DC: Author.

SOURCE: Robert J. Marzano and John S. Kendall, *Essential Knowledge: The Debate Over What American Students Should Know,* Advance Briefing: www.mcrel.org/standards/articles/advbriefing.asp, pp. 6–8, accessed March 31, 1999. Reprinted by permission.

from the 1960s is a planned, state- and federal-government-driven move toward establishing national content standards followed by national assessment programs which will, in effect, produce a national curriculum from Maine to Washington State. Educators, columnists, and laypeople are lined up on both sides of the issue: Shall we/can we establish a national curriculum with national standards and national assessment? One extreme maintains that national standards are a menace, contrary to the historic American system of education, and destructive of growth of individual schools. The other extreme sees national standards as the only solution to America's educational problems. The truth lies somewhere in between a system of national standards and local control. Indeed, a system of national standards that will work in America will require a delicate balance between national and local/state efforts.

Among the arguments against implementing national standards are: they will limit the creativity of local schools, they are likely to be minimal standards, it is impossible to establish a common set of standards in a country so diverse, they will fail without sufficient funding, and they will be limited to core disciplines. Proponents of federal and state standards argue: we need to be competitive educationally with other countries, national standards will encourage school improvement, national standards are necessary in an age of mobility of population, and present standards are too loose. The naysayers contend that national standards will not promote equality of opportunity for all children including minorities while the yea-sayers claim that the opposite is true. Our two major educational associations have taken different sides of the fence with the National Education Association opppsing national standards and assessment whereas the American Federation of Teachers led by Albert Shanker endorsed their development and use. Noting that "there are attractive arguments for federal and state control over curricula—to ensure a set of academic outcomes for all students in America—" Carl D. Glickman joined those opposed to federal and state control, saying:

> the underlying assumption is that local schools lack either the inclination or the capacity to develop and hold themselves to rigorous curricular goals and assessments . . . federal and state controls over local curricula is clearly a statement of skepticism about participatory democracy. . . . Developing curricula and standards "away" from local schools and communities rules out the very flexibility that state and federal policymakers claim to support in their schizophrenic exhortations of "empowerment."[180]

Hirsch, however, faulted the argument for local control, commenting on the "curricular chaos of the American elementary school":

> we assume, quite reasonably, that agreement has been reached locally regarding what shall be taught to children at each grade level—if not within the whole district, then certainly within an individual school. . . . But despite the democratic virtue of that principle, the idea that there exists a coherent plan for teaching content within the local district, or even within the individual school, is a gravely misleading myth[181]

Proposals of the Bush administration's *America 2000* (1991) and later, the Clinton administration's *Goals 2000, Educate America Act* (1994) have led to a complex

---

[180]Carl D. Glickman, *Revolutionizing America's Schools* (San Francisco: Jossey-Bass, 1998), p. 43.
[181]Hirsch, *The Schools We Need*, p. 26.

structure for implementation. The National Education Goals Panel, created by President Bush and the governors was charged with responsibility for monitoring annual progress toward achievement of the national goals. In 1991 the Congress authorized creation of the National Council on Education Standards and Testing (NCEST) whose purposes it was "to advise on the desirability and feasibility of national standards and tests" and "to recommend long-term policies, structures, and mechanisms for setting voluntary education standards and planning an appropriate system of tests."[182] NCEST recommended specification of national content standards and a system of assessments. Although NCEST did not recommend a single national examination, educators were quick to go on record opposing development of any instrument of that nature.[183]

NCEST envisioned national and state standards consisting of four types: content, student-performance, school-delivery (later to be called "opportunity-to-learn" (OTL), and system performance.[184] NCEST stipulated that these standards must:

- reflect high expectations, not expectations of minimal competency
- provide focus and direction, not become a national curriculum
- be national, not federal
- be voluntary, not mandated by the federal government
- be dynamic, not static[185]

A system of assessments, "linked to world-class standards," to be developed by the states and other organizations, would comprise both "individual student assessments and large-scale samples, such as the National Assessment of Educational Progress." They must be multiple, not a single test; voluntary, not mandatory; and developmental, not static.[186]

NCEST recommended creation of a coordinating body, the National Education Standards and Assessments Council (NESAC) to be appointed by the National Education Goals Panel, whose mission it would be "to establish guidelines for standards-setting assessment development and general criteria to determine the appropriateness of standards and assessments recommended."[187] The Congress, however, in 1994 authorized formation of a nineteen-member council to be appointed by the president that they called the National Education Standards and Improvement Council (NESIC).

Through the early 1990s a number of task forces were assembled to develop voluntary national standards. Beginning with the core academic fields English, geography, history, mathematics, and science, standards were developing in the arts, civics and government, economics, foreign language, health, industry skills, physical education, and social studies, as well as the five core areas. Release of the standards began in the

---

[182]The National Council on Education Standards and Testing, *Raising Standards for American Education* (Washington, D.C.: U.S. Government Printing Office, 1992), p. 1.

[183]See Diane Ravitch, *National Standards in American Education*, pp. 143–144.

[184]National Council on Educational Standards and Testing, *Raising Standards*, p. 13.

[185]Ibid., p. 3.

[186]Ibid., p. 4.

[187]Ibid., pp. 35–36.

mid-1990s.[188] That the development of standards has not been an easy task is seen in the case of history standards published in 1994 by the National Center for History in the Schools at the University of California at Los Angeles. The standards met with criticism from some people for its nontraditional interpretation of history.[189]

The simultaneous movement toward outcomes-based education (OBE, see below) required distinction between outcomes as perceived by OBE advocates and national standards. Ravitch described the differences, explaining that both OBE and standards specify what students need to know or perform, standards limit themselves to the cognitive domain, are measureable, and focus on the traditional subjects whereas OBE encompasses the affective domain, may be vague, and is interdisciplinary in nature.[190]

The development of a system of national assessment, to be labeled *American Achievement Tests,* capitalizes on a great deal of work that has been going on for some time. The National Council of Teachers of Mathematics has provided a model of efforts to develop standards in a field of specialization. Some states have assessment programs already in place as, for example, California with its Learning Assessment System. The NAEP has, of course, been assessing student achievement for many years.

Testing is, of course, a concomitant of standards. Determination of attainment of standards is accomplished through measurement techniques. "Discussions of standards tend to turn at once into debates and about testing" said Ravitch.[191] Basically, the issue centers around quantitative, that is, traditional and standardized tests, versus qualitative, that is, authentic, performance techniques and the use of portfolios. Historically and up to the present moment, schools have employed quantitative techniques to assess student achievement. It is not too much of an exaggeration to say that is the way the American public wants it. In colorful prose, however, Maxine Greene questioned the pursuit of quantifiable mastery: "It sometimes appears that the measurement people have joined forces with modern incarnations of the Puritan divines, trying to defend against an impinging wilderness, to keep the demons at bay."[192]

Regarding the current movement toward the creation and use of national assessment instruments, critics like Henry A. Giroux, for example, whose view on testing we noted in Chapter 13,[193] see the end result as the standardization of the curriculum, thereby resulting in ignoring the great diversity among students, schools, and communitites.

Heavily engaged in the development of standards and assessments and with support from the Pew Charitable Trusts and the John D. and Catherine T. MacArthur Foundation is the New Standards Project, a partnership that by spring 1995 involved seventeen states and six school districts. Administered by the Learning Research and

---

[188]See "Status Report on Voluntary National Standards in Education," *The Educational Forum* 58 (Summer 1994): 421–428.

[189]See Philip Cohen, "Challenging History: The Past Remains a Battleground for Schools," *Curriculum Update* (Winter 1995): 1–8.

[190]Ravitch, *National Standards*, p. 163.

[191]Ravitch, *National Standards in American Education*, p. 11.

[192]Maxine Greene, *Releasing the Imagination: Essays on Education, the Arts, and Social Change* (San Francisco: Jossey-Bass, 1995), p. 170.

[193]See p. 404 of this text.

Development Center of the University of Pittsburgh and the National Center on Education and the Economy (NCEE), the New Standards Project issued in 1996 a set of student performance standards for elementary, middle, and high school. The Project has moved away from traditional testing into the "Three P's: performance tasks, projects, and portfolios."[194]

Marc S. Tucker, President of NCEE, has clearly described NCEE's position on the movement to setting standards:

> The hallmark of the National Center's work is standards-based reform. We believe that education and training systems work best when clear standards—standards that match the highest in the world—are set forth for student achievement, accurate measures of progress toward those standards are devised, the people closest to the students are given the authority for figuring out how to get the students to the standards and are then held accountable for student progress.[195]

The New Standards Project has implemented a proposal of the Commission on the Skills of the American Workforce[196] for creation of a Certificate of Initial Mastery that verifies student achievement in the core and vocational subjects. Robert Rothman reported in 1995 that seven states (Indiana, Maine, Massachusetts, New York, Oregon, Texas, and Washington) have adopted some type of certificate of mastery or achievement. The state of Washington in 1993 set the certificate as a requirement to graduate from high school starting in the year 2000.[197] Questioning who has the right to set specific measurable standards for everybody, Theodore R. Sizer's account of *Horace's School* proposed parallel and competing standards shared by the state, the district, the local schools, parents, and students.[198] On the other hand, Albert Shanker, President of the American Federation of Teachers advocated a national curriculum, national standards, and national assessment "with stakes," that is, consequences for passing or failing the assessments.[199]

Whether educators favor a national curriculum, national standards and national assessments, the public clearly supports the idea as they have demonstrated on repeated Phi Delta Kappa/Gallup Polls. The 26th Annual Phi Delta Kappa/Gallup Poll of the Public's Attitudes Toward the Public Schools (1994) found eighty-three percent of those surveyed felt a basic curriculum for all schools to be either very important or quite important and seventy-three percent believed standardized national examinations based on a national curriculum that students must pass for promotion or graduation (as some people say, "with consequences") were either very important or quite

---

[194]See Robert Rothman, "The Certificate of Initial Mastery," *Educational Leadership* 58, no. 8 (May 1995): 41–45. See also John O'Neil, "National System of Standards, Exams Piloted," *ASCD Update* 34, no. 8 (October 1992): 1, 3–5.

[195]Marc S. Tucker, *Who We Are*, Web site: http://www.ncee.org/WhoWeAre/WhoPage.html, accessed May 7, 1999. See also Marc S. Tucker and Judy B. Codding, *Standards for Our Schools: How to Set Them, Measure Them, and Reach Them* (San Francisco: Jossey-Bass, 1998).

[196]Commission on the Skills of the American Workforce, *America's Choice: High Skills or Low Wages!* (Rochester, N.Y.: National Center on Education and the Economy, 1990).

[197]Robert Rothman, "The Certificate of Initial Mastery." *Educational Leadership* 52, no. 8 (May 1995): 44.

[198]Theodore R. Sizer, *Horace's School: Redesigning the American High School* (Boston: Houghton Mifflin, 1992), pp. 110, 114.

[199]Albert Shanker, "Making Standards Count," *Ameican Educator* 18, no. 3 (Fall 1994): 14, 16–19.

important.[200] Arguments for local determination of standards appear to run counter to opinions of a large segment of the public.

Speaking of a national curriculum, NCEST said:

> The definition of national standards must include the crafting of state curriculum frameworks. Such frameworks will make clear that we must abandon the minimum skill orientation, the emphasis on coverage not depth of understanding, and the premium that is often placed on students knowing isolated facts. Instead, the curriculum frameworks will be discipline-based, oriented toward thinking, understanding, problem solving, and knowledge integration with connections to the real world. Such frameworks should provide parameters, not prescriptions, for practice.[201]

Advocating a "standards-based education" Peter W. Hill and Carmel A. Crevola of the University of Melbourne concluded, "all students should have a right to an education system that ensures high standards for all."[202] Addressing the issues of national standards and assessments Ravitch provided some thoughtful remarks:

> Do we really want higher standards? Do we want schools where students work hard and take their education seriously? Do we want a society in which everyone is well educated and knowledgeable about history, literature, science, mathematics, and the arts? Or do we want schools where academic studies are no more important, perhaps less important, than athletics and social activities? . . . Finally, a system of standards and assessments, no matter how reliable, will not solve all the problems of American education. It will not substitute for the protection of a loving family, it will not guard children against violence in the streets, it will not alleviate poverty, and it will not turn off the television at night. But a system of standards and assessments might help to focus the priorities of the educational system on teaching and learning, which is no small matter in a world where what you are and what you can aspire to depends increasingly on what you know. As a society our goal must be to see that knowledge is broadly democratized, that *all* children in America have equal educational opportunity, that the work of teachers is valued and respected, that the brainpower of this nation is treated as its most precious resource, and that we do not waste the educational potential of even one of our citizens.[203]

OUTCOMES-BASED EDUCATION

The 1990s saw both the rise and slowing of the movement known as outcome- or outcomes-based education (OBE) that seeks specification of learning "outputs", sometimes referred to as "exit outcomes," accompanied by "authentic" performance assessment of student achievement of the outcomes. William G. Spady defined outcome as "a culminating demonstration of learning."[204] Floyd Boschee and Mark A. Baron spoke of outcome-based education as "a student-centered, results-oriented design

[200]Elam et al., "The 26th Annual Phi Delta Kappa/Gallup Poll," p. 48.

[201]National Council on Educational Standards and Testing, *Raising Standards*, p. G-4.

[202]Peter W. Hill and Carmel A. Crevola, "The Role of Standards in Educational Reform for the 21st Century" in David D. Marsh, ed., *Preparing Our Schools for the 21st Century*, 1999 Yearbook (Alexandria, Va.: Association for Supervision and Curriculum Development, 1999), p. 139.

[203]Ravitch, *National Standards in American Education*, pp. 178, 186.

[204]Ron Brandt, "On Outcome-Based Education: A Conversation with Bill Spady," *Educational Leadership* 50, no 4 (December 1992/January 1993): 66.

premised on the belief that all individuals can learn."[205] The success of a school in OBE terms is the demonstration by students of the accomplishment of the learning outcomes, not the inputs like Carnegie units, number of students graduating, number of awards won, and teacher-pupil ratios.

Contributing to the development of OBE are, among others, the recommendations of Herbert Spencer in the mid-nineteenth century, the curriculum of the Virginia State Curriculum Program in the 1930s, the Seven Cardinal Principles in 1918, the Ten Imperative Needs of Youth in 1944, Ralph Tyler's classification of aspects of life in the late 1950s, Benjamin Bloom's proposals for mastery learning and the competency-based movement of the 1970s. Spady, for example, addressed the "fundamental life performance roles" whereas Spencer, Virginia, Wisconsin, Statemeyer et al. and Tyler classified areas of human activity (see chapter 7).[206] "Outcome domains" identified by the National Center on Educational Outcomes, for example, physical health, contribution and citizenship, remind the curriculum planner of the Seven Cardinal Principles and the Ten Imperative Needs of Youth that were discussed in Chapter 3.[207] *Performance-based education* is sometimes substituted for *outcomes-based education* as it was in the 1970s in the case of *competency-based education*.

As of 1994 some forty-two states were at varying stages in considering or developing models of outcomes-based education. Among these were Arizona, Colorado, Kentucky, Missouri, Minnesota, Pennsylvania, Utah, and Virginia. Pennsylvania had under consideration a plan to abandon the Carnegie unit. An early exponent of outcomes-based education is Johnson City, New York which inaugurated its Outcomes-Driven Developmental Model (ODDM) in 1972 under the leadership of the superintendent Albert Mamary.[208] William Glasser labeled the Johnson City public schools as "probably the best model in the U.S. of what could be called quality schools."[209] Aurora, Colorado has achieved recognition as it attempts to devise a means of assessing the Five Outcomes that they expect their students to achieve: "self-directed learners, collaborative workers, complex thinkers, quality producers, community contributors." These outcomes, according to Nora Redding, High School Curriculum Coordinator, Aurora, Colorado Public Schools, are "nontraditional, future-oriented abilities students will need to be productive citizens of the twenty-first century."[210]

Boschee and Baron listed four characteristics of outcome-based education:

---

[205]Floyd Boschee and Mark A. Baron, *Outcome-Based Education: Developing Programs Through Strategis Planning* (Lancaster, Pa.: Technomic Publishing Co., 1993), p. 1.

[206]For discussion of Fundamental Life Performance Roles see William G. Spady, "Choosing Outcomes of Significance," *Educational Leadership* 51, no. 6 ((March 1994): 18–22.

[207]See James G. Shriner, James E. Ysseldyke, Martha L. Thurlow, and Dean Honetschlager, "'All' Means 'All'- Including Students with Disabilities," *Educational Leadership* 51, no. 6 (March 1994): 41.

[208]Ron Brandt, "On Creating an Environment Where All Students Learn: A Conversation with Al Mamary, *Educational Leadership* 51, no. 6 (March 1994): 24–28. See also Albert Mamary, "14 Principles of Outcomes-Based Education," *Principal* 73, no.1 (January 1994): 19–23.

[209]William Glasser, "The Quality School," *Phi Delta Kappan* 71, no. 6 (February 1990): 434.

[210]Nora Redding, "Assessing Big Outcomes," *Educational Leadership* 9, no. 8 (May 1992): 49. See also Robert J. Marzano, "Lessons from the Field About Outcome-Based Performance Assessments," *Educational Leadership* 51, no., 6 (March 1994): 51.

What a student is to learn is clearly identified.

Each student's progress is based on his or her demonstrated achievement.

Each student's needs are accommodated through multiple instructional strategies and assessment tools.

Each student is provided time and assistance to realize his or her potential.[211]

Outcomes-based education which on the surface appears to be a very reasonable concept has encountered problems that has impeded its development. Like many concepts in education its lack of precision results in a variety of interpretations. Some people equate outcomes-based education with Bloom's concept of mastery learning, a conclusion rejected by many experts in outcomes-based education. Their perceptions can but do not necessarily include mastery learning (breaking content into small pieces, testing progress) as an instructional technique within the framework of OBE. In that context mastery learning is an instructional approach whereas outcomes-based education is a curricular approach.

Outcomes-based education carries within it preference for interdisciplinary approaches, that is, integration of the disciplines (see Chapter 13), an approach unacceptable to traditionalists who wish to maintain discrete disciplines. It subscribes to site-based management, which, although generally accepted, encounters problems of implementation as in the selection and operation of school advisory committees. Not all teachers are convinced that performance, often referred to as *authentic,* assessments like papers, projects, portfolios, should replace traditional testing techniques. They question whether there can be time for them to do an effective job of performance assessment.

Outcomes-based education could have been equivalent to standards-based education had OBE adhered to subject matter standards. Characterizing OBE as "a term of uncertain meaning which during the 1990s became a symbolic cause of verbal warfare between political liberals and conservatives," Hirsch noted that planners of OBE "tended not to emphasize knowledge so much as various tool metaphors for education and virtue in the form of democratic attitudes and emotions."[212] However, OBE proponents went beyond academic content. OBE has been criticized for specification of both value-laden and vague goal-like outcomes. As a result, it encountered strong opposition in Georgia, Pennsylvania, Michigan, Minnesota, and Virginia. Strong objections have arisen from the religious right and others who raise objections to affective outcomes that introduce values with which they may not agree, appear to intrude on family privacy, call for changes in the community, and appear to promote politically correct solutions to social problems. One fundamentalist, however, commented, "OBE is, first and foremost, a common-sense curricular design that specifies what is to be taught to students."[213] As students graduate from outcomes-based programs we may anticipate some of the same type of problems as were experienced in 1950s and 1960s with core programs, the problem of certifying to college admissions officers what students have achieved. Admissions officers understand Carnegie units and letter grades. They may be less ready to accept a list of achieved outcomes and portfolios.

---

[211]Boschee and Baron, *Outcome-Based Education,* pp. 3–4.

[212]Hirsch, *The Schools We Need,* p. 262.

[213]Randy Zitterkopf, "A Fundamentalist's Defense of OBE," *Educational Leadership* 51, no. 6 (March 1994): 77.

In practice, outcomes-based education establishes a common set of outcomes for all. Some would question whether it is realistic or possible for all students to achieve all outcomes. Outcomes-based education has fared like many innovations, gathering its champions, for example, the National Center for Outcomes-Based Education, and its detractors both within and outside of the teaching profession. It is worthy of note that at the tail end of the 1990s a search through the literature finds fewer articles and books promoting outcomes-based education.

PROVISION FOR EXCEPTIONALITIES

One of the earmarks of restructured schools is the effort to include as many pupils as possible who evidence special needs within the framework of the regular class. In this category are students with learning difficulties, emotional disorders, educational deficiencies, and physical and mental impairment. Although *special education* often takes on the connotation of programs for students with disabilities of one type or another, the broader concept of special needs today encompasses the gifted.

Early one-room schools functioned on a multi-age, multi-grade principle. As schools grew larger and graded they cared for the needs of pupils in heterogeneous groups retaining age of students as the primary form of grouping.

Through mid-twentieth century ability or homogeneous grouping became popular. Schools grouped students by intelligence and, in isolated cases, by achievement. Proponents of ability grouping, also known as tracking, claimed advantages for the teacher in handling groups where the range of abilities was narrowed. They felt brighter students would not be held back by slower students and each group could move at its own pace. Critics maintained that ability grouping denies students the opportunity to associate with all kinds of students and leads to lowering of self-esteem of those placed in the slower sections. Whether we call the lower groups Section *A* or The Bluebirds, students know that they have been placed in those groups because they are less able academically than pupils in the higher groups. Nor were the academic achievement results of ability grouping so superior to heterogenous grouping as to merit this form of curriculum organization.

Ability grouping has been debated for many years. Jeannie Oakes, Adam Gamoran, and Reba Page remarked, "Findings about students' assignments to ability-grouped classes and curriculum tracks not only are contradictory but also have been variously interpreted."[214] Today tracking of students is generally frowned on for both philosophical and pedagogical reasons. Schools that have been tracking students are derailing those tracks in favor of heterogeneous models. This movement applies even to gifted students who formerly were placed in separate classes for all or part of a day or even in separate schools. In one respect magnet schools continue a form of homogeneous grouping, not based on ability, of course, but on academic and vocational interests.

Key concepts in the handling of students with special needs are *mainstreaming* and *inclusion*. What curriculum worker has not yet encountered Public Law 94-192? This enactment of the U.S. Congress, *the Education for All Handicapped Children Act of*

---

[214]Jeannie Oakes, Adam Gamoran, and Reba N. Page, "Curriculum Differentiation: Opportunities, Outcomes, and Meanings," in Philip W. Jackson, ed., *Handbook of Research on Curriculum* (New York: Macmillan, 1992), p. 577.

1975, supplementing *Section 504 of the Rehabilitation Act of 1973,* was structured to eliminate discrimination against the physically or mentally handicapped including those with behavior disorders.[215]

Schools must make special provisions to ensure that all handicapped children receive a "free and appropriate" education. To accomplish this goal, schools must develop an individualized educational plan (IEP) for every handicapped child. IEP's, which contain annual performance objectives for each child and must be reviewed each year, require a considerable amount of the faculty's time. Determining the appropriate educational program and the best placement for each child requires difficult judgments by teachers and administrators.

Until *Education for All Handicapped,* amended in 1990, and the retitled (and reauthorized in 1997) *Individuals with Disabilities Education Act,* the common plan for treating students with special needs was pulling them out of classes or segregating them in their own classes. *Education for All Handicapped* called for placement of students in "the least restrictive environment." One manifestation of that principle is "mainstreaming"—that is, placement of students in regular classrooms with nonhandicapped children—unless their handicaps require special treatment or equipment or are so severe that they cannot be taught effectively in the regular classroom.

Educators still disagree, however, as to whether handicapped youngsters are best taught by placement in regular or special classes, in regular or special schools. An analysis of special education by *U.S. News and World Report* revealed a disproportionately high cost for special education programs, a disproportionately high number of blacks placed in special education, misclassification of students, and inconsistencies among the state in number of students mainstreamed.[216]

A decade ago Susan Ohanian described the dilemma teachers face, and to some extent still face, with mainstreaming.[217] She noted that students are mainstreamed primarily for purposes of socialization rather than of academic achievement. Said Ohanian:

> So-called liberal doctrine holds that "special classes"—a relic of education's dark ages—produce demoralization, low self-esteem, and inferior education. And I have seen plenty of evidence that they do. In the worst cases, the special education room is just a holding tank with a curriculum of movies and M & M's; even in the best cases, the curriculum has never taken a direction very different from mainstream academics.[218]

Mainstreaming, however, may not solve the problem of providing appropriate education for all handicapped students. Ohanian concluded:

> We are good at accumulating labels: minimal brain dysfunction, perceptual-motor aberration, impaired learning efficiency, sensory deficit, delayed interpretation of input, and so on. Maybe we should spend less time on labels and more time providing meaningful alternatives to all students who do not flourish in the mainstream.[219]

---

[215]See Robert W. Cole and Rita Dunn, "A New Lease on Life for the Handicapped: Ohio Copes with 94–142," *Phi Delta Kappan* 59, no. 1 (September 1977): 3–6ff.

[216]"Separate and Unequal," *U.S. News and World Report* 115, no. 23, (December 13, 1993): 46–60.

[217]Susan Ohanian, "Pl 94–142: Mainstream or Quicksand?" *Phi Delta Kappan* 72, no. 3 (November 1990): 217–222.

[218]Ibid., p. 222.

[219]Ibid.

At the present time the popular term for organizing the curriculum for students with special needs is *inclusion*, which broadens the concept of *mainstreaming*. Noting the controversy over means of providing for exceptionalities, Jean B. Crockett and James M. Kauffman made the comment:

> Special education's hottest topic over the past decade has been where, not how, special education students should be taught. *Inclusion*, a colloquial term applied to educating students with and without disabilities together within classes in neighborhood schools, has become the topical flash point.[220]

Kay Woelfel defined inclusion as "a way of meeting a child's special needs in a regular, age-appropriate classroom, with the school providing a full continuum of support services and no prerequisites for admittance."[221] Marilyn Friend and Lynne Cook noted that school districts define *inclusion* in different ways. They stated, however:

> Inclusion is most often used to describe programs for students with disabilities, but it also pertains to students from different cultures whose first language is not English, students at risk for failure because of alcohol or drug abuse, and other students with special needs.[222]

Friend and Cook explained that students in inclusive classrooms may be working on different materials and at a different rate, that teachers make use of resource specialists to help them, and that pulling students out of class is still an option if a student is unmanageable or needs special treatment that cannot be provided in the regular class setting. Inclusive programs vary from placement of all students with disabilities in regular classes full-time, to including students with special needs in regular classes part-time, to admitting to regular classes those exceptional students whom the school deems able to profit from being included. In the last case the school system may retain special classes or even special schools for those who are not included.

Some educators are concerned that parents of nonhandicapped pupils might charge that their children are being discriminated against by not having individualized educational programs designed for them. In fact, further restructuring could well bring on not only individualized education plans for all students but also individualized schedules like those that were subject to experimentation in the 1960s.

Mainstreaming and inclusion have met with mixed reviews from educators. Teachers accept the premise that students with special needs can learn from each other—a premise of another restructuring program, cooperative learning. On the other hand, teachers point out the difficulties in differentiating instruction in the light of class loads, lack of help, and lack of time. Crockett and Kauffman expressed the concern that efforts at inclusion might place too great an emphasis on the location where inclusion takes place rather than on instruction.[223]

Laws providing for special needs of students furnish an excellent illustration of the impact that federal legislation can have on the curriculum planner.

---

[220]Jean B. Crockett and James M. Kauffman, "Taking Inclusion Back to Its Roots," *Educational Leadership* 56, no. 2 (October 1998): 74

[221]Kay Woelfel, "Inclusion, Exclusion, Confusion, and Infusion," *Principal* 73, no. 4 (March 1994): 48.

[222]Marilyn Friend and Lynne Cook, "Inclusion: What it takes to make it work, why it sometimes fails, and how teachers really feel about it," *Instructor* 103, no. 4 (November-December 1993): 52–56.

[223]Crockett and Kauffman, *Taking Inclusion Back to Its Roots,* p. 77.

RELIGION IN THE SCHOOLS

In colonial America religion and education were symbiotic. The Latin grammar school prepared young men to teach and to preach. Protestants of various creeds settled in most of the colonies, and Roman Catholics settled in Maryland; clashes over Christian religious beliefs among the early colonists were inevitable. Conflicts were exacerbated over the years as immigrants of all faiths came to the New World, adding beliefs such as Judaism, Islam, Confucianism, Buddhism, Bahaism, and Shinto to those of the Native Americans and the early-arriving Christians.

There are so many varieties of Christians in the United States that it is difficult to count them. They include Baptists, Christian Scientists, Episcopalians, Greek Orthodox, Jehovah's Witnesses, Lutherans, Methodists, Mormons, Presbyterians, Roman Catholics, and Seventh-Day Adventists. Other religions also contain divisions: Judaism has Orthodox, Reform, Hasidic, and Sephardic groups. Sunni Moslem doctrine conflicts with Shiite doctrine. The Christian denominations have divided even further. For example, Lutherans of the Missouri Synod hold differing beliefs from the Evangelical Lutherans. The Free Will, Missionary, and Southern Baptists are but three segments of that large denomination. America also is home to agnostics, deists, humanists, Unitarians, and atheists.

Forty-five simple words, written in 1791, have generated hundreds of disputes over their meaning. Disagreements over these words continue to this day and may very well continue as long as the republic of the United States lasts. The words referred to are as follows:

> Congress shall make no law respecting an establishment of religion, or prohibiting the free exercise thereof, or abridging the freedom of speech, or of the press, or the right of the people peaceably to assemble, and to petition the Government for a redress of grievances.

These powerful words, known as the First Amendment to the U.S. Constitution, are the center of conflicts over freedom of religion, speech, press, and assembly. Almost daily there is news of a lawsuit that contends infringement of one or more of these freedoms. The question of whether religion should be included in the public schools has evoked fiery debates over the years. Time and again the U.S. Supreme Court has reaffirmed the doctrine of separation of church and state. This doctrine has been attributed to Thomas Jefferson and James Madison in particular; it was Thomas Jefferson who wrote of the "wall of separation between church and state."

The question of how high and how impregnable that wall should be has yet to be completely resolved. Decisions of the U.S. Supreme Court, the ultimate arbiter of constitutional issues, have kept that wall relatively high—much to the chagrin of those Americans who would like to see it fall and those who would fortify it even more.

Those practices with religious connotations in the school that have most often necessitated court adjudication are prayer or reading of *Bible* passages in the classroom and at school-sponsored events, *Bible* study, use of public moneys to aid sectarian schools, released time for religious instruction off school grounds, celebration of religious holidays, teaching of evolution, values education, saluting the American flag, permitting religious groups to meet in the school, and extracurricular activities that require a religious test for participation.

Decisions on the constitutionality of religious practices in the schools have frequently invoked the Fourteenth Amendment (due process), which has made the First Amendment binding on the states and had figured so prominently in early racial discrimination cases. From the wealth of U.S. Supreme Court decisions, the following appear to have special relevance for the public school curriculum. (The state of origin of each case is indicated in parentheses.)

- *West Virginia Board of Education v. Barnette*, 319 U.S. 624 (1943) (West Virginia). Ruled that Jehovah's Witnesses would not be required to salute the American flag.
- *People of the State of Illinois ex rel. McCollum v. Board of Education of School District No. 71, Champaign, Ill.*, 333 U.S. 203 (1948) (Illinois). Ruled that released time for religious instruction in the school was unconstitutional.
- *Zorach v. Clauson*, 343 U.S. 306 (1952) (New York). Ruled that released time for religious instruction off school grounds was permissible.
- *Engle v. Vitale*, 370 U.S. 421 (1962) (New York). Ruled that the prayer that originated with the New York State Board of Regents for use in the schools violated the principle of separation of church and state.
- *School District of Abington Township v. Schempp, (Pennsylvania) and Murray v. Curlett* (Maryland), 374 U.S. 203 (1963). Ruled that readings from the Bible and recitation of the Lord's Prayer in the school were unconstitutional.
- *Wallace v. Jaffree*, 105 S. Ct. 2479 (1985) (Alabama). The U.S. Supreme Court affirmed the decision of the U.S. Court of Appeals, which had reversed an earlier ruling by the U.S. District Court that had allowed Alabama schools to hold a period of silence for meditation or voluntary prayer.
- *Bender v. Williamsport Area School District*, 475 U.S. 534 (1986) (Pennsylvania). The U.S. Supreme Court let stand the federal district court's decision that under PL 98-377, the Equal Access Act of 1984, religious groups made up of students in the high school could meet at that school if other student groups also had access to the school's facilities. The Supreme Court in June 1993 ruled in *Lamb's Chapel v. Center Moriches Union Free School District*, 124 L Ed 2d 352 (1993) (Long Island, New York), that religious groups could meet after school hours if the schools were open to other groups from the community.

Prayer, *Bible* reading, and *Bible* study, held unconstitutional practices, remain volatile issues in the mid- and late 1990s. In June 1992 the U.S. Supreme Court in *Lee v. Weisman*, 120 L Ed 2d 467 (1992) (Rhode Island) upheld an appellate court ban on school-sponsored, clergy-delivered prayer at graduation, even though the prayer was nonsectarian and attendance was voluntary. Hailing the decision were the American Civil Liberties Union and Americans United for Separation of Church and State. Critical of the decision were the Christian Coalition and Liberty Counsel. A flurry of court cases followed *Lee v. Weisman*. In early June 1993 the Supreme Court refused to hear the Texas case *Jones v. Clear Creek Independent School District*, 977 F 2d 963 (5th Curcuit, 1992), in which the appellate court had ruled in favor of student-led school prayer. Later that same month a federal district judge in New Jersey allowed student-led prayer. The ACLU immediately appealed to the Third Circuit Court in Philadelphia which blocked student-led prayer at two high schools in Camden County, New Jersey.

Pat Robertson's American Center for Law and Justice, among other organizations, has sought to gain acceptance of the position that prayer at graduation is legal if the student body votes for it. Since the Supreme Court did not rule on the issue, it will no doubt continue to be litigated.

Members of the U.S. Congress, mainly Republicans, in 1995 and again in 1999 considered launching an amendment to the U.S. Constitution that would sanction prayer in the public schools, a move opposed by the American Bar Association among others. Efforts to find substitutes for organized, school-sanctioned prayer are a moment of silence for reflection or silent prayer; voluntary, student-planned, student-led prayer at athletic events, graduation, and nonmandatory events; prayer and *Bible* reading before school in the school building or around the flagpole. Released time for religious instruction off campus remains a viable option in some states. The distribution of Bibles by Gideons International in school has been held unconstitutional.

Glickman contrasted the protagonists in the battles over religion in the schools:

> One group, identified as the secular humanists, says that public education and religion should never be mixed . . . The other group, identified as religious fundamantalists, argue that America is a Christian nation and that Christian values are essential for a moral, ethical, and responsible society.224

Proponents of prayer and Bible reading in the public schools find it difficult to understand why a government founded on religious principles would declare religious practices in the schools unconstitutional. They maintain that the founding fathers had no antagonism toward religion, but rather sought to prevent the federal government from establishing a national religion. They point out that state and national legislatures make references to God, the *Declaration of Independence* addresses "Divine Providence," the *Pledge of Allegiance* contains the phrase "under God." Those who argue for religious practices in the schools, however, often assume a largely Protestant ethic. They downplay the pluralistic nature of our society and the fact that many beliefs—including non-Christian religions—are now represented in the public schools. Jewish parents and children find the New Testament unacceptable. Catholics read from Catholic versions of the Bible, such as the Douay-Rheims, rather than the Protestant King James Version. Furthermore, the wall of separation between church and state protects not only the freedom of religion but also the freedom from religion. Advocates of the separation of church and state note that *Pierce v. Society of Sisters* gave believers the right to send their children to private parochial schools where a religiously homogeneous student population can be instructed in the beliefs of that particular sect.

Decisions of the Supreme Court notwithstanding, supporters of the inclusion of religion in the public schools continue to press their case. Former President Ronald Reagan and President George Bush are both advocates of conducting prayer in the public schools. In 1991 George Bush's Justice Department urged the Supreme Court to permit prayers at public school graduation ceremonies. Organizations are lined up on both sides of the issue of the separation of church and state.

224Glickman, *Revolutionizing America's Schools*, p. 93.

Numerous conflicts over the separation of church and state can be found in the annual listing of such incidents published by Americans United for Separation of Church and State. In the fall of 1995 this organization recorded 205 incidents in forty-nine states.[225]

Prayer, Bible reading, and Bible study remained volatile issues in the mid- and late-1990s. For example, spring 1996 saw the Pontotoc County, Mississippi, school district responding to a suit brought by People for the American Way and the American Civil Liberties Union in 1994 contesting the reading of Bible passages and prayers by students over the school public address system.

As noted earlier in this chapter, the use of taxpayer moneys to provide vouchers for use in religious schools is under legal challenge as a violation of the principle of separation of church and state.

We can cite additional examples of continuing controversies over religion in education at the very end of the 1990s:

- Supported by the Christian Coalition the Lee County, Florida school board required, in its high school curricula, Bible study based on a curriculum developed in North Carolina featuring the New Testament.
- Classes in Bible history were to be taught in a secular, objective manner in several Florida high schools reportedly at the beginning of the year 2000 presenting a Christian fundamentalist view of the Bible as historical fact.
- Student religious clubs have been granted by federal law access to school facilities equal to that enjoyed by other clubs, which could include, according to a ruling in South Carolina, Bible clubs meeting during periods of the school day set aside for club meetings generally.
- The Wisconsin Supreme Court sanctioned the use of taxpayer money to allow Milwaukee children through its Parent Choice Program to attend religious schools, overturning a ruling of the Fourth District Court of Appeals.
- The U.S. Supreme Court overturned a 1985 ruling that prohibited New York City from permitting and paying public school teachers to offer remedial insruction in religious schools, a decision supported by the Clinton administration.
- The U.S. Supreme Court in the winter of 1999 disallowed Maine and Vermont from making payments for tuition of pupils in religious schools while permitting payments in private, nonreligious schools.
- A school bus driver in Indiana was suspended for playing Christian music on the bus.
- The U.S. House of Representatives voted in 1999 to permit posting of the Ten Commandments in schools. One of the questions raised about the posting was which of the varying versions of the Ten Commandments—Jewish, Protestant, or Catholic-Lutheran—should be selected.
- Public display of the Ten Commandments served as a flashpoint from Kentucky to California in late 1999 and early 2000 with the Famiy Research Council distribut-

---

[225]Americans United for Separation of Church and State, *Americans United Seventh Annual Report on Church-State Conflict in the United States* (Washington, D.C.: Americans United for Separation of Church and State, 1995). These annual reports were discontinued after this year.

ing Ten Commandments book covers and the American Civil Liberties Union filing suit over posting of the Ten Commandments in public offices and schools.

- After first banning the wearing of religious symbols such as the six-pointed Jewish Star of David, a Mississippi school board in 1999 reversed itself.
- The Virginia Senate approved a bill in February 2000 requiring a minute of silent meditation daily in its schools.
- Both voluntary, student-led and school-initiated prayer in the schools, during the day, before or after school, and at school events, remained a hot button topic in several states.

Increasingly, educators and others are expressing concern over the schools' failure to include instruction about the contributions and effects of religion throughout the history of the United States and the world. Some teachers and authors of textbooks fearful that they may offend people's sensitivities, veer away from religion entirely. Many students, therefore, are to a large extent ignorant of the importance of religion in the development of this country. Glickman expressed the concern that "we haven't acknowledged that there is a common core of virtue for American education, routed in religious, spiritual, and private conscience."[226]

A relevant curriculum would incorporate the study of comparative religions as a part of the general education of every student. Such a curriculum would focus on teaching about religion, not the teaching of religion. A person cannot fully appreciate the arts, literature, history, psychology, philosophy, or sociology—or even science, with which religion is often at odds—without studying the influence of religion on these areas of human endeavor. Certainly, students should gain familiarity with the world's great masterpieces of religious literature, such as the Bible, the Talmud, the Koran, and the Bhagavad-Gita. A knowledge about religion is one attribute of the culturally literate person.

Curriculum planners must be mindful, however, that many of those who claim the schools advocate "secular humanism" would not be satisfied with teaching about religion. Secular humanism implies faith in humankind and subscription to social and moral values that are not necessarily derived from belief in a divine being. Though the public schools do not, in reality, promote a doctrine of secular humanism, the absence of sectarian practices in itself provokes some people to accuse the schools of promoting secular humanism.

Controversy continues over curriculum content. Values-dimensions of outcomes-based education are subject to attack as we have already noted. Creationism has been a curriculum issue in Alabama, California, Louisiana, and Tennessee, among other states. Robert L. Simonds, president of the National Association of Christian Educators and Citizens for Excellence in Education, sharply criticized the school curriculum when he wrote:

> While claiming to teach our students critical thinking, schools have trained them in the anti-American principles of atheistic socialism. In the process, our nation has outdone even the Soviets in the subtle but systematic destruction of children's faith in God and their sense of right and wrong.[227]

---

[226]Glickman, *Revolutionizing America's Schools*, p. 98.
[227]Robert L. Simonds, "A Plea for Children." *Educational Leadership* 51, no. 4 (December 1993/January 1994): 12.

What does the American public think about the place of character and values education and religion in the public school? Sixty-nine percent of the American public endorsed development of a set of values like honesty, democracy, and patriotism to be taught in the public schools.[228] Seventy-four percent would allow prayers at graduation.[229] Although forty-nine percent thought that courses in character education consisting of values and ethics should be taught in public schools, when confronted with a list of values over ninety percent endorsed character traits like respect for others, hard work, and fairness [230] This same study revealed that 69% would favor nondevotional instruction about the various religions of the world.[231]

Although some people fear that values that run counter to their own may be imposed on young people, Nel Noddings argued for critical examination of values and discovery of shared values and individual commitments, concluding that "teaching in the domain of values need not be dogmatic."[232]

President Clinton, responding to the public's generally religious orientation, in a move to derail efforts to amend the Constitution to permit prayer in the schools, in the summer of 1995 ordered the Department of Education to compile and transmit to the nation's schools a list of religious practices that are already legally permitted by the Constitution and judicial decisions. Guidelines recommended to the local schools by the Department of Education would allow students to (1) pray individually or in informal groups if they do not cause disruption, (2) carry and read the *Bible* or other religious literature, (3) distribute religious literature, and (4) wear religious clothing. The recommendations would not allow prayer in classes or assemblies conducted by students or school personnel. Since the guidelines, a third set of which were issued in December 1999, are not law, they are not binding on the schools nor, if implemented, are they free of legal challenge.

Charles C. Haynes observed that avoidance of religion in the curriculum is far from neutral. Editing a thoughtful guide from The Freedom Forum First Amendment Center at Vanderbilt University with legal editor Oliver Thomas, Haynes commented, "Students need to learn that religious and philosophical beliefs and practices are central to lives of many people."[233] The guide, addressed to school leaders and parents, contains useful material for dealing with the thorny issue of religion in the schools.

Addressing both religious and existential issues in both the curriculum and the preparation of teachers, Noddings advocated teaching *about* religion and discussion of the beliefs of the various religions.[234] Noddings took the position that "Professional programs must make it clear to teachers that the study and discussion of religious and existential questions is legitimate."[235] She commented, "The best teachers will be pre-

---

[228]Elam et al., "The 25th Annual Phi Delta Kappa/Gallup Poll," p. 145

[229]Ibid., p. 150.

[230]Elam et al, "The 26th Annual Phi Delta Kappa/Gallup Poll," pp. 49–50.

[231]Ibid., p. 50.

[232]Nel Noddings, *Educating for Intelligent Belief and Unbelief* (New York: Teachers College Press, 1993), p. 139.

[233]Charles C. Haynes and Oliver Thomas, eds. *Finding Common Ground: A First Amendment Guide to Religion and Public Education* (Nashville, Tenn.: The Freedom Forum First Amendment Center, 1994): 1.3.

[234]Noddings, *Educating for Intelligent Belief and Unbelief,* p. xv.

[235]Ibid., p. 137.

pared to present not only the full spectrum of belief but also the variety of plausible ways in which people have tried to reconcile their religious and scientific beliefs."[236]

The debate over secular versus sectarian curricula for the public schools will be difficult to resolve because strong emotions, values, and fundamental beliefs about life and death underscore the controversy. Haynes wrote that the Freedom Forum guide was based

> on the conviction that finding common ground on many of the issues that divide us is possible within the civic framework provided by the Religious Liberty clauses of the First Amendment to the U.S. Constitution. The key is for all sides to step back from the debate and to give fresh consideration to the democratic first principles that bind us together as a people.[237]

SCHEDULE REVISION

Can you remember when the school year started in late August or right after Labor Day and ended in early or late June? Can you remember when children had two weeks off in the winter and spring and almost three months of what the French call "les grandes vacances." During vacation periods the schools sat like silent sentinels. Was it only yesterday that children attended school 180 days a year, about six hours a day, five days a week, following the same class schedule every day? Do you remember when you encountered school-age children out of school on a school day they were either sick or truant. Not so any more. They may be on the blue track while those in school are on the green track.

Remember when gleeful children greeted the long summer holiday with the doggerel, "no more pencils, no more books, no more teacher's sassy looks"; when the nuclear WASP family (Mom, Dad, brother, sister, and Rover) piled into the station wagon (few vans then) and took off for an experience in family togetherness at the seashore or in the mountains or just motoring (gasoline was cheaper then). No longer. Restructuring has wrought radical changes in scheduling of time. Some changes draw from the past, others are creative present-day innovations. No dimensions of time have been left untouched, not the hour, not the day, not the week, not the year. Let's review some of these changes.

School Hours, Day, and Week.
Changes in the daily hourly schedule have affected primarily the secondary school. Look at the bell schedule of many high schools today and you'll fast discover that periods have been lengthened and courses no longer meet five days a week for equal amounts of time according to the time-honored Carnegie unit.

Where secondary schools' classes formerly met for some fifty to fifty-fives minute daily, they may now meet eighty-five minutes, five periods per day for one semester, as, for example, at Hatboro-Horsham Senior High School (Horsham, Pennsylvania)[238]

---

[236]Ibid., p. 144.

[237]Haynes and Thomas, eds., *Finding Common Ground*, p. 1.1

[238]See Gerald E. Strock and David S. Hottenstein, "The First-Year Experience: A High School Restructures Through the Copernican Plan," *The School Administrator* 51, no. 3 (March 1994): 30–31.

or on a plan such as we saw in Chapter 9 in the case of Lyman High School (Longwood, Florida) with its 103-minute and 53-minute periods alternating over each two weeks.

In 1983 Joseph M. Carroll proposed what he called the *Copernican Plan,* a systemwide approach to school reform. Named after the famed astronomer of the late fifteenth and early sixteenth centuries who, contrary to church teachings, held that the earth revolved around the sun rather than vice versa, fomented a revolution in how the heavens were perceived. The *Copernican Plan* comprised a number of reform features among which is "block scheduling." Carroll stated, "no research supports continuing with the Carnegie unit; it actually impairs effective instruction."[239] Reminiscent of scheduling innovations of the 1950s, extended periods meeting less than five days per week are becoming increasingly more common. Longer periods meeting fewer times a week permit teachers to work with fewer students in a day and allow more time for confronting content in greater depth.

Boschee and Baron described the Copernican Plan as

a major restructuring of high school organization in which . . . students are given the option of either enrolling in one four-hour class each day for a period of thirty days or enrolling in two two-hour classes each day for sixty days. Under the first option, each student would enroll in six of these four-hour classes each year, while the second option requires students to enroll in three two-course trimesters each year (totalling 180 instructional days per year for both options). In both options, the remainder of the day is composed of a seminar, an elective class, and a lunch period.[240]

Carroll noted that the Copernican Plan can have different formats structured to the needs of the school. Whereas six periods per day were the norm, Thomas Jefferson High School of Science and Technology (Alexandria, Virginia)[241] has an eighth period during which students may pursue individual interests. The school day itself has been lengthened. Murfreesboro, Tennessee, for example, keeps its K–8 schools open from 6 A.M. to 7:30 P.M. for both educational services starting at 8 A.M. and ending at 5:30 P.M. (3:00–5:30 P.M. by small parental fee) and extended services 6 A.M.–8 A.M. and 5:30 P.M.–7:30 P.M. (also with small parental fee).[242] The National Education Commission on Time and Learning recommended that those schools that stay on the existing schedule devote that time exclusively to core academic subjects and to lengthen the school day if they wish to maintain clubs, athletics, and other activities. The Commission on Time and Learning further saw value in flexible and block scheduling.[243]

Not even the five-day week is sacred. In order to reduce energy and transportation costs some schools in Colorado and New Mexico have operated four-day weeks since the 1980s in more rural areas. Cimarron, New Mexico is credited as a forerunner of the four-day week. Hawaii's Ma'ili Elementary School on the island of Oahu schedules

[239]Joseph M. Carroll, "Organizing Time to Support Learning," *The School Administrator* 51, no. 3 (March 1994): 26–28, 30–32. See also James M. Carroll, "The Copernican Plan Evaluated: The Evolution of a Revolution," *Phi Delta Kappan* 76, no. 2 (October 1994): 104–113.

[240]Boschee and Baron, *Outcome-Based Education,* p. 133.

[241]National Education Commission on Time and Learning, *Prisoners of Time,* (Washington, D.C.: National Commission on Time and Learning, April 1994). ERIC document ED366115.

[242]Ibid.

[243]Ibid.

a four-day week. The Ma'ili school is open from 7:30 A.M.–2:30 P.M. Monday, Tuesday, Wednesday, and Thursday with Friday as optional for enrichment.[244] The five-day week, however, remains the standard throughout the country. Schools on a four-day week are few in number and we hear no serious advocacy of a six-day week, a very unlikely event since five working days in the norm in the business world, although some segments like police and firefighters are often on four-day, ten- hour shifts.

School Year.   Two major changes are impacting school schedules: lengthening of the school year and year-round education.

Lengthening the School Year.   Children in the United States average six hours per day in school whereas children in some other countries average as many as eight hours. In the United States 180 days per year is the norm for students (although we find 170 in Minnesota, 175 in Louisiana, and 182 in Ohio) whereas students in Russia are in attendance 210 days; Japan, 240 days. American pupils meet an average of five and one-half hours for instruction, including physical education and electives. German and Japanese children devote five and one-half hours to core academic subjects. Hours dedicated to core subjects in the final four years of secondary education by American students are 1,460 per year; 3,170 for Japanese students; 3,280 for French students; and 3,528 for German students.[245] It is little wonder that the National Commission on Excellence in Education in its 1983 publication *A Nation at Risk* recommended schools schedule a seven-hour day 200 to 220 days per year.[246] Charles Ballinger, Executive Director of the National Association for Year-Round Education, reported twenty public and eleven private schools on lengthened school year in 1993.[247] Don Glines noted that as early as 1840 urban schools were open 240 to 250 days, although few students attended that length of time.[248]

As a follow-up to *America 2000,* the U.S. Congress passed the Education Council Act of 1991 authorizing appointment of a nine-member National Education Commission on Time and Learning whose charge it was to examine the quality and adequacy of time U.S. students spend on study and learning. In its April 1994 report the Commission on Time and Learning made the following eight recommendations:

- reinvent schools around learning, not time
- change the fixed clock and calendar to better use students' time in school
- organize the school day so that students spend at least five and a half hours learning core academic subjects
- keep schools open for expanded services and activities
- give teachers more time to prepare for their classes
- seize the promise of new technologies to increase productivity, enhance student achievement, and expand learning time

---

[244]Stan Koki, "Modified School Schedules: A Look at the Research and the Pacific," ERIC document ED354630, November 1992.

[245]National Education Commission on Time and Learning, *Prisoners of Time,* p. 24.

[246]National Commission on Excellence in Education, *A Nation at Risk: The Imperative for Educational Reform* (Washington, D.C.: U.S. Government Printing Office, 1983), p. 29.

[247]Charles Ballinger, *Annual Report to the Association on the Status of Year-Round Education.* ERIC document ED358551 (1993).

[248]Don Glines, *Philosophical Rationale for Year-Round Education.* ERIC document ED368075 (1994).

- develop local action plans to transform schools
- build coalitions of policymakers, community leaders, educators, and parents to make learning a "national obsession."[249]

Although there is strong logic for a longer school year, the major deterrent is cost. Louisiana, for example, gave up the idea of lenghtening its school year from 175 to 180 days primarily because of added costs. Rejecting a lengthened school year, Sizer's fictitious Franklin Middle and High Schools would extend the school year from 36 to 42 weeks, divide the year into four terms with each term preceded by one week for varied activities, and would lengthen the school day from 8 A.M. to 4 P.M.[250] Interest in and discussion of lengthening the school year to 210 days, although not necessarily implemented, continues to surface as it did, for example, in Florida in 1999.

Year-Round Education(YRE).   More subject to debate than lengthening the school period or day is the movement toward year-round education, a reaction to the traditional schedule. Ballinger made clear his opinion of the traditional nine-month schedule: "The traditional school calendar is not educational now, has never been, and never will be."[251]

Most proponents point out that the traditional calendar is a product of an agrarian society which required young people to work on farms in the summers. Consequently, advocates claim new responses must be made in an industrial, technological age.

The concept of year-round education is not brand new. Bluffton, Indiana is credited with operating a year-round school as early as 1904. Several other schools systems conducted year-round programs in the early 1900s, among them Aliquippa, Pennsylvania; Minot, North Dakota; Nashville, Tennessee; Newark, New Jersey; and Omaha, Nebraska. The Christa McAuliffe Elementary School at Oxnard California, opened in 1987, is named as the first school built specifically in year-round education.[252]

Vicki T. Howell pointed out that year-round education died out before World War II, was reborn in the late 1960s and early 1970s.[253] Ballinger's enthusiastic report of 1993 cited the rapid growth of year-round schools, primarily public. Whereas 1,350,000 children in 1,668 schools in twenty-three states were enrolled in year-round schools in 1992, by 1993 that number had increased to 1,575,000 students in 2,049 schools in twenty-six states, a Canadian province, and Palau. California accounts for the largest number of students and schools in year-round plans.[254] The National Association for Year-Round Education numbered 1.9 million students in 2,800 schools in more than forty states on year-round schedules during the school-year 1997–98.[255]

When speakers discuss year-round schooling they should be questioned as to whether they refer to single track or multitrack plans. The difference is significant. Single track plans divide the number of attendance days into learning periods with op-

---

[249]National Education Commission on Time and Learning, *Prisoners of Time.*

[250]Sizer, *Horace's School,* p. 146.

[251]Ballinger, *Annual Report.*

[252]Vicki T. Howell, *An Examination of Year-Round Education: Pros and Cons that Challenge Schooling in America.* ERIC document ED 298602 (1988).

[253]Ibid.

[254]Ballinger, *Annual Report.*

[255]National Association for Year-Round Education Web site: http://www.NAYRE.org, accessed April 9, 1999.

tional intervals called intersessions (often three weeks of which one is vacation time) between the learning periods. Programs during the intersession may be either for enrichment or remediation, most commonly, the latter. Teachers may opt to be off during the intersessions or work and receive extra pay.

Multitrack systems were a response to overcrowded schools. Francis Howell School District in St. Charles, Missouri is credited with creating the first multiple track program in the United States in 1969.[256] Students are divided into tracks (A, B, C, D; red, green, blue, yellow). By staggering the school year for each group and having one group out at all times, schools can increase the capacity accommodated in the same school by twenty to twenty-five percent Multitracking year-round education has proved an attractive alternative for financially strapped communities that do not wish to enter into constructing new schools.

Ballinger reported that in 1990 seventy-five percent of the year-round schools were multitrack. By 1993 fifty-one percent were single track and forty-nine percent multitrack.[257]

Many schools have implemented and maintained plans for year-round schooling. Others have experimented with year-round plans and abandoned them. A significant number of school systems that experimented with year-round schedules have reverted to traditional schedules, including Albuquerque, Los Angeles, San Diego, and several districts in central Florida. Advocates maintain, however, that schools coming on line will replace the ones that have dropped out.

It is difficult to generalize on YRE until we know what type of plan is in operation. There are almost as many permutations and combinations as creative minds can conceive. We will not tax the reader with a description of the many existing plans which include 45–15 (four 9-week periods, 45 days each, 180 days total plus four 3-week optional intersessions, 15 days each), 60-20, 60-15, 90-30, quarter system, quinmesters, Concept 6, and others.[258]

What are the purported advantages and disadvantages of year-round schooling? Among the many reported advantages are improved retention of learning since breaks are shorter, improved attendance of both students and teachers, fewer dropouts, chance for remediation (single track), increased capacity (multitrack), financial savings (multitrack, but single track can cost more), reduced vandalism, accommodation to parental jobs which provide short vacation periods; and diminished teacher burnout. Those who object to year-round education cite disruption of family vacation schedules, especially if parents have children in schools on different tracks, ineffective intersessions (single track), increased teacher stress, problems of organizing and administering.

The jury is out on teacher burnout and stress. Burnout may diminish because of more frequent breaks but if teachers contract year-round, stress and burnout may increase. Blaine R. Worthen concluded, "Teacher 'burnout' on YRE programs will be somewhat less, although they may report more stress when in session."[259]

---

[256]Ibid.

[257]Ballinger, *Annual Report*.

[258]See Howell, *An Examination of Year-Round Education* for description of various plans. See also David J. Mussatti, *Year-Round Education: Calendar Options*. ERIC document 343278 (1992).

[259]Blaine R. Worthen, *What Twenty Years of Educational Studies Reveal about Year-Round Education*. ERIC document ED 373413 (1994), p. 23.

Whether year-round education enhances learning is problematic. Quinn Rasberry concluded that there is no proof of increase in students' learning as a result of year-round education.[260] In reviewing a number of studies of year-round education, Worthen supported some of the claims of proponents of YRE like better attitudes of students, fewer dropouts, better teacher attitudes, , decreased vandalism, and better student attendance.[261] Regarding the effect of YRE on academic learning, Worthen commented, "Overall, there appears to be a slight but not overwhelming advantage for YRE students in learning basic content. What is clear is that well-implemented YRE programs do not result in any lessening of learning. . . .Students on YRE will do as well or better in academic achievement."[262] Howell cautioned, however, "In actuality there are no long-range studies to prove the superiority of traditional or YRE calendars in relation to knowledge retention or achievement."[263]

While educators are making their beliefs known, what is the public's attitude toward YRE? The 24th Annual Phi Delta Kappa/Gallup Poll found fifty-five percent of the public favoring an increase of thirty days, making a school year of ten months or 210 days. Fifty-nine percent of the public favored dividing the 210-day year into four or five segments with three-week vacation breaks.[264] Of those studies which surveyed parental attitudes toward YRE, according to Worthen, a majority of parents favored YRE.[265] Most experts reaffirm the necessity in the case of Year-Round Education as with any innovation to build consensus among the constituencies of the school in advance of implementation.

WHOLE LANGUAGE

Literacy education—that is, the development of the linguistic skills of reading, writing, speaking, and listening—has gone through a number of transformations in curriculum and instruction. Local, state, and national assessments have consistently revealed that our pupils have deficiencies in language skills. Students' poor achievement in the fundamental processes has evoked parental and general dissatisfaction with the public school's curriculum. Pressure for reform in this area resulted in the "back-to-basics" movement.

Reading, the sine qua non of education, has been at the center of controversies over what methods are most effective and which programs most successful. The continuing controversy over methods of teaching reading can readily be found in the professional literature.[266]

---

[260]Quinn Rasberry, *Year-Round Schools May Not Be the Answers.* ERIC document ED353658 (1992).

[261]Worthen, *What Twenty Years of Educational Studies Reveal*, p. 23.

[262]Ibid., pp. 11, 23.

[263]Howell, *An Examination of Year-Round Education*, p. 25.

[264]Stanley M. Elam, Lowell C. Rose, and Alec M. Gallup, "The 24th Annual Gallup/Phi Delta Kappa Poll," *Phi Delta Kappan* 74, no. 1 (September 1992): 49.

[265]Worthen, *What Twenty Years of Educational Studies Reveal*, p. 15.

[266]See, for example, Marie Carbo, "Debunking the Great Phonics Myth," *Phi Delta Kappan* 70, no. 3 (November 1988): 226–240 and Jeanne S. Chall, "Learning to Read: The Great Debate 20 Years Later–A Response to 'Debunking the Great Phonics Myth,'" *Phi Delta Kappan* 70, no. 7 (March 1989): 521–538.

Somehow the profession has managed to survive the controversy over the "look-say" methods versus phonics. Educators have argued eloquently about the use of worksheets, preprimers, primers, and basal readers. Although one goal of reading instruction is to interest children in reading for pleasure, the profession notes that, in spite of commendable sales of books, magazines, and newspapers, there is still a continued disinterest in—even dislike for—reading among a sizable portion of the American population.

The whole-language movement is a response to the failure of the schools to produce literate citizens. In one sense, whole-language challenges the skills approach to the teaching of reading. In another sense, it is more than just a reaction against old methods. Looming large in the 1980s the whole-language movement has rapidly gained champions and, as with any educational development, critics. P. David Pearson declared, "never have I witnessed anything like the rapid spread of the whole-language movement."[267]

Dorothy J. Watson observed:

> Never in the history of literacy education has there been more genuine excitement on the part of educators. Teachers, many discouraged and burned out, are ignited by a new professionalism. . . . This new professionalism, movement, philosophy, spirit is called whole language.[268]

These comments reflect the intensity of interest in the whole-language movement.

On one level, the whole-language movement is a development of a concept about language learning. On another level, whole language is a perspective on learning in general. Whole-language advocates caution teachers against viewing whole language as a specific program or set of techniques or materials. Programs, materials, and techniques for a whole-language approach will vary from school to school, teacher to teacher, pupil to pupil.

No longer a new development but still controversial whole language borrows concepts from the progressive education movement with its premises of child-centeredness, learning by doing, and project instruction; from individualized learning with its appeal to individual needs and interests; from cooperative learning with its emphasis on collaboration; from the principle of the integration of subject matter with its fusion of various disciplines; from the principle of the integration of content within the learner with its emphasis on pupil choice and creativity; and from instructional methodology, which casts the teacher in the role of facilitator. Based on such concepts, whole language challenges the language arts curriculum per se, "look-say" methods, phonics, mastery learning, direct instruction, large-group instruction, and standardized tests. In some of the whole-language literature, pupils are referred to as "curricu-

---

[267]P. David Pearson, "Commentary: Reading the Whole-Language Movement," *The Elementary School Journal* 90, no. 2 (November 1989): 231.

[268]Dorothy J. Watson, "Defining and Describing Whole Language," *The Elementary School Journal* 90, no. 2 (November 1989): 141.

lum informants" with whom the teacher "collaborates."[269] The current buzzword "empowerment" that appears in the literature on whole language refers to the espousal of pupils' control over their own learning and teachers' control over their own teaching.[270]

The whole-language approach allows pupils to learn to read by reading, to write by writing, to speak by speaking, and to listen by listening. The students create their own stories. They speak on matters that concern them. They listen to stories that they like having read to them by their teachers and their peers. They tell what the stories mean to them. "Authenticity" is a key word for whole-language instructors. Whole-language proponents point to the success of literacy education in New Zealand, where basal texts are not used and where teachers possess considerable latitude in the selection of materials and methods based on pupils' needs and interests.[271]

Teachers who use a whole-language approach seek to develop students' self-concept and confidence by deemphasizing mastery and accepting errors and partial mastery. By tolerating error, teachers encourage pupils to take the type of risks that in a more structured situation might be met with disapproval and censure. Whole-language advocates believe that pupils often lose interest in reading due to picayune criticism of their spelling, grammar, and syntax. Students learn language skills by using materials of the real (rather than the academic) world. Whole-language methods require teachers to become proficient in assessing pupils' needs and interests—a skill Yetta M. Goodman calls "kid watching"[272]—in order to ascertain the most appropriate form of instruction.

Pupils' linguistic activities cannot take place in a vacuum because they must use those skills in many disciplines beyond the confines of the language class. Kenneth S. Goodman stated, "The whole-language curriculum is a dual curriculum; every activity, experience, or unit is an opportunity for both linguistic and cognitive development."[273]

Writing at the beginning of the 1990s several proponents of whole language saw it as a theory that is concerned with much more than communication skills. Watson clearly expressed this sentiment: "Whole language is a perspective on education that is supported by beliefs about learners and learning, teachers and teaching, language, and curriculum."[274] In a rebuttal to an article in which Michael C. McKenna, Richard D. Robinson, and John W. Miller recommended a research agenda on whole language, Carole Edelsky argued that whole language is definitely not "another way to teach reading and/or language arts." "Whole language," Edelsky stressed, is "a theory in practice about education generally. It takes seriously a distinction between using lan-

---

[269]Jerome C. Harste, "The Future of Whole Language," *The Elementary School Journal* 90, no. 2 (November 1989): 247.
[270]Ibid.
[271]See Barbara Mabbett, "The New Zealand Story," *Educational Leadership* 47, no. 6 (March 1990): 59–61.
[272]Yetta M. Goodman, "Kid Watching: An Alternative to Testing," *The National Elementary Principal* 57, no. 4 (June 1978): 41–45.
[273]Kenneth S. Goodman, "Whole-Language Research: Foundations and Development," *The Elementary School Journal* 90, no. 2 (November 1989): 210.
[274]Watson, "Defining and Describing." p. 133.

guage and doing language exercises;" it is "a set of beliefs and not methods;" it "entails congruent practice in its richest sense (not just methods and materials but research, evaluation, curriculum design, interpretive norms, preferred classroom organization, and so on)."[275] Harste commented, "All this means that although whole language developed as a theory of language, it rapidly became a theory of learning."[276]

Questions about whole language remain to be answered. Can such a high degree of individualization, no matter how commendable, be attained universally throughout our educational system, which is always strapped for funds? Can teachers successfully follow the whole-language approach when they have large classes? Will schools be able to furnish the wide variety of materials needed? You will recall that one of the major deficiencies of the defunct secondary school core curriculum approach, which integrated subject areas, was the lack of a large assortment of materials. Will schools be able to secure teachers who have been trained in the whole-language approach? The lack of trained teachers was one of the problems of the core curriculum approach.

Research has already shown that some pupils learn better by one method than another and for certain purposes than for others. Will a phonics approach that emphasizes word-attack skills result in higher achievement in language learning than the whole language approach? Will an approach that integrates phonics in instruction with other methods produce better results in some or most circumstances? What will longitudinal studies reveal about the achievement of youngsters exposed to the whole-language approach when they reach high school and beyond? Taking note of the polarization of phonics supporters on one hand and whole language advocates on the other, Hirsch asserted that research conducted by mainline departments of psychology supports a middle-of-the road approach which includes both phonics and a whole-language approach.[277]

Because testing is a reality of education, we must ascertain how well students who have been taught by the whole-language approach will perform on the inevitable SATs and ACTs as well as on international, national, state, and local criterion- and norm-referenced assessments. Will teachers and parents who have been satisfied with the many positive aspects of whole language maintain a high level of approval if assessment results fall short? Will they be willing to accept other indices of achievement that may be more compatible to the whole-language philosophy?

In examining the issue of whole language Scott Willis observed that the debate "shows signs of heating up rather than abating." Willis cited both advocates and opponents of whole language, research that shows "no clear advantage on either side," disagreements over whether research on whole language should be quantitative or

---

[275]Carole Edelsky, "Whose Agenda Is This Anyway?" A Response to McKenna, Robinson, and Miller," *Educational Researcher* 19, no. 8 (November 1990): 8. Copyright 1990 by the American Educational Research Association. Reprinted by permission of the publisher. See ibid., pp. 7–11; Michael C. McKenna, Richard D. Robinson, and John W. Miller, "Whole Language: A Research Agenda for the Nineties," *Educational Researcher* 19, no. 8 (November 1990): 3–6 to which Edelsky was responding; and Mckenna, Robinson, and Miller, "Whole Language and the Need for Open Inquiry: A Rejoinder to Edelsky," *Educational Researcher* 19, no. 8 (November 1990): 12–13. These three articles offer insights into the disagreements among educators about some aspects of whole language.

[276]Harste, "The Future of Whole Language," p. 246.

[277]Hirsch, *The Schools We Need*, p. 67.

qualitative, arguments over whether whole language taught constructively can be blended with the phonics approach and direct instruction, and concerns about the future of whole language.[278]

Elfrieda H. Hiebert and Charles W. Fisher made a thoughtful observation about the future of whole language:

> Since whole language represents the vanguard of a broader set of influences on education, the experiences of students, teachers, and others as they encounter it can either support a transformation or constitute yet another short-lived pendulum swing in educational practice.[279]

To promote the movement, whole-language advocates have established a network affiliated under the aegis of The Whole Language Umbrella, which held its first conference in August 1990 (at the University of Missouri-Columbia).

The late 1990s witnessed a resurgence of phonics and a call for a balanced program of teaching reading, for example, in California.[280] As we enter the twenty-first century the pendulum has clearly swung away from whole language and toward increased emphasis on phonics, to which proponents of whole language take issue.

In Defense of Good Teaching: What Teachers Need to Know About the "Reading Wars,"[281] copyrighted by the Whole Language Umbrella, for example, rebutted criticism of whole language. Kenneth S. Goodman stated, "the underlying objective of those who attack whole language is to bring down public education itself."[282] Carole Edelsky and Ellen H. Brinkley attributed attacks coming from the political and religious right. Wrote Edelsky, "It is important not to confuse the tactics of the far right with its goals. One of its tactics is to smear whole language. But its goal is to eliminate public schools entirely."[283] Noting objections to whole language on the part of some religious sects, Brinkley explained, "what turns fundamentalist Christian parents into whole language attackers, is their perception that literacy learning in their children's classroom fails to recognize the parents' religious worldview."[284] Bess Altwerger linked attacks on whole language to "political ideology, positions on class, race, and gender."[285]

Nevertheless, at the tail end of 1998 California's Board of Education released a set of voluntary guidelines for the teaching of reading that moved away from whole lan-

---

[278]Scott, Willis, "Whole Language: Finding the Surest Way to Literacy," *Curriculum Update* (Fall 1995), pp. 1–8.

[279]Elfrieda H. Hiebert and Charles W. Fisher, "Whole Language: Three Themes for the Future," *Educational Leadership* 47, no. 6 (March 1990): 62.

[280]California Department of Education, *Teaching Reading: A Balanced, Comprehensive Approach in Teaching Reading in Prekindergarten Through Grade Three* (Sacramento: California Department of Education, 1996).

[281]Kenneth S. Goodman, ed. *In Defense of Good Teaching: What Teachers Need to Know About the "Reading Wars"* (York, Maine: Stenhouse Publishers, 1998).

[282]Ibid., p. 35.

[283]Carole Edelsky, "It's a Long Story–And It's Not Done Yet," in Kenneth S. Goodman, ed., *In Defense of Good Teaching: What Teachers Need to Know About the "Reading Wars"* (York, Maine: Stenhouse Publishers, 1998), p. 39.

[284]Ellen H. Brinkley, "What's Religion Got to Do with Attacks on Whole Language," in Kenneth S. Goodman, *In Defense of Good Teaching: What Teachers Need to Know About the "Religious Wars"* (York, Maine: Stenhouse Publishers, 1998), p. 60.

[285]Bess Altwerger, "Whole Language as Decoy: The Real Agenda Behind the Attacks," in Kenneth S. Goodman, ed., *In Defense of Good Teaching: What Teachers Need to Know About the "Reading Wars,"* (York: Maine: Stenhouse Publishers, 1998), p. 179.

guage and renewed an emphasis on phonics. Perhaps the success or failure of California's students who must take the annual statewide tests that include questions on language standards will shed light on whether a phonics, a whole-language, or a middle-of-the-road approach will be best. Experience throughout the country will demonstrate whether the whole-language approach to language and learning will supplant, supplement, or be replaced by other older or newer approaches.

THE IMPACT OF PROFESSIONAL PROBLEMS UPON CURRICULUM

TEACHER ORGANIZATIONS

Teachers' associations and unions wield considerable influence in the schools. Many years ago Robert M. McClure spoke of the positive impact of teachers' organizations on school improvement, citing as examples, the National Education Association's (NEA) Project on the Academically Talented Student; the NEA Project on Educational Implications of Automation; the Contemporary Music Project of the Music Educators National Conference; the Staff Utilization Studies of the National Association of Secondary School Principals; and the NEA Project on the Instructional Program of the Public Schools.[286]

To these examples we could add the many contributions to curriculum research and study of such professional organizations as the American Association of School Administrators, the American Educational Research Association, the Association for Supervision and Curriculum Development, the Association of Teacher Educators, the national associations of elementary, middle, and secondary school principals, and associations in the specific disciplines.

The two most powerful organizations that represent the interests of teachers are the National Education Association (NEA) and the American Federation of Teachers (AFT), which is affiliated with the AFL-CIO. Although the NEA is not a union in the sense of being affiliated with organized labor, the missions of the NEA and the AFT often coincide. In fact, the two organizations on more than one occasion have talked seriously of merger.

Teachers' organizations influence the curriculum both directly and indirectly. Some curriculum decisions are made not at the customary curriculum council table but at the bargaining table, in negotiations between teachers (labor) and the school district (management). Ordinarily, these negotiations are concerned with working conditions, rights of teachers, salary, benefits, and the like. However, as we noted elsewhere in this text the National Education Association opposes legislative proposals for voucher systems and the establishment of charter schools.

Some items of negotiation are clearly curricular in nature. In communities in which school management and a teachers' organization have effected a contract, the

[286]Robert M. McClure, "The Reforms of th Fifties and Sixties: A Historical Look at the Near Past," in *The Curriculum: Retrospect and Prospect.* 70th Yearbook of the National Society for the Study of Education, Part I (Chicago: University of Chicago Press, 1971), pp. 61–62.

process of curriculum planning will likely need to be modified from that of school systems without formal contracts. Regardless of their personal desires, school administrators are bound by the terms of a negotiated contract.

Ways need to be established to integrate efforts of the teachers' organizations into the school district model for curriculum development. As members of the teachers' organizations themselves, curriculum planners can strive to enlist the teachers' organizations in the cause of continuous curriculum improvement.

IMPROVED DISSEMINATION

The curriculum workers' efforts would be greatly enhanced if we had better ways of disseminating results of research and experience with innovative programs. Though we have the Educational Resources Information Center (ERIC),[287] regional educational laboratories,[288] national research and development centers,[289] national institutes within the Office of Educational Research and Improvement of the U.S. Department of Education,[290] the National Diffusion Network,[291] and many professional journals, the results of research and experimentation do not reach the classroom teacher to the degree they should.

The rapid spread of concepts, programs, and practices such as mastery learning, critical thinking, cooperative learning, and whole language would seem to refute the premise that dissemination of curriculum innovations is slow. However, speed is a relative concept. Forty-five miles per hour may be too slow on a four-laned interstate highway but too fast on a country road. Innovations still take a considerable amount of time to permeate some 15,000 public school districts with their 59,000 elementary and middle schools, their 21,000 secondary schools, their 1.3 million elementary school teachers and their one million secondary school teachers.

Curriculum decisions are still made on the basis of limited information and without all currently available data. Curriculum leaders must take special responsibility to stay informed of current research so that they can channel essential information to the classroom teacher and other curriculum workers.

Since so many agencies and associations now have Web ites and the computer has become a way-of-life, we may anticipate more rapid dissemination of research and ideas on every aspect of life, including education.

IMPROVED RESEARCH

Not only do the results of research need to be disseminated, but both quantity and quality of educational research need to be expanded. The school systems need to be

---

[287]See Appendix B.

[288]See Appendix C.

[289]See Appendix D.

[290]See Appendix E.

[291]National Diffusion Network Division, U.S. Department of Education, 555 New Jersey Ave., N.W., Washington, D.C. 20208-1525.

close partners with institutions of higher learning in the conduct of research. For instance, the National Council for Accreditation of Teacher Education (NCATE)—the voluntary accrediting agency to which schools of education may belong—promotes cooperative research between school systems and schools and colleges of education.[292]

The profession is in particular need of more experimental research and more longitudinal studies. We have many status studies and surveys of opinions and practices (favored by doctoral candidates in education) but not enough controlled research or, for that matter, less controlled action research. Curriculum planners should encourage teachers to participate in controlled research studies and to engage in their own unsophisticated action research to determine answers to simple problems that may be applicable only in their own classrooms.

IMPROVED CONSENSUS BUILDING

Looking at the plethora of proposals for reform and restructuring of the schools, even educators, let alone the public, from time to time must express bewilderment. Shall schools go in the direction of core kowledge or constructivism? Is outcomes-based education the answer? Shall we mainstream the gifted? Shall we create national standards? Shall we change the school calendar? Is the effective teaching research passé? Shall we introduce character, values, and ethics education? Should we cease stressing the basic skills?

We find individuals and like-minded groups advocating their own measures to reform and restructure schools. Whom should administrators, teachers, and parents heed? Who has the "right" solution or can we buy all solutions? Is the curriculum for the twenty-first century found in a full-service school with an outcomes-based education and an integrated, interdisciplinary curriculum; its pupils in inclusive classrooms learning cooperatively, following whole-language techniques, using multicultural materials; without common national academic standards; employing authentic assessment?

With the empowerment of teachers and parents the building of consensus becomes a paramount concern. Studies conducted by Public Agenda confirm the fact that the public tends to be more conservative than many educators. Safety, order, high standards, basic skills, and common knowledge head the list of the public's concerns.[293] Borrowing a leaf from the perceptual psychologists, reformers must deal first with perceptions of the public and gain commitment before they can effect lasting change.

Our informed public is well aware of repeated efforts at reforming the public schools. Curriculum workers cannot express impatience if the public asks why we have had to engage repeatedly in reform efforts. When, they ask, will we come up with solutions that will be both effective and reasonably permanent? Curriculum workers today must demonstrate the interpersonal and technical skills necessary to building

[292]National Council for the Accreditation of Teacher Education, *Standards, Procedures, and Policies for the Accreditation of Professional Education Units*, rev. (Washington, D.C.: National Council for the Accreditation of Teacher Education, 1990), p. 51.

[293]See Jean Johnson and John Immerwahr, *First Things First: What Americans Expect from the Public Schools* (New York: Public Agenda, 1994). See also Stephen Farkas, Principal Researcher, *Effective Public Engagement* (Washington, D.C.: New Standards Project, 1993).

consensus among constituencies of the school. They must lay a groundwork, experiment, and demonstrate results to gain acceptance. Assertions to the effect that "research shows" when, indeed, that research may or may not show, will not satisfy a tradition-oriented public, nor for that matter, tradition-oriented teachers and administrators. Researchers and pioneers must encourage teachers and administrators to try out new ways without making them feel that everything they have been doing, possibly for many years, is wrong. In fact, innovators have a heavy responsibility for demonstrating that the newer programs they advocate are indeed superior to the ones they would replace.

IMPROVED PREPARATION

Better programs are needed to prepare curriculum leaders and planners. To gain some perception of the preparation needed by curriculum developers, we might refer to Chapter 1 on the areas of learning from which the field of curriculum is derived, to Chapter 3 on the multiple levels and sectors of curriculum planning, and to Chapter 4 on the roles of various personnel in curriculum development. States might reasonably institute certificates in curriculum development. Such certificates would parallel those now offered in administration, supervision, guidance, and other specialities. Such a certificate would go a long way toward establishing curriculum as a field of specialization in its own right. Furthermore, teacher education institutions should assure that their graduates gain what might be called "curriculum literacy"—that is, knowledge about the curriculum field and basic skills in curriculum development.

Solutions to all of these problems could help to improve the efficacy of curriculum development.

CURRICULUM FUTURE—AN AFTERTHOUGHT

Among the various problems discussed in this chapter are a number of current curricular practices and programs. Some of these will remain with us for many years. If past is prologue, however, some will become universal practice, some will continue to exist in certain localities and certain schools, some will be modified, some will be abandoned, and some newer developments will take the place of some of the older.

SUMMARY

This chapter is, in effect, a continuation of Curriculum Present, a theme we began in Chapter 9 where we discussed some generally accepted curricular programs and practices. This chapter presents a number of current and controversial curricular problems and a few professional problems that have an impact upon the curriculum.

Fifteen current problems of direct concern to curriculum planners were examined. These problems, brought about by social and political forces, are alternative schooling, bilingual education, censorship, community service, cultural literacy, educational management organizations, gender discrimination, multiculturalism, health education, national standards, outcomes-based education, provision for exceptionalities, religion in the schools, schedule revisions, and whole language. Curriculum workers must be aware of the dimensions of these and other current problems as they attempt to develop curricula.

The chapter concluded with a brief discussion of five professional problems that have an impact upon the curriculum: the need to clarify the role of teacher organizations in respect to curriculum improvement, the need for better means of disseminating the results of curriculum research and experimentation, the need for more and better research, the need for improved consensus building, and the need for improved training programs for curriculum developers.

Curriculum development today is a blend of many practices and programs both innovative and time-honored. Illustrative of the phenomenon of déjà vu are recent efforts at integrating the curriculum, block and rotating scheduling, performance-based education, and nongraded schools. As we enter the twenty-first century our schools will be buoyed up by a judicious mixture of the old and the new.

QUESTIONS FOR DISCUSSION

1. What general guidelines would you recommend for curriculum planners to follow in dealing with controversial curriculum issues?
2. What current curriculum developments do you predict will be universally accepted ten years from now?
3. What are some current controversial curricular problems not included in this chapter?
4. How do you account for repeated efforts to reform the public schools?
5. What measures would you recommend in reforming and restructuring the public schools?

SUPPLEMENTARY EXERCISES

1. Take each of the fiteen curriculum problems discussed in this chapter and state your position on each. Give reasons for your position.
2. Select one of the current curriculum problems, search the literature, review local practices, and document with references the degree to which it appears to be a problem both nationally and locally. Show your position on the problem and suggest ways for solving it.
3. Document any instances of the following curriculum problems within the past three years in the school district you know best:
   a. racial conflicts
   b. religious conflicts
   c. gender discrimination
   d. schoolbook protests

4. Prepare a position paper on including the following in regular classes:
   a. physically handicapped (Note: Comment on whether they should be referred to as "physically challenged" instead of physically handicapped.)
   b. children with behavior disorders
   c. the gifted
5. Refer in this chapter to the list of U.S. Supreme Court decisions on church-state disputes, consult references in school law, and report the significance of these cases.
6. Select any current curriculum program, locate one or more research studies on this program, and draw conclusions on its effectiveness.
7. Find out your state's guidelines, curricula, and/or policies regarding sexuality education.
8. Tell how a school system you know well handles protests about books and other materials.
9. Report on any alternative education available in your school district.
10. Either from the literature or from a field visit, assemble data on the success or failure of a charter school.
11. Write a report on the extent of home schooling in a district you know well.
12. Prepare a report on a successful multicultural education program at any level of a school district with which you are familiar.
13. Poll a group of secondary school students and determine whether they believe gender discrimination exists in their school.
14. Prepare a position paper on one of the following:
    a. year-round schools (single track)
    b. year-round schools (multi-track)
    c. lengthened school year .
15. Report on any departures from traditional scheduling you can find in your region.
16. Locate examples of stated outcomes of any Outcomes-Based Education program.
17. Locate and critique any set of national standards in any discipline.
18. Report on the purposes and effectiveness of any bilingual education program in your region.
19. Describe any community service program for secondary school students.
20. Explain to the class how whole language differs from other approaches to teaching the language arts.
21. Report on any activities of a teachers' organization that have had an impact on the curriculum of a school you know well.
22. Explain the purposes of the Educational Resources Information Center (ERIC) and show how the system works. Explain how to use ERIC, giving examples. (See Appendix B).
23. Write the National Diffusion Network Facilitator for your state and report on exemplary programs that exist. (See footnote 291 this chapter.)
24. Report on the work of one or more of the regional educational laboratories or national research and development centers. Give illustrations of their impact on the curriculum. (See Appendices C and D).
25. Prepare a report showing your position on enforcing "high stakes," that is, setting consequences for students' high or low achievement.

26. Prepare a report showing your position on the question whether gender discrimination exists in the schools and, if so, whether one gender or the other suffers disproportionately.

BIBLIOGRAPHY

In order to assist those who wish to do research on a given topic discussed in this chapter this bibliography includes a number in parenthesis to indicate the number to be found in the list of fifteen contemporary problems set forth at the beginning of this chapter. A G after the bibliographical reference signifies *General*.

"Adolescent Health: Reducing Risk," *NASSP Bulletin* 77, no. 557 (December 1993): 1–76. (8)

Alan Guttmacher Institute. *Sex and America's Teenagers.* New York: The Alan Guttmacher Institute, 1994. (8)

Alexander, Elizabeth. "School-Based Clinics: Questions to be Answered in Planning Stages." *The High School Journal* 73, no. 2 (December 1989–January 1990): 133–138. (8)

Altwerger, Bess. "Whole Language as Decoy: The Real Agenda Behind the Attacks" in Kenneth S. Goodman, ed., *In Defense of Good Teaching: What Teachers Need to Know About the "Reading Wars."* York, Maine: Stenhouse Publishers, 1998, pp. 175–181. (15)

Americans United for *Separation of Church and State, American United Seventh Annual Report on Church-State Conflict in the United States.* Washington, D.C.: Americans United for Separation of Church and State, 1995. (13)

"America's Holy War." TIME 138, no. 23 (December 9, 1991): 60–68. (13)

American Association of University Women and American Institutes for Research. *Gender Gaps: Where Schools Fail Our Children.* New York: Marlowe & Co., 1999. (7)

American Association of University Women Educational Foundation and Wellesley College Center for Research on Women. *How Schools Shortchange Girls: The AAUW Report: A Study of Major Findings on Girls and Education.* Washington, D.C.: American Association for University Women; National Education Association, 1992. Trade ed.: New York: Marlowe & Co., 1995. (7)

Anderson, Julie. "Alternative Approaches to Organizing the School Day and Year." *The School Administrator* 51, no. 3 (March 1994): 8–11, 15. (14)

Anne E. Casey Foundation. *When Teens Have Sex: Issues and Trends.* Baltimore: Anne E. Casey Foundation, 1999. (8)

Aronowitz, Stanley and Giroux, Henry A. *Education Under Siege: The Conservative, Liberal, and Radical De-*bate over Schooling. South Hadley, Mass.: Bergin & Garvey, 1985. (G)

Ascher, Carol, Fruchter, Norm, and Berne, Robert. *Hard Lessons: Public Schools and Privatization.* New York: The Twentieth Century Fund, 1996. (6)

Association for Supervision and Curriculum Development. "Plan for 'African-American Immersion Schools' Raises Questions." *Update* 33, no. 2 (February 1991): 6, 8. (9)

————. *Public Schools of Choice.* Alexandria, Va.: Association for Supervision and Curriculum Development, 1990. (1)

————. *Religion in the Curriculum: A Report from the ASCD Panel on Religion in the Curriculum.* Alexandria, Va.: Association for Supervision and Curriculum Development, 1987. (13)

August, Diane and Hakuta, Kenji, eds. *Educating Language-Minority Children.* Washington, D.C.: National Research Council, 1998. (2) (9)

Ballinger, Charles. *Annual Report to the Association on the Status of Year-Round Education, 1993.* ERIC document ED358551. (14)

————. "Rethinking the School Calendar." *Educational Leadership* 45, no. 5 (February 1988): 57–61. (14)

Banks, James A. *Educating Citizens in a Multicultural Society.* New York: Teachers College Press, 1997. (9)

Banks, James A., ed. *Multicultural Education, Transformative Knowledge, and Action: Historical and Contemporary Perpectives.* New York: Teachers College Press, 1996. (9)

————, Guest Editor. "A Special Issue on Multicultural Education," *Phi Delta Kappan* 75, no. 1 (September 1993): 8–54. (9)

Banks, James A. and Banks, Cherry A. McGee, eds. *Handbook of Research on Multicultural Education.* New York: Macmillan, 1995. (9)

————. *Multicultural Education: Issues and Perspectives,* 2nd ed. Boston: Allyn and Bacon, 1993. (9)

Barr, Robert D. and Parrett, William. *How to Create Alternative, Magnet, and Charter Schools That Work.* Bloomington, Ind.: National Educational Service, 1997. (1)

Bennett, William J. *Our Children and Our Country: Improving America's Schools and Affirming the Common Culture.* New York: Simon and Schuster, 1988. (9)

Berliner, David and Biddle, Bruce. *The Manufactured Crisis: Myths, Fraud, and the Attack on America's Public*

Schools. Reading, Mass.: Addison-Wesley-Longman, 1996. (10)

Bloom, Allan. *The Closing of the American Mind.* New York: Simon and Schuster, 1987. (G)

Boschee, Floyd and Baron, Mark A. *Outcome-Based Education: Developing Programs Through Strategic Planning.* Lancaster, Pa.: Technomic Publishing Co., 1993. (11) (14)

Bracey, Gerald W. "Against Ability Grouping . . . Again." *Phi Delta Kappan* 70, no. 1 (March 1993): 573–574. (12)

———. *Setting the Record Straight: Responses to Misconception About Public Education in the United States.* Alexandria, Va.: Association for Supervision and Curriculum Development, 1997. (10)

Brandt, Ron. "An Outcome-Based Education.: A Conversation with Bill Spady." *Educational Leadership* 50, no. 4 (December 1992–January 1993): 66–70. (11)

Breivik, Patricia Senn and Senn, J. A. *Information Literacy: Educating Children for the 21st Century.* New York: Scholastic, 1994. (5)

Brian, Ray. *Home Education Across the United States.* Washington, D.C.: Home School Legal Defense Association, 1997. (1)

Brinkley, Ellen H. "What's Religion Got to Do with Attacks on Whole Language?" in Kenneth S. Goodman, ed., *In Defense of Good Teaching: What Teachers Need to Know About the Reading Wars."* York, Maine: Stenhouse Publishers, 1998, pp. 57–71. (15)

Britzman, Deborah P. *Lost Causes: Contested Objects: Toward a Psychoanalytic Inquiry of Learning.* Albany, N.Y.: State University of New York Press, 1998. (8)

———. *Practice Makes Practice: A Critical Study of Learning to Teach.* Albany, N.Y.: State University of New York Press, 1991. (9)

Butts, R. Freeman. *The American Tradition in Religion and Education.* Boston: Beacon Press, 1950. (13)

Caldas, Stephen J. "Teen Pregnancy: Why It Remains a Serious Social, Economic, and Educational Problem in the U.S." *Phi Delta Kappan* 75, no. 5 (January 1944): 402–406. (8)

Carbo, Marie. "Debunking the Great Phonics Myth." *Phi Delta Kappan* 70, no. 3 (November 1988): 226–240. (15)

Carnegie Foundation for the Advancement of Teaching. *School Choice.* Princeton, N.J.: Carnegie Foundation for the Advancement of Teaching, 1993. (1)

Carroll, Joseph M. "The Copernican Plan Evaluated: The Evolution of a Revolution. *Phi Delta Kappan* 76, no. 2 (October 1994): 104–113. (14)

———. "Organizing Time to Support Learning." *The School Administrator* 51, no. 3 (March 1994): 26–28, 30–33. (14)

Centers for Disease Control and Prevention, "Summary of Notifiable Diseases, United States, 1993," *Mor-bidity and Mortality Weekly Report* 42, no. 53 (October 20, 1994). (8)

———. "Summary of Notifiable Diseases, United States, 1997," *Morbidity and Mortality Weekly Report* 46, no. 54 (November 20, 1998). (8)

Chall, Jeanne S. "Learning to Read: The Great Debate 20 Years Later—A Response to 'Debunking the Great Phonics Myth.'" *Phi Delta Kappan* 70, no. 7 (March 1989): 521–538. (15)

"The Challenge of Higher Standards." *Educational Leadership* 50, no. 5 (February 1993): 4–77. (10)

"The Challenge of Outcome-Based Education." *Educational Leadership* 51, no. 6 (March 1994): 6–84. (11)

"The Charter Schools Movement." *Phi Delta Kappan* 79, no. 7 (March 1998): 488–511. (1)

Cobb, Nina, ed. *The Future of Education: Perspectives on National Standards in America.* New York: College Entrance Examination Board, 1994. (10)

Commission on the Skills of the American Workforce. *America's Choice: High Skills or Low Wages!* Rochester, N.Y.: National Center on Education and the Economy, 1990. (11)

Cordasco, Francesco. *Bilingual Schooling in the United States: A Sourcebook for Educational Personnel.* New York: Webster Division, McGraw-Hill, 1976. (2)

Cornbleth, Catherine and Waugh, Dexter. *The Great Speckled Bird: Multicultural Politics and Education Policymaking.* New York: St. Martin's Press, 1995. (9)

Cornett, Claudia E. and Blankenship, Lesley A. *Whole Language-Whole Learning.* Fastback 307. Bloomington, Ind.: Phi Delta Kappa Foundation, 1990. (15)

Crawford, James. *Bilingual Education: History, Politics, Theory, and Practice,* 3rd ed. Los Angeles: Bilingual Educational Services, 1995. (2)

———, ed. *Language Loyalties: A Source Book on the Offical English Controversy.* Chicago: University of Chicago Press, 1992. (2)

Crockett, Jean B. and Kauffman, James M. "Taking Inclusion Back to Its Roots." *Educational Leadership* 56, no. 2 (October 1998): 74–77. (12)

Darling-Hammond, Linda. *The Right to Learn: A Blueprint for Creating Schools That Work.* San Francisco: Jossey-Bass, 1997. (5)

"Dealing with Diversity." Educational Leadership 46, no. 5 (February 1989): 2–81. (9)

Doyle, Robert P. *Books Challenged or Banned in 1993–94.* Chicago: Office of Intellectual Freedom, American Library Association, 1995. (3)

Dryfoos, Joy G. "Full-Service Schools: What They Are and How to Get One." *NASSP Bulletin* 77, no. 557 (December 1993): 29–35. (12)

Eccles, Jacquelynne S. and Harold, Rena D. *Gender Differences in Sport Involvement: Applying the Eccles' Expectancy-Value Model.* Ann Arbor, Mich.: University Press, n.d., pp. 28–29. (7)

Edelsky, Carole. "It's a Long Story-And It's Not Done Yet" in Kenneth S. Goodman, ed., *In Defense of Good Teaching: What Teachers Need to Know About the "Reading Wars."* York, Maine: Stenhouse Publishers, 1998, pp. 39–55. (15)

————. "Whose Agenda Is This Anyway?: Response to McKenna, Robinson, and Miller." *Educational Researcher* 19, no. 8 (November 1990): 8. (15)

"Education for Diversity." *Educational Leadership* 51, no. 8 (May 1994): 4–54. (9)

Elam, Stanley M. "The 22nd Annual Gallup Poll of the Public's Attitudes Toward the Public Schools." *Phi Delta Kappan* 72, no. 1 (September 1990): 41–55. (G)

Elam, Stanley M. and Rose, Lowell C. "The 27th Annual Poll of the Public's Attitudes Toward the Public Schools," *Phi Delta Kappan* 77, no. 1 (September 1995): 41–56. (G)

Elam, Stanley M., Rose, Lowell C., and Gallup, Alec M. "The 23rd Annual Gallup Poll of the Public's Attitudes Toward the Public Schools." *Phi Delta Kappan* 73, no. 1 (September 1991): 41–56. (G)

————. "The 24th Annual Gallup/Phi Delta Kappa Poll of the Public's Attitudes Toward the Public Schools." *Phi Delta Kappan* 74, no. 1 (September 1992): 41–53. (G)

————. "The 25 Annual Phi Delta Kappa/Gallup Poll of the Public's Attitudes Toward the Public Schools." *Phi Delta Kappan* 75, no. 2 (October 1993): 137–152. (G)

————. "The 26th Annual Phi Delta Kappa/Gallup Poll of the Public's Attitudes Toward the Public Schools." *Phi Delta Kappan* 76, no. 1 (September 1994): 41–56. (G)

————. "The 28th Annual Phi Delta Kappan/Gallup Poll of the Public's Attitudes Toward the Public Schools." *Phi Delta Kappan* 78, no. 1 (September 1996): 41–59. (G)

Elmer-Dewitt, Philip. "Making the Case for Abstinence." *Time* 141, no. 21 (May 24, 1993): 64–65. (8)

Farkas, Stephen, Principal Researcher. *Effective Public Engagement.* Washington, D.C.: New Standards Project, 1993. (10)

Finn, Chester E., Manno, Bruno V., and Bierlien, Louann. *Charter Schools in Action: What Have We Learned?* Indianapolis, Ind.: Hudson Institute, 1996. Gov. doucment ED 399 671. (1)

Forbes, Michael J. "Legality of a High School Condom Distribution Program to Prevent HIV Infection: *Alfonso v. Fernandez.*" *Journal of Law and Education* 22, no. 1 (Winter 1993): 134–138. (8)

Foriska, Terry J. *Restructuring Around Standards: A Practitioner's Guide to Design and Implementation.* Thousand Oaks, Calif.: Corwin Press, 1998. (10)

Friend, Marilyn and Cook, Lynne. "Inclusion." *Instructor* 103, no. 4 (November/December 1993): 53–56. (12)

Fuchs, Douglas, Guest Editor. "A Special Issue on Special Education." *Phi Delta Kappan* 76, no. 7 (March 1995): 522–540. (12)

Furtwengler, Carol B. "Heads Up! The EMOs Are Coming." *Educational Leadership* 56, no. 2 (October 1998): 44–47. (6)

Gagnon, Paul, ed and the Bradley Commission on History in Schools. *Historical Literacy: The Case for History in American Education.* New York: Macmillan, 1989. (5)

Gay, Geneva. *At the Essence of Learning: Multicultural Education.* West Lafayette, Ind.: Kappa Delta Pi, 1994. (9)

George, Paul. *How to Untrack Your School.* Alexandria, Va.: Association for Supervision and Curriculum Development, 1992. (12)

Gibbs, Nancy. "How Should We Teach Our Children About Sex?" *TIME* 141, no. 21 (May 24, 1993): 60–66. (8)

Gibson, Joyce Taylor. *Developing Strategies and Practices for Culturally Diverse Classrooms.* Norwood, Mass.: Christopher-Gordon, 1998. (9)

Giroux, Henry A. *Living Dangerously: Multiculturalism and the Politics of Difference.* New York: Peter Lang, 1993. (9) (10)

Giroux, Henry A. and McLaren, Peter, eds. *Between Borders: Pedagogy and the Politics of Cultural Studies.* New York: Routledge, 1994. (9)

Glasser, William. "The Quality School," *Phi Delta Kappan* 71, no. 6 (February 1990): 424–435. (G)

————. *The Quality School: Managing Students Without Coercion,* 2nd, expanded ed. New York: HarperPerennial, 1992. (G)

Glickman, Carl D. *Revolutionizing America's Schools.* San Francisco: Jossey-Bass, 1998. (10) (13)

Glines, Don. *YRE Basics: History, Methods, Concerns, Future.* ERIC document ED369104, 1994. (14)

Goldberg, David Theo, ed. *Multiculturalism: A Critical Reader.* Cambridge, Mass.: Blackwell, 1994. (9)

Goodman, Kenneth S. "Whole-Language Research: Foundations and Development." *The Elementary School Journal* 90, no. 2 (November 1989): 210. (15)

Goodman, Kenneth S., ed. *In Defense of Good Teaching: What Teachers Need to Know About the "Reading Wars."* York, Maine: Stenhouse Publishers, 1998. (15)

Goodman, Yetta M. "Kid Watching: An Alternative to Testing." *The National Elementary Principal* 57, no. 4 (June 1978): 41–45. (15)

Gramlich, Edward M. and Koshel, Patricia P. *Educational Performance Contracting: An Evaluation of an Experiment.* Washington, D.C.: The Brookings Institution, 1975. (6)

Grant, Carl A. and Sleeer, Christine E. *Turning on Learning: Five Approaches for Multicultural Teaching Plans for Race, Class, Gender, and Disabilities,* 2nd ed. Upper Saddle River, N.J.: Merrill, 1998. (9)

Greene, Maxine. *Releasing the Imagination: Essays on Education, the Arts, and Social Change.* San Francisco: Jossey-Bass, 1995. (9) (10)

————. *Teacher as Stranger: Educational Philosophy for the Modern Era.* Belmont, Calif.: Wadsworth, 1973. (9)

Grumet, Madeleine R. *Bitter Milk: Women and Teaching.* Amherst, Mass.: University of Massachusetts Press, 1988. (7)

Haffner, Debra W., ed. *Facing Facts: Sexual Health for America's Adolescents.* New York: Sex Information and Education Council of the United States, 1995. (8)

Handlin, Oscar and Handlin, Lilian. "America and Its Discontents: A Great Society Legacy." *The American Scholar* 64, no. 1 (Winter 1995): 15–37. (12)

Harrington-Lueker, Donna, "Charter 'Profit'." *The American School Board Journal* 181, no. 9 (September 1994): 27–28. (1)

————. "Charter Schools." *The American School Board Journal* 181. no. 9 (September 1994): 22–26. (1)

Harste, Jerome C. "The Future of Whole Language." *The Elementary School Journal* 90, no. 2 (November 1989): 247. (15)

Haynes, Charles C. and Thomas, Oliver. *Finding Common Ground.* Nashville, Tenn.: The Freedom Forum First Amendment Center at Vanderbilt University, 1994. (13)

Henshaw, S. K. and Van Vort, J., eds. *Abortion Factbook 1992 Edition: Readings, Trends, and State and Local Data.* New York: The Alan Guttmacher Institute, 1992. (8)

Hill, Peter W. and Crevola, Carmel A. "The Role of Standards in Educational Reform for the 21st Century." In David D. Marsh, ed. *Preparing Our Schools for the 21st Century.* 1999 Yearbok. Alexandria, Va.: Association for Supervision and Curriculum Development, 1999, pp. 117–142. (10)

Hirsch, E. D., Jr. "Core Knowledge." *Newsweek* 120, no. 12 (September 12, 1992): A8–9. (5)

————. "The Core Knowledge Curriculum—What's Behind Its Success?" *Educational Leadership* 50, no. 8 (May 1993): 23–25. (5)

————. *Cultural Literacy: What Every American Needs to Know.* Boston: Houghton Mifflin, 1987. (5)

————. *The Schools We Need: Why We Don't Have Them.* New York: Doubleday, 1997. (5) (10)

————., ed. *What Your Kindergartner Needs to Know: Fundamentals of a Good Kindergarten Education.* New York: Doubleday, 1996. *First Grader,* rev. ed., 1997. *Second Grader,* rev. ed. with John Holdren, ed., 1998; *Third Grader,* 1992; *Fourth Grader,* 1992; *Fifth Grader,* 1993; *Sixth Grader,* 1993. (The Core Knowledge Series) (5)

Holland, Robert. *Not With My Child You Don't: A Citizen's Guide to Eradicating OBE and Restoring Education.* Richmond, Va.: Chesapeake Capital Services, 1995. (11)

Horatio Alger Association. *The State of Our Nation's Youth.* Alexandria, Va.: Horatio Alger Association, 1997. (7)

Hudson, Kathi. *Reinventing America's Schools: A Practical Guide to Components of Restructuring and Non-Traditional Education.* Costa Mesa, Calif.: National Association of Christian Educators/Citizens for Excellence in Education, 1992–93. (G)

Hughes, Robert. "The Fraying of America." *Time* 139, no. 5 (February 3, 1992): 44–49. (9)

"The Inclusive School." *Educational Leadership* 52, no. 4 (December 1994/January 1995): 4–87. (12)

Irvine, Janice M. *Sexuality Education Across Cultures: Working with Differences.* San Francisco: Josey-Bass, 1995. (7)

Irvine, Janice M., ed. *Sexual Cultures and the Construction of Adolescent Identities.* Philadelphia: Temple University Press, 1994. (8)

Johnson, Jean and Immerwahr. *First Things First: What Americans Expect from the Public Schools.* New York: Public Agenda, 1994. (G)

Johnston, Lloyd D., O'Malley, Patrick M., and Bachman, Jerald G. *National Survey Results on Drug Use from Monitoring the Future Study, 1975–1998. Vol. 1 Secondary School Students.* Rockville, Md.: National Institute on Drug Abuse, 1998. (8)

Kane, Cheryl. *Prisoners of Time: Research: What We Know and What We Need to Know.* Washington, D.C.: National Education Commission on Time and Learning, 1994. ERIC document ED378685. (14)

Kantrowitz, Barbara and Wingert, Pat. " Learning at Home: Does It Pass the Test?" *Newsweek* 132, no. 14 (0ctober 5, 1998): 64–70. (1)

"A Kappan Special Section on Standards." *Phi Delta Kappan* 76, no. 10 (January 1995): 744–769. (10)

Kendall, John S. and Marzano, Robert J. *Content Knowledge: A Compendium of Standards and Benchmarks for K–12 Education,* 2nd ed. Aurora, Col.: Mid-Continent Regional Educational Laboratory and Alexandria, Va.: Association for Supervision and Curriculum Development, 1997. (10)

————. *The Systematic Identification and Articulation of Content Standards and Benchmarks: Update.* Aurora, Col.: Mid-Continent Regional Educational Laboratory, 1995. (10)

Kinsley, Carol W. and McPherson, Kate. *Enriching the Curriculum Through Service Learning.* Alexandria, Va.: Association for Supervision and Curriculum Development, 1995. (4)

Kleinfeld, Judith. "Student Performance: Males versus Females." *The Public Interest* 134 (1999). (7)

Kluger, Richard. *Simple Justice.* New York: Knopf, 1975. (9)

Koerner, Brendan I. "Where the Boys Aren't." *U.S.News & World Report* 126, no. 5 (February 8, 1999): 46–55. (7)

Kunen, James S. "The End of Segregation." *TIME* 147, no. 18 (April 29, 1996): 39–45. (9)

Latham, Andrew S. "School Vouchers: Much Debate, Little Research." *Educational Leadership* 56, no. 2 (October 1998): 82–83. (1)

Lickona, Thomas. "Where Sex Education Went Wrong." Educational Leadership 54, no. 3 (November 1993): 84–89. (8)

Lieberman, Myron. Privatization and Educational Choice. New York: St. Martin's Press, 1989. (1) (6)

Lockwood, Anne Turnbaugh. Standards: From Policy to Practice. Thousand Oaks, Calif.: Corwin Press, 1998. (10)

McCarthy, Martha M. "Challenges to the Public School Curriculum: New Targets and Strategies. Phi Delta Kappan 75, no. 1 (September 1993): 55–60. (G)

———. "Much Ado over Graduation Prayer." Phi Delta Kappan 76, no. 2 (October 1993): 120–125. (13)

McKenna, Michael C., Robinson, Richartd D., and Miller, John W. "Whole Language: A Research Agenda for the Nineties." Educational Researcher 19, no. 8 (November 1990): 3–6. (15)

Mabbett, Barbara. "The New Zealand Story." Educational Leadership 47, no. 7 (March 1990): 59–61. (15)

Males, Mike. "Schools, Society, and 'Teen' Pregnancy." Phi Delta Kappan 74, no. 7 (March 1993): 566–572. (8)

Mamary, Albert. "14 Principles of Outcomes-Based Education," Principal 76, no. 1 (January 1994): 19–23. (11)

Marzano, Robert J. and Kendall, John S. Essential Knowledge: The Debate Over What American Students Should Know. Aurora, Col.: McRel Institute, 1999. (10)

Mulholland, Lori A. and Bierlein, Louann A. Understanding Charter Schools. Fastback 383. Bloomington, Ind.: Phi Delta Kappa Educational Foundation, 1995. (1)

"Multicultural Issues." Phi Delta Kappan 74, no. 3 (November 1993): 208–227. (9)

Murphy, Joseph. The Privatization of Schooling: Problems and Possibilities. Thousand Oaks, Calif.: Corwin Press, 1996. (6)

Nathan, Joe. Charter Schools: Creating Hope and Opportunity for American Education. San Francisco: Jossey-Bass, 1996. (1)

———. and Kielsmeier, Jim, Guest Editors. "A Special Section on Youth Services. Phi Delta Kappan 72, no. 10 (June 1991): 738–773. (4)

National Association of State Boards of Education. Winners All: A Call for Inclusive Schools. Alexandria, Va.: National Association of State Boards of Education, 1992. (12)

National Center for Education Statistics. The Condition of Education 1998. Washington, D.C.: U.S. Department of Education, 1998. (4)

National Commission on Excellence in Education. A Nation at Risk: The Imperative for Educational Reform. Washington, D.C.: U.S. Government Printing Office, 1983. (G)

National Council on Education and Standards. Raising Standards for American Education. Washington, D.C.: U.S. Government Printing Office, 1992. (10)

National Education Commission on Time and Learning. Prisoners of Time. Washington, D.C.: National Education Commission on Time and Learning, April 1994. (14)

———. Prisoners of Time: Schools and Programs Making Time Work for Students and Teachers. Washington, D.C.: National Education Commission on Time and Learning, September 1994. (14)

———. Research Findings. Washington, D.C.: National Education Commission on Time and Learning, 1993. (14)

Nelkin, Dorothy. The Creation Controversy: Science or Scripture in the Schools?. New York: W. W. Norton, 1982. (13)

"The New Alternative Schools." Educational Leadership 52, no. 1 (September 1994): 4–79. (1)

Nieto, Sonia. Affirming Diversity. White Plains, N.Y.: Longman, 1992. (9)

Noddings, Nell. Educating for Intelligent Belief or Unbelief. New York: Teachers College Press, 1993. (13)

Nord, Warren A. and Haynes, Charles C. Taking Religion Seriously Across the Curriculum. Alexandria, Va.: Association for Supervision and Curriculum Development, 1998. (13).

Oakes, Jeannie. Keeping Track: How Schols Structure Inequality. New Haven, Conn.: Yale University Press, 1985. (9)

Oakes, Jeannie, Gamoran, Adam, and Page, Reba N. "Curriculum Differentiation: Opportunities, Outcomes, and Meanings." in Philip W. Jackson, ed., Handbook of Research on Curriculum, New York: Macmillan, 1992. (12)

Orfield, Gary et al. "The Growth of Segregation in American Schools: Changing Patterns of Separation and Poverty Since 1968." Equity & Excellence in Education 27, no. 1 (April 1994): 5–8. (9)

Ornstein, Allan C. and Behar, Linda S., eds. Contemporary Issues in Curriculum. Boston: Allyn and Bacon, 1995. (G)

Pearson, P. David. "Commentary: Reading the Whole-Language Movement." The Elementary School Journal 90, no. 2 (November 1989): 231. (15)

People for the American Way. Attacks on the Freedom to Learn. Washington, D.C.: People for the American Way, 1995. (3)

Phillips, Lynn. The Girls Report. New York: National Council for Research on Women, 1998. (7)

Powe, Karen. Private Options for Public Schools: Ways Public Schools Are Exploring Privatization. Alexandria, Va.: National School Boards Association, 1995. (6)

Price, Hugh B. "Multiculturalism: Myths and Realities." Phi Delta Kappan 74, no. 3 (November 1992): 208–213. (9)

"Public Schools and the Christian Fundamentalists." Educational Leadership 51, no. 4 (December 1993/January 1994): 4–43. (13)

"The Quest for Higher Standards." *Educational Leadership* 487, no. 5 (February 1991): 4–69. (10)

"Race, Class, and Culture." *Educational Leadership* 56, no. 7 (April 1999): 8–82. (9)

Randall, Ruth E. and Geiger, Keith. *School Choice: Issues and Answers.* Bloomington, Ind.: National Educational Service, 1991. (1)

Ravitch, Diane. *National Standards in American Education: A Citizen's Guide.* Washington, D.C.: The Brookings Institution, 1995. (10)

"Religion and the Schools." *Phi Delt Kappan* 81, no. 1 (September 1999): 14–40, 58. (13)

"Reorganizing Time: Alternative Approaches to the School Day and Year." *The School Administrator* 51, no. 3 (March 1994): 8–33. (14)

Reissman, Rose. *The Evolving Multicultural Classroom.* Alexandria, Va.: Association for Supervision and Curriculum Development, 1994. (9)

Rogers, Spence and Dana, Bonnie. *Outcomes-Based Education: Concerns and Responses.* Fastback 388. Bloomington, Ind.: Phi Delta Kappa Educational Foundation, 1995. (11)

Rose, Lowell C. and Gallup, Alec M. "The 30th Annual Phi Delta Kappa/Gallup Poll of the Public's Attitudes Toward the Public Schools," *Phi Delta Kappan* 80, no. 1 (September 1998): 41–56. (G)

———. "The 31st Annual Phi Delta Kappa/Gallup Poll of the Public's Attitudes Toward the Public Schools." *Phi Delta Kappan* 81, no. 1 (September 1999): 45–56. (G)

———, Gallup, Alec M, and Elam, Stanley M. "The 29th Annual Phi Delta Kappa/Gallup Poll of the Public's Attitudes Toward the Public Schools," *Phi Delta Kappan* 79, no. 1 (September 1997): 41–56. (G)

Samuels, Sarah E., ed. *Condoms in the Schools.* Menlo Park, Calif.: Henry J. Kaiser Family Foundation, 1993. (8)

Sarason, Seymour B. *Charter Schools: Another Flawed Educatinoal Reform.* New York: Teachers College Press, 1998. (1)

Schlesinger, Arthur M., Jr. *The Disuniting of America: Reflections on a Multicultural Society.* New York: W. W. Norton, 1992. (9)

"Schools of Choice?" *Educational Leadership* 48, no. 4 (December 1990/January 1991): 4–72. (1)

Schuster, Mark A., Bell Robert M., Berry, Sandra H., and Kenouse, David E. "Impact of High School Condom Availability on Sexual Attitudes and Behaviors." *Family Planning Perspectives* 30, no. 6 (March/April 1998): 67–72, 88. (8)

Sears, James T., ed. *The Politics and Practices of Sexuality Education: Sexuality and the Curriculum.* New York: Teachers College Press, 1992. (8)

Sedlak, Michael W. et al. *Selling Students Short: Classroom Bargains and Academic Reform in the American High School.* New York: Teachers College Press, 1986. (G)

"Service-Learning," *Phi Delta Kappan* 81, no. 9 (May 2000): 652–680. (4)

Sex Information and Education Council of the United States. *Unfinished Busines: A SIECUS Assessment of State Sexuality Education Programs.* New York: Sex Information and Education Council of the United States, 1993. (8)

Shapiro, Joseph P. et al. "Separate and Unequal." *U.S. News and World Report* 115, no. 23 (December 13, 1993): 46–60. (9)

Singham, Mano. "Race and Intelligence: What Are the Issues?" *Phi Delta Kappan* 77, no. 4 (December 1995): 271–278. (9)

———. "The Science and Religion Wars." *Phi Delta Kappan* 81, no. 6 (February 2000): 425–432. (3, 13)

Sizer, Theodore R. *Horace's School: Redesigning the American High School.* Boston: Houghton Mifflin, 1992. (G)

Sleeter, Christine E. *Multicultural Education as Social Activitism.* Albany, N.Y.: State University of New York Press, 1996. (9)

Spady, William G. "Choosing Outcomes of Significance." *Educational Leadership* 51, no. 6 (March 1994): 18–22. (11)

"A Special Section on Inclusion." *Phi Delta Kappan* 77, no. 4 (December 1995): 281–306. (12)

"A Special Section on Multicultural Education." *Phi Delta Kappan* 76, no. 4 (December 1994): 284–299. (9)

Steffy, Betty E. *The Kentucky Education Reform: Lessons for America.* Lancaster, Pa.: Technomic Publishing Co., 1993. (10)

Stodghill, Ron II. "Where Did You Learn That?" *TIME* 151, no. 23 (June 15, 1998): 52–59. (8)

Stromquist, Nelly P. "Sex Equity Legislation in Education: The State as Promoter of Women's Rights." *Review of Educational Research* 63, no. 4 (Winter 1993): 379–407. (7)

Subcommittee on Oversight and Investigations of the Committee on Education and the Workforce in the United States. *Education at a Crossroads: What Works and What's Wanted Today."* Washington, D.C.: U.S. Government Printing Office, 1998. (1)

Sykes, Charles J. *Dumbing Down Our Kids: Why American Children Feel Good About Themselves But Can't Read, Write, or Add.* New York: St. Martin's Griffin, 1996. (11)

Takaki, Ronald T. *A Different Mirror: A History of Multicultural America.* Boston: Little, Brown, 1993. (9)

Tanner, Laurel N., ed. *Critical Issues in Curriculum.* 87th Yearbook of the National Society for the Study of Education. Part I. Chicago: University of Chicago Press, 1988. (G)

"Teaching Kids About Sex," *TIME* 141, no. 21 (May 24, 1993): 60–66. (8)

Toch, Thomas. "The New Education Bazaar." *U.S. News & World Report* 124, no. 16 (April 27, 1998): 34–46. (1)

Tucker, Marc S. and Codding, Judy B. *Standards for Our Schools: How to Set Them, Measure Them, and Reach Them.* San Francisco: Jossey-Bass, 1998. (10)

Uchitelle, Susan. *School Choice: Issues and Answers.* Bloomington, Ind.: Phi Delta Kappa Educational Foundation, 1993. (1)

Underwood, Julie K. and Mead, Julie F. *Legal Aspects of Special Education and Pupil Services.* Boston: Allyn and Bacon, 1995. (12)

U.S. Bureau of the Census. Statistical Abstract of the United States. Washington, D.C.: U.S. Government Printing Office, 1998. (8)

"Using Standards and Assessments." *Educational Leadership* 56, no. 6 (March 1999): 8–77. (14)

Villa, Richard A. and Thousand, Jacqueline S., eds. *Creating the Inclusive School.* Alexandria, Va.: Association for Supervision and Curriculum Development, 1995. (12)

Watson, Dorothy J. "Defining and Describing Whole Language." The *Elementary School Journal* 90, no. 2 (November 1989): 141. (15)

Weinman, Janmice and Kleinfeld, Judith. *Do Public Schools Shortchange Girls on Educational Opportunities? Insight* 14, no. 46 (December 14, 1998). (7)

White, Forrest R. "Brown Revisited." *Phi Delta Kappan* 76, no. 1 (September 1994): 12–20. (9)

"Whose Culture?" *Educational Leadership* 49, no. 4 (December 1991/January 1992): 4–81. (9)

"Whose Schools?" *Educational Leadership* 56, no. 2 (October 1998): 8–81 (1) (6) (12)

Williams, Juan. "Integration Turns 40: The New Segregation." *Modern Maturity* 37, no. 2 (April-May 1994): 24–33. (9)

Williams, Paul, Lazer, Stephen, Reese, Clyde M., and Carr, Peggy. *NAEP 1994 U.S. History: A First Look: Findings from the National Assessment of Educational Progress.* Washington, D.C.: Office of Educational Research and Improvement, U.S. Department of Education, 1995. (10)

Willis, Scott. "Mainstreaming the Gifted." *Education Update* 37, no. 2, (February 1995): 1, 3–4. (12)

———. "Whole Language: Finding the Surest Way to Literacy," *Curriculum Update* (Fall l995), pp. 1–8. (15)

Wingert, Pat. "The Battle Over Falling Birthrates." *Newsweek* 131, no. 19 (May 11, 1998): 40. (8)

Winn, Deanna D., Menlove, Ronda Rudd, and Zsiray, Stephen, Jr. *Rethinking the Scheduling of School Time.* Fastback 412. Bloomington, Ind.: Phi Delta Kappa Educational Foundation, 1997. (14)

Witmer, Judith and Anderson, Carolyn S. *How to Establish a High School Service Learning Program.* Alexandria, Va.: Association for Supervision and Curriculum Development, 1994. (4)

Woelfel, Kay. "Inclusion, Exclusion, Confusion, and Infusion." *Principal* 73, no. 4 (March 1994): 48, 50. (12)

Worthen, Blaine R. *What Twenty Years of Educational Studies Reveal About Year-Round Education.* ERIC document ED373413, 1994. (14)

Wyman, Sarah. *How to Respond to Your Culturally Diverse Student Population.* Alexandria, Va.: Association for Supervision and Curriculum Development, 1993. (9)

Yell, Mitchell L. "The Legal Basis of Inclusion." *Educational Leadership* 56, no. 2 (October 1998): 70–73. (12)

AUDIOTAPES

Association for Supervision and Curriculum Development, 1703 N. Beauregard St., Alexandria, Va. 22311–1714.

Key Issues in Family Life Planning. Responding to the New Jersey State Mandate for Family Life Education. A House Divided: Religion and the Public Schools. Two tapes. 2 hrs. (Charles Haynes, Chester Finn, Stephen Bates, and Linda Page). 1995.

Tracking: Road to Success or Dead End? Two 90–minute tapes 1993.

Understanding the Conflict over Outcome-Based Education. Two 90–minute tapes. 1995.

Understanding Whole Language to Develop Strategies for Learning. 1990.

CD-ROM

Standards for Excellence in Education. Standards and benchmarks in eight subject areas. Available from Association for Supervision and Curriculum Development, P.O. Box 79760, Baltimore, MD 21279–0760.

ESSAY

African-American Baseline Essays. 1989. Six essays (focusing on art, language arts, mathematics, science, social studies) on the contribution of people of African descent from ancient times to the present. Portland Public Schools, Portland, Ore.

FEATURE FILMS

The Ernest Green Story. 2 hrs. Walt Disney Co., 1992. Story of integration of Central High School, Little Rock, Ark. in 1957. Stars Morris Chestnut, CCH Pounder, Ruby Dee, and Ossie Davis.

Inherit the Wind. 127 min. Black and white. United Artists, 1960. Based on the Scopes trial in Tennessee in 1925 on the teaching of the theory of evolution. Stars Frederic March, Spencer Tracy, and Gene Kelly.

Separate but Equal. 4 hrs. ABC mini-series, 1991. Sidney Poitier plays Thurgood Marshall, attorney in the landmark case of *Brown v. Board of Education,* in which the U.S. Supreme Court ruled segregation unconstitutional.

Simple Justice. 135 min. Television program on Thurgood Marshall and the 1954 U.S. Supreme Court decision *Brown v. Board of Education.* Produced by New Images Production, Inc. From the 1975 book by Richard Kluger, N.Y.: Knopf. Alexandria, Va.: PBS Video, 1993.

KIT

Banned Books Week Kit. Posters, book, bookmarks. Office of Intellectual Freedom, American Library Association, 50 East Huron St., Chicago, IL 60611.

LESSON PLANS

K–5 AFRICAN-AMERICAN LESSON PLANS. Sixty lesson plans in five disciplines. Portland Public Schools, Portland, Ore.

NEWSLETTERS

American Library Association, 50 East Huron St., Chicago, Ill. 60611.

Americans United for Separation of Church and State, 1816 Jefferson Pl., N.W., Washington, D.C. 20036.

Core Knowledge Foundation (formerly Cultural Literacy Foundation). 2012–B Morton Dr., Charlottesville, Va. 22901.

National Association for Bilingual Education, 1220 L St., N.W., Suite 605, Washington, D.C. 20005–4018.

U.S. English, 818 Connecticut Ave., N.W., Suite 200, Washington, D.C. 20006.

PACKAGE

Block Scheduling: Time to Learn. One 30–min. and two 15–min. videotapes, articles edited by Robin Fogarty. *The Copernican Plan Evaluated: The Evolution of a Revolution* by Jospeh M. Caroll, and a facilitator's guide. Phi Delta Kappa Center for Professional Development and Services, P.O. Box 789, Bloomington, Ind. 47402–0789.

SUBSCRIPTION SERVICE

The ASCD Curriculum Handbook. Annual subscription. K–12. Case studies, reports of research and surveys, analyses of curriculum issues, updates on curriculum programs and trends. Association for Supervision and Curriculm Development, 1703 N. Beauregard t., Alexandria, Va. 22311-1714.

VIDEOTAPES

Association for Supervision and Curriculum Development, 1703 N. Beauregard St., Alexandria, Va. 22311-1714.

Challenging the Gifted in the Regular Classroom. 50–min. Facilitator's Guide.

Inclusion. 3 tapes.

Inclusion: *Educating All Students.* 35 min.

Inclusion: *Strategies for the Classroom.* 25 min.

Inclusion: *Profiles of Successful Students.* 25 min.

Facilitator's Guide.

Managing Meaning: Integrated Language Arts Series. 5 tapes. 20–23 min. 1992. Series on whole-language approach to teaching language arts in K–5. Features Marie Clay, Jane Hansen, Ann McCallum, and Dorothy Strickland. Facilitator's Guide. Book: *When Writers Read* by Jane Hansen. Made in cooperation with the International Reading Association.

Multicultural Education. 40 min. *Facilitator's Guide.* Book: Leonard Davidman and Patricia T. Davidman, *Teaching with a Multicultural Perspective: A Practical Guide,* New York: Longman, 1993.

Outcome-Based Education. 4 tapes.

Four Guiding Principles of Outcome-Based Education. 40 min.

How Outcome-Based Education Changes Classroom Instruction. 20 min.

The District Director's Role in Outcome-Based Education. 30 min.

Outcome-Based Education: Executive Overview. 10 min.

Facilitator's Guide.

Core Knowledge Foundation, 801 E. High St., Charlottesville, Va. 22902.

The Uncommon Classroom. Videotape showing schools in Florida, New York, and Texas using the Core Knowledge Sequence.

Kent State University, Audio-Visual Services, P.O. Box 5190, Kent, Ohio 44242–0001.

The Public Schools. Color. 58 min. 1984. Discussion of problems of equity and reforms in education. Features Jeannie Oakes, Lee McMurrin, and Ruth Randall.

Pennsylvania State University Audio-Visual Services, University Division of Media & Learning, Resources Special Services Bldg., University Park, PA 16802.

Cultural Illiteracy (Films for the Humanities, Princeton, N.J.). Color. 28 min. 1988. Discussion of needs for teaching of common knowledge required of literate Americans. Features E. D. Hirsch, Jr., Robert MacNeil, Maya Angelou, Patrick Welsh, and Robert Coles.

Web Sites

The Alan Guttmacher Institute: http://www.agi-usa.org

American Federation of Teachers: http://www.aft.org

American Library Association: http://www.ala.org

Americans United for Separation of Church and State: http://www.au.org/default.htm

Anne E. Casey Foundation: http://www.aecf.org

Association for Supervision and Curriculum Development: http://www.ascd.org.

Brown v. Board of Education, 347 U.S. 483 (1954): http://www.nationalcenter.inter.net/brown.html

Center for Education Reform: http://www.edreform.com/charters.htm

Center for Equal Opportunity: http://www.ceusa.org

Centers for Disease Control and Prevention: http://www.cdc.gov

Core Knowledge Foundation: http://www.coreknowledge.org

Edison Project: http://www.edisonproject.com

Educational Excellence Network: http://www.edexcellence.net

Educational Sites. Numerous links to Educational Sites; General Resources; Educational Oganizations; Think Tanks; and Federal, State, and International Agencies: http://www.cybercollege.com/ed12.htm#organizations

Hudson Institute: http://www.hudson.org/hudson

International Association for the Evaluation of Educational Achievement: http://www.exit109.com/~learn/iea.htm

Kaiser Family Foundation: http://www.kff.org

Making the Grade: http://www.gwu.edu/~mtg

Mid-Continent Regional Educational Laboratory: http://www.mcrel.org/standards

Monitoring the Future, National Institute on Drug Abuse: http://www.isr.umich.edu/src/mtf; http://www.MonitoringtheFuture.org

National Assessment of Educational Progress: http://www.nces.ed.gov/nationsreportcard

National Association for Bilingual Education: http://www.nabe.org

National Association for Year-Round Education: http://www.NAYRE.org.

National Campaign to Prevent Teen Pregnancy: http://www.teenpregnancy.org

National Center for Education Statistics: http://www.nces.ed.gov

National Center for Health Statistics: http://www.cdc.gov/nchswww/default.htm

National Center on Education and the Economy: http://www.ncee.org/OurPrograms/nsPage.html

National Clearinghouse for Alcohol and Drug Information: http://www.health.org/pubs/nhsda

National Coalition Against Censorship: http://www.ncac.org

National Education Association: http://www.nea.org

National Home Education Research Institute, http://www.nheri.org

National Institute on Drug Abuse: http://www.nida.nih.gov/NIDAhome.html

National Service-Learning Clearinghouse: http://www.nicsl.coled.umn.edu

Office of Educational Research and Improvement: http://www.oeri.ed.gov

Parents' Resource Institute for Drug Education: http://www.prideusa.org

People for the American Way: http://www.pfaw.org

Public Agenda: http://www.public agenda.org

Sex Information and Education Council of the United States: http://www.siecus.org

TesseracT: http://www.tesseract.pvt.k12.mn.us

U.S. Charter: http//www.uscharterschools.org

U.S. Department of Education: http://www.ed.gov

U.S. Department of Health and Human Services: http://www.hhs.gov

U.S. English: http://www.us-english.org

CHAPTER 15
CURRICULUM PRODUCTS

After studying this chapter you should be able to:

1. Construct a curriculum guide.
2. Construct a resource unit.
3. Identify sources of curriculum materials.

TANGIBLE PRODUCTS

The Biblical expression "By their fruits ye shall know them" can certainly be applied to curriculum workers. Walk into the curriculum laboratory of any public school or university and you may be surprised, perhaps even overwhelmed, by the evidence of the productivity of curriculum development workers. The products of their efforts are there for all to see—tangible, printed, and often packaged in eye-catching style.

Curriculum workers have been turning out products for many years. Unfortunately, some curriculum developers view the creation of products as the final rather than the intermediate phase of curriculum improvement. The products are meant to be put into practice, tried out, revised, tried again, revised again, and so on.

Creating curriculum products not only has a functional value—the production of a plan or tool for implementing or evaluating the curriculum—but also gives the planners a great psychological boost. In producing tangible materials, they are able to feel some sense of accomplishment.

Throughout this text we have already seen a number of kinds of curriculum products. Chapter 6 contained examples of statements of philosophy and aims of education. Chapter 7 included needs assessment surveys and reports, sections of courses of study and curriculum guides, and portions of a state's statement of minimal standards. In Chapter 8 we saw statements of curriculum goals and objectives. Statements of instructional goals and objectives formed a part of Chapter 10. Unit and lesson plans were outlined in Chapter 11. Chapter 12 discussed instruments for evaluating instruction, and Chapter 13, instruments for evaluating the curriculum.

Judging from the tasks that curriculum coordinators, consultants, directors, and other workers are called on to do in the schools, there is a healthy demand for training in the production of curriculum materials. In this chapter we will discuss the creation and use of several of the more common products found in the schools.

The content, the form, and the names by which curriculum materials are known are almost as varied as the number of groups that author them. Curriculum bulletins, curriculum guides, courses of study, syllabi, resource units, and source units can be found in the curriculum libraries of school systems.

Because curriculum materials are impermanent—nonstandardized products made primarily for local use—the variations among them are considerable. To put the creation of curriculum products into perspective, we must visualize curriculum committees and individuals in thousands of school districts all over the United States constructing materials that they feel will be of most help to their teachers. Terms for these types of curriculum materials may signal quite different products or may be used synonymously. A curriculum guide, for example, may be quite different from a course of study. On the other hand, what is called a curriculum guide in one locality may be called a course of study in another. For this reason it is difficult to predict what will be discovered in any particular curriculum product until it is examined.

The curriculum products that we will consider in this chapter are:

1. curriculum guides, courses of study, and syllabi
2. resource units

We will not discuss curriculum materials that have been discussed in preceding chapters, such as unit plans, lesson plans, and tests. All curriculum materials share the common purpose of serving as aids to teachers and planners in organizing, implementing, and evaluating curriculum and instruction.

CURRICULUM GUIDES, COURSES OF STUDY, AND SYLLABI

Three kinds of curriculum products are clearly related.

These are (1) curriculum guides, (2) courses of study, and (3) syllabi. As already noted, some curriculum workers make no distinction among the three types. The following are definitions of the terms used in this chapter:

1. A *curriculum guide* is the most general of the three types of materials. It may cover a single course or subject area at a particular grade level (e.g., ninth-grade English); all subjects at a particular grade level (e.g., ninth-grade); a sequence in a discipline (e.g., language arts), or an area of interest applicable to two or more courses or grade levels (e.g., occupational safety). When a curriculum guide covers a single course, it may also be called a course of study. However, a curriculum guide is a teaching aid with helpful suggestions rather than a complete course of study in itself.

2. A *course of study* is a detailed plan for a single course, including text materials (content). A well-known example of a curriculum product of this nature is *Man: A*

Course of Study, which has been widely used in the schools and seen on televi-sion.[1] A course of study includes both what is to be taught (content)—in summary or in complete text—and suggestions for how to teach the course. A course of study usually specifies what must be taught, whereas a curriculum guide may offer alternatives to the teacher.

3. A *syllabus* is an outline of topics to be covered in a single course or grade level.

Curriculum Guide Formats

Let's look more closely at the creation of a curriculum guide. What is its purpose? Who should be included in the task? Curriculum guides are used in at least two ways. In less structured situations where teachers have a great deal of flexibility in planning, a curriculum guide provides many suggestions to teachers who wish to use it. In that case the curriculum guide is one source from which teachers may derive ideas for de-veloping their own resource units, learning units, and lesson plans. In more structured situations a curriculum guide specifies minimal objectives that students must master in the discipline. It may spell out objectives for each marking period. The guide may iden-tify teaching materials and suggest learning activities. It may be accompanied by pretests and posttests for each unit or marking period.

A curriculum guide may be written by a group of teachers or planners or by an in-dividual. In the latter case, the guide is often reviewed by other specialists before it is disseminated within the school system. For those who write a curriculum guide, the process is almost as important as the product. The task of constructing a guide forces the writers to clarify their ideas, to gather data, to demonstrate creativity, to select content, to determine sequence, and to organize their thoughts.

Examination of curriculum guides from various school districts will reveal a vari-ety of formats. Some school systems that develop curriculum guides follow a single format. Because the substance of guides varies from format to format, some school dis-tricts find it useful to prepare more than one type of guide. Many curriculum guides are lengthy documents, so I will not attempt to reproduce examples in this text. In-stead we will look at the formats that are often employed.

From the many formats for curriculum guides we may select three that we will call, for lack of better labels, the comprehensive, sequencing, and test-coding formats.

The Comprehensive Format. Curriculum planners following a comprehensive for-mat would include the following components in a curriculum guide for a particular level of a discipline—for example, ninth-grade social studies.

1. *Introduction.* The introduction includes the title of the guide, the subject and grade level for which the guide is designated, and any suggestions that might help users. Some statement should be included as to how the curriculum guide relates to pre-specified statements of philosophy and aims and curriculum goals and objectives

2. *Instructional goals.* In this section, instructional goals (called general objectives by some planners) are stated in nonbehavioral terms. Instructional goals should relate to the schools' curriculum goals and objectives.

---

[1] See Jerome S. Bruner, *Man: A Course of Study* (Cambridge, Mass.: Educational Services, 1965).

TOPIC	GOALS	OBJECTIVES	ACTIVITIES	EVALUATION TECHNIQUES	RESOURCES

Figure 15.1   Comprehensive curriculum guide format

3. *Instructional objectives.* Instructional objectives (called specific, performance, or behavioral objectives by some planners) for the particular grade level of the subject should be stated in behavioral terms and should encompass all three domains of learning, if all are applicable.
4. *Learning activities.* Learning experiences that might be used by the teacher with pupils should be suggested and placed in preferred sequence.
5. *Evaluation techniques.* Suggestions should be given to teachers on how to evaluate student achievement. This section of the guide could include general suggestions on evaluating, sample test items, or even complete tests.
6. *Resources.* Attention should be given to human resources—persons who might be called on to assist with the content of the guide—and to material resources, including books, audiovisual aids, equipment and facilities.

Some writers of comprehensive guides also include a topical outline of the content. No effort is made to separate the goals and objectives into time periods, nor are the components sequenced for the teacher. This format is not prescriptive. Guides of this nature are supplementary aids for the professional teacher. They offer the maximum flexibility to the teacher, who may choose or reject any of the suggested goals, objectives, activities, evaluation techniques, or resources. You will note this format is similar to a unit plan which we discussed in Chapter 11.[2] The curriculum guide, however, is broader in scope than the unit plan and offers more alternatives.

Some curriculum planners prefer to cast their comprehensive guides in the following format:

The Sequencing Format.   Guides of this nature

1. specify behavioral objectives for each competency area
2. indicate at what guide level(s), K–12, each competency will be taught
3. code objectives at each grade level as to whether they are introduced (I), developed (D), mastered (M), reinforced (R), or extended (E) at that level

This format provides an overall view of the sequencing of the objectives of the discipline. Teachers retain the opportunity for making decisions on when and how the

---

[2]See pp. 382–386.

objectives will be taught at each grade level. Georgia's list of thinking skills (Table 15.1), developed in the 1980s and keyed to the Bloom taxonomy, furnishes an example of this type of curriculum product.[3]

The Test-Coding Format.   Offering teachers the least flexibility is the test-coding format, which

1. lists objectives to be mastered by the learners at each marking period of each grade level of a given discipline.
2. codes each objective to district, state, and national criterion-referenced and/or norm-referenced tests that are administered by the school district.

Let's say, for example, a district has developed a set of ten instructional objectives to be accomplished in Health at the second-grade level. The district has further developed tests at the end of each marking period (sometimes as well as comprehensive tests at the end of the year) to determine whether these objectives have been achieved by pupils. Following a test-coding format teachers would specify which objectives were to be pursued during which marking period. Teachers may follow a similar procedure in dealing with state-specified instructional objectives and state assessment tests.

Though teachers may exercise choice of learning activities and supplementary resources, they are held accountable for student achievement every marking period. Locally written tests to assess student mastery of the objectives are administered at the end of each marking period.

The three formats can, of course, be combined and expanded. Test-coding can be added to the comprehensive format. Behavioral or performance indicators may be included to refine the behavioral or performance objectives. For example, one indicator for the instructional objective "The student will describe the effects of freon released in the environment" might be "The student will specify principal uses of freon." Reference is made to criteria for instructional objectives discussed in Chapter 10. Criticizing the lack of specificity of "typical instructions" (that is, objectives) found in curriculum guides, Hirsch mused, "It might be wondered how it is possible for states and localities to produce lengthy curriculum guides that, for all their bulk, fail to define specific knowledge for specific grade levels."[4]

No matter what format is followed by a school system, curriculum guides should be used and revised periodically. It is an open secret that curriculum guides are often written to satisfy a local or state mandate. Having completed the task of writing the documents, teachers set them aside and allow them to accumulate dust. Teachers' failure to use the curriculum guides demonstrates once again that commitment to the process is an essential ingredient. Curriculum guides that are handed down, for example, generate little commitment. They may be followed out of necessity but without enthusiasm. Even those guides that are written by teachers rather than by curriculum consultants will be accepted only if teachers perceive the task as useful to them rather than as a response to directives from superordinates.[5]

---

[3]See Chapter 10 for discussion of the Bloom taxonomy.

[4]E.D. Hirsch, Jr., *The Schools We Need: And Why We Don't Have Them* (New York: Doubleday, 1996): 28.

[5]For a critical view of conventional curriculum guides see Fenwick W. English, "It's Time to Abolish Conventional Curriculum Guides," *Educational Leadership* 44, no. 4 (December 1986–January 1987): 50–52.

TABLE 15.1

GEORGIA'S LIST OF THINKING SKILLS

TOPIC	CONCEPT/SKILL	K-4	5-8	9-12
A. Recall	The learner will recognize information previously encountered such as facts, concepts or specific elements in a subject area.	ID	DR	R
1. Identification	ascertain the origin, nature or definitive characteristics of an item.	ID	DR	R
2. Observation	obtain information by noting, perceiving, noticing and describing. Observation may involve looking, listening, touching, feeling, smelling or tasting.	ID	DR	R
3. Perception	become aware of objects through using the senses, especially seeing or hearing.	ID	DR	R
B. Comprehension	The learner will understand information that has been communicated.	ID	D	R
1. Translation	change information from one form to another, maintaining accuracy of the original communication.	ID	DR	DR
2. Analogy Recognition	infer that if two things are known to be alike in some respects then they may be alike in others.	ID	DR	DR
C. Hypothesizing	The learner will assume, making a tentative explanation.	I	DR	DR
1. Prediction	tell or declare beforehand.	I	DR	DR
2. Imagination	form a mental image of, represent or picture to oneself.	I	DR	DR
D. Application	The learner will put information to use.	I	DR	DR
1. Clarification	make something easier to understand.		ID	DR
2. Hypothesis Testing	try out ideas for possible solutions.	I	ID	DR
3. Operational Definition	order ideas into a step by step plan.		ID	DR
4. Decision-making	choose the best or most desirable alternative.	I	ID	DR
5. Consequence Projection	define further steps toward probable solutions or identify cause/effect relationships.	I	ID	DR
E. Analysis	The learner will break down a concept, problem, pattern or whole into its component parts, systematically or sequentially, so that the relations between parts are expressed explicitly.	ID	DR	
1. Comparison	determine similarities and differences on the basis of given criteria.	ID	DR	R
2. Classification	place elements into arbitrarily established systems of groupings and subgroupings on the basis of common characteristics.	ID	DR	R
3. Selection	choose an element from a set of elements on the basis of given criteria.	ID	DR	R

(Continued)

Table 15.1 Continued

TOPIC	CONCEPT/SKILL	K–4	5–8	9–12
4. Association	relate elements either given or as they come to mind.	ID	DR	R
5. Inference	draw a conclusion based on facts or evidence	I	ID	DR
6. Interpretation	express meaning of or reaction to an experience.	I	ID	DR
7. Qualification	describe by enumerating characteristics.	I	ID	R
F. Synthesis	The learner will arrange and combine elements to form a structure, pattern or product.	I	ID	DR
1. Summarization	express a brief or concise restatement.	I	ID	DR
2. Generalization	formulate or derive from specifics (to make universally applicable) a class, form or statement.	I	ID	DR
3. Formulation of Concepts	originate or express ideas.		ID	DR
4. Integration	form into a whole and unite information.		ID	DR
G. Evaluation	The learner will make judgments regarding quantity and quality on the basis of given criteria.		ID	DR
1. Justification	show adequate reason(s) for something done.	I	ID	DR
2. Imposition of Standards	assure equal comparison with established criteria.		ID	DR
3 Judgment	form an idea or opinion about any matter.		ID	DR
4. Internal Consistency	understand that all the parts of a process fit together.		ID	DR
5. Value	establish worth or esteem.	I	ID	DR

SOURCE: Georgia Department of Education, *Essential Skills for Georgia Schools* (Atlanta: Division of Curriculum Services, Georgia Department of Education, 1980), pp. 87–88. Reprinted by permission.

RESOURCE UNIT

A resource unit, called a source unit by some curriculum workers, is "an arrangement of materials and activities around a particular topic or problem."[6] The resource unit is a curriculum product that falls somewhere between a teacher's learning unit and a course of study or curriculum guide. I explained elsewhere:

> The resource unit is a source of information and ideas for teachers to use. . . . The major purpose of the resource unit is to provide ideas for a teacher who wishes to create his [or her] own learning unit on the same topic. . . . The resource unit contains a wealth of suggestions and information which will aid the teacher in supplementing material found in the basic textbook. The resource unit shortens the busy teacher's planning time and simplifies his [or her] work in the construction of learning units for his [or her] classes.[7]

---

[6]Peter F. Oliva, *The Secondary School Today,* 1st ed. (Scranton, Pa.: International Textbook Company, 1967), p. 176.
[7]Ibid.

In essence, the resource unit serves the same general purpose as a course of study or curriculum guide. The major distinction between these types of products is that the resource unit is much narrower in scope, focusing on a particular topic rather than on an entire year, course, subject area, or sequence. Although we may encounter a course of study or curriculum guide for eleventh-grade American history, for example, we may also find resource units on topics within American history, such as the Age of Jackson, the Great Depression, or the Persian Gulf War.

The same outline that was suggested for a comprehensive curriculum guide applies to the resource unit. An example of a resource unit is given in Box 15.1.

SOURCES OF CURRICULUM MATERIALS

These illustrations of curriculum products barely suggest the types that are already available or can be constructed. In every state of the union, curriculum committees have created a wide variety of useful materials. Curriculum developers and others who are searching for curriculum materials beyond the textbooks and accompanying teachers' manuals may locate examples in several places: curriculum libraries of colleges and universities, particularly those of schools and departments of education; curriculum centers of the public school systems; teacher education centers; the offices of curriculum consultants; state departments of education; and regional educational service agencies.

Professional organizations such as the Association for Supervision and Curriculum Development[8] and its state affiliates produce many helpful materials. Commercial firms are another source of curriculum materials that may be useful to the teacher. Many publishing firms display curriculum materials at major professional conferences. Several sources of curriculum guides are listed in the bibliography at the end of this chapter.

Great variation can be found in both the format of printed curriculum materials and in the types of available materials. Beyond typical curriculum guides, we can find curriculum materials packaged into multimedia kits consisting of films, filmstrips, charts, audiotapes, videotapes, records, CD-ROMs, and so on.

SUMMARY

Curriculum planners and teachers frequently engage in developing curriculum products that will be of use to teachers in their school systems. In this chapter we looked at these types of products: curriculum guides, courses of study, syllabi, and resource units.

Curriculum guides should provide many suggestions to teachers for teaching a single course, a subject area at a particular grade level, an entire sequence, or an area of interest. Curriculum guides should include instructional goals, instructional objectives, activities, evaluation techniques, and resources. Sometimes curriculum planners incorporate an outline of the content. Courses of study cover single courses and often contain a considerable amount of content material. Syllabi list topics to be covered.

---

[8]Association for Supervision and Curriculum Development, 1703 North Beuregard Street, Alexandria, Va. 22311-1714.

BOX 15.1

A RESOURCE UNIT

Grade Level/Course:
Senior High School/Problems of American Democracy
Topic: Education in the United States

A. Introduction

   The enterprise of education in the United States consumes close to 500 billion dollars per year, nearly 250 billion of which are spent on public elementary and secondary schools. About 25 percent of the population is enrolled in schools from nursery through graduate level. In some way, schooling touches the lives of every person in the country, yet schooling itself is rarely studied in the schools. Although most people have their own ideas about education, their data base is often limited or lacking. The purpose of this resource unit is to provide students with facts, insights, and understandings about the American educational system.

B. Instructional Goals
   1. Cognitive
   The student will become familiar with
      a.   the purposes of education in the United States
      b.   the general structure of education in the United States
      c.   the ways in which education in the United States is administered and financed
      d.   major differences between the U.S. system of education and systems of other countries
   2. Affective
   The student will appreciate
      a.   the complexity of the U.S. educational system
      b.   our decentralized system of education
      c.   the extent and complexity of problems facing education in the United States
      d.   the achievements of American schools

C. Instructional Objectives
   1. Cognitive
   The student will be able to
      a.   identify sources of funding for education
      b.   explain local, state, and federal responsibilities for education
      c.   state purposes of levels of education: elementary, middle, junior high, senior high, community college, senior college, and university
      d.   tell the strengths and weaknesses of our decentralized system of education
      e.   explain how teachers are prepared and hired
      f.   describe how the educational dollar is spent
      g.   account for differences in the support of education by the various states
      h.   identify problems facing the schools and tell what efforts are being made to solve them
      i.   account for the growth of private schools
      j.   compare the American system of education with the system in another country

(Continued)

Table 15.1 Continued

    2. Affective

    The student will

      a. write a statement of purposes of education as he or she sees them

      b. state what he or she feels constitutes a good education

      c. state with reasons whether he or she believes compulsory education is desirable

      d. describe how he or she feels education should be funded

      e. take a position on whether public school education or private school education is better

      f. take a position on whether American education or European (or Russian or Japanese) education is better

      g. show his or her position by written reports on some controversial issues such as prayer in the schools, the teaching of the theory of evolution, censorship of textbooks and library books, busing of students for purposes of integrating the races, and bilingual education

    3. Psychomotor

    None

D. Learning Activities

    1. Read provisions of the United States Constitution regarding education, especially the First, Tenth, and Fourteenth Amendments.

    2. Read provisions of the state constitution regarding education.

    3. Examine recent state and federal legislation on education.

    4. Prepare a chart showing the percentages of funding for education from local, state, and federal sources.

    5. Prepare a diagram showing overall dollars spent in any one year for education by local, state, and federal sources in the students' home state.

    6. Observe an elementary, middle/junior high, and secondary class in action, and afterward compare such aspects as objectives, materials, methods of teaching, and student conduct.

    7. Visit a community college and interview one of the administrators on the purposes and programs of the community college.

    8. Invite a private and/or parochial school administrator to come to class to talk on purposes and programs of his or her school.

    9. Invite a panel of public school principals at elementary, middle/junior high, and secondary levels to come to class to talk on problems they face in administering their schools.

    10. Critique the requirements for a teacher's certificate in the students' home state.

    11. Gather and present data on the funding of higher education in both the United States and in the students' home state.

    12. Read and evaluate several statements of purposes of education.

    13. Read and evaluate a book or article critical of American public education.

    14. Report on pressure groups that influence education.

    15. Read a book or several articles on the educational system of one foreign country and describe major characteristics of that system.

    16. Find out how teachers are trained, certified, and employed in the students' home state.

    17. Find out how school administrators are trained, certified, and employed in the students' home state.

(Continued)

Table 15.1 Continued

18. Attend a school board meeting and discuss it in class.
19. Visit the superintendent's office and hear the superintendent (or his or her deputy) explain the role of the superintendent.
20. Find out what the school tax rate is in the students' home community, how moneys are raised for the schools, and how much money is expended in the community for schools.
21. Find out how much teachers and administrators are paid in the students' home community and what fringe benefits they receive.
22. Examine the staffing patterns of an elementary, middle, or secondary school and determine types of employees needed to run the school.
23. Find out how serious the dropout problem is in the students' home community and what is being done to solve it.
24. Determine whether or not student achievement in schools of the students' home district is satisfactory. If not, account for reasons for unsatisfactory achievement and report on measures that are being taken to improve the situation.
25. Debate whether teachers should have the right to strike.
26. Choose a controversial educational issue and write a paper showing positions of several prominent persons or groups and the students' own positions.

E. Evaluation Techniques
    1. Give a pretest consisting of objective test items to survey students' factual knowledge about education in the United States.
       Sample test items:
       a. Responsibility for state control of education in the United States is derived from the U.S. Constitution's
           (1) First Amendment
           (2) Fifth Amendment
           (3) Tenth Amendment
           (4) Fourteenth Amendment
       b. Policies for local school districts are promulgated by
           (1) advisory councils
           (2) school boards
           (3) teachers' unions
           (4) school principals
    2. Evaluate students' oral reports.
    3. Evaluate students' written work—reports, charts, etc.
    4. Observe students' reactions and comments in class discussion.
    5. Give a posttest of objective items similar to those of the pretest.

F. Resources
    Armstrong, David G., Henson, Kenneth T., and Savage, Tom V. *Teaching Today: An Introduction to Education,* 5th ed.: Upper Saddle River, N.J.: Merrill, 1997.
    Educational Leadership. Alexandria, Va.: Association for Supervision and Curriculum Development, monthly.
    Educational Testing Service. Reports of the National Assessment of Educational Progress.
    Gerald, Debra E. and Hussar, William J. *Projections of Educational Statistics to 2003.* Washington, D.C.: U.S. Government Printing Office. Biennially.

(Continued)

Table 15.1 Continued

Goodlad, John. *A Place Called School: Prospects for the Future.* New York: McGraw Hill, 1984.

Johnson, James A. et al. *Introduction to the Foundations of American Education,* 10th ed. Boston: Allyn and Bacon, 1996.

National Center for Education Statistics. *The Condition of Education: A Statistical Report.* Washington, D.C.: U.S. Government Printing Office, annually.

————. *Digest of Education Statistics.* Washington, D.C.: U.S. Government Printing Office, annually.

Phi Delta Kappan. Bloomington, Ind. Phi Delta Kappa, monthly.

Schultz, Fred. *Education.* Guilford, Conn.: Dushkin Publishing Group, annually.

Sizer, Theodore R. *Horace's School: Redesigning the American High School.* Boston: Houghton Mifflin, 1992.

Standard Education Almanac. Chicago: Marquis Who's Who, annually.

United States Bureau of the Census. *Statistical Abstract of the United States.* Washington, D.C.: U.S. Government Printing Office, annually.

The World Almanac and Book of Facts. Mahwah, N.J.: PRIMEDIA Reference Inc., annually.

Films*

Education in America: The 17th and 18th Centuries. 16 min. black and white. Coronet Instructional Films, 1958. Part of the History of Education in America series.

Education in America: The 19th Century. 16 min. black and white. Coronet Instructional Films, 1958. Part of the History of Education in America series.

Education in America: The 20th Century. 16 min. black and white. Coronet Instructional Films, 1958. Part of the History of Education in America series.

*Old but useful overview of the history of American education from Colonial days to mid-20th century. Available from Audio-Visual Services, Kent State University, Kent, Ohio.

Resource units are, in essence, minicurriculum guides for teaching particular topics or problems. Limited to single topics or problems, resource units offer types of suggestions similar to those found in curriculum guides.

In the creation of curriculum materials, both the process and product are important. Examples of curriculum materials can be found in school systems, colleges and universities, state departments of education, and regional educational service agencies. Professional organizations produce curriculum materials as do some business and industrial concerns.

QUESTIONS FOR DISCUSSION

1. Should writing curriculum guides be the job of the curriculum director or coordinator? Explain.
2. Should schools borrow curriculum guides from each other?
3. How do curriculum guides, resource units, and teaching units differ from each other?
4. What effect should the eight perennial principles of curriculum construction discussed in Chapter 13 have on the production of curriculum guides?
5. Where would you place the production of curriculum guides, courses of study, resource units, and the like in the model for curriculum development presented by the author of this text?

SUPPLEMENTARY EXERCISES

1. List various curriculum products and state values you see in each.
2. List various curriculum products and state problems you see in each.
3. Locate and critique samples of curriculum guides, courses of study, syllabi, and resource units.
4. Survey opinions of teachers on the value of curriculum guides and other products listed in exercise 3.
5. Locate and describe types of curriculum products other than those mentioned in this text.
6. Determine to what extent teachers in a school system you know well use their curriculum products. Account for their use or lack of use.
7. Locate and report on a curriculum product called a "scope and sequence chart."
8. Locate and list sources of curriculum materials available (1) in the school system, (2) in nearby colleges or universities, (3) from state departments of education, (4) from regional educational service agencies, (5) from professional associations, and (6) from business and industry.
10. Report on Fenwick W. English's alternative to the conventional curriculum guide. (See bibliography.)
11. Analyze a curriculum guide and determine whether its instructional objectives meet criteria discussed in Chapter 10.
12. Analyze a curriculum guide and determine whether it allows teachers enough flexibility or too much flexibility.

BIBLIOGRAPHY

English, Fenwick W. "It's Time to Abolish Conventional Curriculum Guides." *Educational Leadership* 44, no. 4 (December 1986–January 1987): 50–52.

Glatthorn, Allan A. *Curriculum Renewal.* Alexandria, Va.: Association for Supervision and Curriculum Development, 1987.

———. Developing a Quality Curriculum. Alexandria, Va.: Association for Supervision and Curriculum Development, 1994.

Henson, Kenneth T. *Curriculum Development in an Age of Reform.* New York: HarperCollins, 1995.

Hirsch, E. D., Jr. *The Schools We Need: And Why We Don't Have Them.* New York: Doubleday, 1996.

Kemp, Jerrold E. *Instructional Design: A Plan for Unit and Course Development.* Belmont, Calif.: Fearon, 1971.

Oliva, Peter F. *The Secondary School Today,* 1st ed. Scranton, Pa.: International Textbook, 1967. Chapter 8.

Posner, George J. and Rudnitsky, Alan N. *Course Design: A Guide to Curriculum Development,* 2nd ed. White Plains, N.Y.: Longman, 1982.

Van Til, William, Vars, Gordon F., and Lounsbury, John H. Modern *Education for the Junior High School Years.* Indianapolis: Bobbs-Merrill, 1967. Chapter 11.

Winters, Marilyn. *Designing Your Curriculum Guide: A Step-by-Step Approach.* Westlake, Calif.: Las Virgines Unified School District, 1980.

Zenger, William F. and Zenger, Sharon K. *Curriculum Planning: A Ten-Step Process.* Palo Alto, Calif.: R & E Research Associates, 1982.

MATERIALS DIRECTORY

The ASCD Curriculum Materials Directory. Annual publication on newest curriculum materials and programs. Also available on diskette. Annually. Association for Supervision and Curriculum Development, 1703 N. Beauregard St., Alexandria, Va. 22311-1714.

Appendix A
Exit Competencies

After studying the chapters of this book you should be able to:

1. Define curriculum development.
2. Distinguish between curriculum and instruction.
3. Describe roles of teachers, students, curriculum specialists, administrators, and parents in curriculum development.
4. Describe, giving examples, types of curriculum planning that are done at the local school, the school district, and the state levels.
5. Design and describe staff roles in a central curriculum office in a given school district.
6. Explain responsibilities and duties of a curriculum leader.
7. List skills needed by a curriculum leader.
8. Explain, identifying appropriate principles, how to go about effecting change in the curriculum.
9. Demonstrate communication skills.
10. Draw and explain a model for curriculum improvement.
11. Demonstrate skills in leading a group.
12. Write a statement of aims of education.
13. Write a school philosophy.
14. Contrast the major beliefs of essentialism and progressivism as they apply to the curriculum.
15. Conduct a curriculum needs assessment.
16. Write curriculum goals and objectives.
17. Develop a plan for organizing the curriculum of a school you know well, supporting the plan with appropriate references from the professional literature.
18. Write instructional goals and objectives in each of the three domains of learning.
19. Identify the most frequently used strategies of instruction and describe the strengths and weaknesses of each.
20. Write a unit plan.
21. Write a lesson plan.
22. Devise ways to preassess achievement of students.
23. Devise formative and summative methods of evaluating instruction.
24. Devise means of evaluating the curriculum.

25. Define and suggest ways to achieve each of the following: scope, relevance, balance, integration, sequence, continuity, articulation, and transferability.
26. Identify several controversial curriculum problems and explain their significance for curriculum development.
27. Identify several professional problems and explain their significance for curriculum planners.
28. Write a curriculum guide.
29. Write a resource unit.

APPENDIX B
ERIC NETWORK COMPONENTS

There are currently sixteen (16) ERIC Clearinghouses, each responsible for a major area of the field of education. Clearinghouses acquire, select, catalog, abstract, and index the documents announced in *Resources in Education* (RIE). They also prepare interpretive summaries and annotated bibliographies dealing with high interest topics and based on the documents analyzed for RIE. These information analysis products are also announced in RIE.

ERIC CLEARINGHOUSES:

Adult, Career, and Vocational Education (CE)
Ohio State University
Center on Education and Training
for Employment
1900 Kenny Road
Columbus, Ohio 43210-1090
Telephone: (614) 292-4353; (800) 848-4815
Fax: (614) 292-1260

Assessment and Evaluation (TM)
University of Maryland, College Park
Schriver Hall
College Park, Maryland 20742-5701
Telephone: (301) 405-7449; (800) 464-3742
Fax: (301) 405-8134

Community Colleges (JC)
University of California at Los Angeles
(UCLA)
405 Hilgard Avenue, P. O. Box 951521
3051 Moore Hall
Los Angeles, California 90024-1521
Telephone: (310) 825-3931; (800) 832-8256
Fax: (310) 206-8095

Counseling and Student Services (CG)
University of North Carolina at Greensboro
School of Education
201 Ferguson, P.O. Box 26171
Greensboro, North Carolina 27402-6171
Telephone: (336) 334-4114; (800) 414-9769
Fax: (336) 334-4116

Disabilities and Gifted Education (EC)
Council for Exceptional Children (CEC)
1920 Association Drive
Reston, Virginia 20191-1589
Telephone: (703) 264-9474; (800) 328-0272
Fax: (703) 620-2521

Educational Management (EA)
University of Oregon (Dept. 5207)
1787 Agate Street
Eugene, Oregon 97403-5307
Telephone: (541) 346-5043; (800) 438-8841
Fax: (541) 346-2334

Elementary and Early Childhood Education (PS)
University of Illinois at Urbana-Champaign

Children's Research Center, Room 13
51 Gerty Drive
Champaign, Illinois 61820-7469
Telephone: (217) 333-1386; (800) 583-4135
Fax: (217) 333-3767

Higher Education (HE)
George Washington University
One Dupont Circle, N.W., Suite 630
Washington, D.C. 20036-1183
Telephone: (202) 296-2597; (800) 773-3742
Fax: (202) 452-1844

Information and Technology (IR)
Syracuse University
Center for Science and Technology
4th Floor, Room 194
Syracuse, New York 13244-4100
Telephone: (315) 443-3640; (800) 464-9107
Fax: (315) 443-5448

Languages and Linguistics (FL)
Center for Applied Linguistics (CAL)
1118 22nd Street, N.W.
Washington, D.C. 20037-1214
Telephone: (202) 429-9292; (800) 276-9834
Fax: (202) 659-5641

Reading, English, and Communication (CS)
Indiana University
Smith Research Center, Suite 150
2805 East 10th Street
Bloomington, Indiana 47408-2698
Telephone: (812) 855-5847; (800) 759-4723
Fax: (812) 855-4220

Rural Education and Small Schools (RC)
Appalachia Educational Laboratory (AEL)
1031 Quarrier Street, Suite 607
P.O. Box 1348
Charleston, West Virginia 25325-1348
Telephone: (304) 347-0461; (800) 624-9120
Fax: (304) 347-0487

Science, Mathematics, and Environmental Education (SE)
Ohio State University
1929 Kenny Road
Columbus, Ohio 43210-1080

Telephone: (614) 292-6717; (800) 276-0462
Fax: (614) 292-0263

Social Studies/Social Science Education (SO)
Indiana University
Social Studies Development Center
Suite 120, 2805 East 10th Street
Bloomington, Indiana 47408-2698
Telephone: (812) 855-3838; (800) 266-3815
Fax: (812) 855-0455

Teaching and Teacher Education (SP)
American Association of Colleges for Teacher Education
1307 New York Avenue, N.W., Suite 300
Washington, D.C. 20005-4701
Telephone: (202) 293-2450; (800) 822-9229
Fax: (202) 457-8095

Urban Education (UD)
Teachers College, Columbia University
Institute for Urban and Minority Education
Main Hall, Room 303, Box 40
525 West 120th Street
New York, New York 10027-6696
Telephone: (212) 678-3433; (800) 601-4868
Fax: (212) 678-4012

SPONSOR:
Educational Resources Information Center (ERIC)
National Library of Education (NLE)
Office of Educational Research and Improvement (OERI)
555 New Jersey Avenue, N.W.
Washington, DC 20208-5721
Telephone: (202) 219-2221
Fax: (202) 219-1817

CENTRALIZED DATABASE MANAGEMENT:
ERIC Processing and Reference Facility
Computer Sciences Corporation (CSC)
1100 West Street, 2nd Floor
Laurel, Maryland 20707-3598
Telephone: (301) 497-4080; (800) 799-3742
Fax: (301) 953-0263

DOCUMENT DELIVERY:
ERIC Document Reproduction Service (EDRS)
DynEDRS, Inc.

7420 Fullerton Road, Suite 110
Springfield, Virginia 22153-2852
Telephone: (703) 440-1400; (800) 443-3742
Fax: (703) 440-1408

COMMERCIAL PUBLISHING:
Oryx Press
4041 North Central Ave. at Indian School
Road, Suite 700
Phoenix, Arizona 85012-3397
Telephone: (602) 265-2651; (800) 279-6799
Fax: (800) 279-4663; (602) 265-6250

OUTREACH:
ACCESS ERIC
Aspen Systems Corporation
2277 Research Boulevard, 7A
Rockville, Maryland 20850
Telephone: (301) 519-5157; (800) 538-3742
Fax: (301) 519-6760

APPENDIX C
REGIONAL EDUCATION LABORATORY CONTRACTORS

The Regional Education Laboratory contractors are educational research and development organizations supported by contracts with the U.S. Education Department, Office of Educational Research and Improvement (OERI).

AEL Appalachia Educational Laboratory
Specialty Area: Rural Education
P.O. Box 1348
Charleston, WV 25325-1348
Voice: (304) 347-0400; (800) 624-9120
Fax: (304) 347-0487
Terry L. Eidell, Executive Director
eidellt@ael.org
Web site | FTP

LAB The Laboratory at Brown University
(includes Puerto Rico and the Virgin Islands)
Specialty Area: Language and Cultural Diversity
222 Richmond Street, Suite 300
Providence, RI 02903-4226
Voice: (401) 274-9548
Fax: (401) 421-7650
Philip Zarlengo, Executive Director
Phil_Zarlengo@Brown.edu
Web site | FTP (n/a)

LSS Laboratory for Student Success at Temple University
Specialty Area: Urban Education

933 Ritte Annex, 13th St. & Cecil B. Moore
Philadephia, PA 19122
Voice: (215) 204-3030
Fax: (215) 204-5130
Margaret C. Wang, Executive Director
lss@vm.temple.edu
Web site | FTP (n/a)

McREL Mid-Continent Regional Educational Laboratory
Specialty Area: Curriculum, Learning, and Instruction
2550 S. Parker Rd., Suite 500
Aurora, CO 80014
Voice: (303) 337-0990
Fax: (303) 337-3005
Tim Waters, Executive Director
twaters@mcrel.org
Web site | FTP

NCREL North Central Regional Educational Laboratory
Specialty Area: Technology
1900 Spring Road, Suite 300
Oak Brook, IL 60521-1480

Voice: (630) 571-4700
Fax: (630) 571-4716
Jeri Nowakowski, Executive Director
nowakows@ncrel.org
Web site | FTP (n/a)

NWREL Northwest Regional Educational Laboratory
(includes Alaska)
Specialty Area: School Change Processes
101 S. W. Main Ave., Suite 500
Portland, OR 97204
Voice: (503) 275-9500
Fax: (503) 275-9489
Ethel Simon-McWilliams, Executive Director
simone@nwrel.org
Web site | FTP (n/a)

PREL Pacific Resources for Education and Learning
(includes Hawaii and all U.S. affiliates in the Pacific Basin)
Specialty Area: Language and Cultural Diversity
828 Fort Street Mall, Suite 500
Honolulu, HI 96813
Voice: (808) 533-6000
Fax: (808) 533-7599
John W. Kofel, Executive Director
kofelj@prel.hawaii.org
Web site | FTP (n/a)

SEDL Southwest Educational Development Laboratory
Specialty Area: Language and Cultural Diversity

211 E. Seventh St.
Austin, TX 78701-3281
Voice: (512) 476-6861
Fax: (512) 476-2286
Wesley A. Hoover, President & CEO
whoover@sedl.org
Web site | FTP

SERVE Southeastern Regional Vision for Education
Specialty Area: Early Childhood Education
P.O. Box 5367
Greensboro, NC 27435
Voice: (910) 334-3211; (800) 755-3277
Fax: (910) 334-3268
Don Holznagel, Interim Executive Director
dholznag@serve.org
Web site | FTP (n/a)

WestEd (Far West Laboratory and Southwest Regional Laboratory)
Specialty Area: Assessment and Accountability
730 Harrison Street
San Francisco, CA 94107-1242
Voice: (415) 565-3000
Fax: (415) 565-3012
Glen Harvey, Executive Director
gharvey@wested.org
Web site | FTP/Gopher

Appendix D

National Research and Development Centers

Web site: http://www.ed.gov/offices/OERI/ResCtr.html

To address nationally significant problems and issues in education, the U.S. Department of Education's Office of Educational Research and Improvement, through its five National Institutes, supports university-based national educational research and development centers. The centers address specific topics such as early childhood development and learning, student learning and achievement, cultural and linguistic diversity and second language learning, and postsecondary improvement. In addition, each center has collaborating partners, and many work with elementary and secondary schools. Centers may be contacted directly for a catalog of their publications and services.

Center for Research on Education, Diversity and Excellence (CREDE)
University of California, Santa Cruz
1156 High Street
Santa Cruz, CA 95064
(408) 459-3500
Director: Roland Tharp
Web site: http://www.crede.ucsc.edu
OERI Contact: Gilbert N. Garcia
(202) 219-2144, National Institute on the Education of At-Risk Students

Center for Research on the Education of Students Placed At-Risk (CRESPAR)
Johns Hopkins University, CSOS
3505 North Charles Street
Baltimore, MD 21218
(410) 516-8800

and
Howard University
Department of Psychology
Washington, DC 20059
(202) 806-8484
Co-directors: Robert Slavin (Johns Hopkins) and A. Wade Boykin (Howard)
Web site: http://scov.csos.jhu.edu/crespar/CReSPaR.html
OERI Contact: Ron Pedone
(202) 219-2247, National Institute on the Education of At-Risk Students

Center for Research on Evaluation, Standards, and Student Testing (CRESST)
University of California, Los Angeles
Graduate School of Education
1339 Moore Hall

405 Hilgard Avenue
Los Angeles, CA 90024
(310) 206-1530
Co-directors: Eva L. Baker and Robert Linn
Web site: http://cresst96.cse.ucla.edu
OERI Contact: David Sweet
(202) 219-1748, National Institute on Student Achievement, Curriculum, and Assessment

Center for the Improvement of Early Reading Achievement (CIERA)
University of Michigan
School of Education
610 E. University Avenue, Rm. 1600 SEB
Ann Arbor, MI 48109-1259
(734) 647-6940
Director: Elfrieda H. Hiebert
Web site: http://www.ciera.org/
OERI Contact: Anne P. Sweet
(202) 219-2043, National Institute on Student Achievement, Curriculum, and Assessment

Center for the Study of Teaching and Policy (CTP)
University of Washington
College of Education Box 353600
Seattle, Washington 98195
(206) 221-4114
Director: Michael Knapp
Web site: http://depts.washington.edu/ctpmail
OERI Contact: Ron Anson
(202) 219-2214, National Institute on Educational Governance, Finance, Policy-Making, and Management

National Center for Early Development and Learning (NCEDL)
University of North Carolina-Chapel Hill
Frank Porter Graham Child Development Center
CB #4100
Chapel Hill, NC 27599-4100
(919) 966-4250
Director: Don Bailey
Web site: http://www.fpg.unc.edu/~ncedl/

OERI Contact; Naomi Karp
(202) 219-1586, National Institute on Early Childhood Development and Education

National Center for Improving Student Learning and Achievement in Mathematics and Science
Wisconsin Center for Education Research, School of Education
University of Wisconsin
1025 West Johnson Street
Madison, WI 53706
(608) 263-4285
Director: Thomas A. Romberg
Web site: http://www.wcer.wisc.edu/NCISLA/
OERI Contacts: Wanda Chambers
(202) 219-2035; Ram Singh (202) 219-2025, National Institute on Student Achievement, Curriculum, and Assessment

National Center for Postsecondary Improvement (NCPI)
CERAS 508, School of Education
520 Galvez Mall
Stanford University
Stanford, CA 94305-3084
(650) 723-7724
Director: Patricia J. Gumport
Web site: http://ncpi.stanford.edu
OERI Contact: Gregory Henschel
(202) 219-2082, National Institute on Post-Secondary Education, Libraries, and Lifelong Learning

National Center for the Study of Adult Learning and Literacy (NCSALL)
Harvard Graduate School of Education
101 Nichols House, Appian Way
Cambridge, MA 02138
(617) 495-4843
Director: John P. Comings
Web site: http://hugse1.harvard.edu/~ncsall
OERI Contact: Harold Himmelfarb
(202) 219-2031, National Institute on Post-Secondary Education, Libraries, and Lifelong Learning

National Center on Increasing the Effectiveness of State and Local Education Reform Efforts

Consortium for Policy Research in Education (CPRE)
Graduate School of Education
University of Pennsylvania
3440 Market Street, Suite 560
Philadephia, PA 19104-3325
(215) 573-0700
Director: Susan Fuhrman
Web site: http://www.upenn.edu/gse/cpre
OERI Contact: Betty Demarest
(202) 219-2217, National Institute on Educational Governance, Finance, Policy-Making, and Management

National Research & Development Center on English Learning & Achievement (CELA)

University of Albany, State University of New York
School of Education

1400 Washington Avenue
Albany, NY 12222
(518) 442-5026
Co-directors: Judith Langer, Arthur Applebee, and Martin Nystrand
Web site: http://www.albany.edu/cela/
OERI Contact: Rita Foy (202) 219-2027;
Anne Sweet (202) 219-2043, National Institute on Student Achievement, Curriculum, and Assessment

National Research Center on the Gifted and Talented (NRC/GT)

University of Connecticut
362 Fairfield Road U-7
Storrs, CT 06269-2007
(860) 486-4676
Director: Joseph S. Renzulli
Web site: http://www.gifted.uconn.edu/nrcgt.html
OERI Contact: Beverly E. Coleman
(202) 219-2280

APPENDIX E

NATIONAL INSTITUTES, OFFICE OF EDUCATIONAL RESEARCH AND IMPROVEMENT

In 1994, the Office of Educational Research and Improvement (OERI) was reauthorized by the U.S. Congress in the Educational Research, Development, Dissemination, and Improvement Act. The act established five research institutes within OERI to help provide a "deeper understanding of the processes of learning and schooling" and new ideas "to make a substantial difference in the lives of every student in the United States." All of the institutes are to carry out a coordinated and comprehensive program of research and development to provide research-based leadership to the United States on each of the themes.[1]

NATIONAL INSTITUTE ON STUDENT ACHIEVEMENT, CURRICULUM, AND ASSESSMENT

Purpose: to seek to improve student achievement in core content areas and the integration of these areas; to identify, develop, and evaluate innovative and exemplary methods to improve student knowledge; to conduct research in human learning, cognition, and performance; to identify, develop, and evaluate programs designed to narrow racial and gender performance gaps; and to support a research and development program in assessment.

U.S. Department of Education/OERI
Student Achievement Institute, Room 510
555 New Jersey Avenue NW
Washington, DC 20208-5573
Phone: (202) 219-2079
Fax: (202) 219-2135
Email: sai@ed.gov

---

[1]SOURCE: Office of Educational Research and Improvement, U.S. Department of Education, Washington, D.C.

Joseph C. Conaty, Director
Phone: (202) 219-2079
Email: Joseph_Conaty@ed.gov

NATIONAL INSTITUTE ON THE EDUCATION OF AT-RISK STUDENTS

Purpose: to support research and development designed to improve educational opportunities for students placed at risk of educational failure; to provide a sound basis from which to identify programs and models, which promote greater educational success of students who have a high likelihood of failure; and to maximize the effectiveness of schools that serve the greatest number of students who are at risk of failing.

U.S. Department of Education/OERI
Room 610
555 New Jersey Avenue NW
Washington, DC 20208-5521
Our fax is (202) 219-2030
Ed Fuentes, Director
Telephone: (202) 219-2239
Email: Edward_Fuentes@ed.gov

NATIONAL INSTITUTE ON EARLY CHILDHOOD DEVELOPMENT AND EDUCATION

Purpose: to support research that will investigate the factors, including services and supports, that will improve the learning, cognitive, and social-emotional development and general well-being of young children and their families.

U.S. Department of Education/OERI
555 New Jersey Avenue NW
Washington, DC 20208
Phone: (202) 219-1935
Fax: (202) 273-4768
Email: eci@inet.ed.gov
Naomi Karp, Acting Director
(202) 219-1935

NATIONAL INSTITUTE ON EDUCATIONAL GOVERNANCE, FINANCE, POLICY-MAKING, AND MANAGEMENT

Purpose: to seek to improve student achievement through education reform and to provide a sound basis of research from which to identify, develop, and evaluate approaches in elementary and secondary education governance, finance, policymaking, and management at state, local, tribal, school building, classroom, and community levels which promise to advance high levels of learning by all students.

U.S. Department of Education/OERI
555 New Jersey Avenue NW
Washington, DC 20208-5510
Phone: (202) 219-2032
Fax: (202) 219-2159
Email: gfi@ed.gov
C. Kent McGuire, Acting Director
(202) 219-2032

NATIONAL INSTITUTE ON POSTSECONDARY EDUCATION, LIBRARIES, AND LIFELONG LEARNING

Purpose: to expand knowledge about the education and training of adults in a variety of contexts, including 2- and 4-year postsecondary institutions, adult literacy programs, community-based education programs, special mission institutions, and libraries and to explore adults' acquisition of the skills and knowledge necessary to compete in a global economy and participate as responsible citizens.

U.S. Department of Education/OERI
555 New Jersey Avenue NW
Washington, DC 20208-5531
Phone: (202) 219-2207
Fax: (202) 501-3005
Carole Lacampagne, Director
(202) 219-2207
Email: carole_lacampagne@ed.gov

Appendix F
Curriculum Journals

Curriculum Inquiry
Ontario Institute for Studies
in Education
Blackwell Publishers
350 Main Street
Malden, Massachusetts 02148
Telephone: (800) 835-6770
URL: http://www.blackwellpub.com

Curriculum Review
W D & S Publishing
20 Highland Ave.
Suite 4
Metuchen, NJ 08840-1949
URL: http://www.dealersedge.com

Educational Leadership
Association for Supervision and
Curriculum Development
1703 N. Beauregard St.

Alexandria, Virginia 22311-1714
Telephone: (703) 578-9600
URL: http://www.ascd.org

*Journal of Curriculum and
Supervision*
Association for Supervision and
Curriculum Development
1703 N. Beauregard St.
Alexandria, Virginia 22311-1714
Telephone: (703) 578-9600
URL: http://www.ascd.org

Journal of Curriculum Studies
Taylor & Francis, Inc.
47 Runway Rd.
Suite G
Levittown, Pennsylvania 19057-4700
Telephone: (215) 269-0363
URL: http://www.tandf.co.uk

CREDITS

dria, Va.: Association for Supervision and Curriculum Development, 1962). Reprinted with permission of the Association for Supervision and Curriculum Development. Copyright © 1962 by the Association for Supervision and Curriculum Development. All rights reserved.

John Henry Martin, "Reconsidering the Goals of High School Education," *Educational Leadership* 37, no. 4 (January 1980). Reprinted with permission of the Association for Supervision and Curriculum Development. Copyright © 1980 by the Association for Supervision and Curriculum Development. All rights reserved.

Abraham H. Maslow, "Some Basic Propositions of a Growth and Self-Actualization Psychology." in *Perceiving, Behaving, Becoming,* 1962 Yearbook (Alexandria, Va.: Association for Supervision and Curriculum Development, 1962). Reprinted with permission of the Association for Supervision and Curriculum Development. Copyright © 1962 by the Association for Supervision and Curriculum Development. All rights reserved.

James D. Raths, "Teaching Without Specific Objectives," *Educational Leadership* 28, no. 7 (April 1971). Reprinted with permission of the Association for Supervision and Curriculum Development. Copyright © 1971 by the Association for Supervision and Curriculum Development. All rights reserved.

Richard L. Turner, "The Value of Variety in Teaching Styles," *Educational Leadership* 36, no. 4 (January 1979). Reprinted with permission of the Association for Supervision and Curriculum Development. Copyright © 1979 by the Association for Supervision and Curriculum Development. All rights reserved.

David Turney, "Sisyphus Revisited," *Perspective on Curriculum Development 1776-1976*, 1976 Yearbook. Reprinted with permission of the Association for Supervision and Curriculum Development. Copyright © 1976 by the Association for Supervision and Curriculum Development. All rights reserved.

Kimball Wiles and Franklin Patterson, *The High School We Need* (Alexandria, Va.: Association for Supervision and Curriculum Development, 1959). Reprinted with permission of the Association for Supervision and Curriculum Development. Copyright © 1959 by the Association for Supervision and Curriculum Development. All rights reserved.

Excerpts from Howard Gardner, *Multiple Intelligences: Theory in Practice* (New York: Basic Books, 1993). Reprinted with permission.

Kenneth D. Benne and Paul Sheats, "Functional Roles of Group Members," *Journal of Social Issues,* Vol. IV, No. 2 (Spring 1948). Reprinted by permission of the author and Blackwell Publishers.

Excerpts from Diane Ravitch, *National Standards in American Education: A Citizen's Guide* (Washington, D.C.: The Brookings Institution, 1995). Reprinted with permission.

From Ruth Manning Hackett, ed. *Teachers' Guide to Curriculum Development: Manual for Kindergarten and Primary Teachers* (Sacramento, California Department of Education, 1930). Reprinted by permission.

Gary W. Orwig and Donna J. Baumbach, *What Every Educator Needs to Know About the New Technologies: Interactive Video I* (Orlando, Fla.: University of Central Florida, undated). Reprinted by permission.

Excerpts from *The Child and the Curriculum* by John Dewey. Copyright © 1902 by the University of Chicago. Reprinted by permission of The University of Chicago Press. All rights reserved.

Excerpts from *Basic Principles of Curriculum and Instruction* by Ralph W. Tyler. Copyright © 1949 by The University of Chicago. Reprinted by permission of The University of Chicago Press. All rights reserved.

From Ralph W. Tyler, *Basic Principles of Curriculum and Instruction,* (Copyright © 1949 by The University of Chicago), as adapted by W. James Popham and Eva L. Baker, *Establishing Instructional Goals,* Prentice-Hall, Inc., Copyright © 1970. Reprinted by permission of The University of Chicago Press. All rights reserved.

Decker F. Walker, "A Naturalistic Model for Curriculum Development," *School Review*, Vol. 80, No. 1 November 1971. Copyright © 1971 and 1972 by The University of Chicago. Reprinted by permission of The University of Chicago Press. All rights reserved.

Dorothy J. Watson, "Defining and Describing Whole Language," *The Elementary School Journal* 90, no. 2 (November 1989). Copyright © 1989 by The University of Chicago Press. Reprinted by permission of The University of Chicago Press. All rights reserved.

From James B. Conant. *Recommendations for Education in the Junior High School Years* (Princeton, N.J.: Educational Testing Service, 1960). Reprinted by permission of Educational Testing Service.

Elizabeth Jane Simpson, *The Psychomotor Domain* (Mt. Rainier, Md.: Gryphon House, 1972). Reprinted by permission.

Excerpts from *Fundamentals of Curriculum Development,* Revised Edition by B. Othanel Smith, William O. Stanley, and J. Harlan Shores, copyright © 1957 by Harcourt, Inc. and renewed 1985 by B. Othanel Smith, William O. Stanley, J. Harlan Shores, reprinted by permission of the publisher.

Excerpts from *Curriculum Development: Theory and Practice* by Hilda Taba and Willard B. Spalding,

NAME INDEX

Subject Index